SPSS® for UNIX®
Base System User's Guide
Release 5.0

SPSS Inc.

SPSS Inc.
444 N. Michigan Avenue
Chicago, Illinois 60611
Tel: (312) 329-2400
Fax: (312) 329-3668

SPSS Federal Systems (U.S.)
SPSS Latin America
SPSS Benelux BV
SPSS UK Ltd.
SPSS UK Ltd., New Delhi
SPSS GmbH Software
SPSS Scandinavia AB
SPSS Asia Pacific Pte. Ltd.
SPSS Japan Inc.
SPSS Australasia Pty. Ltd.

For more information about SPSS® software products, please write or call

Marketing Department
SPSS Inc.
444 North Michigan Avenue
Chicago, IL 60611
Tel: (312) 329-2400
Fax: (312) 329-3668

SPSS is a registered trademark and the other product names are the trademarks of SPSS Inc. for its proprietary computer software. No material describing such software may be produced or distributed without the written permission of the owners of the trademark and license rights in the software and the copyrights in the published materials.

The SOFTWARE and documentation are provided with RESTRICTED RIGHTS. Use, duplication, or disclosure by the Government is subject to restrictions as set forth in subdivision (c)(1)(ii) of The Rights in Technical Data and Computer Software clause at 52.227-7013. Contractor/manufacturer is SPSS Inc., 444 N. Michigan Avenue, Chicago, IL, 60611.

General notice: Other product names mentioned herein are used for identification purposes only and may be trademarks of their respective companies.

UNIX is a registered trademark of AT&T.

SPSS® for UNIX®: Base System User's Guide, Release 5.0
Copyright © 1993 by SPSS Inc.
All rights reserved.
Printed in the United States of America.

No part of this publication may be reproduced, stored in a retrieval system, or transmitted, in any form or by any means, electronic, mechanical, photocopying, recording, or otherwise, without the prior written permission of the publisher.

1 2 3 4 5 6 7 8 9 0   94 93

ISBN 0-923967-86-9

Library of Congress Catalog Card Number: 93-083410

Preface

SPSS is a comprehensive and flexible statistical analysis and data management system. SPSS can take data from almost any type of file and use them to generate tabulated reports, charts and plots of distributions and trends, descriptive statistics, and complex statistical analyses.

SPSS for UNIX provides a Motif interface that makes statistical analysis more accessible for the casual user and more convenient for the experienced user. Simple menus and dialog box selections make it possible to perform complex analyses without typing a single line of command syntax. The Data Editor offers a simple and efficient spreadsheet-like facility for entering data and browsing the working data file. High-resolution, presentation-quality charts and plots are included as part of the Base system.

The *SPSS for UNIX Base System User's Guide* documents the Motif graphical user interface. Beneath the menus and dialog boxes, SPSS uses a command language, and some features of the system can be accessed only via command syntax. Appendix A lists the commands available only with command syntax. Complete command syntax is documented in the *SPSS Base System Syntax Reference Guide*.

SPSS Options

The following options are available as add-on enhancements to the SPSS Base system:

- **SPSS Professional Statistics**™ provides techniques to measure the similarities and differences in data, classify data, identify underlying dimensions, and more. It includes procedures for these analyses: cluster, k-means cluster, discriminant, factor, multidimensional scaling, proximity, and reliability.
- **SPSS Advanced Statistics**™ includes sophisticated techniques such as logistic regression, loglinear analysis, multivariate analysis of variance, constrained nonlinear regression, probit analysis, Cox regression, Kaplan-Meier and actuarial survival analysis.
- **SPSS Tables**™ creates a variety of presentation-quality tabular reports, including complex tables and displays of multiple-response data.

- **SPSS Trends**™ performs comprehensive forecasting and time-series analyses with multiple curve-fitting models, smoothing models, and methods for estimating autoregressive functions.
- **SPSS Categories**™ performs conjoint analysis and optimal scaling procedures, including correspondence analysis.
- **SPSS LISREL**® **7** analyzes linear structural models and simultaneous equation models. It provides sophisticated techniques for formulating, estimating, and testing causal models for nonexperimental data and for confirmatory factor analysis. SPSS LISREL 7 is not available on all platforms.

Training Seminars

SPSS Inc. provides both public and onsite training seminars for SPSS for UNIX. All seminars feature hands-on workshops. SPSS for UNIX seminars will be offered in major U.S. and European cities on a regular basis. For more information on these seminars, call the SPSS Inc. Training Department toll-free at 1-800-543-6607.

Technical Support

The services of SPSS Technical Support are available to registered customers of SPSS for UNIX. Customers may call Technical Support for assistance in using SPSS products or for installation help for one of the warranted hardware environments.

To reach Technical Support, call 1-312-329-3410. Be prepared to identify yourself, your organization, and the serial number of your system or your SPSS ID number.

Additional Publications

Additional copies of all SPSS product manuals may be purchased separately. To order additional manuals, just fill out the Publications order form included with your system and send it to SPSS Publications Sales, 444 N. Michigan Avenue, Chicago IL, 60611.

Note: In Europe, additional copies of publications can be purchased by site-licensed customers only. Please contact your local office at the address listed at the end of this preface for more information.

Lend Us Your Thoughts

Your comments are important. So send us a letter and let us know about your experiences with SPSS products. We especially like to hear about new and interesting applications using the SPSS for UNIX system. Write to SPSS Inc. Marketing Department, 444 N. Michigan Avenue, Chicago IL, 60611.

Contacting SPSS Inc.

If you would like to be on our mailing list, write to us at one of the addresses below. We will send you a copy of our newsletter and let you know about SPSS Inc. activities in your area.

SPSS Inc.
444 North Michigan Ave.
Chicago, IL 60611
Tel: (312) 329-2400
Fax: (312) 329-3668

SPSS Federal Systems
12030 Sunrise Valley Dr.
Suite 300
Reston, VA 22091
Tel: (703) 391-6020
Fax (703) 391-6002

SPSS Latin America
444 North Michigan Ave.
Chicago, IL 60611
Tel: (312) 329-3556
Fax: (312) 329-3668

SPSS Benelux BV
P.O. Box 115
4200 AC Gorinchem
The Netherlands
Tel: +31.1830.36711
Fax: +31.1830.35839

SPSS UK Ltd.
SPSS House
5 London Street
Chertsey
Surrey KT16 8AP
United Kingdom
Tel: +44.932.566262
Fax: +44.932.567020

SPSS UK Ltd., New Delhi
c/o Ashok Business Centre
Ashok Hotel
50B Chanakyapuri
New Delhi 110 021
India
Tel: +91.11.600121 x1029
Fax: +91.11.6873216

SPSS GmbH Software
Steinsdorfstrasse 19
D-8000 Munich 22
Germany
Tel:+49.89.2283008
Fax: +49.89.2285413

SPSS Scandinavia AB
Sjöängsvägen 7
S-191 72 Sollentuna
Sweden
Tel: +46.8.7549450
Fax: +46.8.7548816

SPSS Asia Pacific Pte. Ltd.
10 Anson Road, #34-07
International Plaza
Singapore 0207
Singapore
Tel: +65.221.2577
Fax: +65.221.9920

SPSS Japan Inc.
Gyoen Sky Bldg.
2-1-11, Shinjuku
Shinjuku-ku
Tokyo 160
Japan
Tel: +81.3.33505261
Fax: +81.3.33505245

SPSS Australasia Pty. Ltd.
121 Walker Street
North Sydney, NSW 2060
Australia
Tel: +61.2.954.5660
Fax: +61.2.954.5616

Contents

1 Overview 1

SPSS Motif Interface 1
Starting SPSS 1
SPSS Windows 3
  Designated versus Active Window 4
  Moving between Windows 4
Menus 4
  Data Editor Menus 5
Status Bar 5
  Turning the Status Bar Off and On 6
Icon Bars 6
  Output Window Icon Bar 6
  Syntax Window Icon Bar 6
  Chart Window Icon Bar 7
  Turning Icon Bars Off and On 7
Statistical Analysis with the Dialog Box Interface 7
  Before You Start 7
  Choosing a Data File 8
  Choosing a Statistical Procedure 9
  Main Dialog Box 10
  Subdialog Boxes 14
  Persistence of Settings 17
  Order of Operations 18
Data Editor 18
  Entering Data 18
  Editing Data 20
Creating and Editing Charts 21
Pasting and Editing Command Syntax 24
Saving Results 26
Getting Help 27
Ending an SPSS Session 27

Decimal Indicator and the LANG Environment Variable Setting 27
Keyboard Movement 28
  Menus 28
  Dialog Boxes 28

2 Data Files 29

Creating a New Data File 29
Opening an SPSS Data File 29
  Filename and Location 30
  File Type 31
  Multiple User Access 31
SQL Databases 31
  Variable Names and Labels 31
  Reading Databases 32
  Tables and Fields 33
  Selecting a Subset of Cases 33
  Time-saving Tip 35
Reading Text Files 36
  Define Fixed Variables 39
  Define Freefield Variables 44
Data Editor Window 45
File Information 46
  Working Data File 46
  Other SPSS Data Files 47
Saving Data Files 48
  Multiple User Access 48
  Save As New File or Different Format 48
  Filename and Location 49
  File Type 50
Closing a Data File 50

3 Data Editor 51

Defining Variables 52
  Variable Names 53
  Variable Type 54
  Labels 56
  Missing Values 58
  Column Format 59
  Templates 60

Entering Data 63
  Entering Data in a Selected Area 64
  Data Value Restrictions 65

Editing Data 65
  Changing Data Values 65
  Cutting, Copying, and Pasting Values 66
  Inserting New Cases 69
  Inserting New Variables 69
  Deleting Cases and Variables 70
  Moving Variables 71
  Changing Data Type 71

Finding Variables 72

Finding Cases 72

Finding Data Values 72

Display Options 73
  Display Value Labels 73
  Grid Lines 74
  Fonts 74

Printing 75

Pending Transformations and the Data Editor 75

Saving Data Files 75
  Save As New File or Different Format 75

Closing a Data File and Opening a Different One 76

Keyboard Movement 76

4 Output and Syntax Windows 79

Output Windows 79
  Opening a New Text File in an Output Window 79
  Opening an Existing Text File in an Output Window 80
  Multiple Output Windows 81
  Output Window Icon Bar 81
  Output Page Titles 82

Syntax Windows 83
  Opening a New Text File in a Syntax Window 83
  Opening an Existing File in a Syntax Window 83
  Using SPSS Command Syntax in a Syntax Window 84
  Multiple Syntax Windows 86
  Syntax Window Icon Bar 86

Editing Text Files 86
  Basic Text-editing Concepts 87
  Edit Menu 87
  Font Control 90

Saving Text Files 90
  Save As New File 91
  Saving Selected Areas of Text Files 92

5 Data Transformations 93

Computing Values 93
  Calculator Pad 94
  Functions 95
  Conditional Expressions 98
  Variable Type and Label 99
  Syntax Rules for Expressions 100

Random Number Seed 101

Counting Occurrences 101
  Defining Values to Count 103
  Selecting Subsets of Cases 104

Recoding Values   104
  Recode into Same Variables   104
  Recode into Different Variables   107
Ranking Data   110
  Ranking Method   111
  Rank Ties   113
Creating Consecutive Integers from Numeric and String Values   114
Pending Transformations   115

6 File Handling and File Transformations   117

Sorting Data   117
Transposing Cases and Variables   118
  Missing Values in Transposed Data Files   119
Combining Data Files   119
  Merging Files That Contain Different Cases   120
  Merging Files That Contain Different Variables   126
Applying a Data Dictionary   132
  Weighted Files   133
Aggregating Data   134
  Aggregate Functions   135
  New Variable Names and Labels   137
  Aggregate Filename and Location   137
Split-File Processing   138
  Turning Split-File Processing On and Off   139
  Sorting Cases for Split-File Processing   139
Selecting Subsets of Cases   139
  Selecting Cases Based on Conditional Expressions   141
  Selecting a Random Sample   142
Weighting Cases   143
  Turning Weights On and Off   143
  Weights in Scatterplots and Histograms   144

7 Data Tabulation   145

A Frequency Table   145
  Visual Displays   146
  What Day?   148
  Histograms   148
  Percentiles   149
  Screening Data   150
How to Obtain Frequency Tables   150
  Frequencies Statistics   151
  Frequencies Charts   153
  Frequencies Format   154
  Additional Features Available with Command Syntax   155

8 Descriptive Statistics   157

Examining the Data   157
Summarizing the Data   159
  Levels of Measurement   159
  Summary Statistics   161
  The Normal Distribution   164
  Who Lies?   167
How to Obtain Descriptive Statistics   167
  Descriptives Options   168
  Additional Features Available with Command Syntax   170

9 Exploring Data   171

Reasons for Exploring Data   171
  Identifying Mistakes   171
  Exploring the Data   172
  Preparing for Hypothesis Testing   172
Ways of Displaying Data   172
  The Histogram   172
  The Stem-and-Leaf Plot   173
  The Boxplot   175

Evaluating Assumptions   177
  The Levene Test   177
  Spread-versus-Level Plots   178
  Tests of Normality   179
Estimating Location with Robust Estimators   181
  The Trimmed Mean   182
  M-Estimators   182
How to Explore Your Data   185
  Explore Statistics   186
  Explore Plots   187
  Explore Options   189
  Additional Features Available with Command Syntax   189

10 Crosstabulation and Measures of Association   191

Crosstabulation   191
  Cell Contents and Marginals   192
  Choosing Percentages   193
  Adding a Control Variable   193
Graphical Representation of Crosstabulations   195
Using Crosstabulation for Data Screening   195
Crosstabulation Statistics   196
  The Chi-Square Test of Independence   196
  Measures of Association   199
  Nominal Measures   199
  Ordinal Measures   205
  Measures Involving Interval Data   208
  Estimating Risk in Cohort Studies   208
  Estimating Risk in Case-Control Studies   210
How to Obtain Crosstabulations   211
  Crosstabs Statistics   212
  Crosstabs Cell Display   213
  Crosstabs Table Format   215
  Additional Features Available with Command Syntax   216

11 Describing Subpopulation Differences   217

Searching for Discrimination   217
  Who Does What?   218
  Level of Education   219
  Beginning Salaries   220
  Introducing More Variables   222
How to Obtain Subgroup Means   222
  Means Options Dialog Box   223
  Additional Features Available with Command Syntax   224

12 Multiple Response Analysis   225

Introduction to Multiple Response Data   225
  Set Definition   226
  Crosstabulations   228
Analyzing Multiple Response Data   231
How to Define Multiple Response Sets   231
How to Obtain Multiple Response Frequencies   232
  Additional Features Available with Command Syntax   234
How to Crosstabulate Multiple Response Sets   234
  Define Value Ranges   236
  Options   236
  Additional Features Available with Command Syntax   238

13 Testing Hypotheses about Differences in Means   239

Testing Hypotheses   239
  Samples and Populations   240
  Sampling Distributions   241
  Sampling Distribution of the Mean   242

The Two-Sample T Test 244
  Significance Levels 246
  One-tailed versus Two-tailed Tests 246
  What's the Difference? 246

Using Crosstabulation to Test Hypotheses 247

Independent versus Paired Samples 248
  Analysis of Paired Data 248

Hypothesis Testing: A Review 249
  The Importance of Assumptions 250

How to Obtain an Independent-Samples T Test 250
  Define Groups for Numeric Variables 251
  Define Groups for String Variables 252
  Independent-Samples T Test Options 252

How to Obtain a Paired-Samples T Test 253
  Paired-Samples T Test Options 254
  Additional Features Available with Command Syntax 255

14 One-Way Analysis of Variance 257

Examining the Data 257
  Sample Means and Confidence Intervals 258

Testing the Null Hypothesis 259

Assumptions Needed for Analysis of Variance 260
  The Levene Test 260

Analyzing the Variability 260
  Between-Groups Variability 261
  Within-Groups Variability 261
  Calculating the F Ratio 262

Multiple Comparison Procedures 262

How to Obtain One-Way Analysis of Variance 264
  One-Way ANOVA Define Range 265
  One-Way ANOVA Contrasts 266
  One-Way ANOVA Post Hoc Multiple Comparisons 267
  One-Way ANOVA Options 268
  Additional Features Available with Command Syntax 270

15 Analysis of Variance 271

Descriptive Statistics 271

Analysis of Variance 272
  Testing for Interaction 274
  Tests for Sex and Attractiveness 275

Explanations 275

Extensions 275

How to Obtain a Simple Factorial Analysis of Variance 276
  Simple Factorial ANOVA Define Range 277
  Simple Factorial ANOVA Options 277
  Additional Features Available with Command Syntax 280

16 Measuring Linear Association 281

Examining Relationships 281

The Correlation Coefficient 282
  Some Properties of the Correlation Coefficient 284
  Calculating Correlation Coefficients 284
  Hypothesis Tests about the Correlation Coefficient 285
  Correlation Matrices and Missing Data 286
  Choosing Pairwise Missing-Value Treatment 287
  The Rank Correlation Coefficient 287

How to Obtain Bivariate Correlations 288
  Bivariate Correlations Options 289
  Additional Features Available with Command Syntax 290

17 Partial Correlation Analysis 291

Computing a Partial Correlation Coefficient 291
   The Order of the Coefficient 292
   Tests of Statistical Significance 292
Detecting Spurious Relationships 292
Detecting Hidden Relationships 294
Interpreting the Results of Partial Correlation Analysis 295
How to Obtain Partial Correlations 295
   Partial Correlations Options 296
   Additional Features Available with Command Syntax 297

18 Multiple Linear Regression Analysis 299

Linear Regression 299
   Outliers 300
   Choosing a Regression Line 301
   From Samples to Populations 302
   Goodness of Fit 305
   Predicted Values and Their Standard Errors 308
   Searching for Violations of Assumptions 312
   Locating Outliers 318
   When Assumptions Appear to Be Violated 322
Multiple Regression Models 326
   Predictors of Beginning Salary 326
   Determining Important Variables 329
   Building a Model 331
   Procedures for Selecting Variables 334
   Checking for Violations of Assumptions 339
   Looking for Influential Points 341
   Measures of Collinearity 343
   Interpreting the Equation 345

How to Obtain a Linear Regression Analysis 346
   Linear Regression Statistics 347
   Linear Regression Plots 348
   Linear Regression Save New Variables 350
   Linear Regression Options 352
   Additional Features Available with Command Syntax 353

19 Distribution-Free or Nonparametric Tests 355

The Mann-Whitney Test 355
   Ranking the Data 356
   Calculating the Test 356
   Which Diet? 357
   Assumptions 358
Nonparametric Tests 358
   One-Sample Tests 358
   Tests for Two or More Independent Samples 364
How to Obtain the Chi-Square Test 367
   Chi-Square Test Options 369
   Additional Features Available with Command Syntax 370
How to Obtain the Binomial Test 370
   Binomial Test Options 371
   Additional Features Available with Command Syntax 372
How to Obtain the Runs Test 372
   Runs Test Options 373
   Additional Features Available with Command Syntax 374
How to Obtain the One-Sample Kolmogorov-Smirnov Test 374
   One-Sample Kolmogorov-Smirnov Options 376
   Additional Features Available with Command Syntax 376

How to Obtain Two-Independent-Samples Tests   377
  Two-Independent-Samples Define Groups   378
  Two-Independent-Samples Options   379
  Additional Features Available with Command Syntax   379

How to Obtain Tests for Several Independent Samples   379
  Several Independent Samples Define Range   381
  Several Independent Samples Options   381
  Additional Features Available with Command Syntax   382

How to Obtain Two-Related-Samples Tests   382
  Two-Related-Samples Options   384
  Additional Features Available with Command Syntax   385

How to Obtain Tests for Several Related Samples   385
  Several Related Samples Statistics   386

20 Listing Cases   387

How to Obtain Case Listings   387
  Additional Features Available with Command Syntax   389

21 Reporting Results   391

Basic Report Concepts   391
  Summary Reports   391
  Listing Reports   392
  Combined Reports   393
  Multiple Break Variables   394
  Grand Total Summary Statistics   394

Formatting Reports   395
  Titles and Footnotes   396
  Column Headings   396
  Displaying Value Labels   397

How to Obtain Listing Reports and Reports with Summaries in Rows   397
  Data Column Format   399
  Break Category Summary Statistics   400
  Break Spacing and Page Options   402
  Break Column Format   402
  Report Total Summary Statistics   403
  Report Options   403
  Report Layout   404
  Titles and Footers   405
  Additional Features Available with Command Syntax   406

22 Overview of the SPSS Chart Facility   407

How to Create and Modify a Chart   407
  Entering the Data   408
  Creating the Chart   409
  Modifying the Chart   411

Chart Carousel   419
  Chart Carousel Menus   419
  Chart Carousel Pushbuttons   420
  Saving Charts in the Chart Carousel   421

Chart Definition Global Options   421
  Titles, Subtitles, and Footnotes   422
  Missing Values   423
  Chart Templates   426

23 Bar, Line, Area, and Pie Charts   429

Chicago Uniform Crime Reports Data   429

Simple Charts   430

Clustered Bar and Multiple Line Charts   432

Stacked Bar and Area Charts   433

Variations on Bar, Line, and Area Charts   434
  100% Stacked Bar and Area Charts   434
  Hanging Bar Charts   435
  Drop-Line Charts   436
  Mixed Charts   436

How to Obtain Bar, Line, Area,
and Pie Charts   437
   Bar Charts   438
   Line Charts   448
   Area Charts   456
   Pie Charts   464

Transposed Charts   469
   Summary Functions   470

24 Boxplots   475

How to Obtain a Boxplot   477
   Defining Boxplots   479

25 Scatterplots and Histograms   483

A Simple Scatterplot   483
   Profits, Growth, and Compensation   485

Scatterplot Matrices   487
   Smoothing the Data   488

Plotting in Three Dimensions   488

How to Obtain a Scatterplot   490
   Defining Simple Scatterplots   491
   Defining Scatterplot Matrices   492
   Defining Overlay Scatterplots   494
   Defining 3-D Scatterplots   495

How to Obtain a Histogram   496

26 Modifying Charts   499

Exploring Data with the Chart Editor   499

Enhancing Charts for Presentation   501

Editing in a Chart Window   503
   Chart Menus   503
   Selecting Objects to Modify   504

Changing Chart Types (Gallery Menu)   506
   Additional Chart Types   506
   Changing Types   509

Modifying Chart Elements
(Chart Menu)   510
   Accessing Chart Options   511
   Bar/Line/Area Options   511
   Pie Options   514
   Boxplot Options   517
   Scatterplot Options: Simple and Matrix   518
   Overlay Scatterplot Options   523
   3-D Scatterplot Options   524
   Histogram Options   526
   Axis Characteristics   527
   Bar Spacing   540
   Adding or Changing Explanatory Text   541
   Adding Reference Lines   546
   Inner and Outer Frames   547

Selecting and Arranging Data (Series
Menu)   548
   Bar, Line, and Area Chart
   Displayed Data   549
   Pie Chart Displayed Data   550
   Simple Scatterplot Displayed Data   551
   Overlay Scatterplot Displayed Data   553
   Scatterplot Matrix Displayed Data   554
   3-D Scatterplot Displayed Data   554
   Histogram Displayed Data   555
   Transposing Data   555

Modifying Attributes (Attributes Menu)   556
   Palettes   557
   Exploding Pie Chart Slices   567
   Changing or Rotating the Axes   567

27 Printing   573

Printers   573

Printing a Syntax or Output File   573
   Text Printer Setup   574
   Determining the Correct Width and Length
   for Printed Output   575
   Using Page Headers to Format Printed
   Output Pages   575

Printing a Data File   575
  Options for Data Files   575
Printing a Chart File   576
  Chart Printer Setup   578
Font Mapping   579

28 Utilities   581

Command Index   581
Variable Information   582
Variable Sets   583
  Defining Variable Sets   583
  Using Variable Sets   585
File Information   585
Reordering Target Variable Lists   586
Stopping the SPSS Processor   586

29 Preferences   587

Preferences Dialog Boxes   587
  Session Journal   588
  Working Memory   590
  Opening a Syntax Window at Startup   590
  Transformation and Merge Options   590
  Display Order for Variable Lists   591
  Display Format for New Variables   591
  Graphics   591
  Custom Currency Formats   593
  Output   594
Using SPSS Graphical Characters   596
Saving Preferences   597
  Preferences File (.spssrc)   597
  Editing the Preferences File (.spssrc)   598
  SET Command Specifications   598
  Preferences and Profile (.profile.sps)   599
Multiple Sessions   599
  Preferences   599
  Journal File (spss.jnl)   599

30 Getting Help   601

The Help Menu   601
Help Text   603
  Hypertext Links   603
  Pushbuttons   603
The Help Window Menu   605
  Copying Help Text   605
  Annotating a Help Topic   605
  Marking Most Frequently Consulted Topics   606
SPSS Command Syntax Charts   607
Output Glossary   607

Appendix A
Command Syntax   609

A Few Useful Terms   609
Syntax Rules   609
  Batch Mode and Include Files   610
Commands Available Only with Syntax   611

Appendix B
Commands Not Available in SPSS for UNIX   613

Appendix C
Batch Processing   615

Running SPSS in Batch Mode   615
  Syntax Rules   615
  Output File   615
  Chart Files   616
Building a Command Syntax File   616
  Pasting Syntax from Dialog Boxes   616
  Editing Syntax in an Output File   617
  Editing Syntax in a Journal File   618

Appendix D
Keyboard Movement and Accelerator Keys 619

Menus 619

Dialog Boxes 619

Data Editor 620

Syntax and Output Windows 621

Chart Carousel 622

Chart Window 622

Window Control 622

Appendix E
Command Line Switches 623

Motif Graphical User Interface 623

Manager Mode 625

Prompted Mode 627

Batch Processing 627

Appendix F
Customizing the SPSS Resource File 629

The SPSS Resource File 629
  Window Size and Position 630
  Fonts 631
  Accelerator Keys 631
  Source Variable List Length 632
  Default Printer 632
  Colors 632
  Other Settings 632

Applications Resources Directory 633
  Setting the XAPPLRESDIR or XUSERFILESEARCHPATH Environment Variable 633
  Using the .Xdefaults File 633

Appendix G
Running SPSS through the Manager 635

SPSS Manager 635

Mini-Menus and Keyboard Shortcuts 636
  Choosing an Option from Mini-Menus 637
  Accelerator Keys 637

Edit Mode and Menu Mode 638
  Editing with the Manager 638
  Using Menus 641

Windows 645
  Input and Output Windows 645
  Files Window 646
  Variables Window 648

Online Help 649
  Manager Help 649
  Syntax Help 650
  Glossary Help 651

Other Functions 652

Status Line Messages 654

Running an SPSS Manager Session 655
  Beginning the Session 655
  Running SPSS Commands 656
  Running Commands 657
  Viewing Output 658
  Interrupting Commands that are Running 659
  Executing UNIX Commands during an SPSS Manager Session 659
  Ending an SPSS Session 659

Command and Output Files 660
  Opening Files 660
  Deleting Files 661
  Inserting from Files 661
  Saving Files 661
  Saving the Journal File 662

Appendix H
  Running an SPSS
  Prompted Session 663

  An SPSS Prompted Session 663

  Starting a Prompted Session 663
    Using an Automatic Profile 663

  Output Files 664

  Journal File 664

  SPSS Prompts 665

  Command Line Continuation 665

  Command Terminator 665

  Using UNIX Commands 666

  Interrupting a Prompted Session 666

  Ending a Prompted Session 666

Bibliography 667

Index 671

1 Overview

SPSS for UNIX, Release 5, provides a new Motif graphical user interface. This manual is a guide to using the SPSS Motif interface. You can also run SPSS with the character-based Manager or in a prompted interactive session, both of which require some knowledge of SPSS command syntax. For more information on the SPSS Manager, see Appendix G. For more information on prompted sessions, see Appendix H.

SPSS Motif Interface

The SPSS Motif interface provides a powerful statistical analysis and data management system in a graphical environment, using descriptive menus and simple dialog boxes to do most of the work for you. Most tasks can be accomplished simply by pointing and clicking the mouse.

In addition to the menu-driven, dialog-box interface, this release of SPSS offers several new features:

- **Data Editor.** A versatile spreadsheet-like system for defining, entering, editing, and displaying data.
- **High-resolution graphics.** High-resolution, full-color pie charts, bar charts, histograms, scatterplots, 3-D graphics, and more are now included as a standard feature in the SPSS Base system.
- **Chart Editor.** A highly visual, object-oriented facility for manipulating and customizing the many charts and graphs produced by SPSS.

Starting SPSS

To start an SPSS session:

● At the UNIX prompt (in an X window) type:

```
spss
```

If you want to use the same X window for other tasks, type:

```
spss &
```

② The first time you start an SPSS session, the Startup Preferences dialog box opens. Click on OK to accept the default settings. (See Chapter 29 for information on startup preferences.)

This opens the SPSS Data Editor window and an output window, as shown in Figure 1.1.

Figure 1.1   Data Editor and output windows

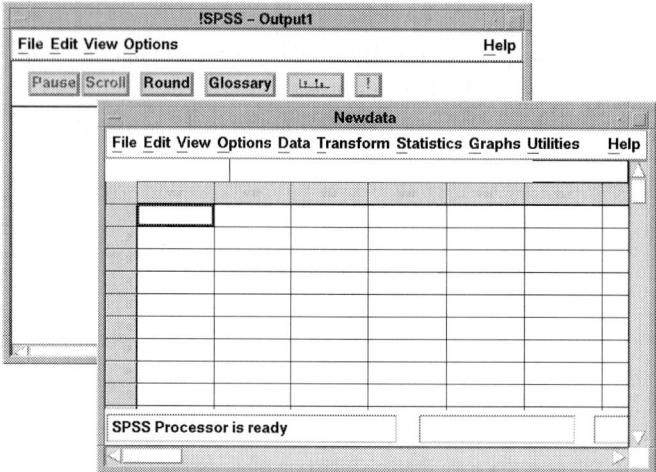

Note: If you iconize the Data Editor window before it is fully displayed on the screen, the SPSS startup process will "freeze" at that point and will not continue until you restore the Data Editor window. In general, you should avoid iconizing windows before they are fully displayed.

You can also begin a session with specific SPSS data, chart, output, or syntax files.

Data files. For data files in SPSS format, use the -data switch followed by the data file directory path and filename, as in:

```
spss -data /spss/data/bank.sav
```

The contents of the data file are displayed in the Data Editor window. You can omit the -data switch if the file has the extension *.sav*, as in:

```
spss /spss/data/bank.sav
```

Chart files. For SPSS chart files, use the -C (capital C) switch followed by the chart file directory path and filename, as in:

```
spss -C /spss/results/bank1.chart
```

The chart is displayed in a chart window. You can omit the -chart switch if the file has the extension *.cht*, as in:

```
spss /spss/results/bank1.cht
```

Output files. For SPSS output files, use the -O (capital O) switch followed by the output file directory path and filename, as in:

```
spss -O /spss/results/bank1.lst
```

The contents of the output file are displayed in an output window. You can omit the -O switch if the file has the extension *.lst*, as in:

```
spss /spss/results/bank1.lst
```

Syntax files. For SPSS syntax files, use the -S (capital S) switch followed by the syntax file directory path and filename, as in:

```
spss -S /spss/jobs/bank1.sps
```

The contents of the syntax file are displayed in a syntax window. You can omit the -S switch if the file has the extension *.sps*, as in:

```
spss /spss/jobs/bank1.sps
```

You can specify multiple chart, output, and syntax files on the command line (each file must be preceded by the appropriate switch). You can specify only one data file.

Command line switches are also available for controlling mode of operation, fonts used on menus and in dialog boxes, and colors used in windows. See Appendix E for more information on command line switches.

SPSS Windows

SPSS uses several different windows:

Data Editor window. This window displays the contents of the working data file. You can create new data files or modify existing ones with the Data Editor. The Data Editor window opens automatically when you start an SPSS session.

Output window. As you make selections from the menus and dialog boxes, relevant system information and the text-based results of your work—such as descriptive statistics, crosstabulations, or correlation matrices—appear in an output window. You can edit this output and save it for later use. An output window opens automatically when you start an SPSS session. You can also open additional output windows.

Chart Carousel window. All of the charts and graphs produced in your SPSS session are accessed through the Chart Carousel, which opens automatically the first time you generate a chart during the session. If you produce multiple charts, you can view them in the Chart Carousel before modifying, saving, or discarding them.

Chart window. You can modify and save high-resolution charts and plots in chart windows. You can change the colors, select different type fonts or sizes, switch the horizontal and vertical axes, rotate 3-D scatterplots, and even change the chart type.

Syntax window. You can paste your dialog box choices into a syntax window, where your selections appear in the form of command syntax. You can then edit the command syntax to utilize special features of SPSS not available through dialog boxes. You can save these commands in a file for use in subsequent SPSS sessions. You can open multiple syntax windows.

Designated versus Active Window

If you have more than one open output window, the text-based results of your work are routed to the **designated** output window. If you have more than one open syntax window, command syntax is pasted into the designated syntax window. The designated windows are indicated by an exclamation point (!) before the word Syntax or Output on the title bar. You can change the designated windows at any time (see "Icon Bars" on p. 6).

The designated window should not be confused with the **active** window, which is the currently selected window. The active window has a different border and title bar color or shade than the other windows. If you have overlapping windows, the active window usually appears in the foreground. If you open a new syntax or output window, that window automatically becomes the active window; but it does not become the designated window until you instruct SPSS to make it the designated window.

Moving between Windows

You can move between SPSS windows simply by moving the mouse pointer from one window to another (and clicking the left mouse button in the window if you are using explicit focus policy). If you have a lot of open windows, however, it may sometimes be hard to find the window you want. SPSS provides an easy alternative for going directly to the window you want. The View menu in every SPSS window displays a list of all open SPSS windows. Just select Raise Document Window from the View menu, pick the window (or document filename) from the list, and you go directly to that window.

Menus

The SPSS Motif interface is **menu-driven**. Most of the features are accessed by making selections from the menus. Each window has its own set of menus. The following menus appear on all windows:

File. Use the File menu to open, close, save, and print files.

Edit. Use the Edit menu to cut, copy, and paste data and text.

View. Use the View menus to turn grid lines on and off in the Data Editor, display value labels instead of values, and make other changes that alter the display of information in a window without affecting the contents. You can also use the View menu to move to any open SPSS window.

Options. Use the Options menu to display or hide the status bar and icon bars, change the designated syntax or output window, or change Preferences settings (see Chapter 29).

Help. This opens a hypertext help window containing information on how to use the many features of SPSS. Context-sensitive help is also available through the dialog boxes.

Data Editor Menus

The Data Editor window contains the menus that you use to analyze and modify data and create charts and plots.

Data. Use the Data menu to make global changes to SPSS data files, such as merging files, transposing variables and cases, or creating subsets of cases for analysis. These changes are only temporary unless you save the file after making the changes.

Transform. Use the Transform menu to make changes to selected variables in the data file and to compute new variables based on the values of existing ones. These changes are only temporary unless you save the file after making the changes.

Statistics. Use the Statistics menu to select the various statistical procedures you want to use, such as crosstabulation, analysis of variance, correlation, and linear regression.

Graphs. Use the Graphs menu to create bar charts, pie charts, histograms, scatterplots, and other full-color, high-resolution graphs. Some statistical procedures also generate graphs. All graphs can be customized with the Chart Editor.

Utilities. Use the Utilities menu to display information on the contents of SPSS data files, open an index of SPSS commands, or define subsets of variables to use in dialog boxes.

Status Bar

At the bottom of the Data Editor window there is a **status bar** that indicates the current status of the SPSS processor. If the processor is running a command, it displays the command name and a case counter indicating the current case number being processed. When you first begin an SPSS session, the status bar displays the message *Starting SPSS Processor*. When SPSS is ready, the message changes to *SPSS Processor is ready*. The status bar also provides the following information:

- **Command status.** For each procedure or command you run, a case counter indicates the number of cases processed so far. For statistical procedures that require iterative processing, the number of iterations is displayed.
- **Filter status.** If you have selected a random sample or a subset of cases for analysis, the message *Filter on* indicates that some type of case filtering is currently in effect and that not all cases in the data file are included in the analysis.
- **Weight status.** The message *Weight on* indicates that a weight variable is being used to weight cases for analysis.
- **Split File status.** The message *Split File on* indicates that the data file has been split into separate groups for analysis, based on the values of one or more grouping variables.

Turning the Status Bar Off and On

By default, the status bar is on. To turn the status bar off or on, select Status Bar from the Data Editor window's Options menu.

Icon Bars

At the top of the output, syntax, and chart windows there is an **icon bar** that provides quick, easy access to the special features of these windows.

Output Window Icon Bar

Pause. Pauses the output display. By default, the display of output scrolls through the output window as it is generated. You can pause the display at any point.

Scroll. Scrolls the output display as it is generated.

Round. Rounds numbers in the highlighted area.

Glossary. Opens the glossary of SPSS terms.

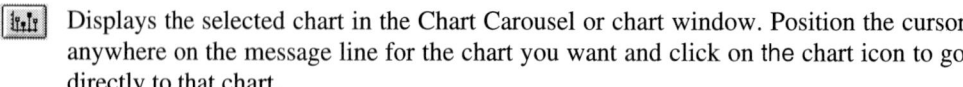 Displays the selected chart in the Chart Carousel or chart window. Position the cursor anywhere on the message line for the chart you want and click on the chart icon to go directly to that chart.

Sends output results to this output window (if you have multiple output windows open). This setting is disabled in the designated output window.

Syntax Window Icon Bar

Run. Runs the highlighted SPSS commands or the command at the current cursor location if there isn't a highlighted block of commands.

Syntax. Opens a Help window containing the SPSS command syntax for the current command line in the syntax window.

 Pastes command syntax generated by dialog box choices to this syntax window (if you have multiple syntax windows open). This setting is disabled in the designated syntax window.

Chart Window Icon Bar

Many of the features for viewing and editing charts and plots can be accessed through the pushbuttons on the chart window icon bar. (For more information, see Chapter 26.)

Turning Icon Bars Off and On

By default, icon bars are on. To turn a window's icon bar off or on, click on Icon Bar on the window's Options menu.

Statistical Analysis with the Dialog Box Interface

There are three basic steps in performing statistical analysis with SPSS:

- Choose a data file. This can be a file you create with the Data Editor, a previously defined SPSS data file, a database file, or a text file.
- Choose a statistical procedure from the menus.
- Choose the variables to include in the analysis and any additional parameters from the dialog boxes.

Before You Start

Before you start the following tutorial, you need to copy the SPSS data file, *bank.sav*, into your home directory (or into one of your sub-directories). To copy this file into your directory:

① If you haven't already started SPSS, at the UNIX prompt type:

```
spss
```

or

```
spss &
```

This should be entered in all lowercase letters. Do not use any capital letters.

② Click on File on the Data Editor menu bar.

③ Click on New on the File menu.

④ Click on Syntax on the New submenu. This opens a new syntax window.

⑤ In the syntax window, type the following SPSS command:

`host cp $SPSS_ROOT/data/bank.sav [your directory path].`

⑥ Click on Run on the syntax window icon bar or press Ctrl-A.

For example,

`host cp $SPSS_ROOT/data/bank.sav /dan/quayle/potatoe.`

copies the file into the */dan/quayle/potatoe* directory. Pay close attention to case because UNIX filenames are case-sensitive, and make sure to put a period (.) at the end of the SPSS command.

⑦ Click on File on the syntax window icon bar.

⑧ Click on Close to close the syntax window.

⑨ Click on Discard when SPSS asks if you want to save the changes to the syntax window.

Choosing a Data File

To select a data file for analysis:

① Click on File on the Data Editor menu bar.

② Click on Open on the File menu.

③ Click on Data on the Open submenu. This opens the Open Data File dialog box, as shown in Figure 1.2.

Figure 1.2 Open Data File dialog box

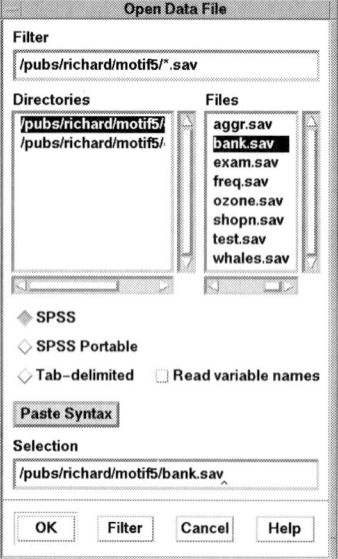

Overview   9

By default, all files in the current directory with the extension *.sav* are displayed on the Files list. If you copied the SPSS data file *bank.sav* into the same directory from which you started SPSS, it should appear on the Files list.

④ If *bank.sav* does not appear on the Files list, enter the correct directory path followed by /*.sav in the Filter text box and then click on Filter.

⑤ Click on the file *bank.sav* on the Files list or type the filename in the Selection text box.

⑥ Click on OK.

The contents of the data file are displayed in the Data Editor window, as shown in Figure 1.3.

Figure 1.3   Data file displayed in Data Editor

	id	salbeg	sex	time	age	salnow	edlevel	work	jobcat
1	628	8400	0	81	28.50	16080	16	.25	4
2	630	24000	0	73	40.33	41400	16	12.50	5
3	632	10200	0	83	31.08	21960	15	4.08	5
4	633	8700	0	93	31.17	19200	16	1.83	4
5	635	17400	0	83	41.92	28350	19	13.00	5
6	637	12996	0	80	29.50	27250	18	2.42	4
7	641	6900	0	79	28.00	16080	15	3.17	1
8	649	5400	0	67	28.75	14100	15	.50	1
9	650	5040	0	96	27.42	12420	15	1.17	1
10	652	6300	0	77	52.92	12300	12	26.42	3

Choosing a Statistical Procedure

The Statistics menu, shown in Figure 1.4, contains a list of general statistical categories. Each of these is followed by an arrow (▶), which indicates that there is another menu level. The individual statistical procedures are listed at this submenu level.

For example, to produce frequency tables:

① Click on Statistics on the Data Editor menu bar.

② Click on Summarize ▶ on the Statistics menu.

③ Click on Frequencies... on the Summarize submenu.

Figure 1.4 Statistics menu and Summarize submenu

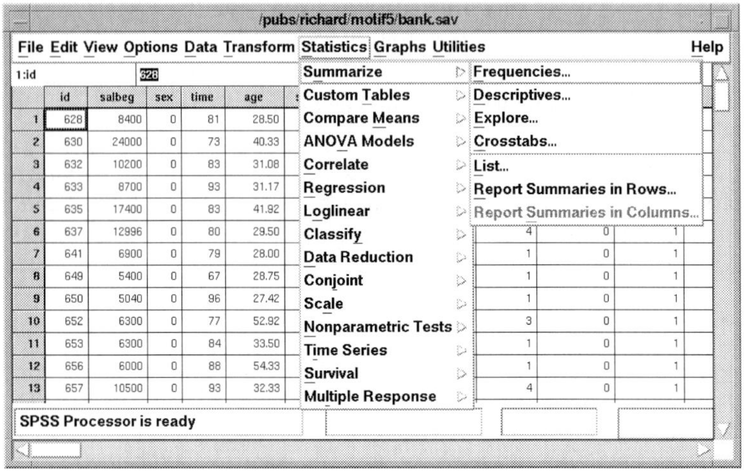

Throughout the rest of this book, we'll use the following shorthand method to indicate menu selections:

Statistics
 Summarize ▶
  Frequencies...

Main Dialog Box

When you choose a statistical procedure from the menus, a dialog box appears on the screen. Figure 1.5 shows the Frequencies dialog box.

Figure 1.5 Frequencies main dialog box

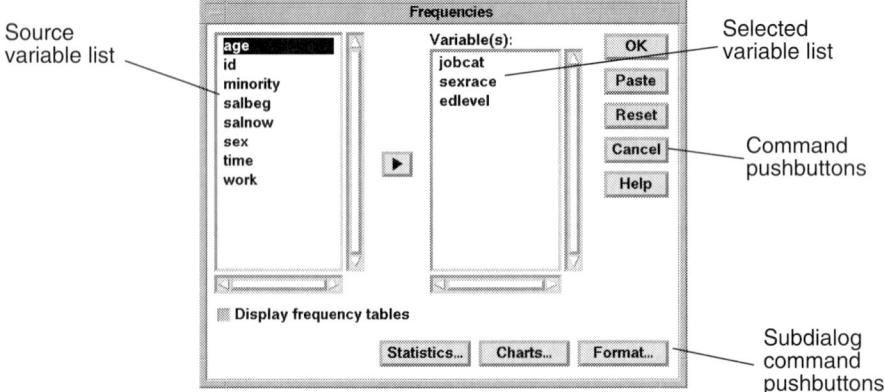

The main dialog box for each statistical procedure has three basic components:

Source variable list. A list of variables in the data file.

Selected variable list(s). One or more lists indicating the variables you have chosen for the analysis, such as dependent and independent variable lists. This is sometimes referred to as the target variable list.

Command pushbuttons. Action buttons that tell SPSS to do something, such as run the procedure, get help, or go to a subdialog box for additional specifications.

Source Variable List

The source variable list contains any variables in the data file that can be used by that procedure. There are three basic types of variables:

- **Numeric variables.** This includes any variables that use a numeric coding scheme, even if the underlying "real" values are not numeric. Date and time format variables are also considered numeric because they are stored internally as a number of seconds.
- **Short string variables.** Alphanumeric string values up to eight characters long. These are identified with a "less than" symbol (<).
- **Long string variables.** Alphanumeric string values more than eight characters long. These are identified with a "greater than" symbol (>).

Command Pushbuttons

There is a column of pushbuttons on the right side of the dialog box (see Figure 1.5). These are often referred to as **command** or **action pushbuttons** because they tell the system to do something immediately, such as run a procedure or get help. There are five standard command pushbuttons in the main dialog box:

OK. Runs the procedure. After you select your variables and choose any additional specifications, click on OK to run the procedure. This also closes the dialog box.

Paste. Generates command syntax from the dialog box selections and pastes the syntax into a syntax window. You can then customize the commands with additional SPSS features not available from dialog boxes.

Reset. Deselects any variables on the selected variable list(s) and resets all specifications in the dialog box and any subdialog boxes to the default state.

Cancel. Cancels any changes in the dialog box settings since the last time it was opened and closes the dialog box. Within an SPSS session, dialog box settings are persistent. A dialog box retains your last set of specifications until you override them. (See "Persistence of Settings" on p. 17.)

Help. Context-sensitive help. This takes you to a hypertext help window that contains information about the current dialog box.

Selecting Variables

To select a single variable, you simply highlight it on the source variable list and click on the ▶ button next to the selected variable list box. If there is only one selected variable list (as in the Frequencies dialog box), you can double-click individual variables to move them from the source list to the selected list.

You can also select multiple variables:

- To highlight multiple variables that are grouped together on the variable list, as in Figure 1.6, use the click-and-drag technique. Alternatively, you can click on the first one and then shift-click on the last one in the group.

- To highlight multiple variables that are not grouped together on the variable list, as in Figure 1.7, use the ctrl-click method. Click on the first variable, then ctrl-click on the next variable, and so on.

For example:

① Click on the variable *jobcat* on the source variable list. It is now highlighted.

② Click on the ▶ pushbutton. The variable *jobcat* moves from the source variable list to the selected variable list labeled Variable(s).

③ Click on variable *salbeg* on the source variable list, hold down the mouse button and drag the pointer down to *time*. Alternatively, click on *salbeg* and then shift-click on *time*. All the variables from *salbeg* to *time* are highlighted, as in Figure 1.6.

④ Click on the ▶ pushbutton. All the highlighted variables move to the Variable(s) list.

⑤ Click on *edlevel* on the source variable list. Then ctrl-click on *work*. The two variables are highlighted without affecting the variables between them, as in Figure 1.7.

⑥ Click on the ▶ pushbutton. The two variables move to the Variable(s) list.

Figure 1.6 Selecting a group of variables with shift-click or click-and-drag

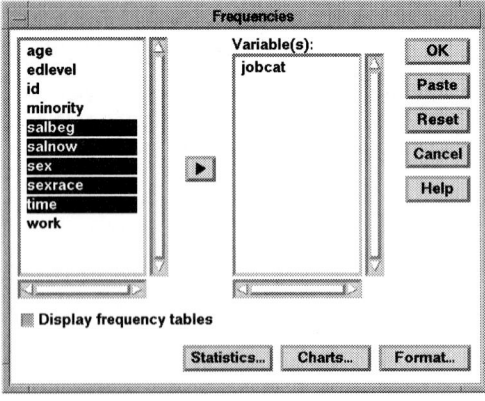

Figure 1.7 Selecting noncontiguous multiple variables with ctrl-click

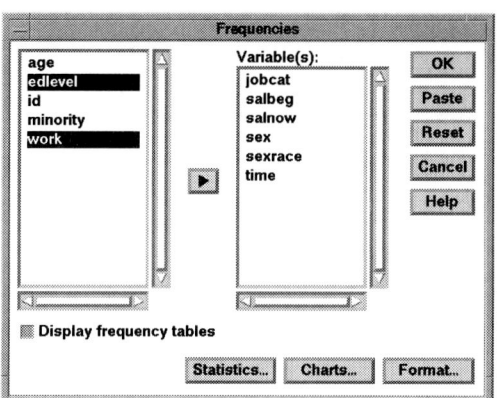

Deselecting Variables

You can also deselect variables, removing them from the selected list and putting them back on the source list. Deselecting variables works just like selecting them. When you highlight variables on the selected variable list, the ▶ pushbutton changes direction, pointing back to the source variable list.

Running a Procedure

In many instances, all you need to do to run a statistical procedure is select your variables and click on OK. The results then appear in the output window. For example:

❶ Click on Reset in the Frequencies dialog box to clear anything you have entered.

❷ Click on the variable *jobcat* on the source variable list. The variable is now highlighted.

❸ Click on the ▶ pushbutton. The variable moves to the Variable(s) list.

❹ Click on OK. This runs the procedure and closes the dialog box. The results are displayed in the output window, as shown in Figure 1.8.

Figure 1.8   Results displayed in the output window

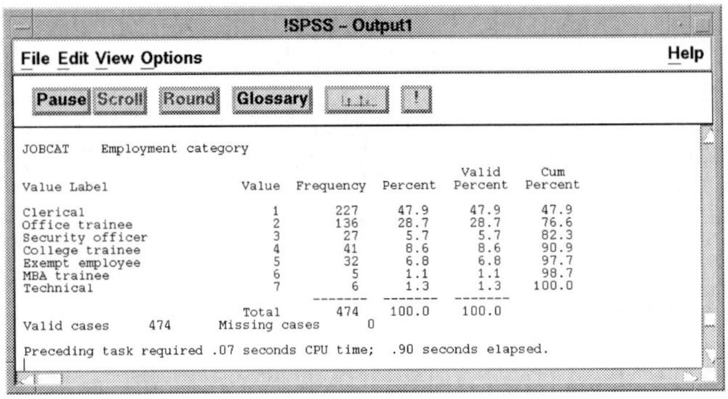

```
                            !SPSS - Output1
 File Edit View Options                                          Help
 Pause Scroll Round Glossary

 JOBCAT     Employment category
                                              Valid     Cum
 Value Label           Value  Frequency Percent Percent Percent
 Clerical                1      227     47.9    47.9    47.9
 Office trainee          2      136     28.7    28.7    76.6
 Security officer        3       27      5.7     5.7    82.3
 College trainee         4       41      8.6     8.6    90.9
 Exempt employee         5       32      6.8     6.8    97.7
 MBA trainee             6        5      1.1     1.1    98.7
 Technical               7        6      1.3     1.3   100.0
                              -------  ------  ------
                       Total    474    100.0   100.0
 Valid cases     474  Missing cases     0

 Preceding task required .07 seconds CPU time;  .90 seconds elapsed.
```

You can use the scroll bars to view portions of the output not visible in the window, or you can resize the window to show more of the output.

Subdialog Boxes

Since most SPSS procedures provide a great deal of flexibility, not all of the possible choices can be contained in a single dialog box. The main dialog box usually contains the minimum information required to run a procedure. Additional specifications are made in subdialog boxes.

In the main dialog box, pushbuttons with an ellipsis (…) after the name indicate a subdialog box. For example, the Frequencies main dialog box has three associated subdialog boxes: Statistics, Charts, and Format.

① Open the Frequencies dialog box again.

② Click on Statistics… in the Frequencies dialog box. This opens the Frequencies Statistics subdialog box, as shown in Figure 1.9.

Figure 1.9 Subdialog box with check buttons

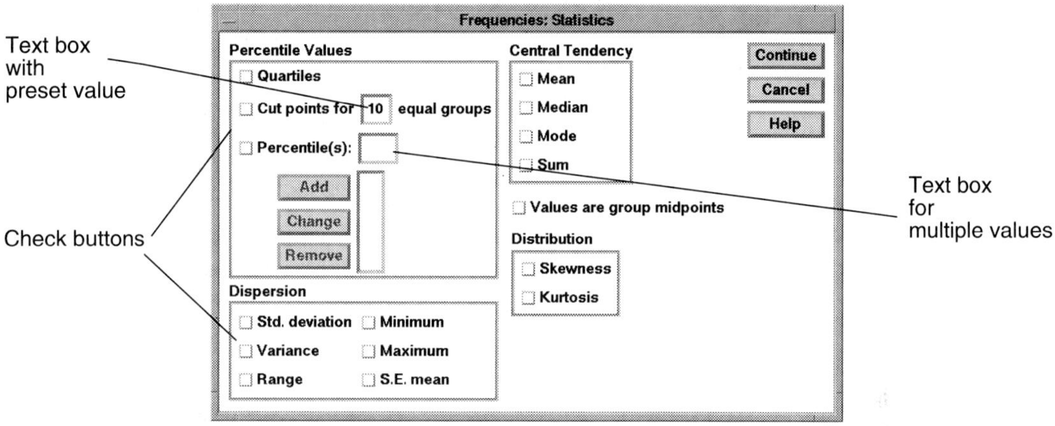

Text box with preset value — *Check buttons* — *Text box for multiple values*

(Frequencies: Statistics dialog showing Percentile Values [Quartiles, Cut points for 10 equal groups, Percentile(s)], Central Tendency [Mean, Median, Mode, Sum], Dispersion [Std. deviation, Variance, Range, Minimum, Maximum, S.E. mean], Distribution [Skewness, Kurtosis], Values are group midpoints, with Add/Change/Remove and Continue/Cancel/Help buttons.)

Subdialog Box Command Pushbuttons

The subdialog box contains three command pushbuttons:

Continue. Saves any changes to the settings and returns to the main dialog box.

Cancel. Ignores any changes, restores the previous settings, and returns to the main dialog box.

Help. Provides context-sensitive help for the subdialog box.

Multiple Selections with Check Buttons

In the Frequencies Statistics subdialog box, there is a variety of summary statistics available. The **check buttons** next to each one indicate that you can choose one or more of these statistics in any combination. For convenience, they are grouped by type of summary measure (central tendency, dispersion), but there is no restriction on how many you can choose from each group.

To select an item, simply click on the check button next to it. You deselect items the same way. For example:

① Click on Mean, Median, and Mode in the Central Tendency group.

② Click on Mode again to deselect it.

User-Defined Specifications with Text Boxes

Sometimes there are **text boxes** associated with selections that provide additional control over the specifications. There are three basic types of text boxes:

Preset text boxes. Some text boxes have a preset default value already entered. If you choose the item without entering a new value in the text box, the default value is used.

Blank text boxes. There is no default setting. If you choose an item with an associated blank text box, you must enter a value (or deselect the item) before you can continue.

Multiple-entry text boxes. If an item can have multiple values (such as percentile specifications), the text box is accompanied by a list box and a group of pushbuttons. Enter each value in the text box, click on Add, and it appears in the list box. You can also change and delete values. For example:

1. Click on Percentile(s) in the Frequencies Statistics subdialog box. A flashing cursor appears in the text box.
2. Type in the value 25 and click on Add. The value appears in the list box.
3. Type in the value 40 in the text box and click on Add. The value is added to the list.
4. Type in the value 75 in the text box and click on Add. The value is added to the list.
5. Click on the value 40 on the list. The value is highlighted on the list, and it also appears in the Percentiles text box.
6. Highlight the entire value in the text box, type in the value 50, and click on Change. The new value replaces the old one on the list.
7. Click on the value 75 on the list. The value is highlighted on the list.
8. Click on Remove. The value is deleted from the list.
9. Click on Continue to save the new settings and return to the main dialog box.

Single Selections with Radio Buttons

Some selections are mutually exclusive and you can choose only one from a list of alternatives. **Radio buttons** next to each choice in a group, as in Figure 1.10, indicate that you can choose only one item in the group. (Radio buttons are diamond-shaped, while check buttons are square.)

Figure 1.10 Subdialog box with radio buttons

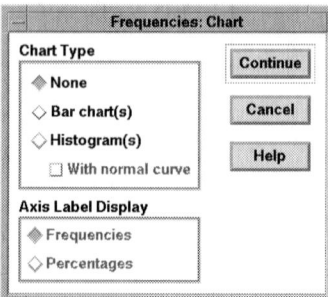

In a radio button group, there is always a default selection. To change the selected alternative, you simply click on a different radio button in the group. For example:

① Click on Charts... in the Frequencies dialog box. This opens the Frequencies Charts subdialog box, as shown in Figure 1.10.

② Click on the Bar chart(s) radio button in the Chart Type group. This selection replaces the default selection of None.

③ Click on Continue to save the new setting and return to the Frequencies dialog box.

④ Click on Cancel to close the Frequencies dialog box without running the procedure.

Single Selection with Drop-down Option Menus

In some dialog boxes, drop-down **option menus** are used instead of radio buttons for single selections from a list of alternatives. The current selection appears in a box with a small rectangular icon next to it, as shown in Figure 1.11. Click on the box to open the drop-down option menu and change the selection.

Figure 1.11 Single selection from a drop-down option menu (Linear Regression dialog box)

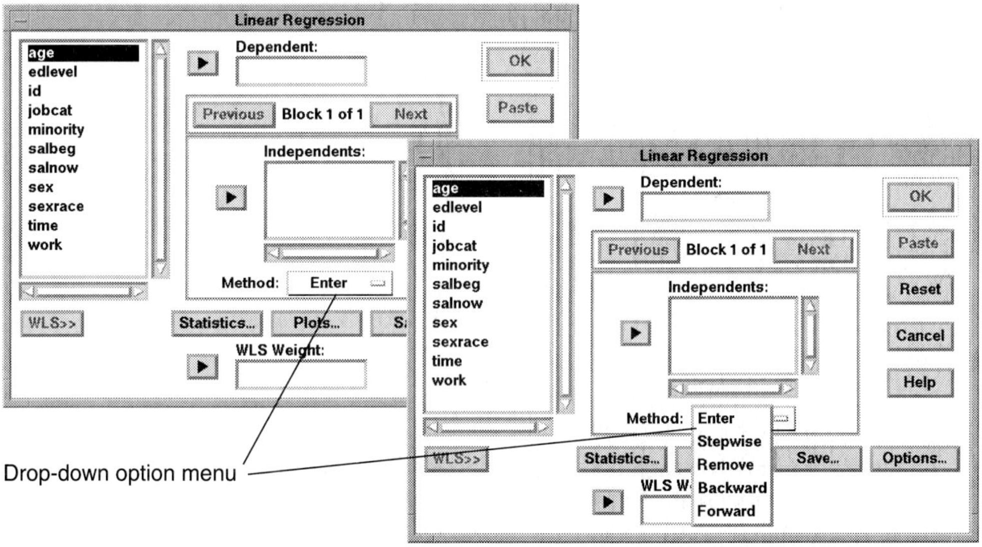

Drop-down option menu

Persistence of Settings

You may have noticed that the variable *jobcat* was still selected when you reopened the dialog box after running the procedure. That's because dialog box settings are **persistent** within an SPSS session. Once you click on OK or Paste, the current dialog and subdialog selections are saved. The next time you open that dialog box, those are the settings in effect.

At the subdialog box level, any changes you make are temporarily saved when you click on Continue. If, however, you then click on Cancel in the main dialog box, the subdialog selections revert to their former settings. As with the main dialog box, the subdialog box selections are persistent only after you click on OK or Paste.

The Reset button always returns all dialog and subdialog settings to the default state. You cannot undo this action. (The Cancel button has no effect on Reset.)

Dialog box settings are not persistent for different data files in the same SPSS session. If you make dialog box selections using one data file and then open a different data file, all dialog boxes are reset to the default state with no selected variables.

Order of Operations

For most procedures, you can make your dialog box selections in virtually any order. You can change the selected variable list (or any other setting) in the main dialog box after you make selections in the subdialog boxes, and you can go to subdialog boxes in any sequence. You can even make subdialog box selections before you choose any variables for analysis.

Data Editor

The Data Editor provides a convenient spreadsheet-like facility for entering, editing, and displaying the contents of your data file.

The Data Editor opens automatically when you start an SPSS session. If there isn't an open data file, you can use the Data Editor to create one. If there is an open data file, you can use the Data Editor to change data values and add or delete cases and variables.

The Data Editor has many similarities to a spreadsheet program, but there are several important distinctions:

- Cases are represented in rows.
- Variables are represented in columns.
- There are no "empty" cells within the boundaries of the data file. For numeric variables, blank cells are converted to the system-missing value (represented by a period). For string variables, a blank is considered a valid value.

Entering Data

Basic data entry in the Data Editor is simple:

① Click on the Data Editor title bar to make it the active window. (You may have to move the output window first.) The contents of the data file (*bank.sav*) are displayed. A heavy border appears around the currently selected cell (this should be the first cell in the Data Editor—row 1, column 1).

❷ Use the → key to move the cursor to the first empty column (the column to the right of the variable *sexrace*). Empty columns with the dimmed title *var* indicate **potential variables**.

❸ Beginning with the first data cell (below the variable name) in the column, type the following:

123.4 (⏎Enter)

123.45 (⏎Enter)

123.456 (⏎Enter)

123 (⏎Enter)

As you type, the value appears in the cell editor at the top of the Data Editor window. Each time you press (⏎Enter), the value is entered in the cell and you move down to the next row. The values appear in the default numeric format, with two decimal places. Thus, 123.456 is displayed as 123.46, but the complete value is stored internally and used in any calculations.

By entering data in the column, you automatically create a variable, and SPSS gives it the default variable name *var00001*. The variable name at the top of the column is no longer dimmed, indicating that it is now a real variable rather than a potential one. Since there are no "empty" cells within the boundaries of the data file, SPSS supplies the system-missing value (represented by a period) for the new variable for all the remaining cases in the data file.

❹ Select the first cell in the next column (the next potential variable). You can use the mouse to click on the cell or use the arrow keys on the keyboard to move to the cell. (Make sure the selected cell is in row 1.)

❺ Type

223.4 (⏎Enter)

By entering a value in the column, you automatically create a new variable with the default name *var00002*. Once again, SPSS supplies the system-missing value to all the remaining cases.

❻ Select the first cell in the next column (the next potential variable). You can use the mouse to click on the cell or use the arrow keys on the keyboard to move to the cell.

❼ Type

323.4 (⏎Enter)

SPSS automatically creates another new variable, *var00003*, and assigns the system-missing value to the remaining cases. At this point, the Data Editor window should look like Figure 1.12.

Figure 1.12 Data Editor window with missing data

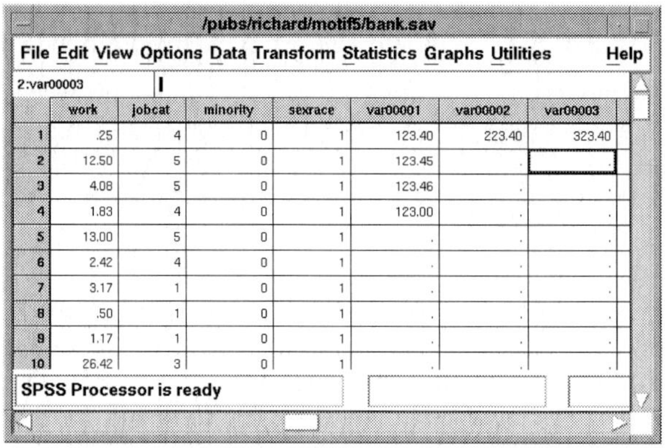
/pubs/richard/motif5/bank.sav
File Edit View Options Data Transform Statistics Graphs Utilities Help
2:var00003
work jobcat minority sexrace var00001 var00002 var00003
1 .25 4 0 1 123.40 223.40 323.40
2 12.50 5 0 1 123.45 . .
3 4.08 5 0 1 123.46 . .
4 1.83 4 0 1 123.00 . .
5 13.00 5 0 1 . . .
6 2.42 4 0 1 . . .
7 3.17 1 0 1 . . .
8 .50 1 0 1 . . .
9 1.17 1 0 1 . . .
10 26.42 3 0 1 . . .
SPSS Processor is ready

Editing Data

You can change, delete, copy, and move data values in the Data Editor.

1. In the column for the new variable *var00001*, click on the second cell (row 2) or use the arrow keys to move to the cell. The highlighted value appears in the cell editor at the top of the Data Editor.

2. Type

   `234.56` [↵Enter]

   The new value of 234.56 replaces the old value of 123.45.

3. Select the first cell (row 1) for the variable *var00001* again. If you use the mouse, click on the cell. If you use the keyboard, use the arrow keys to move to the cell.

4. Select the first four values for the variable. If you use the mouse, click and drag to case 4 (row 4) in the same column. If you use the keyboard, press and hold the [⇧Shift] key and use the [↓] key to move down to the fourth row. The first four values in the column are highlighted, indicating that they are selected.

5. From the menus choose:

   Edit
    Copy

6. Select the first cell for variable *var00002*.

⑦ From the menus choose:

Edit
  Paste

The four values for variable *var00001* are duplicated in the column for *var00002*.

⑧ Select the fourth cell in the column for *var00002* (row 4). This cell should contain the value 123.00.

⑨ From the menus choose:

Edit
  Copy

⑩ Select the first four cells for *var00003*.

⑪ From the menus choose:

Edit
  Paste

The value 123.00 is duplicated in all four cells for variable *var00003*, and the Data Editor window should look like Figure 1.13.

Figure 1.13 Data Editor window with copied data

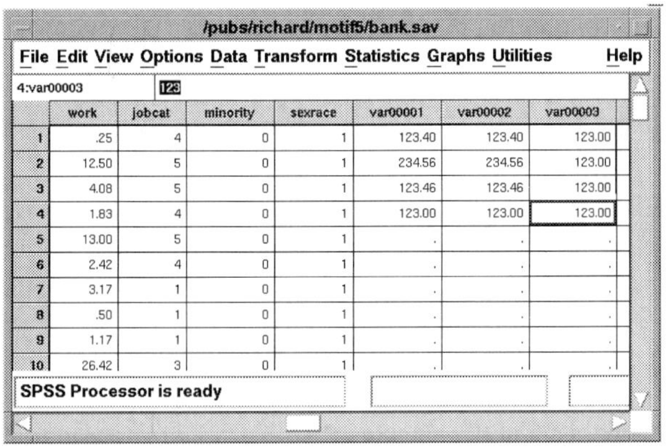

	work	jobcat	minority	sexrace	var00001	var00002	var00003
1	.25	4	0	1	123.40	123.40	123.00
2	12.50	5	0	1	234.56	234.56	123.00
3	4.08	5	0	1	123.46	123.46	123.00
4	1.83	4	0	1	123.00	123.00	123.00
5	13.00	5	0	1	.	.	.
6	2.42	4	0	1	.	.	.
7	3.17	1	0	1	.	.	.
8	.50	1	0	1	.	.	.
9	1.17	1	0	1	.	.	.
10	26.42	3	0	1	.	.	.

For a complete discussion of the Data Editor, see Chapter 3.

Creating and Editing Charts

If you run a procedure that produces charts or graphs, SPSS displays the results in the Chart Carousel. You can then select the chart and edit it in a chart window.

① Open the Frequencies dialog box again.

② Click on Reset to clear any previous settings.

③ Click on the variable *jobcat* on the source variable list and click on the ▶ pushbutton to move it to the Variable(s) list.
④ Click on Charts... to open the Frequency Charts subdialog box.
⑤ Click on Bar Chart(s).
⑥ Click on Continue or press ⏎Enter to save the new setting and return to the Frequencies dialog box.
⑦ Click on the Display frequency tables check button in the Frequencies dialog box to deselect this default setting and suppress the display of frequency tables.
⑧ Click on OK or press ⏎Enter to run the Frequencies procedure. The bar chart is displayed in the Chart Carousel, as shown in Figure 1.14, which opens automatically.

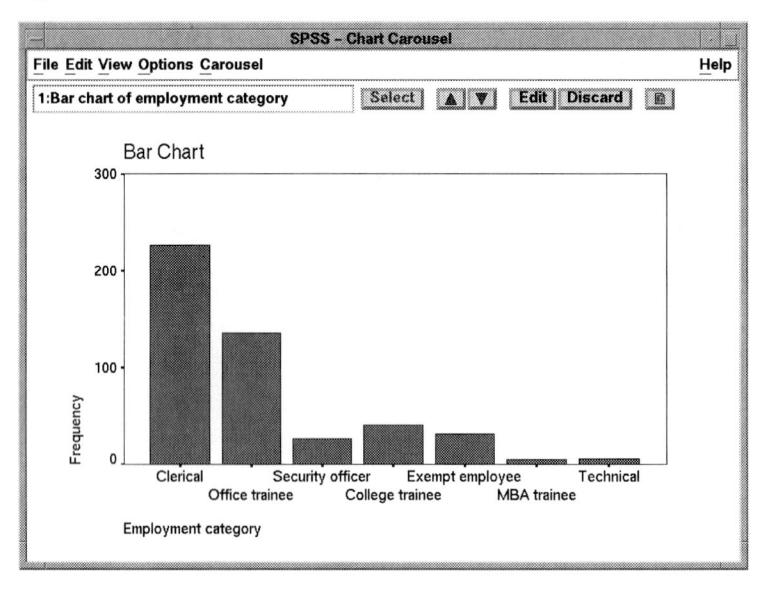

Figure 1.14 Chart Carousel

⑨ Click on Edit on the Chart Carousel icon bar or press Ctrl-E. The chart is displayed in a chart window, as shown in Figure 1.15.

Figure 1.15 Chart window

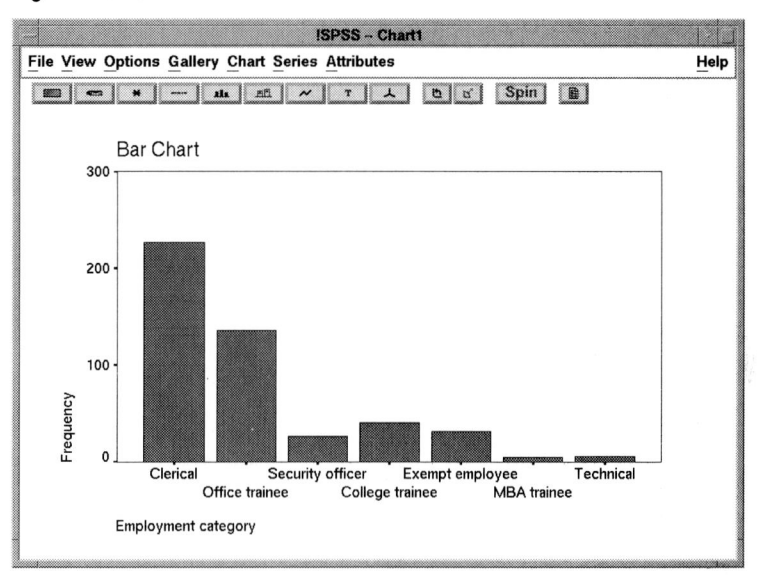

⑩ From the menus choose:

Attributes
  Bar Style...

This opens the Bar Styles dialog box, as shown in Figure 1.16.

Figure 1.16 Bar Styles dialog box

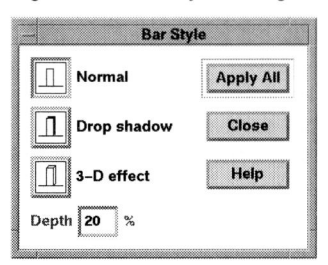

⑪ Click on 3-D effect in the Bar Styles dialog box.
⑫ Type 40 in the Depth text box.

⑬ Click on Apply All or press ⏎Enter and then click on Close in the Bar Styles dialog box. The chart now looks like Figure 1.17.

Figure 1.17 Bar chart with 3-D effects

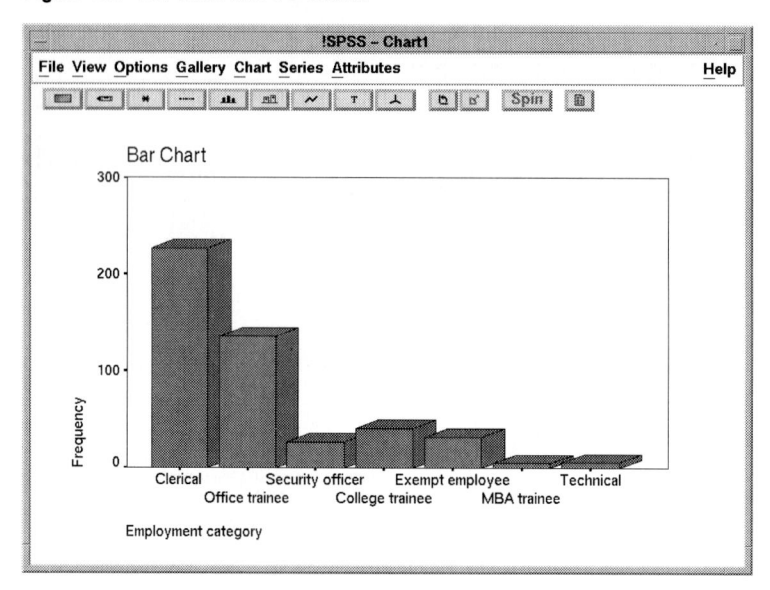

For more information on creating and editing charts and plots, see Chapter 22 through Chapter 26.

Pasting and Editing Command Syntax

The dialog box interface is designed to handle most of the capabilities of SPSS. Beneath the dialog boxes, there is a command language that you can use to access additional features and customize your analysis.

The SPSS command language consists of descriptive and usually self-explanatory commands. For example, the command to obtain frequency tables is FREQUENCIES.

After you make your dialog box selections, you can paste the underlying command syntax into a syntax window. You can then edit the resulting text like any text file and run the modified commands.

- Use the Paste pushbutton in the main dialog box to paste the command syntax into a syntax window.
- Use the Run pushbutton on the icon bar at the top of the syntax window to run the modified commands.

For example:

① Open the Frequencies dialog box again.

② Click on Reset to clear any previous settings.

③ Click on the variable *jobcat* on the source variable list and click on the ▶ pushbutton to move it to the Variable(s) list.

④ Click on Paste.

If you don't have an open syntax window, one opens automatically. The FREQUENCIES command syntax appears in the syntax window, as in Figure 1.18.

Figure 1.18 Command syntax pasted into a syntax window

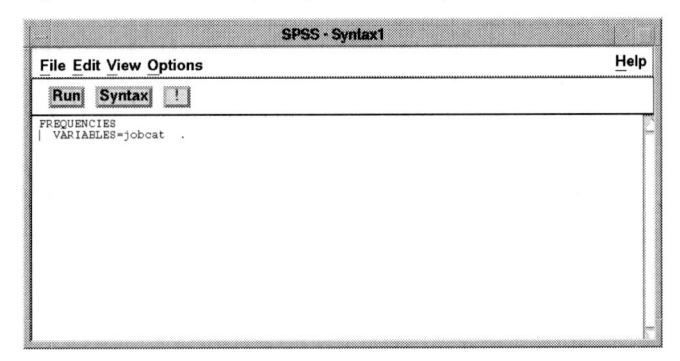

```
SPSS - Syntax1
File Edit View Options                                    Help
Run  Syntax  !
FREQUENCIES
  VARIABLES=jobcat  .
```

⑤ Using the mouse or the arrow keys, position the blinking cursor between the word *jobcat* and the period at the end of the second line.

⑥ Type in

`(5, 7)`

This indicates a value range for the frequency table, a specification not available in the dialog boxes. The entire command should now look like this:

```
FREQUENCIES
  VARIABLES = jobcat (5, 7).
```

⑦ Click on the Run pushbutton on the icon bar at the top of the syntax window or press Ctrl-A. This runs the command, and the frequency table for the modified command appears in the output window. The results are shown in Figure 1.19.

Figure 1.19 Results from modified command syntax

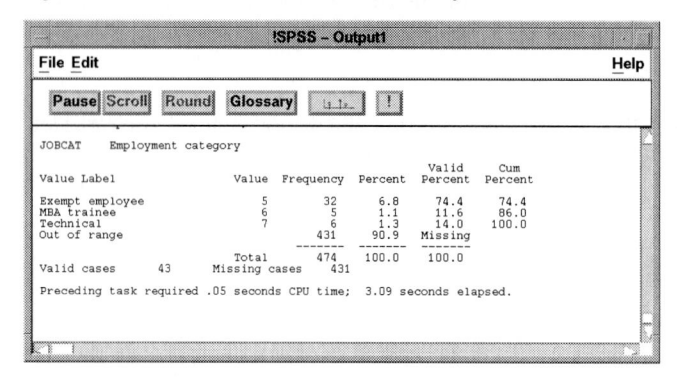

```
                                     !SPSS - Output1
 File Edit                                                                   Help
 Pause  Scroll  Round  Glossary

 JOBCAT     Employment category
                                                  Valid    Cum
 Value Label              Value  Frequency  Percent  Percent  Percent
 Exempt employee            5         32       6.8     74.4    74.4
 MBA trainee                6          5       1.1     11.6    86.0
 Technical                  7          6       1.3     14.0   100.0
 Out of range                        431      90.9   Missing
                                   -------  -------  -------
                         Total       474     100.0   100.0
 Valid cases    43   Missing cases   431
 Preceding task required .05 seconds CPU time;  3.09 seconds elapsed.
```

For a complete discussion on editing text files with SPSS and running commands from a syntax window, see Chapter 4.

Saving Results

Data Files. You can save data files in SPSS format, SPSS portable format for use on other operating systems, or fixed ASCII text format (see Chapter 2).

Output window results. The output window contains the text-based results of your SPSS session. You can edit this output and save it in text files for later use (see Chapter 4). Since the results are saved as text, you can easily cut and paste portions of the output into other applications, such as a word processing program.

Syntax window commands. You can edit and save the command syntax that you paste into a syntax window. You can then recall and rerun these commands in other SPSS sessions or run the command file from the UNIX prompt (see Appendix C).

Charts and plots. You can save charts and plots from the Chart Carousel or from chart windows and then recall and edit them in other sessions (see Chapter 22).

Getting Help

SPSS uses a hypertext-based help system. The best way to find out more about the help system is to use it. You can ask for help in any of the following ways:
- Select a topic from the Help menu in an SPSS window.
- Click on the Help pushbutton in an SPSS dialog box.
- Press F1 at any time in SPSS.
- For specialized help, click on the Glossary pushbutton in an SPSS output window or the Syntax pushbutton in a syntax window.

For an overview of how to use the help system, from the menus select:
Help
  On Help

For more information on the SPSS help system, see Chapter 30.

Ending an SPSS Session

To end an SPSS session:

1. From the menu bar in any SPSS window choose:

   File
     Exit

2. For each open window, SPSS asks if you want to save the contents before it ends the session. To end the session without saving any changes, click on Discard for each window. If you click on Yes or press ↵Enter, SPSS opens the appropriate dialog box for saving each type of file (data, output, syntax, chart).

Decimal Indicator and the LANG Environment Variable Setting

The decimal indicator used in the Data Editor and in results displayed in output windows is determined by the environment variable, *LANG*. If the decimal indicator defined by this environment variable is anything other than a period, SPSS uses a comma as the decimal indicator.

The decimal indicator defined by the *LANG* setting also affects the display of the system-missing value in the Data Editor and in output windows. If a period is the decimal indicator, a period is also used to represent the system-missing value. If anything other than a period is the decimal indicator, a comma is used to represent the system-missing value.

Regardless of the defined decimal indicator, a period must be used as the decimal indicator in command syntax and in transformation expressions.

Keyboard Movement

If you don't have a mouse, you can use the keyboard to navigate the menus and dialog boxes. The following general rules apply:

Menus

For selecting items from menus:
- (Alt) used with the underlined letter in a menu name opens that menu. For example, (Alt)-(S) opens the Statistics menu.
- (↑) and (↓) move up and down an open menu.
- (←) and (→) move between menus and submenus.
- (↵Enter) selects the highlighted menu item and takes you to the corresponding submenu or dialog box.
- (Esc) cancels the selection and takes you back up one level, closing the open menu or submenu.

Dialog Boxes

For selecting items from dialog boxes:
- (↑) and (↓) move up and down variable lists and between group items (for example, a group of radio button alternatives).
- (Tab→) and (⇧Shift)-(Tab→) move between selections.
- (Space) selects the highlighted item.
- (↵Enter) is equivalent to OK or Continue or the default pushbutton selection for the dialog box (the pushbutton with the border around it).
- (Esc) is equivalent to Cancel.

For a complete guide to navigating the system with the keyboard, see Appendix D.

2 Data Files

Data files come in a wide variety of formats, and SPSS is designed to handle many of them, including:
- Database files created with various SQL formats.
- ASCII text data files.
- SPSS data files created on other operating systems.

Creating a New Data File

If your data are not already in computer files, you can use the Data Editor to enter the data and create an SPSS data file. The Data Editor is a simple, efficient spreadsheet-like facility that opens automatically when you start an SPSS session. For information on the Data Editor, see Chapter 3.

Opening an SPSS Data File

To open an SPSS data file, from the Data Editor menus choose:

File
  Open ▶
    Data...

This opens the Open Data File dialog box, as shown in Figure 2.1.

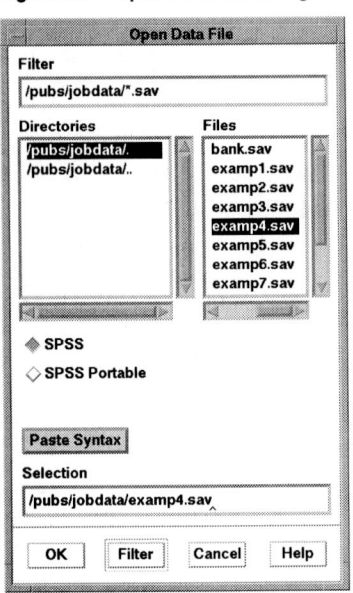

Figure 2.1 Open Data File dialog box

Filename and Location

Filter. To display a list of files that match a wildcard search or change the directory location, enter the directory path and wildcard specification and press Filter. By default, SPSS looks for all SPSS data files in the current directory (files with the extension *.sav*) and displays them on the Files list.

Directories. You can also use the Directories list to change the directory location. To change directories, select the name of the directory on the Directories list and press Filter or double-click on the directory name. To move up a directory level, select the directory path that ends with a slash and two periods (/..).

Files. All files in the directory that match the wildcard search appear on the Files list. Select the file you want and press OK or double-click on the filename.

Selection. Enter the directory path and filename and press OK. If you select a directory and file from the lists, this information is entered automatically. If you enter the information directly, you can bypass the filter process.

File Type

Before you can open a data file, you need to tell SPSS what type of file it is. In the Open Data File dialog box, choose one of the following alternatives:

◇ **SPSS.** Data files created and/or saved in SPSS for UNIX or SPSS for Windows.

◇ **SPSS portable.** SPSS data files created on other operating systems (for example, Macintosh, Windows) and saved in SPSS portable format.

Multiple User Access

More than one user can access the same SPSS data file at the same time. This doesn't present any problems for normal operations—provided you don't save any changes to the data file. If you save changes to the data file, these changes will be lost if another user who had the file open at the same time saves subsequent changes.

SPSS does *not* provide any alert messages when a data file is already in use.

SQL Databases

SPSS can read the following types of SQL databases:

- Oracle (version 6.0)
- Sybase (version 4.2)
- Ingres (version 6.4)
- Informix (version 5.0)

Variable Names and Labels

The complete database column name is used as the variable label. SPSS assigns variable names to each column from the database in one of two ways:

- If the name of the database column (or the first eight characters) forms a valid, unique SPSS variable name, it is used as the variable name.
- If the name of the database column does not form a valid, unique SPSS variable name, SPSS creates a name by using the first few characters from the column name and adding a numeric suffix, based on the column's position number in the SQL SELECT statement (Fields to Retrieve in the Select Table and Fields dialog box). If the first few characters of the column name are not valid characters for SPSS variable names, the prefix *col* is used with a numeric suffix.

Reading Databases

To read a database into SPSS, from the Data Editor menus choose:

File
　Open ▶
　　[database type]

Informix. For Informix, this opens a dialog box in which you enter the database name.

Ingres. For Ingres, this opens a dialog box in which you enter the following information:

Login. The database login name. This is optional. By default, the current user ID name is used.

Database. The name of the database you want to access.

Oracle and **Sybase**. For Oracle and Sybase, this opens a dialog box in which you enter the following information:

Login. The database login name. This is required. SPSS does not read the environment variable *dblogin* from the login string.

Password. The password that accesses the database. Depending on how the database system is set up, this may be required or optional. As a security precaution, asterisks are displayed instead of the password you enter.

Server. Enter the name of the server that contains the database.

For Sybase, there is an additional dialog box in which you select a database after you select the server.

Tables and Fields

The Open dialog boxes lead to the Select Table and Fields dialog box, like the one in Figure 2.2.

Figure 2.2 Select Table and Fields dialog box

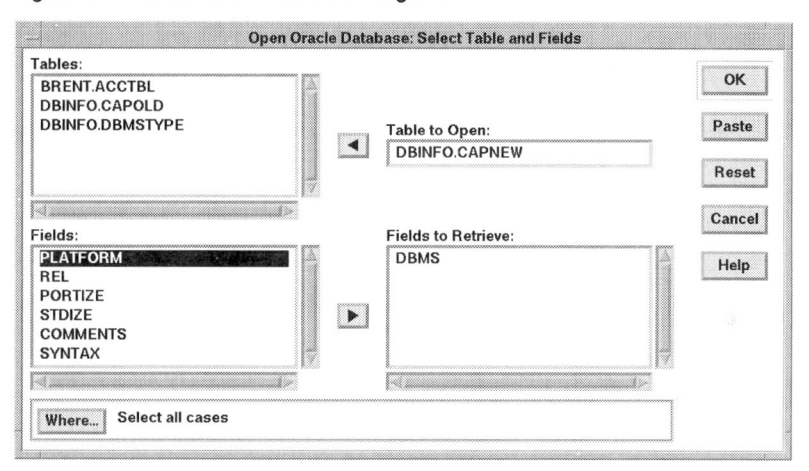

Tables. A list of tables and views in the database.

Table to Open. Select a table or view from the Tables list. You can select only one.

Fields. A list of fields in the selected table. If there is no currently selected table, the Fields list is empty.

Fields to Retrieve. Select one or more fields to retrieve. Fields are columns in the database. They are read as variables by SPSS.

Selecting a Subset of Cases

To select a subset of cases from the database, click on Where... in the Select Table and Fields dialog box. This opens the Where Cases dialog box, as shown in Figure 2.3.

You can choose one of the following alternatives:

- ◇ **Select all cases.** This is the default. Values are calculated for all cases, and any WHERE clause is ignored.
- ◇ **Select where case satisfies condition.** Enter an SQL WHERE clause in the text box. (Do not include the actual word "where.") If you change the selected table in the SQL Server Select Tables and Fields dialog box, the current WHERE clause is deleted.

Figure 2.3 Where Cases dialog box

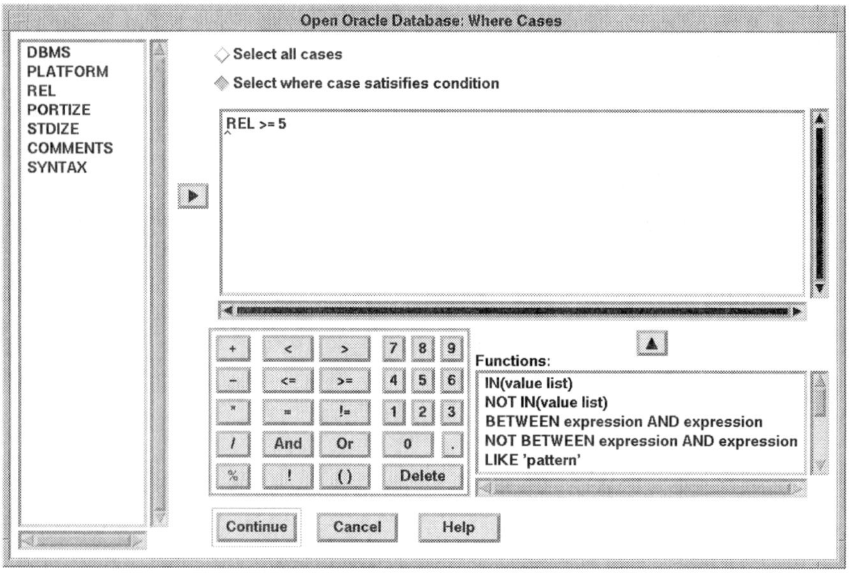

Calculator Pad

The calculator pad contains numbers and arithmetic, relational, and logical operators (see Table 2.1). You can use it like a calculator (using the mouse to point and click on keys) or simply as a reference for the correct symbols to use for various operators.

Since fairly complex expressions are possible, it is important to keep in mind the order in which operations are performed. Functions are evaluated first, followed by multiplication and division, and finally addition and subtraction. You can control the order of operations by enclosing the operation you want executed first in parentheses.

Table 2.1 Calculator pad operators

Arithmetic Operators	Relational Operators*	Logical Operators[†]
+ Addition	< Less than	And Both relations must be true.
- Subtraction	> Greater than	Or Either relation can be true.
* Multiplication	<= Less than or equal to	! Not. Reverses the true/false outcome of the expression.
/ Division	>= Greater than or equal to	
% Modulus (remainder)[†]	= Equal to	
( ) Order of operations	!= Not equal to	

*A relation is a logical expression that compares two values using a relational operator.

[†]A logical operator joins two relations or reverses the true/false outcome of an expression.

[†]Available only for Sybase.

Functions

The available SQL functions are different for each type of database. You can paste functions from the list or type in any valid SQL functions.

Pasting and Editing Functions

Pasting a Function into an Expression. To paste a function into an expression:

1. Position the cursor in the expression at the point where you want the function to appear.
2. Double-click on the function on the Functions list (or select the function and click on the ▲ pushbutton).

The function is inserted in the expression.

Editing a Function in an Expression. The function isn't complete until you enter the **arguments**, represented by question marks in the pasted function. The number of question marks indicates the minimum number of arguments required to complete the function. To edit a function:

1. Highlight the question mark(s) in the pasted function.
2. Enter the arguments. If the arguments are field (variable) names, you can paste them from the source list.

Time-saving Tip

By default, SPSS automatically reads the entire data file when you click on OK in the Select Table and Fields dialog box. This may take some time if it is a large database. To avoid this potentially time-consuming data pass, there are two options:

- Change your Preferences setting for Transformation and Merge Options to Calculate values before used.

or

- Paste the command syntax to a syntax window and delete the EXECUTE command.

To paste and edit the underlying command syntax:

1. Click on Paste to paste the underlying command syntax into a syntax window.
2. Delete the EXECUTE command in the syntax window, as shown in Figure 2.4.
3. Click on Run on the syntax window icon bar.

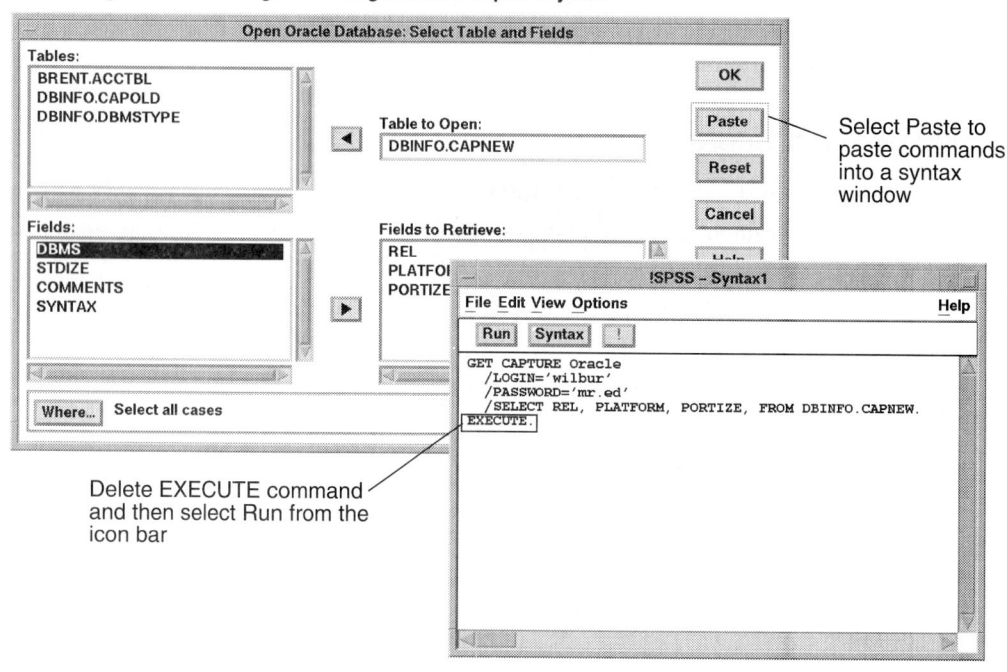

Figure 2.4 Pasting and editing database capture syntax

```
Open Oracle Database: Select Table and Fields
Tables:
  BRENT.ACCTBL
  DBINFO.CAPOLD
  DBINFO.DBMSTYPE          Table to Open:        OK
                           DBINFO.CAPNEW         Paste      ← Select Paste to
                                                 Reset        paste commands
                                                              into a syntax
                                                 Cancel       window
Fields:                    Fields to Retrieve:
  DBMS                       REL
  STDIZE                     PLATFO       !SPSS - Syntax1
  COMMENTS                   PORTIZE  File Edit View Options                 Help
  SYNTAX                              Run  Syntax  !
                                      GET CAPTURE Oracle
  Where...  Select all cases            /LOGIN='wilbur'
                                        /PASSWORD='mr.ed'
                                        /SELECT REL, PLATFORM, PORTIZE, FROM DBINFO.CAPNEW.
                                      EXECUTE.
```

Delete EXECUTE command and then select Run from the icon bar

The variable names will appear in the Data Editor, but no data values will appear in the cells until SPSS runs a command that requires a data pass, such as a statistical procedure.

Reading Text Files

If your raw data are in simple text files (standard ASCII format), you can read the data in SPSS and assign variable names and data formats. To read a text file, from the Data Editor menus choose:

File
  Read ASCII Data...

This opens the Read ASCII Data File dialog box, as shown in Figure 2.5.

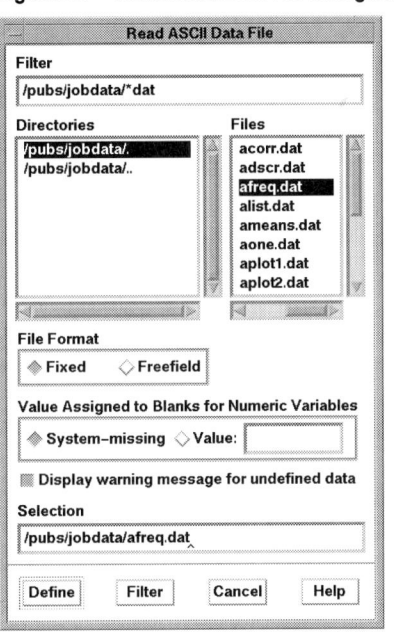

Figure 2.5 Read ASCII Data File dialog box

Filter. To display a list of files that match a wildcard search or change the directory location, enter the directory path and wildcard specification and press Filter. By default, SPSS looks for all files in the current directory with the extension *.dat* and displays them on the Files list.

Directories. You can also use the Directories list to change the directory location. To change directories, select the name of the directory in the Directories list and press Filter or double-click on the directory name. To move up a directory level, select the directory path that ends with a slash and two periods (/..).

Files. All files in the directory that match the wildcard search appear on the Files list. Select the file you want and press Define or double-click on the filename.

Selection. Enter the directory path and filename and press Define. If you select a directory and file from the lists, this information is entered automatically. If you enter the information directly, you can bypass the filter process.

File Format. You can choose one of the following alternatives:

- **Fixed.** Each variable is recorded in the same column location on the same record (line) for each case in the data file. This is the default.
- **Freefield.** The variables are recorded in the same order for each case, but not necessarily in the same locations. Spaces are interpreted as delimiters between values. More than one case can be recorded on a single line. After reading the value for the last defined variable for a case, SPSS reads the next value encountered as the first variable for the next case.

Value Assigned to Blanks for Numeric Variables. For fixed-format data, you can choose one of the following alternatives for the treatment of blank numeric fields:

- **System-missing.** Blank numeric fields are treated as missing data. This is the default.
- **Value.** Blank numeric fields receive a user-specified value. For example, blanks may represent a value of 0 instead of missing data. Enter the value in the text box.

The following option is also available:

- **Display warning message for undefined data.** If anything other than a number is encountered in a numeric field, the system-missing value is assigned and a warning message is displayed in the output. To suppress the warning message, deselect this default setting.

Define Fixed Variables

To define fixed-format data, select Fixed for the File Format in the Read ASCII Data File dialog box and click on Define. This opens the Define Fixed Variables dialog box, as shown in Figure 2.6.

Figure 2.6   Define Fixed Variables dialog box

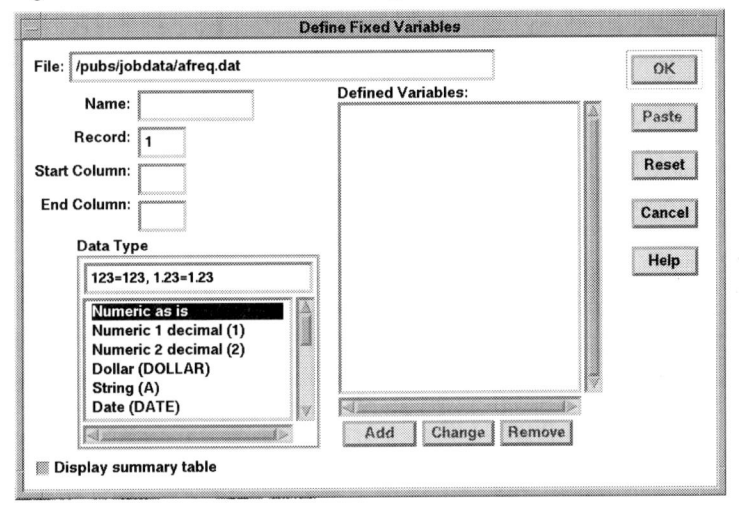

For each variable, you must specify the following:

Name. The following rules apply to variable names:

- The name must begin with a letter. The remaining characters can be any letter, any digit, a period, or the symbols @, #, _, or $.
- Variable names cannot end with a period.
- The length of the name cannot exceed eight characters.
- Blanks and special characters (for example, !, ?, ', and *) cannot be used.
- Each variable name must be unique; duplication is not allowed. Variable names are not case-sensitive. The names *NEWVAR*, *NewVar*, and *newvar* are all identical in SPSS.
- The following reserved keywords cannot be used:

ALL	NE	EQ	TO	LE
LT	BY	OR	GT	
AND	NOT	GE	WITH	

Record. A case can have data on more than one line. The **record number** indicates the line within the case where the variable is located.

Start Column/End Column. These two column specifications indicate the location of the variable within the record. The value for a variable can appear anywhere within the range of columns. With the exception of string variables, leading blank spaces in the column range are ignored.

Data Type. You can choose one of the following alternatives:

▢ **Numeric as is.** Valid values include numbers, a leading plus or minus sign, and a decimal indicator.

Numeric 1 decimal (1). If there is not an explicitly coded decimal indicator, one **implied decimal position** is assigned. For example, 123 is read as 12.3. A value with more than one explicitly coded decimal position (for example, 1.23) is read correctly but is rounded to one decimal position in output unless you change the variable definition (see Chapter 3).

Numeric 2 decimals (2). If there is not an explicitly coded decimal indicator, two implied decimal positions are assigned. For example, 123 is read as 1.23. A value with more than two explicitly coded decimal positions (for example, 1.234) is read correctly but is rounded to two decimal positions in output unless you change the variable definition (see Chapter 3).

Dollar (DOLLAR). Valid values are numbers with an optional leading dollar sign and optional commas as thousands separators. If you don't enter the dollar sign or commas, they are automatically inserted in output. Decimal positions are read but do not appear in output unless you change the variable definition (see Chapter 3). For example, $10.95 would be displayed as $11.

String (A). Valid values include virtually any keyboard characters and imbedded blanks. Leading blanks are treated as part of the value. Internally, string values are right-padded to the total width of the field defined by the Start and End columns. If the defined width is eight or fewer characters, it is a **short string variable**. If the defined width is more than eight characters, it is a **long string variable**. Short string variables can be used in many SPSS procedures; long string variables can be used in fewer procedures.

Date (DATE). Dates of the general format dd-mmm-yyyy. The following conventions apply:
- Dashes, periods, commas, slashes, or blanks can be used as delimiters. For example, 28-10-90, 28/10/1990, 28.OCT.90, and October 28, 1990 are all acceptable.
- Months may be represented in digits, Roman numerals, three-letter abbreviations, or fully spelled out. For example, 10, X, OCT, and October are all acceptable.
- Two-digit years are assumed to have the prefix 19.

Date format variables are displayed with dashes as delimiters and three-letter abbreviations for the month values. Internally, dates are stored as the number of seconds from October 14, 1582.

European Date (EDATE). Dates of the general format dd.mm.yyyy. The conventions for Date format also apply to European Date format. Edate format variables are displayed with periods as delimiters and numbers for the month values.

American Date (ADATE). Dates of the general format mm/dd/yyyy. The conventions for Date format also apply to American Date. Adate format variables are displayed with slashes as delimiters and numbers for the month values.

Julian Date (JDATE). Dates of the general format yyyyddd. The following rules apply:
- If the input value contains only five digits, a two-digit year is assumed and 1900 is added.
- Year values can be two or four digits. Two-digit year values less than 10 must contain a leading zero.
- All day values must be three digits. Leading zeros are required for day values less than 100.

Quarter and Year (QYR). Dates of the general format qQyyyy. The quarter is expressed as 1, 2, 3, or 4, and the year is represented by two or four digits. If two digits are used, 1900 is added. The quarter and the year are separated by the letter Q. Blanks may be used as additional delimiters. For example, 4Q90, 4Q1990, 4 Q 90, and 4 Q 1990 are all acceptable.

Month and Year (MOYR). Dates of the general format mm/yyyy. The Date format conventions for month and year apply.

Week and Year (WKYR). Dates of the general form wkWKyyyy. A week is expressed as a number from 1 to 53. Week 1 begins on January 1, week 2 on January 8, and so forth. The year is a two- or four-digit number. If it is a two-digit number, 1900 is added. The week and year are separated by the string WK. Blanks can be used as additional delimiters. For example, 43WK90, 43WK1990, and 43 WK 1990 are all acceptable.

Date and Time (DATETIME). Values containing a date and a time. The following conventions apply:
- The date must be written as an international date (dd-mmm-yyyy) followed by a blank and then a time value in the form hh:mm:ss.ss.
- The time conforms to a 24-hour clock. Thus, the maximum hour value is 23; the maximum minute value is 59; and the seconds value must be less than 60.
- Fractional seconds must have the decimal indicator explicitly coded in the data value.

For example, the input values 25/1/90 1 2, 25-JAN-1990 1:02, and 25 January 1990 01:02:00 are all acceptable variations for the same value.

Time (TIME). Time of day or time interval values of the general form hh:mm:ss.ss. The following conventions apply:
- Colons, blanks, or periods may be used as delimiters between hours, minutes, and seconds. A period is required to separate seconds from fractional seconds.
- Data values must contain hours and minutes. Seconds and fractional seconds may be omitted.
- Data values may contain a sign.
- Hours may be of unlimited magnitude. The maximum for minutes is 59, and seconds must be less than 60 (for example, 59.99 is acceptable).

Internally, times are stored as the number of seconds.

Day and Time (DTIME). Time interval that includes days in the form ddd hh:mm:ss.ss. The following conventions apply:
- The number of days is separated from the hours by an acceptable Time delimiter: a blank, a period, or a colon. A preceding sign (+ or –) may be used.
- The maximum value for hours is 23.
- The remainder of the field must conform to required specifications for Time format. Fractional seconds must have the decimal indicator explicitly coded in the data value.

Day of week (WKDAY). The day of the week expressed as a character string. Only the first two characters are significant. The remaining characters are optional. For example, Sunday can be expressed as Sunday, Sun, or Su. Internally, values are stored as integers from 1 to 7 (Sunday=1).

Month (MONTH). Month of the year expressed as an integer or a character string. Only the first three characters are significant. The remaining characters are optional. For example, January can be expressed as 1, January, or Jan. Internally, values are stored as integers from 1 to 12 (January=1).

Other Formats. Using SPSS syntax in a syntax window (see Chapter 4), you can specify different widths for many of the above formats, plus numerous other formats, including:
- Comma format: commas as thousands separators.
- Dot format: Commas as decimal indicators and periods as thousands separators.
- Scientific notation.
- Percent.
- Hexadecimal.
- Column binary.

- Packed decimal.

For a complete list of data format types, see the *SPSS Base System Syntax Reference Guide*.

The following display option is also available:

❏ **Display summary table.** Displays a summary table of defined variables, including data type and column location, in the output window.

Entering Variable Definitions

To enter a variable definition:

1. Specify the variable name, record and column locations, and data type.
2. Click on Add. The record number, start and end columns, variable name, and data type appear on the Defined Variables list, as shown in Figure 2.7.

Figure 2.7 Defined Variables

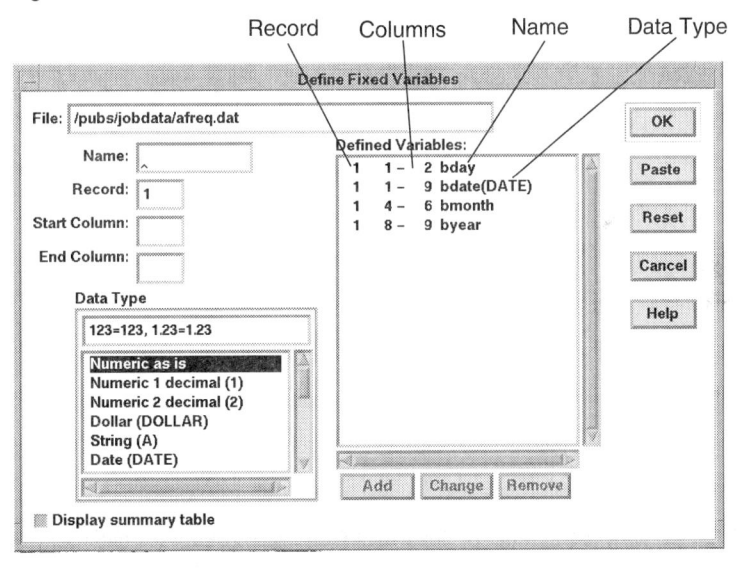

The following general rules apply:

- You can enter variables in any order. They are automatically sorted by record and start column on the list.
- You can specify multiple variables in the same or overlapping column locations. For example, in Figure 2.7, *bday* is in columns 1–2, *bmonth* in columns 4–6, *byear* in columns 8–9, and *bdate* in columns 1–9.

- You can read selective data fields and/or records. You don't have to define or read all the data in the file. SPSS reads only the columns and records you specify and skips over any data you don't define.

Changing and Deleting Variable Definitions

To change a variable definition, highlight the variable on the Defined Variables list, make the changes, and then click on Change. To delete a variable, highlight the variable on the Defined Variables list and click on Remove.

Define Freefield Variables

To define freefield format data, select Freefield for the File Format in the Read ASCII Data File dialog box and click on Define. This opens the Define Freefield Variables dialog box, as shown in Figure 2.8.

Figure 2.8   Define Freefield Variables dialog box

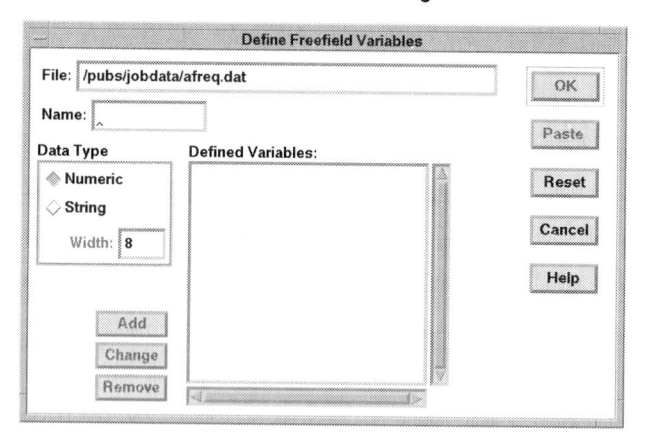

For each variable, you must specify the following:

Name. Variable names must begin with a letter and cannot exceed eight characters. Additional variable-naming rules are given in "Define Fixed Variables" on p. 39.

Data Type. For freefield data, there are only two alternatives for data type:

◇ **Numeric.** Valid values include numbers, a leading plus or minus sign, and a decimal indicator. Imbedded thousands separators are not allowed in data values.

◇ **String.** Valid values include virtually any keyboard characters and imbedded blanks. For width, specify the *maximum* width of the string. Internally, shorter string values are right-padded to the defined width. If the defined width is eight or fewer characters, it is a short string variable. If the defined width is more than eight characters, it is a long string variable. Short string variables can be used in many SPSS procedures; long string variables can be used in fewer procedures. If a value contains blanks, the entire string must be enclosed in apostrophes or quotes.

Entering Variable Definitions

To enter a variable definition, specify the variable name and data type and click on Add. The variable appears on the Defined Variables list. If it is a string variable, the letter A and the defined width appear in parentheses next to the variable name.

While defining data in freefield format is relatively simple and easy, it is also easy to make mistakes. Keep the following rules in mind:

- You must enter variables in the order in which they appear in the data file. Each new variable definition is added to the bottom of the list, and SPSS reads the variables in that order.
- You must provide definitions for all variables in the file. If you omit any, the data file will be read incorrectly. SPSS determines the end of one case and the beginning of the next based on the number of defined variables.
- The data file cannot contain any missing data. Blank fields are read as delimiters between variables, and SPSS does not distinguish between single and multiple blanks. If a single observation is missing, the entire remainder of the data file will be read incorrectly.
- If your system is configured to use a period as the decimal indicator, SPSS interprets commas as delimiters between values in freefield format. For example, a value of 1,234 is read as two separate values: 1 and 234.

Changing and Deleting Variable Definitions

To change a variable definition, highlight the variable on the Defined Variables list, make the changes and then click on Change. To delete a variable, highlight the variable on the Defined Variables list and click on Remove.

Data Editor Window

When you open a data file, the data appear in the Data Editor window, as shown in Figure 2.9. You can then use the Data Editor to change variable definitions, add or delete cases or variables, and modify data values. For more information on the Data Editor, see Chapter 3.

Figure 2.9 Data Editor window

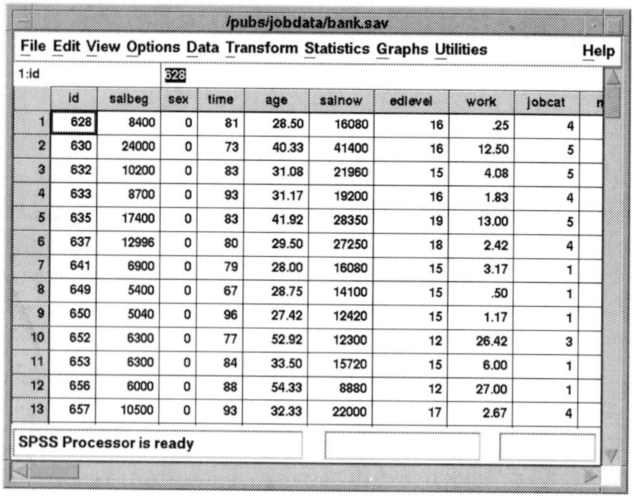

	id	salbeg	sex	time	age	salnow	edlevel	work	jobcat
1	628	8400	0	81	28.50	16080	16	.25	4
2	630	24000	0	73	40.33	41400	16	12.50	5
3	632	10200	0	83	31.08	21960	15	4.08	5
4	633	8700	0	93	31.17	19200	16	1.83	4
5	635	17400	0	83	41.92	28350	19	13.00	5
6	637	12996	0	80	29.50	27250	18	2.42	4
7	641	6900	0	79	28.00	16080	15	3.17	1
8	649	5400	0	67	28.75	14100	15	.50	1
9	650	5040	0	96	27.42	12420	15	1.17	1
10	652	6300	0	77	52.92	12300	12	26.42	3
11	653	6300	0	84	33.50	15720	15	6.00	1
12	656	6000	0	88	54.33	8880	12	27.00	1
13	657	10500	0	93	32.33	22000	17	2.67	4

File Information

An SPSS data file contains much more than raw data. It also contains any variable definition information, including:

- Variable names
- Variable formats
- Descriptive variable and value labels

This information is stored in the dictionary portion of the SPSS data file. The Data Editor provides one way to view the variable definition information (see Chapter 3). You can also display complete dictionary information for the working data file or any other SPSS data file.

Working Data File

To display complete dictionary information for every variable in the working data file, from the menus choose:

Utilities
  File Info

The following information is displayed in the output window:

- Variable names.
- Descriptive variable label (if any).
- Print and write formats. The data type is followed by a number indicating the maximum width and the number of decimal positions (if any). For example, F8.2 indicates a numeric variable with a maximum width of eight columns, including one column for the decimal indicator and two columns for decimal positions.
- Descriptive value labels (if any) for different values of the variable. Both the value and the corresponding label are displayed.

You can also obtain dictionary information on individual variables using the Variables dialog box (see Chapter 28).

Other SPSS Data Files

To display dictionary information for SPSS data files not currently open, from the Data Editor menus choose:

File
  Display Data Info...

This opens the Display Data Info dialog box, as shown in Figure 2.10.

Figure 2.10 Display Data Info dialog box

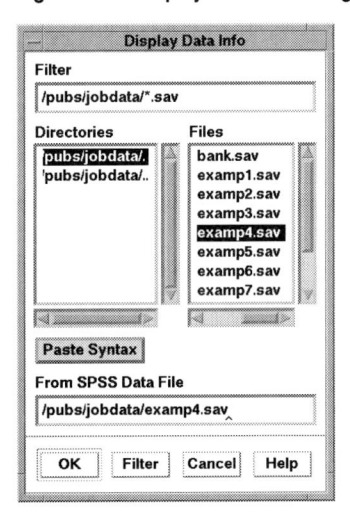

Filter. To display a list of files that match a wildcard search or change the directory location, enter the directory path and wildcard specification and press Filter. By default,

SPSS looks for all files in the current directory with the extension *.sav* and displays them in the Files list.

Directories. You can also use the Directories list to change the directory location. To change directories, select the name of the directory on the Directories list and press Filter or double-click on the directory name. To move up a directory level, select the directory path that ends with a slash and two periods (/..).

Files. All files in the directory that match the wildcard search appear on the Files list. Select the file you want and press OK or double-click on the filename.

Selection. Enter the directory path and filename and press OK. If you select a directory and file from the lists, this information is entered automatically. If you enter the information directly, you can bypass the filter process.

The dictionary information for the specified file is displayed in the output window.

Saving Data Files

Any changes you make in a data file last only for the duration of the SPSS session—unless you explicitly save the changes. To save any changes to a previously defined SPSS data file, from the Data Editor menus choose:

File
 Save

The modified data file is saved, overwriting the previous version of the file.

Multiple User Access

More than one user can access the same SPSS data file at the same time. If you save changes to the data file, these changes will be lost if another user who had the file open at the same time saves subsequent changes.

SPSS does *not* provide any alert messages when a data file is already in use.

Save As New File or Different Format

To save a new SPSS data file or save the data in a different file format, from the Data Editor menus choose:

File
 Save As...

This opens the Save As Data File dialog box, as shown in Figure 2.11.

Figure 2.11 Save As Data File dialog box

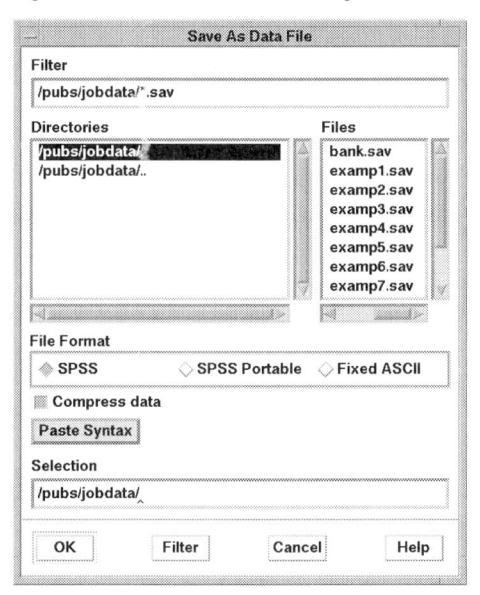

Filename and Location

Filter. To display a list of files that match a wildcard search or change the directory location, enter the directory path and wildcard specification and press Filter. By default, SPSS looks for all files in the current directory with the extension *.sav* and displays them on the Files list.

Directories. You can also use the Directories list to change the directory location. To change directories, select the name of the directory on the Directories list and press Filter or double-click on the directory name. To move up a directory level, select the directory path that ends with a slash and two periods (/..).

Files. All files in the directory that match the wildcard search appear on the Files list. If you select a file from the list, SPSS asks you if you want to replace the existing file.

Selection. Enter the directory path and filename and press OK. If you select a directory and file from the lists, this information is entered automatically. If you enter the information directly, you can bypass the filter process.

File Type

Before you can save a data file, you need to specify a file format. You can choose one of the following alternatives:

◇ **SPSS.** SPSS 5.0 for UNIX. The default file extension is *.sav*. Files saved in this format can also be read by SPSS for Windows.

◇ **SPSS portable.** Portable SPSS file that can be read by other versions of SPSS on other operating systems (for example, Macintosh, OS/2).

◇ **Fixed ASCII.** ASCII text file in fixed format, using the default write formats for all variables. There are no tabs or spaces between variable fields.

If you save as SPSS format, the new file becomes the working data file and the new filename is displayed on the title bar of the Data Editor window. If you save as any other format, the working data file is unaffected.

Closing a Data File

Since only one data file can be open at a time, SPSS automatically closes the working data file before it opens another one. If there have been any changes to the data file since it was last saved, SPSS asks if you want to save the changes before it closes the file and opens the next one.

3 Data Editor

The Data Editor provides a convenient, spreadsheet-like method for creating and editing SPSS data files. The Data Editor window, shown in Figure 3.1, opens automatically when you start an SPSS session.

Figure 3.1 Data Editor window

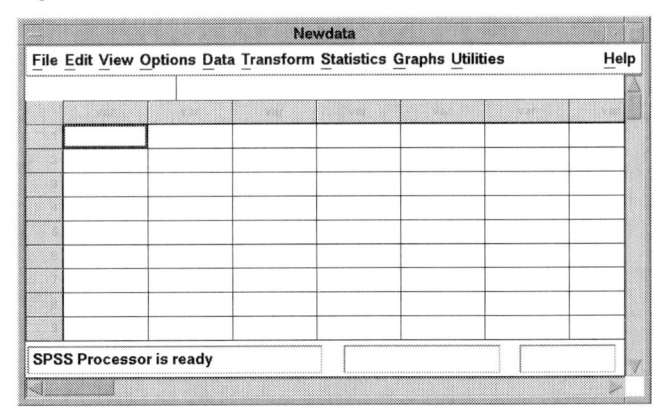

If you have previous experience with spreadsheet programs, many of the features of the Data Editor should be familiar. There are, however, several important distinctions.

- **Rows are cases**. Each row represents a **case** or observation. For example, each individual respondent to a questionnaire is a case.
- **Columns are variables**. Each column represents a **variable** or characteristic being measured. For example, each item on a questionnaire is a variable.
- **Cells contain values**. Each cell contains a single value of a variable for a case. The cell is the intersection of the case and variable. Cells contain only data values. Unlike spreadsheet programs, cells in the Data Editor cannot contain formulas.
- **The data file is rectangular**. The dimensions of the data file are determined by the number of cases and variables. You can enter data in any cell. If you enter data in a cell outside the boundaries of the defined data file, SPSS extends the data rectangle to include any rows and/or columns between that cell and the file boundaries. There

are no "empty" cells within the boundaries of the data file. For numeric variables, blank cells are converted to the system-missing value (see "Missing Values" on p. 58). For string variables, a blank is considered a valid value.

Defining Variables

When you open an existing data file (see Chapter 2), the data are displayed in the Data Editor, as shown in Figure 3.2. Any existing data definition recognized by SPSS (that is, variable names, formats, etc.) is reflected in the display. Beyond the boundaries of the defined data file, the Data Editor displays dimmed row numbers and dimmed column headings to indicate potential cases and variables.

Figure 3.2   Data file displayed in the Data Editor

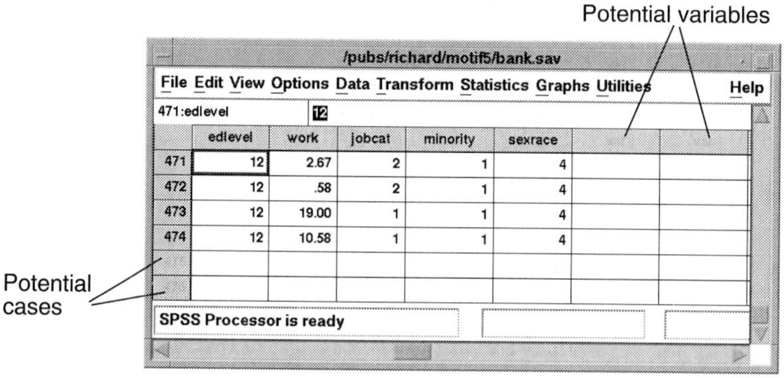

You can replace existing or default data definition with your own specifications. You can:

- Create your own variable names.
- Provide descriptive variable and value labels.
- Use special codes for missing values.
- Assign different formats (such as string, date, and time).

To change the name, format, and other attributes of a variable:

- Double-click on the current variable name at the top of the column

   or

- Select any cell in the column for the variable and from the menus choose:
   Data
     Define Variable...

This opens the Define Variable dialog box, as shown in Figure 3.3.

Figure 3.3   Define Variable dialog box

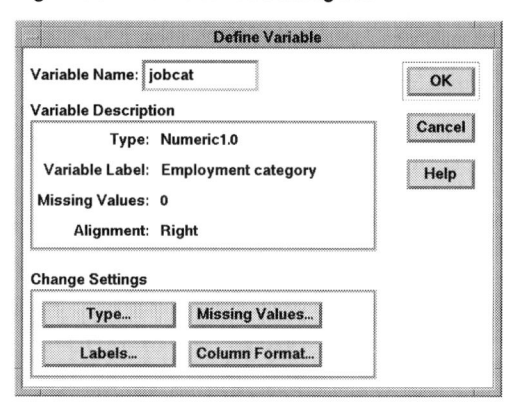

[Define Variable dialog box showing Variable Name: jobcat; Variable Description — Type: Numeric1.0, Variable Label: Employment category, Missing Values: 0, Alignment: Right; Change Settings buttons: Type..., Missing Values..., Labels..., Column Format...; OK, Cancel, Help buttons]

The variable name, type, label, missing values (if any), and alignment for the selected variable are displayed.

Variable Names

The default name for new variables is the prefix *var* and a sequential five-digit number (*var00001*, *var00002*, etc.). To change the variable name, simply enter the new name in the Variable Name text box. The following rules apply to valid variable names:

- The name must begin with a letter. The remaining characters can be any letter, any digit, a period, or the symbols @, #, _, or $.
- Variable names cannot end with a period.
- The length of the name cannot exceed eight characters.
- Blanks and special characters (for example, !, ?, ', and *) cannot be used.
- Each variable name must be unique; duplication is not allowed.
- Variable names are not case-sensitive. The names *NEWVAR*, *NewVar*, and *newvar* are all identical in SPSS.
- The following reserved keywords cannot be used:

ALL	NE	EQ	TO	LE
LT	BY	OR	GT	
AND	NOT	GE	WITH	

The following are all valid variable names: *location*, *loc#5*, *x.1*, and *over$500*.

Renamed Variables in Dialog Boxes

Source variable lists in dialog boxes are updated to reflect new variable names, but, in some cases, selected variable lists may not be updated. If a selected variable list contains an old variable name and you want to run the procedure again during the same session, you should remove the variable name from the selected variable list or an error will result.

To remove an old variable name from a selected variable list, select the variable and click on the ◄ pushbutton. This removes the variable name without placing it back on the source variable list.

Variable Type

By default, SPSS assumes that all new variables are numeric. To change the variable type, click on Type... in the Define Variable dialog box. This opens the Define Variable Type dialog box, as shown in Figure 3.4.

Figure 3.4 Define Variable Type dialog box

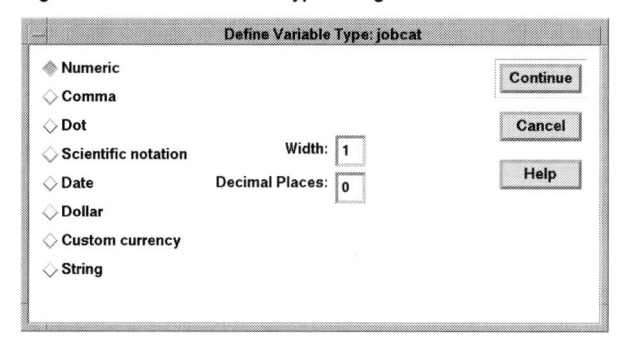

The contents of the Define Variable Type dialog box depend on the data type selected. For some data types, there are text boxes for width and number of decimals; for others, you can simply select a format from a scrollable list of examples. You can choose one of the following alternatives:

- **Numeric**. Valid values include numerals, a leading plus or minus sign, and a decimal indicator. For width, enter the maximum number of characters, including one position for the decimal indicator. For decimal places, enter the number of decimal positions for display purposes. The maximum width for numeric variables is 40 characters; the maximum number of decimal positions is 16.

- **Comma**. Valid values include numerals, a leading plus or minus sign, one period for the decimal indicator, and multiple imbedded commas as thousands separators. If you don't include the commas when you enter data values, they are automatically inserted. For width, enter the maximum number of characters, including the decimal point and imbedded commas. For decimal places, enter the number of decimal positions for display purposes.

◇ **Dot**. Valid values include numerals, a leading plus or minus sign, one comma for the decimal indicator, and multiple imbedded periods as thousands separators. If you don't include the periods when you enter data values, they are automatically inserted. For width, enter the maximum number of characters, including the decimal indicator and imbedded periods. For decimal places, enter the number of decimal positions for display purposes.

◇ **Scientific notation**. Valid values include all valid numeric values plus scientific notation indicated with an imbedded E, D, plus sign, or minus sign. For example, 123, 123E3, 123D3, 123+3, 123–3, and 123E+3 are all acceptable.

◇ **Date**. Valid values are dates and/or times. Choose a format from the list.

◇ **Dollar**. Valid values include a dollar sign, one period for the decimal indicator, and multiple commas as thousands separators. Choose a format from the list or enter values for width and number of decimal places. If you don't include the dollar sign or the commas when you enter data values, they are automatically inserted.

◇ **Custom currency**. If you have created any custom currency formats (see Chapter 29), you can specify them as display formats. For width, enter the maximum number of characters, including any custom currency characters. For decimal places, enter the number of decimal positions for display purposes. You cannot include custom currency characters when you enter data values. They are automatically inserted after you enter the value.

◇ **String**. Valid values include letters, numerals, and other characters. Enter the maximum number of characters (that is, the longest valid string value for the variable). String variables with a defined width of eight or less characters are **short strings**. String variables with a width of more than eight characters are **long strings**. Short string variables can be used in many SPSS procedures. The use of long string variables is severely restricted or not allowed in most SPSS procedures.

Other Formats

SPSS data files created on other operating systems or generated by command syntax in a syntax window may contain other data formats. If the selected variable uses one of these other formats, the format appears as an additional alternative at the bottom of the list. You can change the format to one of the standard format alternatives—but once you apply the change, you cannot change the variable back to its original format. Other formats recognized by SPSS include:

- Implied decimal
- Percent
- Hexadecimal
- Column binary

Input versus Display Formats

Depending on the format, the display of values in the Data Editor may differ from the actual value as entered and stored internally. Here are some general guidelines:

- For numeric, comma, and dot formats, you can enter values with any number of decimal positions (up to 16), and the entire value is stored internally. The Data Editor displays only the defined number of decimal places, and it rounds values with more decimals. However, the complete value is used in any computations.

- For string variables, all values are right-padded to the maximum width. For a string variable with a width of 6, a value of 'No' is stored internally as 'No   ' and is not equivalent to ' No '.

- For date formats, you can use slashes, dashes, spaces, commas, or periods as delimiters between day, month, and year values, and you can enter numbers, three-letter abbreviations, or complete names for month values. Dates of the general format dd-mmm-yy are displayed with dashes as delimiters and three-letter abbreviations for the month. Dates of the general format dd/mm/yy and mm/dd/yy are displayed with slashes for delimiters and numbers for the month. Internally, dates are stored as the number of seconds from October 14, 1582.

- For time formats, you can use colons, periods, or spaces as delimiters between hours, minutes, and seconds. Times are displayed with colons as delimiters. Internally, times are stored as the number of seconds.

See the *SPSS Base System Syntax Reference Guide* for more information on input and display data formats.

Decimal Indicators and the LANG Environment Variable

The decimal indicator used in the Data Editor is determined by the environment variable, *LANG*. If the decimal indicator defined by this environment variable is anything other than a period, SPSS uses a comma as the decimal indicator.

The decimal indicator defined by the *LANG* setting also affects the display of the system-missing value in the Data Editor. If a period is the decimal indicator, a period is also used to represent the system-missing value. If anything other than a period is the decimal indicator, a comma is used to represent the system-missing value. Comma, dollar, dot, and custom currency formats are not affected by the *LANG* setting.

Labels

To provide descriptive variable and value labels, click on Labels... in the Define Variable dialog box. This opens the Define Labels dialog box, as shown in Figure 3.5.

Figure 3.5 Define Labels dialog box

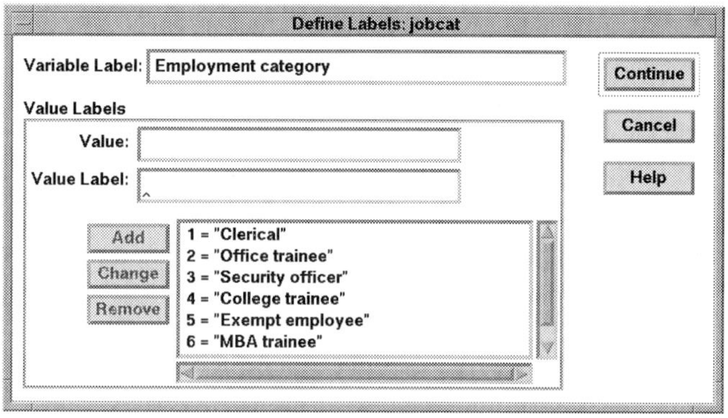

```
┌─────────────── Define Labels: jobcat ───────────────┐
│ Variable Label: Employment category      [Continue] │
│ Value Labels                                        │
│         Value: [            ]            [ Cancel ] │
│   Value Label: [            ]                       │
│                                          [  Help  ] │
│         ┌─────┐  1 = "Clerical"                     │
│         │ Add │  2 = "Office trainee"               │
│         ├─────┤  3 = "Security officer"             │
│         │Change│  4 = "College trainee"             │
│         ├─────┤  5 = "Exempt employee"              │
│         │Remove│  6 = "MBA trainee"                 │
│         └─────┘                                     │
└─────────────────────────────────────────────────────┘
```

Variable Label

Variable labels can be up to 120 characters long, although most procedures display fewer than 120 characters in output. Variable labels are case-sensitive; they are displayed exactly as entered.

Value Labels

You can assign a label for each value of a variable. This is particularly useful if your data file uses numeric codes to represent non-numeric categories (for example, codes of 1 and 2 for male and female). Value labels can be up to 60 characters long, although most procedures display fewer than 60 characters in output. Value labels are case-sensitive; they are displayed exactly as entered. Value labels are not available for long string variables.

Assign a label. To assign value labels:

1. Enter the value in the Value text box. The value can be numeric or string.
2. Enter a label in the Value Label text box.
3. Click on Add. The value label is added to the list.

Modify a label. To modify a value label:

1. Highlight the label on the list.
2. Enter the new label (or value) in the text box.
3. Click on Change. The new label appears on the list.

Delete a label. To delete a value label:

1. Highlight the value label.
2. Click on Remove. The label is removed from the list.

You can display value labels instead of values in the Data Editor window. You can also use value label lists for data entry. (See "Display Value Labels" on p. 73.)

Missing Values

In SPSS, there are two types of missing values:

- **System-missing values.** Any blank numeric cells in the data rectangle are assigned the system-missing value, which is indicated with a period (.).
- **User-missing values.** It is often useful to be able to distinguish why information is missing. You can assign values that identify information missing for specific reasons and then instruct SPSS to flag these values as missing. SPSS statistical procedures and data transformations recognize this flag, and those cases with user-missing values are handled specially. Figure 3.6 shows how user-missing values are treated by the Frequencies procedure.

Figure 3.6 User-missing values

```
OZONE     Concern About Ozone Depletion

                                                   Valid     Cum
Value Label              Value  Frequency  Percent Percent   Percent

Very concerned            1.00      237      51.3    54.4     54.4
Somewhat concerned        2.00      144      31.2    33.0     87.4
Not concerned             3.00       55      11.9    12.6    100.0
Never use ozone           8.00        9       1.9  Missing            User-missing
No answer                 9.00       17       3.7  Missing            values
                                  -------  -------  -------
                         Total      462     100.0   100.0

Valid cases    436    Missing cases    26
```

User-missing Values

To specify user-missing values, click on Missing Values... in the Define Variable dialog box. This opens the Define Missing Values dialog box, as shown in Figure 3.7.

Figure 3.7 Define Missing Values dialog box

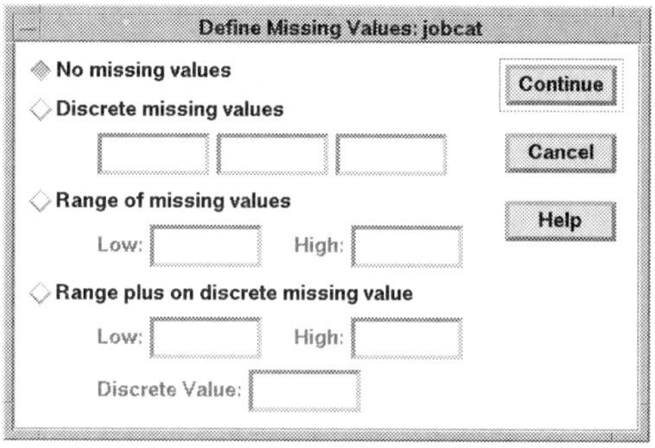

User-missing values can be assigned to variables of any format type except long string (see "Variable Type" on p. 54). You can choose one of the following alternatives:

- **No missing values.** No user-missing values. All values are treated as valid. This is the default.
- **Discrete missing values.** You can enter up to three discrete (individual) user-missing values for a variable. You can define discrete missing values for numeric or short string variables.
- **Range of missing values.** All values between and including the low and high values are flagged as missing. Not available for short string variables.
- **Range plus one discrete missing value.** All values between the low and high values and one additional value outside the range are flagged as missing. Not available for short string variables.

If you want to include all values below or above a certain value in a range but you don't know what the lowest or highest possible value is, you can enter an asterisk (*) for Low or High.

Column Format

To adjust the width of the Data Editor columns or change the alignment of data in the column, click on Column Format... in the Define Variable dialog box. This opens the Define Column Format dialog box, as shown in Figure 3.8.

Figure 3.8   Define Column Format dialog box

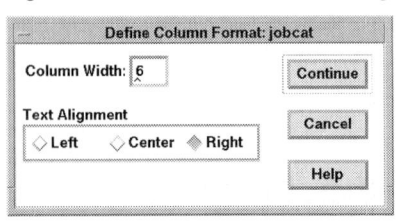

Column Width. The default column width is determined by the defined width of the variable (see "Variable Type" on p. 54). To change the column width, enter a new value. You can also change the column width in the Data Editor window. Position the mouse pointer on the border between two variable names at the top of the Data Editor window and use the click-and-drag technique to move the column border.

New column widths remain in effect as long as the data file is open or until they are changed again. They are not saved with the data file. The next time you open the file, the default column widths are used.

Text Alignment. The default alignment depends on the data type. You can choose one of the following alternatives:

◇ **Left.** Text is left-aligned. This is the default for string variables.

◇ **Center.** Text is centered.

◇ **Right.** Text is right-aligned. This is the default for nonstring variables.

Column Width versus Variable Width

Column formats affect only the display of values in the Data Editor. Changing the column width does not change the defined width of a variable. If the defined and actual width of a value are wider than the column, the value appears truncated in the Data Editor window.

Templates

You can assign the same variable definition information to multiple variables with variable templates. For example, if you have a group of variables that all use the numeric codes 1 and 2 to represent "yes" and "no" responses and 9 to represent missing responses, you can create a template that contains those value labels and missing value specifications and apply the template to the entire group of variables.

To create, apply, or modify a template, from the menus choose:

Data
　Templates...

This opens the Template dialog box, as shown in Figure 3.9.

Figure 3.9　Template dialog box

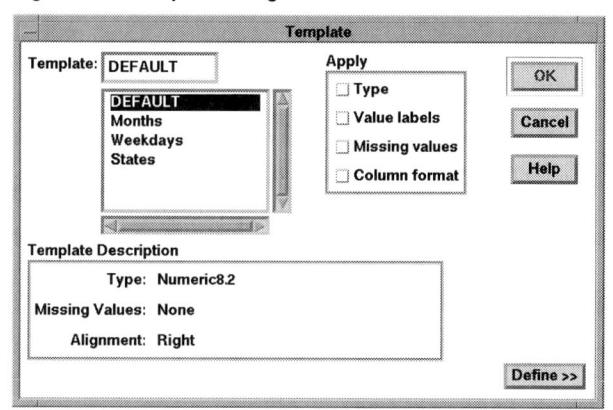

![Template dialog box showing Template field with DEFAULT, a list containing DEFAULT, Months, Weekdays, States; Apply checkboxes for Type, Value labels, Missing values, Column format; OK, Cancel, Help, Define>> buttons; and Template Description showing Type: Numeric8.2, Missing Values: None, Alignment: Right]

You can select and apply one of the existing templates from the Template list, modify it, or create a new template.

Applying Templates

To apply an existing template, select a template from the list and specify the template characteristics to be applied.

Template. SPSS comes with the following predefined templates:

Default. Numeric, eight characters wide, two decimal positions.

Months. A numeric variable with the month names as value labels for the values 1 through 12.

Weekdays. A numeric variable with the weekday names as value labels for the values 1 through 7.

States. A two-character string variable with the full state names as value labels for the corresponding two-character zip code abbreviation.

Template Description. The currently selected template name, variable type, user-missing values, and alignment are displayed.

Apply. You can apply any or all of the template characteristics to the selected variables. Choose one or more of the following alternatives:

- **Type.** Variable type (for example, numeric, string, date).
- **Value labels.** Descriptive labels for value categories (for example, labels of *No* and *Yes* for values coded 0 and 1).
- **Missing values.** User-missing values (See "Missing Values" on p. 58).
- **Column format.** Column width and alignment for display in the Data Editor (see "Column Format" on p. 59).

Creating and Modifying Templates

To modify an existing template or create a new one, click on Define>>. This expands the Template dialog box, as shown in Figure 3.10.

Figure 3.10 Expanded Template dialog box

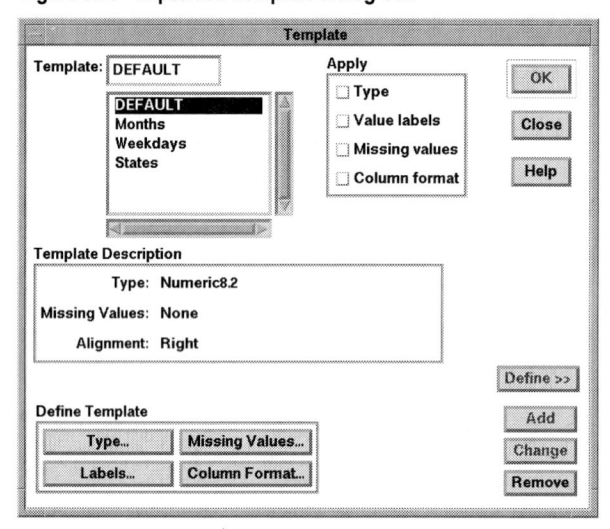

Defining a template is almost identical to defining a variable and uses the same dialog boxes for variable type, labels, missing values, and column format (see "Variable Type" on p. 54 through "Column Format" on p. 59).

Modify a template. To modify an existing template:

1. Select the template from the Template list.
2. Make the changes using the Define Template options.

3. Click on Change.

4. Click on OK to apply the template to the selected variables or click on Close to save the modified template without applying it to any variables. Any variables defined with the template but not currently selected remain unchanged.

Create a new template. To create a new template:

1. Select an existing template from the Template list. (If possible, select a template similar to the one you want to create.)

2. Use the Define Template options to create the template.

3. Enter a name for the template in the Template text box.

4. Click on Add.

5. Click on OK to apply the template to the selected variables or click on Close to save the modified template without applying it to any variables.

Saving Templates

Templates are saved in a file named *.spss.tpl* in your home directory. If this file is not found, a new template file is automatically created.

Entering Data

You can enter data in virtually any order. You can enter data by case or by variable, for selected areas or individual cells. To enter a value in a cell:

1. Click on the cell or use the arrow keys to move to the cell. As shown in Figure 3.11, a heavy border appears around the cell, indicating that it is the active cell. The variable name and the row number are displayed in the upper left corner of the Data Editor window.

2. Type in the value. The value is displayed in the cell editor at the top of the Data Editor window. (See "Data Value Restrictions" on p. 65 for data value restrictions.)

3. Press (←Enter) (or select another cell). The data value from the cell editor appears in the cell.

If you select a single cell, the (←Enter) and (Tab→) keys move down and right one cell, respectively. (↑Shift)-(Tab→) moves left one cell. If you enter a value in a column outside the boundaries of the defined data file, you automatically create a new variable. If you enter a value in a row outside the boundaries of the data file, you automatically create a new case.

Figure 3.11 Active cell and cell editor

Variable name
Row number
Cell editor
Active cell

Entering Data in a Selected Area

You can restrict and control the flow of movement by selecting an area for data entry.

- **Select a case (row).** Click on the case number on the left side of the row or select any cell in the row and press ⇧Shift-Space. This highlights the entire row. Both the ↵Enter and Tab→ keys are restricted to movement between variables (columns) for that case.

- **Select a variable (column).** Click on the variable name at the top of the column or select any cell in the column and press Ctrl-Space. This highlights the entire column. Both the ↵Enter and Tab→ keys are restricted to movement between cases for that variable.

- **Select an area of cases and variables.** Click and drag the mouse diagonally from one corner of the area to the far corner (for example, upper left to lower right) or select a cell in one corner of the area, press and hold the ⇧Shift key, and use the arrow keys to define the area. The Tab→ key moves from left to right through the variables for each case in the selected area. The ↵Enter key moves from top to bottom through the cases for each variable in the selected area. (See Figure 3.12.)

Figure 3.12 Moving in a selected area

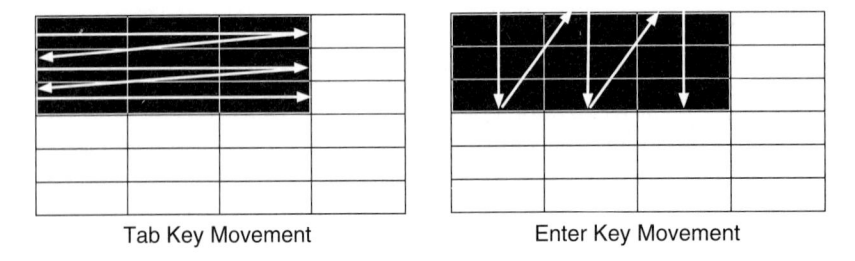

Tab Key Movement

Enter Key Movement

Data Value Restrictions

The defined variable type and width determine the type of value that can be entered in the cell.

- If you type a character not allowed by the defined variable type, the Data Editor beeps and does not enter the character.
- For string variables, characters beyond the defined width are not allowed.
- For numeric variables, integer values that exceed the defined width can be entered, but the Data Editor displays either scientific notation or asterisks in the cell to indicate that the value is wider than the defined width. To display the value in the cell, change the defined width of the variable. (*Note*: Changing the *column* width does not affect the *variable* width.)

Editing Data

With the Data Editor, you can modify a data file in many ways. You can:
- Change data values.
- Cut, copy, and paste data values.
- Add and delete cases.
- Add and delete variables.
- Change the order of variables.
- Change variable definitions.

Changing Data Values

To change a data value, you can either replace the entire value or modify part of it.

Replace a value. To delete the old value and enter a new value:

1. Click on the cell or use the arrow keys to move to the cell. The cell value is displayed in the cell editor.
2. Enter the new value. It replaces the old value in the cell editor.
3. Press ⏎Enter (or select another cell). The new value appears in the cell.

Modify a value. To modify a data value using the mouse:

1. Click on the cell. The cell value appears in the cell editor.
2. Click on the cell editor. A cursor appears at the position where you clicked the mouse. To reposition the cursor, simply aim and click the mouse again.

3. Edit the data value as you would any other text (see Chapter 4).
4. Press ⏎Enter (or select another cell). The modified value appears in the cell.

To modify a data value using the keyboard:

1. Use the arrow keys to move to the cell. The cell value is displayed in the cell editor.
2. Press F2 to switch to edit mode. A blinking cursor appears at the end of the value in the cell editor. The left and right arrow keys now move between characters in the value, and the ⇧Shift key used with the arrow keys selects blocks of text.
3. Edit the data value as you would any other text (see Chapter 4).
4. Press ⏎Enter (or press F2 to switch out of edit mode and select another cell). The modified value appears in the cell.

Cutting, Copying, and Pasting Values

You can cut, copy, and paste individual cell values or groups of values. You can:
- Move or copy a single cell value to another cell.
- Move or copy a single cell value to a group of cells.
- Move or copy the values for a single case (row) to multiple cases.
- Move or copy the values for a single variable (column) to multiple variables.
- Move or copy a group of cell values to another group of cells.

Move or Copy Cell Values

To move or copy cell values:

1. Select the cell value(s) you want to cut or copy.
2. From the menus choose:

    Edit
     Cut

    or

    Edit
     Copy

3. Select the target cell(s).
4. From the menus choose:

    Edit
     Paste

The pasted values appear in the cells unless the defined variable types are not the same and no conversion is possible.

Data Conversion

If the defined variable types of the source and target cells are not the same, SPSS attempts to convert the value. If no conversion is possible, SPSS inserts the system-missing value in the target cell.

- **Numeric or Date into String.** Numeric (for example, numeric, dollar, dot, comma) and date formats are converted to strings if they are pasted into a string variable cell. The string value is the numeric value as displayed in the cell. For example, for a dollar format variable, the displayed dollar sign becomes part of the string value. Values that exceed the defined string variable width are truncated.

- **String into Numeric or Date.** String values that contain acceptable characters for the numeric or date format of the target cell are converted to the equivalent numeric or date value. For example, a string value of 25/12/91 is converted to a valid date if the format type of the target cell is one of the day-month-year formats, but it is converted to system-missing if the format type of the target cell is one of the month-day-year formats.

- **Date into Numeric.** Date and time values are converted to a number of seconds if the target cell is one of the numeric formats (for example, numeric, dollar, dot, comma). Since dates are stored internally as the number of seconds since October 14, 1582, converting dates to numeric values can yield some extremely large numbers. For example, the date 10/29/91 is converted to a numeric value of 12,908,073,600.

- **Numeric into Date or Time.** Numeric values are converted to dates or times if the value represents a number of seconds that can produce a valid date or time. For dates, numeric values of less than 86,400 are converted to the system-missing value.

Pasting into Areas with Different Dimensions

If the target area does not have the same number of rows and columns as the source area, the pasting rules shown in Figure 3.13 apply:

Figure 3.13 Pasting into areas with different dimensions

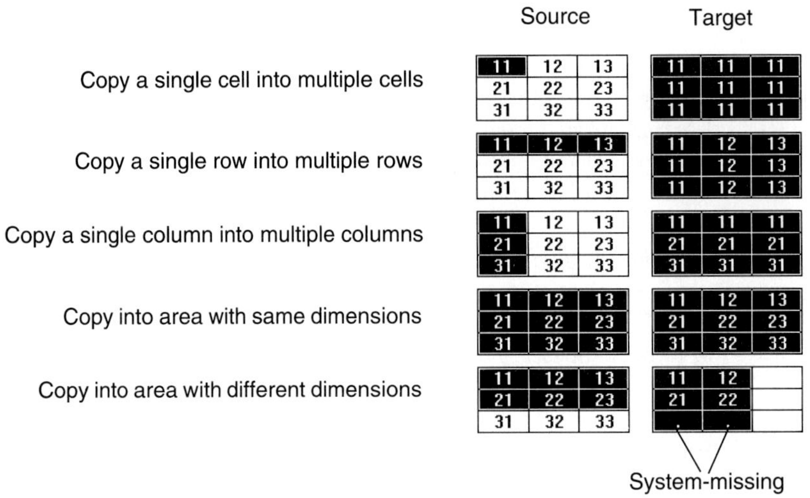

Pasting Outside the Defined Data File

If you paste values outside the boundaries of the defined data file, SPSS extends the data file to include the pasted area and creates new cases and/or new variables as needed with system-missing values for new cells outside the pasted area (see Figure 3.14).

Figure 3.14 Pasting outside the defined data file

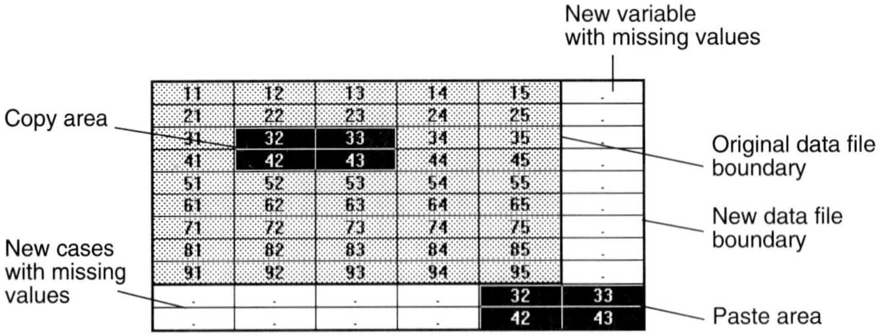

Pasting Outside the Data Editor

You can paste data from the Data Editor into a syntax or output window or into another application. If you paste data values outside the Data Editor, what you see displayed in the cell is what is pasted. For example, if the real value of a cell is 1.29 but it is displayed as 1.3, the value 1.3 is pasted. If you display value labels instead of values (see "Display Value Labels" on p. 73), the value labels are pasted, not the actual values.

Inserting New Cases

Entering data in a cell on a blank row automatically creates a new case. SPSS inserts the system-missing value for all the other variables for that case. If there are any blank rows between the new case and the existing cases, the blank rows also become new cases with the system-missing value for all variables.

Insert a new case between existing cases. To insert a new case between existing cases:

1. Select any cell in the case (row) below the position where you want to insert the new case.

2. From the menus choose:

    Data
      Insert Case

A new row is inserted for the case and all variables receive the system-missing value.

Auto New Case

By default, a new case is automatically created if you move down a row from the last defined case by pressing the ⏎Enter key. To turn this feature on and off, from the menus choose:

Options
  Auto New Case

Inserting New Variables

Entering data in a blank column automatically creates a new variable with a default variable name (the prefix *var* and a sequential five-digit number) and a default data format type (numeric). SPSS inserts the system-missing value for all cases for the new variable. If there are any blank columns between the new variable and the existing ones, these columns also become new variables with the system-missing value for all cases.

Insert a new variable between existing variables. To insert a new variable between existing variables:

1. Select any cell in the variable (column) to the right of the position where you want to insert the new variable.

2. From the menus choose:

   Data
     Insert Variable

   A new variable is inserted with the system-missing value for all cases.

Deleting Cases and Variables

Delete a case. To delete a case (row):

1. Click on the case number on the left side of the row or select any cell in the row and press ⇧Shift-Space. The entire row is highlighted. To delete multiple cases, use the click-and-drag method or use the ⇧Shift key with the arrow keys to extend the selection.

2. From the menus choose:

   Edit
     Clear

The selected cases are deleted. Any cases below them shift up.

Delete a variable. To delete a variable (column):

1. Click on the variable name at the top of the column or select any cell in the column and press Ctrl-Space. The entire column is highlighted.

   To delete multiple variables, use the click-and-drag method or use the ⇧Shift key with the arrow keys to extend the selection.

2. From the menus choose:

   Edit
     Clear

The selected variables are deleted. Any variables to the right of the deleted variables shift left.

Deleted Variables in Dialog Boxes

Source variable lists in dialog boxes are updated when variables are deleted, but, in some cases, selected variable lists may not be updated. If a selected variable list contains a deleted variable and you want to run the procedure again during the same session, you should remove the variable name from the selected variable list or an error will result.

To remove a deleted variable name from a selected variable list, select the variable and click on the ◄ pushbutton. This removes the variable name without placing it back on the source variable list.

Moving Variables

To move a variable by cutting and pasting in the Data Editor:

1. Insert a new variable in the position where you want to move the existing variable (see "Inserting New Variables" on p. 69).

2. For the variable you want to move, click on the variable name at the top of the column or select any cell in the column and press Ctrl-Space. The entire column is highlighted.

3. From the menus choose:

    Edit
     Cut

    The selected variable is cut. Any variables to the right of the cut variables shift left.

4. Click on the variable name of the new, inserted variable or select any cell in the columns and press Ctrl-Space. The entire variable is highlighted.

5. From the menus choose:

    Edit
     Paste

The cut variable is pasted into the new variable space. All dictionary information for the variable is retained

Changing Data Type

You can change the data type for a variable at any time using the Define Variable Type dialog box (see "Variable Type" on p. 54), and SPSS will attempt to convert existing values to the new type. If no conversion is possible, SPSS assigns the system-missing value. The conversion rules are the same as those for pasting data values to a variable with a different format type (see "Cutting, Copying, and Pasting Values" on p. 66). If the change in data format may result in the loss of missing value specifications or value labels, SPSS displays an alert box and asks if you want to proceed with the change or cancel it.

Finding Variables

Since variables are not always sorted in alphabetical order, it can sometimes be difficult to find a specific variable, particularly if the data file contains a large number of variables. You can use the Go To pushbutton in the Variables dialog box to find the selected variable in the Data Editor window. For more information about the Variables dialog box, see Chapter 28.

Finding Cases

To find a specific case (row) in the Data Editor, from the menus choose:

Data
  Go to Case...

This opens the Go to Case dialog box, as shown in Figure 3.15.

Figure 3.15 Go to Case dialog box

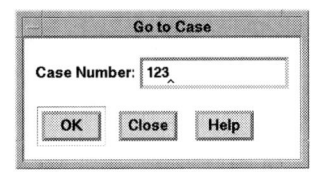

For Case Number, enter the row number for the case in the Data Editor. This value reflects the current position of the case in the data file. It is not a fixed value of a case ID variable. If you change the position of the case by inserting or deleting cases above it or by sorting the data file, the case number value changes.

Finding Data Values

Within a variable, you can search for specific data values or value labels in the Data Editor. To search for a data value:

1. Select any cell in the column of the variable you want to search.

2. From the menus choose:

   Edit
     Search for Data...

This opens the Search for Data dialog box, as shown in Figure 3.16.

Figure 3.16 Search for Data dialog box

The name of the selected variable is displayed in the title bar. You can search forward or backward within the selected variable from the active cell location. To search for a value label, value labels must be turned on (see "Display Value Labels," below).

The following option is also available:

❏ **Ignore case in strings.** By default, the search for string values in string variables and value labels ignores case. Deselect this default setting for a case-sensitive search.

Display Options

The View menu contains several options for controlling the Data Editor display:
- Display value labels instead of values.
- Turn the grid lines on and off for display and/or printing.

Display Value Labels

If you have defined descriptive value labels for any variables, you can display these labels in the Data Editor instead of the actual values. From the menus choose:

View
  Value Labels

Data Entry with Value Labels

The Value Labels option also provides a list of value labels for data entry, as shown in Figure 3.17. To use the value label list for data entry:

1. Use the mouse or the arrow keys to select the cell. The actual value (not the label) is displayed in the cell editor.

2. Press and hold the Ctrl key and click the left mouse button or press ⇧Shift-F2 to display the list of value labels for that variable. If value labels have not been defined for the variable, no list appears.

3. Select the value label you want to enter from the list. You can use the arrow keys or the scroll bar to scroll through the list, or you can type the first letter of the value label to sequentially search the list for all value labels that start with that letter.

4. Double-click the left mouse button or press ↵Enter to enter the value that corresponds to the selected value label. When you leave the cell, the selected value label appears in the cell. (To cancel the operation and leave the original value in the cell, use the mouse to select another cell or press Esc.)

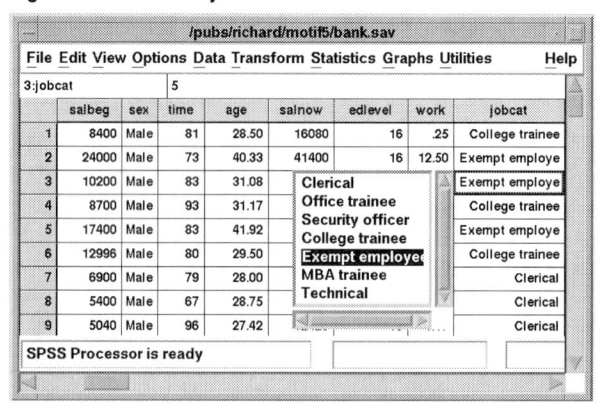

Figure 3.17 Data entry with value labels

Grid Lines

You can turn the Data Editor grid lines on and off for both display and printing. From the menus choose:

View
  Grid Lines

Fonts

To change the display font in the Data Editor, change the SPSS resource file setting for SPSS*DataWindow.fontList. See Appendix F for more information about the SPSS resource file.

Printing

To print the contents of the Data Editor, from the Data Editor menus choose:

File
  Print...

This opens the Print dialog box. You can print the entire data file or a selected area. For more information on printing, see Chapter 27.

Pending Transformations and the Data Editor

If you have pending transformations (see Chapter 29), the following limitations apply to the Data Editor:

- Variables cannot be inserted or deleted.
- Variable names and format type cannot be changed.
- Variables cannot be reordered.
- Templates cannot be applied to potential variables.
- If you change any data values, the changes may be overwritten when the transformations are executed. An alert box asks if you want to run the pending transformations.

Saving Data Files

Any changes you make to a data file in the Data Editor window last only for the duration of the SPSS session or until you open another data file—unless you explicitly save the changes. To save a previously defined SPSS data file, from the Data Editor menus choose:

File
  Save

The modified data file is saved, overwriting the previous version of the file.

Save As New File or Different Format

To save a new SPSS data file or save the data in a different file format, from the Data Editor menus choose:

File
  Save As...

This opens the Save As Data File dialog box. See Chapter 2 for more information on saving data files.

Closing a Data File and Opening a Different One

Only one data file can be open at any time. If you have an open data file and then open a different one, SPSS automatically closes the open data file first. If there have been any changes to the data file since it was last saved, SPSS asks if you want to save the changes before it closes the file and opens the next one.

Keyboard Movement

If you don't have a mouse, you can use the keyboard to navigate the Data Editor window and select cells. Table 3.1 and Table 3.2 provide a list of the basic keyboard actions. A more complete list is provided in Appendix D.

Table 3.1 Keyboard movement

Action	Keys
Move and select one cell down	↓ or ↵Enter
Move and select one cell up	↑
Move and select once cell right or left	→ ← or Tab→ / ⇧Shift+Tab→
Select first cell in case (row) or selected area	Home
Select last cell in case (row) or selected area	End
Select first case (row) for a variable (column)	Ctrl+↑
Select last case (row) for a variable (column)	Ctrl+↓
Select entire case (row)	⇧Shift+Space
Select entire variable (column)	Ctrl+Space
Extend selection	⇧Shift + arrow keys
Scroll up or down the height of the window	PgUp PgDn
Scroll left or right the width of the window	Ctrl+PgUp / Ctrl+PgDn
Copy from selected cells	Ctrl+Ins
Cut from selected cells	⇧Shift+Del
Paste into selected cells	⇧Shift+Ins

Table 3.2 Edit Mode keyboard movement

Edit Mode	Keys
Switch to Edit Mode	F2
Move one character right or left	→ ←
Extend selection	⇧Shift + arrow keys

Table 3.2 Edit Mode keyboard movement (Continued)

Edit Mode	Keys
Move to beginning of value	Home
Move to end of value	End
Select to beginning of value	Shift+Home
Select to end of value	Shift+End

4 Output and Syntax Windows

In SPSS, there are two types of text windows:

Output windows. The text-based results of your SPSS session are displayed in output windows. This includes any nongraphic statistical results, such as a crosstabulation or a correlation matrix. You can edit and save the output in text files.

Syntax windows. Syntax windows are text windows that you can use to run SPSS commands with command syntax. You can generate SPSS command syntax by pasting your dialog box choices into a syntax window. You can then edit the command syntax to take advantage of features not available in the dialog box interface. You can save the commands in text files and run them again in other SPSS sessions. If you have existing command files, you can open these in a syntax window and run the commands.

You can open any text file in an output or a syntax window. However, output generated during the session is always displayed in an output window, and you can run command syntax only from a syntax window.

Output Windows

An output window opens automatically when you start an SPSS session. This output window opens a new, untitled text file. You can have more than one open output window. These windows can contain new or existing text files.

Opening a New Text File in an Output Window

There are two ways to open an output window for a new text file:

- From the Data Editor menus choose:

    File
    New ▶
      SPSS Output

- From the menus in an open output window choose:

    File
    New

This opens an output window for a new text file.

Opening an Existing Text File in an Output Window

To open an existing text file in an output window:

- From the Data Editor menus choose:

File
　Open ▶
　　SPSS Output ...

- From the menus in an open output window choose:

File
　Open...

This opens the Open Output dialog box, as shown in Figure 4.1.

Figure 4.1　Open Output dialog box

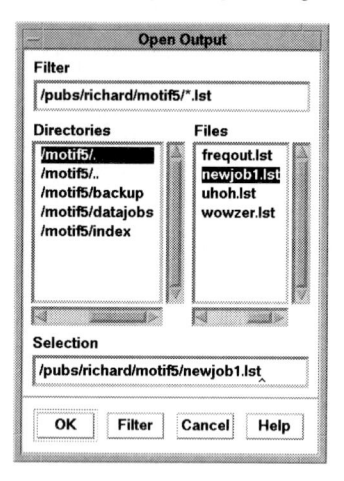

Filter. To display a list of files that match a wildcard search or change the directory location, enter the directory path and wildcard specification and press Filter. By default, SPSS looks for all files in the current directory with the extension *.lst* and displays them on the Files list.

Directories. You can also use the Directories list to change the directory location. To change directories, select the name of the directory on the Directories list and press Filter or double-click on the directory name. To move up a directory level, select the directory path that ends with a slash and two periods (/..).

Files. All files in the directory that match the wildcard search appear on the Files list. Select the file you want and press OK or double-click on the filename.

Selection. Enter the directory path and filename and press OK. If you select a directory and file from the lists, this information is entered automatically. If you enter the information directly, you can bypass the filter process.

Multiple Output Windows

If you have more than one output window open, SPSS sends output results to the **designated output window**. Although you can open multiple output windows, there can be only one designated output window. By default, the output window that opens automatically at the start of the session is the designated output window.

To designate a different output window, click on the [!] pushbutton on the icon bar at the top of the output window where you want to send the output, or make the output window the active window and choose Designate Window from the Utilities menu.

All new output is appended to the bottom of the text file in the designated output window. The window remains the designated output window until you select another. You cannot close the designated output window. There is always at least one open output window in an SPSS session.

Output Window Icon Bar

As shown in Figure 4.2, an icon bar at the top of each output window provides the following features:

Pause. Pauses the output display. By default, the display of output scrolls through the output window as it is generated. You can pause the display at any point.

Scroll. Scrolls the output display as it is generated.

Round. Rounds numbers in the highlighted area. By default, the Round pushbutton rounds numbers to integers (0 decimal positions). Use the Edit menu to specify a number of decimals for rounding (see "Round" on p. 89).

Glossary. This opens a hypertext-based help system with an index of SPSS glossary terms. Click on Search... and enter the term in the Search dialog box (see Chapter 30).

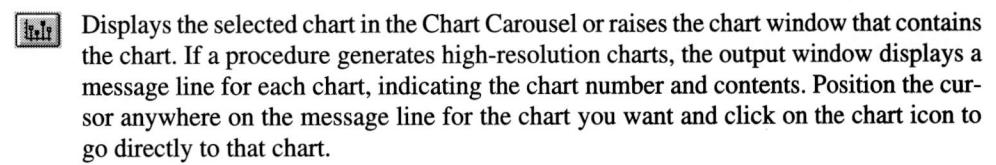

Displays the selected chart in the Chart Carousel or raises the chart window that contains the chart. If a procedure generates high-resolution charts, the output window displays a message line for each chart, indicating the chart number and contents. Position the cursor anywhere on the message line for the chart you want and click on the chart icon to go directly to that chart.

Makes this output window the designated output window. This pushbutton is enabled only if you have more than one output window open and is disabled for the currently designated output window.

Figure 4.2   Output window icon bar

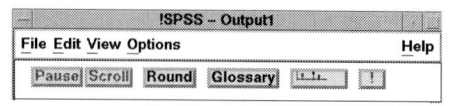

Output Page Titles

SPSS can place a heading at the top of each page in output files. The default heading includes the date, page number, and the version of SPSS being used. To add a title or subtitle to the output page heading, from the Data Editor menus choose:

Options
  Output Page Title...

This opens the Output Page Title dialog box, as shown in Figure 4.3.

Figure 4.3   Output Page Title dialog box

Page Title. The title can be up to 60 characters in length.

Page Subtitle. The subtitle can be up to 60 characters in length.

You can use quotation marks or apostrophes in your title or subtitle, but not both.

New titles and subtitles affect only new output and take effect on the next display page. If you want different titles for different analyses, enter a new title before running each analysis. Titles affect all output windows.

Displaying Output Page Titles

Output page titles and subtitles appear only on output pages if you choose to display page headers. To turn the display of page headers on or off, from the Data Editor menus choose:

Options
  Preferences...

This opens the Preferences dialog box. Click on Output... to open the Preferences Output dialog box, and click on Page headers to display or suppress page headers and titles. For more information on output preferences, see Chapter 29.

Syntax Windows

The dialog box interface is designed to handle most of the capabilities of SPSS. Underlying the dialog boxes, there is a command language that you can use to access additional features and customize your analysis. After you make your dialog box selections, you can use the Paste pushbutton to paste this underlying command syntax into a syntax window. You can then edit the resulting text and run the modified commands from the syntax window (see "Using SPSS Command Syntax in a Syntax Window" on p. 84).

Opening a New Text File in a Syntax Window

If you don't have an open syntax window, one opens automatically the first time you use the Paste pushbutton. You can also use the menus to open a new text file in a syntax window.

- From the Data Editor menus choose:

  File
    New ▶
      SPSS Syntax

- From the menus in an open syntax window choose:

  File
    New

This opens a syntax window for a new text file.

Opening an Existing File in a Syntax Window

To open an existing text file in a syntax window:

- From the Data Editor menus choose:

  File
    Open ▶
      SPSS Syntax

- From the menus in an open syntax window choose:

  File
    Open

This opens the Open SPSS Syntax dialog box, as shown in Figure 4.4.

Figure 4.4   Open SPSS Syntax dialog box

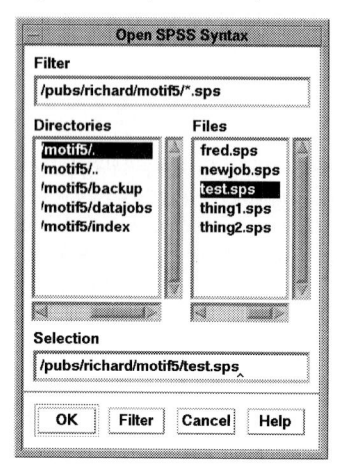

Filter. To display a list of files that match a wildcard search or to change the directory location, enter the directory path and wildcard specification and press Filter. By default, SPSS looks for all files in the current directory with the extension *.sps* and displays them on the Files list.

Directories. You can also use the Directories list to change the directory location. To change directories, select the name of the directory on the Directories list and press Filter or double-click on the directory name. To move up a directory level, select the directory path that ends with a slash and two periods (/..).

Files. All files in the directory that match the wildcard search appear on the Files list. Select the file you want and press OK or double-click on the filename.

Selection. Enter the directory path and filename and press OK. If you select a directory and file from the lists, this information is entered automatically. If you enter the information directly, you can bypass the filter process.

Using SPSS Command Syntax in a Syntax Window

You can use any text editor or word processing software that saves files in text format to create a file of SPSS command syntax and then open the file in a syntax window. You can also use the dialog box interface to generate the basic command syntax and then edit the commands in the syntax window.

Pasting Command Syntax from Dialog Boxes

Use the Paste pushbutton to paste your dialog box selections into a syntax window. If you don't have an open syntax window, one opens automatically the first time you paste from a dialog box.

Pasting Variable Names from the Variables Dialog Box

You can use the Variables dialog box to copy variable names and then paste them into command syntax. For more information, see Chapter 28.

Running SPSS Commands

You can run single commands or groups of commands in the syntax window.

1. Select the commands you want to run.

    Using the mouse, use the click-and-drag method to highlight the commands. Using the keyboard, press and hold the ⇧Shift key and use the up and down arrow keys to highlight the commands. The highlighted area can begin anywhere in the first command and end anywhere in the last command, as shown in Figure 4.5.

    If you want to run only a single command, you can position the cursor anywhere in the command line. If you want to run all the commands in the syntax window, you can choose Select All from the Edit menu.

2. Click on the Run pushbutton on the icon bar at the top of the syntax window (or press Ctrl-A).

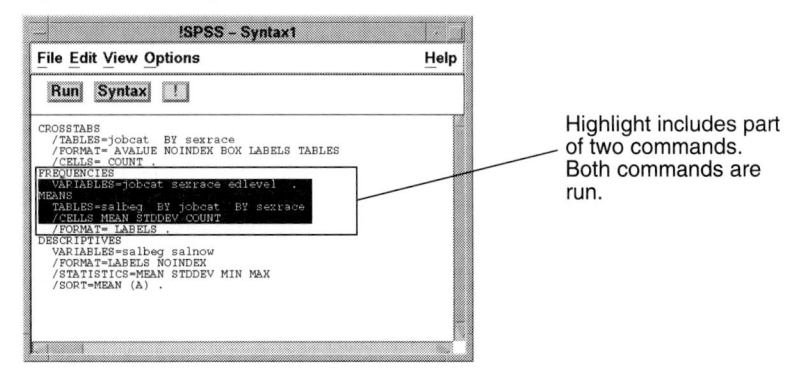

Figure 4.5 Running selected commands

Highlight includes part of two commands. Both commands are run.

Multiple Syntax Windows

You can have multiple syntax windows, and you can run commands from any open syntax window—but there is only one **designated syntax window**. If you have more than one syntax window open, the Paste pushbutton pastes command syntax into the designated syntax window. By default, the first syntax window opened is the designated syntax window. To designate a different syntax window, click on the [!] pushbutton on the icon bar at the top of the syntax window where you want to paste the commands, or make the syntax window the active window and choose Designate Window from the Utilities menu.

All new commands that you paste are appended to the bottom of the text file in the designated syntax window. The window remains the designated syntax window until you select another. If you close the designated syntax window, there is no designated syntax window until you select one. If there is no designated syntax window, a new one is automatically opened the next time you click on the Paste pushbutton.

Syntax Window Icon Bar

An icon bar at the top of each syntax window provides the following features:

Run. Runs the highlighted commands. If there is no highlighted text, SPSS runs the command line where the cursor is located.

Syntax. Opens a Help window containing a syntax chart for the command line where the cursor is located.

Makes this syntax window the designated syntax window. This pushbutton is enabled only if you have more than one syntax window open and it is disabled for the currently designated syntax window.

Editing Text Files

You can edit text in syntax and output windows using text-editing features similar to those used in word processing software. You can:

- Insert or overtype text.
- Cut, copy, and paste blocks of text within and between text files and windows.
- Copy text to and from the Data Editor and other software applications.
- Search for and replace text strings.

Basic Text-editing Concepts

SPSS follows standard graphical user interface conventions for editing text. It also provides features for copying tables in tab-delimited form (see "Edit Menu," below) and rounding numbers (see "Round" on p. 89). The following is a brief overview of some basic text-editing concepts.

- **Insertion point.** A cursor (a vertical bar) in the active window indicates where text will be inserted or deleted.
- **Insert mode.** By default, new text is inserted between existing text at the insertion point. Text to the right of the insertion point moves as new text is entered.
- **Overtype mode.** To overtype text to the right of the insertion point, press the [Ins] key. The vertical bar at the insertion point changes to a rectangular cursor. To change back to insert mode, press the [Ins] key again.
- **Deleting text.** The [←Backspace] key deletes one character to the left of the cursor. The [Del] key deletes one character to the right of the cursor. Both the [←Backspace] and [Del] keys delete highlighted blocks of text (without putting the text on the clipboard).
- **Highlighting text.** To highlight entire lines of text, use the click-and-drag method with the left mouse button (or press and hold the [⇧Shift] key and use the arrow keys). To select a rectangular area of text, press and hold the control key ([Ctrl]) and use the click-and-drag method with the left mouse button.
- **Cutting, copying, and pasting.** You can cut or copy highlighted text to the clipboard and paste the contents of the clipboard to another area of the same file, to another text file in another syntax or output window, to the Data Editor, or to another software application (for example, a spreadsheet or a word processing program).

Edit Menu

The following text-editing options are available with the Edit menu:

Cut. Cuts the highlighted text and puts it on the clipboard.

Copy. Copies the highlighted text onto the clipboard.

Copy Table. Copies the highlighted columns onto the clipboard in tab-delimited format. This is useful for copying output tables (for example, frequency distributions, means tables, etc.) into spreadsheet or word processing files.

Paste. Pastes the contents of the clipboard into the file at the insertion point. In insert mode, the text is inserted between existing text, and text to the right of the cursor moves over. In overtype mode, text to the right of the cursor is replaced with the pasted text. Paste is enabled only if there is something on the clipboard.

Clear. Cuts the highlighted text without putting it on the clipboard. (You cannot paste the text anywhere else.)

Select All. Selects the entire contents of the active syntax or output window.

Search for Text. Searches for a text string in the active syntax or output window. This opens the Search dialog box.

Replace Text. Searches for and replaces a text string with a new text string. This opens the Replace dialog box.

Round. Rounds any numbers in the highlighted area. This opens the Round dialog box.

Shortcut for Copying and Pasting

To copy and paste text without using the Edit menu or the clipboard:

1. Use the click-and-drag method with the left mouse button to highlight the area of text you want to copy.

2. Use the *middle* mouse button to paste the text where you want it.

Search for Text

To search for a text string in a syntax or output window, from the menus choose:

Edit
  Search for Text...

This opens the Search for Text dialog box, as shown in Figure 4.6.

Figure 4.6   Search for Text dialog box

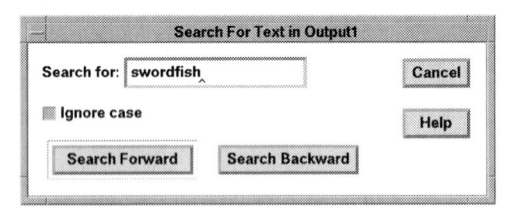

Search Forward. Searches forward from the cursor location to the end of the file.

Search Backward. Searches backward from the cursor location to the beginning of the file.

The following option is also available:

❑ **Ignore case.** By default, SPSS searches for any occurrence of the specified text string, regardless of case. If you want to restrict the search to occurrences that match the case as entered, deselect this default setting.

Replace Text

To search for a text string and replace it with another text string, from the menus choose:

Edit
　Replace Text...

This opens the Replace Text dialog box, as shown in Figure 4.7.

Figure 4.7　Replace Text dialog box

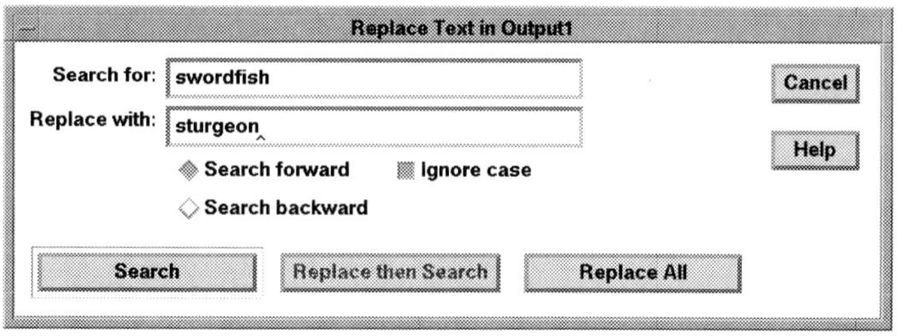

Search. Finds the next occurrence of the text string.

Replace then Search. Replaces the current occurrence of the text string and searches for the next one. If an occurrence of the text string is not currently highlighted in the syntax or output window, click on Search to find and highlight the text string.

Replace All. Replaces all occurrences of the text string from the cursor location to the end (or beginning) of the file.

For search direction, you can choose one of the following alternatives:

- **Search forward.** Searches forward from the cursor location to the end of the file.
- **Search backward.** Searches backward from the cursor location to the beginning of the file.

The following option is also available:

- **Ignore case.** By default, SPSS searches for any occurrence of the specified text string, regardless of case. If you want to restrict the search to occurrences that match the case as entered, deselect this default setting.

Round

To round or truncate highlighted values in a syntax or output window, from the menus choose:

Edit
　Round...

This opens the Round dialog box, as shown in Figure 4.8.

Figure 4.8 Round dialog box

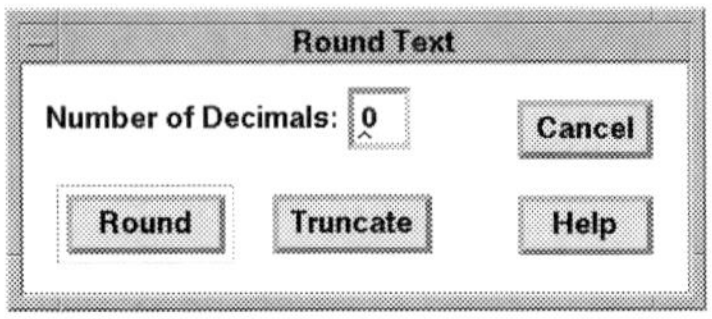

Number of decimals. Enter an integer value from 0 to 9. The default value is 0.

Round. Rounds values in the highlighted area to the specified number of decimals.

Truncate. Truncates values in the highlighted area at the specified number of decimals.

You can also round values in an output window with the Round pushbutton on the icon bar. This rounds numeric values based on the number of decimals currently specified in the Round dialog box. By default, it rounds values to integers.

Font Control

To change the font type, style, and size of text in a syntax or output window, modify the settings for SPSS*.SyntaxWindow.fontList and SPSS*.OutputWindow.fontList in the SPSS resource file. The specified font must be a fixed-pitch font. See Appendix F for more information about the SPSS resource file.

Saving Text Files

New syntax and output files and changes to existing text files are not saved unless you explicitly save them. To save changes to an existing text file:

1. Make the syntax or output window containing the file the active window.

2. From the menus choose:

    File
      Save

The modified text file is saved, overwriting the previous version of the file.

Save As New File

To save a new syntax or output text file or to save changes to an existing file as a new file:

1. Make the syntax or output window containing the file the active window.
2. From the menus choose:

   File
     Save As...

3. This opens the Save As Output dialog box for output windows, as shown in Figure 4.9, or the Save as Syntax dialog box for syntax windows. Enter a name for the file in the Selection text box and click on OK.

Figure 4.9   Save As Output dialog box

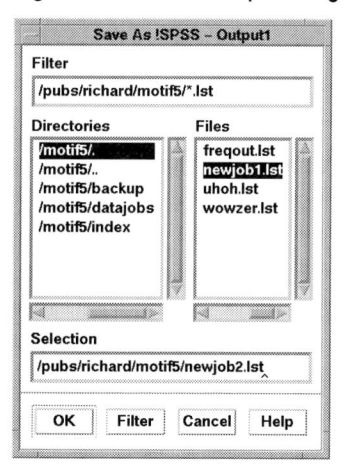

Filter. To display a list of files that match a wildcard search or change the directory location, enter the directory path and wildcard specification and press Filter. By default, SPSS looks for all files in the current directory with the extension *.lst* for output files (the *.lst* extension stands for *listing* file) and *.sps* for syntax files and displays them on the Files list.

Directories. You can also use the Directories list to change the directory location. To change directories, select the name of the directory on the Directories list and press Filter or double-click on the directory name. To move up a directory level, select the directory path that ends with a slash and two periods (/..).

Files. All files in the directory that match the wildcard search appear on the Files list. If you select a file from the list, SPSS asks you if you want to replace the existing file.

Selection. Enter the directory path and filename and press OK. If you select a directory and file from the lists, the information is entered automatically. If you enter the information directly, you can bypass the filter process.

Saving Selected Areas of Text Files

To save a selected area of an output or a syntax file, highlight the area you want to save before choosing Save or Save As from the File menu. An alert box will ask if you want to save the selected area only. Click on Yes to save the selected area, or click on No to save the entire file.

5 Data Transformations

In an ideal situation, your raw data are perfectly suitable for the type of analysis you want to perform, and any relationships between variables are either conveniently linear or neatly orthogonal. Unfortunately, this is rarely the case. Preliminary analysis may reveal inconvenient coding schemes or coding errors, or data transformations may be required in order to coax out the true relationship between variables.

With SPSS, you can perform data transformations ranging from simple tasks, such as collapsing categories for analysis, to creating new variables based on complex equations and conditional statements.

Computing Values

To compute values for a variable based on numeric transformations of other variables, from the menus choose:

Transform
  Compute...

This opens the Compute Variable dialog box, as shown in Figure 5.1.

Figure 5.1 Compute Variable dialog box

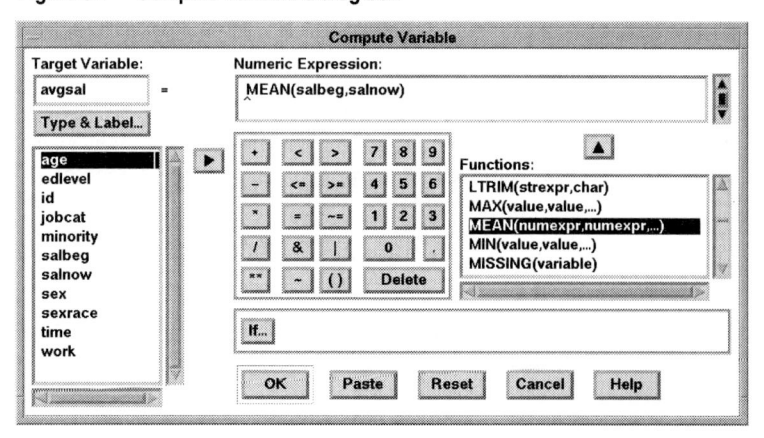

Target Variable. The name of the variable that receives the computed value. The target variable can be an existing variable or a new one. New variable names must begin with a letter and cannot exceed eight characters. (See Chapter 2 for complete variable naming rules.) By default, new computed variables are numeric (see "Variable Type and Label" on p. 99 for information on computing new string variables).

Numeric Expression. The expression used to compute the value of the target variable. The expression can use existing variable names, constants, arithmetic operators, and functions. You can type and edit the expression in the text box just like text in a syntax or output window (see Chapter 4). You can also use the calculator pad, variable list, and function list to paste elements into the expression.

Calculator Pad

The calculator pad contains numbers, arithmetic operators, and relational operators (Table 5.1). You can use it like a calculator (using the mouse to point and click on keys) or simply as a reference for the correct symbols to use for various operators.

Table 5.1 Calculator pad operators

Arithmetic Operators	Relational Operators	Logical Operators
+ Addition	< Less than	& And. Both relations must be true.
− Subtraction	> Greater than	
* Multiplication	<= Less than or equal to	| Or. Either relation can be true.
/ Division	>= Greater than or equal to	
** Exponentiation	= Equal to	~ Not. Reverses the true/false outcome of the expression.
( ) Order of operations	~= Not equal to	

Arithmetic Operators

Since fairly complex expressions are possible, it is important to keep in mind the order in which operations are performed. Functions are evaluated first, followed by exponentiation, then multiplication and division, and finally addition and subtraction. You can control the order of operations by enclosing the operation you want executed first in parentheses. You can use the ( ) key on the calculator pad to enclose a highlighted portion of the expression in parentheses.

Relational Operators

A relation is a logical expression that compares two values using a relational operator. They are primarily used in conditional transformations (see "Relational and Logical Operators in Conditional Expressions" on p. 99).

Logical Operators

You can use logical operators to join two relations or reverse the true/false outcome of a conditional expression. They are primarily used in conditional transformations (see "Relational and Logical Operators in Conditional Expressions" on p. 99).

Functions

The function list contains over seventy built-in functions, including:
- Arithmetic functions
- Statistical functions
- Logical functions
- Date and time aggregation and extraction functions
- Missing value functions
- Cross-case functions
- String functions

The following sections provide descriptions of some of the more commonly used functions. A complete list of functions is provided in the *SPSS Base System Syntax Reference Guide*.

Arithmetic Functions

ABS(numexpr). Absolute value. If the value of variable *scale* is –4.7, ABS(scale) results in a value of 4.7, and ABS(scale - 5) results in a value of 9.7.

RND(numexpr). Round to the nearest integer. If the value of *scale* is 4.7, RND(scale) results in a value of 5, and RND(scale + 5) results in a value of 10.

TRUNC(numexpr). Truncate to an integer. If the value of *scale* is 4.7, TRUNC(scale) results in a value of 4, and TRUNC(scale + 5) results in a value of 9.

MOD(numexpr,modulus). Remainder of the first argument (numexpr) divided by the second argument (modulus). If the value of *year* is 1983, MOD(year, 100) results in a value of 83. The two arguments must be separated by a comma.

SQRT(numexpr). Square root. If *scale* is 4.7, SQRT(scale) results in a value of 2.17, and SQRT(scale - 0.7) results in a value of 2.

EXP(numexpr). Exponential. *e* is raised to the power of the argument (numexpr). If the value of *scale* is 2, EXP(scale) results in a value of 7.39.

LG10(numexpr). Base 10 logarithm. If the value of *scale* is 4.7, LG10(scale) results in a value of 0.67.

LN(numexpr). Natural or Naperian logarithm (base *e*). If the value of *scale* is 10, LN(scale) results in a value of 2.3.

ARSIN(numexpr). Arcsine. The result is expressed in radians.

ARTAN(numexpr). Arctangent. The result is given in radians.

SIN(radians). Sine. The argument must be specified in radians.

COS(radians). Cosine. The argument must be specified in radians.

All arithmetic functions except MOD have a single argument enclosed in parentheses. MOD has two arguments which must be separated by a comma. Arguments can be variables, constants, or expressions.

Statistical Functions

SUM(numexpr,numexpr,...). Sum of the values across the argument list. For example, SUM(var1, var2, var3) computes the sum of the three variables.

MEAN(numexpr, numexpr,...). Mean of the values across the argument list. For example, MEAN(var1, var2, 5) computes the mean of the two variables and the constant 5.

SD(numexpr, numexpr,...). Standard deviation of the values across the argument list. For example, SD(var1, var2, var3**2) computes a standard deviation based on the values of *var1* and *var2* and the squared value of *var3*.

VARIANCE(numexpr,numexpr,...). Variance of the values across the argument list.

CFVAR(numexpr,numexpr,...). Coefficient of variance of the values across the argument list.

MIN(value,value,...). Minimum value across the argument list.

MAX(value,value,...). Maximum value across the argument list.

All statistical functions have at least two arguments enclosed in parentheses. Arguments must be separated by commas. Arguments can be numeric variables, constants, or expressions.

Logical Functions

RANGE(test,lo,hi...). True if the value of the first argument is within the inclusive range(s) defined by the remaining arguments. The first argument (test) is usually a variable name. The other arguments are pairs of values defining ranges. You can have more than one pair of low and high values. For example, RANGE(year, 1900, 1949, 1960, 1999) is true if the value of *year* is between 1900 and 1949 or between 1960 and 1999, and it is false for the values 1950 through 1959.

ANY(test,value,value...). True if the value of the first argument matches the value of any of the remaining arguments in the list. The first argument (test) is usually a variable name, as in ANY(year, 1951, 1958, 1986, 1987).

Random Number Functions

NORMAL(stddev). Each case is assigned a pseudo-random number from a normal distribution with a mean of 0 and a user-specified standard deviation.

UNIFORM (max). Each case is assigned a pseudo-random number from a uniform distribution with a minimum of 0 and a user-specified maximum.

Nested Functions

A function can be used as an argument in another function, as in

```
MEAN(RND(var1),TRUNC(var2))
```

or even

```
MEAN(RND(SD(var1)),TRUNC(SQRT(var2)))
```

Missing Values with Functions

Functions and simple arithmetic expression treat missing values in different ways. In the expression

```
(var1+var2+var3)/3
```

the result is missing if a case has a missing value for *any* of the three variables. However, in the expression

```
MEAN(var1, var2, var3)
```

the result is missing only if the case has missing values for *all* three variables. For statistical functions, you can specify the minimum number of arguments that must have nonmissing values. To do so, type a period and the number after the function name (before the argument list), as in

```
MEAN.2(var1, var2, var3)
```

In this example, at least two of the three variables in the argument list must contain a nonmissing value for the function to return a nonmissing result.

Pasting and Editing Functions

Pasting a Function into an Expression. To paste a function into an expression:

1. Position the cursor in the expression at the point where you want the function to appear.

2. Double-click on the function in the Functions list (or select the function and click on the ▲ pushbutton).

The function is inserted in the expression. If you highlight part of the expression and then insert the function, the highlighted portion of the expression is used as the first argument in the function.

Editing a Function in an Expression. The function isn't complete until you enter the **arguments**, represented by question marks in the pasted function. The number of question marks indicates the minimum number of arguments required to complete the function. To edit a function:

1. Highlight the question mark(s) in the pasted function.
2. Enter the arguments. If the arguments are variable names, you can paste them from the source variable list.

Conditional Expressions

You can use **conditional expressions** (also called logical expressions) to apply transformations to selected subsets of cases. A conditional expression returns a value of true, false, or missing for each case. If the result of a conditional expression is true, the transformation is applied to that case. If the result is false or missing, the transformation is not applied to the case.

To specify a conditional expression, click on If... in the Compute Variable dialog box. This opens the If Cases dialog box, as shown in Figure 5.2.

Figure 5.2   If Cases dialog box

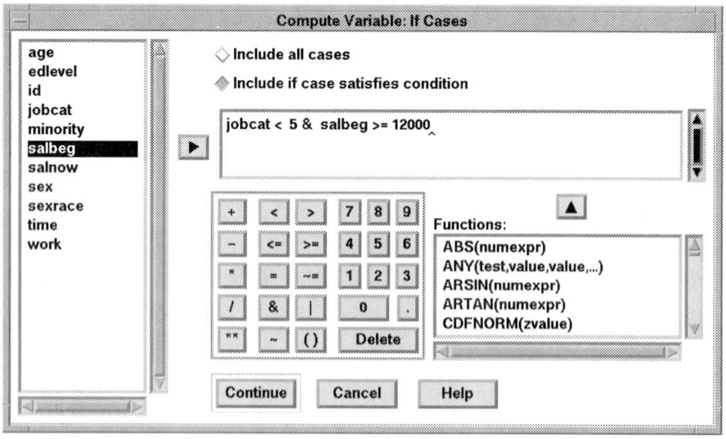

You can choose one of the following alternatives:

◇ **Include all cases**. This is the default. Values are calculated for all cases, and any conditional expressions are ignored.
◇ **Include if case satisfies condition**. Enter the conditional expression in the text box. The expression can include variable names, constants, arithmetic operators, numeric and other functions, logical variables, and relational operators.

Calculator Pad and Function List

These are identical to those described for the Compute Variable dialog box. See "Calculator Pad" on p. 94 and "Functions" on p. 95.

Relational and Logical Operators in Conditional Expressions

Most conditional expressions contain at least one relational operator, as in

```
age>=21
```

or

```
salary*3<100000
```

In the first example, only cases with a value of 21 or greater for *age* are selected. In the second, *salary* multiplied by 3 must be less than 100,000 for a case to be selected.

You can also link two or more conditional expressions using logical operators, as in

```
age>=21 | educat=1
```

or

```
salary*3<100000 & jobcat~=5
```

In the first example, cases that meet either the *age* condition or the *educat* condition are selected. In the second, both the *salary* and *jobcat* conditions must be met for a case to be selected.

Variable Type and Label

By default, new computed variables are numeric. To compute new string variables or assign descriptive variable labels, click on Type & Label.... in the Compute Variable dialog box. This opens the Type and Label dialog box, as shown in Figure 5.3.

Figure 5.3 Type and Label dialog box

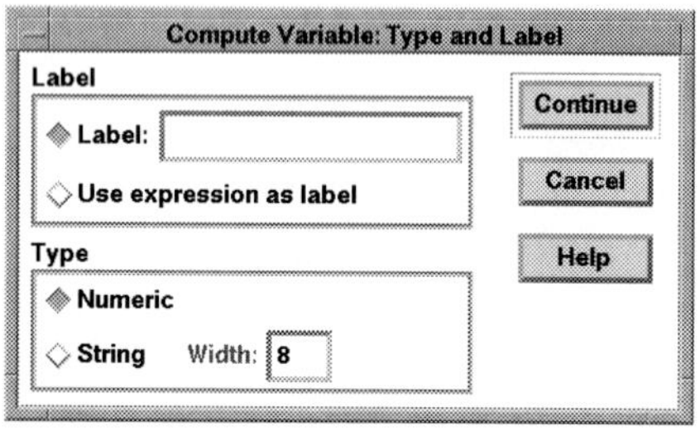

Label. Descriptive variable label. You can choose one of the following alternatives:
- Label. Enter a label up to 120 characters long.
- Use expression as label. The first 110 characters of the expression are used as the label.

Type. Variable format type. You can choose one of the following alternatives:
- Numeric. This is the default setting.
- String. Alphanumeric string.

   Width. Enter the maximum width. A width specification is required for string variables.

Syntax Rules for Expressions

Items selected from the calculator pad, function list, and source variable list are pasted with correct syntax. If you type an expression in the text box or edit part of it (such as arguments for a function), remember the following simple syntax rules:

- String variable values must be enclosed in apostrophes or quotation marks, as in NAME='Fred'. If the string value includes an apostrophe, enclose the string in quotation marks.
- The argument list for a function must be enclosed in parentheses. You can insert a space between the argument name and the parentheses, but none is required.
- Multiple arguments in a function must be separated by commas. You can insert spaces between arguments, but none is required.
- Each relation in a complex expression must be complete by itself. For example, age>=18 & age<35 is correct, while age>=18 & <35 generates an error.
- A period (.) is the only valid decimal indicator in expressions, regardless of your *LANG* environment variable setting.

Random Number Seed

Computations or conditional expressions that include random numbers (for example, the NORM and UNIFORM distribution functions) use the SPSS pseudo-random number generator, which begins with a **seed**, a very large integer value. Within a session, SPSS uses a different seed each time you generate a set of random numbers, producing different results. If you want to duplicate the same random numbers, you can reset the seed value. From the menus choose:

Transform
　Random Number Seed...

This opens the Random Number Seed dialog box, as shown in Figure 5.4.

Figure 5.4　Random Number Seed dialog box

The seed can be any positive integer value up to 999,999,999. SPSS resets the seed to the specified value each time you open the dialog box and click on OK.

To duplicate the same series of random numbers, you should set the seed *before* you generate the series for the first time. Since SPSS resets the seed as it generates a series of random numbers, it is virtually impossible to determine what seed value was used previously unless you specified the value yourself.

Counting Occurrences

To count occurrences of the same value(s) across a list of variables within cases, from the menus choose:

Transform
　Count Occurrences...

This opens the Count Occurrences dialog box, as shown in Figure 5.5.

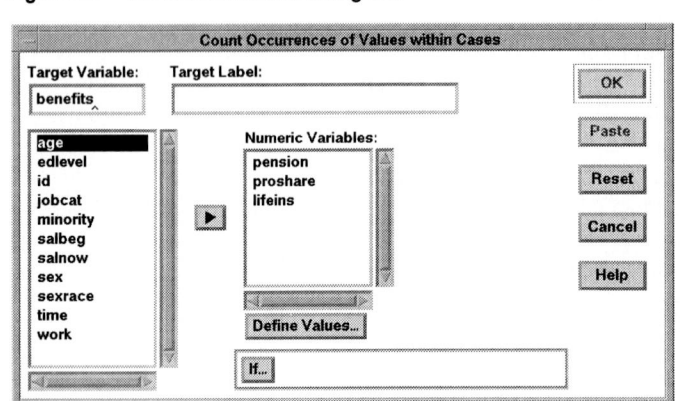

Figure 5.5   Count Occurrences dialog box

Target Variable. The name of the variable that receives the counted value. The target variable can be an existing numeric variable or a new one. New variable names must begin with a letter and cannot exceed eight characters. (See Chapter 2 for complete variable naming rules.) The target variable must be numeric.

Target Label. Descriptive variable label for the target variable. The label can be up to 120 characters. If the target variable already exists, the current label (if any) is displayed.

Variables. The selected numeric or string variables from the source list for which you want to count occurrences of certain values. The list cannot contain both numeric and string variables.

Defining Values to Count

To specify the values to count, highlight a variable in the selected variables list and click on Define Values... in the Count Occurrences dialog box. This opens the Values to Count dialog box, as shown in Figure 5.6.

Figure 5.6   Values to Count dialog box

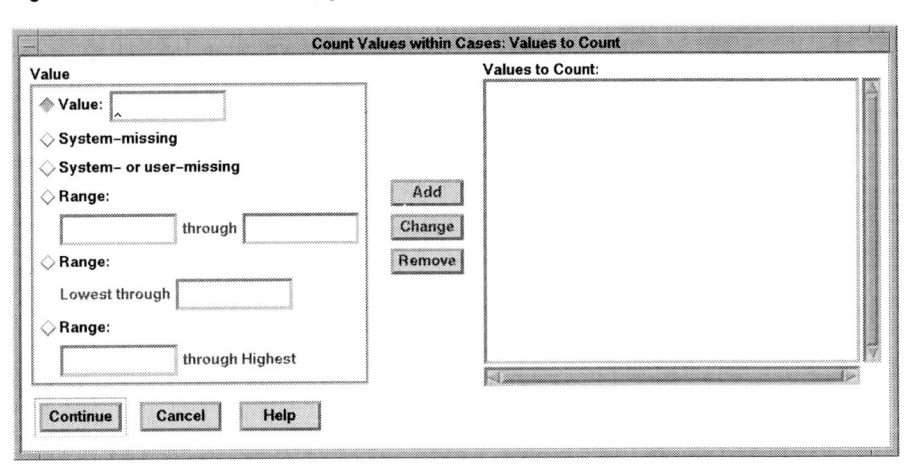

You can specify a single value, a range, or a combination of the two. To build a list of values to count, make selections from the Value alternatives and click on Add after each selection. Each occurrence of any value in the list across the variable list is counted.

Value. You can choose one of the following alternatives:

◇ **Value.** Counts occurrences of the value you have specified.

◇ **System-missing.** Counts occurrences of the system-missing value. This appears as SYSMIS in the list of values to count. Not available for string variables.

◇ **System- or user-missing.** Counts occurrences of any missing values, both system-missing and user-missing values. This appears as MISSING in the list of values to count.

◇ **Range.** Counts occurrences of values within the specified range. Not available for string variables.

◇ **Range: Lowest through n.** Counts occurrences of any value from the lowest observed value to the specified value. Not available for string variables.

◇ **Range: N through highest.** Counts occurrences from the specified value to the highest observed value. Not available for string variables.

All range specifications include any user-specified missing values that fall within the range.

Selecting Subsets of Cases

You can count occurrences of values for selected subsets of cases using conditional expressions. To specify a conditional expression, click on If... in the Count Occurrences dialog box. This opens the If Cases dialog box, as shown in Figure 5.2. (See "Conditional Expressions" on p. 98 for a description of this dialog box and instructions on how to specify conditional expressions. See "Calculator Pad" on p. 94, "Functions" on p. 95, and "Syntax Rules for Expressions" on p. 100 for additional information.)

Recoding Values

You can modify data values by recoding them. This is particularly useful for collapsing or combining categories. You can recode the values within existing variables or you can create new variables based on the recoded values of existing variables.

Recode into Same Variables

To recode the values of an existing variable, from the menus choose:

Transform
  Recode ▶
    Into Same Variables...

This opens the Recode into Same Variables dialog box, as shown in Figure 5.7.

Figure 5.7 Recode into Same Variables dialog box

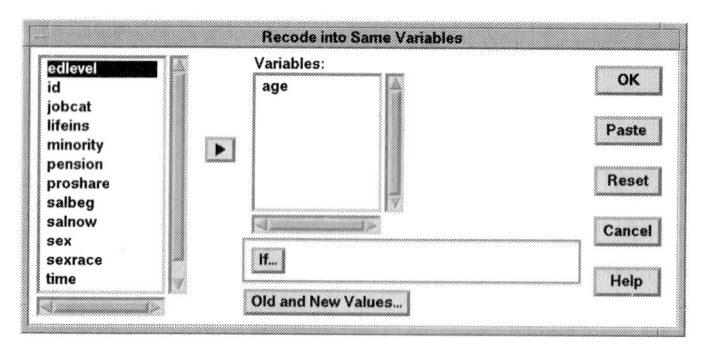

The source variable list contains the numeric and string variables in the data file. Select one or more variables for recoding. If you select multiple variables, they must all be the same type. You cannot recode numeric and string variables together.

Defining Values to Recode

To define the values to recode, click on Old and New Values... in the Recode into Same Variables dialog box. This opens the Old and New Values dialog box, as shown in Figure 5.8.

Figure 5.8   Old and New Values dialog box

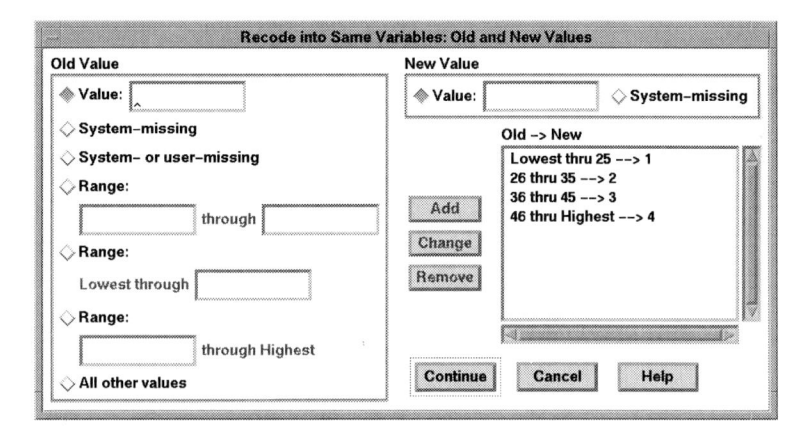

For each value (or range) that you want to recode, specify the old value and the new value, and then click on Add. You can recode multiple old values into a single new value. You cannot, however, recode a single old value into multiple new values.

Old Value. The current values for the variable that you want to recode into new values. You can choose one of the following alternatives:

- ◇ **Value**. Enter a single value. String values are automatically enclosed in apostrophes or quotes when they appear in the value list. If you enter quotation marks or apostrophes, they are considered part of the string value.
- ◇ **System-missing**. The system-missing value. This appears as SYSMIS in the value list. Not available for string variables.
- ◇ **System- or user-missing**. All missing values, including user-missing values. This appears as MISSING in the value list.
- ◇ **Range**. Enter an inclusive range of values. Not available for string variables.

- ◇ **Range: Lowest through n.** Any value from the lowest observed value to the specified value. Not available for string variables.
- ◇ **Range: N through highest.** Any value from the specified value to the highest observed value. Not available for string variables.
- ◇ **All other values.** Any remaining values not previously specified. This appears as ELSE in the value list.

New Value. The recoded value. You can choose one of the following alternatives:

- ◇ **Value.** Enter a value. String values are automatically enclosed in apostrophes or quotes when they appear in the value list. If you enter quotation marks or apostrophes, they are considered part of the string value.
- ◇ **System-missing.** The system-missing value. This appears as SYSMIS in the value list. Not available for string variables.

You can use the same new value with multiple old value specifications. This is particularly useful for combining noncontiguous categories that can't be defined in a range.

Recode Order

Recode specifications are automatically sorted in the value list, based on the old value specification, using the following order:

- Single values
- Missing values
- Ranges
- All other values

If you change a recode specification in the list, SPSS automatically re-sorts the list, if necessary, to maintain this order.

Selecting Subsets of Cases

You can recode values for selected subsets of cases using conditional expressions. To specify a conditional expression, click on If... in the Recode into Same Variables dialog box. This opens the If Cases dialog box, as shown in Figure 5.2. (See "Conditional Expressions" on p. 98 for a description of this dialog box and instructions on how to specify conditional expressions. See "Calculator Pad" on p. 94, "Functions" on p. 95, and "Syntax Rules for Expressions" on p. 100 for additional information.)

Recode into Different Variables

To create new variables based on the recoded values of existing variables, from the menus choose:

Transform
 Recode ▶
  Into Different Variables...

This opens the Recode into Different Variables dialog box, as shown in Figure 5.9.

Figure 5.9   Recode into Different Variables dialog box

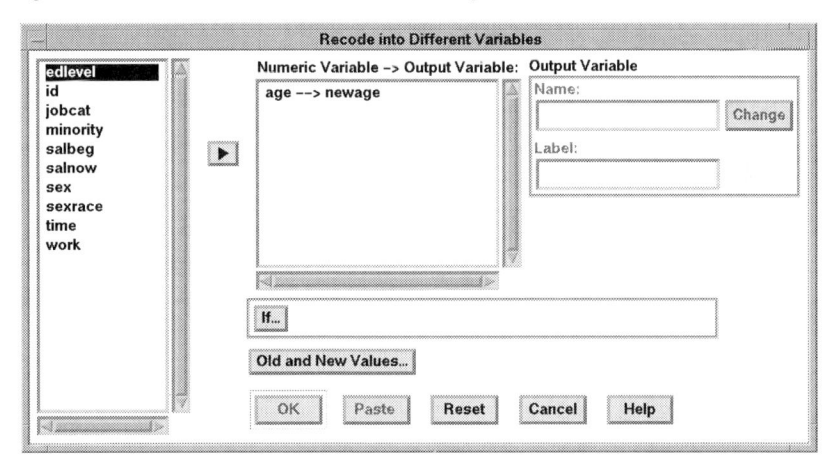

The source variable list contains the numeric and string variables in the data file. Select one or more variables for recoding. If you select multiple variables, they must all be the same type. You cannot recode numeric and string variables together.

Input Variable –> Output Variable. Selected variables from the source list appear in the input variable column. (The word Input changes to Numeric or String depending on the type of variables selected.) A question mark in the output variable column indicates that a name needs to be supplied for the output variable. You must provide output variable names for all selected input variables.

Output Variable. The new variable that receives the recoded values.

> **Name.** An output variable name is required for each input variable. Highlight the input variable in the selected variable list and then type a name for the corresponding output variable. Variable names must start with a letter and cannot exceed eight characters. (See Chapter 2 for complete variable naming rules.)
>
> **Label.** Optional descriptive variable label, up to 120 characters long.

After entering the output variable name and the optional label, click on Change to put the name in the output variable list, next to the corresponding input variable name.

Defining Values to Recode

To define the values to recode, click on Old and New Values... in the Recode into Different Variables dialog box. This opens the Old and New Values dialog box, as shown in Figure 5.10.

Figure 5.10 Old and New Values dialog box

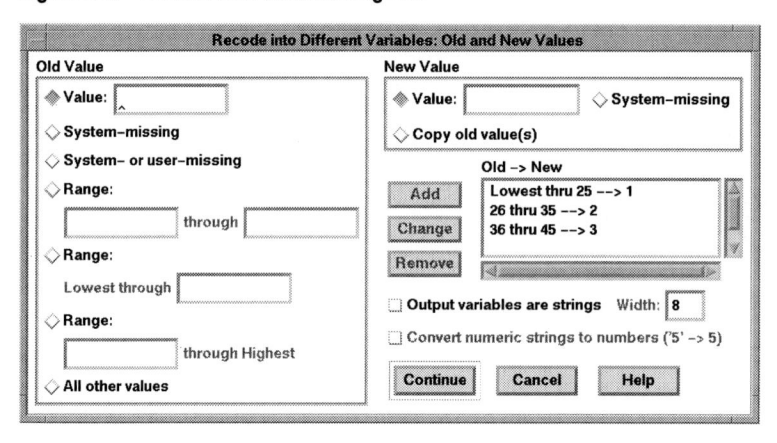

For each value (or range) that you want to recode, specify the old value from the input variable and the new value for the output variable, and then click on Add. You can recode multiple old values into a single new value. You cannot, however, recode a single old value into multiple new values.

Old Value. The values for the input variable that you want to recode for the output variable. You can choose one of the following alternatives:

- **Value.** Enter a value. String values are automatically enclosed in apostrophes or quotes when they appear in the value list. If you enter quotation marks or apostrophes, they are considered part of the string value.
- **System-missing.** The system-missing value. This appears as SYSMIS in the value list. Not available for string variables.
- **System- or user-missing.** All missing values, including user-missing values. This appears as MISSING in the value list.
- **Range.** Enter an inclusive range of values. Not available for string variables.

- **Range: Lowest through n.** Any value from the lowest observed value to the specified value. Not available for string variables.
- **Range: N through highest.** Any value from the specified value to the highest observed value. Not available for string variables.
- **All other values.** Any remaining values not previously specified. This appears as ELSE in the value list.

New Value. The recoded value for the output variable. You can choose one of the following alternatives:

- **Value.** Enter a value. String values are automatically enclosed in apostrophes or quotes when they appear in the value list. If you enter quotation marks or apostrophes, they are considered part of the string value.
- **System-missing.** The system-missing value. This appears as SYSMIS in the value list. Not available for string variables.
- **Copy old value(s).** Retains the input variable value.

You can use the same new value with multiple old value specifications. This is particularly useful for combining noncontiguous categories that can't be defined in a range.

For string variables, there are two additional parameters:

- ❏ **Output variables are strings.** Select this item if your new output variables are string variables. This is required for new string variables.

    Width. Enter an integer between 1 and 255 for the maximum width of the string.

- ❏ **Convert numeric strings to numbers.** Valid values are numbers with an optional leading sign (+ or –) and a single period for a decimal point. Alphanumeric strings are assigned the system-missing value.

Missing Values

Any unspecified old values for the input variable are undefined for the new output variable and are assigned the system-missing value. To make sure unspecified old values for the input variable receive a nonmissing value for the output variable, do the following:

1. For the old value, select All other values.
2. For the new value, select Copy old value(s).
3. Click on Add.

ELSE –> COPY appears in the value list. Any unspecified values for the input variable are retained for the output variable.

Selecting Subsets of Cases

You can recode values for selected subsets of cases using conditional expressions. To specify a conditional expression, click on If... in the Recode into Different Variables dialog box. This opens the If Cases dialog box, as shown in Figure 5.2. (See "Conditional Expressions" on p. 98 for a description of this dialog box and instructions on how to specify conditional expressions. See "Calculator Pad" on p. 94, "Functions" on p. 95, and "Syntax Rules for Expressions" on p. 100 for additional information.)

Ranking Data

To compute ranks, normal and savage scores, or classify cases into groups based on percentile values, from the menus choose:

Transform
  Rank Cases...

This opens the Rank Cases dialog box, as shown in Figure 5.11.

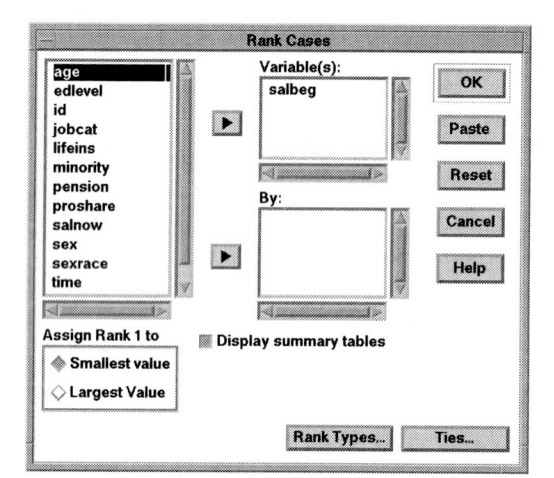

Figure 5.11 Rank Cases dialog box

The numeric variables in the data file are displayed in the source variable list. Select one or more variables for which you want to compute ranks. To obtain the default simple ranking in ascending order with the mean rank assigned to ties, click on OK. SPSS creates a new variable that contains the rankings. The original variable is unaffected.

Optionally, you can organize rankings into subgroups by selecting one or more **grouping variables** for the By list. Ranks are computed within each group. Groups are defined by the combination of values of the grouping variables. For example, if you select *sex* and *minority* as grouping variables, ranks are computed for each combination of *sex* and *minority*.

Assign Rank 1 to. There are two options for the order in which values are ranked:

◇ **Smallest value.** Assigns ranks by ascending order, with the smallest value receiving a rank of 1. This is the default.

◇ **Largest value.** Assigns ranks by descending order, with the largest value receiving a rank of 1.

SPSS automatically creates a new variable name and a descriptive variable label for each variable ranked and each ranking method (see "Ranking Method" on p. 111). The following option is available for displaying a summary table of new variable names:

❑ **Display summary tables.** Displays a table of new variable names and labels that describe the variable ranked, ranking method, and any grouping variables. This is displayed by default. Deselect this item to suppress the summary table.

Ranking Method

Simple ranks are computed by default. To choose other ranking methods, click on Rank Types... in the Rank Cases dialog box. This opens the Rank Types dialog box, as shown in Figure 5.12.

Figure 5.12 Rank Types dialog box

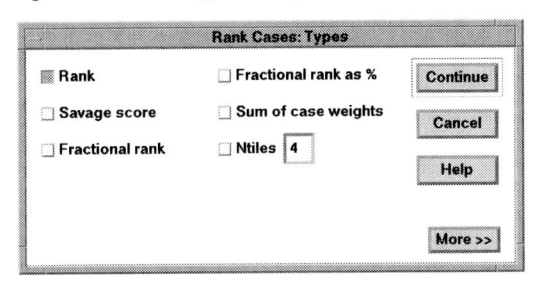

You can select multiple methods. A separate ranking variable is created for each method. You can choose one or more of the following methods:

❑ **Rank.** Simple rank. This is the default.

❑ **Savage score.** Scores based on an exponential distribution.

❑ **Fractional rank.** Each rank is divided by the number of cases with valid values or by the sum of any weighting variables (see Chapter 6).

❑ **Fractional rank as percent.** Each rank is divided by the number of cases with valid values and multiplied by 100.

❏ **Sum of cases weights.** The value of the variable is a constant for cases in the same group.
❏ **Ntiles.** A user-specified number of percentiles, each with approximately the same number of cases.

Proportion Estimates and Normal Scores

To create new ranking variables based on proportion estimates and normal scores, click on More>> in the Rank Types dialog box. The dialog box expands, as shown in Figure 5.13.

Figure 5.13 Expanded Rank Types dialog box

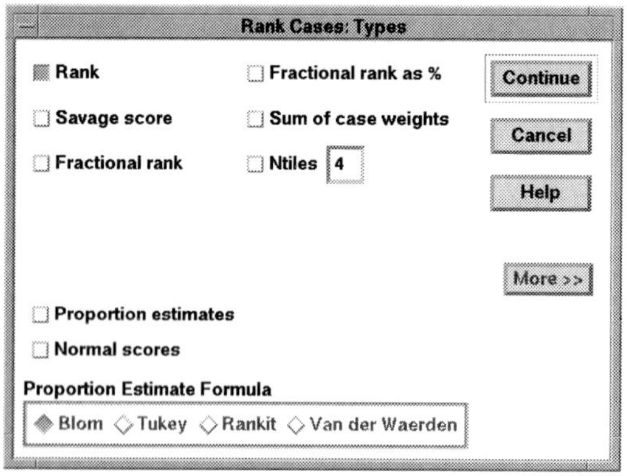

You can choose one or both of the following:

❏ **Proportion estimates.** The estimate of the cumulative proportion (area) of the distribution corresponding to a particular rank.
❏ **Normal scores.** The new variable contains the Z scores from the standard normal distribution that correspond to the estimated cumulative proportion. For example, if the estimated cumulative proportion is 0.50, the normal score is 0.

Proportion Estimate Formula. You can choose one of the following formula methods:

◇ **Blom.** Blom's transformation, defined by the formula $(r - 3/8) / (w + 1/4)$, where w is the number of observations and r is rank, ranging from 1 to w (see Blom, 1958). This is the default.
◇ **Tukey.** Tukey's transformation, defined by the formula $(r - 1/3) / (w + 1/3)$, where w is the sum of case weights and r is the rank, ranging from 1 to w (see Tukey, 1962).
◇ **Rankit.** Uses the formula $(r - 1/2) / w$, where w is the number of observations and r is the rank, ranging from 1 to w (see Chambers et al., 1983).

◇ **Van der Waerden**. Van der Waerden's transformation, defined by the formula $r/(w+1)$, where w is the sum of case weights and r is the rank, ranging from 1 to w (see Lehmann, 1975).

Rank Ties

By default, cases with the same values for a variable are assigned the average (mean) of the ranks for the tied values. To choose an alternate method for handling ties, click on Ties... in the Rank Cases dialog box. This opens the Rank Ties dialog box, as shown in Figure 5.14.

Figure 5.14 Rank Ties dialog box

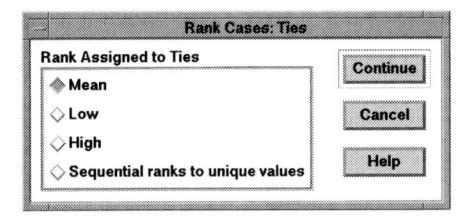

Rank Assigned to Ties. You can choose one of the following alternatives for assigning ranks to tied values:

◇ **Mean**. Average rank assigned to tied values. This is the default.

◇ **Low**. Lowest rank assigned to tied values.

◇ **High**. Highest rank assigned to ties.

◇ **Sequential ranks to unique values**. Ranks are assigned from 1 to D, where D is the number of unique values. Cases with the same value receive the same rank.

Table 5.2 shows the effects of each method on a group of data values.

Table 5.2 Alternatives for ranking ties

Value	Mean	Low	High	Sequential
10	1	1	1	1
15	3	2	4	2
15	3	2	4	2
15	3	2	4	2
16	5	5	5	3
20	6	6	6	4

Creating Consecutive Integers from Numeric and String Values

When category codes are not sequential, the resulting empty cells reduce performance and increase memory requirements for many SPSS procedures. Additionally, some procedures cannot use long string variables, and some require consecutive integer values for factor levels.

To recode string and numeric variables into consecutive integers, from the menus choose:

Transform
 Automatic Recode...

This opens the Automatic Recode dialog box, as shown in Figure 5.15.

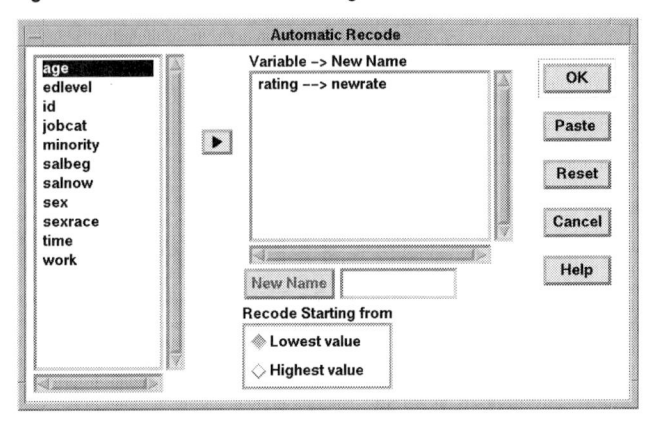

Figure 5.15   Automatic Recode dialog box

The variables in the working data file are displayed in the source variable list. Select one or more variables for which you want to recode values into consecutive integers. SPSS creates new variables containing the recoded values. The original variables are not affected. Any existing variable or value labels are retained for the new variables. If the original value doesn't have a value label, the original value is used as the value label for the recoded value.

Variable –> New Name. You must specify a new variable name to receive the recoded values for each selected variable. To specify a new variable name, highlight the original variable in the selected list, enter the new variable name in the text box, and click on New Name. The new variable name is displayed next to the original variable name. Variable names must begin with a letter and cannot exceed eight characters. (See Chapter 2 for complete variable naming rules.)

Recode Starting from. There are two alternatives for the order in which new values are assigned:

- ◇ **Lowest value.** Assigns values by ascending order, with the lowest value receiving a recoded value of 1. This is the default.
- ◇ **Highest value.** Assigns values by descending order, with the highest value receiving a recoded value of 1.

String values are recoded in alphabetical order, with uppercase letters preceding their lowercase counterparts. Missing values are recoded into missing values higher than any nonmissing values, with their order preserved. For example, if the original variable has ten nonmissing values, the lowest missing value would be recoded to 11, and the value 11 would be a missing value for the new variable.

Pending Transformations

To run pending transformations, from the menus choose:

Transform
  Run Pending Transforms

By default, data transformations are executed immediately. If you have a large number of transformations or you are working with a large data file, you can save processing time by changing your Preferences settings to delay the execution of transformations until SPSS encounters a command that requires a data pass (see Chapter 29). If you choose to delay the execution of data transformations, they are automatically executed as soon as you run any statistical procedure that requires a data pass. You can also run pending transformations at any time without running any statistical procedure.

6 File Handling and File Transformations

Data files are not always organized in the ideal form for your specific needs. You may want to combine data files, sort the data in a different order, select a subset of cases, or change the unit of analysis by grouping cases together. SPSS offers a wide range of file transformation capabilities, including the ability to:

- **Sort data**. You can sort cases based on the value of one or more variables.
- **Transpose cases and variables**. SPSS reads rows as cases and columns as variables. For data files in which this order is reversed, you can switch the rows and columns and read the data in the correct format.
- **Merge files**. You can merge two or more data files together. You can combine files with the same variables but different cases, or files with the same cases but different variables.
- **Select subsets of cases**. You can restrict your analysis to a subset of cases or perform simultaneous analyses on different subsets.
- **Aggregate data**. You can change the unit of analysis by aggregating cases based on the value of one or more grouping variables.
- **Weight data**. Weight cases for analysis based on the value of a weight variable.

Sorting Data

Sorting cases (sorting rows of the data file) is often useful—and sometimes necessary—in conjunction with merging files (see "Combining Data Files" on p. 119), split-file processing (see "Sorting Cases for Split-File Processing" on p. 139), and generating summary reports (see Chapter 21).

To reorder the sequence of cases in the data file based on the value of one or more sorting variables, from the menus choose:

Data
 Sort Cases...

This opens the Sort Cases dialog box, as shown in Figure 6.1.

Figure 6.1 Sort Cases dialog box

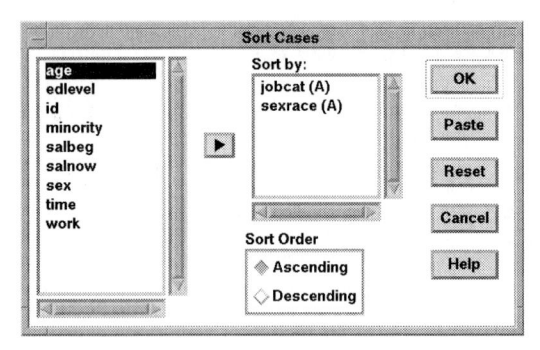

The variables in the data file appear on the source variable list. Select one or more sort variables. If you select multiple sort variables, the order in which they appear on the sort list determines the order in which cases are sorted. For example, based on the sort list in Figure 6.1, cases will be sorted by the value of *sexrace* within sorted categories of *jobcat*. For string variables, uppercase letters precede their lowercase counterparts in sort order (for example, the string value "Yes" comes before "yes" in sort order).

Sort Order. There are two alternatives for sort order:

◇ **Ascending.** Sort cases by ascending order of the values of the sort variable(s). This is the default.

◇ **Descending.** Sort case by descending order of the values of the sort variable(s).

Transposing Cases and Variables

SPSS assumes a file structure in which cases are represented in rows and variables are represented in columns. Sometimes, however, data are recorded in the opposite fashion. You might, for example, find this to be the case with spreadsheet data. To switch the columns and rows in the data file, from the menus choose:

Data
    Transpose...

This opens the Transpose dialog box, as shown in Figure 6.2.

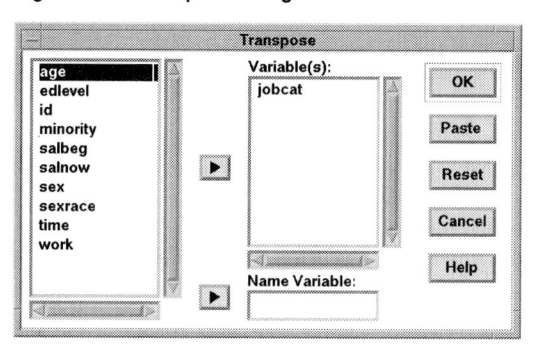

Figure 6.2   Transpose dialog box

The variables in the data file appear on the source variable list. Select one or more variables. The selected variables become cases, and all cases become variables.

Name Variable. By default, SPSS assigns the new variable names *var001*, *var002*, and so on, to the transposed data. Optionally, you can use the values of an existing variable in the untransposed file as the variable names for the transposed file. If the name variable is numeric, the new variable names begin with the letter V followed by the numeric values. If values exceed eight characters, they are truncated. If values are not unique, SPSS creates unique variable names by adding a sequential number to the end of the value. A table of the new variable names is displayed in the output window.

Missing Values in Transposed Data Files

Any user-missing values are converted to the system-missing value when the data file is transposed. If you want to retain the original data values in the transposed file, before transposing the file, change the variable definition so that there are no user-missing values (see Chapter 3).

Combining Data Files

With SPSS, you can combine data from two files in two different ways. You can:
- Merge files containing the same variables but different cases.
- Merge files containing the same cases but different variables.

Merging Files That Contain Different Cases

The Add Cases procedure merges two data files that contain the same variables but different cases. For example, you might record the same information for customers in two different sales regions and maintain the data for each region in separate files. The variables can be in any order in the two files. Variables are matched by name. The procedure also provides a facility to match variables that contain the same information but different variable names in the two files.

The Add Cases procedure adds cases to the working data file from a second, external SPSS data file. So, before you can merge the files, one of them must already be open, and both files must be SPSS data files.

To add cases to the working data file from an external SPSS data file, from the menus choose:

Data
  Merge Files ▶
    Add Cases...

This opens the Add Cases Read File dialog box, as shown in Figure 6.3.

Figure 6.3   Add Cases Read File dialog box

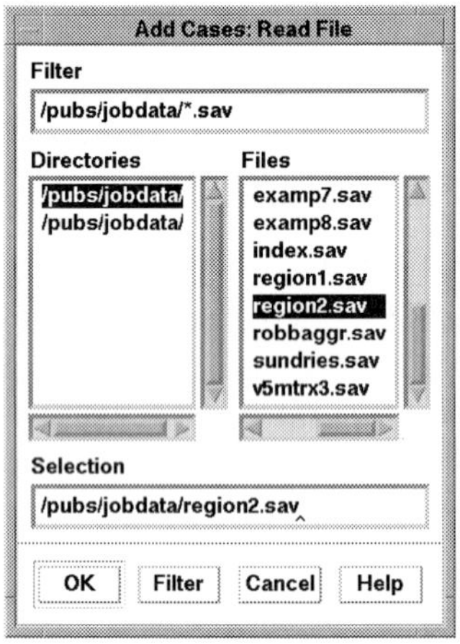

Filter. To display a list of files that match a wildcard search or to change the directory location, enter the directory path and wildcard specification and press Filter. By default, SPSS looks for all files in the current directory with the extension *.sav* and displays them on the Files list.

Directories. You can also use the Directories list to change the directory location. To change directories, select the name of the directory on the Directories list and press Filter or double-click on the directory name. To move up a directory level, select the directory path that ends with a slash and two periods (/..).

Files. All files in the directory that match the wildcard search appear on the Files list. Select the file you want and press OK or double-click on the filename.

Selection. Enter the directory path and filename and press OK. If you select a directory and file from the lists, this information is entered automatically. If you enter the information directly, you can bypass the filter process.

Select the external data file you want to merge with the working data file and click on OK. This opens the Add Cases From dialog box, as shown in Figure 6.4.

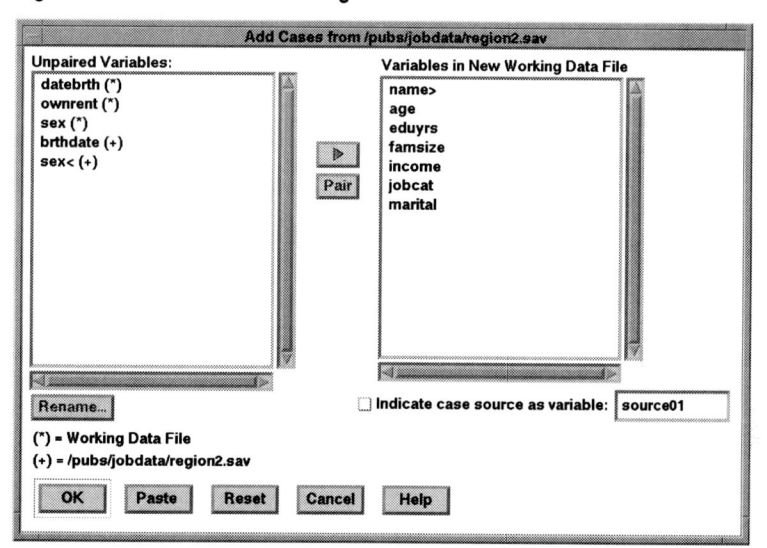

Figure 6.4   Add Cases From dialog box

Unpaired Variables. Variables to be excluded from the new, merged data file. Variables from the working data file are identified with an asterisk (*). Variables from the external data file are identified with a plus sign (+). By default, this list contains:

- Variables from either data file that do not match a variable name in the other file. You can create pairs from unpaired variables and include them in the new, merged file (see below).
- Variables defined as numeric data in one file and string data in the other file. Numeric variables cannot be merged with string variables. For example, in Figure 6.4, *sex* is a numeric variable in the working data file, but it is a short string variable in the external data file.

- String variables of unequal width. The defined width of a string variable must be the same in both data files.

Variables in the New Working Data File. Variables to be included in the new, merged data file. By default, all the variables that match both name and data type (numeric or string) are included on the list. You can remove variables from the list if you don't want them included in the merged file.

The following option is also available:

❑ **Indicate case source as variable**. Creates an **indicator variable** that indicates the source data file for each case in the merged file. For cases from the working data file, the value of this variable is 0; for cases from the external data file, the value of this variable is 1. The default name of the variable is *source01*. You can enter a variable name up to eight characters long. The name cannot be the same as one of the variables on the list to be included in the merged file.

Selecting Variables

If the same information is recorded under different variable names in the two files, you can create a pair from the Unpaired Variables list. Select the two variables on the Unpaired Variables list and click on Pair. (Use the ctrl-click method to select noncontiguous pairs of variables.) Both variable names appear together in the same line on the list of variables to be included in the merged file, as shown in Figure 6.5. By default, the name of the variable in the working data file is used as the name of the variable in the merged file.

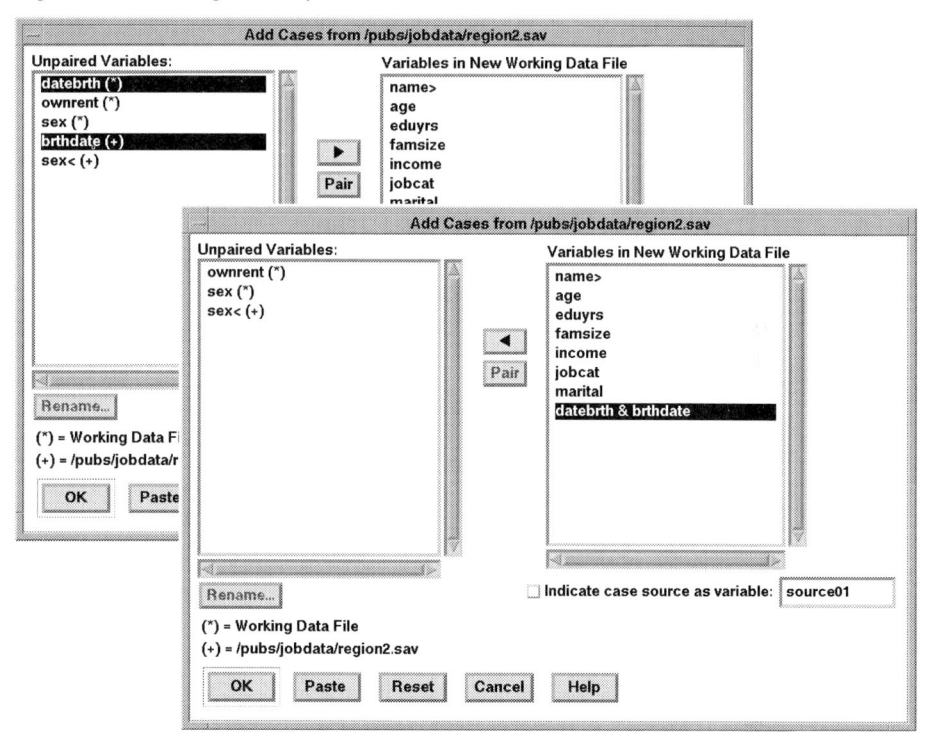

Figure 6.5   Selecting variable pairs

To include an unpaired variable from one file without pairing it with a variable from the other file, select the variable on the Unpaired Variables list and click on ▶. Any unpaired variables included in the merged file will contain missing data for cases from the file that does not contain that variable. For example, the variable *ownrent* exists in the working data file but not in the external data file. If this variable is included in the merged file, cases from the external file will contain the system-missing value for this variable in the merged file.

Removing Variables

To remove a variable from the list of variables to be included in the merged file, select the variable on the list and click on ◀. The variable is moved to the Unpaired Variables list. The variable name is displayed twice on the Unpaired Variables list, once for the working data file, and once for the external file. To move the variable back to the list of variables to be included in the merged file, select both variable names on the Unpaired Variables list and click on Pair.

Renaming Variables

You can rename variables from either the working data file or the external file before moving them from the Unpaired Variables list to the list of variables to be included in the merged data file. Renaming variables enables you to:

- Use the variable name from the external file rather than the name from the working data file for variable pairs—for example, to use *brthdate* instead of *datebrth* for the variable pair in Figure 6.7.
- Include two variables with the same name but of unmatched types or different string widths. For example, to include both the numeric variable *sex* from the working data file and the string variable *sex* from the external file, one of them must be renamed first.

To rename a variable on the Unpaired Variables list, highlight the variable and click on Rename... in the Add Cases From dialog box. This opens the Rename dialog box, as shown in Figure 6.6. The new variable name can be up to eight characters long. (See Chapter 3 for complete variable-naming rules.)

Figure 6.6   Rename dialog box

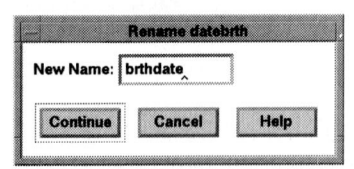

Both the original variable name and the new name are displayed on the Unpaired Variables list. If the new variable name is the same as the other variable in the pair, only one variable name appears on the list of variables to be included in the merged file, as shown in Figure 6.7.

To undo variable renaming, simply go back to the Rename dialog box and delete the new variable name.

Figure 6.7   Selecting renamed variables

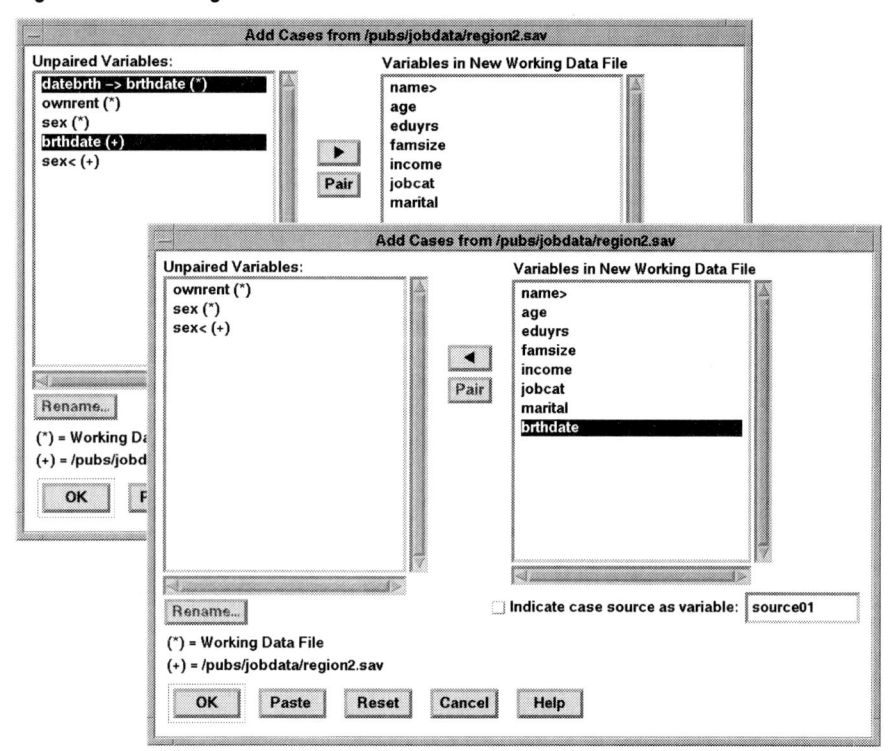

[Screenshot of "Add Cases from /pubs/jobdata/region2.sav" dialog boxes showing Unpaired Variables and Variables in New Working Data File lists]

Dictionary Information

Any existing dictionary information (variable and value labels, user-missing values, display formats) in the working data file is applied to the merged data file. If any dictionary information for a variable is undefined in the working data file, dictionary information from the external data file is used.

If the working data file contains any defined value labels or user-missing values for a variable, any additional value labels or user-missing values for that variable in the external file are ignored.

Merging Files That Contain Different Variables

With the Add Variables procedure, you can:
- Merge two SPSS data files that contain the same cases but different variables.
- Use a table lookup file to add data to multiple cases in another file.

The two data files to be merged must meet the following requirements:
- Files must be in SPSS or SPSS/PC+ format.
- Cases must be sorted in the same order in both data files.
- If one or more key variables are used to match cases, the two data files must be sorted by ascending order of the key variable(s).

The Add Variables procedure merges the working data file with an external SPSS data file. Both files must be sorted in the same case order, so, before you can merge the files, you must complete any necessary sorting. One of the files must already be open when you start the procedure (see "Sorting Data" on p. 117).

To add variables to the working data file from an external SPSS data file or to use data from a table lookup file, from the menus choose:

Data
  Merge Files ▶
    Add Variables...

This opens the Add Variables Read File dialog box, as shown in Figure 6.8.

Figure 6.8 Add Variables Read File dialog box

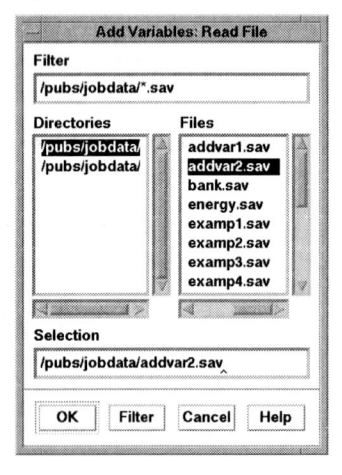

Filter. To display a list of files that match a wildcard search or to change the directory location, enter the directory path and wildcard specification and press Filter. By default, SPSS looks for all files in the current directory with the extension *.sav* and displays them on the Files list.

Directories. You can also use the Directories list to change the directory location. To change directories, select the name of the directory on the Directories list and press Filter or double-click on the directory name. To move up a directory level, select the directory path that ends with a slash and two periods (/..).

Files. All files in the directory that match the wildcard search appear on the Files list. Select the file you want and press OK or double-click on the filename.

Selection. Enter the directory path and filename and press OK. If you select a directory and file from the lists, this information is entered automatically. If you enter the information directly, you can bypass the filter process.

Select the external data file you want to merge with the working data file and click on OK. This opens the Add Variables From dialog box, as shown in Figure 6.9.

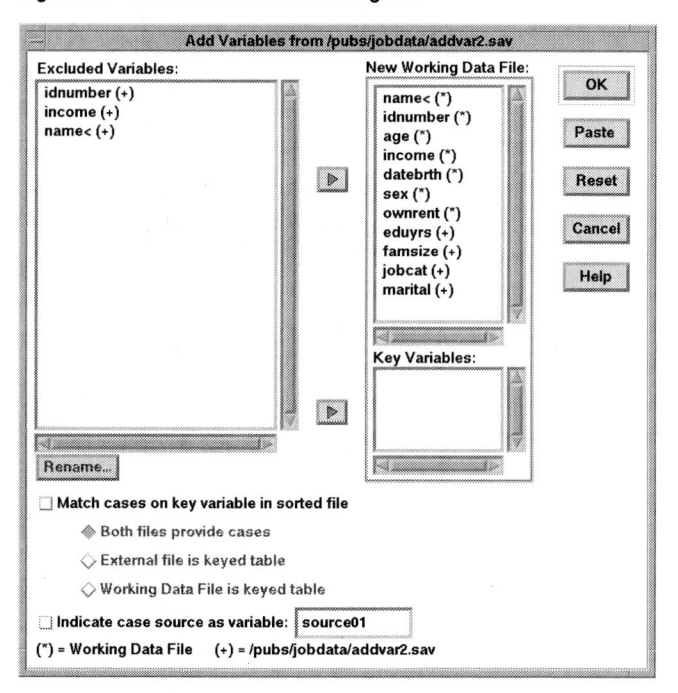

Figure 6.9   Add Variables From dialog box

Excluded Variables. Variables to be excluded from the new, merged data file. By default, this list contains any variable names from the external data file that duplicate variable names in the working data file. If you want to include the variable with the duplicate name in the merged file, you can rename it and add it to the list of variables to be included (see "Renaming Variables" on p. 130). Variables from the working data file are identified with an asterisk (*). Variables from the external data file are identified with a plus sign (+).

New Working Data File. Variables to be included in the new, merged data file. By default, all unique variable names in both data files are included on the list.

The following options are also available:

- **Match cases on key variables in sorted files.** If some cases in one file do not have matching cases in the other file (that is, some cases are missing in one file), use **key variables** to identify and correctly match cases from the two files. You can also use key variables with table lookup files. The key variables must have the same names in both data files. Both data files must be sorted by ascending order of the key variables, and the order of variables on the Key Variables list must be the same as their sort sequence. Key variables are included in the new, merged file.

  Cases that do not match on the key variables are included in the merged file but are not merged with cases from the other file. Unmatched cases contain values only for the variables in the file from which they are taken; variables from the other file contain the system-missing value.

  You can choose one of the following alternatives for the key variable matching method:

  ◇ **Both files provide cases.** Cases in one file correspond to cases in the other file on a one-to-one basis. This is the default. The key variables should uniquely identify each case. If two or more cases have the same values for all the key variables, SPSS merges those cases in sequential order and issues a warning message.

  ◇ **External file is keyed table.** The external data file is a table lookup file.

  ◇ **Working data file is keyed table.** The working data file is a table lookup file.

  A **keyed table** or **table lookup file** is a file in which data for each "case" can be applied to multiple cases in the other data file. For example, if one file contains information on individual family members (for example, sex, age, education) and the other file contains overall family information (for example, total income, family size, location), you can use the file of family data as a table lookup file and apply the common family data to each individual family member in the merged data file.

The following option is also available:

- **Indicate case source as variable.** Creates an indicator variable that indicates the source data file for each case in the merged file. For cases from the working data file that are missing from the external file, the value of this variable is 0; for cases from the external data file that are missing from the working file and cases present in both files, the value of this variable is 1. The default name of the variable is *source01*. You can enter a variable name up to eight characters long. The name cannot be the same as one of the variables on the list to be included in the merged file.

Selecting Key Variables

Key variables are selected from the Excluded Variables list. The key variables must be present in both data files. By default, any variables in the external file that duplicate variable names in the working data file are placed on the Excluded Variables list. For example, in Figure 6.10, *idnumber* and *name* are the key variables.

To select a key variable, highlight the variable on the Excluded Variables list, select Match cases on key variables in sorted files, and click on the ▶ pushbutton next to the Key Variables list. You can select multiple key variables. Both files must be sorted by ascending order of the key variables, and the order of variables on the Key Variables list must be the same as their sort sequence.

Key variables must have the same variable names in both data files. If the names differ, you can rename the variable in one file to match the variable name in the other file (see "Renaming Variables" on p. 130).

Figure 6.10 Selecting key variables

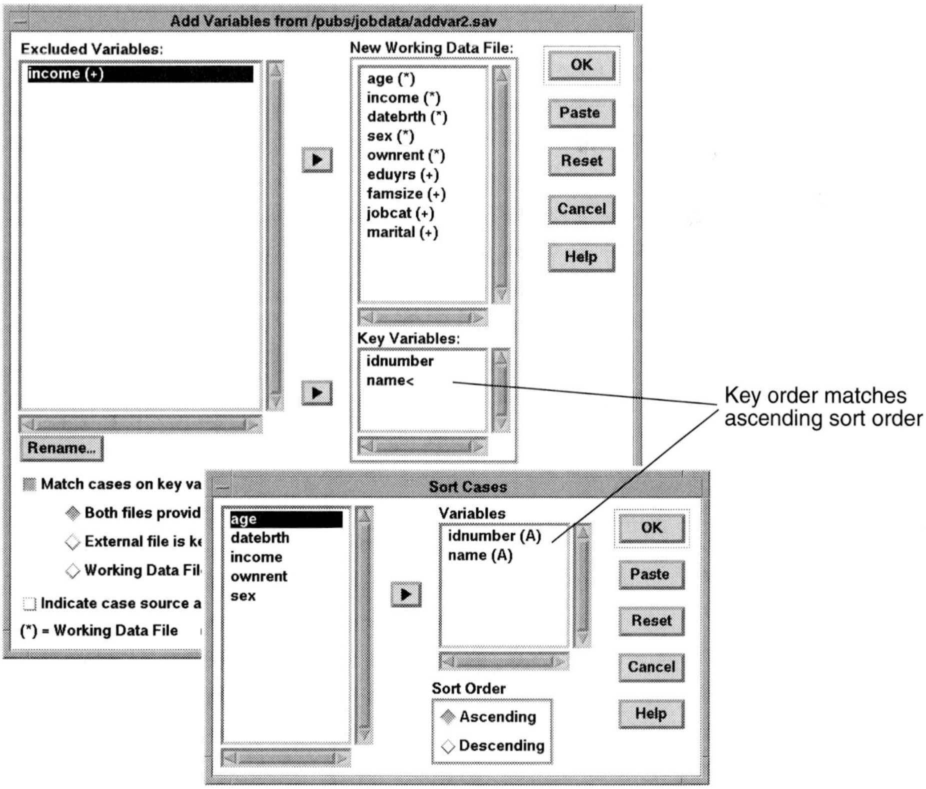

Renaming Variables

There are several reasons for renaming variables before merging two files that contain different variables:

- You want to include a variable from the external file that has the same name as a variable in the working data file but contains different data.
- You want to select a key variable that does not have the same name in both data files.
- You don't like a variable name and want to change it.

To rename a variable, highlight the variable on the Excluded Variables list and click on Rename... in the Add Variables From dialog box. This opens the Rename dialog box, as shown in Figure 6.11. The new variable name can be up to eight characters long. (See Chapter 3 for complete variable-naming rules.)

Figure 6.11 Rename dialog box

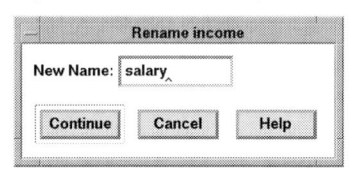

Both the original variable name and the new name are displayed on the Excluded Variables list. If you move the renamed variable to the new working data file list or the Key Variables list, only the new variable name is displayed, as shown in Figure 6.12.

To undo variable renaming, simply go back to the Rename dialog box and delete the new variable name.

Figure 6.12 Selecting renamed variables

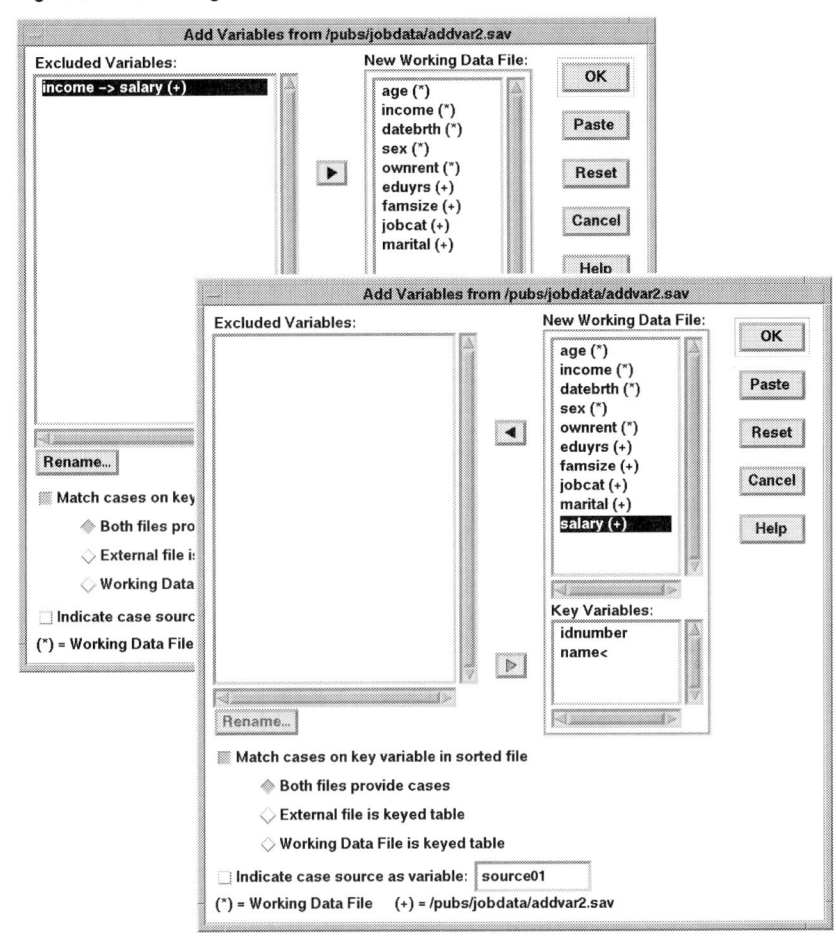

Applying a Data Dictionary

An SPSS data dictionary can contain extensive data definition information, including:
- Data type (numeric, string, etc.) and width
- Display format
- Descriptive variable and value labels
- User-missing value specifications

To apply the data dictionary information from another SPSS data file to the working data file, from the menus choose:

Data
　Apply Dictionary...

This opens the Apply SPSS Dictionary dialog box, as shown in Figure 6.13.

Figure 6.13　Apply SPSS Dictionary dialog box

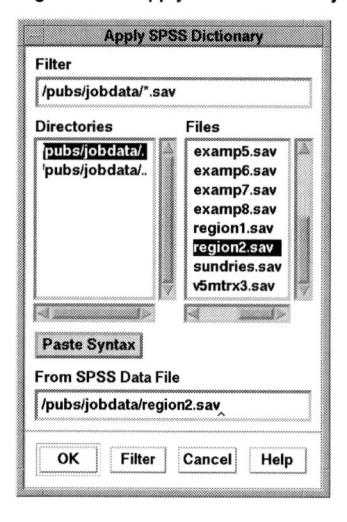

Filter. To display a list of files that match a wildcard search or to change the directory location, enter the directory path and wildcard specification and press Filter. By default, SPSS looks for all files in the current directory with the extension *.sav* and displays them on the Files list.

Directories. You can also use the Directories list to change the directory location. To change directories, select the name of the directory on the Directories list and press Filter or double-click on the directory name. To move up a directory level, select the directory path that ends with a slash and two periods (/..).

Files. All files in the directory that match the wildcard search appear on the Files list. Select the file you want and press OK or double-click on the filename.

Selection. Enter the directory path and filename and press OK. If you select a directory and file from the lists, this information is entered automatically. If you enter the information directly, you can bypass the filter process.

Dictionary information is applied based on matching variable names. The variables don't have to be in the same order in both files, and variables that aren't present in both files are unaffected. The following rules apply:

- If the variable type (numeric or string) is the same in both files, all the dictionary information is applied.
- If the variable type is not the same for both files, or if it is a long string (more than eight characters), only the variable label is applied.
- Numeric, Dollar, Dot, Comma, Date, and Time formats are all considered numeric, and all dictionary information is applied.
- String variable widths are not affected by the applied dictionary.
- For short string variables (eight characters or less), missing values and specified values for value labels are truncated if they exceed the defined width of the variable in the working data file.
- Any applied dictionary information overwrites existing dictionary information.

Weighted Files

The following rules apply to weighted files (see "Weighting Cases" on p. 143):

- If the working data file is weighted and the file containing the dictionary is unweighted, the working data file remains weighted.
- If the working data file is unweighted and the file containing the dictionary is weighted by a variable that exists in the working data file, the working data file is weighted by that variable.
- If both files are weighted but they are not weighted by the same variable, the weight is changed in the working data file if the weight variable in the file containing the dictionary also exists in the working data file.

The status bar at the bottom of the SPSS application window displays the message Weight on if weighting is in effect in the working data file.

Aggregating Data

You can aggregate cases based on the value of one or more grouping variables and create a new data file containing one case for each group. For example, you can aggregate county data by state and create a new data file in which state is the unit of analysis. To aggregate cases, from the menus choose:

Data
  Aggregate...

This opens the Aggregate Data dialog box, as shown in Figure 6.14.

Figure 6.14 Aggregate Data dialog box

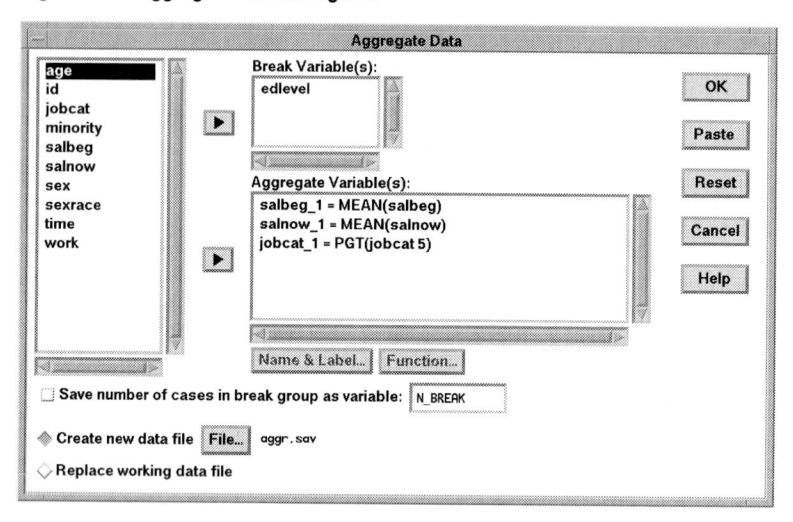

The variables in the data file appear on the source variable list. You must select at least one break variable and define at least one new variable based on an aggregate variable and an aggregate function. SPSS automatically creates a new file with the default name *aggr.sav* unless you specify a different filename.

Break Variable(s). Cases are grouped together based on the values of the break variables. Each unique combination of break variable values defines a group and generates one case in the new aggregated file. All break variables are saved in the new file with their existing names and dictionary information. The break variable can be either numeric or string.

Aggregate Variable(s). Variables are used with aggregate functions (see "Aggregate Functions" on p. 135) to create the new variables for the aggregated file. By default, SPSS creates new aggregate variable names using the first several characters of the source variable name followed by an underscore and a sequential number. For example, *salbeg* on the source list becomes *salbeg_1* on the Aggregate Variable(s) list. The aggregate variable name is followed by an optional variable label (see "New Variable Names and Labels" on p. 137) in quotes, the name of the aggregate function, and the source variable name in parentheses. Source variables for aggregate functions must be numeric.

To create a variable containing the number of cases in each break group, select:

❑ **Save number of cases in break group as variable.** The default variable name is *N_BREAK*. Enter a new name to override the default. Variable names must begin with a letter and cannot exceed eight characters.

To specify the filename and location of the aggregated data file, choose one of the following alternatives:

◇ **Create new data file.** By default, a file called *aggr.sav* is created in the current directory. To change the file name or directory, click on File... (see "Aggregate Filename and Location" on p. 137).

◇ **Replace working data file.** Replaces the working data file with the new aggregated data file. This creates a temporary aggregated file unless you explicitly save the file.

Aggregate Functions

New variables in the aggregated file are created by applying aggregate functions to existing variables. By default, the mean of values across cases is used as the value of the new aggregated variable. To specify a different aggregate function, highlight the variable on the Aggregate Variable(s) list and click on Function... in the Aggregate Data dialog box. This opens the Aggregate Function dialog box, as shown in Figure 6.15.

Figure 6.15 Aggregate Function dialog box

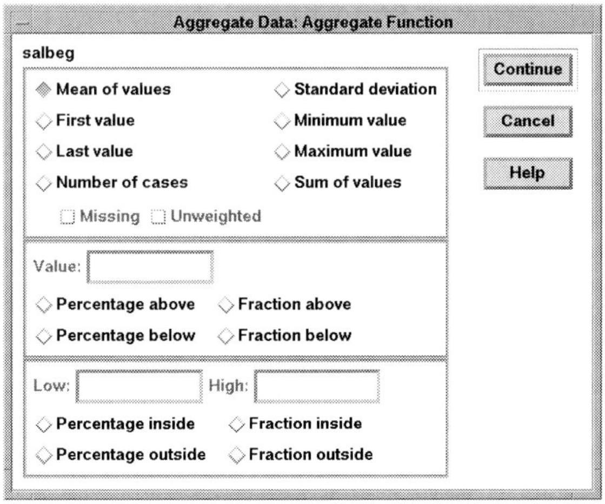

For each variable, you can choose one of the aggregate functions described below. When a function is performed, the resulting value is displayed on the Aggregate Variable(s) list in the Aggregate Data dialog box.

- **Mean of values.** Mean across cases in the break group. This is displayed as MEAN.
- **First value.** First nonmissing observed value in the break group. This is displayed as FIRST.
- **Last value.** Last nonmissing observed value in the break group. This is displayed as LAST.
- **Number of cases.** Number of cases in the break group. This is displayed as N. You can also choose one or both of the following:
  - **Missing.** Number of missing cases in the break group. This is displayed as NMISS.
  - **Unweighted.** Number of unweighted cases in the break group. This is displayed as NU.

  If you select both Missing and Unweighted, the result is the number of unweighted missing values in the break group. This is displayed as NUMISS.
- **Standard deviation.** Standard deviation across cases in the break group. This is displayed as SD.
- **Minimum value.** Minimum value across cases in the break group. This is displayed as MIN.
- **Maximum value.** Maximum value across cases in the break group. This is displayed as MAX.
- **Sum of values.** Sum of values across cases in the break group. This is displayed as SUM.
- **Percentage above.** Percentage of cases in the break group greater than a user-specified value. This is displayed as PGT.
- **Percentage below.** Percentage of cases in the break group less than a user-specified value. This is displayed as PLT.
- **Fraction above.** Fraction of cases in the break group greater than a user-specified value. This is displayed as FGT.
- **Fraction below.** Fraction of cases in the break group less than a user-specified value. This is displayed as FLT.
- **Percentage inside.** Percentage of cases in the break group with values within the inclusive range defined by Low and High. This is displayed as PIN.
- **Percentage outside.** Percentage of cases in the break group with values outside the inclusive range defined by Low and High. This is displayed as POUT.
- **Fraction inside.** Fraction of cases in the break group with values within the inclusive range defined by Low and High. This is displayed as FIN.
- **Fraction outside.** Fraction of cases in the break group with values outside the inclusive range defined by Low and High. This is displayed as FOUT.

New Variable Names and Labels

SPSS provides default variable names for the variables in the new aggregated data file. To specify a different variable name and an optional descriptive label for a new variable, highlight the variable on the Aggregate Variable(s) list and click on Name and Label... in the Aggregate Data dialog box. This opens the Variable Name and Label dialog box, as shown in Figure 6.16.

Figure 6.16   Variable Name and Label dialog box

The aggregate function name, the original variable name, and any related value specifications are displayed for reference purposes. To specify a different aggregate function, return to the main dialog box and click on Function... (see "Aggregate Functions" on p. 135).

Name. Variable names must begin with a letter and cannot exceed eight characters. (See Chapter 3 for complete variable-naming rules.)

Label. Optional, descriptive variable label, up to 120 characters long.

Aggregate Filename and Location

By default, SPSS creates a new aggregated data file named *aggr.sav* in the current directory. To specify a different filename or directory, click on File... in the Aggregate Data dialog box. This opens the Output File Specification dialog box, as shown in Figure 6.17.

Figure 6.17   Output File Specification dialog box

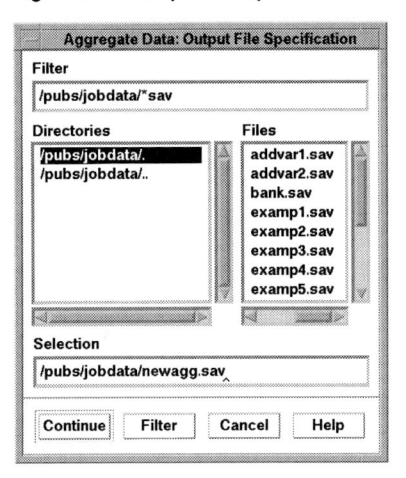

Filter. To display a list of files that match a wildcard search or to change the directory location, enter the directory path and wildcard specification and press Filter. By default, SPSS looks for all files in the current directory with the extension *.sav* and displays them on the Files list.

Directories. You can also use the Directories list to change the directory location. To change directories, select the name of the directory on the Directories list and press Filter or double-click on the directory name. To move up a directory level, select the directory path that ends with a slash and two periods (/..).

Files. All files in the directory that match the wildcard search appear on the Files list. If you select a file from the list, SPSS asks you if you want to replace the existing file.

Selection. Enter the directory path and filename and press Continue. If you select a directory and file from the lists, the information is entered automatically. If you enter the information directly, you can bypass the filter process.

Split-File Processing

To split your data file into separate groups for analysis, from the menus choose:
Data
  Split File...

This opens the Split File dialog box, as shown in Figure 6.18.

Figure 6.18 Split File dialog box

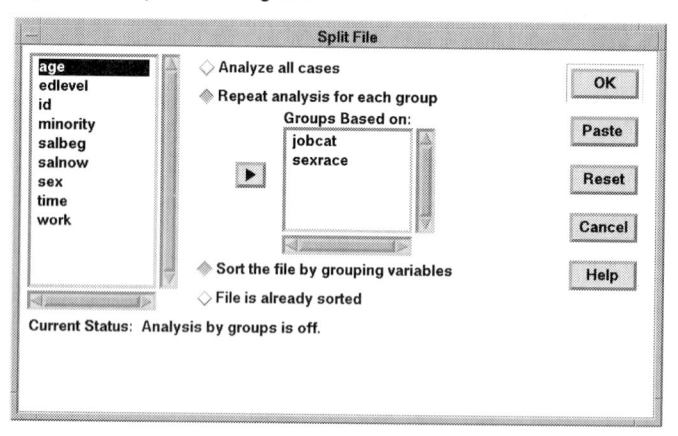

The numeric and short string variables in the data file appear on the source variable list. Select Repeat analysis for each group and choose one or more variables to use as grouping variables. The maximum number of grouping variables is eight. You can use numeric, short string, and long string variables as grouping variables. A separate analysis is performed for each subgroup.

If you select multiple grouping variables, the order in which they appear on the Groups list determines the manner in which cases are grouped. For example, based on the Groups list in Figure 6.18, cases will be grouped by the value of *sexrace* within categories of *jobcat*.

Turning Split-File Processing On and Off

Once you invoke split-file processing, it remains in effect for the rest of the session unless you turn it off. You can choose one of the following alternatives for the status of split-file processing:

- ◇ **Analyze all cases.** Split-file processing is off. All cases are analyzed together. Any split-file grouping variables are ignored. This is the default.

- ◇ **Repeat analysis for each group.** Split-file processing is on. A separate analysis is performed for each subgroup.

If split-file processing is in effect, the message Split File on appears in the status bar at the bottom of the SPSS application window.

Sorting Cases for Split-File Processing

The Split File procedure creates a new subgroup each time it encounters a different value for one of the grouping variables. Therefore, it is important to sort cases based on the values of the grouping variables before invoking split-file processing. You can choose one of the following alternatives for file sorting:

- ◇ **Sort the file by grouping variables.** This is the default. If the file isn't already sorted, this sorts the cases by the values of the grouping variables before splitting the file for analysis.

- ◇ **File is already sorted.** If the file is already sorted in the proper order, this alternative can save processing time.

Selecting Subsets of Cases

You can restrict your analysis to a specific subgroup based on criteria that include variables and complex expressions. You can also select a random sample of cases. The criteria used to define a subgroup can include:

- Variable values and ranges
- Arithmetic expressions
- Logical expressions
- Functions

To select a subset of cases for analysis, from the menus choose:

Data
  Select Cases...

This opens the Select Cases dialog box, as shown in Figure 6.19.

Figure 6.19 Select Cases dialog box

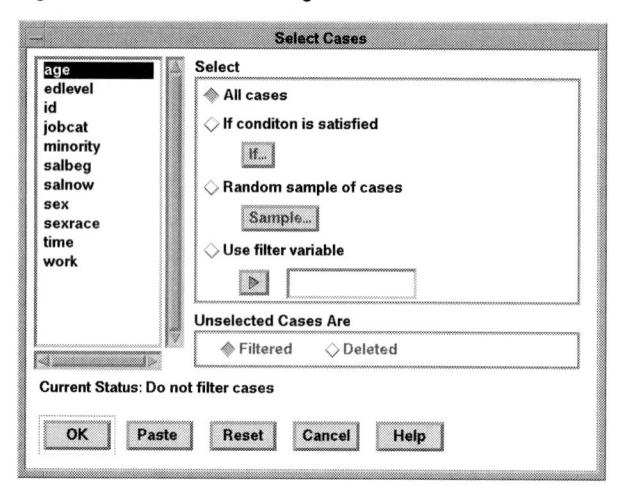

![Select Cases dialog box showing variable list on left (age, edlevel, id, jobcat, minority, salbeg, salnow, sex, sexrace, time, work) and Select options on right: All cases, If condition is satisfied, Random sample of cases, Use filter variable. Unselected Cases Are: Filtered or Deleted. Current Status: Do not filter cases. Buttons: OK, Paste, Reset, Cancel, Help.]

Select. You can choose one of the following alternatives for case selection:

◇ **All cases.** Use all cases in the data file. This is the default. If filtering (discussed below) is in effect, you can use this option to turn it off.

◇ **If condition is satisfied.** You can use conditional expressions to select cases. A **conditional expression** returns a value of true, false, or missing for each case. If the result of a conditional expression is true, the case is selected. If the result is false or missing, the case is not selected. (For information on how to use conditional expressions, see "Selecting Cases Based on Conditional Expressions" on p. 141.)

◇ **Random sample of cases.** You can select a percentage or an exact number of cases. (For more information on random samples, see "Selecting a Random Sample" on p. 142.)

◇ **Use filter variable.** You can select a numeric variable from the data file to use to filter or delete cases. Cases with any value other than 0 or missing for the filter variable are selected.

Unselected Cases. You can choose one of the following alternatives for the treatment of unselected cases:

◇ **Filtered.** Unselected cases are not included in the analysis but remain in the data file. You can use the unselected cases later in the session if you turn filtering off. If you select a random sample or if you select cases based on a conditional expression, this generates a variable named *filter_$* with a value of 1 for selected cases and a value of 0 for unselected cases.

◇ **Deleted.** Unselected cases are deleted from the data file. By reducing the number of cases in the open data file, you can save processing time. The cases can be recovered if you close the data file without saving any changes and then reopen it. The deletion of cases is permanent only if you save the changes to the data file.

Current Status. Status of filtering. There are two possible states:

Do not filter cases. Filtering is off. If All cases is selected or if unselected cases are deleted, filtering is off.

Filter cases by values of [variable name]. Filtering is on. The variable is either a user-specified variable or the system-generated variable *filter_$*. If filtering is on, the message Filter on appears at the bottom of the status bar.

Selecting Cases Based on Conditional Expressions

To select cases based on a conditional expression, select If condition is satisfied and click on If... in the Select Cases dialog box. This opens the Select Cases If dialog box, as shown in Figure 6.20.

Figure 6.20 Select Cases If dialog box

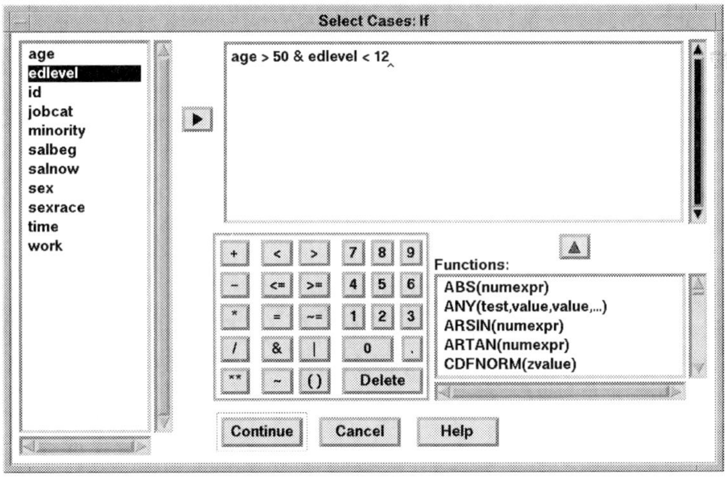

The conditional expression can use existing variable names, constants, arithmetic operators, logical operators, relational operators, and functions. You can type and edit the expression in the text box just like text in a syntax or output window (see Chapter 4). You can also use the calculator pad, variable list, and function list to paste elements into the expression. See Chapter 5 for more information on working with conditional expressions.

Selecting a Random Sample

To obtain a random sample, choose Random sample of cases in the Select Cases dialog box and click on Sample... This opens the Random Sample dialog box, as shown in Figure 6.21.

Figure 6.21 Random Sample dialog box

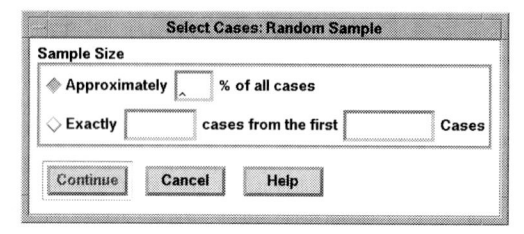

Sample Size. You can choose one of the following alternatives for sample size:

◇ **Approximately.** A user-specified percentage. SPSS generates a random sample of approximately the specified percentage of cases.

◇ **Exactly.** A user-specified number of cases. You must also specify the number of cases from which to generate the sample. This second number should be less than or equal to the total number of cases in the data file. If the number exceeds the total number of cases in the data file, the sample will contain proportionally fewer cases than the requested number.

Setting the Seed for Random Sampling

The SPSS pseudo random-number generator begins with a **seed**, a very large integer value. Within a session, SPSS uses a different seed each time you select a random sample, producing a different sample of cases. If you want to duplicate the same random sample, you can reset the seed value using the Random Number Seed dialog box. See Chapter 5 for more information.

Weighting Cases

If each record in the data file represents more than one case, you can specify the replication factor with the Weight procedure. To apply weights to cases based on the value of a weighting variable, from the menus choose:

Data
  Weight Cases...

This opens the Weight Cases dialog box, as shown in Figure 6.22.

Figure 6.22 Weight Cases dialog box

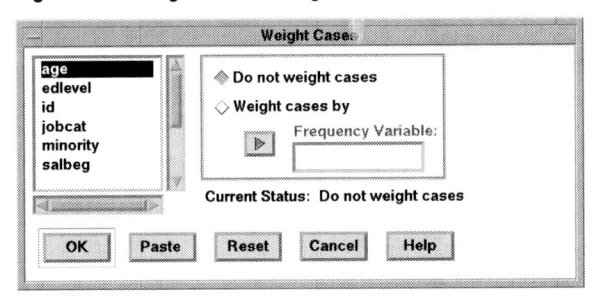

The numeric variables in the data file appear on the source variable list. Select Weight cases by and choose a single variable to use as a weight variable.

Turning Weights On and Off

Once you apply a weight variable, it remains in effect until you select another weight variable or turn weighting off. Cases with a negative value, 0, or a missing value for the weighting variable are excluded from all analyses. You can choose one of the following alternatives for the status of weighting:

- **Do not weight cases.** Weighting is off. Any selected weight variable is ignored. This is the default.
- **Weight cases by.** Weighting is on. Cases are weighted by the selected Frequency Variable.

The status bar at the bottom of the SPSS application window displays the message Weight on if weighting is in effect in the working data file.

Weights in Scatterplots and Histograms

Scatterplots and histograms have an option for turning case weights on and off, but this does not affect cases with a negative value, 0, or a missing value for the weight variable. These cases remain excluded from the chart even if you turn weighting off from within the chart.

7 Data Tabulation

Few people would dispute the effects of "rainy days and Mondays" on the body and spirit. It has long been known that more suicides occur on Mondays than other days of the week. An excess of cardiac deaths on Mondays has also been noted (Rabkin et al., 1980). In this chapter, using a study of coronary heart disease among male Western Electric employees (Paul et al., 1963), we will examine the day of death to see if an excess of deaths occurred on Mondays.

A Frequency Table

The first step in analyzing data on day of death might be to count the number of deaths occurring on each day of the week. Figure 7.1 contains this information.

Figure 7.1 Frequency of death by day of week

```
DAYOFWK    DAY OF DEATH

                                             Valid      Cum
      Value Label          Value  Frequency  Percent  Percent  Percent
      SUNDAY                 1        19       7.9      17.3     17.3
      MONDAY                 2        11       4.6      10.0     27.3
      TUESDAY                3        19       7.9      17.3     44.5
      WEDNESDAY              4        17       7.1      15.5     60.0
      THURSDAY               5        15       6.3      13.6     73.6
      FRIDAY                 6        13       5.4      11.8     85.5
      SATURDAY               7        16       6.7      14.5    100.0
      MISSING                9       130      54.2    Missing
                                   -------   -------  -------
                          Total      240     100.0    100.0

Valid cases      110    Missing cases    130
```

Each row of the frequency table describes a particular day of the week. The last row (labeled *Missing*) represents cases for which the day of death is not known or death has not occurred. For the table in Figure 7.1, there are 110 cases for which day of death is known. The first column (*Value Label*) gives the name of the day, while the second column contains the **value**, which is the numeric or string value given to the computer to represent the day.

The number of people dying on each day (the **frequency**) appears in the third column. Monday is the least-frequent day of death, with 11 deaths. These 11 deaths represent 4.6% (11/240) of all cases. This **percentage** appears in the fourth column. However, of the 240 cases, 130 are **missing cases** (cases for which day of death is unknown or death has not occurred). The 11 deaths on Monday represent 10% of the total deaths for which day of death is known (11/110). This **valid percentage** appears in the fifth column.

The last column of the table contains the **cumulative percentage**. For a particular day, this percentage is the sum of the valid percentages of that day and of all other days that precede it in the table. For example, the cumulative percentage for Tuesday is 44.5, which is the sum of the percentage of deaths that occurred on Sunday, Monday, and Tuesday. It is calculated as:

$$\frac{19}{110} + \frac{11}{110} + \frac{19}{110} = \frac{49}{110} = 44.5\%$$

Equation 7.1

Sometimes it is helpful to look at frequencies for a selected subset of cases. Figure 7.2 is a frequency table of day of death for a subset characterized by sudden cardiac death. This is a particularly interesting category, since it is thought that sudden death may be related to stressful events such as returning to the work environment. In Figure 7.2, deaths do not appear to cluster on any particular day. Twenty-two percent of deaths occurred on Sunday, while 8.3% occurred on Thursday. Since the number of sudden deaths in the table is small, the magnitude of the observed fluctuations is not very large.

Figure 7.2   Frequency of sudden cardiac death by day of week

```
DAYOFWK    DAY OF DEATH

                                                  Valid     Cum
    Value Label          Value  Frequency  Percent Percent  Percent
    SUNDAY                 1         8      22.2    22.2    22.2
    MONDAY                 2         4      11.1    11.1    33.3
    TUESDAY                3         4      11.1    11.1    44.4
    WEDNESDAY              4         7      19.4    19.4    63.9
    THURSDAY               5         3       8.3     8.3    72.2
    FRIDAY                 6         6      16.7    16.7    88.9
    SATURDAY               7         4      11.1    11.1   100.0
                                   -------  ------  ------
                          Total    36      100.0   100.0

    Valid cases    36   Missing cases    0
```

Visual Displays

While the numbers in a frequency table can be studied and compared, it is often useful to present results in a form that can be interpreted visually. Figure 7.3 is a pie chart of the data displayed in Figure 7.1. Each slice represents a day of the week. The size of the slice depends on the frequency of death for that day. Monday is represented by 10% of the pie chart, since 10% of the deaths for which the day is known occurred on Monday.

Figure 7.3   Pie chart of death by day of week

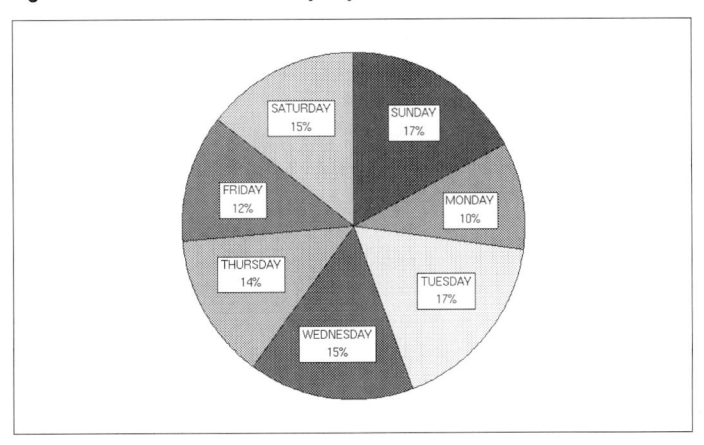

Another way to represent the data is with a bar chart, as shown in Figure 7.4. There is a bar for each day, and the height of the bar is proportional to the number of deaths observed on that day. The number of deaths, or frequency, is displayed at the top of each bar.

Figure 7.4   Bar chart of frequency of death by day of week

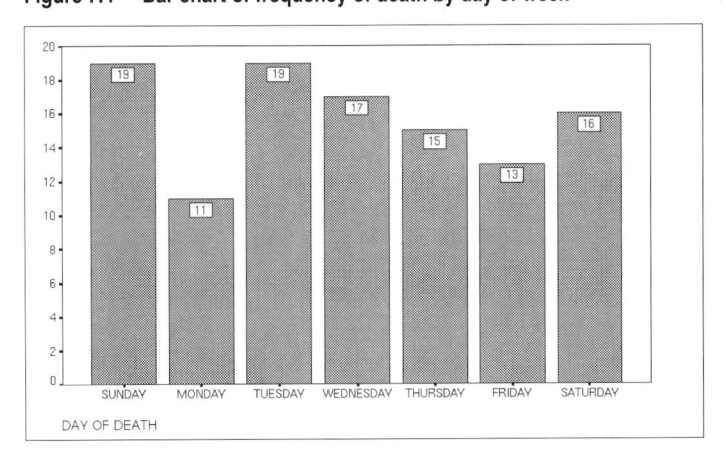

Only values that actually occur in the data are represented in the bar chart. For example, if no deaths occurred on Thursday, no space would be left for Thursday, and the bar for

Wednesday would be followed by the bar for Friday. Likewise, if you charted the number of cars per family, the bar describing 6 cars might be next to the one for 25 cars if no family owned 7 to 24 cars. Therefore, you should pay attention to where categories with no cases may occur.

Although the basic information presented by frequency tables, pie charts, and bar charts is the same, the visual displays enliven the data. Differences among the days of the week are apparent at a glance, eliminating the need to pore over columns of numbers.

What Day?

Although the number of sudden cardiac deaths is small in this study, the data in Figure 7.2 indicate that the number of deaths on Mondays is not particularly large. In fact, the most deaths occurred on Sunday—slightly over 22%. A study of over 1000 sudden cardiac deaths in Rochester, Minnesota, also found a slightly increased incidence of death on weekends for men (Beard et al., 1982). The authors speculate that for men, this might mean that "the home environment is more stressful than the work environment." But you should be wary of explanations that are not directly supported by data. It is only too easy to find a clever explanation for any statistical finding.

Histograms

A frequency table or bar chart of all values for a variable is a convenient way of summarizing a variable that has a relatively small number of distinct values. Variables such as sex, country, and astrological sign are necessarily limited in the number of values they can have. For variables that can take on many different values, such as income to the penny or weight in ounces, a tally of the cases with each observed value may not be very informative. In the worst situation, when all cases have different values, a frequency table is little more than an ordered list of those values.

Variables that have many values can be summarized by grouping the values of the variables into intervals and counting the number of cases with values within each interval. For example, income can be grouped into $5,000 intervals such as 0–4999, 5000–9999, 10000–14999, and so forth, and the number of observations in each group can be tabulated. Such grouping should be done using SPSS during the actual analysis of the data. Whenever possible, the values for variables should be entered into the data file in their original, ungrouped form.

A histogram is a convenient way to display the distribution of such grouped values. Consider Figure 7.5, which is a histogram of body weight in pounds for the sample of 240 men from the Western Electric study. The numbers below the bars indicate the midpoint, or middle value, of each interval. Each bar represents the number of cases having values in the interval. Intervals that have no observations are included in the histogram, but no bars are printed. This differs from a bar chart, which does not leave space for the empty categories.

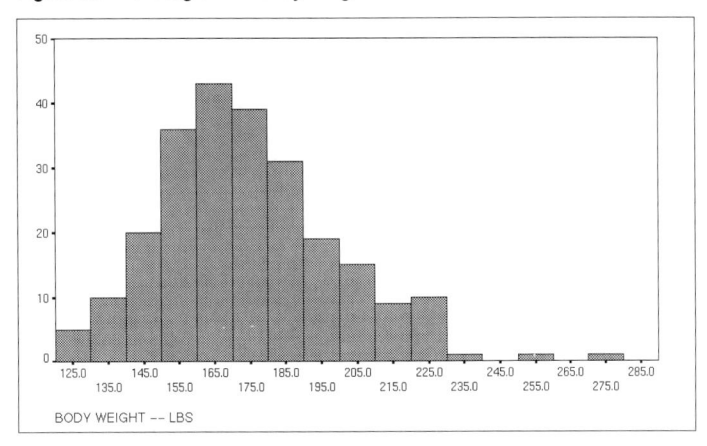

Figure 7.5 Histogram of body weight

[Histogram showing BODY WEIGHT -- LBS on x-axis from 125.0 to 285.0, with frequency on y-axis from 0 to 50]

A histogram can be used whenever it is reasonable to group adjacent values. Histograms should not be used to display variables when there is no underlying order to the values. For example, if 100 different religions are arbitrarily assigned codes of 1 to 100, grouping values into intervals is meaningless. Either a bar chart or a histogram in which each interval corresponds to a single value should be used to display such data.

Percentiles

The information in a histogram can be further summarized by computing values above and below which a specified percentage of cases fall. Such values are called **percentiles**. For example, the 50th percentile, or median, is the value above and below which 50% (or half) of the cases fall. The 25th percentile is the value below which 25% and above which 75% of the cases fall.

Figure 7.6 contains values for the 25th, 50th, and 75th percentiles for the weight data shown in the histogram in Figure 7.5. You see that 25% of the men weigh less than 156 pounds, 50% weigh less than 171 pounds, and 75% weigh less than 187 pounds.

Figure 7.6 Percentiles for body weight

```
WT58        BODY WEIGHT -- LBS

Percentile    Value      Percentile    Value      Percentile    Value
  25.00      156.000       50.00      171.000       75.00      187.000

Valid cases      240     Missing cases      0
```

From these three percentiles, sometimes called **quartiles** (since they divide the distribution into four parts containing the same number of cases), you can tell that 50% of the men weigh between 156 and 187 pounds. (Remember that 25% of the men weigh less than 156 and 25% weigh more than 187. That leaves 50% of the men with weights between those two values.)

Screening Data

Frequency tables, bar charts, and histograms can serve purposes other than summarizing data. Unexpected codes in the tables may indicate errors in data entry or coding. Cases with day of death coded as 0 or 8 are in error if the numbers 1 through 7 represent the days of the week and 9 stands for unknown. Since errors in the data should be eliminated as soon as possible, it is a good idea to run frequency tables as the first step in analyzing data.

Frequency tables and visual displays can also help you identify cases with values that are unusual but possibly correct. For example, a tally of the number of cars in families may show a family with 25 cars. Although such a value is possible, especially if the survey did not specify cars in working condition, it raises suspicion and should be examined to ensure that it is really correct.

Incorrect data values distort the results of statistical analyses, and correct but unusual values may require special treatment. In either case, early identification is valuable.

How to Obtain Frequency Tables

The Frequencies procedure produces frequency tables, measures of central tendency and dispersion, histograms, and bar charts. You can sort frequency tables by value or by count, and you can display frequency tables in condensed format.

The minimum specification is one numeric or short string variable.

To get frequency tables, charts, and related statistics, from the menus choose:

Statistics
  Summarize ▶
    Frequencies...

This opens the Frequencies dialog box, as shown in Figure 7.7.

The numeric and short string variables are displayed on the source list. Select one or more variables for analysis. To get a standard frequency table showing counts, percentages, and valid and cumulative percentages, click on OK. The first 40 characters of any variable labels are shown in the output.

Figure 7.7 Frequencies dialog box

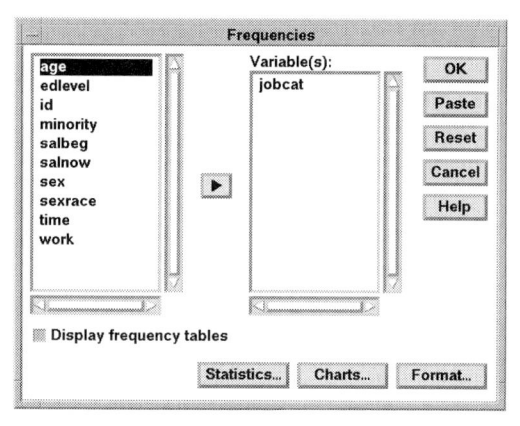

The following option is also available:

❑ **Display frequency tables.** By default, frequency tables are displayed. To suppress tables, deselect this item (for example, if you want to display only selected charts). If you suppress frequency tables without selecting any additional statistics or charts, only counts of cases with valid and missing values are shown.

Frequencies Statistics

To obtain optional descriptive and summary statistics for numeric variables, click on Statistics... in the Frequencies dialog box. This opens the Frequencies Statistics dialog box, as shown in Figure 7.8.

Figure 7.8 Frequencies Statistics dialog box

Percentile Values. You can choose one or more of the following:

- **Quartiles.** Displays the 25th, 50th, and 75th percentiles.
- **Cut points for n equal groups.** Displays percentile values that divide the sample into equal-size groups of cases. The default number of groups is 10. Optionally, you can request a different number of groups. Enter a positive integer between 2 and 100. For example, if you enter 4, quartiles are shown. The number of percentiles displayed is one fewer than the number of groups specified; you need only two values to divide a sample into three groups.
- **Percentile(s).** User-specified percentile values. Enter a percentile value between 0 and 100, and click on Add. Repeat this process for any other percentile values. Values appear in sorted order on the percentile list. To remove a percentile, highlight it on the list and click on Remove. To change a value, highlight it on the list, enter a new value, and click on Change.

If a requested percentile cannot be computed, SPSS displays a period (.) as the value associated with that percentile.

Dispersion. You can choose one or more of the following:

- **Std. deviation.** Standard deviation. A measure of how much observations vary from the mean, expressed in the same units as the data.
- **Variance.** A measure of how much observations vary from the mean, equal to the square of the standard deviation.
- **Range.** The difference between the largest (maximum) and smallest (minimum) values.
- **Minimum.** The smallest value.
- **Maximum.** The largest value.
- **S.E. mean.** Standard error of the mean. A measure of variability of the sample mean.

Central Tendency. You can choose one or more of the following:

- **Mean.** The arithmetic average.
- **Median.** The median is defined as the value below which half the cases fall. If there is an even number of cases, the median is the average of the two middle cases when the cases are sorted in ascending order. The median is not available if you request sorting by frequency counts (see "Frequencies Format" on p. 154).
- **Mode.** The most frequently occurring value. If several values are tied for the highest frequency, only the smallest value is displayed.
- **Sum.** The sum of all the values.

Distribution. You can choose one or more of the following:

- **Skewness.** An index of the degree to which a distribution is not symmetric. The standard error of the skewness statistic is also displayed.
- **Kurtosis.** A measure of the extent to which observations cluster around a central point. The standard error of the kurtosis statistic is also displayed.

For grouped or collapsed data, the following option is also available:

- **Values are group midpoints.** If the values represent midpoints of groups (for example, all people in their thirties are coded as 35), you can estimate percentiles for the original, ungrouped data, assuming that cases are uniformly distributed in each interval. Since this affects the values of the median and the percentiles for *all* variables, you should not select this option if any variable on the variable list contains ungrouped data.

Frequencies Charts

To get bar charts or histograms, click on Charts... in the Frequencies dialog box. This opens the Frequencies Charts dialog box, as shown in Figure 7.9.

Figure 7.9   Frequencies Charts dialog box

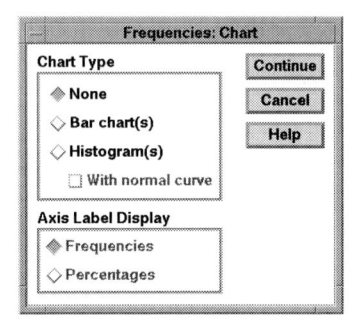

Chart Type. You can choose one of the following alternatives:

- **None.** No charts. This is the default setting.
- **Bar chart(s).** The scale is determined by the frequency count of the largest category plotted.
- **Histogram(s).** Histograms are available for numeric variables only. The number of intervals plotted is 21 (or fewer if the range of values is less than 21).
  - **With normal curve.** This option superimposes a normal curve over the histogram(s).

Axis Label Display. For bar charts, you can control labeling of the vertical axis. Choose one of the following alternatives:

◇ **Frequencies.** The axis is labeled with frequencies. This is the default setting.
◇ **Percentages.** The axis is labeled with percentages.

Frequencies Format

To modify the format of the frequency table output, select Display frequency tables in the Frequencies dialog box and click on Format... to open the Frequencies Format dialog box, as shown in Figure 7.10.

Figure 7.10 Frequencies Format dialog box

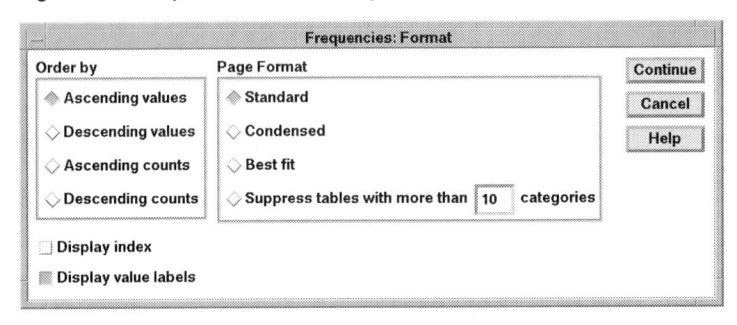

Order by. Order selection determines the order by which data values are sorted and displayed in a frequency table. You can choose one of the following alternatives:

◇ **Ascending values.** Sorts categories by ascending order of values. This is the default setting.
◇ **Descending values.** Sorts categories by descending order of values.
◇ **Ascending counts.** Sorts categories by ascending order of frequency counts.
◇ **Descending counts.** Sorts categories by descending order of frequency counts.

If you request a histogram or percentiles, categories of the frequency table are sorted by ascending order, regardless of your order selection.

Page Format. You can choose one of the following alternatives:

◇ **Standard.** Displays as many frequency tables on a page as will fit. This is the default.
◇ **Condensed.** Condensed format. This format displays frequency counts in three columns. It does not display value labels or percentages that include cases with missing values, and it rounds valid and cumulative percentages to integers.

◇ **Best fit.** Conditional condensed format. If a table cannot fit on one page in default format, condensed format is used.

◇ **Suppress tables with more than n categories.** Does not display tables for variables with more categories than specified. To override the default value of 10, enter an integer value greater than or equal to 1. This item is particularly useful if your variable list includes continuous variables for which summary statistics or histograms are requested, but for which a frequency table would be long and uninformative. For example, the frequency table that would accompany the histogram of weight in Figure 7.5 would have a separate entry for each one-pound weight increment.

The following format choices are also available:

❏ **Display index.** Displays a positional and alphabetic index of frequency tables. This is particularly useful if you have a large number of variables.

❏ **Display value labels.** The first 20 characters of the value labels are shown. This is the default setting. To suppress value labels, deselect this item. Value labels are automatically suppressed when condensed format is chosen.

Additional Features Available with Command Syntax

You can customize your frequencies if you paste your selections into a syntax window and edit the resulting FREQUENCIES command syntax (see Chapter 4). Additional features include:

- The ability to exclude ranges of data values from analysis (with the VARIABLES subcommand).
- Additional formatting options, such as the ability to begin each frequency table on a new page, double-space tables, or write tables to a file (with the FORMAT subcommand).
- For bar charts, user-specified lower and upper data bounds and maximum scale axis value (with the BARCHART subcommand).
- For histograms, user-specified lower and upper data bounds, maximum horizontal axis value, and interval width (with the HISTOGRAM subcommand).
- Additional options for processing of grouped data (with the GROUPED subcommand).

See Appendix A for command syntax rules. See the *SPSS Base System Syntax Reference Guide* for complete FREQUENCIES command syntax.

8 Descriptive Statistics

Survey data that rely on voluntary information are subject to many sources of error. People fail to recall events correctly, deliberately distort the truth, or refuse to participate. Refusals influence survey results by failing to provide information about certain types of people—those who refuse to answer surveys at all and those who avoid certain questions. For example, if college graduates tend to be unwilling to answer polls, results of surveys will be biased.

One possible way to examine the veracity of survey responses is to compare them with similar data recorded in official records. Systematic differences between actual data and self-reported responses jeopardize the usefulness of the survey. Unfortunately, in many sensitive areas—illicit drug use, abortion history, or even income—official records are usually unavailable.

Wyner (1980) examined the differences between the actual and self-reported numbers of arrests obtained from 79 former heroin addicts enrolled in the Vera Institute of Justice Supported Employment Experiment. As part of their regular quarterly interviews, participants were asked about their arrest histories in New York City. The self-reported number of arrests was compared with arrest-record data coded from New York City Police Department arrest sheets. The goal of the study was not only to quantify the extent of error but also to identify factors related to inaccurate responses.

Examining the Data

Figure 8.1 shows histograms for the following three variables—actual number of arrests, self-reported number of arrests, and the difference of the two. From a histogram, it is possible to see the shape of the distribution; that is, how likely the different values are, how much spread, or **variability**, there is among the values, and where typical values are concentrated. Such characteristics are important because of the direct insight they provide into the data and because many statistical procedures are based on assumptions about the underlying distributions of variables.

Figure 8.1   Self-reported and actual arrests

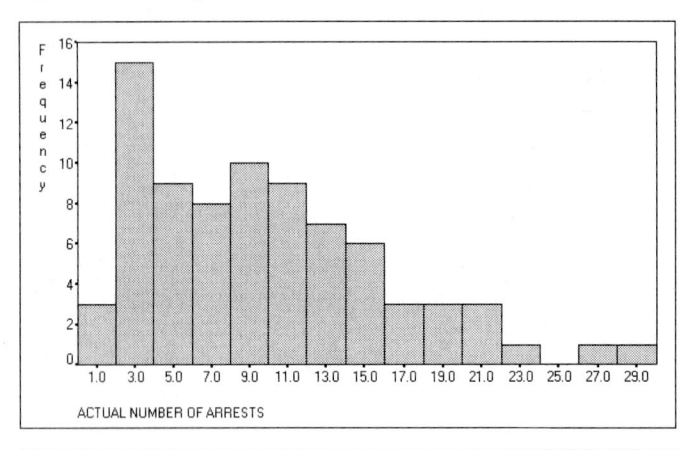

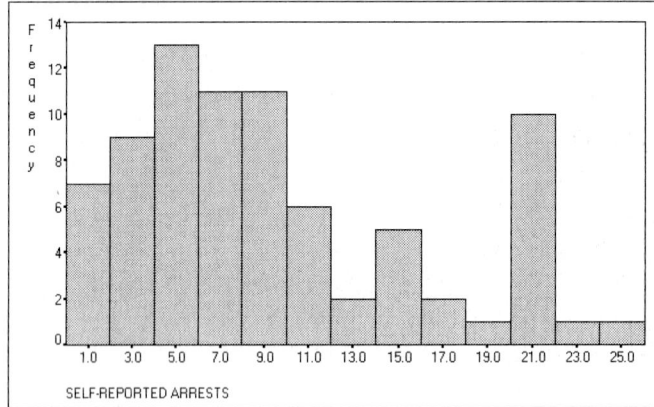

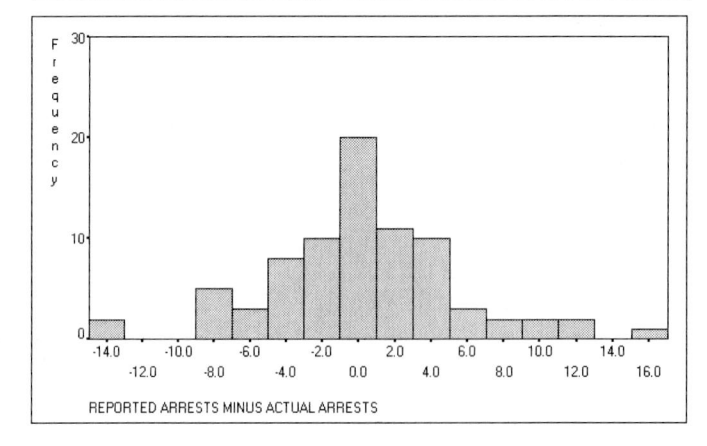

The distributions of the self-reported and actual number of arrests have a somewhat similar shape. Neither distribution has an obvious central value, although the self-reported values peak at 4 to 5 arrests, while the actual number of arrests peaks at 2 to 3 arrests. The distribution of self-reported arrests peaks again at 20 to 21 arrests. The peaks corresponding to intervals containing 5, 15, and 20 arrests arouse suspicion that people may be more likely to report their arrest records as round numbers. Examination of the actual number of arrests shows no corresponding peaks at multiples of five.

The distribution of the differences between reported and actual number of arrests is not as irregularly shaped as the two distributions from which it is derived. It has a peak at the interval with a midpoint of 0. Most cases cluster around the peak values, and cases far from these values are infrequent.

Summarizing the Data

Although frequency tables and bar charts are useful for summarizing and displaying data (see Chapter 7), further condensation and description are often desirable. A variety of summary measures that convey information about the data in single numbers can be computed. The choice of a summary measure, or statistic, depends upon characteristics of both the data and the statistic. One important characteristic of the data that must be considered is the level of measurement of each variable being studied.

Levels of Measurement

Measurement is the assignment of numbers or codes to observations. **Levels of measurement** are distinguished by ordering and distance properties. A computer does not know what measurement underlies the values it is given. You must determine the level of measurement of your data and apply appropriate statistical techniques.

The traditional classification of levels of measurement into nominal, ordinal, interval, and ratio scales was developed by S. S. Stevens (1946). This remains the basic typology and is the one used throughout this manual. Variations exist, however, and issues concerning the statistical effect of ignoring levels of measurement have been debated (for example, see Borgatta & Bohrnstedt, 1980).

Nominal Measurement

The **nominal** level of measurement is the "lowest" in the typology because no assumptions are made about relations between values. Each value defines a distinct category and serves merely as a label or name (hence, *nominal* level) for the category. For instance, the birthplace of an individual is a nominal variable. For most purposes, there is no inherent ordering among cities or towns. Although cities can be ordered according to size, density, or air pollution, as birthplaces they cannot be ordered or ranked against other cities. When numeric values are attached to nominal categories, they are merely identifiers. None of the properties of numbers, such as relative size, addition, or multiplication, can be applied to these numerically coded categories. Therefore, statistics that assume ordering or meaningful numerical distances between the values do not ordinarily give useful information about nominal variables.

Ordinal Measurement

When it is possible to rank or order all categories according to some criterion, the **ordinal** level of measurement is achieved. For instance, classifying employees into clerical, supervisory, and managerial categories is an ordering according to responsibilities or skills. Each category has a position lower or higher than another category. Furthermore, knowing that supervisory is higher than clerical and that managerial is higher than supervisory automatically means that managerial is higher than clerical. However, nothing is known about how much higher; no distance is measured. Ordering is the sole mathematical property applicable to ordinal measurements, and the use of numeric values does not imply that any other property of numbers is applicable.

Interval Measurement

In addition to order, **interval** measurements have the property of meaningful distance between values. A thermometer, for example, measures temperature in degrees that are the same size at any point on the scale. The difference between 20°C and 21°C is the same as the difference between 5°C and 6°C. However, an interval scale does not have an inherently determined zero point. In the familiar Celsius and Fahrenheit systems, 0° is determined by an agreed-upon definition, not by the absence of heat. Consequently, interval-level measurement allows us to study differences between items but not their proportionate magnitudes. For example, it is incorrect to say that 80°F is twice as hot as 40°F.

Ratio Measurement

Ratio measurements have all the ordering and distance properties of an interval scale. In addition, a zero point can be meaningfully designated. In measuring physical distances between objects using feet or meters, a zero distance is naturally defined as the absence of any distance. The existence of a zero point means that ratio comparisons can be made. For example, it is quite meaningful to say that a 6-foot-tall adult is twice as tall as a 3-foot-tall child or that a 500-meter race is five times as long as a 100-meter race.

Because ratio measurements satisfy all the properties of the real number system, any mathematical manipulations appropriate for real numbers can be applied to ratio measures. However, the existence of a zero point is seldom critical for statistical analyses.

Summary Statistics

Figure 8.2 and Figure 8.3 contain a variety of summary statistics that are useful in describing the distributions of self-reported and actual numbers of arrests and their difference. The statistics can be grouped into three categories according to what they quantify: central tendency, dispersion, and shape.

Figure 8.2 was obtained with the Descriptives procedure; Figure 8.3, with the Frequencies procedure. If your computer has a math coprocessor, the Descriptives procedure is faster than the Frequencies procedure. However, the median and mode are not available with Descriptives.

Figure 8.2 Summary statistics from the Descriptives procedure

```
Variable  ACTUAL     ACTUAL NUMBER OF ARRESTS

Mean              9.253             S.E. Mean           .703
Std Dev           6.248             Variance         39.038
Kurtosis           .597             S.E. Kurt           .535
Skewness           .908             S.E. Skew           .271
Range           28.000              Minimum               1
Maximum             29              Sum             731.000

Valid observations -      79        Missing observations -      0
- - - - - - - - - - - - - - - - - - - - - - - - - - - - - - - -
Variable  SELF       SELF-REPORTED ARRESTS

Mean              8.962             S.E. Mean           .727
Std Dev           6.458             Variance         41.704
Kurtosis          -.485             S.E. Kurt           .535
Skewness           .750             S.E. Skew           .271
Range           25.000              Minimum               0
Maximum             25              Sum             708.000

Valid observations -      79        Missing observations -      0
- - - - - - - - - - - - - - - - - - - - - - - - - - - - - - - -
Variable  ERRORS     REPORTED ARRESTS MINUS ACTUAL ARRESTS

Mean              -.291             S.E. Mean           .587
Std Dev           5.216             Variance         27.209
Kurtosis          1.102             S.E. Kurt           .535
Skewness           .125             S.E. Skew           .271
Range           29.000              Minimum         -14.000
Maximum             15              Sum             -23.000

Valid observations -      79        Missing observations -      0
```

Figure 8.3 Summary statistics from the Frequencies procedure

```
ACTUAL     ACTUAL NUMBER OF ARRESTS

Mean         9.253    Std err       .703    Median        8.000
Mode         3.000    Std dev      6.248    Variance     39.038
Kurtosis      .597    S E Kurt      .535    Skewness       .908
S E Skew      .271    Range       28.000    Minimum       1.000
Maximum     29.000    Sum        731.000

Valid cases     79    Missing cases     0
- - - - - - - - - - - - - - - - - - - - - - - - - - - - - -
SELF       SELF-REPORTED ARRESTS

Mean         8.962    Std err       .727    Median        7.000
Mode         5.000    Std dev      6.458    Variance     41.704
Kurtosis     -.485    S E Kurt      .535    Skewness       .750
S E Skew      .271    Range       25.000    Minimum        .000
Maximum     25.000    Sum        708.000

Valid cases     79    Missing cases     0
- - - - - - - - - - - - - - - - - - - - - - - - - - - - - -
ERRORS     REPORTED ARRESTS MINUS ACTUAL ARRESTS

Mean         -.291    Std err       .587    Median         .000
Mode        -1.000    Std dev      5.216    Variance     27.209
Kurtosis     1.102    S E Kurt      .535    Skewness       .125
S E Skew      .271    Range       29.000    Minimum     -14.000
Maximum     15.000    Sum        -23.000

* Multiple modes exist.  The smallest value is shown.

Valid cases     79    Missing cases     0
```

Measures of Central Tendency

The mean, median, and mode are frequently used to describe the location of a distribution. The **mode** is the most frequently occurring value (or values). For the actual number of arrests, the mode is 3; for the self-reported values, it is 5. The distribution of the difference between the actual and self-reported values is multimodal. That is, it has more than one mode, since the values −1 and 0 occur with equal frequency. SPSS, however, displays only one of the modes, the smaller value, as shown in Figure 8.3. The mode can be used for data measured at any level. It is not usually the preferred measure for interval and ordinal data, since it ignores much of the available information.

The **median** is the value above and below which one half of the observations fall. For example, if there are 79 observations, the median is the 40th-largest observation. When there is an even number of observations, no unique center value exists, so the mean of the two middle observations is usually taken as the median value. For the arrest data, the median is 0 for the differences, 8 for the actual arrests, and 7 for self-reported arrests. For ordinal data, the median is usually a good measure of central tendency, since it uses the ranking information. The median should not be used for nominal data, since ranking of the observations is not possible.

The **mean**, also called the **arithmetic average**, is the sum of the values of all observations divided by the number of observations. Thus,

$$\bar{X} = \sum_{i=1}^{N} \frac{X_i}{N}$$

Equation 8.1

where N is the number of cases and X_i is the value of the variable for the ith case. Since the mean utilizes the distance between observations, the measurements should be interval or ratio. Calculating the mean race, religion, and auto color provides no useful information. For dichotomous variables coded as 0 and 1, the mean has a special interpretation: it is the proportion of cases coded 1 in the data.

The three measures of central tendency need not be the same. For example, the mean number of actual arrests is 9.25, the median is 8, and the mode is 3. The arithmetic mean is greatly influenced by outlying observations, while the median is not. Adding a single case with 400 arrests would increase the mean from 9.25 to 14.1, but it would not affect the median. Therefore, if there are values far removed from the rest of the observations, the median may be a better measure of central tendency than the mean.

For symmetric distributions, the observed mean, median, and mode are usually close in value. For example, the mean of the differences between self-reported and actual arrest values is −0.291, the median is 0, and the modes are −1 and 0. All three measures give similar estimates of central tendency in this case.

Measures of Dispersion

Two distributions can have the same values for measures of central tendency and yet be very dissimilar in other respects. For example, if the actual number of arrests for five cases in two methadone clinics is 0, 1, 10, 14, 20 for clinic A, and 8, 8, 9, 10, 10 for clinic B, the mean number of arrests (9) is the same in both. However, even a cursory examination of the data indicates that the two clinics are different. In clinic B, all cases have fairly comparable arrest records, while in clinic A, the records are quite disparate. A quick and useful index of dissimilarity, or dispersion, is the **range**. It is the difference between the maximum and minimum observed values. For clinic B the range is 2, while for clinic A it is 20. Since the range is computed from only the minimum and maximum values, it is sensitive to extremes.

Although the range is a useful index of dispersion, especially for ordinal data, it does not take into account the distribution of observations between the maximum and minimum. A commonly used measure of variation that is based on all observations is the **variance**. For a sample, the variance is computed by summing the squared differences from the mean for all observations and then dividing by one less than the number of observations. In mathematical notation, this is:

$$S^2 = \sum_{i=1}^{N} \frac{(X_i - \bar{X})^2}{N-1}$$

Equation 8.2

If all observations are identical—that is, if there is no variation—the variance is 0. The more spread out they are, the greater the variance. For the methadone clinic example above, the sample variance for clinic A is 73, while for clinic B it is 1.

The square root of the variance is termed the **standard deviation**. While the variance is expressed in squared units, the standard deviation is expressed in the same units of measurement as the observations. This is an appealing property, since it is much clearer to think of variability in terms of the number of arrests rather than the number of arrests squared.

The Normal Distribution

For many variables, most observations are concentrated near the middle of the distribution. As distance from the central concentration increases, the frequency of observation decreases. Such distributions are often described as "bell-shaped." An example is the **normal distribution** (see Figure 8.4). A broad range of observed phenomena in nature and in society is approximately normally distributed. For example, the distributions of variables such as height, weight, and blood pressure are approximately normal. The normal distribution is by far the most important theoretical distribution in statistics and serves as a reference point for describing the form of many distributions of sample data.

The normal distribution is symmetric: each half is a mirror image of the other. Three measures of central tendency—the mean, median, and mode—coincide exactly. As shown in Figure 8.4, 95% of all observations fall within two standard deviations (σ) of the mean (μ) and 68% fall within one standard deviation. The exact theoretical proportion of cases falling into various regions of the normal curve can be found in tables included in most introductory statistics textbooks.

Figure 8.4 Normal curve

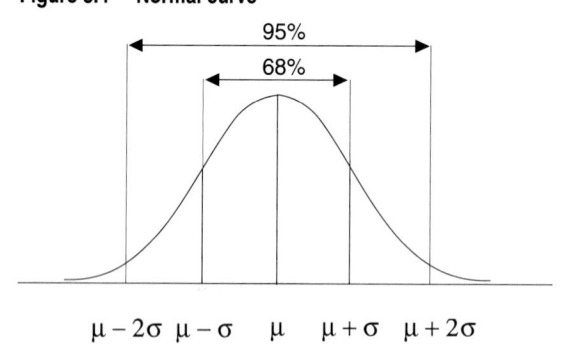

In SPSS, you can superimpose a normal distribution on a histogram. Consider Figure 8.5, a histogram of the differences in self-reported and actual arrests. The curved line indicates what the distribution of cases would be if the variable had a normal distribution with the same mean and variance. Tests for normality are available in the Explore procedure (see Chapter 9).

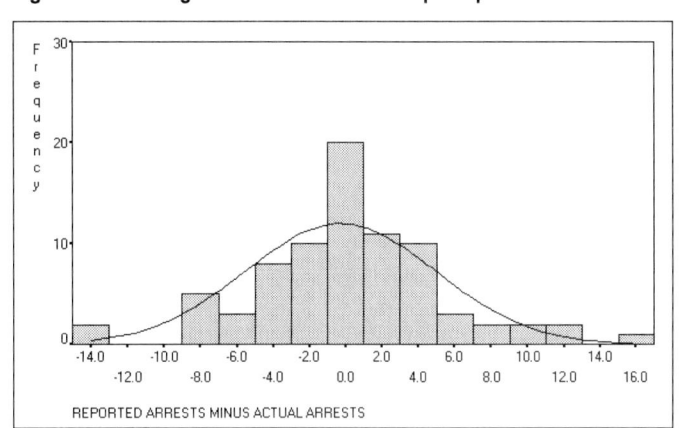

Figure 8.5   Histogram with normal curve superimposed

Measures of Shape

A distribution that is not symmetric but has more cases (more of a "tail") toward one end of the distribution than the other is said to be **skewed**. If the tail is toward larger values, the distribution is **positively skewed**, or skewed to the right. If the tail is toward smaller values, the distribution is **negatively skewed**, or skewed to the left.

Another characteristic of the form of a distribution is called **kurtosis**—the extent to which, for a given standard deviation, observations cluster around a central point. If cases within a distribution cluster more than those in the normal distribution (that is, the distribution is more peaked), the distribution is called **leptokurtic**. A leptokurtic distribution also tends to have more observations straggling into the extreme tails than does a normal distribution. If cases cluster less than in the normal distribution (that is, it is flatter), the distribution is termed **platykurtic**.

Although examination of a histogram provides some indication of possible skewness and kurtosis, it is often desirable to compute formal indexes that measure these properties. Values for skewness and kurtosis are 0 if the observed distribution is exactly normal. Positive values for skewness indicate a positive skew, while positive values for kurtosis indicate a distribution that is more peaked than normal. For samples from a normal distribution, measures of skewness and kurtosis typically will not be exactly zero but will fluctuate around zero because of sampling variation.

Standard Scores

It is often desirable to describe the relative position of an observation within a distribution. Knowing that a person achieved a score of 80 in a competitive examination conveys little information about performance. Judgment of performance would depend on whether 80 is the lowest, the median, or the highest score.

One way of describing the location of a case in a distribution is to calculate its **standard score**. This score, sometimes called the **Z score**, indicates how many standard deviations above or below the mean an observation falls. It is calculated by finding the difference between the value of a particular observation X_i and the mean of the distribution, and dividing this difference by the standard deviation:

$$Z_i = \frac{X_i - \bar{X}}{S}$$

Equation 8.3

The mean of Z scores is 0 and the standard deviation is 1. For example, a participant with five actual arrests would have a Z score of $(5 - 9.25)/6.25$, or -0.68. Since the score is negative, the case had fewer arrests than the average for the individuals studied. Figure 8.6 shows summary statistics for Z scores based on the difference between actual and self-reported arrests.

Figure 8.6 Summary statistics for Z scores

```
Variable   ZERRORS    Zscore:  REPORTED ARRESTS MINUS ACTUAL

Mean                 .000          S.E. Mean          .113
Std Dev             1.000          Variance          1.000
Kurtosis            1.102          S.E. Kurt          .535
Skewness             .125          S.E. Skew          .271
Range               5.560          Minimum        -2.62812
Maximum           2.93146          Sum                .000
```

Standardization permits comparison of scores from different distributions. For example, an individual with Z scores of -0.68 for actual arrests and 1.01 for the difference between self-reported and actual arrests had fewer arrests than the average but exaggerated more than the average.

When the distribution of a variable is approximately normal and the mean and variance are known or are estimated from large samples, the Z score of an observation provides more specific information about its location. For example, if actual arrests and response error were normally distributed, 75% of cases would have more arrests than the example individual, but only 16% would have exaggerated as much as the example individual (75% of a standard normal curve lies above a Z score of -0.68, and 16% lies above a score of 1.01).

Who Lies?

The distribution of the difference between self-reported and actual arrests indicates that response error exists. Although observing a mean close to zero is comforting, misrepresentation is obvious. What, then, are the characteristics that influence willingness to be truthful?

Wyner identifies three factors that are related to inaccuracies: the number of arrests before 1960, the number of multiple-charge arrests, and the perceived desirability of being arrested. The first factor is related to a frequently encountered difficulty—the more distant an event in time, the less likely it is to be correctly recalled. The second factor, underreporting of multiple-charge arrests, is probably caused by the general social undesirability of serious arrests. Finally, persons who view arrest records as laudatory are likely to inflate their accomplishments.

How to Obtain Descriptive Statistics

The Descriptives procedure computes univariate summary statistics and saves standardized variables. Although it computes statistics also available in the Frequencies procedure, Descriptives computes descriptive statistics for continuous variables more efficiently because it does not sort values into a frequencies table.

The minimum specification is one or more numeric variables.

To obtain descriptive statistics and Z scores, from the menus choose:

Statistics
  Summarize ▶
    Descriptives...

This opens the Descriptives dialog box, as shown in Figure 8.7.

Figure 8.7   Descriptives dialog box

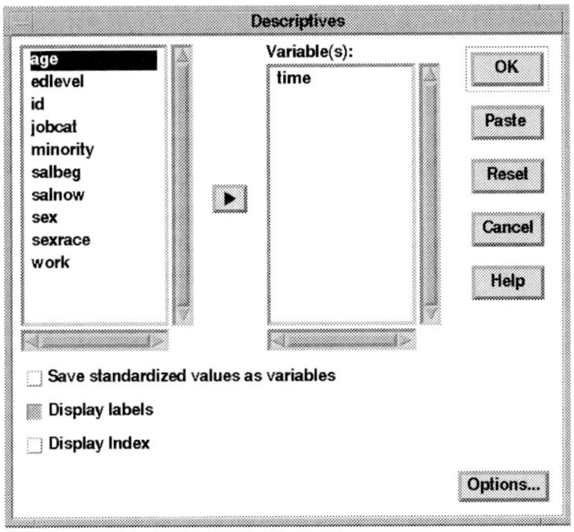

The numeric variables in your data file appear on the source list. Select one or more variables for which you want descriptive statistics. To obtain the default statistics (mean, standard deviation, minimum, and maximum) and display variable labels, click on OK.

You can also choose one or more of the following:

- **Save standardized values as variables.** Creates one Z-score variable for each variable. New variable names are created by prefixing the letter *z* to the first seven characters of original variable names. For example, *zsalnow* is the Z-score variable for *salnow*. If this naming convention would produce duplicate names, an alternate naming convention is used: first *zsc001* through *zsc099*, then *stdz01* through *stdz09*, then *zzzz01* through *zzzz09*, and then *zqzq01* through *zqzq09*.

  Variable labels for Z-score variables are generated by prefixing *zscore* to the first 31 characters of the original variable label. If SPSS assigns a variable name that does not contain part of the original variable name, it prefixes *zscore(original variable name)* to the first 31 characters of the original variable's label. If the original variable has no label, it uses *zscore(original variable name)* for the label.

  SPSS displays a table in the output showing the original variable name, the new variable name and its label, and the number of cases for which the Z score is computed.

- **Display labels.** Displays 40-character variable labels in the output. If requested statistics do not fit in the available page width, labels are truncated to 21 characters and then, if necessary, a serial output format is used. Labels are displayed by default.

- **Display index.** Displays a positional and alphabetical reference index showing the page location in the statistics output for each variable. The variables are listed by their position in the data file and alphabetically.

Descriptives Options

To obtain additional descriptive statistics or control the order by which variables appear in the output, click on Options... in the Descriptives dialog box. This opens the Descriptives Options dialog box, as shown in Figure 8.8.

Figure 8.8 Descriptives Options dialog box

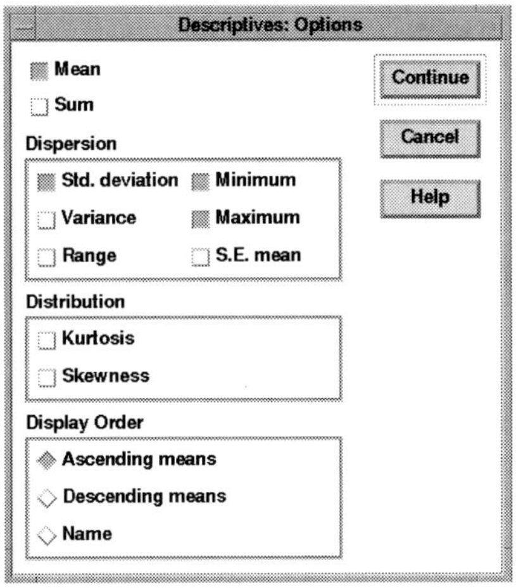

At least one statistic must be selected.

You can choose one or both of the following:

- **Mean.** The arithmetic average. Displayed by default.
- **Sum.** The sum of all the values.

Dispersion. You can choose one or more of the following dispersion statistics:

- **Std. deviation.** Standard deviation. Displayed by default. A measure of how much observations vary from the mean, expressed in the same units as the data.
- **Variance.** A measure of how much observations vary from the mean, equal to the square of the standard deviation.
- **Range.** The difference between the largest (maximum) and smallest (minimum) values.
- **Minimum.** The smallest value. Displayed by default.
- **Maximum.** The largest value. Displayed by default.
- **S. E. mean.** Standard error of the mean. A measure of variability of the sample mean.

Distribution. You can choose one or both of the following distribution statistics:

- **Kurtosis.** A measure of the extent to which observations cluster around a central point, given their standard deviation. The standard error of the kurtosis statistic is also displayed.
- **Skewness.** An index of the degree to which a distribution is not symmetric. The standard error of the skewness statistic is also displayed.

Display Order. You can choose one of the following:

- **Ascending means.** Displays variables by order of ascending means. This is the default setting.
- **Descending means.** Displays variables by order of descending means.
- **Name.** Displays variables in alphabetical order by name.

Additional Features Available with Command Syntax

You can customize your descriptive statistics if you paste your selections to a syntax window and edit the resulting DESCRIPTIVES command syntax (see Chapter 4). Additional features include:

- Z scores for a subset of variables (with the VARIABLES subcommand).
- User-specified names for Z-score variables (with the VARIABLES subcommand).
- Exclusion from the analysis of cases with missing values for any variable (with the MISSING subcommand).
- Additional display order options such as sorting by variance (with the SORT subcommand).

See Appendix A for command syntax rules. See the *SPSS Base System Syntax Reference Guide* for complete DESCRIPTIVES command syntax.

9 Exploring Data

The first step of data analysis should always be a detailed examination of the data. Whether the problem you're solving is simple or complex, whether you're planning to do a *t* test or a multivariate repeated measures analysis of variance, you should first take a careful look at the data. In this chapter, we'll consider a variety of descriptive statistics and displays that are useful as a preliminary step in data analysis. Using the SPSS Explore procedure, you can screen your data, visually examine the distributions of values for various groups, and test for normality and homogeneity of variance.

Reasons for Exploring Data

There are several important reasons for examining your data carefully before you begin your analysis. Let's start with the simplest.

Identifying Mistakes

Data must make a hazardous journey before finding final rest in a computer file. First, a measurement is made or a response is elicited, sometimes with a faulty instrument or by a careless experimenter. The result is then recorded, often barely legibly, in a lab notebook, medical chart, or personnel record. Often this information is not actually coded and entered onto a data form until much later. From this form, the numbers must find their way into their designated slot in the computer file. Then they must be properly introduced to a computer program. Their correct location and missing values must be specified.

Errors can be introduced at any step. Some errors are easy to spot. For example, forgetting to declare a value as missing, using an invalid code, or entering the value 701 for age will be apparent from a frequency table. Other errors, such as entering an age of 54 instead of 45, may be difficult, if not impossible, to spot. Unless your first step is to carefully check your data for mistakes, errors may contaminate all of your analyses.

Exploring the Data

After completing data acquisition, entry, and checking, it's time to look at the data—not to search haphazardly for statistical significance, but to examine the data systematically using simple exploratory techniques. Why bother, you might ask? Why not just begin your analysis?

Data analysis has often been compared to detective work. Before the actual trial of a hypothesis, there is much evidence to be gathered and sifted. Based on the clues, the hypothesis itself may be altered, or the methods for testing it may have to be changed. For example, if the distribution of data values reveals a gap—that is, a range where no values occur—we must ask why. If some values are extreme (far removed from the other values), we must look for reasons. If the pattern of numbers is strange (for example, if all values are even), we must determine why. If we see unexpected variability in the data, we must look for possible explanations; perhaps there are additional variables that may explain it.

Preparing for Hypothesis Testing

Looking at the distribution of the values is also important for evaluating the appropriateness of the statistical techniques we are planning to use for hypothesis testing or model building. Perhaps the data must be transformed so that the distribution is approximately normal or so that the variances in the groups are similar; or perhaps a nonparametric technique is needed.

Ways of Displaying Data

Now that we've established why it's important to look at data, we'll consider some of the techniques available for exploring data. One technique is to create a graphical representation of the data. To illustrate, we'll use data from a study of coronary heart disease among male employees of Western Electric and salary data from a study of employees of a bank engaged in Equal Employment Opportunity litigation.

The Histogram

The **histogram** is commonly used to represent data graphically. The range of observed values is subdivided into equal intervals, and the number of cases in each interval is obtained. Each bar in a histogram represents the number of cases with values within the interval.

Figure 9.1 is a histogram of diastolic blood pressure for a sample of 239 men from the Western Electric study. The values on the vertical axis indicate the number of cases. The values on the horizontal axis are midpoints of value ranges. For example, the midpoint of the first bar is 65 and the midpoint of the second bar is 75, indicating that each bar covers a value range of 10. Thus, the first bar contains cases with diastolic blood pressures in the 60's. Cases with diastolic blood pressures in the 70's go into the next bar, and so on.

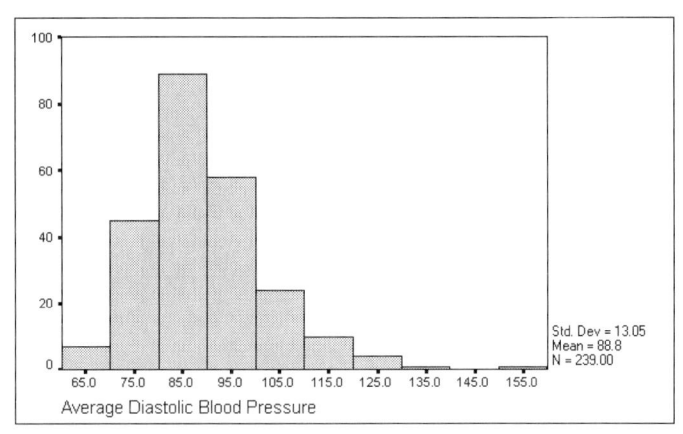

Figure 9.1 Histogram of diastolic blood pressure

The Stem-and-Leaf Plot

A display closely related to the histogram is the stem-and-leaf plot. A **stem-and-leaf plot** provides more information about the actual values than does a histogram. Consider Figure 9.2, which is a stem-and-leaf plot of the diastolic blood pressures. As in a histogram, the length of each row corresponds to the number of cases that fall into a particular interval. However, the stem-and-leaf plot represents each case with a numeric value that corresponds to the actual observed value. This is done by dividing observed values into two components—the leading digit or digits, called the **stem**, and a trailing digit, called the **leaf**. For example, the value 75 has a stem of 7 and a leaf of 5.

Figure 9.2 Stem-and-leaf plot of diastolic blood pressure

```
Frequency    Stem &  Leaf

      .00      6  *
     7.00      6  .  5558889
    13.00      7  *  0000111223344
    32.00      7  .  55555555667777777777788888889999
    44.00      8  *  00000000000000000000011112222233333334444
    45.00      8  .  555555555566666667777777777777788888999999999
    31.00      9  *  0000000001111111122222222333334
    27.00      9  .  556666677777788888888899999
    13.00     10  *  0000122233333
    11.00     10  .  55555577899
     5.00     11  *  00003
     5.00     11  .  55789
     2.00     12  *  01
     4.00  Extremes    (125), (133), (160)

Stem width:     10
Each leaf:       1 case(s)
```

In this example, each stem is divided into two rows. The first row of each pair has cases with leaves of 0 through 4, while the second row has cases with leaves of 5 through 9. Consider the two rows that correspond to the stem of 11. In the first row, we can see that there are four cases with diastolic blood pressure of 110 and one case with a reading of 113. In the second row, there are two cases with a value of 115 and one case each with a value of 117, 118, and 119.

The last row of the stem-and-leaf plot is for cases with extreme values (values far removed from the rest). In this row, the actual values are displayed in parentheses. In the frequency column, we see that there are four extreme cases. Their values are 125, 133, and 160. Only distinct values are listed.

To identify cases with extreme values, you can generate a table identifying cases with the largest and smallest values. Figure 9.3 shows the five cases with the largest and smallest values for diastolic blood pressure. Values of a case-labeling variable can be used to identify cases. Otherwise, the sequence of the case in the data file is reported.

Figure 9.3   Cases with extreme values

```
                        Extreme Values
                        -------  ------

    5   Highest   Case #          5   Lowest   Case #
          160     Case: 120            65      Case: 73
          133     Case: 56             65      Case: 156
          125     Case: 163            65      Case: 157
          125     Case: 42             68      Case: 153
          121     Case: 26             68      Case: 175
```

Other Stems

In Figure 9.2, each stem was divided into two parts—one for leaves of 0 through 4, and the other for leaves of 5 through 9. When there are few stems, it is sometimes useful to subdivide each stem even further. Consider Figure 9.4, a stem-and-leaf plot of cholesterol levels for the men in the Western Electric study. In this figure, stems 2 and 3 are divided into five parts, each representing two leaf values. The first row, designated by an asterisk, is for leaves of 0 and 1; the next, designated by *t*, is for leaves of 2's and 3's; the third, designated by *f*, is for leaves of 4's and 5's; the fourth, designated by *s*, is for leaves of 6's and 7's; and the fifth, designated by a period, is for leaves of 8's and 9's. Rows without cases are not represented in the plot. For example, in Figure 9.4, the first two rows for stem 1 (corresponding to 0–1 and 2–3) are omitted.

This stem-and-leaf plot differs from the previous one in another way. Since cholesterol values have a wide range—from 106 to 515 in this example—using the first two digits for the stem would result in an unnecessarily detailed plot. Therefore, we will use only the hundreds digit as the stem, rather than the first two digits. The stem setting of 100 appears in the column labeled *Stem width*. The leaf is then the tens digit. The last digit is ignored.

Thus, from this stem-and-leaf plot, it is not possible to determine the exact cholesterol level for a case. Instead, each case is classified by its first two digits only.

Figure 9.4 Stem-and-leaf plot of cholesterol levels

```
Frequency     Stem & Leaf

    1.00 Extremes    (106)
    2.00         1 f  55
    6.00         1 s  677777
   12.00         1 .  888889999999
   23.00         2 *  00000000000001111111111
   36.00         2 t  222222222222222223333333333333333333
   35.00         2 f  44444444444444444455555555555555555
   42.00         2 s  666666666666666666667777777777777777777777
   28.00         2 .  8888888888888889999999999999
   18.00         3 *  000000011111111111
   17.00         3 t  22222222222233333
    9.00         3 f  444445555
    6.00         3 s  666777
    1.00         3 .  8
    3.00 Extremes    (393), (425), (515)

Stem width:     100
Each leaf:      1 case(s)
```

The Boxplot

Both the histogram and the stem-and-leaf plot provide useful information about the distribution of observed values. We can see how tightly cases cluster together. We can see if there is a single peak or several peaks. We can determine if there are extreme values.

A display that further summarizes information about the distribution of the values is the boxplot. Instead of plotting the actual values, a **boxplot** displays summary statistics for the distribution. It plots the median, the 25th percentile, the 75th percentile, and values that are far removed from the rest.

Figure 9.5 shows an annotated sketch of a boxplot. The lower boundary of the box is the 25th percentile and the upper boundary is the 75th percentile. (These percentiles, sometimes called Tukey's hinges, are calculated a little differently from ordinary percentiles.) The horizontal line inside the box represents the median. Fifty percent of the cases have values within the box. The length of the box corresponds to the interquartile range, which is the difference between the 75th and 25th percentiles.

The boxplot includes two categories of cases with outlying values. Cases with values that are more than 3 box-lengths from the upper or lower edge of the box are called **extreme values**. On the boxplot, these are designated with an asterisk (*). Cases with values that are between 1.5 and 3 box-lengths from the upper or lower edge of the box are called **outliers** and are designated with a circle. The largest and smallest observed values that aren't outliers are also shown. Lines are drawn from the ends of the box to these values. (These lines are sometimes called **whiskers** and the plot is called a **box-and-whiskers plot**.)

Figure 9.5 Annotated sketch of a boxplot

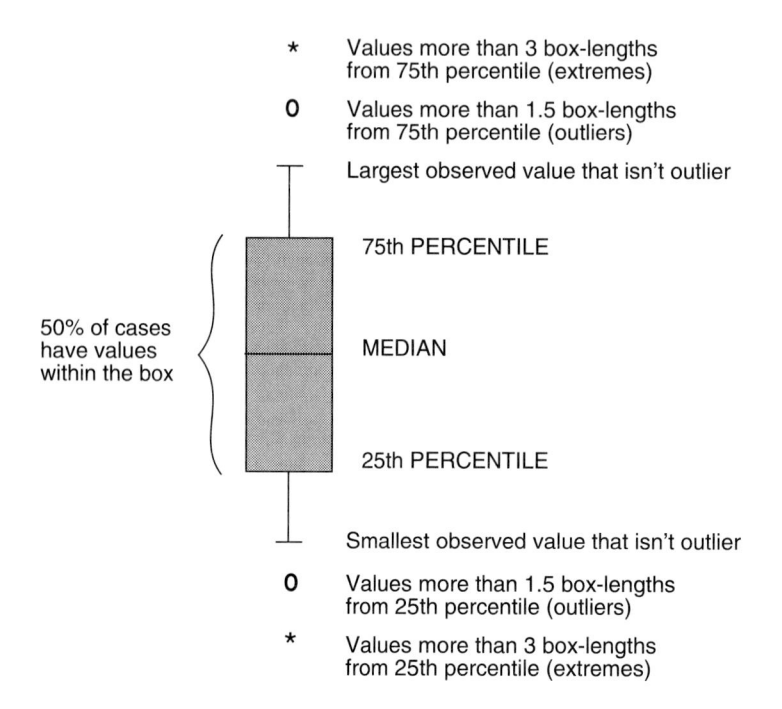

```
*      Values more than 3 box-lengths
       from 75th percentile (extremes)

O      Values more than 1.5 box-lengths
       from 75th percentile (outliers)

       Largest observed value that isn't outlier

       75th PERCENTILE

50% of cases
have values        MEDIAN
within the box

       25th PERCENTILE

       Smallest observed value that isn't outlier

O      Values more than 1.5 box-lengths
       from 25th percentile (outliers)

*      Values more than 3 box-lengths
       from 25th percentile (extremes)
```

What can you tell about your data from a boxplot? From the median, you can determine the central tendency, or location. From the length of the box, you can determine the spread, or variability, of your observations. If the median is not in the center of the box, you know that the observed values are skewed. If the median is closer to the bottom of the box than to the top, the data are positively skewed. If the median is closer to the top of the box than to the bottom, the opposite is true: the distribution is negatively skewed. The length of the tail is shown by the whiskers and the outlying and extreme points.

Boxplots are particularly useful for comparing the distribution of values in several groups. For example, suppose you want to compare the distribution of beginning salaries for people employed in several different positions at a bank. Figure 9.6 contains boxplots of the bank salary data. From these plots, you can see that the first two job categories have similar distributions for salary, although the first category has several extreme values. The third job category has little variability; all 27 people in this category earn similar amounts of money. The last two groups have much higher median salaries than the other groups, and a larger spread as well.

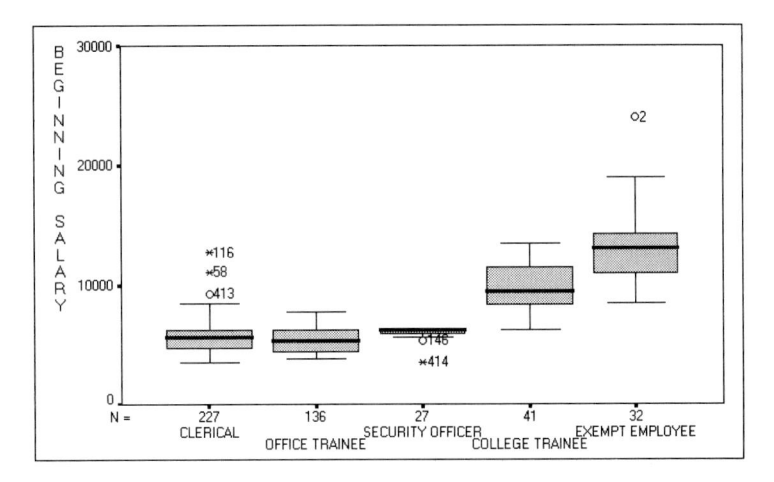

Figure 9.6   Boxplots for bank salary data

[Boxplot figure showing beginning salary by employment category: Clerical (N=227), Office Trainee (N=136), Security Officer (N=27), College Trainee (N=41), Exempt Employee (N=32). Outliers noted: *116, *58, o413 for clerical; *414 for security officer; o146 for college trainee; o2 for exempt employee.]

Evaluating Assumptions

Many statistical procedures, such as analysis of variance, require that all groups come from normal populations with the same variance. Therefore, before choosing a statistical hypothesis, we need to test the hypothesis that all the group variances are equal or that the samples come from normal populations. If it appears that the assumptions are violated, we may want to determine appropriate transformations.

The Levene Test

Numerous tests are available for evaluating the assumption that all groups come from populations with equal variances. Many of these tests, however, are heavily dependent on the data being from normal populations. Analysis-of-variance procedures, on the other hand, are reasonably robust to departures from normality. The **Levene test** is a homogeneity-of-variance test that is less dependent on the assumption of normality than most tests and thus is particularly useful with analysis of variance. It is obtained by computing, for each case, the absolute difference from its cell mean and performing a one-way analysis of variance on these differences.

From Figure 9.7, you can see that for the salary data, the null hypothesis that all group variances are equal is rejected. We should consider transforming the data if we plan to use a statistical procedure that requires equality of variance. Next we'll consider how to select a transformation.

Figure 9.7 The Levene test

```
Test of homogeneity of variance                df1      df2     Significance
Levene Statistic                     28.9200     4       458          .0000
```

Spread-versus-Level Plots

Often there is a relationship between the average value, or level, of a variable and the variability, or spread, associated with it. For example, we can see in Figure 9.6 that as salaries increase, so does the variability.

One way of studying the relationship between spread and level is to plot the values of spread and level for each group. If there is no relationship, the points should cluster around a horizontal line. If this is not the case, we can use the observed relationship between the two variables to choose an appropriate transformation.

Determining the Transformation

A power transformation is frequently used to stabilize variances. A power transformation raises each data value to a specified power. For example, a power transformation of 2 squares all of the data values. A transformation of 1/2 calculates the square root of all the values. If the power is 0, the log of the numbers is used.

To determine an appropriate power for transforming the data, we can plot, for each group, the log of the median against the log of the interquartile range. Figure 9.8 shows such a plot for the salary data shown in Figure 9.6. You see that there is a fairly strong

Figure 9.8 Spread-versus-level plot of bank data

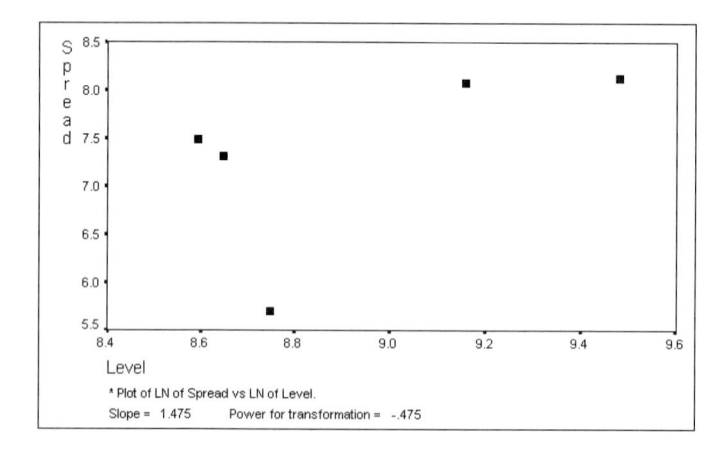

* Plot of LN of Spread vs LN of Level.
Slope = 1.475   Power for transformation = -.475

linear relationship between spread and level. From the slope of the line, we can estimate the power value that will eliminate or lessen this relationship. The power is obtained by subtracting the slope from 1. That is,

Power = 1 − slope **Equation 9.1**

Although this formula can result in all sorts of powers, for simplicity and clarity we usually choose the closest powers that are multiples of 1/2. Table 9.1 shows the most commonly used transformations.

Table 9.1 Commonly used transformations

Power	Transformation
3	Cube
2	Square
1	No change
1/2	Square root
0	Logarithm
−1/2	Reciprocal of the square root
−1	Reciprocal

As shown in Figure 9.8, the slope of the least-squares line for the bank data is 1.475, so the power for the transformation is −0.475. Rounding to the nearest multiple of a half, we will use the reciprocal of the square root.

After applying the power transformation, it is wise to obtain a spread-versus-level plot for the transformed data. From this plot, you can judge the success of the transformation.

Tests of Normality

Since the normal distribution is very important to statistical inference, we often want to examine the assumption that our data come from a normal distribution. One way to do this is with a normal probability plot. In a **normal probability plot**, each observed value is paired with its expected value from the normal distribution. (The expected value from the normal distribution is based on the number of cases in the sample and the rank order of the case in the sample.) If the sample is from a normal distribution, we expect that the points will fall more or less on a straight line.

The first plot in Figure 9.9 is a normal probability plot of a sample of 200 points from a normal distribution. Note how the points cluster around a straight line. You can also plot the actual deviations of the points from a straight line. This is called a detrended normal plot and is shown in the second plot in Figure 9.9. If the sample is from a normal population, the points should cluster around a horizontal line through 0, and there should be no pattern. A striking pattern suggests departure from normality.

Figure 9.9 Normal plots for a normal distribution

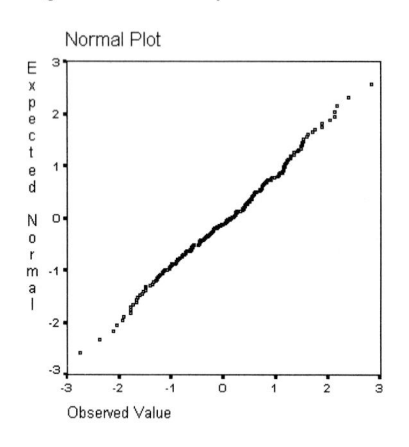

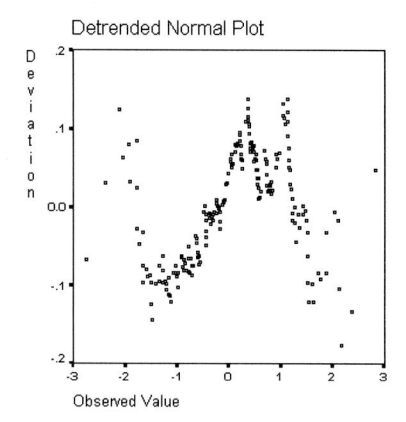

Figure 9.10 shows a normal probability plot and a detrended plot for data from a uniform distribution. The points do not cluster around a straight line, and the deviations from a straight line are not randomly distributed around 0.

Figure 9.10 Normal plots for a uniform distribution

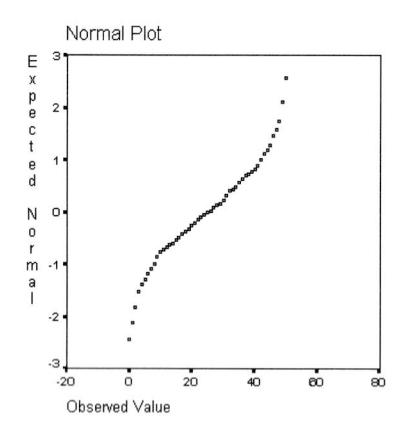

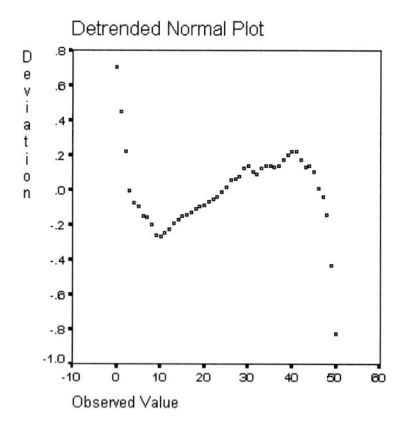

Although normal probability plots provide a visual basis for checking normality, it is often desirable to compute a statistical test of the hypothesis that the data are from a normal distribution. Two commonly used tests are the Shapiro-Wilks' test and the Lilliefors test. The **Lilliefors test**, based on a modification of the Kolmogorov-Smirnov test, is used when means and variances are not known but must be estimated from the data. The **Shapiro-Wilks' test** shows good power in many situations compared to other tests of normality (Conover, 1980).

Figure 9.11 contains normal probability plots and Figure 9.12 contains the Lilliefors test of normality for the diastolic blood pressure data. From the small observed significance levels, you see that the hypothesis of normality can be rejected. However, it is important to remember that whenever the sample size is large, almost any goodness-of-fit test will result in rejection of the null hypothesis. It is almost impossible to find data that are *exactly* normally distributed. For most statistical tests, it is sufficient that the data are approximately normally distributed. Thus, for large data sets, you should look not only at the observed significance level but also at the actual departure from normality.

Figure 9.11 Normal plots for diastolic blood pressure

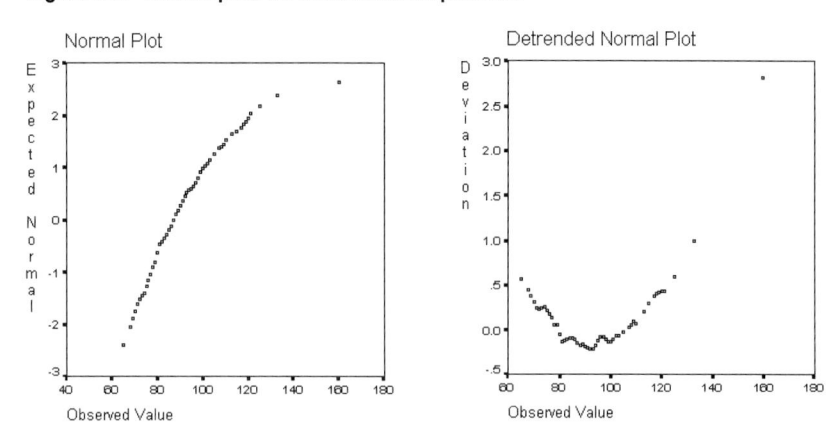

Figure 9.12 Normality test

```
                       Statistic        df       Significance
K-S (Lilliefors)          .0974        239           .0000
```

Estimating Location with Robust Estimators

We often use the arithmetic mean to estimate central tendency, or location. We know, however, that the mean is heavily influenced by outliers. One very large or very small value can change the mean dramatically. The median, on the other hand, is insensitive to outliers; addition or removal of extreme values has little effect on it. The median is called a **resistant measure**, since its value depends on the main body of the data and not on outliers. The advantages of resistant measures are obvious: their values are not unduly influenced by a few observations, and they don't change much if small amounts of data are added or removed.

Although the median is an intuitive, simple measure of location, there are better estimators of location if we are willing to make some assumptions about the population from which our data originate. Estimators that depend on simple, fairly nonrestrictive assumptions about the underlying distribution and are not sensitive to these assumptions are called **robust estimators**. In the following sections, we will consider some robust estimators of central tendency that depend only on the assumption that the data are from a symmetric population.

The Trimmed Mean

A simple robust estimator of location can be obtained by "trimming" the data to exclude values that are far removed from the others. For example, a 20% trimmed mean disregards the smallest 20% and the largest 20% of all observations. The estimate is based on only the 60% of data values that are in the middle. What's the advantage of a trimmed mean? Like the median, it results in an estimate that is not influenced by extreme values. However, unlike the median, it is not based solely on a single value, or two values, that are in the middle. It is based on a much larger number of middle values. (The median can be considered a 50% trimmed mean, since half of the values above and below the median are ignored.) In general, a trimmed mean makes better use of the data than does the median.

M-Estimators

When calculating a trimmed mean, we divide our cases into two groups: those included and those excluded from the computation of the mean. We can consider the trimmed mean as a weighted mean in which cases have weights of 0 or 1, depending on whether they are included or excluded from the computations. A weighted mean is calculated by assigning a weight to each case and then using the formula $\bar{X} = (\Sigma w_i x_i) / (\Sigma w_i)$. In calculating the trimmed mean, we treat observations that are far from most of the others by excluding them altogether. A less extreme alternative is to include them but give them smaller weights than cases closer to the center, which we can do using the **M-estimator**, or generalized *m*aximum-likelihood estimator.

Since many different schemes can be used to assign weights to cases, there are many different M-estimators. (The usual mean can be viewed as an M-estimator with all cases having a weight of 1.) All commonly used M-estimators assign weights so that they decrease as distance from the center of the distribution increases. Figure 9.13 through Figure 9.16 show the weights used by four common M-estimators.

Common M-Estimators

Figure 9.13 Huber's (c = 1.339)

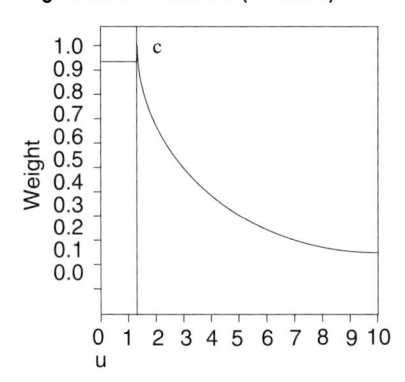

Figure 9.14 Tukey's biweight (c = 4.685)

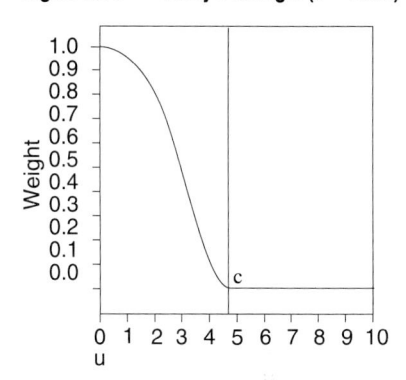

Figure 9.15 Hampel's (a = 1.7, b = 3.4, c = 8.5)

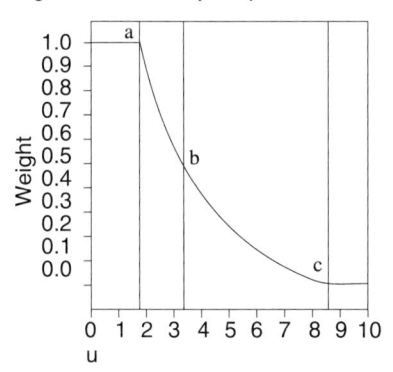

Figure 9.16 Andrew's (c = 1.339π)

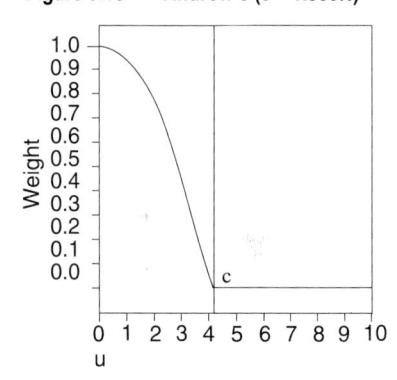

Consider Figure 9.13, which shows Huber's M-estimator. The value on the horizontal axis is a standardized distance from the estimate of location. It is computed using the following formula:

$$u_i = \frac{|\text{value for } i\text{th case} - \text{estimate of location}|}{\text{estimate of spread}}$$

Equation 9.2

The estimate of spread used is the median of the absolute deviations from the sample median, commonly known as MAD. It is calculated by first finding the median for the sample and then computing for each case the absolute value of the deviation from the median. The MAD is then the median of these absolute values. Since the weights for cases depend on the value of the estimate of central location, M-estimators must be computed iteratively.

From Figure 9.13, you can see that cases have weights of 1 up to a certain critical point, labeled c. After the critical point, the weights decrease as u, the standardized distance from the location estimate, increases. The SPSS values for these critical points are given in parentheses in Figure 9.13 through Figure 9.16.

The four M-estimators in Figure 9.13 through Figure 9.16 differ from each other in the way they assign weights. The Tukey biweight (Figure 9.14) does not have a point at which weights shift abruptly from 1. Instead, weights gradually decline to 0. Cases with values greater than c standardized units from the estimate are assigned weights of 0.

Hampel's three-part redescending M-estimator (Figure 9.15) has a more complicated weighting scheme than the Huber or the Tukey biweight. It uses four schemes for assigning weights. Cases with values less than a receive a weight of 1, cases with values between a and b receive a weight of a/u, while cases between b and c receive a weight of:

$$\frac{a}{u} \times \frac{c-u}{c-b}$$
Equation 9.3

Cases with values greater than c receive a weight of 0. With Andrew's M-estimator (Figure 9.16), there is no abrupt change in the assignment of weights. A smooth function replaces the separate pieces.

Figure 9.17 contains basic descriptive statistics and values for the M-estimators for the diastolic blood pressure data. As expected, the estimates of location differ for the various methods. The mean produces the largest estimate: 88.79. That's because we have a positively skewed distribution and the mean is heavily influenced by the large values. Of the M-estimators, the Huber and Hampel estimates have the largest values. They too are influenced by the large data values. The remaining two M-estimates are fairly close in value.

Figure 9.17 M-estimates for blood pressure variable

```
     DBP58      AVERAGE DIAST BLOOD PRESS

Valid cases:        239.0   Missing cases:      1.0   Percent missing:      .4

Mean       88.7908  Std Err        .8441  Min       65.0000  Skewness    1.2557
Median     87.0000  Variance   170.3006  Max      160.0000  S E Skew     .1575
5% Trim    88.0065  Std Dev     13.0499  Range     95.0000  Kurtosis    3.5958
                                          IQR       17.0000  S E Kurt     .3137

                              M-Estimators
                              ------------

Huber   (1.339)              87.1219      Tukey  (4.685)              86.4269
Hampel  (1.700,3.400,8.500)  87.1404      Andrew (1.340 * pi)         86.4105
```

In summary, M-estimators are good alternatives to the usual mean and median. The Huber M-estimator is good if the distribution is close to normal but is not recommended if there are extreme values. For further discussion of robust estimators, see Hogg (1979) and Hoaglin et al. (1983).

How to Explore Your Data

The Explore procedure provides a variety of descriptive plots and statistics, including stem-and-leaf plots, boxplots, normal probability plots, and spread-versus-level plots. Also available are the Levene test for homogeneity of variance, Shapiro-Wilks' and Lilliefors tests for normality, and several robust maximum-likelihood estimators of location. Cases can be subdivided into groups and statistics can be obtained for each group.

The minimum specification is one or more numeric dependent variables.

To obtain exploratory plots and statistics, from the menus choose:

Statistics
  Summarize ▶
    Explore...

This opens the Explore dialog box, as shown in Figure 9.18.

Figure 9.18 Explore dialog box

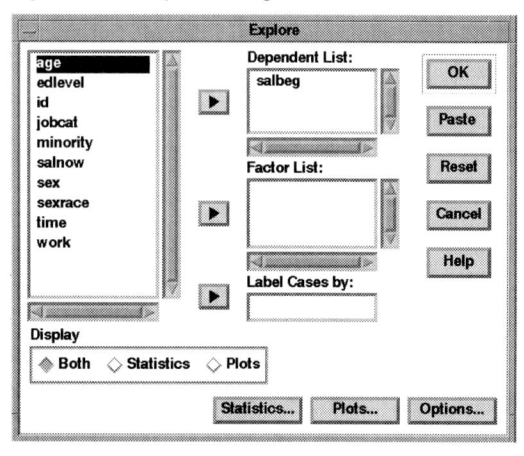

The variables in your data file appear on the source list. Select one or more numeric dependent variables and click on OK to get the default analysis, which includes boxplots, stem-and-leaf plots, and basic descriptive statistics for each variable. By default, cases with missing values for any dependent or factor variable are excluded from all summaries.

By default, output is produced for all cases. Optionally, you can obtain separate analyses for groups of cases based on their values for one or more numeric or short string **factor** variables. (For example, *jobcat* is the factor variable in Figure 9.6.) If you select more than one factor variable, separate summaries of each dependent variable are produced for each factor variable.

When output is produced showing individual cases (such as outliers), cases are identified by default by their sequence in the data file. Optionally, you can label cases with their values for a variable, such as a case ID variable. It can be a long string, short string, or numeric variable. For long string variables, the first 15 characters are used.

Display. You can also choose one of the following display options:

◇ **Both**. Displays plots and statistics. This is the default.

◇ **Statistics**. Displays statistics only (suppresses all plots).

◇ **Plots**. Displays plots only (suppresses all statistics).

Explore Statistics

To obtain robust estimators or display outliers, percentiles, or frequency tables, select Both or Statistics under Display and click on Statistics... in the Explore dialog box to open the Explore Statistics dialog box, as shown in Figure 9.19.

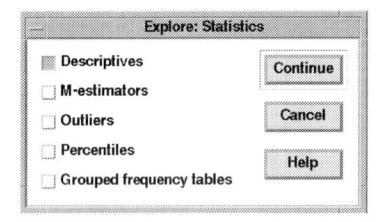

Figure 9.19   Explore Statistics dialog box

At least one statistic must be selected. You can choose one or more of the following statistics:

❏ **Descriptives**. Includes the mean, median, 5% trimmed mean, standard error, variance, standard deviation, minimum, maximum, range, and interquartile range. Skewness and kurtosis and their standard errors are also shown. This is the default. Interquartile ranges are computed according to the HAVERAGE method.

❏ **M-estimators**. Robust maximum-likelihood estimators of location. Displays Huber's M-estimator ($c = 1.339$), Andrew's wave estimator ($c = 1.34\pi$), Hampel's redescending M-estimator ($a = 1.7$, $b = 3.4$, and $c = 8.5$), and Tukey's biweight estimator ($c = 4.685$). (See "M-Estimators" on p. 182.)

❏ **Outliers**. Displays cases with the five largest and five smallest values. These are labeled *Extreme Values* in the output (see Figure 9.3).

❏ **Percentiles**. Displays the following percentiles: 5, 10, 25, 50, 75, 90, and 95. The weighted average at $X_{(W+1)p}$ (HAVERAGE) is used to calculate percentiles, where W is the sum of the weights for all cases with nonmissing values, p is the percentile divided by 100, i is the rank of the case when cases are sorted in ascending order, and

X_i is the value for the ith case. The percentile value is the weighted average of X_i and X_{i+1} using the formula $(1-f) X_i + f X_{i+1}$, where $(W+1)p$ is decomposed into an integer part i and fractional part f. Also displays Tukey's hinges (25th, 50th, and 75th percentiles).

❑ **Grouped frequency tables.** Displays tables for the total sample and broken down by any factor variables. Starting value and increment are selected on the basis of observed data values.

Explore Plots

To obtain histograms, normality plots and tests, or spread-versus-level plots with Levene's statistic, select Both or Plots under Display and click on Plots... in the Explore dialog box to open the Explore Plots dialog box, as shown in Figure 9.20.

Figure 9.20 Explore Plots dialog box

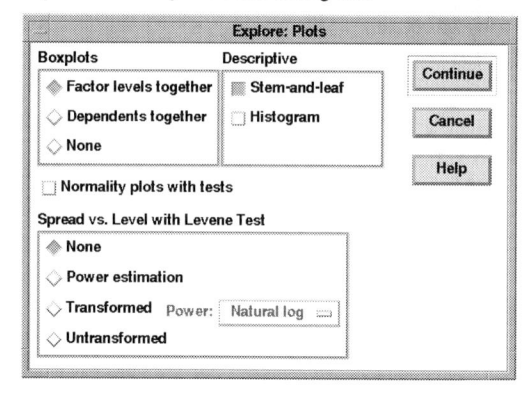

At least one plot must be selected.

Boxplots. You can choose one of the following boxplot display alternatives:

◇ **Factor levels together.** For a given dependent variable, displays boxplots for each group side by side. This is the default. Select this display method when you want to compare groups for a variable. If no factor variable is selected, only a boxplot for the total sample is shown.

◇ **Dependents together.** For a given group, displays boxplots for each dependent variable side by side. Select this display method when you want to compare variables for a particular group.

◇ **None.** Suppresses boxplot.

Descriptive. You can choose one or both of the following descriptive plots:

- **Stem-and-leaf.** Displayed by default. Each observed value is divided into two components—the leading digits (stem) and trailing digits (leaf). To suppress stem-and-leaf plots, deselect this item.
- **Histogram.** The range of observed values is divided into equal intervals and the number of cases in each interval is displayed.

Spread vs. Level with Levene Test. For all spread-versus-level plots, the slope of the regression line and Levene's test for homogeneity of variance are displayed. Levene's test is based on the original data if no transformation is specified and on the transformed data if a transformation is specified. If no factor variable is selected, spread-versus-level plots are not produced.

You can choose one of the following alternatives:

- **None.** Suppresses spread-versus-level plots and Levene's statistic. This is the default.
- **Power estimation.** For each group, the natural log of the median is plotted against the log of the interquartile range. Estimated power is also displayed. Use this method to determine an appropriate transformation for your data.
- **Transformed.** Data are transformed according to a user-specified power. The interquartile range and median of the transformed data are plotted. (See "Determining the Transformation" on p. 178.)
  - **Power.** To transform data, you must select a power for the transformation. You can choose one of the following alternatives:

    Natural log. Natural log transformation. This is the default.

    1/square root. For each data value, the reciprocal of the square root is calculated.

    Reciprocal. Reciprocal transformation.

    Square root. Square root transformation.

    Square. Data values are squared.

    Cube. Data values are cubed.
- **Untransformed.** No transformation of the data is performed. *(Power value is 1.)*

The following option is available for normal probability and detrended probability plots:

- **Normality plots with tests.** Normal probability and detrended probability plots are produced, and the Shapiro-Wilks' statistic and the Kolmogorov-Smirnov statistic with a Lilliefors significance level for testing normality are calculated. The Shapiro-Wilks' statistic is not calculated if the sample size exceeds 50.

Explore Options

To modify the handling of missing values, click on Options... in the Explore dialog box. This opens the Explore Options dialog box, as shown in Figure 9.21.

Figure 9.21 Explore Options dialog box

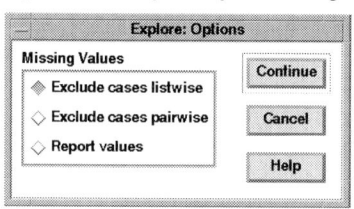

Missing Values. You can choose one of the following alternatives:

◇ **Exclude cases listwise.** Cases with missing values for any dependent or factor variable are excluded from all analyses. This is the default.

◇ **Exclude cases pairwise.** Cases with no missing values for variables in a cell are included in the analysis of that cell. The case may have missing values for variables used in other cells.

◇ **Report values.** Missing values for factor variables are treated as a separate category. All output is produced for this additional category. Frequency tables include categories for missing values.

Additional Features Available with Command Syntax

You can customize your exploratory data analysis if you paste your selections into a syntax window and edit the resulting EXAMINE command syntax (see Chapter 4). Additional features include:

- Output for cells formed by *combinations* of factor variables (using the keyword BY).
- User-specified number of outliers displayed (with the STATISTICS subcommand).
- User-specified starting and increment values for frequency tables (with the FREQUENCIES subcommand).
- Alternative methods of percentile estimation and user-specified percentiles (using the PERCENTILES subcommand).
- Additional user-specified power values for spread-versus-level plot transformations (with the PLOT subcommand).
- User-specified critical points for M-estimators (with the MESTIMATORS subcommand).

See Appendix A for command syntax rules. See the *SPSS Base System Syntax Reference Guide* for complete EXAMINE command syntax.

10 Crosstabulation and Measures of Association

Newspapers headline murders in subway stations, robberies on crowded main streets, suicides cheered by onlookers. All are indications of the social irresponsibility and apathy said to characterize city residents. Since overcrowding, decreased sense of community, and other urban problems are usually blamed, you might ask whether small-town residents are more responsible and less apathetic than their urban counterparts.

Hansson and Slade (1977) used the "lost letter technique" to test the hypothesis that altruism is higher in small towns than in cities, unless the person needing assistance is a social deviant. In this technique, stamped and addressed letters are "lost," and the rate at which they are returned is examined. A total of 216 letters were lost in Hansson and Slade's experiment. Half were dropped within the city limits of Tulsa, Oklahoma, the others in 51 small towns within a 50-mile radius of Tulsa. The letters were addressed to three fictitious people at a post-office box in Tulsa: M. J. Davis; Dandee Davis, c/o Pink Panther Lounge; and M. J. Davis, c/o Friends of the Communist Party. The first person is considered a normal "control," the second, a person whose occupation is questionable, and the third, a subversive or political deviant.

Crosstabulation

To see whether the return rate is similar for the three addresses, the letters found and mailed and those not mailed must be tallied separately for each address. Figure 10.1 is a crosstabulation of address type and response. The number of cases (letters) for each combination of values of the two variables is displayed in a **cell** in the table, together with various percentages. These cell entries provide information about relationships between the variables.

Figure 10.1 Crosstabulation of status of letter by address

```
RETURNED  FOUND AND MAILED  by  ADDRESS  ADDRESS ON LETTER
                    ADDRESS                        Page 1 of 1
          Count
          Row Pct  CONTROL  DANDEE   COMMUNIS
          Col Pct                    T            Row
          Tot Pct       1        2          3     Total
RETURNED
               1         35       32         10      77
    YES              45.5     41.6       13.0     35.6
                    48.6     44.4       13.9
                    16.2     14.8        4.6

               2         37       40         62     139
    NO               26.6     28.8       44.6     64.4
                    51.4     55.6       86.1
                    17.1     18.5       28.7

          Column       72       72         72     216
          Total      33.3     33.3       33.3    100.0

Number of Missing Observations:  0
```

In Figure 10.1, the address is called the **column variable**, since each address is displayed in a column of the table. Similarly, the status of the letter (whether it was returned or not) is called the **row variable**. With three categories of the column variable and two of the row, there are six cells in the table.

Cell Contents and Marginals

The first entry in the table is the number of cases, or **frequency**, in that cell. It is labeled as *Count* in the key displayed in the upper left corner of the table. For example, 35 letters addressed to the control were returned, and 62 letters addressed to the Communist were not returned. The second entry in the table is the **row percentage** (*Row Pct*). It is the percentage of all cases in a row that fall into a particular cell. Of the 77 letters returned, 45.5% were addressed to the control, 41.6% to Dandee, and 13.0% to the Communist.

The **column percentage** (*Col Pct*), the third item in each cell, is the percentage of all cases in a column that occur in a cell. For example, 48.6% of the letters addressed to the control were returned and 51.4% were not. The return rate for Dandee is similar (44.4%), while that for the Communist is markedly lower (13.9%).

The last entry in the table is the **table percentage** (*Tot Pct*). The number of cases in the cell is expressed as a percentage of the total number of cases in the table. For example, the 35 letters returned to the control represent 16.2% of the 216 letters in the experiment.

The numbers to the right and below the table are known as **marginals**. They are the counts and percentages for the row and column variables taken separately. In Figure 10.1, the row marginals show that 77 (35.6%) of the letters were returned, while 139 (64.4%) were not.

Choosing Percentages

Row, column, and table percentages convey different types of information, so it is important to choose carefully among them.

In this example, the row percentage indicates the distribution of address types for returned and "lost" letters. It conveys no direct information about the return rate. For example, if twice as many letters were addressed to the control, an identical return rate for all letters would give row percentages of 50%, 25%, and 25%. However, this does not indicate that the return rate is higher for the control. In addition, if each category had the same number of returned letters, the row percentages would have been 33.3%, 33.3%, and 33.3%, regardless of whether one or all letters were returned.

The column percentage is the percentage of letters returned and not returned for each address. By looking at column percentages across rows, you can compare return rates for the address types. Interpretation of this comparison is not affected if unequal numbers of letters are addressed to each category.

Since it is always possible to interchange the rows and columns of any table, general rules about when to use row and column percentages cannot be given. The percentages to use depend on the nature of the two variables. If one of the two variables is under experimental control, it is termed an **independent variable**. This variable is hypothesized to affect the response, or **dependent variable**. If variables can be classified as dependent and independent, the following guideline may be helpful: if the independent variable is the row variable, select row percentages; if the independent variable is the column variable, select column percentages. In this example the dependent variable is the status of the letter, whether it was mailed or not. The type of address is the independent variable. Since the independent variable is the column variable in Figure 10.1, column percentages should be used for comparisons of return rates.

Adding a Control Variable

Since Figure 10.1 combines results from both the city and the towns, differences between the locations are obscured. Two separate tables, one for the city and one for the towns, are required. Figure 10.2 shows crosstabulations of response and address for each of the locations. SPSS produces a separate table for each value of the location (control) variable.

Figure 10.2 Crosstabulations of status of letter by address controlled for location

```
RETURNED  FOUND AND MAILED  by  ADDRESS   ADDRESS ON LETTER
Controlling for..
LOCATION  LOCATION LOST  Value = 1   CITY
```

	ADDRESS			Page 1 of 1
Count Col Pct	CONTROL	DANDEE	COMMUNIST	Row Total
	1	2	3	
RETURNED				
YES 1	16 44.4	14 38.9	9 25.0	39 36.1
NO 2	20 55.6	22 61.1	27 75.0	69 63.9
Column Total	36 33.3	36 33.3	36 33.3	108 100.0

Chi-Square	Value	DF	Significance
Pearson	3.13043	2	.20904
Likelihood Ratio	3.21258	2	.20063
Mantel-Haenszel test for linear association	2.92252	1	.08735

Minimum Expected Frequency - 13.000

```
RETURNED  FOUND AND MAILED  by  ADDRESS   ADDRESS ON LETTER
Controlling for..
LOCATION  LOCATION LOST  Value = 2   TOWN
```

	ADDRESS			Page 1 of 1
Count Col Pct	CONTROL	DANDEE	COMMUNIST	Row Total
	1	2	3	
RETURNED				
YES 1	19 52.8	18 50.0	1 2.8	38 35.2
NO 2	17 47.2	18 50.0	35 97.2	70 64.8
Column Total	36 33.3	36 33.3	36 33.3	108 100.0

Chi-Square	Value	DF	Significance
Pearson	24.92932	2	.00000
Likelihood Ratio	31.25344	2	.00000
Mantel-Haenszel test for linear association	19.54962	1	.00001

Minimum Expected Frequency - 12.667

Number of Missing Observations: 0

These tables show interesting differences between cities and towns. Although the overall return rates are close, 36.1% for the city and 35.2% for the towns, there are striking differences between the addresses. Only 2.8% of the Communist letters were returned in towns, while 25.0% of them were returned in Tulsa. (At least two of the Communist letters were forwarded by small-town residents to the FBI for punitive action.) The return rates for both the control (52.8%) and Dandee (50.0%) are higher in towns.

The results support the hypothesis that suspected social deviance influences the response more in small towns than in big cities, although it is surprising that Dandee and the Pink Panther Lounge were deemed worthy of as much assistance as they received. If the Communist letter is excluded, inhabitants of small towns are somewhat more helpful than city residents, returning 51% of the other letters, in comparison with the city's 42%.

Graphical Representation of Crosstabulations

As with frequency tables, visual representation of a crosstabulation often simplifies the search for associations. Figure 10.3 is a **bar chart** of letters returned from the crosstabulations shown in Figure 10.2. In a bar chart, the height of each bar represents the frequencies or percentages for each category of a variable. In Figure 10.3, the percentages plotted are the column percentages shown in Figure 10.2 for the returned letters only. This chart clearly shows that the return rates for the control and Dandee are high compared with the return rate for the Communist. Also, it demonstrates more vividly than the crosstabulation that the town residents' return rates for the control and Dandee are higher than city residents' return rates, but that the reverse is true for the Communist.

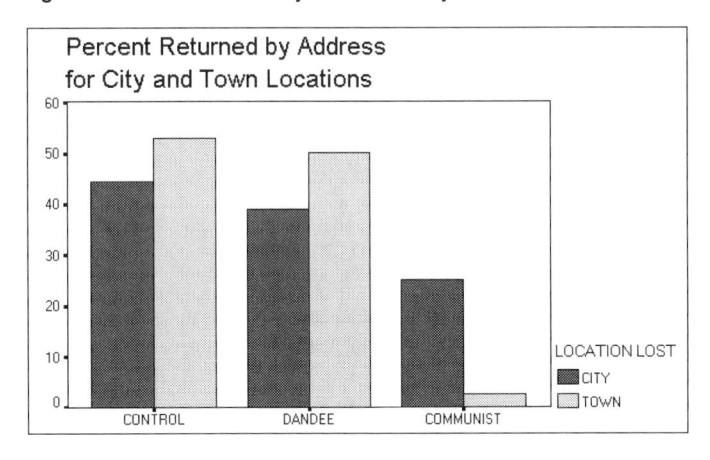

Figure 10.3 Status of letter by address and by location

Using Crosstabulation for Data Screening

Errors and unusual values in data entry that cannot be spotted with frequency tables can sometimes be identified using crosstabulation. For example, a case coded as a male with a history of three pregnancies would not be identified as suspicious in frequency tables of sex and number of pregnancies. When considered separately, the code *male* is acceptable for sex and the value 3 is acceptable for number of pregnancies. The combination, however, is unexpected.

Whenever possible, crosstabulations of related variables should be obtained so that anomalies can be identified and corrected before further statistical analysis of the data.

Crosstabulation Statistics

Although examination of the various row and column percentages in a crosstabulation is a useful first step in studying the relationship between two variables, row and column percentages do not allow for quantification or testing of that relationship. For these purposes, it is useful to consider various indexes that measure the extent of association as well as statistical tests of the hypothesis that there is no association.

The Chi-Square Test of Independence

The hypothesis that two variables of a crosstabulation are independent of each other is often of interest to researchers. Two variables are by definition **independent** if the probability that a case falls into a given cell is simply the product of the marginal probabilities of the two categories defining the cell.

In Figure 10.1, for example, if returns of the letter and address type are independent, the probability of a letter being returned to a Communist is the product of the probability of a letter being returned and the probability of a letter being addressed to a Communist. From the table, 35.6% of the letters were returned, and 33.3% of the letters were addressed to a friend of the Communist Party. Thus, if address type and status of the letter are independent, the probability of a letter being returned to the Communist is estimated to be:

$$P(\text{return})\, P(\text{Communist}) = 0.356 \times 0.333 = 0.119 \qquad \text{Equation 10.1}$$

The **expected** number of cases in that cell is 25.7, which is 11.9% of the 216 cases in the sample. From the table, the **observed** number of letters returned to the Communist is 10 (4.6%), nearly 16 fewer than expected if the two variables are independent.

To construct a statistical test of the independence hypothesis, you repeat the above calculations for each cell in the table. The probability under independence of an observation falling into cell (ij) is estimated by:

$$P(\text{row} = i \text{ and column} = j) = \left(\frac{\text{count in row } i}{N}\right)\left(\frac{\text{count in column } j}{N}\right) \qquad \text{Equation 10.2}$$

To obtain the expected number of observations in cell (*ij*), the probability is multiplied by the total sample size:

$$E_{ij} = N\left(\left(\frac{\text{count in row } i}{N}\right)\left(\frac{\text{count in column } j}{N}\right)\right)$$
$$= \frac{(\text{count in row } i)(\text{count in column } j)}{N}$$

Equation 10.3

Figure 10.4 contains the observed and expected frequencies and the **residuals**, which are the observed minus the expected frequencies for the data in Figure 10.1.

Figure 10.4 Observed, expected, and residual values

```
RETURNED   FOUND AND MAILED   by   ADDRESS   ADDRESS ON LETTER
                      ADDRESS                        Page 1 of 1
           Count
           Exp Val  CONTROL    DANDEE   COMMUNIS
           Residual                     T                Row
                         1         2         3         Total
RETURNED
              1         35        32        10           77
   YES                 25.7      25.7      25.7        35.6%
                       9.3        6.3     -15.7

              2         37        40        62          139
   NO                  46.3      46.3      46.3        64.4%
                       -9.3      -6.3      15.7

          Column        72        72        72          216
          Total       33.3%     33.3%     33.3%       100.0%

    Chi-Square                     Value                DF       Significance
    ----------                     -----                --       ------------

Pearson                          22.56265               2          .00001
Likelihood Ratio                 24.68683               2          .00000
Mantel-Haenszel test for         18.83234               1          .00001
    linear association

Minimum Expected Frequency -     25.667

Number of Missing Observations:  0
```

A statistic often used to test the hypothesis that the row and column variables are independent is the **Pearson chi-square**. It is calculated by summing over all cells the squared residuals divided by the expected frequencies:

$$\chi^2 = \sum_i \sum_j \frac{(O_{ij} - E_{ij})^2}{E_{ij}}$$

Equation 10.4

The calculated chi-square is compared to the critical points of the theoretical chi-square distribution to produce an estimate of how likely (or unlikely) this calculated value is if the two variables are in fact independent. Since the value of the chi-square depends on the number of rows and columns in the table being examined, you must know the **degrees of freedom** for the table. The degrees of freedom can be viewed as the number of cells of a table that can be arbitrarily filled when the row and column totals (marginals) are fixed. For an $r \times c$ table, the degrees of freedom are $(r-1) \times (c-1)$, since once $(r-1)$ rows and $(c-1)$ columns are filled, frequencies in the remaining row and column cells must be chosen so that marginal totals are maintained.

In this example, there are two degrees of freedom (1×2) and the Pearson chi-square value is 22.56 (see Figure 10.4). If type of address and return rate are independent, the probability that a random sample would result in a chi-square value of at least that magnitude is 0.00001. This probability is also known as the **observed significance level** of the test. If the probability is small enough (usually less than 0.05 or 0.01), the hypothesis that the two variables are independent is rejected.

Since the observed significance level in Figure 10.1 is very small (based on the combined city and town data), the hypothesis that address type and return rate are independent is rejected. When the chi-square test is calculated for the city and town data separately (Figure 10.2), different results are obtained. The observed significance level of the city data is 0.209, so the independence hypothesis is not rejected. For the towns, the observed significance level is less than 0.000005, and the hypothesis that address and return rate are independent is rejected. These results support the theory that city and town residents respond differently.

An alternative to the commonly used Pearson chi-square is the **likelihood-ratio chi-square** (see Figure 10.4). This test is based on maximum-likelihood theory and is often used in the analysis of categorical data. For large samples, the Pearson and likelihood-ratio chi-square statistics give very similar results. (The Mantel-Haenszel test is discussed under "Ordinal Measures" on p. 205.)

The chi-square test is a test of independence; it provides little information about the strength or form of the association between two variables. The magnitude of the observed chi-square depends not only on the goodness of fit of the independence model but also on the sample size. If the sample size for a particular table increases n-fold, so does the chi-square value. Thus, large chi-square values can arise in applications where residuals are small relative to expected frequencies but where the sample size is large.

Certain conditions must be met for the chi-square distribution to be a good approximation of the distribution of the statistic in the equation given above. The data must be random samples from multinomial distributions and the expected values must not be too small. While it has been recommended that all expected frequencies be at least 5, studies indicate that this is probably too stringent and can be relaxed (Everitt, 1977). SPSS displays the number of cells with expected frequencies less than 5 and the minimum expected cell value.

To improve the approximation for a 2×2 table, **Yates' correction for continuity** is sometimes applied. Yates' correction for continuity involves subtracting 0.5 from positive differences between observed and expected frequencies (the residuals) and adding 0.5 to negative differences before squaring. For a discussion of the controversy over the merits of this correction, see Conover (1974) and Mantel (1974).

Fisher's exact test, based on the hypergeometric distribution, is an alternative test for the 2×2 table. It calculates exact probabilities of obtaining the observed results if the two variables are independent and the marginals are fixed. It is most useful when the total sample size and the expected values are small. SPSS calculates Fisher's exact test if any expected cell value in a 2×2 table is less than 5.

Measures of Association

In many research situations, the strength and nature of the dependence of variables are of central concern. Indexes that attempt to quantify the relationship between variables in a cross-classification are called **measures of association**. No single measure adequately summarizes all possible types of association. Measures vary in their interpretation and in the way they define perfect and intermediate association. These measures also differ in the way they are affected by various factors such as marginals. For example, many measures are "margin sensitive" in that they are influenced by the marginal distributions of the rows and columns. Such measures reflect information about the marginals along with information about association.

A particular measure may have a low value for a given table, not because the two variables are not related but because they are not related in the way to which the measure is sensitive. No single measure is best for all situations. The type of data, the hypothesis of interest, and the properties of the various measures must all be considered when selecting an index of association for a given table. It is not, however, reasonable to compute a large number of measures and then to report the most impressive as if it were the only one examined.

The measures of association available with crosstabulation in SPSS are computed only from bivariate tables. For example, if three dichotomous variables are specified in the table, two sets of measures are computed, one for each subtable produced by the values of the controlling variable. In general, if relationships among more than two variables are to be studied, examination of bivariate tables is only a first step. For an extensive discussion of more sophisticated multivariate procedures for the analysis of qualitative data, see Fienberg (1977), Everitt (1977), and Haberman (1978).

Nominal Measures

Consider measures that assume only that both variables in the table are nominally measured. As such, these measures can provide only some indication of the strength of association between variables; they cannot indicate direction or anything about the nature of the relationship. The measures provided are of two types: those based on the chi-square statistic and those that follow the logic of proportional reduction in error, denoted PRE.

Chi-Square-based Measures

As explained above, the chi-square statistic itself is not a good measure of the degree of association between two variables. But its widespread use in tests of independence has encouraged the use of measures of association based upon it. Each of these measures based on the chi-square attempts to modify the chi-square statistic to minimize the influence of sample size and degrees of freedom as well as to restrict the range of values of the measure to those between 0 and 1. Without such adjustments, comparison of chi-square values from tables with varying dimensions and sample sizes is meaningless.

The **phi coefficient** modifies the Pearson chi-square by dividing it by the sample size and taking the square root of the result:

$$\phi = \sqrt{\frac{\chi^2}{N}}$$ Equation 10.5

For a 2×2 table only, the phi coefficient is equal to the Pearson correlation coefficient, so the sign of phi matches that of the correlation coefficient. For tables in which one dimension is greater than 2, phi may not lie between 0 and 1, since the chi-square value can be greater than the sample size. To obtain a measure that must lie between 0 and 1, Pearson suggested the use of

$$C = \sqrt{\frac{\chi^2}{\chi^2 + N}}$$ Equation 10.6

which is called the **coefficient of contingency**. Although the value of this measure is always between 0 and 1, it cannot generally attain the upper limit of 1. The maximum value possible depends upon the number of rows and columns. For example, in a 4×4 table, the maximum value of C is 0.87.

Cramér introduced the following variant

$$V = \sqrt{\frac{\chi^2}{N(k-1)}}$$ Equation 10.7

where k is the smaller of the number of rows and columns. This statistic, known as **Cramér's V**, can attain the maximum of 1 for tables of any dimension. If one of the table dimensions is 2, V and phi are identical.

Figure 10.5 shows the values of the chi-square-based measures for the letter data. The test of the null hypothesis that a measure is 0 is based on the Pearson chi-square probability.

Figure 10.5 Chi-square-based measures

```
RETURNED  FOUND AND MAILED  by  ADDRESS  ADDRESS ON LETTER
                   ADDRESS                   Page 1 of 1
            Count
                  CONTROL  DANDEE  COMMUNIS
                                      T         Row
                     1        2       3        Total
RETURNED
              1     35       32      10          77
   YES                                          35.6

              2     37       40      62         139
   NO                                           64.4

           Column   72       72      72         216
           Total   33.3     33.3    33.3       100.0


                                                          Approximate
     Statistic              Value      ASE1    Val/ASE0   Significance
  -------------------       -----      ----    --------   ------------
Phi                        .32320                          .00001 *1
Cramer's V                 .32320                          .00001 *1
Contingency Coefficient    .30753                          .00001 *1

*1 Pearson chi-square probability

Number of Missing Observations:  0
```

The chi-square-based measures are hard to interpret. Although when properly standardized they can be used to compare strength of association in several tables, the strength of association being compared is not easily related to an intuitive concept of association.

Proportional Reduction in Error

Common alternatives to chi-square-based measurements are those based on the idea of **proportional reduction in error (PRE)**, introduced by Goodman and Kruskal (1954). With PRE measures, the meaning of association is clearer. These measures are all essentially ratios of a measure of error in predicting the values of one variable based on knowledge of that variable alone and the same measure of error applied to predictions based on knowledge of an additional variable.

For example, Figure 10.6 is a crosstabulation of depth of hypnosis and success in treatment of migraine headaches by suggestion (Cedercreutz, 1978). The best guess of the results of treatment when no other information is available is the outcome category with the largest proportion of observations (the modal category).

Figure 10.6 Depth of hypnosis and success of treatment

```
HYPNOSIS  DEPTH OF HYPNOSIS  by  MIGRAINE  OUTCOME

                    MIGRAINE                       Page 1 of 1
            Count
            Col Pct  CURED    BETTER   NO
            Tot Pct                    CHANGE
                       1.00     2.00     3.00    Row
                                                 Total
HYPNOSIS
            1.00        13        5                18
   DEEP               56.5     15.6              18.0
                     13.0      5.0

            2.00        10       26       17       53
   MEDIUM             43.5     81.3     37.8     53.0
                     10.0     26.0     17.0

            3.00                  1       28       29
   LIGHT                         3.1     62.2     29.0
                                 1.0    28.0

            Column      23       32       45      100
            Total     23.0     32.0     45.0    100.0


                                                              Approximate
     Statistic                  Value     ASE1    Val/ASE0   Significance
     ---------                  -----     ----    --------   ------------

Lambda :
    symmetric                   .35294   .11335   2.75267
    with HYPNOSIS dependent     .29787   .14702   1.72276
    with MIGRAINE dependent     .40000   .10539   3.07580
Goodman & Kruskal Tau :
    with HYPNOSIS dependent     .29435   .06304                .00000 *2
    with MIGRAINE dependent     .34508   .04863                .00000 *2

*2 Based on chi-square approximation

Number of Missing Observations:  0
```

In Figure 10.6, *no change* is the largest outcome category, with 45% of the subjects. The estimate of the probability of incorrect classification is 1 minus the probability of the modal category:

$$P(1) = 1 - 0.45 = 0.55 \qquad \textbf{Equation 10.8}$$

Information about the depth of hypnosis can be used to improve the classification rule. For each hypnosis category, the outcome category that occurs most frequently for that hypnosis level is predicted. Thus, *no change* is predicted for participants achieving a light level of hypnosis, *better* for those achieving a medium level, and *cured* for those achieving a deep level. The probability of error when depth of hypnosis is used to predict outcome is the sum of the probabilities of all the cells that are not row modes:

$$P(2) = 0.05 + 0.10 + 0.17 + 0.01 = 0.33 \qquad \textbf{Equation 10.9}$$

Goodman and Kruskal's **lambda**, with outcome as the predicted (dependent) variable, is calculated as:

$$\lambda_{outcome} = \frac{P(1) - P(2)}{P(1)} = \frac{0.55 - 0.33}{0.55} = 0.40 \qquad \text{Equation 10.10}$$

Thus, a 40% reduction in error is obtained when depth of hypnosis is used to predict outcome.

Lambda always ranges between 0 and 1. A value of 0 means the independent variable is of no help in predicting the dependent variable. A value of 1 means that the independent variable perfectly specifies the categories of the dependent variable (perfection can occur only when each row has at most one non-zero cell). When the two variables are independent, lambda is 0; but a lambda of 0 need not imply statistical independence. As with all measures of association, lambda is constructed to measure association in a very specific way. In particular, lambda reflects the reduction in error when values of one variable are used to predict values of the other. If this particular type of association is absent, lambda is 0. Other measures of association may find association of a different kind even when lambda is 0. A measure of association sensitive to every imaginable type of association does not exist.

For a particular table, two different lambdas can be computed, one using the row variable as the predictor and the other using the column variable. The two do not usually have identical values, so care should be taken to specify which is the dependent variable; that is, the variable whose prediction is of primary interest. In some applications, dependent and independent variables are not clearly distinguished. In those instances, a symmetric version of lambda, which predicts the row variable and column variable with equal frequency, can be computed. When the lambda statistic is requested, SPSS displays the symmetric lambda as well as the two asymmetric lambdas.

Goodman and Kruskal's Tau

When lambda is computed, the same prediction is made for all cases in a particular row or column. Another approach is to consider what happens if the prediction is randomly made in the same proportion as the marginal totals. For example, if you're trying to predict migraine outcome without any information about the depth of the hypnosis, you can use the marginal distributions in Figure 10.6 instead of the modal category to guess *cured* for 23% of the cases, *better* for 32% of the cases, and *no change* for 45% of the cases.

Using these marginals, you would expect to correctly classify 23% of the 23 cases in the *cured* category, 32% of the 32 cases in the *better* category, and 45% of the 45 cases in the *no change* category. This results in the correct classification of 35.78 out of 100 cases. When additional information about the depth of hypnosis is incorporated into the prediction rule, the prediction is based on the probability of the different outcomes for each depth of hypnosis. For example, for those who experienced deep hypnosis, you would predict *cure* 72% of the time (13/18) and *better* 28% of the time (5/18). Similarly, for those with light hypnosis, you would predict *better* 3% of the time and *no change* 97% of the time. This results in correct classification for about 58 of the cases.

Goodman and Kruskal's tau is computed by comparing the probability of error in the two situations. In this example, when predicting only from the column marginal totals, the probability of error is 0.64. When predicting from row information the probability of error is 0.42. Thus,

tau (migraine | hypnosis) = (0.64 − 0.42) / 0.64 = 0.34   **Equation 10.11**

By incorporating information about the depth of hypnosis, we have reduced our error of prediction by about 34%.

A test of the null hypothesis that tau is 0 can be based on the value of $(N-1)(c-1)$ tau (col | row), which has a chi-square distribution with $(c-1) \times (r-1)$ degrees of freedom. In this example, the observed significance level for tau is very small, and you can reject the null hypothesis that tau is 0. The asymptotic standard error for the statistic is shown in the column labeled *ASE1* (see Figure 10.6). The asymptotic standard error can be used to construct confidence intervals.

Measuring Agreement

Measures of agreement allow you to compare the ratings of two observers for the same group of objects. For example, consider the data reported in Bishop et al. (1975), shown in Figure 10.7.

Figure 10.7 Student teachers rated by supervisors

```
SUPRVSR1   Supervisor 1   by   SUPRVSR2   Supervisor 2

                       SUPRVSR2                         Page 1 of 1
             Count
             Tot Pct  Authorit Democrat Permissi
                      arian    ic       ve         Row
                          1.00     2.00     3.00   Total
SUPRVSR1
                1.00       17        4        8      29
         Authoritarian   23.6      5.6     11.1    40.3

                2.00        5       12                17
         Democratic       6.9     16.7              23.6

                3.00       10        3       13      26
         Permissive     13.9      4.2     18.1    36.1

             Column       32       19       21      72
             Total      44.4     26.4     29.2   100.0


                                                          Approximate
        Statistic              Value       ASE1  Val/ASE0  Significance
        ------------------    --------   -------- --------  ------------

        Kappa                  .36227    .09075   4.32902


Number of Missing Observations:  0
```

Two supervisors rated the classroom style of 72 teachers. You are interested in measuring the agreement between the two raters. The simplest measure that comes to mind is just the proportion of cases for which the raters agree. In this case, it is 58.3%. The disadvantage of this measure is that no correction is made for the amount of agreement expected by chance. That is, you would expect the supervisors to agree sometimes even if they were assigning ratings by tossing dice.

To correct for chance agreement, you can compute the proportion of cases that you would expect to be in agreement if the ratings are independent. For example, supervisor 1 rated 40.3% of the teachers as authoritarian, while supervisor 2 rated 44.4% of the teachers as authoritarian. If their rankings are independent, you would expect that 17.9% (40.3% × 44.4%) of the teachers would be rated as authoritarian by both. Similarly, 6.2% (23.6% × 26.4%) would be rated as democratic and 10.5% (36.1% × 29.2%) as permissive. Thus, 34.6% of all the teachers would be classified the same merely by chance.

The difference between the observed proportion of cases in which the raters agree and that expected by chance is 0.237 (0.583 − 0.346). **Cohen's kappa** (Cohen, 1960) normalizes this difference by dividing it by the maximum difference possible for the marginal totals. In this example, the largest possible "non-chance" agreement is 1 − 0.346 (the chance level). Therefore,

$$\text{kappa} = 0.237 / (1 - 0.346) = 0.362 \qquad \text{Equation 10.12}$$

The test of the null hypothesis that kappa is 0 can be based on the ratio of the measure to its standard error, assuming that the null hypothesis is true. (See Benedetti and Brown, 1978, for further discussion of standard errors for measures of association.) This asymptotic error is not the one shown on the output. The asymptotic standard error on the output, *ASE1*, does not assume that the true value is 0.

Since the kappa statistic measures agreement between two raters, the two variables that contain the ratings must have the same range of values. If this is not true, SPSS will not compute kappa.

Ordinal Measures

Although relationships among ordinal variables can be examined using nominal measures, other measures reflect the additional information available from ranking. Consideration of the kind of relationships that may exist between two ordered variables leads to the notion of direction of relationship and to the concept of **correlation**. Variables are positively correlated if cases with low values for one variable also tend to have low values for the other, and cases with high values on one also tend to be high on the other. Negatively correlated variables show the opposite relationship: the higher the first variable, the lower the second tends to be.

The **Spearman correlation coefficient** is a commonly used measure of correlation between two ordinal variables. For all of the cases, the values of each of the variables are ranked from smallest to largest, and the Pearson correlation coefficient is computed on the ranks. The **Mantel-Haenszel chi-square** is another measure of linear association between the row and column variables in a crosstabulation. It is computed by multiplying the square of the Pearson correlation coefficient by the number of cases minus 1. The resulting statistic has one degree of freedom (Mantel & Haenszel, 1959). (Although the Mantel-Haenszel statistic is displayed whenever chi-square is requested, it should not be used for nominal data.)

Ordinal Measures Based on Pairs

For a table of two ordered variables, several measures of association based on a comparison of the values of both variables for all possible *pairs* of cases or observations are available. Cases are first compared to determine if they are concordant, discordant, or tied. A pair of cases is **concordant** if the values of both variables for one case are higher (or both are lower) than the corresponding values for the other case. The pair is **discordant** if the value of one variable for a case is larger than the corresponding value for the other case, and the direction is reversed for the second variable. When the two cases have identical values on one or on both variables, they are **tied**.

Thus, for any given pair of cases with measurements on variables X and Y, the pair may be concordant, discordant, or tied in one of three ways: they may be tied on X but not on Y, they may be tied on Y but not on X, or they may be tied on both variables. When data are arranged in crosstabulated form, the number of concordant, discordant, and tied pairs can be easily calculated, since all possible pairs can be conveniently determined.

If the preponderance of pairs is concordant, the association is said to be positive: as ranks of variable X increase (or decrease), so do ranks of variable Y. If the majority of pairs is discordant, the association is negative: as ranks of one variable increase, those of the other tend to decrease. If concordant and discordant pairs are equally likely, no association is said to exist.

The ordinal measures presented here all have the same numerator: the number of concordant pairs (P) minus the number of discordant pairs (Q) calculated for all distinct pairs of observations. They differ primarily in the way in which $P - Q$ is normalized. The simplest measure involves subtracting Q from P and dividing by the total number of pairs. If there are no pairs with ties, this measure (**Kendall's tau-*a***) is in the range from −1 to +1. If there are ties, the range of possible values is narrower; the actual range depends on the number of ties. Since all observations within the same row are tied, so also are those in the same column, and the resulting tau-*a* measures are difficult to interpret.

A measure that attempts to normalize $P - Q$ by considering ties on each variable in a pair separately but not ties on both variables in a pair is **tau-*b***

$$\tau_b = \frac{P - Q}{\sqrt{(P + Q + T_X)(P + Q + T_Y)}} \qquad \text{Equation 10.13}$$

where T_X is the number of pairs tied on X but not on Y, and T_Y is the number of pairs tied on Y but not on X. If no marginal frequency is 0, tau-b can attain +1 or −1 only for a square table.

A measure that can attain, or nearly attain, +1 or −1 for any $r \times c$ table is **tau-c**

$$\tau_c = \frac{2m(P-Q)}{N^2(m-1)} \qquad \text{Equation 10.14}$$

where m is the smaller of the number of rows and columns. The coefficients tau-b and tau-c do not differ much in value if each margin contains approximately equal frequencies.

Goodman and Kruskal's gamma is closely related to the tau statistics and is calculated as:

$$G = \frac{P-Q}{P+Q} \qquad \text{Equation 10.15}$$

Gamma can be thought of as the probability that a random pair of observations is concordant minus the probability that the pair is discordant, assuming the absence of ties. The absolute value of gamma is the proportional reduction in error between guessing the concordant and discordant ranking of each pair, depending on which occurs more often, and guessing the ranking according to the outcome of a fair toss of a coin. Gamma is 1 if all observations are concentrated in the upper left to lower right diagonal of the table. In the case of independence, gamma is 0. However, the converse (that a gamma of 0 necessarily implies independence) need not be true except in the 2×2 table.

In the computation of gamma, no distinction is made between the independent and dependent variable; the variables are treated symmetrically. Somers (1962) proposed an asymmetric extension of gamma that differs only in the inclusion of the number of pairs not tied on the independent variable (X) in the denominator. **Somers' d** is:

$$d_Y = \frac{P-Q}{P+Q+T_Y} \qquad \text{Equation 10.16}$$

The coefficient d_Y indicates the proportionate excess of concordant pairs over discordant pairs among pairs not tied on the independent variable. The symmetric variant of Somers' d uses for the denominator the average value of the denominators of the two asymmetric coefficients.

These ordinal measures for the migraine data are shown in Figure 10.8. All of the measures indicate that there is a fairly strong positive association between the two variables.

Figure 10.8 Ordinal measures

```
HYPNOSIS  DEPTH OF HYPNOSIS  by  MIGRAINE  OUTCOME
Number of valid observations = 100


                                                              Approximate
       Statistic              Value      ASE1      Val/ASE0   Significance
---------------------                                         ------------


Kendall's Tau-b               .67901    .04445    11.96486
Kendall's Tau-c               .63360    .05296    11.96486
Gamma                         .94034    .02720    11.96486
Somers' D :
   symmetric                  .67866    .04443    11.96486
   with HYPNOSIS dependent    .65774    .05440    11.96486
   with MIGRAINE dependent    .70096    .03996    11.96486

Pearson's R                   .71739    .04484    10.19392    .00000 *4
Spearman Correlation          .72442    .04317    10.40311    .00000 *4

*4 VAL/ASE0 is a t-value based on a normal approximation, as is the significance
Number of Missing Observations:  0
```

Measures Involving Interval Data

If the two variables in the table are measured on an interval scale, various coefficients that make use of this additional information can be calculated. A useful symmetric coefficient that measures the strength of the *linear* relationship is the **Pearson correlation coefficient (r)**. It can take on values from −1 to +1, indicating negative or positive linear correlation.

The **eta coefficient** is appropriate for data in which the dependent variable is measured on an interval scale and the independent variable on a nominal or ordinal scale. When squared, eta can be interpreted as the proportion of the total variability in the dependent variable that can be accounted for by knowing the values of the independent variable. The measure is asymmetric and does not assume a linear relationship between the variables.

Estimating Risk in Cohort Studies

Often you want to identify variables that are related to the occurrence of a particular event. For example, you may want to determine if smoking is related to heart disease. A commonly used index that measures the strength of the association between presence of a factor and occurrence of an event is the **relative risk ratio**. It is estimated as the ratio of two incidence rates; for example, the incidence rate of heart disease in those who smoke and the incidence rate of heart disease in those who do not smoke.

For example, suppose you observe for five years 1000 smokers without a history of heart disease and 1000 nonsmokers without a history of heart disease, and you determine how many of each group develop heart disease during this time period. (Studies in which a group of disease-free people are studied to see who develops the disease are called **cohort** or **prospective studies**.) Figure 10.9 contains hypothetical results from such a cohort study.

Figure 10.9 Hypothetical cohorts

```
SMOKING   Smoking  by  HDISEASE   Heart Disease

                   HDISEASE          Page 1 of 1
            Count
                   Yes       No
                                         Row
                     1.00     2.00     Total
SMOKING
              1.00    100      900      1000
Yes                                     50.0

              2.00     50      950      1000
No                                      50.0

            Column    150     1850      2000
            Total     7.5     92.5     100.0


         Statistic                    Value          95% Confidence Bounds
---------------------                --------       -----------------------
Relative Risk Estimate (SMOKING 1.0 / SMOKING 2.0) :
   case control                      2.11111         1.48544        3.00032
   cohort (HDISEASE 1.0 Risk)        2.00000         1.44078        2.77628
   cohort (HDISEASE 2.0 Risk)         .94737          .92390         .97143

Number of Missing Observations:  0
```

The five-year incidence rate for smokers is 100/1000, while the incidence rate for nonsmokers is 50/1000. The relative risk ratio is 2 (100/1000 divided by 50/1000). This indicates that, in the sample, smokers are twice as likely to develop heart disease as nonsmokers.

The estimated relative risk and its 95% confidence interval are in the row labeled *cohort (HDISEASE 1.0 Risk)* in Figure 10.9. In SPSS, the ratio is always computed by taking the incidence in the first row and dividing it by the incidence in the second row. Since either column can represent the event, separate estimates are displayed for each column. The 95% confidence interval does not include the value of 1, so you can reject the null hypothesis that the two incidence rates are the same.

Estimating Risk in Case-Control Studies

In the cohort study described above, we took a group of disease-free people (the cohort) and watched what happened to them. Another type of study that is commonly used is called a **retrospective** or **case-control study**. In this type of study, we take a group of people with the disease of interest (the cases) and a comparable group of people without the disease (the controls) and see how they differ. For example, we could take 100 people with documented coronary heart disease and 100 controls without heart disease and establish how many in each group smoked. The hypothetical results are shown in Figure 10.10.

Figure 10.10 Hypothetical smoking control

```
GROUP   by  SMOKING

                       SMOKING        Page 1 of 1
              Count
              Row Pct |Yes       No
                      |                       Row
                      |    1.00|    2.00|   Total
GROUP         ────────
              1.00    |    30  |    70  |    100
      Cases           |   30.0 |   70.0 |   50.0

              2.00    |    10  |    90  |    100
      Control         |   10.0 |   90.0 |   50.0

              Column        40      160      200
              Total       20.0     80.0    100.0


       Statistic                     Value         95% Confidence Bounds
────────────────────────            ────────      ─────────────────────
Relative Risk Estimate (GROUP 1.0 / GROUP 2.0) :
   case control                     3.85714       1.76660       8.42156
   cohort (SMOKING 1.0 Risk)        3.00000       1.55083       5.80335
   cohort (SMOKING 2.0 Risk)         .77778        .67348        .89823

Number of Missing Observations:   0
```

From a case-control study, we cannot estimate incidence rates. Thus, we cannot compute the relative risk ratio. Instead, we estimate relative risk using what is called an **odds ratio**. We compute the odds that a case smokes and divide it by the odds that a control smokes.

For example, from Figure 10.10, the odds that a case smokes are 30/70. The odds that a control smokes are 10/90. The odds ratio is then 30/70 divided by 10/90, or 3.85. The odds ratio and its confidence interval are in the row labeled *case control* in Figure 10.10. SPSS expects the cases to be in the first row and the controls in the second. Similarly, the event of interest must be in the first column. For further discussion of measures of risk, see Kleinbaum et al. (1982).

How to Obtain Crosstabulations

The Crosstabs procedure produces two-way to n-way crosstabulations and related statistics for numeric and short string variables. In addition to cell counts, you can obtain cell percentages, expected values, and residuals.

The minimum specifications are:
- One numeric or short string row variable.
- One numeric or short string column variable.

To obtain crosstabulations and related statistics as well as measures of association, from the menus choose:

Statistics
 Summarize ▶
  Crosstabs...

This opens the Crosstabs dialog box, as shown in Figure 10.11.

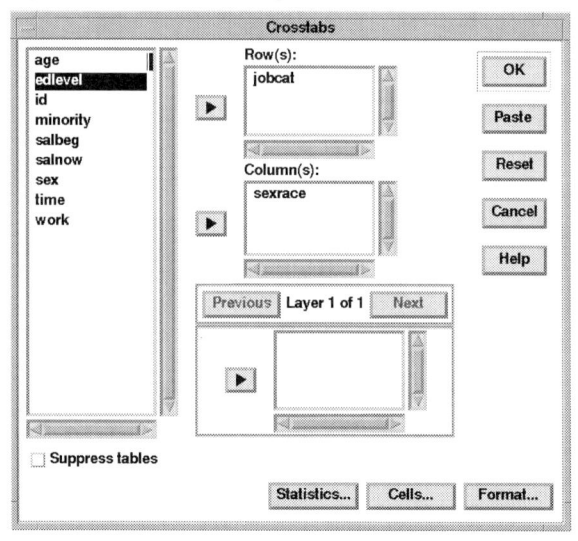

Figure 10.11 Crosstabs dialog box

The numeric and short string variables in your data file are displayed in the source variable list. Select the variables you want to use as the row and column variables. A crosstabulation is produced for each combination of row and column variables. For example, if there are four variables in the Row(s) list and three variables in the Column(s) list, you will get 12 crosstabulations. To get a crosstabulation in default format (cell counts only and no measures of association), click on OK.

Optionally, you can select one or more layers of control variables. A separate crosstabulation is produced for each category of each control variable. For example, if you have one row variable, one column variable, and one control variable with two categories, you will get two crosstabulations, as in Figure 10.2.

You can add additional layers of control variables by clicking on Next. Each layer divides the crosstabulation into smaller subgroups. For example, if *jobcat* is the row variable, *sexrace* is the column variable, *edlevel* is the layer 1 control variable, and *age* is the layer 2 control variable, you will get separate crosstabulations of *jobcat* and *sexrace* for each category of *age* within each category of *edlevel*. If *age* and *edlevel* each have six categories, you will get 36 crosstabulations (probably not what you want).

You can add up to eight layers of control variables. Use Next and Previous to move between the control variables for the different layers.

The following option is also available:

❑ **Suppress tables.** If you are interested in crosstabulation statistical measures but don't want to display the actual tables, you can choose Suppress tables. However, if you haven't selected any statistics from the Crosstabs Statistics dialog box, no output will be generated.

Crosstabs Statistics

To obtain statistics and measures of association, click on Statistics... in the Crosstabs dialog box. This opens the Crosstabs Statistics dialog box, as shown in Figure 10.12.

Figure 10.12 Crosstabs Statistics dialog box

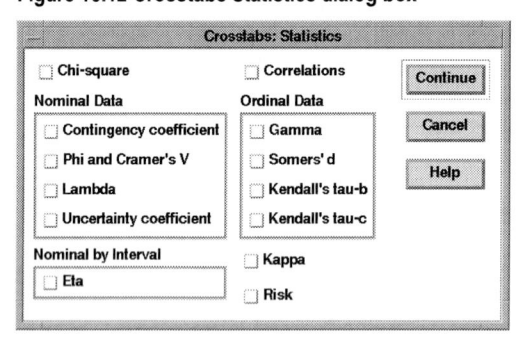

You can choose one or more of the following statistics:

❑ **Chi-square.** Pearson chi-square, likelihood-ratio chi-square, and Mantel-Haenszel linear association chi-square. For 2×2 tables, Fisher's exact test is computed when a table that does not result from missing rows or columns in a larger table has a cell with an expected frequency of less than 5. Yates' corrected chi-square is computed for all other 2×2 tables.

- **Correlations.** Pearson's *r* and Spearman's correlation coefficient. These are available for numeric data only.
- **Kappa.** Cohen's kappa. The kappa coefficient can only be computed for square tables in which the row and column values are identical (Kraemer, 1982).
- **Risk.** Relative risk ratio. This can only be calculated for 2×2 tables (Kleinbaum et al., 1982).

Nominal Data. Nominal measures assume that variables have values with no intrinsic order (such as *Catholic, Protestant,* and *Jewish*). You can choose one or more of the following:

- **Contingency coefficient.**
- **Phi and Cramér's V.**
- **Lambda.** Symmetric and asymmetric lambda, and Goodman and Kruskal's tau.
- **Uncertainty coefficient.** Symmetric and asymmetric uncertainty coefficient.

Nominal by Interval. It is assumed that one variable is measured on a nominal scale, and the other is measured on an interval scale.

- **Eta.** Eta is not available for short string variables. The nominal variable must be coded numerically. Two eta values are computed: one treats the column variable as the nominal variable; the other treats the row variable as the nominal variable.

Ordinal Data. Ordinal measures assume that variables have values with some intrinsic order (such as *None, Some,* and *A lot*). You can choose one or more of the following:

- **Gamma.** Zero-order gammas are displayed for 2-way tables, and conditional gammas are displayed for 3-way to 10-way tables.
- **Somers' d.** Symmetric and asymmetric Somers' *d*.
- **Kendall's tau-b.**
- **Kendall's tau-c.**

Crosstabs Cell Display

The default crosstabulation displays only the number of cases in each cell. You can also display row, column, and total percentages, expected values, and residuals. To change the cell display, click on Cells... in the Crosstabs dialog box. This opens the Crosstabs Cell Display dialog box, as shown in Figure 10.13.

Figure 10.13 Crosstabs Cell Display dialog box

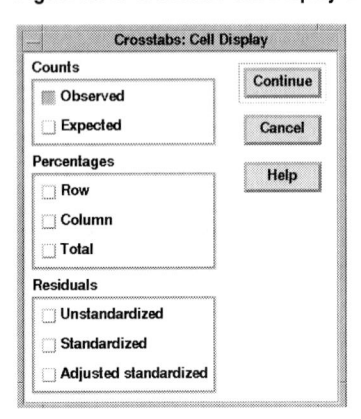

You can choose any combination of cell displays. For example, Figure 10.1 was produced by selecting row, column, and total percentages, in addition to the default observed count. At least one item must be selected.

Counts. You can choose one or more of the following:

- **Observed.** Observed frequencies. This is the default. To suppress observed frequencies, deselect this item.
- **Expected.** Expected frequencies. The number of cases expected in each cell if the two variables in the subtable are statistically independent.

Percentages. You can choose one or more of the following:

- **Row.** The number of cases in each cell expressed as a percentage of all cases in that row.
- **Column.** The number of cases in each cell expressed as a percentage of all cases in that column.
- **Total.** The number of cases in each cell expressed as a percentage of all cases in the subtable.

Residuals. You can choose one or more of the following:

- **Unstandardized.** The value of the observed cell count minus the expected value.
- **Standardized.** Standardized residuals (Haberman, 1978).
- **Adjusted standardized.** Adjusted standardized residuals (Haberman, 1978).

Crosstabs Table Format

You can modify the table format by clicking on Format... in the Crosstabs dialog box. This opens the Crosstabs Table Format dialog box, as shown in Figure 10.14.

Figure 10.14 Crosstabs Table Format dialog box

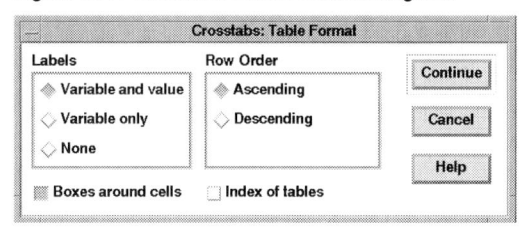

Labels. You can choose one of the following alternatives:

- ◇ **Variable and value.** Displays both variable and value labels for each table. This is the default. Only the first 16 characters of the value labels are used. Value labels for the columns are displayed on two lines with eight characters per line.
- ◇ **Variable only.** Displays variable labels but suppresses value labels.
- ◇ **None.** Suppresses both variable and value labels.

Row Order. You can choose one of the following alternatives:

- ◇ **Ascending.** Displays row variable values in ascending order from lowest to highest. This is the default.
- ◇ **Descending.** Displays row variable values in descending order from highest to lowest.

The following format choices are also available:

- ❏ **Boxes around cells.** This is the default. To produce tables without boxes, deselect this item.
- ❏ **Index of tables.** The index lists all crosstabulations produced and the page number on which each table begins.

Additional Features Available with Command Syntax

You can customize your crosstabulation if you paste your selections to a syntax window and edit the resulting CROSSTABS command syntax (see Chapter 4). An additional feature is the option of using integer mode (with the VARIABLES subcommand). Integer mode, although not significantly faster, conserves memory when variables are coded as adjacent integers and allows you to display cells containing missing data. See Appendix A for command syntax rules. See the *SPSS Base System Syntax Reference Guide* for complete CROSSTABS command syntax.

11 Describing Subpopulation Differences

The 1964 Civil Rights Act prohibits discrimination in the workplace based on sex or race; employers who violate the act are liable to prosecution. Since passage of this legislation, women, blacks, and other groups have filed numerous lawsuits charging unfair hiring or advancement practices.

The courts have ruled that statistics can be used as *prima facie* evidence of discrimination, and many lawsuits depend heavily on complex statistical analyses to demonstrate that similarly qualified individuals are not treated equally. Identifying and measuring all variables that legitimately influence promotion and hiring is difficult, if not impossible, especially for nonroutine jobs. Years of schooling and prior work experience can be quantified, but what about the more intangible attributes such as enthusiasm and creativity? How are they to be objectively measured so as not to become convenient smoke screens for concealing discrimination?

Searching for Discrimination

In this chapter, we analyze employee records for 474 individuals hired between 1969 and 1971 by a bank engaged in Equal Employment Opportunity litigation. Two types of unfair employment practices are of particular interest: shunting (placing some employees in lower job categories than other employees with similar qualifications) and salary and promotion inequities.

Although extensive and intricate statistical analyses are usually involved in studies of this kind (for example, see Roberts, 1980), the discussion here is necessarily limited. The SPSS Means procedure is used to calculate average salaries for groups of employees based on race and sex. Additional grouping variables are introduced to help "explain" some of the observed variability in salary.

Who Does What?

Figure 11.1 is a crosstabulation of job category at the time of hiring by sex and race characteristics. The first three job classifications contain 64% of white males (adding column percentages), 94% of both minority males and white females, and 100% of minority females. Among white males, 17% are in the college trainee program, compared with 4% of white females.

Figure 11.1 Crosstabulation of job category by sex–race

```
JOBCAT   EMPLOYMENT CATEGORY   by   SEXRACE   SEX & RACE CLASSIFICATION
```

		SEXRACE				
	Count Col Pct Tot Pct	WHITE MA LES 1	MINORITY MALES 2	WHITE FE MALES 3	MINORITY FEMALES 4	Row Total
JOBCAT						
CLERICAL	1	75 38.7 15.8	35 54.7 7.4	85 48.3 17.9	32 80.0 6.8	227 47.9
OFFICE TRAINEE	2	35 18.0 7.4	12 18.8 2.5	81 46.0 17.1	8 20.0 1.7	136 28.7
SECURITY OFFICER	3	14 7.2 3.0	13 20.3 2.7			27 5.7
COLLEGE TRAINEE	4	33 17.0 7.0	1 1.6 .2	7 4.0 1.5		41 8.6
EXEMPT EMPLOYEE	5	28 14.4 5.9	2 3.1 .4	2 1.1 .4		32 6.8
MBA TRAINEE	6	3 1.5 .6	1 1.6 .2	1 .6 .2		5 1.1
TECHNICAL	7	6 3.1 1.3				6 1.3
Column Total		194 40.9	64 13.5	176 37.1	40 8.4	474 100.0

```
Number of Missing Observations:  0
```

Although these observations are interesting, they do not imply discriminatory placement into beginning job categories because the qualifications of the various groups are not necessarily similar. If women and nonwhites are more qualified than white males in the same beginning job categories, discrimination may be suspected.

Level of Education

One easily measured employment qualification is years of education. Figure 11.2 shows the average years of education for the entire sample (labeled *For Entire Population*), for each of the two sexes (labeled *Sex, Males* or *Females*), and for each of the two race categories within each sex category (labeled *Minority, White* or *Nonwhite*).

Figure 11.2 Education by sex and race

```
- - Description of Subpopulations - -

Summaries of    EDLEVEL      EDUCATIONAL LEVEL
By levels of    SEX          SEX OF EMPLOYEE
                MINORITY     MINORITY CLASSIFICATION

Variable          Value  Label                 Mean    Std Dev   Cases

For Entire Population                        13.4916   2.8848     474

SEX                 0    MALES               14.4302   2.9793     258
  MINORITY          0    WHITE               14.9227   2.8484     194
  MINORITY          1    NONWHITE            12.9375   2.8888      64

SEX                 1    FEMALES             12.3704   2.3192     216
  MINORITY          0    WHITE               12.3409   2.4066     176
  MINORITY          1    NONWHITE            12.5000   1.9081      40

Total Cases = 474
```

The entire sample has an average of 13.49 years of education. Males have more years of education than females—an average of 14.43 years compared with 12.37. White males have the highest level of education, almost 15 years, which is 2 years more than nonwhite males and approximately 2.5 years more than either group of females.

In Figure 11.3, the cases are further subdivided by their combined sex–race characteristics and by their initial job category. For each cell in the table, the average years of education, the standard deviation, and number of cases are displayed. White males have the highest average years of education in all job categories except MBA trainees, where the single minority male MBA trainee has 19 years of education. From this table, it does not appear that females and minorities are overeducated when compared to white males in similar job categories. However, it is important to note that group means provide information about a particular class of employees. While discrimination may not exist for a class as a whole, some individuals within that class may be victims (or beneficiaries) of discrimination.

Figure 11.3 Education by sex–race and job category

```
- - Description of Subpopulations - -

Summaries of     EDLEVEL    EDUCATIONAL LEVEL
By levels of     JOBCAT     EMPLOYMENT CATEGORY
                 SEXRACE    SEX & RACE CLASSIFICATION

Variable        Value  Label                   Mean     Std Dev    Cases

For Entire Population                        13.4916    2.8848      474

JOBCAT            1    CLERICAL              12.7753    2.5621      227
  SEXRACE         1    WHITE MALES           13.8667    2.3035       75
  SEXRACE         2    MINORITY MALES        13.7714    2.3147       35
  SEXRACE         3    WHITE FEMALES         11.4588    2.4327       85
  SEXRACE         4    MINORITY FEMALES      12.6250    2.1213       32

JOBCAT            2    OFFICE TRAINEE        13.0221    1.8875      136
  SEXRACE         1    WHITE MALES           13.8857    1.4095       35
  SEXRACE         2    MINORITY MALES        12.5833    2.6097       12
  SEXRACE         3    WHITE FEMALES         12.8148    1.9307       81
  SEXRACE         4    MINORITY FEMALES      12.0000     .0000        8

JOBCAT            3    SECURITY OFFICER      10.1852    2.2194       27
  SEXRACE         1    WHITE MALES           10.2857    2.0542       14
  SEXRACE         2    MINORITY MALES        10.0769    2.4651       13

JOBCAT            4    COLLEGE TRAINEE       17.0000    1.2845       41
  SEXRACE         1    WHITE MALES           17.2121    1.3407       33
  SEXRACE         2    MINORITY MALES        17.0000       .          1
  SEXRACE         3    WHITE FEMALES         16.0000     .0000        7

JOBCAT            5    EXEMPT EMPLOYEE       17.2813    1.9713       32
  SEXRACE         1    WHITE MALES           17.6071    1.7709       28
  SEXRACE         2    MINORITY MALES        14.0000    2.8284        2
  SEXRACE         3    WHITE FEMALES         16.0000     .0000        2

JOBCAT            6    MBA TRAINEE           18.0000    1.4142        5
  SEXRACE         1    WHITE MALES           18.3333    1.1547        3
  SEXRACE         2    MINORITY MALES        19.0000       .          1
  SEXRACE         3    WHITE FEMALES         16.0000       .          1

JOBCAT            7    TECHNICAL             18.1667    1.4720        6
  SEXRACE         1    WHITE MALES           18.1667    1.4720        6

Total Cases = 474
```

Beginning Salaries

The average beginning salary for the 474 persons hired between 1969 and 1971 is $6,806. The distribution by the four sex–race categories is shown in Figure 11.4.

Figure 11.4 Beginning salary by sex–race

```
- - Description of Subpopulations - -

Summaries of     SALBEG     BEGINNING SALARY
By levels of     SEXRACE    SEX & RACE CLASSIFICATION

Variable        Value  Label                   Mean     Std Dev    Cases

For Entire Population                        6806.4346  3148.2553    474

SEXRACE           1    WHITE   MALES         8637.5258  3871.1017    194
SEXRACE           2    MINORITY MALES        6553.5000  2228.1436     64
SEXRACE           3    WHITE   FEMALES       5340.4886  1225.9605    176
SEXRACE           4    MINORITY FEMALES      4780.5000   771.4188     40

Total Cases = 474
```

White males have the highest beginning salaries—an average of $8,638—followed by minority males. Since males are in higher job categories than females, this difference is not surprising.

Figure 11.5 shows beginning salaries subdivided by race, sex, and job category. For most of the job categories, white males have higher beginning salaries than the other groups. There is a $1,400 salary difference between white males and white females in the clerical jobs and a $1,000 difference in the general office trainee classification. In the college trainee program, white males averaged over $3,000 more than white females. However, Figure 11.3 shows that white females in the college trainee program had only an undergraduate degree, while white males had an average of 17.2 years of schooling.

Figure 11.5 Beginning salary by sex–race and job category

```
                    - - Description of Subpopulations - -

Summaries of         SALBEG      BEGINNING SALARY
By levels of         JOBCAT      EMPLOYMENT CATEGORY
                     SEXRACE     SEX & RACE CLASSIFICATION


Variable          Value  Label                    Mean

For Entire Population                          6806.4346

JOBCAT              1    CLERICAL               5733.9471
    SEXRACE         1    WHITE MALES            6553.4400
    SEXRACE         2    MINORITY MALES         6230.7429
    SEXRACE         3    WHITE FEMALES          5147.3176
    SEXRACE         4    MINORITY FEMALES       4828.1250

JOBCAT              2    OFFICE TRAINEE         5478.9706
    SEXRACE         1    WHITE MALES            6262.2857
    SEXRACE         2    MINORITY MALES         5610.0000
    SEXRACE         3    WHITE FEMALES          5208.8889
    SEXRACE         4    MINORITY FEMALES       4590.0000

JOBCAT              3    SECURITY OFFICER       6031.1111
    SEXRACE         1    WHITE MALES            6102.8571
    SEXRACE         2    MINORITY MALES         5953.8462

JOBCAT              4    COLLEGE TRAINEE        9956.4878
    SEXRACE         1    WHITE MALES           10467.6364
    SEXRACE         2    MINORITY MALES        11496.0000
    SEXRACE         3    WHITE FEMALES          7326.8571

JOBCAT              5    EXEMPT EMPLOYEE       13258.8750
    SEXRACE         1    WHITE MALES           13255.2857
    SEXRACE         2    MINORITY MALES        15570.0000
    SEXRACE         3    WHITE FEMALES         10998.0000

JOBCAT              6    MBA TRAINEE           12837.6000
    SEXRACE         1    WHITE MALES           14332.0000
    SEXRACE         2    MINORITY MALES        13992.0000
    SEXRACE         3    WHITE FEMALES          7200.0000

JOBCAT              7    TECHNICAL             19996.0000
    SEXRACE         1    WHITE MALES           19996.0000

Total Cases = 474
```

Introducing More Variables

The differences in mean beginning salaries between males and females are somewhat suspect. It is, however, unwise to conclude that salary discrimination exists, since several important variables, such as years of prior experience, have not been considered. It is necessary to control (or adjust statistically) for other relevant variables. Cross-classifying cases by the variables of interest and comparing salaries across the subgroups is one way of achieving control. However, as the number of variables increases, the number of cases in each cell rapidly diminishes, making statistically meaningful comparisons difficult. To circumvent these problems, you can use regression methods, which achieve control by specifying certain statistical relations that may describe what is happening. Regression methods are described in Chapter 18.

How to Obtain Subgroup Means

The Means procedure calculates subgroup means and related univariate statistics for dependent variables within categories of one or more independent variables. Optionally, you can also obtain one-way analysis of variance, eta, and a test of linearity.

The minimum specifications are:

- One numeric dependent variable.
- One numeric or short string independent variable.

To obtain subgroup means and related univariate statistics, from the menus choose:

Statistics
  Compare Means ▶
    Means...

This opens the Means dialog box, as shown in Figure 11.6.

Figure 11.6 Means dialog box

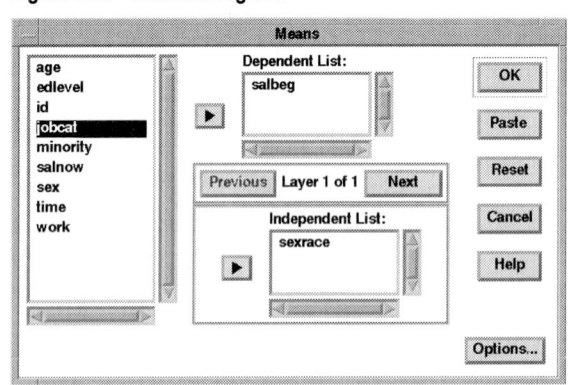

The numeric and short string variables in your data file appear in the source variable list. Select one or more numeric variables for the Dependent List, and select one or more numeric or short string variables for the Independent List. To obtain the default table of means and number of cases, click on OK. Subgroup means for each dependent variable are calculated for each category of each independent variable, as in Figure 11.4.

Optionally, you can specify additional layers of independent variables. Each layer further subdivides the sample. For example, Figure 11.2 was produced by using *edlevel* as the dependent variable, *sex* as the layer 1 independent variable, and *minority* as the layer 2 independent variable. Subgroup means of *edlevel* are calculated for each category of *minority* within each category of *sex*.

You can specify up to five layers of independent variables. Use Next and Previous to move between the independent variable lists for the different layers.

Means Options Dialog Box

To obtain additional univariate statistics, control the display of variable and value labels, or generate an analysis of variance for the first layer, click on Options... in the Means dialog box. This opens the Means Options dialog box, as shown in Figure 11.7.

Figure 11.7 Means Options dialog box

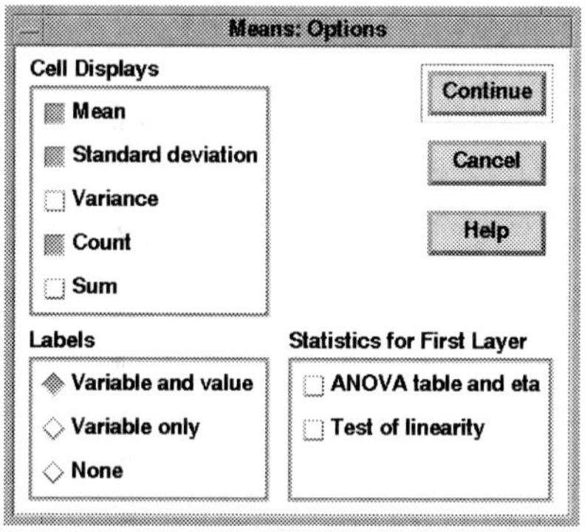

Cell Displays. You can choose one or more of the following subgroup statistics for the dependent variable(s) within each category (cell) of each independent variable:

- **Mean.** The arithmetic mean. Displayed by default.
- **Standard deviation.** A measure of how much observations vary from the mean, expressed in the same units as the data. Displayed by default.
- **Variance.** A measure of how much observations vary from the mean, equal to the square of the standard deviation. The units are the square of those of the variable itself.
- **Count.** The number of cases in each subgroup. Displayed by default.

❑ **Sum.** The sum of all the values in each subgroup.

Labels. You can choose one of the following alternatives:

◇ **Variable and value.** Displays variable and value labels. This is the default.

◇ **Variable only.** Displays variable labels but suppresses value labels.

◇ **None.** Suppresses both variable and value labels.

Statistics for First Layer. For subgroups based on categories of the independent variables in the first layer only, you can choose one or more of the following additional statistics:

❑ **ANOVA table and eta.** Displays a one-way analysis-of-variance table and calculates eta and eta^2 for each independent variable in the first layer.

❑ **Test of linearity.** Calculates the sums of squares, degrees of freedom, and mean square associated with linear and nonlinear components, as well as the F ratio, R, and R^2. Linearity is not calculated if the independent variable is a short string.

Additional Features Available with Command Syntax

You can customize the Means procedure if you paste your selections to a syntax window and edit the resulting MEANS command syntax (see Chapter 4). An additional feature is the option to generate output in crosstabular format (with the CROSSBREAK subcommand). See Appendix A for command syntax rules. See the *SPSS Base System Syntax Reference Guide* for complete MEANS command syntax.

12 Multiple Response Analysis

Introduction to Multiple Response Data

The example in this section illustrates the use of multiple response items in a market research survey. The data in these tables are fictitious and should not be interpreted as real.

An airline might survey passengers flying a particular route to evaluate competing carriers. In this example, American Airlines wants to know about its passengers' use of other airlines on the Chicago–New York route and the relative importance of schedule and service in selecting an airline. The flight attendant hands each passenger a brief questionnaire upon boarding similar to the one shown in Figure 12.1. The first question is a multiple response question because the passenger can circle more than one response. However, this question cannot be coded directly because an SPSS variable can have only one value for each case. You must use several variables to map responses to the question. There are two ways to do this. One is to define a variable corresponding to each of the choices (for example, American, United, TWA, Eastern, and Other). If the passenger circles United, the variable *united* is assigned a code of 1—otherwise, 0. This is the **multiple dichotomy method** of mapping variables.

Figure 12.1 An in-flight questionnaire

```
Circle all airlines that you have flown at least one time
in the last six months on this route:


   American   United   TWA   Eastern   Other:_____


Which is more important in selecting a flight?
   Schedule             Service
(Circle only one.)


Thank you for your cooperation.
```

The other way to map the responses is the **multiple category method**, in which you estimate the maximum number of possible responses to the question and set up the same number of variables, with codes used to specify the airline flown. By perusing a sample of the questionnaires, you might discover that no user has flown more than three different airlines on this route in the last six months. Further, you find that due to the deregulation of airlines, 10 other airlines are named in the *Other* category. Using the multiple response method, you would define three variables, coded as 1 = *american*, 2 = *united*, 3 = *twa*, 4 = *eastern*, 5 = *republic*, 6 = *usair*, and so on. If a given passenger circles American and TWA, the first variable has a code of 1, the second has a code of 3, and the third has some missing-value code. Another passenger might have circled American and entered USAir. Thus, the first variable has a code of 1, the second a code of 6, and the third a missing-value code. If you use the multiple dichotomy method, on the other hand, you end up with 14 separate variables. Although either method of mapping is feasible for this survey, the method you choose depends on the distribution of responses.

Set Definition

Each SPSS variable created from the survey question is an elementary variable. To analyze a multiple response item, you must combine the variables into one of two types of multiple response sets: a multiple dichotomy set or a multiple category set. For example, if the airline survey asked about only three airlines (American, United, and TWA) and you used dichotomous variables to account for multiple responses, the separate frequency tables would resemble Table 12.1. When you define a **multiple dichotomy set**, each of the three variables in the set becomes a category of the group variable. The counted values represent the *Have flown* category of each elementary variable. Table 12.2 shows the frequencies for this multiple dichotomy set. The 75 people using American Airlines are the 75 cases with code 1 for the variable representing American Airlines in Table 12.1. Because some people circled more than one response, 120 responses are recorded for 100 respondents.

Table 12.1 Dichotomous variables tabulated separately

American

Category Label	Code	Frequency	Relative Frequency
Have flown	1	75	75.0
Have not flown	0	25	25.0
	Total	100	100.0

United

Category Label	Code	Frequency	Relative Frequency
Have flown	1	30	30.0
Have not flown	0	70	70.0
	Total	100	100.0

TWA

Category Label	Code	Frequency	Relative Frequency
Have flown	1	15	15.0
Have not flown	0	85	85.0
	Total	100	100.0

Table 12.2 Dichotomous variables tabulated as a group

Airlines

Variable	Frequency	Relative Frequency
American	75	62.5
United	30	25.0
TWA	15	12.5
Total	120	100.0

If you discover that no respondent mentioned more than two airlines, you could create two variables, each having three codes, one for each airline. The frequency tables for these elementary variables would resemble Table 12.3. When you define a **multiple category set**, the values are tabulated by adding the same codes in the elementary variables together. The resulting set of values is the same as those for each of the elementary variables. Table 12.4 shows the frequencies for this multiple category set. For example, the 30 responses for United are the sum of the 25 United responses for airline 1 and the five United responses for airline 2.

Table 12.3 Multiple response items tabulated separately

Airline 1

Category Label	Code	Frequency	Relative Frequency
American	1	75	75.0
United	2	25	25.0
	Total	100	100.0

Airline 2

Category Label	Code	Frequency	Relative Frequency
United	2	5	5.0
TWA	3	15	15.0
Missing	99	80	80.0
	Total	100	100.0

Table 12.4 Multiple response items tabulated as a group

Airlines

Category Label	Code	Frequency	Relative Frequency
American	1	75	62.5
United	2	30	25.0
TWA	3	15	12.5
	Total	120	100.0

Crosstabulations

Both multiple dichotomy and multiple category sets can be crosstabulated with other variables in the SPSS Multiple Response Crosstabs procedure. In the airline passenger survey, the airline choices can be crosstabulated with the question asking why people chose different airlines. If you have organized the first question into dichotomies as in Table 12.1, the three crosstabulations of the dichotomous variables with the schedule/service question would resemble Figure 12.2. If you had chosen the multiple category set method and created two variables, the two crosstabulations would resemble Figure 12.3 (cases with missing values are omitted from the table for airline 2). With either method, the crosstabulation of the elementary variable and the group variable would resemble Figure 12.4. Each row in Figure 12.4 represents the *Have flown* information for the three dichotomous variables. Like codes are added together for the multiple category set. For example, 21 respondents have flown United and think schedule is the most important consideration in selecting a flight. The 21 cases are a combination of 20 people who flew United as airline 1 and circled Schedule plus one person who flew United as airline 2 and circled Schedule.

Figure 12.2 Dichotomous variables crosstabulated separately

```
   AMERICAN
by SELECT
```

	Count	SELECT Schedule Service 0	1	Row Total
AMERICAN Have not flown	0	20	5	25 25.0
Have flown	1	41	34	75 75.0
	Column Total	61 61.0	39 39.0	100 100.0

```
   UNITED
by SELECT
```

	Count	SELECT Schedule Service 0	1	Row Total
UNITED Have not flown	0	40	30	70 70.0
Have flown	1	21	9	30 30.0
	Column Total	61 61.0	39 39.0	100 100.0

```
   TWA
by SELECT
```

	Count	SELECT Schedule Service 0	1	Row Total
TWA Have not flown	0	53	32	85 85.0
Have flown	1	8	7	15 15.0
	Column Total	61 61.0	39 39.0	100 100.0

Figure 12.3 Multiple response variables crosstabulated separately

```
    AIRLINE1
by  SELECT
```

		SELECT		
	Count	Schedule	Service	Row Total
		0	1	
AIRLINE1				
American	1	41	34	75 75.0
United	2	20	5	25 25.0
Column Total		61 61.0	39 39.0	100 100.0

```
    AIRLINE2
by  SELECT
```

		SELECT		
	Count	Schedule	Service	Row Total
		0	1	
AIRLINE2				
United	2	1	4	5 25.0
TWA	3	8	7	15 75.0
Column Total		9 45.0	11 55.0	20 100.0

Figure 12.4 A group crosstabulated

```
    AIRLINES (group)
by  SELECT
```

		SELECT		
	Count	Schedule	Service	Row Total
		0	1	
AIRLINES				
American	1	41	34	75 62.5
United	2	21	9	30 25.0
TWA	3	8	7	15 12.5
Column Total		70 58.3	50 41.7	120 100.0

Analyzing Multiple Response Data

Two procedures are available for analyzing multiple dichotomy and multiple category sets (see "Introduction to Multiple Response Data" on p. 225). The Multiple Response Frequencies procedure displays frequency tables. The Multiple Response Crosstabs procedure displays two- and three-dimensional crosstabulations. Before using either procedure, you must first define your multiple response sets.

How to Define Multiple Response Sets

The Define Multiple Response Sets procedure groups elementary variables into multiple dichotomy and multiple category sets, for which you can obtain frequency tables and crosstabulations.

The minimum specifications are:
- Two or more numeric variables.
- Value(s) to be counted.
- A name for the multiple response set.

To define one or more multiple response sets, from the menus choose:

Statistics
 Multiple Response ▶
  Define Sets...

This opens the Define Multiple Response Sets dialog box, as shown in Figure 12.5.

Figure 12.5 Define Multiple Response Sets dialog box

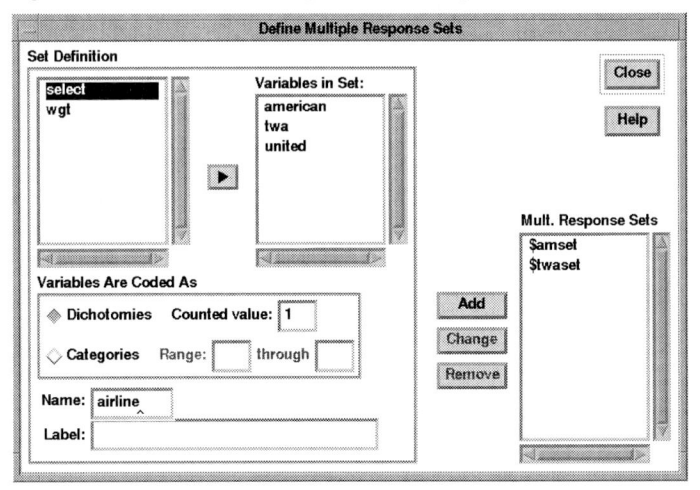

The numeric variables in your data file appear in the source list. To define a multiple response set, select two or more variables, indicate how variables are coded, and supply a set name; then click on Add to add the multiple response set to the list of defined sets. You can use the same variables in more than one set. After you define each set, all selected variables move back to the source variable list.

Variables Are Coded As. You can choose one of the following alternatives:

- **Dichotomies.** Elementary variables having two categories. This is the default. Select this item to create a multiple dichotomy set. Enter an integer value for Counted value. Each variable having at least one occurrence of the counted value becomes a category of the multiple dichotomy set.

- **Categories.** Elementary variables having more than two categories. Select this item to create a multiple category set having the same range of values as the component variables. Enter integer values for the minimum and maximum values of the range for categories of the multiple category set. SPSS totals each distinct integer value in the inclusive range across all component variables. Empty categories are not tabulated.

Name. The name for the multiple response set. Enter up to seven characters for the name. SPSS prefixes a dollar sign ($) to the name you assign. You cannot use the following reserved names: *casenum, sysmis, jdate, date, time, length,* and *width*. The name of the multiple response set exists only for use in multiple response procedures. You cannot refer to multiple response set names in other procedures.

Label. Enter an optional descriptive variable label for the multiple response set. The label can be up to 40 characters long.

You can define up to 20 multiple response sets. Each set must have a unique name. To remove a set, highlight it in the list of multiple response sets and click on Remove. To change a set, highlight it in the list, modify any set definition characteristics, and click on Change.

How to Obtain Multiple Response Frequencies

The Multiple Response Frequencies procedure produces frequency tables for multiple response sets.

The minimum specification is one or more defined multiple response sets.

To obtain multiple response frequencies for defined multiple response sets, you must first define one or more multiple response sets (see "How to Define Multiple Response Sets" on p. 231). Then, from the menus choose:

Statistics
  Multiple Response▶
    Frequencies...

This opens the Multiple Response Frequencies dialog box, as shown in Figure 12.6.

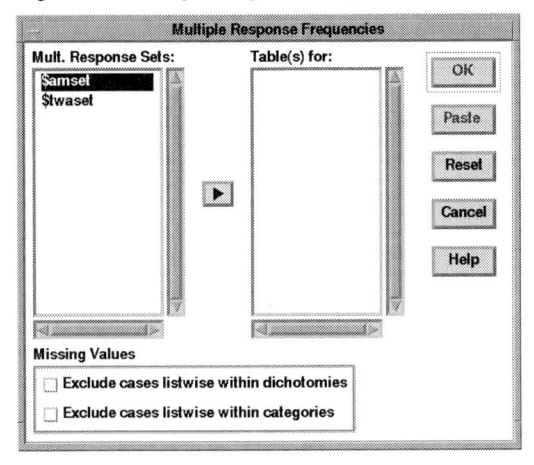

Figure 12.6 Multiple Response Frequencies dialog box

The currently defined multiple response sets appear in the source list. Select one or more sets for frequency tables. Click on OK to get the default frequency tables showing counts and percentages. Cases with missing values are excluded on a table-by-table basis.

For multiple dichotomy sets, category names shown in the output come from variable labels defined for elementary variables in the group. If variable labels are not defined, variable names are used as labels. For multiple category sets, category labels come from the value labels of the first variable in the group. If categories missing for the first variable are present for other variables in the group, define a value label for the missing categories.

Missing Values. You can choose one or both of the following:

- **Exclude cases listwise within dichotomies.** Excludes cases with missing values for any variable from the tabulation of the multiple dichotomy set. This applies only to multiple response sets defined as dichotomy sets. By default, a case is considered missing for a multiple dichotomy set if none of its component variables contains the counted value. Cases with missing values for some but not all variables are included in tabulations of the group if at least one variable contains the counted value.

❏ **Exclude cases listwise within categories.** Excludes cases with missing values for any variable from tabulation of the multiple category set. This applies only to multiple response sets defined as category sets. By default, a case is considered missing for a multiple category set only if none of its components has valid values within the defined range.

Additional Features Available with Command Syntax

You can customize your multiple response frequencies if you paste your selections to a syntax window and edit the resulting MULT RESPONSE command syntax. Additional features include output format options such as suppression of value labels (with the FORMAT subcommand).

See Appendix A for command syntax rules. See the *SPSS Base System Syntax Reference Guide* for complete MULT RESPONSE command syntax.

How to Crosstabulate Multiple Response Sets

The Multiple Response Crosstabs procedure crosstabulates defined multiple response sets, elementary variables, or a combination. You can also obtain cell percentages based on cases or responses, modify the handling of missing values, or get paired crosstabulations.

The minimum specifications are:
- One numeric variable or multiple response set for each dimension of the crosstabulation.
- Category ranges for any elementary variables.

To obtain crosstabulation tables for multiple response sets, you must first define one or more multiple response sets (see "How to Define Multiple Response Sets" on p. 231). Then, from the menus choose:

Statistics
  Multiple Response ▶
    Crosstabs...

This opens the Multiple Response Crosstabs dialog box, as shown in Figure 12.7.

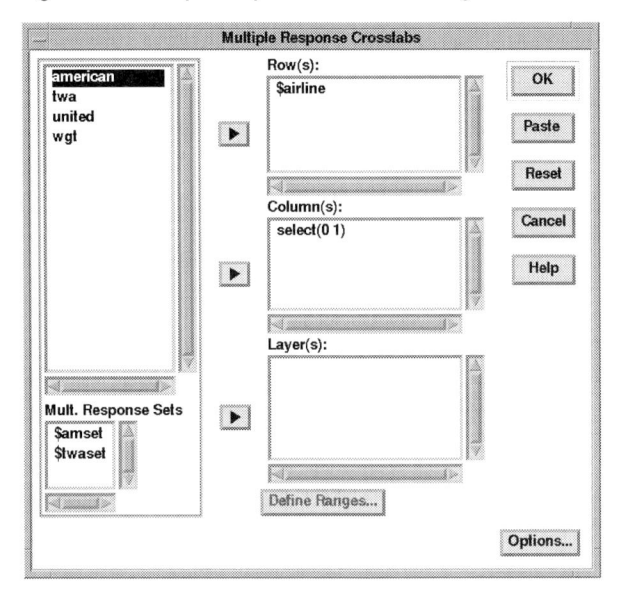

Figure 12.7 Multiple Response Crosstabs dialog box

The numeric elementary variables in your data file appear in the source list. The currently defined multiple response sets appear in the list of multiple response sets. Select row and column items for the crosstabulation. A table is produced for each combination of row and column items.

After defining the value ranges of any elementary variables (see "Define Value Ranges" below), click on OK to get the default tables displaying cell counts. Cases with missing values are excluded on a table-by-table basis.

For multiple dichotomy sets, category names shown in the output come from variable labels defined for elementary variables in the group. If variable labels are not defined, variable names are used as labels. For multiple category sets, category labels come from the value labels of the first variable in the group. If categories missing for the first variable are present for other variables in the group, define a value label for the missing categories. SPSS displays category labels for columns on three lines, with up to eight characters per line. To avoid splitting words, you can reverse row and column items or redefine labels.

Optionally, you can obtain a two-way crosstabulation for each category of a control variable or multiple response set. Select one or more items for the layer list.

Define Value Ranges

Value ranges must be defined for any elementary variables in the crosstabulation. To define value ranges for an elementary variable, highlight the variable in the Row(s), Column(s), or Layer(s) list and click on Define Ranges... in the Multiple Response Crosstabs dialog box. This opens the Multiple Response Crosstabs Define Variable Ranges dialog box, as shown in Figure 12.8.

Figure 12.8   Multiple Response Crosstabs Define Variable Ranges dialog box

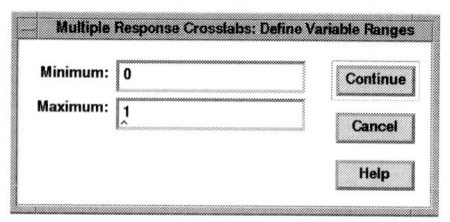

Enter integer minimum and maximum category values that you want to tabulate. Categories outside the range are excluded from analysis. Values within the inclusive range are assumed to be integers (non-integers are truncated).

Options

To obtain cell percentages, control the computation of percentages, modify the handling of missing values, or get a paired crosstabulation, click on Options... in the Multiple Response Crosstabs dialog box. This opens the Multiple Response Crosstabs Options dialog box, as shown in Figure 12.9.

Figure 12.9   Multiple Response Crosstabs Options dialog box

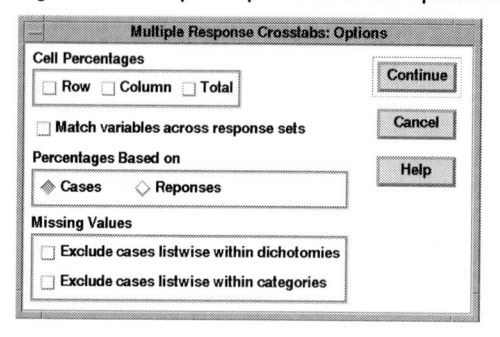

Cell Percentages. Cell counts are always displayed. You can also choose one or more of the following:

- **Row.** Displays row percentages.
- **Column.** Displays column percentages.
- **Total.** Displays two-way table total percentages.

Percentages Based on. You can choose one of the following alternatives:

- **Cases.** Bases cell percentages on cases, or respondents. This is the default. This item is not available if you select matching of variables across multiple category sets.
- **Responses.** Bases cell percentages on responses. For multiple dichotomy sets, the number of responses is equal to the number of counted values across cases. For multiple category sets, the number of responses is the number of values in the defined range (see "Define Value Ranges" on p. 236).

Missing Values. You can choose one or both of the following:

- **Exclude cases listwise within dichotomies.** Excludes cases with missing values for any variable from the tabulation of the multiple dichotomy set. This applies only to multiple response sets defined as dichotomy sets. By default, a case is considered missing for a multiple dichotomy set only if none of its elementary variables contains the counted value.
- **Exclude cases listwise within categories.** Excludes cases with missing values for any component variable from tabulation of the multiple category set. This applies only to multiple response sets defined as category sets. By default, a case is considered missing for a multiple category set only if none of its elementary variables has valid values falling within the defined range.

By default, when crosstabulating two multiple category sets, SPSS tabulates each variable in the first group with each variable in the second group and sums the counts for each cell. So, some responses can appear more than once in a table. You can choose the following option:

- **Match variables across response sets.** Pairs the first variable in the first group with the first variable in the second group, the second variable in the first group with the second variable in the second group, etc. If you select this option, SPSS bases cell percentages on responses rather than respondents. Pairing is not available for multiple dichotomy sets or elementary variables.

Additional Features Available with Command Syntax

You can customize your multiple response crosstabulation if you paste your selections to a syntax window and edit the resulting MULT RESPONSE command syntax. Additional features include:

- Crosstabulation tables with up to five dimensions (with the BY subcommand).
- Output formatting options, including suppression of value labels (with the FORMAT subcommand).

See Appendix A for command syntax rules. See the *SPSS Base System Syntax Reference Guide* for complete MULT RESPONSE command syntax.

13 Testing Hypotheses about Differences in Means

Would you buy a disposable raincoat, vegetables in pop-top cans, or investment counseling via closed-circuit television? These products and 17 others were described in questionnaires administered to 100 married couples (Davis & Ragsdale, 1983). Respondents were asked to rate on a scale of 1 (definitely want to buy) to 7 (definitely do not want to buy) their likelihood of buying the product. Of the 100 couples, 50 received questionnaires with pictures of the products and 50 received questionnaires without pictures. In this chapter, we will examine whether pictures affect consumer preferences and whether husbands' and wives' responses differ.

Testing Hypotheses

The first part of the table in Figure 13.1 contains basic descriptive statistics for the buying scores of couples receiving questionnaires with and without pictures. A couple's buying score is simply the sum of all ratings assigned to products by the husband and wife individually. Low scores indicate buyers, while high scores indicate reluctance to buy. The 50 couples who received questionnaires without pictures (group 1) had a mean score of 168, while the 48 couples who received forms with pictures had an average score of 159. (Two couples did not complete the questionnaire and are not included in the analysis.) The standard deviations show that scores for the second group were somewhat more variable than those for the first.

If you are willing to restrict the conclusions to the 98 couples included in the study, it is safe to say that couples who received forms with pictures indicated a greater willingness to purchase the products than couples who received forms without pictures. However, this statement is not very satisfying. What is needed is some type of statement about the effect of the two questionnaire types for all couples—or at least some larger group of couples—not just those actually studied.

Figure 13.1 Family buying scores by questionnaire type

Variable	Number of Cases	Mean	SD	SE of Mean
FAMSCORE FAMILY BUYING SCORE				
NO PICTURES	50	168.0000	21.787	3.081
PICTURES	48	159.0833	27.564	3.979

Mean Difference = 8.9167

Levene's Test for Equality of Variances: F= 1.382 P= .243

t-test for Equality of Means

Variances	t-value	df	2-Tail Sig	SE of Diff	95% CI for Diff
Equal	1.78	96	.078	5.008	(-1.027, 18.860)
Unequal	1.77	89.43	.080	5.032	(-1.084, 18.918)

Samples and Populations

The totality of cases about which conclusions are desired is called the **population**, while the cases actually included in the study constitute the **sample**. The couples in this experiment can be considered a sample from the population of couples in the United States.

The field of statistics helps us draw inferences about populations based on observations obtained from **random samples**, or samples in which the characteristics and relationships of interest are independent of the probabilities of being included in the sample. The necessity of a good research design cannot be overemphasized. Unless precautions are taken to ensure that the sample is from the population of interest and that the cases are chosen and observed without bias, the results obtained from statistical analyses may be misleading. For example, if a sample contains only affluent suburban couples, conclusions about all couples may be unwarranted.

If measurements are obtained from an entire population, the population can be characterized by the various measures of central tendency, dispersion, and shape described in Chapter 8. The results describe the population exactly. If, however, you obtain information from a random sample—the usual case—the results serve as **estimates** of the unknown population values. Special notation is used to identify population values, termed **parameters**, and to distinguish them from sample values, termed **statistics**. The mean of a population is denoted by μ, and the variance by σ^2. The symbols $\bar{X}$ and S^2 are reserved for the mean and variance of samples.

Sampling Distributions

The observations actually included in a study are just one of many random samples that could have been selected from a population. For example, if the population consists of married couples in the United States, the number of different samples that could be chosen for inclusion in a study is mind boggling. The estimated value of a population parameter depends on the particular sample chosen. Different samples usually produce different estimates.

Figure 13.2 is a histogram of 400 means produced by the SPSS Frequencies procedure. Each mean is calculated from a random sample of 25 observations from a population that has a normal distribution with a mean value of 0 and a standard deviation of 1. The estimated means are not all the same. Instead, they have a distribution. Most sample means are fairly close to 0, the population mean. The mean of the 400 means is 0, and the standard deviation of these means is 0.2. In fact, the distribution of the means appears approximately normal.

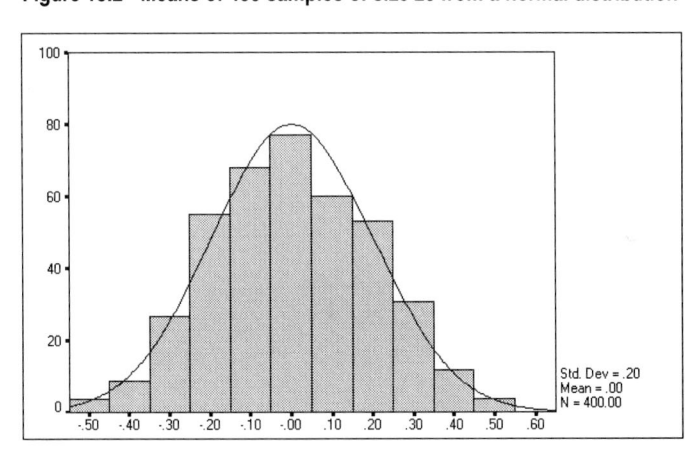

Figure 13.2 Means of 400 samples of size 25 from a normal distribution

Although Figure 13.2 gives some idea of the appearance of the distribution of sample means of size 25 from a standard normal population, it is only an approximation because all possible samples of size 25 have not been taken. If the number of samples taken is increased to 1000, an even better picture of the distribution could be obtained. As the number of samples of a fixed size increases, the observed (or empirical) distribution of the means approaches the underlying or theoretical distribution.

The theoretical distribution of all possible values of a statistic obtained from a population is called the **sampling distribution** of the statistic. The mean of the sampling distribution is called the **expected value** of the statistic. The standard deviation is termed the **standard error**. The sampling distributions of most commonly used statistics calculated from random samples are tabulated and readily accessible. Knowing the sampling distribution of a statistic is very important for hypothesis testing, since from it you can calculate the probability of obtaining an observed sample value if a particular hypothesis is true. For example, from Figure 13.2, it appears quite unlikely that a sample mean based on a sample of size 25 from a standard normal distribution would be greater than 0.5 if the population mean were 0.

Sampling Distribution of the Mean

Since hypotheses about population means are often of interest, the sampling distribution of the mean is particularly important. If samples are taken from a normal population, the sampling distribution of the sample mean is also normal. As expected, the observed distribution of the 400 means in Figure 13.2 is approximately normal. The theoretical distribution of the sample mean, based on all possible samples of size 25, is exactly normal.

Even when samples are taken from a non-normal population, the distribution of the sample means will be approximately normal for sufficiently large samples. This is one reason for the importance of the normal distribution in statistical inference. Consider Figure 13.3, which shows a sample from a uniform distribution. In a **uniform distribution**, all values of a variable are equally likely; hence, the proportion of cases in each bin of the histogram is roughly the same.

Figure 13.3 Values from a uniform distribution

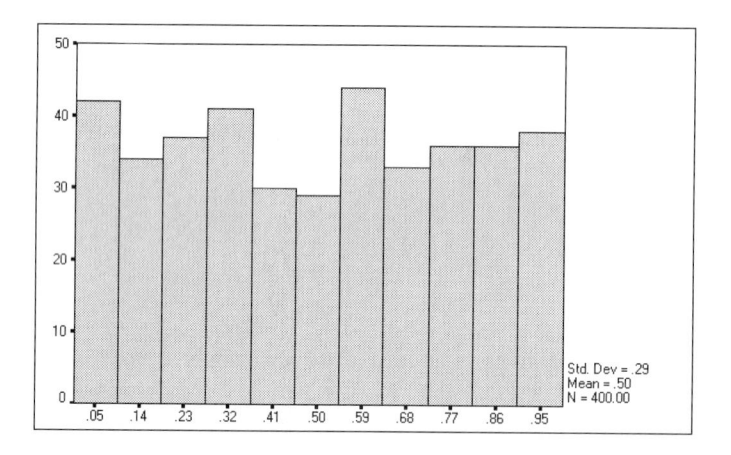

Figure 13.4 is a histogram of 400 means calculated from samples of size 25 from a uniform distribution. Note that the observed distribution is approximately normal even though the distribution from which the samples were taken is markedly non-normal.

Both the size of a sample and the shape of the distribution from which samples are taken affect the shape of the sampling distribution of the mean. If samples are small and come from distributions that are far from normal, the distribution of the means will not be even approximately normal. As the size of the sample increases, the sampling distribution of the mean will approach normality.

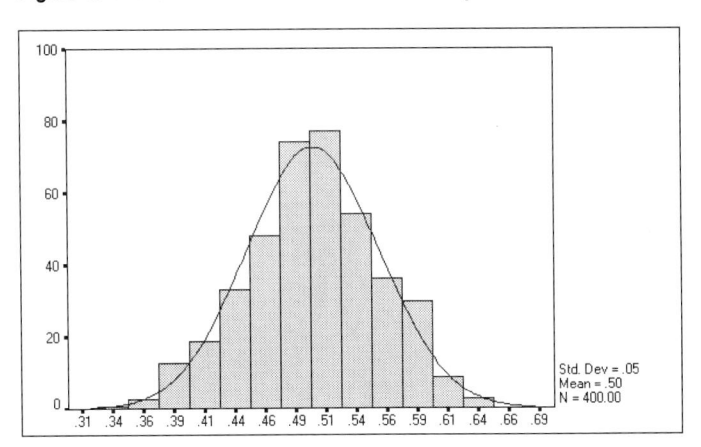

Figure 13.4 Distribution of 400 means from samples of size 25 from a uniform distribution

The mean of the theoretical sampling distribution of the means of samples of size N is m, the population mean. The standard error, which is another name for the standard deviation of the sampling distribution of the mean, is

$$\sigma_{\bar{X}} = \frac{\sigma}{\sqrt{N}}$$ Equation 13.1

where σ is the standard deviation of the population and N is the sample size.

The standard deviation of the observed sampling distribution of means in Figure 13.2 is 0.20. This is the same as the value of the standard error for the theoretical distribution, which, from the previous formula, is $1/5$, or 0.20.

Usually, the value of the standard error is unknown and is estimated from a single sample using

$$S_{\bar{X}} = \frac{S}{\sqrt{N}}$$ Equation 13.2

where S is the *sample* standard deviation. The estimated standard error is displayed in the SPSS Frequencies procedure and is also part of the output shown in Figure 13.1. For example, for group 1, the estimated standard error of the mean is:

$$\frac{21.787}{\sqrt{50}} = 3.081$$ Equation 13.3

This value is displayed in the column labeled *SE of Mean* in Figure 13.1.

The standard error of the mean depends on both the sample standard deviation and the sample size. For a fixed standard deviation, the size of a sample increases, and the standard error decreases. This is intuitively clear, since the more data that are gathered, the more confident you can be that the sample mean is not too far from the population mean. Also, as the standard deviation of the observations decreases, the standard error decreases as well. Small standard deviations occur when observations are fairly homogeneous. In this case, means based on different samples should also not vary much.

The Two-Sample T Test

Consider again whether there is evidence that the type of form administered influences couples' buying decisions. The question is not whether the two sample means are equal, but whether the two population means are equal.

To test the hypothesis that, in the population, buying scores for the two questionnaire types are the same, the following statistic can be calculated:

$$t = \frac{\bar{X}_1 - \bar{X}_2}{\sqrt{\frac{S_1^2}{N_1} + \frac{S_2^2}{N_2}}}$$

Equation 13.4

where $\bar{X}_1$ is the sample mean of group 1, S_1^2 is the variance, and N_1 is the sample size.

Based on the sampling distribution of the above statistic, you can calculate the probability that a difference at least as large as the one observed would occur if the two population means (μ_1 and μ_2) are equal. This probability is called the **observed significance level**. If the observed significance level is small enough (usually less than 0.05, or 0.01), the hypothesis that the population means are equal is rejected.

The t value and its associated probability are given in Figure 13.1 in the row labeled *Unequal*. The t value is:

$$t = \frac{168.0 - 159.08}{\sqrt{\frac{21.787^2}{50} + \frac{27.564^2}{48}}} = 1.77$$

Equation 13.5

If $\mu_1 = \mu_2$, the probability of observing a difference at least as large as the one in the sample is estimated to be about 0.08. Since this probability is greater than 0.05, the hypothesis that mean buying scores in the population are equal for the two types of forms is not rejected. The entry under *df* in Figure 13.1 is a function of the sample size in the two groups and is used together with the *t* value in establishing the observed significance level.

Another statistic based on the *t* distribution can be used to test the equality-of-means hypothesis. This statistic, known as the **pooled-variance *t* test**, is based on the assumption that the population variances in the two groups are equal and is obtained using a pooled estimate of that common variance. The test statistic is identical to the equation for *t* given previously, except that the individual group variances are replaced by a pooled estimate, S_p^2. That is,

$$t = \frac{\bar{X}_1 - \bar{X}_2}{\sqrt{\frac{S_p^2}{N_1} + \frac{S_p^2}{N_2}}}$$

Equation 13.6

where S_p^2, the pooled variance, is a weighted average of the individual variances and is calculated as:

$$S_p^2 = \frac{(N_1 - 1) S_1^2 + (N_2 - 1) S_2^2}{N_1 + N_2 - 2}$$

Equation 13.7

From the output in Figure 13.1, the pooled *t* test value for the study is 1.78. The degrees of freedom for the pooled *t* test are 96, the sum of the sample sizes in both groups minus 2. If the pooled-variance *t* test is used when the population variances are not equal, the probability level associated with the statistic may be in error. The amount of error depends on the inequality of the sample sizes and the variances. However, using the separate-variance *t* value when the population variances are equal will usually result in an observed significance level somewhat larger than it should be. For large samples, the discrepancy between the two methods is small. In general, it is a good idea to use the separate-variance *t* test whenever you suspect that the variances are unequal.

Levene's test is used to test the hypothesis that the two population variances are equal. This test is less dependent on the assumption of normality than most tests of equality of variance. It is obtained by computing for each case the absolute difference from its group mean and then performing a one-way analysis of variance on these differences. In Figure 13.1, the value of the Levene statistic is 1.382. If the observed significance level for this test is small, the hypothesis that the population variances are equal is rejected, and the separate-variance *t* test for means should be used. In this example, the significance level for the Levene statistic is large, and thus the pooled-variance *t* test is appropriate.

Significance Levels

The commonsense interpretation of a small observed significance level is straightforward: it appears unlikely that the two population means are equal. Of course, there is a possibility that the means are equal and the observed difference is due to chance. The observed significance level is the probability that a difference at least as large as the one observed would have arisen if the means were really equal.

When the observed significance level is too large to reject the equality hypothesis, the two population means may indeed be equal, or they may be unequal, but the difference cannot be detected. Failure to detect can be due to a true difference that is very small. For example, if a new cancer drug prolongs survival time by only one day when compared to the standard treatment, it is unlikely that such a difference will be detected, especially if survival times vary substantially and the additional day represents a small increment.

There are other reasons why true differences may not be found. If the sample sizes in the two groups are small or the variability is large, even substantial differences may not be detected. Significant *t* values are obtained when the numerator of the *t* statistic is large compared to the denominator. The numerator is the difference between the sample means, and the denominator depends on the standard deviations and sample sizes of the two groups. For a given standard deviation, the larger the sample size, the smaller the denominator. Thus, a difference of a given magnitude may be significant if obtained with a sample size of 100 but not significant with a sample size of 25.

One-tailed versus Two-tailed Tests

A two-tailed test is used to detect a difference in means between two populations regardless of the direction of the difference. For example, in the study of buying scores presented in this chapter, we are interested in whether buying scores for products without pictures are larger *or* smaller than buying scores for products with pictures. In applications where you are interested in detecting a difference in one direction—such as whether a new drug is better than the current treatment—a so-called one-tailed test can be performed. The procedure is the same as for the two-tailed test, but the resulting probability value is divided by 2, adjusting for the fact that the equality hypothesis is rejected only when the difference between the two means is sufficiently large and in the direction of interest. In a two-tailed test, the equality hypothesis is rejected for large positive or negative values of the statistic.

What's the Difference?

It appears that the questionnaire type has no significant effect on couples' willingness to purchase products. Overall buying scores for the two conditions are similar. Pictures of the products do not appear to enhance their perceived desirability. In fact, the pictures actually appear to make several products somewhat less desirable. However, since the purpose of the questionnaires is to ascertain buying intent, including a picture of the actual product may help to gauge true product response. Although the concept of disposable raincoats may be attractive, if they make the wearer look like a walking trash bag, their appeal may diminish considerably.

Using Crosstabulation to Test Hypotheses

The SPSS Independent-Samples T Test procedure is used to test hypotheses about the equality of two means for variables measured on an interval or ratio scale. Crosstabulation and the Pearson chi-square statistic can be used to test hypotheses about a dichotomous variable, such as the purchase of a particular product.

Figure 13.5 is an SPSS crosstabulation showing the number of husbands who would definitely want to buy vegetables in pop-top cans when shown a picture and when not shown a picture of the product (value 1 of variable *H2S*). The vegetables in pop-top cans were chosen by 6.0% of the husbands who were tempted with pictures and 16.0% of the husbands who were not shown pictures. The chi-square statistic provides a test of the hypothesis that the proportion of husbands selecting the vegetables in pop-top cans is the same for the picture and no-picture forms.

Figure 13.5 Preference of husbands for vegetables in pop-top cans

```
H2S   POP-TOP CANS HUSB SELF   by   VISUAL   PICTURE ACCOMPANIED QUESTION

                    VISUAL           Page 1 of
           Count
           Col Pct  NO PICTU PICTURES
                    RES                        Ro
                         0         1        Tot
H2S
              1
           DEFINITELY      8         3
                        16.0       6.0        11

              2
           VERY LIKELY    42        47
                        84.0      94.0        89

              Column      50        50         1
              Total     50.0      50.0       100

        Chi-Square              Value          DF         Significance
        -----------             -----         ----        ------------

Pearson                        2.55363         1            .11004
Continuity Correction          1.63432         1            .20111
Likelihood Ratio               2.63933         1            .10425
Mantel-Haenszel test for       2.52809         1            .11184
    linear association

Minimum Expected Frequency -    5.500
```

The probability of 0.11 associated with the Pearson chi-square in Figure 13.5 is the probability that a difference at least as large as the one observed would occur in the sample if in the population there were no difference in the selection of the product between the two formats. Since the probability is large, the hypothesis of no difference between the two formats is not rejected.

Independent versus Paired Samples

Several factors contribute to the observed differences in response between two groups. Part of the observed difference in scores between the picture and no-picture formats may be attributable to form type. Another component is due to differences between individuals. Not all couples have the same buying desires, so even if the type of form does not affect buying, differences between the two groups will probably be observed due to differences between the couples within the two groups.

One method of minimizing the influence of individual variation is to choose the two groups so that the couples within them are comparable on characteristics that can influence buying behavior, such as income, education, family size, and so forth.

It is sometimes possible to obtain pairs of subjects, such as twins, and assign one member of each pair to each of the two treatments. Another frequently used experimental design is to expose the same individual to both types of conditions. (In this design, care must be taken to ensure that the sequential administration of treatments does not influence response by providing practice, decreasing attention span, or affecting the second treatment in other ways.) In both designs, subject-to-subject variability has substantially less effect. These designs are called **paired-samples designs**, since for each subject there is a corresponding pair in the other group. In the second design, a person is paired with himself or herself. In an **independent-samples design**, there is no pairing of cases; all observations are independent.

Analysis of Paired Data

Although the interpretation of the significance of results from paired experiments is the same as those from the two independent samples discussed previously, the actual computations are different. For each pair of cases, the difference in the responses is calculated. The statistic used to test the hypothesis that the mean difference in the population is 0 is

$$t = \frac{\bar{D}}{S_D/\sqrt{N}} \qquad \text{Equation 13.8}$$

where $\bar{D}$ is the observed difference between the two means and S_D is the standard deviation of the differences of the paired observations. The sampling distribution of t, if the differences are normally distributed with a mean of 0, is Student's t with $N-1$ degrees of freedom, where N is the number of pairs. If the pairing is effective, the standard error of the difference will be smaller than the standard error obtained if two independent samples with N subjects each were chosen. However, if the variables chosen for pairing do not affect the responses under study, pairing may result in a test that is less powerful, since true differences can be detected less frequently.

For example, to test the hypothesis that there is no difference between husbands' and wives' buying scores, a paired t test should be calculated. A paired test is appropriate because husbands and wives constitute matched observations. Including both members of a couple helps control for nuisance effects such as socioeconomic status and age. The observed differences are more likely to be attributable to differences in sex.

Figure 13.6 contains output from the paired t test. The entry under *Number of pairs* is the number of pairs of observations. The mean difference is the difference between the mean scores for males and females. The t value is the mean difference divided by the standard error of the difference ($0.55/1.73 = 0.32$). The two-tailed probability for this test is 0.75, so there is insufficient evidence to reject the null hypothesis that married males and females have similar mean buying scores.

Figure 13.6 Husbands' versus wives' buying scores

```
                       - - - t-tests for paired samples - - -

                          Number of           2-tail
     Variable                pairs    Corr     Sig       Mean      SD      SE o

     HSSCALE  HUSBAND SELF SCALE                        82.0918   14.352
                                 98     .367   .000
     WSSCALE  WIFE SELF SCALE                           81.5408   15.942


              Paired Differences
      Mean         SD      SE of Mean       t-value    df    2-tail Sig
      .5510      17.095      1.727            .32      97      .750
     95% CI (-2.877, 3.979)
```

The correlation coefficient between husbands' and wives' scores is 0.367. A positive correlation indicates that pairing has been effective in decreasing the variability of the mean difference. The larger the correlation coefficient, the greater the benefit of pairing.

Hypothesis Testing: A Review

The purpose of hypothesis testing is to help draw conclusions about population parameters based on results observed in a random sample. The procedure remains virtually the same for tests of most hypotheses.

- A hypothesis of no difference (called a **null hypothesis**) and its alternative are formulated.
- A test statistic is chosen to evaluate the null hypothesis.
- For the sample, the test statistic is calculated.

- The probability, if the null hypothesis is true, of obtaining a test value at least as extreme as the one observed is determined.
- If the observed significance level is judged to be small enough, the null hypothesis is rejected.

The Importance of Assumptions

To perform a statistical test of any hypothesis, it is necessary to make certain assumptions about the data. The particular assumptions depend on the statistical test being used. Some procedures require stricter assumptions than others. For parametric tests, some knowledge about the distribution from which samples are selected is required.

The assumptions are necessary to define the sampling distribution of the test statistic. Unless the distribution is defined, correct significance levels cannot be calculated. For the equal-variance *t* test, the assumption is that the observations are random samples from normal distributions with the same variance.

For many procedures, not all assumptions are equally important. Moderate violation of some assumptions may not always be serious. Therefore, it is important to know for each procedure not only what assumptions are needed, but also how severely their violation may influence results.

The responsibility for detecting violations of assumptions rests with the researcher. Unlike the chemist who ignores laboratory safety procedures, the investigator who does not comply with good statistical practice is not threatened by explosions. However, from a research viewpoint, the consequences can be just as severe.

Wherever possible, **tests of assumptions**—often called diagnostic checks of the model—should be incorporated as part of the hypothesis-testing procedures. Throughout SPSS, attempts have been made to provide facilities for examining assumptions. For example, in the Explore procedure, there are several tests for normality. Discussions of other such diagnostics are included with the individual procedures.

How to Obtain an Independent-Samples T Test

The Independent-Samples T Test procedure computes Student's *t* statistic for testing the significance of a difference in means for independent samples. Both equal- and unequal-variance *t* values are provided, as well as the Levene test for equality of variances.

The minimum specifications are:
- One or more numeric test variables.
- One numeric or short string grouping variable.
- Group values for the grouping variable.

To obtain an independent-samples *t* test, from the menus choose:

Statistics
  Compare Means ▶
    Independent-Samples T Test...

This opens the Independent-Samples T Test dialog box, as shown in Figure 13.7.

Figure 13.7 Independent-Samples T Test dialog box

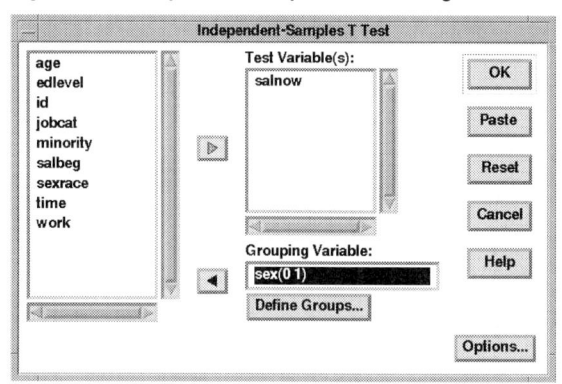

The numeric and short string variables in your data file appear on the source list. Select one or more numeric test variables. Each test variable produces one *t* test. Choose one numeric or short string grouping variable, which splits your file into two groups. After defining the categories of your grouping variable, you can click on OK to get the default independent-samples *t* test with two-tailed probabilities and a 95% confidence interval. (See Figure 13.1.) To obtain one-tailed probabilities, divide the *t* probabilities by 2.

Define Groups for Numeric Variables

You must define the two groups for the grouping variable. The procedure to follow for defining groups depends on whether your grouping variable is string or numeric. For both string and numeric variables, *t* tests are not performed if there are fewer than two non-empty groups.

To define groups, highlight the grouping variable and click on Define Groups... in the Independent-Samples T Test dialog box. For numeric variables, this opens the Define Groups dialog box, as shown in Figure 13.8.

Figure 13.8 Define Groups dialog box for numeric variables

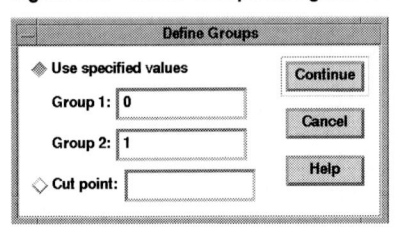

You can choose one of the following:

- **User-specified values.** User-specified group values. This is the default. Enter a group 1 value and a group 2 value that correspond to the two categories of the grouping variable. Cases with other values are excluded from the analysis.

- **Cut point.** User-specified cut point. All cases with values greater than or equal to the specified value are assigned to one group, and the remaining cases are assigned to the other group.

Define Groups for String Variables

The Define Groups dialog box for string variables is shown in Figure 13.9. Enter a group 1 value and a group 2 value that correspond to the two categories of the grouping variable. Cases with other values are excluded from the analysis.

Figure 13.9 Define Groups dialog box for string variables

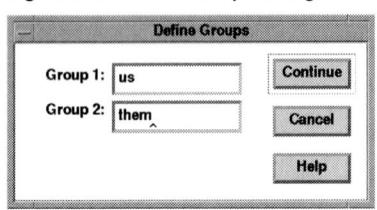

Independent-Samples T Test Options

To change confidence interval bounds or control the handling of cases with missing values, click on Options... in the Independent-Samples T Test dialog box. This opens the Independent-Samples T Test Options dialog box, as shown in Figure 13.10.

Figure 13.10 Independent-Samples T Test Options dialog box

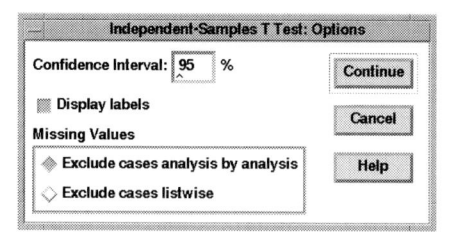

[Dialog box: Independent-Samples T Test: Options — Confidence Interval: 95 %; Display labels; Missing Values: Exclude cases analysis by analysis, Exclude cases listwise; buttons Continue, Cancel, Help]

Confidence Interval. A 95% confidence interval for the difference in means is displayed by default. Optionally, you can request a different confidence level by entering a value between 1 and 99. For example, to obtain a 99% confidence interval, enter 99.

Missing Values. You can choose one of the following:

◇ **Exclude cases analysis by analysis.** Cases with missing values on either the grouping variable or the test variable are excluded from the analysis of that variable. This is the default.

◇ **Exclude cases listwise.** Cases with missing values on either the grouping variable or any test variable are excluded from all analyses.

You can also choose the following display option:

❑ **Display labels.** By default, any variable labels are displayed in the output. To suppress labels, deselect this setting.

How to Obtain a Paired-Samples T Test

The Paired-Samples T Test procedure computes Student's *t* statistic for testing the significance of a difference in means for paired samples.

The minimum specification is a pair of numeric variables.

To obtain a paired-samples *t* test, from the menus choose:

Statistics
  Compare Means ▶
    Paired-Samples T Test...

This opens the Paired-Samples T Test dialog box, as shown in Figure 13.11.

Figure 13.11 Paired-Samples T Test dialog box

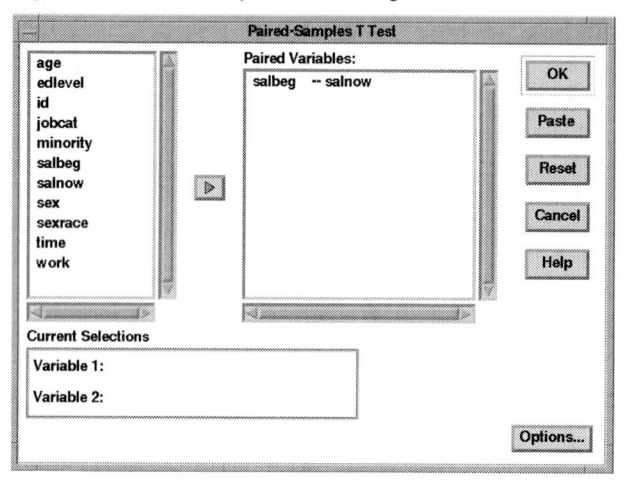

The numeric variables in your data file appear on the source list. Select one or more pairs of variables you want to use in the paired-samples tests. To select a pair:

1. Click on one of the variables. It appears as the first variable under Current Selections.

2. Click on another variable. It appears as the second variable. To remove a variable from Current Selections, click on it again.

3. Click on ▶ to move the pair to the Paired Variables list.

Repeat this process if you have more than one pair of variables.

To obtain the default test for paired samples with two-tailed probabilities and a 95% confidence interval for the mean difference, click on OK. To obtain one-tailed probabilities, divide the *t* probabilities by 2.

Paired-Samples T Test Options

To change confidence interval bounds or to control the handling of cases with missing values, click on Options... in the Paired-Samples T Test dialog box. This opens the Paired-Samples T Test Options dialog box, as shown in Figure 13.12.

Figure 13.12 Paired-Samples T Test Options dialog box

```
┌─────────── Paired-Samples T Test: Options ───────────┐
│                                                       │
│  Confidence Interval: [95] %          ┌──Continue──┐  │
│                                                       │
│  ▪ Display labels                     ┌──Cancel────┐  │
│  Missing Values                                       │
│    ◆ Exclude cases analysis by analysis ┌──Help────┐  │
│    ◇ Exclude cases listwise                           │
│                                                       │
└───────────────────────────────────────────────────────┘
```

Confidence Interval. A 95% confidence interval for the mean difference is displayed by default. Optionally, you can request a different confidence level. Enter a value between 1 and 99. For example, to obtain a 99% confidence interval, enter 99.

Missing Values. You can choose one of the following:

◇ **Exclude cases analysis by analysis.** Cases with missing values for either variable in a given pair are excluded from the analysis of that pair. This is the default.

◇ **Exclude cases listwise.** Cases with missing values for any pair variable are excluded from all analyses.

You can also choose the following display option:

❑ **Display labels.** Displays any variable labels in output. This is the default setting.

Additional Features Available with Command Syntax

You can customize your paired-samples *t* tests if you paste your selections into a syntax window and edit the resulting T-TEST command syntax (see Chapter 4). An additional feature is the ability to test a variable against each variable on a list (with the PAIRS subcommand). See Appendix A for command syntax rules. See the *SPSS Base System Syntax Reference Guide* for complete T-TEST command syntax.

14 One-Way Analysis of Variance

Which of four brands of paper towels is the strongest? Do six models of intermediate-size cars get the same average gasoline mileage? Do graduates of the top ten business schools receive the same average starting salaries? There are many situations in which you want to compare the means of several independent samples and, based on them, draw conclusions about the populations from which they were selected. Consider, for example, the following problem.

You are a manufacturer of paper used for making grocery bags. You suspect that the tensile strength of the bags depends on the pulp hardwood concentration. You currently use 10% hardwood concentration in the pulp and produce paper with an average tensile strength of about 15 pounds per square inch (psi). You want to see what happens if you vary the concentration of the pulp.

In consultation with the process engineer, you decide on four concentrations: 5%, 10%, 15%, and 20%. You measure the tensile strength of six samples at each of the four concentrations. You want to test the null hypothesis that all four concentrations result in the same average tensile strength of the paper.

Examining the Data

As always, before you embark on any statistical analysis, you should look at the distribution of data values to make sure that there is nothing unusual. You can use the Explore procedure (see Chapter 9) to make a boxplot for each group.

From the plots in Figure 14.1, you see that the medians for the four groups differ. It appears that as the concentration increases, so does the tensile strength. The vertical length of the boxes, a measure of the spread or variability of the data values, also seems to differ for the concentrations, but not in any systematic fashion. There are no outlying or extreme values.

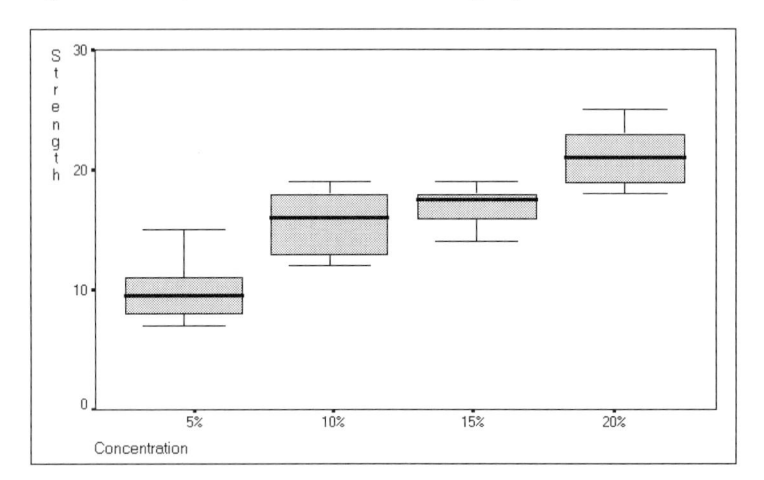

Figure 14.1 Boxplots for the four concentration groups

[Boxplot figure showing Strength vs Concentration (5%, 10%, 15%, 20%)]

Sample Means and Confidence Intervals

The sample mean for a group provides the single best guess for the unknown population value μ_i. However, it is unlikely that the value of the sample mean is exactly equal to the population value. Instead, it is probably not too different. Based on the sample mean, you can calculate a range of values that, with a designated likelihood, includes the population value. Such a range is called a **confidence interval**. For example, as shown in Figure 14.2, the 95% confidence interval for the average tensile strength for a concentration of 10% is 12.72 to 18.61. This means that if you repeated the experiment under the same conditions and with the same sample sizes in each group, and each time you calculated 95% confidence intervals, 95% of these intervals would contain the unknown population parameter value. Since the parameter value is not known, you don't know whether a particular interval contains the population value.

Figure 14.2 also shows descriptive statistics for the tensile strengths for the four concentrations. You see that as the concentration of hardwood increases, so does the mean strength. For a concentration of 5%, the average tensile strength is 10, while for a concentration of 20%, the average strength is 21.17. The group with a hardwood concentration of 15% has the smallest standard deviation. The others differ somewhat.

Figure 14.2 Sample means and confidence intervals for the four concentration groups

```
        Variable  STRENGTH
     By Variable  CONCENT

                              Standard    Standard
     Group    Count    Mean   Deviation   Error      Minimum    Maximum    95 Pct Conf Int for Mean

     5%         6    10.0000   2.8284    1.1547      7.0000    15.0000     7.0318  TO   12.9682
     10%        6    15.6667   2.8048    1.1450     12.0000    19.0000    12.7233  TO   18.6100
     15%        6    17.0000   1.7889     .7303     14.0000    19.0000    15.1227  TO   18.8773
     20%        6    21.1667   2.6394    1.0775     18.0000    25.0000    18.3968  TO   23.9366

     Total     24    15.9583   4.7226     .9640      7.0000    25.0000    13.9642  TO   17.9525
```

Testing the Null Hypothesis

The boxplots in Figure 14.1 and the means in Figure 14.2 suggest that the four concentrations result in different tensile strengths. Now you need to determine whether the observed differences in the four sample means can be attributed to just the natural variability among sample means from the same population or whether it's reasonable to believe that the four concentrations come from populations that have different means. You must determine the probability of seeing results as remote as the ones you've observed when, in fact, all population means are equal.

The statistical technique you'll use to test the null hypothesis that several population means are equal is called **analysis of variance** (abbreviated ANOVA). This technique examines the variability of the observations within each group as well as the variability between the group means. Based on these two estimates of variability, you draw conclusions about the population means.

SPSS for UNIX contains two different analysis-of-variance procedures: One-Way ANOVA and Simple Factorial ANOVA. This chapter discusses the One-Way ANOVA procedure. One-way analysis of variance is needed when only one variable is used to classify cases into different groups. In the example on the tensile strength of paper, cases are assigned to groups based on their values for one variable: hardwood concentration. When two or more variables are used to form the groups, the Simple Factorial ANOVA procedure is required (see Chapter 15).

Note that you can use the One-Way ANOVA procedure only when your groups are independent. If you observe the same person under several conditions, you cannot use this procedure. You need a special class of procedures called *repeated measures analysis of variance*, available in the SPSS Advanced Statistics option.

Assumptions Needed for Analysis of Variance

Analysis-of-variance procedures require the following assumptions:
- Each of the groups is an independent random sample from a normal population.
- In the population, the variances of the groups are equal.

One way to check these assumptions is to use the Explore procedure to make stem-and-leaf plots or histograms for each group and calculate the variances. You can also use formal statistical tests to check the assumptions of normality and equal variances. See Chapter 9 for more information on stem-and-leaf plots and tests for normality.

The Levene Test

To test the null hypothesis that the groups come from populations with the same variance, you can use the **Levene test** (shown in Figure 14.3), which can be obtained with the One-Way ANOVA procedure. If the observed significance level is small, you can reject the null hypothesis that all variances are equal. In this example, since the observed significance level (0.583) is large, you can't reject the null hypothesis. This means you don't have sufficient evidence to suspect that the variances are unequal, confirming what you saw in the plot.

Figure 14.3 Levene test

```
Levene Test for Homogeneity of Variances
   Statistic     df1     df2     2-tail Sig.
      .6651       3      20         .583
```

Analyzing the Variability

Now you're ready to perform the analysis-of-variance test. In analysis of variance, the observed variability in the sample is divided, or partitioned, into two parts: variability of the observations within a group (that is, the variability of the observations around their group mean) and the variability among the group means.

If the null hypothesis is true, the population means for the four groups are equal and the observed data can be considered to be four samples from the same population. In this case, you should be able to estimate how much the four sample means should vary. If your observed sample means vary more than you expect, you have evidence to reject the null hypothesis. The one-way analysis-of-variance table is shown in Figure 14.4.

Figure 14.4 One-way analysis-of-variance table

```
      Variable  STRENGTH
   By Variable  CONCENT

                        Analysis of Variance

                           Sum of       Mean            F       F
       Source      D.F.   Squares      Squares        Ratio   Prob.

Between Groups       3    382.7917    127.5972       19.6052  .0000
Within Groups       20    130.1667      6.5083
Total               23    512.9583
```

Between-Groups Variability

In Figure 14.4, the row labeled *Between Groups* contains an estimate of the variability of the observations based on the variability of the group means. To calculate the entry labeled *Sum of Squares,* start by subtracting the overall mean (the mean of all the observations) from each group mean (the overall and group means are listed in Figure 14.2). Then square each difference and multiply the square by the number of observations in its group. Finally, add the results together. For this example, the between-groups sum of squares is:

$$6 \times (10 - 15.96)^2 + 6 \times (15.67 - 15.96)^2 + 6 \times (17 - 15.96)^2$$
$$+ 6 \times (21.17 - 15.96)^2 = 382.79$$

Equation 14.1

The column labeled *D.F.* contains the degrees of freedom. To calculate the degrees of freedom for the between-groups sum of squares, subtract 1 from the number of groups. In this example, there are four concentrations, so there are three degrees of freedom.

To calculate the between-groups mean square, divide the between-groups sum of squares by its degrees of freedom:

$$\frac{382.79}{3} = 127.60$$

Equation 14.2

Within-Groups Variability

The row labeled *Within Groups* contains an estimate of the variability of the observations based on how much the observations vary from the group mean. The within-groups sum of squares is calculated by multiplying each of the group variances (the square of the standard deviation) by the number of cases in the group minus 1 and then adding up the results. In this example, the within-groups sum of squares is:

$$5 \times 8.0000 + 5 \times 7.8667 + 5 \times 3.2000 + 5 \times 6.9667 = 130.17$$

Equation 14.3

To calculate the degrees of freedom for the within-groups sums of squares, take the number of cases in all groups combined and subtract the number of groups. In this example, there are 24 cases and 4 groups, so there are 20 degrees of freedom. The mean square is then calculated by dividing the sum of squares by the degrees of freedom:

$$\frac{130.17}{20} = 6.51 \qquad \text{Equation 14.4}$$

Calculating the F Ratio

You now have two estimates of the variability in the population: the within-groups mean square and the between-groups mean square. The within-groups mean square is based on how much the observations within each group vary. The between-groups mean square is based on how much the group means vary among themselves. If the null hypothesis is true, the two numbers should be close to each other. If you divide one by the other, the ratio should be close to 1.

The statistical test for the null hypothesis that all groups have the same mean in the population is based on this ratio, called an F statistic. You take the between-groups mean square and divide it by the within-groups mean square. For this example,

$$F = \frac{127.6}{6.51} = 19.6 \qquad \text{Equation 14.5}$$

This number appears in Figure 14.4 in the column labeled F *Ratio*. It certainly doesn't appear to be close to 1. Now you need to obtain the observed significance level. You obtain the observed significance level by comparing the calculated F value to the **F distribution** (the distribution of the F statistic when the null hypothesis is true). The significance level is based on both the actual F value and the degrees of freedom for the two mean squares. In this example, the observed significance level is less than 0.00005, so you can reject the null hypothesis that the four concentrations of pulp result in paper with the same average tensile strength.

Multiple Comparison Procedures

A significant F value tells you only that the population means are probably not all equal. It doesn't tell you which pairs of groups appear to have different means. You reject the null hypothesis that all population means are equal if *any two* means are unequal. You need to use special tests called **multiple comparison procedures** to determine which means are significantly different from each other.

You might wonder why you can't just compare all possible pairs of means using a *t* test. The reason is that when you make many comparisons involving the same means, the probability that one comparison will turn out to be statistically significant increases.

For example, if you have 5 groups and compare all pairs of means, you're making 10 comparisons. When the null hypothesis is true, the probability that at least one of the 10 observed significance levels will be less than 0.05 is about 0.29. The more comparisons you make, the more likely it is that you'll find one or more pairs to be statistically different, even if all population means are equal.

By adjusting for the number of comparisons you're making, multiple comparison procedures protect you from calling too many differences significant. The more comparisons you make, the larger the difference between pairs of means must be for a multiple comparison procedure to find it significant. When you use a multiple comparison procedure, you can be more confident that you are finding true differences.

Many multiple comparison procedures are available. They differ in how they adjust the observed significance level. One of the simplest is the **Bonferroni test**. It adjusts the observed significance level based on the number of comparisons you are making. For example, if you are making 5 comparisons, the observed significance level for the original comparison must be less than 0.05/5, or 0.01, for the difference to be significant at the 0.05 significance level. For further discussion of multiple comparison techniques, see Winer et al. (1991).

Figure 14.5 shows a portion of the Bonferroni test results obtained with the One-Way ANOVA procedure. At the bottom, you see a table that orders the group means from smallest to largest in both the rows and columns. (In this example, the order happens to be the same as the order of the group code numbers.) An asterisk marks a pair of means that are different at the 0.05 level after the Bonferroni correction is made. Differences are marked only once, in the lower diagonal of the table. If the significance level is greater than 0.05, the space is left blank.

Figure 14.5 Bonferroni multiple comparisons

```
     Variable  STRENGTH
  By Variable  CONCENT

Multiple Range Tests:  Modified LSD (Bonferroni) test with significance
                       level .05

The difference between two means is significant if
MEAN(J)-MEAN(I)  >= 1.8039 * RANGE * SQRT(1/N(I) + 1/N(J))
with the following value(s) for RANGE: 4.14

  (*) Indicates significant differences which are shown in the lower triangle

                              1 1 2
                            5 0 5 0
                            % % % %
       Mean       CONCENT

      10.0000      5%
      15.6667     10%       *
      17.0000     15%       *
      21.1667     20%       * *
```

In this example, the asterisks in the first column indicate that the mean of the 5% hardwood concentration group is significantly different from that of every other group. In the second column, the 10% group is different from the 20% group, but not from the

15% group. There are no asterisks in the third column. Thus, you see that all pairs of means are significantly different from each other except for the 10% and 15% groups.

The formula above the table indicates how large an observed difference must be for the multiple comparison procedure to call it significant. If no pairs are found to be significantly different, the table is omitted and a message is printed.

When the sample sizes in all of the groups are the same, you can also use the output of homogeneous subsets to identify subsets of means that are not different from each other. Figure 14.6 shows the homogeneous subsets output.

Figure 14.6 Homogeneous subsets

```
Subset 1

Group       5%

Mean       10.0000
- - - - - - - - -

Subset 2

Group       10%         15%

Mean       15.6667     17.0000
- - - - - - - - - - - - - - -

Subset 3

Group       15%         20%

Mean       17.0000     21.1667
- - - - - - - - - - - - - - - - -
```

Groups that appear in the same subset are not significantly different from each other. In this example, the 10% and 15% hardwood concentration groups are in the same subset, as are the 15% and 20% groups. The 5% group is in a subset of its own, since its mean is significantly different from all of the other means.

How to Obtain One-Way Analysis of Variance

The One-Way ANOVA procedure produces a one-way analysis of variance for an interval-level dependent variable by a single factor (independent) variable. You can test for trends across categories, specify contrasts, and use a variety of range tests.

The minimum specifications are:
- One numeric dependent variable. The variable is assumed to be measured on an interval scale.
- One numeric factor variable. Factor variable values should be integers.
- A defined range for the factor variable.

To obtain one-way analysis of variance, from the menus choose:

Statistics
 Compare Means ▶
  One-Way ANOVA...

This opens the One-Way ANOVA dialog box, as shown in Figure 14.7.

Figure 14.7 One-Way ANOVA dialog box

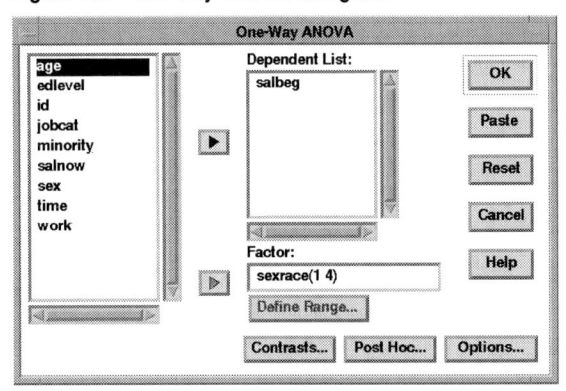

The numeric variables in your data file are displayed on the source variable list. Select your dependent variable(s) and a single factor (independent) variable. After defining a range for the factor variable (see "One-Way ANOVA Define Range," below), click on OK to obtain the default one-way analysis-of-variance table containing the F ratio, F probability, and sum of squares and mean squares for between groups and within groups. (See Figure 14.2.) A separate analysis-of-variance table is generated for each dependent variable.

One-Way ANOVA Define Range

A value range is required for the factor (independent) variable. To define the range, click on Define Range... in the One-Way ANOVA dialog box. This opens the One-Way ANOVA Define Range dialog box, as shown in Figure 14.8.

Figure 14.8 One-Way ANOVA Define Range dialog box

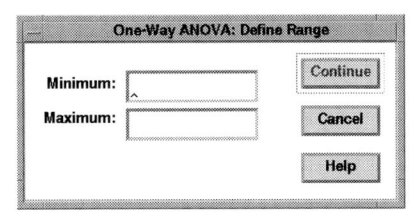

The minimum and maximum values must be integers. If any of the intervening values are non-integers, they are truncated in the analysis. Any empty categories are deleted from the analysis. If there are more than 50 categories of the factor variable, multiple comparison tests are not available.

One-Way ANOVA Contrasts

To partition the between-groups sum of squares into trend components or specify *a priori* contrasts, click on Contrasts... in the One-Way ANOVA dialog box. This opens the One-Way ANOVA Contrasts dialog box, as shown in Figure 14.9.

Figure 14.9 One-Way ANOVA Contrasts dialog box

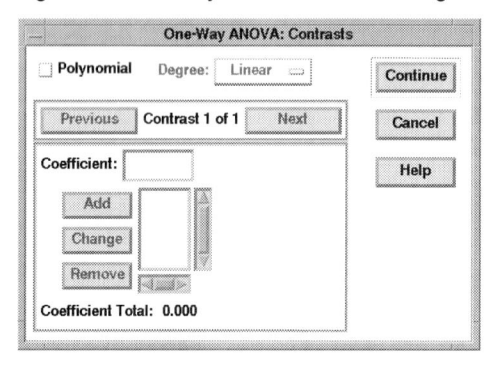

❏ **Polynomial.** Partitions the between-groups sum of squares into trend components. When you choose this option with balanced designs, SPSS computes the sum of squares for each order polynomial from weighted polynomial contrasts, using the group code as the metric. These contrasts are orthogonal; hence, the sum of squares for each order polynomial is statistically independent. If the design is unbalanced and there is equal spacing between groups, SPSS also computes sums of squares using the unweighted polynomial contrasts, which are not orthogonal. The deviation sums of squares are always calculated from the weighted sums of squares (Speed, 1976).

▭ **Degree.** You can choose one of the following alternatives for the polynomial degree:

Linear. 1st-degree polynomial.

Quadratic. 2nd-degree polynomial.

Cubic. 3rd-degree polynomial.

4th. 4th-degree polynomial.

5th. 5th-degree polynomial.

Coefficient. User-specified *a priori* contrasts to be tested by the t statistic. Enter a coefficient value for each group (category) of the factor variable and click on Add after each entry. Each new value is added at the bottom of the coefficient list. To change a value on the list, highlight it, enter the new value in the text box, and click on Change. To remove a value, highlight it and click on Remove. To specify additional sets of contrasts, click on Next. You can specify up to 10 sets of contrasts and up to 50 coefficients for each set. Use Next and Previous to move between sets of contrasts.

The sequential order of the coefficients is important because it corresponds to the ascending order of the category values of the factor variable. The first coefficient on the list corresponds to the lowest group value of the factor variable, and the last coefficient corresponds to the highest value. For example, if there are six categories of the factor variable, the coefficient list $-1, -1, -1, -1, 2, 2$ contrasts the combination of the first four groups with the combination of the last two groups.

You can also specify fractional coefficients and exclude groups by assigning a coefficient of 0. For example, the coefficient list $-1, 0, 0, 0, 0.5, 0.5$ contrasts the first group with the combination of the fifth and sixth groups.

For most applications, the coefficients should sum to 0. Sets that do not sum to 0 can also be used, but a warning message is displayed.

Output for each contrast list includes the value of the contrast, the standard error of the contrast, the t statistic, the degrees of freedom for t, and the two-tailed probability of t. Both pooled- and separate-variance estimates are displayed.

One-Way ANOVA Post Hoc Multiple Comparisons

To produce post hoc multiple comparison tests, click on Post Hoc... in the One-Way ANOVA dialog box. This opens the One-Way ANOVA Post Hoc Multiple Comparisons dialog box, as shown in Figure 14.10.

Figure 14.10 One-Way ANOVA Post Hoc Multiple Comparisons dialog box

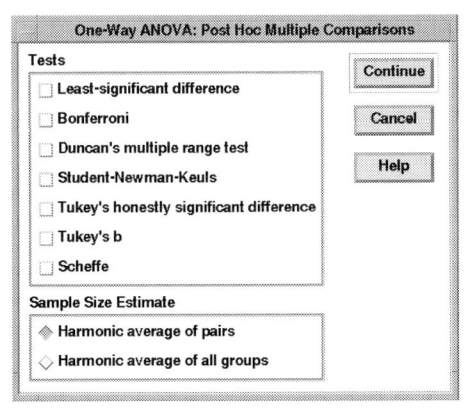

Tests. These tests always produce multiple comparisons between all groups. Non-empty group means are sorted by ascending order. Asterisks in the matrix indicate significantly different group means at an alpha level of 0.05. In addition to this output, homogeneous subsets are calculated for balanced designs if you also choose Harmonic average of all groups. You can choose one or more of the following tests:

- **Least significant difference.** This is equivalent to doing multiple t tests between all pairs of groups. No "multiple comparisons" protection is provided.
- **Bonferroni.** The Bonferroni test is a modified least-significant-difference test.
- **Duncan's multiple range test.**
- **Student-Newman-Keuls.**
- **Tukey's honestly significant difference.**
- **Tukey's b.** Tukey's alternate procedure.
- **Scheffé.** This test is conservative for pairwise comparisons of means and requires larger differences between means for significance than the other multiple comparison tests.

Sample Size Estimate. You can choose one of the following alternatives:

- **Harmonic average of pairs.** If the sample sizes are not equal in all groups, a separate harmonic mean is computed for each pair of groups being compared. This is the default.
- **Harmonic average of all groups.** If the sample sizes are not equal in all groups, a single harmonic mean is computed for all groups. If you choose this alternative, homogeneous subsets are calculated for all multiple comparison tests.

One-Way ANOVA Options

To obtain additional statistics, change the treatment of missing values, or use value labels to identify groups in output, click on Options... in the One-Way ANOVA dialog box. This opens the One-Way ANOVA Options dialog box, as shown in Figure 14.11.

Figure 14.11 One-Way ANOVA Options dialog box

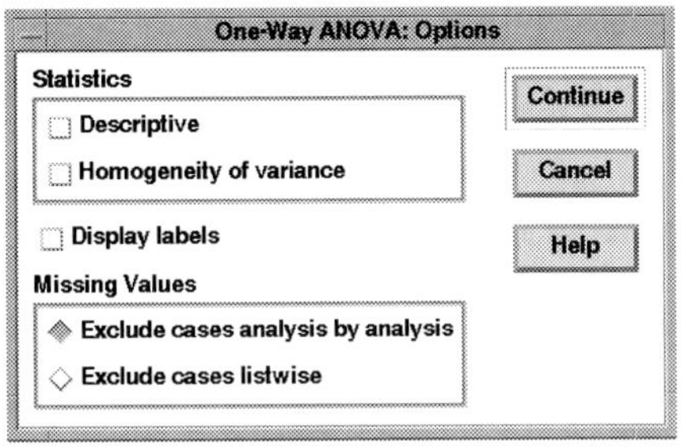

Statistics. You can choose one or more of the following:

- **Descriptive.** Calculates the number of cases, mean, standard deviation, standard error, minimum, maximum, and 95% confidence interval for each dependent variable for each group.
- **Homogeneity of variance.** Calculates the Levene statistic.

Missing Values. You can choose one of the following alternatives:

- **Exclude cases analysis by analysis.** A case with a missing value for either the dependent variable or factor variable for a given analysis is not used in that analysis. Also, a case outside the range specified for the factor variable is not used. This is the default.
- **Exclude cases listwise.** Cases with missing values for the factor variable or for *any* dependent variable included on the dependent list in the main dialog box are excluded from all analyses. If you have not specified multiple dependent variables, this has no effect.

The following labeling option is also available:

- **Display labels.** Uses the first eight characters from the value labels of the factor variable for group labels. By default, groups are labeled *GRP1*, *GRP2*, *GRP3*, etc., where the number indicates the value of the factor variable.

Additional Features Available with Command Syntax

You can customize your one-way analysis of variance if you paste your dialog box selections into a syntax window and edit the resulting ONEWAY command syntax (see Chapter 4). Additional features include:

- Fixed- and random-effects statistics. Standard deviation, standard error, and 95% confidence intervals for the fixed-effects model. Standard error, 95% confidence intervals, and estimate of between-component variance for the random-effects model (using STATISTICS=EFFECTS).
- User-specified alpha levels for the least significant difference, Bonferroni, Duncan, and Scheffé multiple-comparison tests (with the RANGES subcommand).
- Matrix facility to write a matrix of means, standard deviations, and frequencies or to read a matrix of means, frequencies, pooled variances, and degrees of freedom for the pooled variances. These matrixes can be used in place of raw data to obtain a one-way analysis of variance (with the MATRIX subcommand).

See Appendix A for command syntax rules. See the *SPSS Base System Syntax Reference Guide* for complete ONEWAY command syntax.

15 Analysis of Variance

Despite constitutional guarantees, any mirror will testify that all citizens are not created equal. The consequences of this inequity are pervasive. Physically attractive individuals are generally perceived as more desirable social partners, more persuasive communicators, and more likeable and competent. Even cute children and attractive burglars are disciplined more leniently than their homely counterparts (Sigall & Ostrove, 1975).

Much research on physical attractiveness focuses on its impact on heterosexual relationships and evaluations. Its effect on same-sex evaluations has received less attention. Anderson and Nida (1978) examined the influence of attractiveness on the evaluation of writing samples by college students. In the study, 144 male and 144 female students were asked to appraise essays purportedly written by college freshmen. As supplemental information, a slide of the "author" was projected during the evaluation. Half of the slides were of authors of the same sex as the rater; the other half were of authors of the opposite sex. Each author had previously been determined to be of high, medium, or low attractiveness. Each rater evaluated one essay for creativity, ideas, and style. The three scales were combined to form a composite measure of performance.

Descriptive Statistics

Figure 15.1 contains average composite scores for the essays, subdivided by the three categories of physical attractiveness and the two categories of sex similarity. The table is similar to the summary table shown for the one-way analysis of variance in Chapter 14. The difference here is that there are two independent (or grouping) variables: attractiveness and sex similarity. The first mean displayed (25.11) is for the entire sample. The number of cases (288) is shown in parentheses. Then, for each of the independent variables, mean scores are displayed for each of the categories. The attractiveness categories are ordered from low (coded 1) to high (coded 3). Evaluations in which the rater and author are of the same sex are coded as 1, while opposite-sex evaluations are coded as 2. The possible combinations of the values of the two variables result in six cells. Finally, a table of means is displayed for cases classified by both grouping variables. Attractiveness is the row variable, and sex is the column variable. Each mean is based on the responses of 48 subjects.

Figure 15.1 Table of group means

```
                    * * *  C E L L   M E A N S  * * *

                    SCORE         COMPOSITE SCORE
                 BY ATTRACT       ATTRACTIVENESS LEVEL
                    SEX           SEX SIMILARITY

TOTAL POPULATION

       25.11
   (   288)

ATTRACT
         1            2            3

       22.98        25.78        26.59
   (    96)    (    96)    (    96)

SEX
         1            2

       25.52        24.71
   (   144)    (   144)


              SEX
                1            2
ATTRACT
         1    22.79        23.17
          (    48)    (    48)

         2    28.63        22.92
          (    48)    (    48)

         3    25.13        28.04
          (    48)    (    48)
```

The overall average score is 25.11. Highly attractive individuals received the highest average score (26.59), while those rated low in physical appeal had the lowest score (22.98). There doesn't appear to be much difference between the average scores (across attractiveness levels) assigned by same-sex (25.52) and opposite-sex (24.71) evaluators. However, highly attractive individuals received an average rating of 25.13 when evaluated by people of the same sex and 28.04 when evaluated by people of the opposite sex.

Analysis of Variance

Three questions are of interest in the study: Does attractiveness relate to the composite scores? Does sex similarity relate to the scores? Is there an interaction between the effects of attractiveness and sex? The statistical technique used to evaluate these questions is an extension of the one-way analysis of variance outlined in Chapter 14. The same assumptions are needed for correct application; that is, the observations should be independently selected from normal populations with equal variances. Again, discussion here is limited to instances in which both grouping variables are considered **fixed**; that is, they constitute the populations of interest.

The total observed variation in the scores is subdivided into four components: the sums of squares due to attractiveness, sex, their interaction, and the residual. This can be expressed as:

Total SS = Attractiveness SS + Sex SS
+ Interaction SS + Residual SS

Equation 15.1

Figure 15.2 is the analysis-of-variance table for this study. The first column lists the sources of variation. The sums of squares attributable to each of the components are given in the second column. The sums of squares for each independent variable alone are sometimes termed the **main effect** sums of squares. The **explained** sum of squares is the total sum of squares for the main effect and interaction terms in the model.

The degrees of freedom for sex and attractiveness, listed in the third column, are one fewer than the number of categories. For example, since there are three levels of attractiveness, there are two degrees of freedom. Similarly, sex has one degree of freedom. Two degrees of freedom are associated with the interaction term (the product of the degrees of freedom of each of the individual variables). The degrees of freedom for the residual are $N - 1 - k$, where k equals the degrees of freedom for the explained sum of squares.

Figure 15.2 Analysis-of-variance table

```
            * * *  A N A L Y S I S    O F   V A R I A N C E  * * *
            SCORE     COMPOSITE SCORE
      by    ATTRACT   ATTRACTIVENESS LEVEL
            SEX       SEX SIMILARITY

                              Sum of              Mean                Sig
Source of Variation           Squares     DF     Square        F    of F

Main Effects                  733.700      3    244.567    3.276    .022
    ATTRACT                   686.850      2    343.425    4.600    .011
    SEX                        46.850      1     46.850    0.628    .429

2-Way Interactions            942.350      2    471.175    6.311    .002
    ATTRACT   SEX             942.350      2    471.175    6.311    .002

Explained                    1676.050      5    355.210    4.490    .000

Residual                    21053.140    282     74.656

Total                       22729.190    287     79.196
```

The mean squares shown in the fourth column in Figure 15.2 are obtained by dividing each sum of squares by its degrees of freedom. Hypothesis tests are based on the ratios of the mean squares of each source of variation to the mean square for the residual. When the assumptions are met and the true means are in fact equal, the distribution of the ratio is an F with the degrees of freedom for the numerator and denominator terms.

Testing for Interaction

The *F* value associated with the attractiveness and sex interaction is 6.311, as shown in Figure 15.2. The observed significance level is approximately 0.002. Therefore, it appears that there is an interaction between the two variables. What does this mean?

Consider Figure 15.3, which is a plot of the cell, or group, means in Figure 15.1. Notice how the mean scores relate not only to the attractiveness of the individual and to the sex of the rater, but also to the particular combination of the values of the variables. Opposite-sex raters assign the highest scores to highly attractive individuals. Same-sex raters assign the highest scores to individuals of medium attractiveness. Thus, the ratings for each level of attractiveness depend on the sex variable. If there were no interaction between the two variables, a plot similar to the one shown in Figure 15.4 might result, in which the difference between the two types of raters is the same for the three levels of attractiveness.

Figure 15.3 Cell means

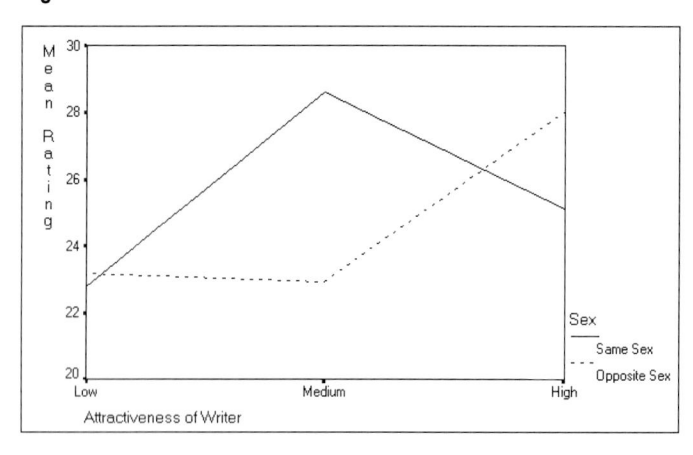

Figure 15.4 Cell means with no interaction

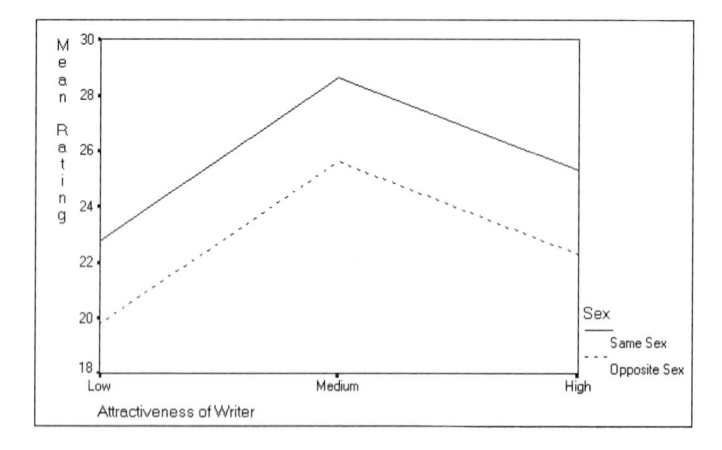

Tests for Sex and Attractiveness

Once the presence of interaction has been established, it is not particularly useful to continue hypothesis testing, since the two variables *jointly* affect the dependent variable. If there is no significant interaction, the grouping variables can be tested individually. The F value associated with attractiveness would provide a test of the hypothesis that attractiveness does not affect the rating. Similarly, the F value associated with sex would test the hypothesis that sex has no main effect on evaluation.

Note that the small F value associated with sex does not indicate that response is unaffected by sex, since sex is included in the significant interaction term. Instead, it shows that when response is averaged over attractiveness levels, the two sex-category means are not significantly different.

Explanations

Several explanations are consistent with the results of this study. Since people generally identify with individuals most like themselves, and since most people consider themselves moderately attractive, the highest degree of identification should be with same-sex individuals of moderate attractiveness. The higher empathy may result in the higher scores. An alternate theory is that moderately attractive individuals are generally perceived as more desirable same-sex friends; they have more favorable personality profiles and don't encourage unfavorable comparisons. Their writing scores may benefit from their perceived popularity.

Although we may not want friends who outshine us, attractive dates can reflect favorably on us and enhance our status. Physical beauty is generally advantageous for heterosexual relationships but may not be for same-sex friendships. This prejudice may affect all evaluations of highly attractive members of the opposite sex.

Extensions

Analysis-of-variance techniques can be used with any number of grouping variables. For example, the data in Figure 15.1 originated from a more complicated experiment than described here. There were four factors—essay quality, physical attractiveness, sex of writer, and sex of subject. The original data were analyzed with a $3 \times 3 \times 2 \times 2$ ANOVA table. (The numbers indicate how many categories each grouping variable has.) The conclusions from our simplified analysis are the same as those from the more elaborate analysis.

Each of the cells in our experiment had the same number of subjects. This greatly simplifies the analysis and its interpretation. When unequal sample sizes occur in the cells, the total sum of squares cannot be partitioned into nice components that sum to the total. Various techniques are available for calculating sums of squares in such **nonorthogonal designs**. The methods differ in the way they adjust the sums of squares to account for other effects in the model. Each method results in different sums of squares and tests different hypotheses. However, when all cell frequencies are equal, the methods yield the same results. For discussion of various procedures for analyzing designs with unequal cell frequencies, see Kleinbaum and Kupper (1978) and Overall and Klett (1972).

How to Obtain a Simple Factorial Analysis of Variance

The Simple Factorial ANOVA procedure tests the hypothesis that the group, or cell, means of the dependent variable are equal.

The minimum specifications are:
- One or more interval-level dependent variables.
- One or more categorical factor variables.
- Minimum and maximum group values for each factor variable.

To obtain a simple factorial ANOVA and optional statistics, from the menus choose:

Statistics
　ANOVA Models ▶
　　Simple Factorial...

This opens the Simple Factorial ANOVA dialog box, as shown in Figure 15.5.

Figure 15.5 Simple Factorial ANOVA dialog box

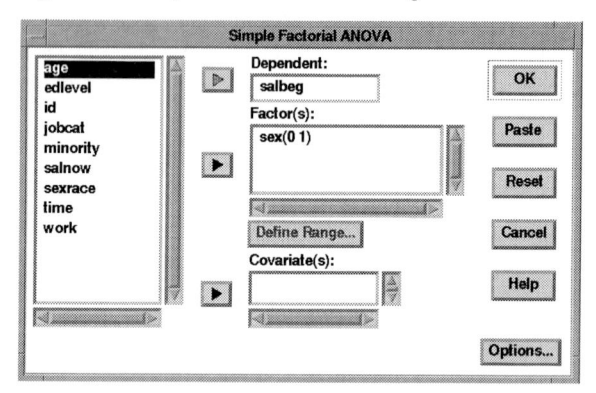

The numeric variables in your data file appear on the source list. Select an interval-level dependent variable. Choose one or more categorical variables, or factors, which split your file into two or more groups. After defining the range of the factor variable(s), click on OK to get the default analysis of variance using unique sums of squares. Cases with missing values for any variable are excluded from the analysis.

If there are five or fewer factors, the default model is **full factorial**, meaning that all factor-by-factor interaction terms are included. If you specify more than five factors, only interaction terms up to order five are included.

Optionally, you can select one or more continuous explanatory variables, or covariates, for the analysis.

Simple Factorial ANOVA Define Range

You must indicate the range of categories for each factor variable. To define categories, highlight a variable or group of variables on the Factor(s) list and click on Define Range... in the Simple Factorial ANOVA dialog box. This opens the Simple Factorial ANOVA Define Range dialog box, as shown in Figure 15.6.

Figure 15.6 Simple Factorial ANOVA Define Range dialog box

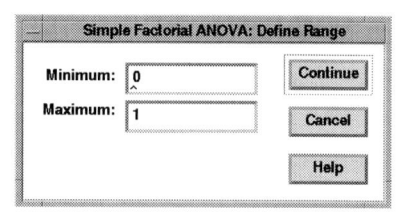

Enter values for minimum and maximum that correspond to the lowest and highest categories of the factor variable. Both values must be positive integers, and the minimum value you specify must be less than the maximum value. Cases with values outside the bounds are excluded. For example, if you specify a minimum value of 0 and a maximum value of 3, only the values 0, 1, 2, and 3 are used.

Repeat this process for each factor variable.

Simple Factorial ANOVA Options

To choose an alternate method for decomposing sums of squares, control the order of entry of covariates, obtain summary statistics, or suppress interaction terms, click on Options... in the Simple Factorial ANOVA dialog box. This opens the Simple Factorial ANOVA Options dialog box, as shown in Figure 15.7.

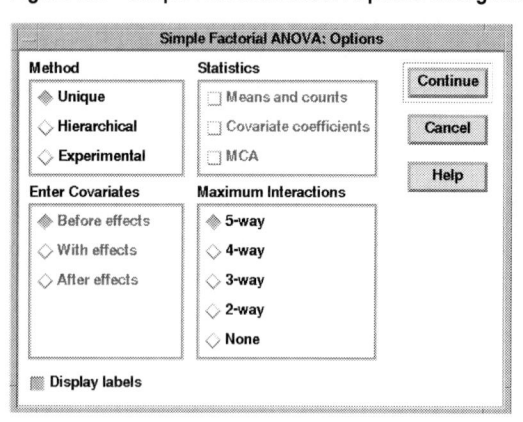

Figure 15.7 Simple Factorial ANOVA Options dialog box

Method. Method selection controls how the effects are assessed. You can choose one of the following alternatives:

◇ **Unique.** All effects are assessed simultaneously for their contribution. That is, each effect is adjusted for all other covariates, main effects, and interaction terms in the model. This is the default.

◇ **Hierarchical.** Factor main effects and covariate effects are assessed hierarchically. If the default treatment of covariates is in effect, covariates are adjusted only for covariates that precede them on the covariate list. Main effects are adjusted for all covariates and for factors that precede them on the factor list. Interactions are not processed hierarchically; they are adjusted for all covariates, factors, and other interactions of the same and lower orders, just as in the experimental approach. Thus, the hierarchical method differs from the experimental method only in the treatment of covariates and main effects.

◇ **Experimental.** If the default treatment of covariates (covariates entered before main effects) is in effect, effects are assessed in the following order: covariates, main effects, two-way interactions, three-way interactions, four-way interactions, and five-way interactions. This means that covariates are not adjusted for any other terms in the model except for other covariates; main effects are adjusted only for covariates and other main effects; and interactions are adjusted for all interactions of the same and lower order, as well as for all main effects and covariates. The effects within each type are adjusted for all other effects of that type and also for the effects of prior types. For example, all two-way interactions are adjusted for other two-way interactions and for all main effects and covariates.

Enter Covariates. Operation of the experimental and hierarchical methods depends on the order of entry of any covariates. If you want to select a covariate entry alternative, there must be at least one covariate on the covariate list. In addition, the experimental or hierarchical method must be specified (with the unique method, covariates are always entered concurrently with all other effects). You can choose one of the following alternatives:

- ◇ **Before effects.** Processes covariates before main effects for factors. This is the default.
- ◇ **With effects.** Processes covariates concurrently with main effects for factors.
- ◇ **After effects.** Processes covariates after main effects for factors.

For example, if the experimental method is selected but you choose After effects, main effects are entered first and adjusted only for other main effects, and covariates are entered after the main effects and adjusted for other covariates and main effects. If, instead, you select the experimental method and With effects, covariates are entered together with main effects. This means that all covariates and main effects are adjusted for each other.

Statistics. You can choose one or more of the following:

- ❑ **Means and counts.** Requests means and counts for each dependent variable for groups defined for each factor and each combination of factors up to the fifth level. Means and counts are not available if you select unique sums of squares.
- ❑ **Covariate coefficients.** Unstandardized regression coefficients for the covariate(s). The coefficients are computed at the point where the covariates are entered into the model. Thus, their values depend on the method you specify. If you want covariate coefficients, there must be at least one covariate on the covariate list.
- ❑ **MCA.** Multiple classification analysis. In the MCA table, effects are expressed as deviations from the grand mean. The table includes a listing of unadjusted category effects for each factor, category effects adjusted for other factors, category effects adjusted for all factors and covariates, and eta and beta values. The MCA table is not available if you specify unique sums of squares.

Maximum Interactions. You can control the effects of various orders of interactions. Any interaction effects that are not computed are pooled into the residual sums of squares. You can choose one of the following alternatives:

- ◇ **5-way.** Displays all interaction terms up to and including the fifth order. This is the default.
- ◇ **4-way.** Displays all interaction effects up to and including the fourth order.
- ◇ **3-way.** Displays all two- and three-way interaction effects.
- ◇ **2-way.** Displays two-way interaction effects.

◇ **None.** Deletes all interaction terms from the model. Only main effects and covariate effects appear in the ANOVA table.

You can also choose the following display option:

❑ **Display labels.** Displays any value and variable labels in the output. This is the default. To suppress labels, deselect this item.

Additional Features Available with Command Syntax

You can customize your analysis of variance if you paste your dialog box selections into a syntax window and edit the resulting ANOVA command syntax (see Chapter 4). An additional feature is the ability to specify more than one dependent variable. See Appendix A for command syntax rules. See the *SPSS Base System Syntax Reference Guide* for complete ANOVA command syntax.

16 Measuring Linear Association

Youthful lemonade-stand entrepreneurs as well as executives of billion-dollar corporations share a common concern—how to increase sales. Hand-lettered signs affixed to neighborhood trees, television campaigns, siblings and friends canvassing local playgrounds, and international sales forces are known to be effective marketing tactics. However, it can be difficult to measure the effectiveness of specific marketing techniques when they are part of an overall marketing strategy, so businesses routinely conduct market research to determine exactly what makes their products sell.

Churchill (1979) describes a study undertaken by the manufacturer of Click ballpoint pens to determine the effectiveness of the firm's marketing efforts. A random sample of 40 sales territories is selected, and sales, amount of advertising, and number of sales representatives are recorded. This chapter looks at the relationship between sales and these variables.

Examining Relationships

A scatterplot can reveal various types of associations between two variables. Some commonly encountered patterns are illustrated in Figure 16.1. In the first example, there appears to be no discernible relationship between the two variables. In the second example, the variables are related exponentially; that is, Y increases very rapidly for increasing values of X. In the third example, the relationship between the two variables is U-shaped. Small and large values of the X variable are associated with large values of the Y variable.

Figure 16.1 Scatterplots showing common relationships

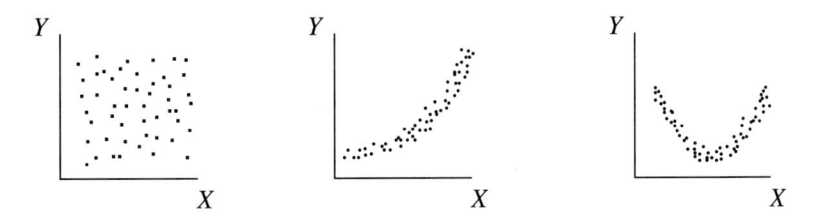

Figure 16.2 is a scatterplot showing the amount of sales and the number of television spots in each of 40 territories from the study. From the figure, it appears there is a positive association between sales and advertising. That is, as the amount of advertising increases, so does the number of sales. The relationship between sales and advertising may be termed **linear**, since the observed points cluster more or less around a straight line.

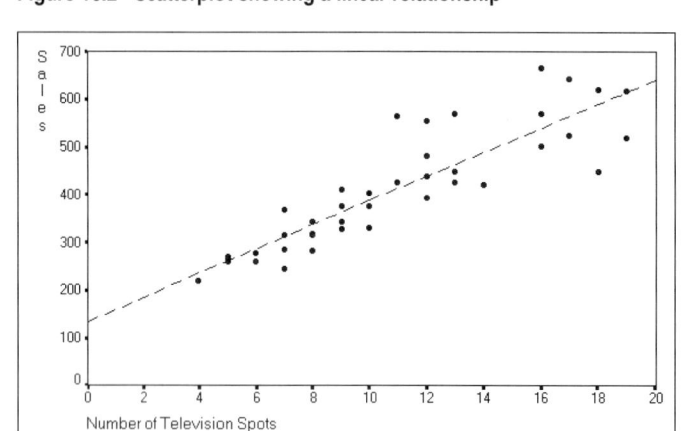

Figure 16.2 Scatterplot showing a linear relationship

The Correlation Coefficient

Although a scatterplot is an essential first step in studying the association between two variables, it is often useful to quantify the strength of the association by calculating a summary index. One commonly used measure is the **Pearson correlation coefficient**, denoted by r. It is defined as

$$r = \frac{\sum_{i=1}^{N} (X_i - \bar{X})(Y_i - \bar{Y})}{(N-1) S_X S_Y}$$

Equation 16.1

where N is the number of cases and S_X and S_Y are the standard deviations of the two variables. The absolute value of r indicates the strength of the linear relationship. The largest possible absolute value is 1, which occurs when all points fall exactly on the line. When the line has a positive slope, the value of r is positive, and when the slope of the line is negative, the value of r is negative (see Figure 16.3).

Figure 16.3 Scatterplots with correlation coefficients of +1 and −1

A value of 0 indicates no *linear* relationship. Two variables can have a strong association but a small correlation coefficient if the relationship is not linear. Figure 16.4 shows two plots with correlation coefficients of 0.

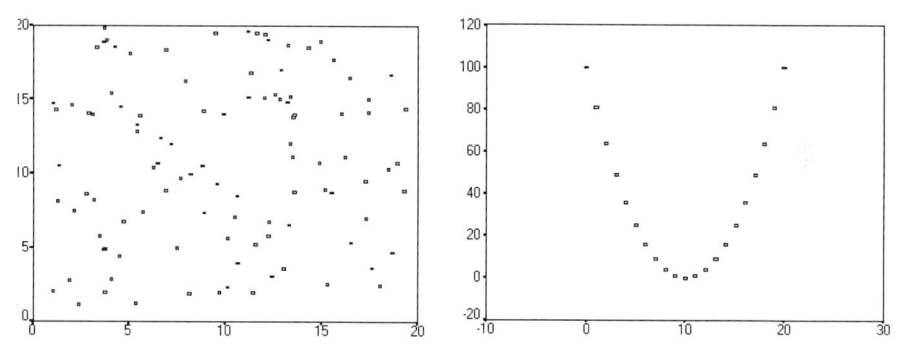

Figure 16.4 Scatterplots with correlation coefficients of 0

It is important to examine correlation coefficients together with scatterplots, since the same coefficient can result from very different underlying relationships. The variables plotted in Figure 16.5 have a correlation coefficient greater than 0.8, as do the variables plotted in Figure 16.2. But note how different the relationships are between the two sets of variables. In Figure 16.5, there is a strong positive linear association for only part of the graph. The relationship between the two variables is basically nonlinear. The scatterplot in Figure 16.2 is very different. The points cluster more or less around a line. Thus, the correlation coefficient should be used only to summarize the strength of linear association.

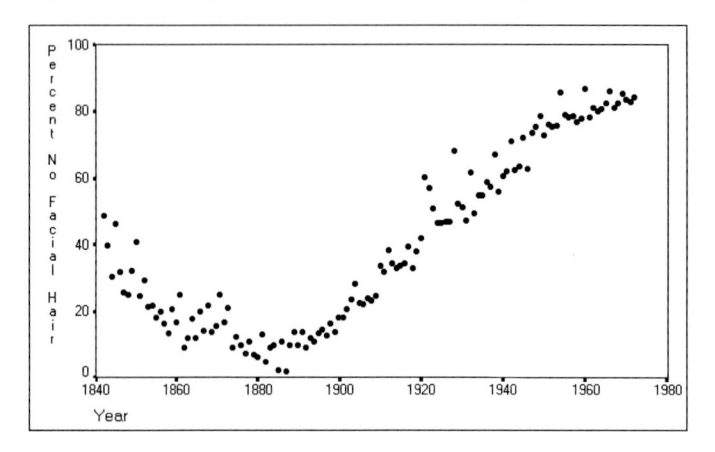

Figure 16.5 Scatterplot showing nonlinear relationship

Some Properties of the Correlation Coefficient

A common mistake in interpreting the correlation coefficient is to assume that correlation implies causation. No such conclusion is automatic. While sales are highly correlated with advertising, they are also highly correlated with other variables, such as the number of sales representatives in a territory. Advertising alone does not necessarily result in increased sales. For example, territories with high sales may simply have more money to spend on TV spots, regardless of whether the spots are effective.

The correlation coefficient is a **symmetric measure**, since interchanging the two variables X and Y in the formula does not change the results. The correlation coefficient is not expressed in any units of measure, and it is not affected by linear transformations such as adding or subtracting constants or multiplying or dividing all values of a variable by a constant.

Calculating Correlation Coefficients

Figure 16.6 is a table of correlation coefficients for the number of television spots, number of sales representatives, and amount of sales. The entry in each cell is the correlation coefficient. For example, the correlation coefficient between advertising and sales is 0.8802. This value indicates that there is a fairly strong linear association between the two variables, as shown in Figure 16.2. The table is symmetric, since the correlation between X and Y is the same as the correlation between Y and X. The correlation values on the diagonal are all 1, since a variable is perfectly related to itself.

Figure 16.6 Correlation coefficients

```
       - - Correlation Coefficients - -

              ADVERTIS     REPS         SALES

ADVERTIS      1.0000       .7763**      .8802**
REPS           .7763**    1.0000        .8818**
SALES          .8802**     .8818**     1.0000

 * - Signif. LE .05     ** - Signif. LE .01    (2-tailed)

 " . " is printed if a coefficient cannot be computed
```

Hypothesis Tests about the Correlation Coefficient

Although the correlation coefficient is sometimes used only as a summary index to describe the observed strength of the association, in some situations description and summary are but a first step. The primary goal may be to test hypotheses about the unknown population correlation coefficient—denoted as ρ—based on its estimate, the sample correlation coefficient r. In order to test such hypotheses, certain assumptions must be made about the underlying joint distribution of the two variables. A common assumption is that independent random samples are taken from a distribution in which the two variables together are distributed normally. If this condition is satisfied, the test that the population coefficient is 0 can be based on the statistic

$$t = r\sqrt{\frac{N-2}{1-r^2}}$$

Equation 16.2

which, if ρ = 0, has a Student's t distribution with $N-2$ degrees of freedom. Either one- or two-tailed tests can be calculated. If nothing is known in advance, a two-tailed test is appropriate. That is, the hypothesis that the coefficient is zero is rejected for both extreme positive and extreme negative values of t. If the direction of the association can be specified in advance, the hypothesis is rejected only for t values that are of sufficient magnitude and in the direction specified.

In SPSS, you can request that coefficients with two-tailed observed significance levels less than 0.05 be identified with a single asterisk and those with two-tailed significance levels less than 0.01 be identified with two asterisks. From Figure 16.6, the probability is less than 0.01 that a correlation coefficient of at least 0.88 in absolute value is obtained when there is no linear association in the population between sales and advertising. Care should be exercised when examining the significance levels for large tables. Even if there is no association between the variables, if many coefficients are computed, some would be expected to be statistically significant by chance alone.

Special procedures must be employed to test more general hypotheses of the form ρ = $ρ_0$, where $ρ_0$ is a constant. If the assumptions of bivariate normality appear unreasonable, nonparametric measures such as Spearman's rho and Kendall's tau-*b* can be calculated. These coefficients make limited assumptions about the underlying distributions of the variables. (See "The Rank Correlation Coefficient" on p. 287.)

Correlation Matrices and Missing Data

For a variety of reasons, data files frequently contain incomplete observations. Respondents in surveys scrawl illegible responses or refuse to answer certain questions. Laboratory animals die before experiments are completed. Patients fail to keep scheduled clinic appointments.

Analysis of data with missing values is troublesome. Before even considering possible strategies, you should determine whether there is evidence that the missing-value pattern is not random. That is, are there reasons to believe that missing values for a variable are related to the values of that variable or other variables? For example, people with low incomes may be less willing to report their financial status than more affluent people. This may be even more pronounced for people who are poor but highly educated.

One simple method of exploring such possibilities is to subdivide the data into two groups—those observations with missing data for a variable and those with complete data—and examine the distributions of the other variables in the file across these two groups. The SPSS crosstabulation and independent-samples *t* test procedures are particularly useful for this. For a discussion of more sophisticated methods for detecting nonrandomness, see Frane (1976).

If it appears that the data are not missing randomly, use great caution in attempting to analyze the data. It may be that no satisfactory analysis is possible, especially if there are only a few cases.

If you are satisfied that the missing data are random, several strategies are available. First, if the same few variables are missing for most cases, exclude those variables from the analysis. Since this luxury is not usually available, alternately you can keep all variables but eliminate the cases with missing values. This is termed **listwise** missing-value treatment, since a case is eliminated if it has a missing value for any variable on the list. If many cases have missing data for some variables, listwise missing-value treatment can eliminate too many cases and leave you with a very small sample. One common technique is to calculate the correlation coefficient between a pair of variables based on all cases with complete information for the two variables, regardless of whether the cases have missing data for any other variable. For example, if a case has values for variables 1, 3, and 5 only, it is used in computations involving only variable pairs 1 and 3, 1 and 5, and 3 and 5. This is **pairwise** missing-value treatment.

Choosing Pairwise Missing-Value Treatment

Several problems can arise with pairwise matrices, one of which is inconsistency. There are some relationships between coefficients that are clearly impossible but may seem to occur when different cases are used to estimate different coefficients. For example, if age and weight and age and height have high positive correlations, it is impossible in the same sample for height and weight to have a high negative correlation. However, if the same cases are not used to estimate all three coefficients, such an anomaly can occur.

There is no single sample size that can be associated with a pairwise matrix, since each coefficient can be based on a different number of cases. Significance levels obtained from analyses based on pairwise matrices must be viewed with caution, since little is known about hypothesis testing in such situations.

It should be emphasized that missing-value problems should not be treated lightly. You should base your decision on careful examination of the data and not leave the choices up to system defaults.

The Rank Correlation Coefficient

The Pearson product-moment correlation is appropriate only for data that attain at least an interval level of measurement, such as the sales and advertising data used in this chapter. Normality is also assumed when testing hypotheses about this correlation coefficient. For ordinal data or interval data that do not satisfy the normality assumption, another measure of the linear relationship between two variables, **Spearman's rank correlation coefficient**, is available.

The rank correlation coefficient is the Pearson correlation coefficient based on the ranks of the data if there are no ties (adjustments are made if some of the data are tied). If the original data for each variable have no ties, the data for each variable are first ranked, and then the Pearson correlation coefficient between the ranks for the two variables is computed. Like the Pearson correlation coefficient, the rank correlation ranges between −1 and +1, where −1 and +1 indicate a perfect linear relationship between the ranks of the two variables. The interpretation is therefore the same except that the relationship between *ranks,* and not values, is examined.

Figure 16.7 shows the matrix of rank correlation coefficients for the sales and advertising data. SPSS displays a lower-triangular matrix in which redundant coefficients and the diagonal are omitted. As expected, these coefficients are similar in sign and magnitude to the Pearson coefficients shown in Figure 16.6.

Figure 16.7 Rank correlation coefficients

```
- - - S P E A R M A N   C O R R E L A T I O N   C O E F F I C I E N T S - - -

REPS            .7733
             N(   40)
             SIG .000

SALES           .9182        .8636
             N(   40)    N(   40)
             SIG .000    SIG .000

             ADVERTIS      REPS

" . " is printed if a coefficient cannot be computed.
```

How to Obtain Bivariate Correlations

The Bivariate Correlations procedure computes Pearson product-moment and two rank-order correlation coefficients, Spearman's rho and Kendall's tau-*b*, with their significance levels. Optionally, you can obtain univariate statistics, covariances, and cross-product deviations.

The minimum specification is two or more numeric variables.

To obtain bivariate correlations, from the menus choose:

Statistics
  Correlate ▶
    Bivariate...

This opens the Bivariate Correlations dialog box, as shown in Figure 16.8.

Figure 16.8 Bivariate Correlations dialog box

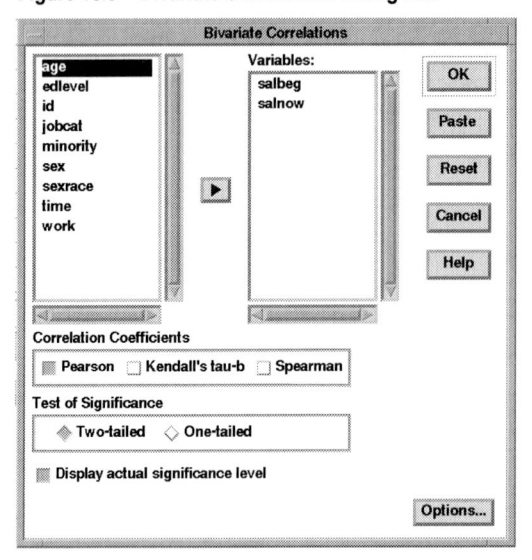

The numeric variables in your data file appear on the source list. Select two or more variables for analysis. To obtain the default Pearson correlations using two-tailed tests of significance, click on OK. If all cases have a missing value for one or both of a given pair of variables, or if they all have the same value for a variable, the coefficient cannot be computed and a period is displayed instead.

Correlation Coefficients. At least one type of correlation must be selected. You can choose one or more of the following:

- **Pearson.** This is the default setting. Displays a square correlation matrix. The correlation of a variable with itself is always 1.0000 and can be found on the diagonal of the matrix. Each variable appears twice in the matrix with identical coefficients, and the upper and lower triangles of the matrix are mirror images.
- **Kendall's tau-b.** A rank-order coefficient. Displays the correlations of each variable with every other variable in a lower-triangular matrix. The correlation of a variable with itself (the diagonal) and redundant coefficients are not displayed.
- **Spearman.** Spearman's rho. A rank-order coefficient. Displays a lower-triangular matrix.

Test of Significance. You can choose one of the following:

- **Two-tailed.** This test is appropriate when the direction of the relationship cannot be determined in advance, as is often the case in exploratory data analysis. This is the default. See "Hypothesis Tests about the Correlation Coefficient" on p. 285.
- **One-tailed.** This test is appropriate when the direction of the relationship between a pair of variables can be specified in advance of the analysis.

The following display option is also available:

- **Display actual significance level.** By default, actual significance levels are displayed. Deselect this item to indicate significance levels with asterisks. Correlation coefficients significant at the 0.05 level are identified with a single asterisk, and those significant at the 0.01 level are identified with two asterisks.

Bivariate Correlations Options

To obtain optional statistics for Pearson correlations or modify the treatment of cases with missing values, click on Options... in the Bivariate Correlations dialog box. This opens the Bivariate Correlations Options dialog box, as shown in Figure 16.9.

Figure 16.9 Bivariate Correlations Options dialog box

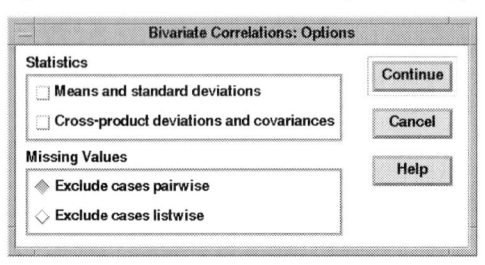

Statistics. For Pearson correlations, you can choose one or both of the following:

- **Means and standard deviations.** Displayed for each variable. The number of cases with nonmissing values is also shown. Missing values are handled on a variable-by-variable basis regardless of your missing values setting (see "Missing Values," below).

- **Cross-product deviations and covariances.** Displayed for each pair of variables. The cross-product deviation is equal to the sum of the products of mean-corrected variables. This is the numerator of the Pearson correlation coefficient, shown in Equation 16.1. The covariance is an unstandardized measure of the relationship between two variables, equal to the cross-product deviation divided by $N-1$.

Missing Values. You can choose one of the following alternatives:

- **Exclude cases pairwise.** Cases with missing values for one or both of a pair of variables for a correlation coefficient are excluded from the analysis. This is the default setting. Since each coefficient is based on all cases that have valid codes on that particular pair of variables, the maximum information available is used in every calculation. This can result in a set of coefficients based on a varying number of cases.

- **Exclude cases listwise.** Cases with missing values for any variable are excluded from all analyses.

Additional Features Available with Command Syntax

You can customize your correlations if you paste your selections to a syntax window and edit the resulting CORRELATIONS (Pearson correlations) or NONPAR CORR (Spearman or Kendall correlations) command syntax (see Chapter 4). Additional features include:

- For Pearson correlations, a matrix facility to write a correlation matrix that can be used in place of raw data to obtain other analyses such as factor analysis (with the MATRIX subcommand).

- Correlations of each variable of a list with each variable of a second list (using the keyword WITH on the VARIABLES subcommand).

See Appendix A for command syntax rules. See the *SPSS Base System Syntax Reference Guide* for complete CORRELATIONS and NONPAR CORR command syntax.

17 Partial Correlation Analysis

Whenever you examine the relationship between two variables, you must be concerned with the effects of other variables on the relationship of interest. For example, if you are studying the relationship between education and income, you must worry about controlling for the effects of age and work experience. It may be that a small observed relationship between education and income is due to younger people being more highly educated but less experienced in the work force. If you control for job experience and age, the relationship between education and income may appear stronger.

The **partial correlation coefficient**, a technique closely related to multiple linear regression, provides us with a single measure of linear association between two variables while adjusting for the linear effects of one or more additional variables. Properly used, partial correlation is a useful technique for uncovering spurious relationships, identifying intervening variables, and detecting hidden relationships.

Computing a Partial Correlation Coefficient

Consider the steps involved in computing a partial correlation coefficient between salary and education, controlling for age. First, two regression equations must be estimated. The first equation predicts salary from age, and the second predicts education from age. For each of the regression equations, we compute the residuals for each case. The partial correlation coefficient between salary and education, controlling for age, is simply the usual Pearson correlation coefficient between the two sets of residuals.

In our example, the first regression equation removes the linear effects of age from salary. The residuals represent salary after the adjustment for age. The second regression equation removes the linear effects of age from education. The residuals represent education after the adjustment for age. The partial correlation coefficient estimates the linear association between the two variables after the effects of age are removed.

Since we used linear regression analysis to control for the age variable, we had to make the assumption that the relationships of interest are linear. If there is reason to suspect that the variables are related in a nonlinear way, the partial correlation coefficient is not an appropriate statistical technique to use.

The Order of the Coefficient

In the previous example, we controlled for the effect of only one variable, age. However, partial correlation analysis is not limited to a single control variable. The same procedure can be applied to several control variables.

The number of control variables determines the order of the partial correlation coefficient. If there is one control variable, the partial correlation coefficient is a **first-order partial**. If there are five control variables, it is a fifth-order partial. Sometimes the ordinary correlation coefficient is called a **zero-order correlation**, since there are no control variables.

(In fact, it is not necessary to keep computing regression equations, since partial correlation coefficients of a particular order can be computed recursively from coefficients of a lower order.)

Tests of Statistical Significance

The assumption of multivariate normality is required to test the null hypothesis that the population partial coefficient is 0. The test statistic is

$$t = r\sqrt{\frac{N - \theta - 2}{1 - r^2}} \qquad \text{Equation 17.1}$$

where θ is the order of the coefficient and r is the partial correlation coefficient. The degrees of freedom for t are $N - \theta - 2$, where N is the number of cases.

Detecting Spurious Relationships

Partial correlation analysis can be used to detect spurious correlations between two variables. A **spurious correlation** is one in which the correlation between two variables results solely from the fact that one of the variables is correlated with a third variable that is the true predictor.

Consider the following example described by Kendall and Stuart (1973). Figure 17.1 is the correlation matrix between four variables measured in 16 large cities: crime rate, percentage of church membership, percentage of foreign-born males, and number of children under 5 per 1000 women between ages 15 and 44.

You can see that the correlation coefficient between crime rate (*crime*) and church membership (*church*) is negative (-0.14). The simplest conclusion is that church membership is a deterrent to crime. Although such a conclusion is no doubt comforting to theologians, let's examine the observed relationship further.

Figure 17.1 Zero-order correlation matrix

```
Zero Order Partials

              CRIME       CHURCH      PCTFRNM      UNDER5

CRIME        1.0000       -.1400      -.3400       -.3100
           (     0)      (    14)    (    14)     (    14)
           P=  .         P=  .605    P=  .198     P=  .243

CHURCH       -.1400       1.0000      .3300        .8500
           (    14)      (     0)    (    14)     (    14)
           P=  .605     P=  .        P=  .212     P=  .000

PCTFRNM      -.3400       .3300       1.0000       .4400
           (    14)      (    14)    (     0)     (    14)
           P=  .198     P=  .212     P=  .        P=  .088

UNDER5       -.3100       .8500       .4400        1.0000
           (    14)      (    14)    (    14)     (     0)
           P=  .243     P=  .000     P=  .088     P=  .

(Coefficient / (D.F.) / 2-tailed Significance)

" . " is printed if a coefficient cannot be computed
```

From Figure 17.1 you see that the crime rate is negatively correlated with the percentage of foreign-born males (*pctfrnm*) and with the number of children per woman (*under5*). Both of these variables are positively correlated with church membership. That is, both foreigners and women with many children tend to be church members.

Let's see what happens to the relationship between crime and church membership when we control for the linear effects of being foreign-born and having many children. Figure 17.2 shows the partial correlation coefficient between crime and church membership when the percentage of foreign-born males is held constant. Note that the correlation coefficient, −0.03, is now close to 0.

Figure 17.2 First-order partials, controlling for percentage of foreign-born males

```
Controlling for..    PCTFRNM

              CRIME       CHURCH

CRIME        1.0000       -.0313
           (     0)      (    13)
           P=  .         P=  .912

CHURCH       -.0313       1.0000
           (    13)      (     0)
           P=  .912     P=  .

(Coefficient / (D.F.) / 2-tailed Significance)

" . " is printed if a coefficient cannot be computed
```

Similarly, Figure 17.3 is the partial correlation coefficient between crime and church membership when the number of young children per woman is held constant. The partial correlation coefficient is now positive, 0.25.

Figure 17.3 First-order partials, controlling for number of children

```
Controlling for..    UNDER5

              CRIME       CHURCH

CRIME        1.0000        .2466
           (     0)      (    13)
           P=  .         P=  .376

CHURCH        .2466       1.0000
           (    13)      (     0)
           P=  .376      P=  .

(Coefficient / (D.F.) / 2-tailed Significance)

" . " is printed if a coefficient cannot be computed
```

The second-order partial correlation coefficient controlling for both foreign-born males and number of children is shown in Figure 17.4. The relationship between church membership and crime is now positive, 0.23.

Figure 17.4 Second-order partial correlations

```
Controlling for..    PCTFRNM    UNDER5

              CRIME       CHURCH

CRIME        1.0000        .2321
           (     0)      (    12)
           P=  .         P=  .425

CHURCH        .2321       1.0000
           (    12)      (     0)
           P=  .425      P=  .

(Coefficient / (D.F.) / 2-tailed Significance)

" . " is printed if a coefficient cannot be computed
```

From examination of the partial coefficients, it appears that the original negative relationship between church membership and crime may be due to the presence of law-abiding foreigners with large families. In 1935, when the study was done, foreigners were less likely to commit crimes and more likely to be church members than the general population. These relationships cause the overall coefficient between the two variables to be negative. However, when these two variables are controlled for, the relationship between church membership and crime changes drastically.

Detecting Hidden Relationships

Theory or intuition sometimes suggests that there should be a relationship between two variables even though the data indicate no correlation. In this situation, it is possible that one or more additional variables are suppressing the expected relationship. For example, it may be that A is not correlated with B because A is negatively related to C, which is positively related to B.

For example, assume that a marketing research company wants to examine the relationship between the need for transmission-rebuilding kits and the intent to purchase such a kit. Initial examination of the data reveals almost no correlation (0.01) between need for such a kit and intent to buy. However, the data show a *negative* relationship (−0.5) between income and need to buy and a *positive* relationship (0.6) between income and intent to buy. If we control for the effect of income using a partial correlation coefficient, the first-order partial between need and intent, controlling for income, is 0.45. Thus, income hid the relationship between need and intent to buy.

Interpreting the Results of Partial Correlation Analysis

Proper interpretation of partial correlation analysis requires knowledge about the way the variables may be related. You must know, for example, the nature of the relationship between need for a transmission and family income; that is, does income influence need, or need influence income? If you assume that need for a transmission influences family income, then need is specified as the control variable. One way of codifying the requisite assumptions in using partials in multivariate analysis is known as **path analysis** (see Wright, 1960, and Duncan, 1966).

How to Obtain Partial Correlations

The Partial Correlations procedure computes partial correlation coefficients that describe the linear relationship between two variables while controlling for the effects of one or more additional variables. The procedure calculates a matrix of zero-order coefficients and bases the partial correlations on this matrix.

The minimum specifications are:
- Two or more numeric variables for which partial correlations are to be computed.
- One or more numeric control variables.

To obtain a partial correlation analysis, from the menus choose:

Statistics
  Correlate ▶
    Partial...

This opens the Partial Correlations dialog box, as shown in Figure 17.5.

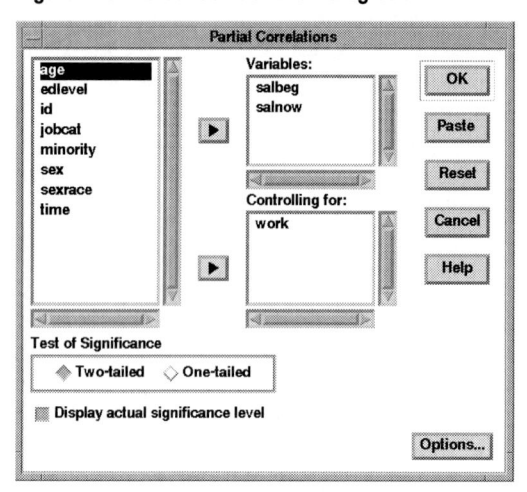

Figure 17.5 Partial Correlations dialog box

The numeric variables in your data file appear in the source list. Select two or more variables to be correlated and at least one control variable. To obtain the default partial correlation analysis with two-tailed probabilities, click on OK. SPSS produces a square matrix of the highest-order partial correlations. Cases with missing values for any of the variables are excluded from all analyses.

Test of Significance. You can choose one of the following alternatives:

- **Two-tailed.** Two-tailed probabilities. This is the default.
- **One-tailed.** One-tailed probabilities.

The following display option is also available:

- **Display actual significance level.** By default, the probability and degrees of freedom are shown for each coefficient. If you deselect this item, coefficients significant at the 0.05 level are identified with a single asterisk, coefficients significant at the 0.01 level are identified with a double asterisk, and degrees of freedom are suppressed. This setting affects both partial and zero-order correlation matrices.

Partial Correlations Options

To obtain optional univariate summary statistics or zero-order correlations, or to modify the handling of missing values, click on Options... in the Partial Correlations dialog box. This opens the Partial Correlations Options dialog box, as shown in Figure 17.6.

Figure 17.6 Partial Correlations Options dialog box

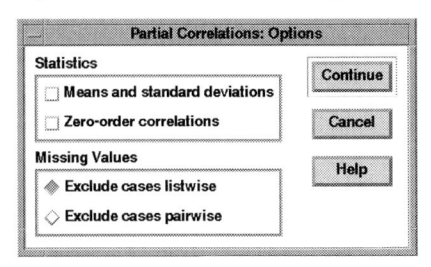

Statistics. You can choose one or both of the following:

- **Means and standard deviations.** Displayed for each variable. The number of cases with nonmissing values is also shown.
- **Zero-order correlations.** A matrix of simple correlations between all variables, including control variables, is displayed (see "The Order of the Coefficient" on p. 292).

Missing Values. You can choose one of the following alternatives:

- **Exclude cases listwise.** Cases having missing values for any variable, including a control variable, are excluded from all computations. This is the default.
- **Exclude cases pairwise.** For computation of the zero-order correlations on which the partial correlations are based, a case having missing values for one or both of a pair of variables is not used. Pairwise deletion uses as much of the data as possible. However, the number of cases may differ across coefficients. When pairwise deletion is in effect, the degrees of freedom for a particular partial coefficient are based on the smallest number of cases used in the calculation of any of the zero-order correlations.

Additional Features Available with Command Syntax

You can customize your partial correlations if you paste your selections to a syntax window and edit the resulting PARTIAL CORR command syntax (see Chapter 4). Additional features include:

- Matrix facility to read a zero-order correlation matrix or write a partial correlation matrix (with the MATRIX subcommand).
- Partial correlations between two lists of variables (using the keyword WITH on the VARIABLES subcommand).
- Multiple analyses (with multiple VARIABLES subcommands).
- User-specified order values to request, for example, both first- and second-order partial correlations when you have two control variables (with the VARIABLES subcommand).

- Ability to suppress redundant coefficients (with the FORMAT subcommand).
- An option to display a matrix of simple correlations when some coefficients cannot be computed (with the STATISTICS subcommand).

See Appendix A for command syntax rules. See the *SPSS Base System Syntax Reference Guide* for complete PARTIAL CORR command syntax.

18 Multiple Linear Regression Analysis

The 1964 Civil Rights Act prohibits discrimination in the workplace based on sex or race; employers who violate the act are liable to prosecution. Since passage of the Civil Rights Act, women, blacks, and other groups have filed numerous lawsuits charging unfair hiring or advancement practices.

The courts have ruled that statistics can be used as *prima facie* evidence of discrimination. Many lawsuits depend heavily on complex statistical analyses to demonstrate that similarly qualified individuals are not treated equally (Roberts, 1980). In this chapter, employee records for 474 individuals hired between 1969 and 1971 by a bank engaged in Equal Employment Opportunity litigation are analyzed. A mathematical model is developed that relates beginning salary and salary progression to employee characteristics such as seniority, education, and previous work experience. One objective is to determine whether sex and race are important predictors of salary.

The technique used to build the model is linear regression analysis, one of the most versatile data analysis procedures. Regression can be used to summarize data as well as to study relations among variables.

Linear Regression

Before examining a model that relates beginning salary to several other variables, consider the relationship between beginning salary and current (as of March, 1977) salary. For employees hired during a similar time period, beginning salary should serve as a reasonably good predictor of salary at a later date. Although superstars and underachievers might progress differently from the group as a whole, salary progression should be similar for the others. The scatterplot of beginning salary and current salary shown in Figure 18.1 supports this hypothesis.

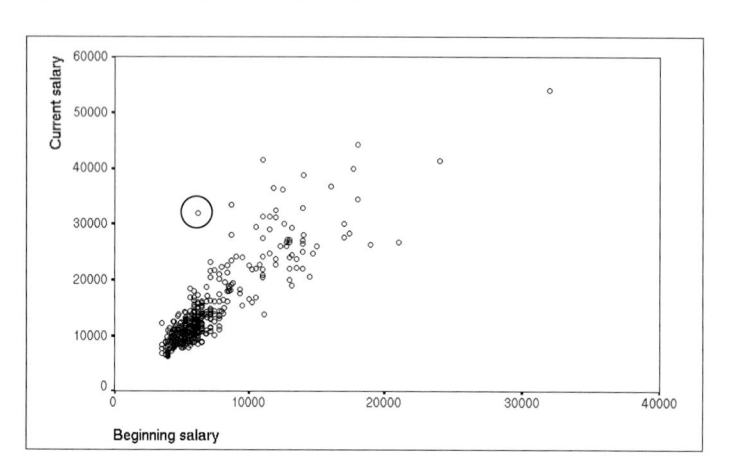

Figure 18.1 Scatterplot of beginning and current salaries

A scatterplot may suggest what type of mathematical functions would be appropriate for summarizing the data. Many functions, including parabolas, hyperbolas, polynomials, and trigonometric functions, are useful in fitting models to data. The scatterplot in Figure 18.1 shows current salaries tending to increase linearly with increases in beginning salary. If the plot indicates that a straight line is not a good summary measure of the relationship, you should consider other methods of analysis, including transforming the data to achieve linearity (see "Coaxing a Nonlinear Relationship to Linearity" on p. 322).

Outliers

A plot may also indicate the presence of points suspiciously different from the others. Examine such observations, termed **outliers**, carefully to see if they result from errors in gathering, coding, or entering data. The circled point in Figure 18.1 appears to be an outlier. Though neither the value of beginning salary ($6,300) nor the value of current salary ($32,000) is unique, jointly they are unusual.

The treatment of outliers can be difficult. If the point is incorrect due to coding or entry problems, you should correct it and rerun the analysis. If there is no apparent explanation for the outlier, consider interactions with other variables as a possible explanation. For example, the outlier may represent an employee who was hired as a low-paid clerical worker while pursuing an MBA degree. After graduation, the employee rose rapidly to a higher position. In this instance, the variable for education explains the unusual salary characteristics.

Choosing a Regression Line

Since current salary tends to increase linearly with beginning salary, a straight line can be used to summarize the relationship. The equation for the line is:

$$\text{predicted current salary} = B_0 + B_1 (\text{beginning salary}) \quad \text{Equation 18.1}$$

The **slope** (B_1) is the change (in dollars) in the fitted current salary for a change in the beginning salary. The **intercept** (B_0) is the theoretical estimate of current salary for a beginning salary of 0.

However, the observed data points do not all fall on a straight line, they cluster around it. Many lines can be drawn through the data points; the problem is to select among the possible lines. The method of **least squares** results in a line that minimizes the sum of squared vertical distances from the observed data points to the line. Any other line has a larger sum. Figure 18.2 shows the least-squares line superimposed on the salary scatterplot. Some vertical distances from points to the line are also shown.

Figure 18.2 Regression line for beginning and current salaries

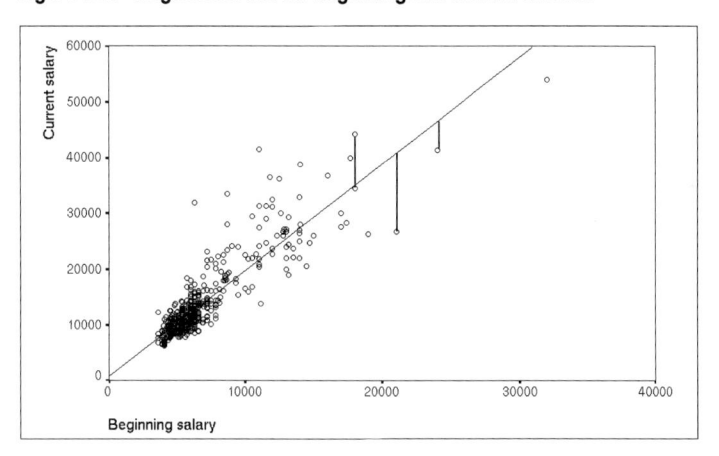

You can use SPSS to calculate the least-squares line. For the data in Figure 18.1, that line is:

$$\text{predicted current salary} = 771.28 + 1.91 (\text{beginning salary}) \quad \text{Equation 18.2}$$

The slope and intercept values are shown in the column labeled *B* in the output shown in Figure 18.3.

Figure 18.3 Statistics for variables in the equation

```
------------------ Variables in the Equation ------------------

Variable              B          SE B        Beta         T    Sig T

SALBEG            1.909450      .047410     .880117    40.276  .0000
(Constant)      771.282303    355.471941                2.170  .0305
```

The Standardized Regression Coefficient

The **standardized regression coefficient**, labeled *Beta* in Figure 18.3, is defined as:

$$\text{beta} = B_1 \frac{S_X}{S_Y} \qquad \text{Equation 18.3}$$

Multiplying the regression coefficient (B_1) by the ratio of the standard deviation of the independent variable (S_X) to the standard deviation of the dependent variable (S_Y) results in a dimensionless coefficient. In fact, the beta coefficient is the slope of the least-squares line when both *X* and *Y* are expressed as *Z* scores. The beta coefficient is discussed further in "Beta Coefficients" on p. 330.

From Samples to Populations

Generally, more is sought in regression analysis than a description of observed data. You usually want to draw inferences about the relationship of the variables in the population from which the sample was taken. How are beginning and current salaries related for all employees, not just those included in the sample? Inferences about population values based on sample results are based on the following assumptions:

Normality and Equality of Variance. For any fixed value of the independent variable *X*, the distribution of the dependent variable *Y* is normal, with mean $\mu_{Y/X}$ (the mean of *Y* for a given *X*) and a constant variance of σ^2 (see Figure 18.4). This assumption specifies that not all employees with the same beginning salary have the same current salary. Instead, there is a normal distribution of current salaries for each beginning salary. Though the distributions have different means, they have the same variance: σ^2.

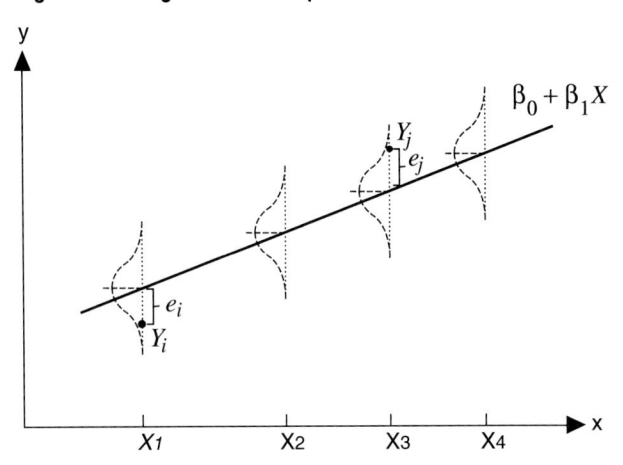

Figure 18.4 Regression assumptions

Independence. The Y's are statistically independent of each other; that is, observations are in no way influenced by other observations. For example, observations are *not* independent if they are based on repeated measurements from the same experimental unit. If three observations are taken from each of four families, the twelve observations are not independent.

Linearity. The mean values $\mu_{Y/X}$ all lie on a straight line, which is the population regression line. This is the line drawn in Figure 18.4. An alternative way of stating this assumption is that the linear model is correct.

When there is a single independent variable, the model can be summarized by:

$$Y_i = \beta_0 + \beta_1 X_i + e_i \qquad \text{Equation 18.4}$$

The population parameters (values) for the slope and intercept are denoted by β_1 and β_0. The term e_i, usually called the **error**, is the difference between the observed value of Y_i and the subpopulation mean at the point X_i. The errors, e_i, are assumed to be normally distributed, independent, random variables with a mean of 0 and variance of σ^2 (see Figure 18.4).

Estimating Population Parameters

Since β_0 and β_1 are unknown population parameters, they must be estimated from the sample. The least-squares coefficients B_0 and B_1, discussed in "Choosing a Regression Line" on p. 301, are used to estimate the population parameters.

However, the slope and intercept estimated from a single sample typically differ from the population values and vary from sample to sample. To use these estimates for inference about the population values, the sampling distributions of the two statistics are needed. When the assumptions of linear regression are met, the sampling distributions of B_0 and B_1 are normal, with means of β_0 and β_1.

The standard error of B_0 is

$$\sigma_{B_0} = \sigma \sqrt{\frac{1}{N} + \frac{\bar{X}^2}{(N-1) S_X^2}} \qquad \text{Equation 18.5}$$

where S_X^2 is the sample variance of the independent variable. The standard error of B_1 is:

$$\sigma_{B_1} = \frac{\sigma}{\sqrt{(N-1) S_X^2}} \qquad \text{Equation 18.6}$$

Since the population variance of the errors, σ^2, is not known, it must also be estimated. The usual estimate of σ^2 is:

$$S^2 = \frac{\sum_{i=1}^{N} (Y_i - B_0 - B_1 X_i)^2}{N-2} \qquad \text{Equation 18.7}$$

The positive square root of S^2 is termed the **standard error of the estimate**, or the standard deviation of the residuals. (The reason for this name is discussed in "Predicting a New Value" on p. 310.) The estimated standard errors of the slope and intercept are displayed in the third column (labeled *SE B*) in Figure 18.3.

Testing Hypotheses

A frequently tested hypothesis is that there is no linear relationship between X and Y—that the slope of the population regression line is 0. The statistic used to test this hypothesis is:

$$t = \frac{B_1}{S_{B_1}} \qquad \text{Equation 18.8}$$

The distribution of the statistic, when the assumptions are met and the hypothesis of no linear relationship is true, is Student's *t* distribution with $N - 2$ degrees of freedom. The statistic for testing the hypothesis that the intercept is 0 is:

$$t = \frac{B_0}{S_{B_0}}$$

Equation 18.9

Its distribution is also Student's *t* with $N - 2$ degrees of freedom.

These *t* statistics and their two-tailed observed significance levels are displayed in the last two columns of Figure 18.3. The small observed significance level (less than 0.00005) associated with the slope for the salary data supports the hypothesis that beginning and current salaries have a linear association.

Confidence Intervals

A statistic calculated from a sample provides a point estimate of the unknown parameter. A point estimate can be thought of as the single best guess for the population value. While the estimated value from the sample is typically different from the value of the unknown population parameter, the hope is that it isn't too far away. Based on the sample estimate, it is possible to calculate a range of values that, within a designated likelihood, includes the population value. Such a range is called a **confidence interval**. For example, as shown in Figure 18.5, the 95% confidence interval for β_1, the population slope, is 1.816 to 2.003.

Figure 18.5 Confidence intervals

```
---- Variables in the Equation -----
Variable        95% Confdnce Intrvl B

SALBEG           1.816290    2.002610
(Constant)      72.778982 1469.785624
```

Ninety-five percent confidence means that if repeated samples are drawn from a population under the same conditions and 95% confidence intervals are calculated, 95% of the intervals will contain the unknown parameter β_1. Since the parameter value is unknown, it is not possible to determine whether a particular interval contains it.

Goodness of Fit

An important part of any statistical procedure that builds models from data is establishing how well the model actually fits, or its **goodness of fit**. This includes the detection of possible violations of the required assumptions in the data being analyzed.

The R-squared Coefficient

A commonly used measure of the goodness of fit of a linear model is R^2, or the **coefficient of determination**. It can be thought of in a variety of ways. Besides being the square of the correlation coefficient between variables X and Y, it is the square of the correlation coefficient between Y (the observed value of the dependent variable) and $\hat{Y}$ (the predicted value of Y from the fitted line). If you compute the predicted salary for each employee (based on the coefficients in the output in Figure 18.3) as follows

$$\text{predicted current salary} = 771.28 + 1.91 \,(\text{beginning salary}) \qquad \text{Equation 18.10}$$

and then calculate the square of the Pearson correlation coefficient between predicted current salary and observed current salary, you will get R^2. If all the observations fall on the regression line, R^2 is 1. If there is no linear relationship between the dependent and independent variables, R^2 is 0.

Note that R^2 is a measure of the goodness of fit of a particular model and that an R^2 of 0 does not necessarily mean that there is no association between the variables. Instead, it indicates that there is no *linear* relationship.

In the output in Figure 18.6, R^2 is labeled *R Square* and its square root is labeled *Multiple R*. The sample R^2 tends to be an optimistic estimate of how well the model fits the population. The model usually does not fit the population as well as it fits the sample from which it is derived. The statistic *adjusted R^2* attempts to correct R^2 to more closely reflect the goodness of fit of the model in the population. Adjusted R^2 is given by

$$R_a^2 = R^2 - \frac{p(1-R^2)}{N-p-1} \qquad \text{Equation 18.11}$$

where p is the number of independent variables in the equation (1 in the salary example).

Figure 18.6 Summary statistics for the equation

```
Multiple R              .88012
R Square                .77461
Adjusted R Square       .77413
Standard Error      3246.14226
```

Analysis of Variance

To test the hypothesis that there is no linear relationship between X and Y, several equivalent statistics can be computed. When there is a single independent variable, the hypothesis that the population R^2 is 0 is identical to the hypothesis that the population slope is 0. The test for $R_{pop}^2 = 0$ is usually obtained from the analysis-of-variance table (see Figure 18.7).

Figure 18.7 Analysis-of-variance table

```
Analysis of Variance
                   DF       Sum of Squares        Mean Square
Regression          1    17092967800.01978    17092967800.0198
Residual          472       4973671469.79454     10537439.55465

F =    1622.11776        Signif F =   .0000
```

The total observed variability in the dependent variable is subdivided into two components—that which is attributable to the regression (labeled *Regression*) and that which is not (labeled *Residual*). Consider Figure 18.8. For a particular point, the distance from Y_i to $\bar{Y}$ (the mean of the Y's) can be subdivided into two parts:

$$Y_i - \bar{Y} = (Y_i - \hat{Y}_i) + (\hat{Y}_i - \bar{Y}) \qquad \text{Equation 18.12}$$

The distance from Y_i (the observed value) to $\hat{Y}_i$ (the value predicted by the regression line), or $Y_i - \hat{Y}_i$, is called the **residual from the regression**. It is zero if the regression line passes through the point. The second component $(\hat{Y}_i - \bar{Y})$ is the distance from the regression line to the mean of the Y's. This distance is "explained" by the regression in

Figure 18.8 Components of variability

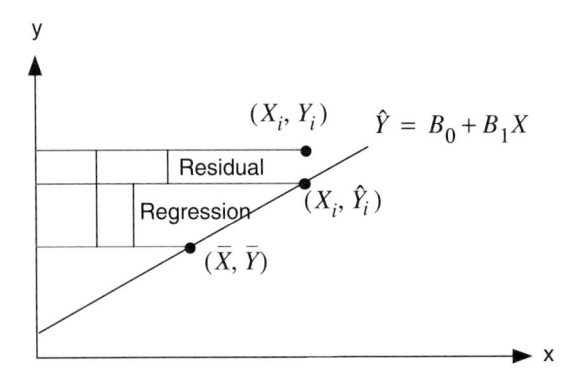

that it represents the improvement in the estimate of the dependent variable achieved by the regression. Without the regression, the mean of the dependent variable $\bar{Y}$ is used as the estimate. It can be shown that:

$$\sum_{i=1}^{N} (Y_i - \bar{Y})^2 = \sum_{i=1}^{N} (Y_i - \hat{Y}_i)^2 + \sum_{i=1}^{N} (\hat{Y}_i - \bar{Y})^2 \qquad \text{Equation 18.13}$$

The first quantity following the equals sign is called the **residual sum of squares** and the second quantity is the **regression sum of squares**. The sum of these is called the **total sum of squares**.

The analysis-of-variance table in Figure 18.7 displays these two sums of squares under the heading *Sum of Squares*. The *Mean Square* for each entry is the sum of squares divided by the degrees of freedom (DF). If the regression assumptions are met, the ratio of the mean square regression to the mean square residual is distributed as an F statistic with p and $N - p - 1$ degrees of freedom. F serves to test how well the regression model fits the data. If the probability associated with the F statistic is small, the hypothesis that $R^2_{pop} = 0$ is rejected. For this example, the F statistic is:

$$F = \frac{\text{mean square regression}}{\text{mean square residual}} = 1622 \qquad \text{Equation 18.14}$$

The observed significance level (*Signif F*) is less than 0.00005.

The square root of the F value (1622) is 40.28, which is the value of the t statistic for the slope in Figure 18.3. The square of a t value with k degrees of freedom is an F value with 1 and k degrees of freedom. Therefore, either t or F values can be computed to test that $\beta_i = 0$. Another useful summary statistic is the standard error of the estimate, S, which can also be calculated as the square root of the residual mean square (see "Predicting a New Value" on p. 310).

Another Interpretation of R-squared

Partitioning the sum of squares of the dependent variable allows another interpretation of R^2. It is the proportion of the variation in the dependent variable "explained" by the model:

$$R^2 = 1 - \frac{\text{residual sum of squares}}{\text{total sum of squares}} = 0.775 \qquad \text{Equation 18.15}$$

Similarly, adjusted R^2 is

$$R^2_a = 1 - \frac{\text{residual sum of squares} / (N - p - 1)}{\text{total sum of squares} / (N - 1)} \qquad \text{Equation 18.16}$$

where p is the number of independent variables in the equation (1 in the salary example).

Predicted Values and Their Standard Errors

By comparing the observed values of the dependent variable with the values predicted by the regression equation, you can learn a good deal about how well a model and the various assumptions fit the data (see the discussion of residuals beginning with "Searching for Violations of Assumptions" on p. 312). Predicted values are also of interest when the results are used to predict new data. You may wish to predict the mean *Y* for all cases with a given value of *X* (denoted X_0) or to predict the value of *Y* for a single case. For example, you can predict either the mean salary for all employees with a beginning salary of $10,000 or the salary for a particular employee with a beginning salary of $10,000. In both situations, the predicted value

$$\hat{Y}_0 = B_0 + B_1 X_0 = 771 + 1.91 \times 10,000 = 19,871 \qquad \text{Equation 18.17}$$

is the same. What differs is the standard error.

Predicting Mean Response

The estimated standard error for the predicted mean *Y* at X_0 is:

$$S_{\hat{Y}} = S \sqrt{\frac{1}{N} + \frac{(X_0 - \bar{X})^2}{(N-1) S_X^2}} \qquad \text{Equation 18.18}$$

The equation for the standard error shows that the smallest value occurs when X_0 is equal to $\bar{X}$, the mean of *X*. The larger the distance from the mean, the greater the standard error. Thus, the mean of *Y* for a given *X* is better estimated for central values of the observed *X*'s than for outlying values. Figure 18.9 is a plot of the standard errors of predicted mean salaries for different values of beginning salary (obtained by saving the standard error as a new variable in the Linear Regression procedure and then using the Scatter option on the Graphs menu).

Figure 18.9 Standard errors for predicted mean responses

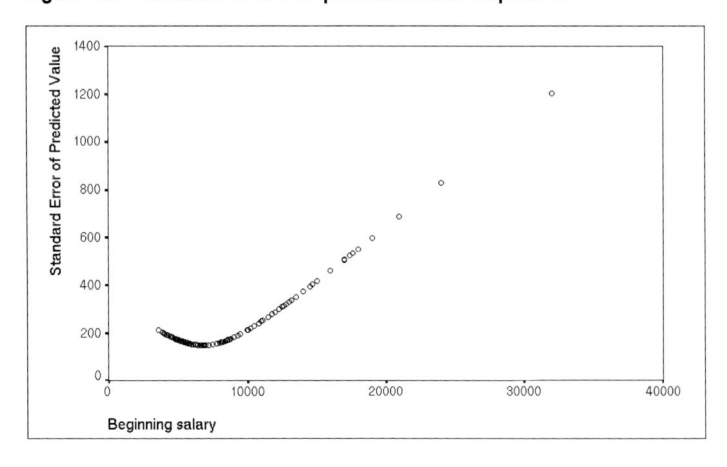

Prediction intervals for the mean predicted salary are calculated in the standard way. The 95% confidence interval at X_0 is:

$$\hat{Y} \pm t_{(1-\frac{\alpha}{2}, N-2)} S_{\hat{Y}}$$

Equation 18.19

Figure 18.10 shows a typical 95% confidence band for predicted mean responses. It is narrowest at the mean of X and widens as the distance from the mean $(X_0 - \bar{X})$ increases.

Figure 18.10 95% confidence band for mean prediction

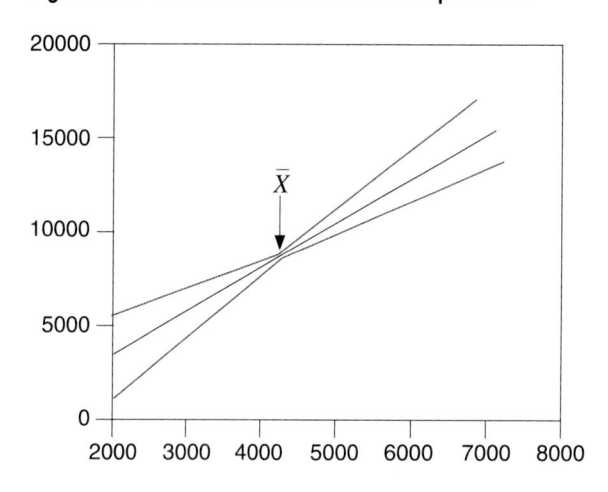

Predicting a New Value

Although the predicted value for a single new observation at X_0 is the same as the predicted value for the mean at X_0, the standard error is not. The two sources of error when predicting an individual observation are:

1. The individual value may differ from the population mean of Y for X_0.

2. The estimate of the population mean at X_0 may differ from the population mean.

The sources of error are illustrated in Figure 18.11.

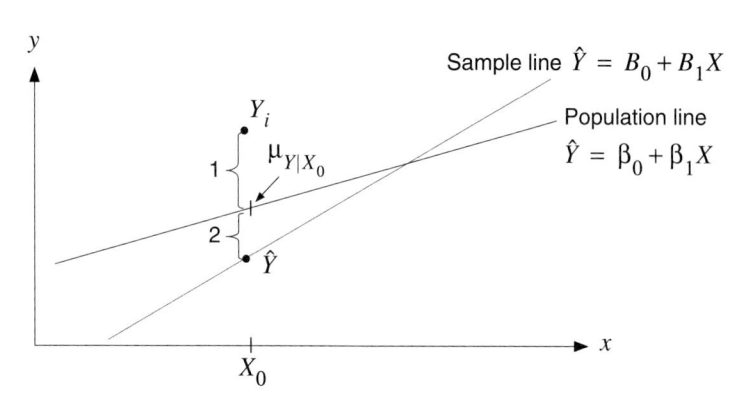

Figure 18.11 Sources of error in predicting individual observations

When estimating the mean response, only the second error component is considered. The variance of the individual prediction is the variance of the mean prediction plus the variance of Y_i for a given X. This can be written as:

$$S^2_{\text{ind } \hat{Y}} = S^2_{\hat{Y}} + S^2 = S^2\left(1 + \frac{1}{N} + \frac{(X_0 - \bar{X})^2}{(N-1)S^2_X}\right)$$

Equation 18.20

Prediction intervals for the new observation are obtained by substituting $S_{\text{ind } \hat{Y}}$ for $S_{\hat{Y}}$ in Equation 18.19. If the sample size is large, the terms $1/N$ and

$$\frac{(X_0 - \bar{X})^2}{(N-1)S^2_X}$$

Equation 18.21

are negligible. In that case, the standard error is simply S, which explains the name standard error of the estimate for S (see "Estimating Population Parameters" on p. 304). You can obtain plots of confidence intervals for predicted values using the Scatter option on the Graphs menu.

Reading the Casewise Plot

Figure 18.12 shows the output from the beginning and end of a plot of the salary data. The sequential number of the case is listed first, followed by the plot of standardized residuals, the observed (*SALNOW*), predicted (**PRED*), and residual (**RESID*) values. In SPSS, you can save predicted values and confidence intervals for the mean responses and for individual responses and use the List Cases procedure to display these values for all cases or for a subset of cases (see Chapter 20).

Figure 18.12 Casewise plot with predicted values

```
Casewise Plot of Standardized Residual
*: Selected    M: Missing

                -3.0            0.0            3.0
     Case #    O:...............:...............:O    SALNOW       *PRED       *RESID
        1      .               *.              .      16080     16810.6600    -730.6600
        2      .         *     .               .      41400     46598.0758   -5198.0758
        3      .               .    *          .      21960     20247.6695    1712.3305
        4      .               .    *          .      19200     17383.4949    1816.5051
        5      .     *         .               .      28350     33995.7076   -5645.7076
        6      .               .   *           .      27250     25586.4910    1663.5090
        7      .               .    *          .      16080     13946.4854    2133.5146
        8      .               .      *        .      14100     11082.3108    3017.6892
        9      .               .   *           .      12420     10394.9089    2025.0911
       10      .              *.               .      12300     12800.8156    -500.8156
       11      .               .    *          .      15720     12800.8156    2919.1844
       12      .        *      .               .       8880     12227.9807   -3347.9807
       ..
       ..
       ..
      470      .               *               .       9420      9592.9401    -172.9401
      471      .              .*               .       9780      9134.6721     645.3279
      472      .          *   .                .       7680      9249.2391   -1569.2391
      473      .           *  .                .       7380      8561.8372   -1181.8372
      474      .        *     .                .       8340     10738.6099   -2398.6099
     Case #    O:...............:...............:O    SALNOW       *PRED       *RESID
                -3.0            0.0            3.0
```

Searching for Violations of Assumptions

You usually don't know in advance whether a model such as linear regression is appropriate. Therefore, it is necessary to conduct a search focused on residuals to look for evidence that the necessary assumptions are violated.

Residuals

In model building, a **residual** is what is left after the model is fit. It is the difference between an observed value and the value predicted by the model:

$$E_i = Y_i - B_0 - B_1 X_i = Y_i - \hat{Y}_i \qquad \text{Equation 18.22}$$

In regression analysis, the true errors, e_i, are assumed to be independent normal values with a mean of 0 and a constant variance of σ^2. If the model is appropriate for the data, the observed residuals, E_i, which are estimates of the true errors, e_i, should have similar characteristics.

If the intercept term is included in the equation, the mean of the residuals is always 0. So, the mean provides no information about the true mean of the errors. Since the sum of the residuals is constrained to be 0, the residuals are *not* strictly independent. However, if the number of residuals is large when compared with the number of independent variables, the dependency among the residuals can be ignored for practical purposes.

The relative magnitudes of residuals are easier to judge when they are divided by estimates of their standard deviations. The resulting **standardized residuals** are expressed in standard deviation units above or below the mean. For example, the fact that a particular residual is −5198.1 provides little information. If you know that its standardized form is −3.1, you know not only that the observed value is less than the predicted value but also that the residual is larger than most in absolute value.

Residuals are sometimes adjusted in one of two ways. The standardized residual for case i is the residual divided by the sample standard deviation of the residuals. Standardized residuals have a mean of 0 and a standard deviation of 1. The **Studentized residual** is the residual divided by an estimate of its standard deviation that varies from point to point, depending on the distance of X_i from the mean of X. Usually, standardized and Studentized residuals are close in value, but not always. The Studentized residual reflects more precisely differences in the true error variances from point to point.

Linearity

For the bivariate situation, a scatterplot is a good means for judging how well a straight line fits the data. Another convenient method is to plot the residuals against the predicted values. If the assumptions of linearity and homogeneity of variance are met, there should be no relationship between the predicted and residual values. You should be suspicious of any observable pattern.

For example, fitting a least-squares line to the data in the plots shown in Figure 18.13 yields the residual plots shown in Figure 18.14. The two residual plots show patterns, since straight lines do not fit the data well. Systematic patterns between the predicted values and the residuals suggest possible violations of the assumption of linearity. If the assumption were met, the residuals would be randomly distributed in a band clustered around the horizontal line through 0, as shown in Figure 18.15.

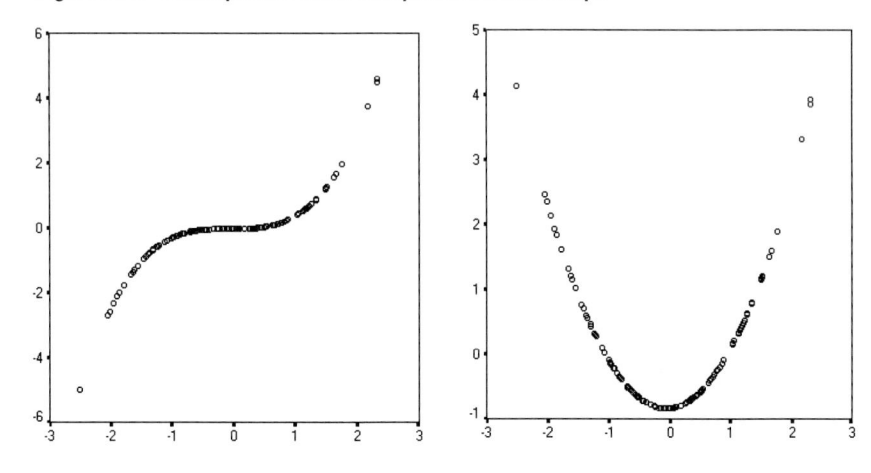

Figure 18.13 Scatterplots of cubic and quadratic relationships

Figure 18.14 Standardized residuals scatterplots—cubic and quadratic relationships

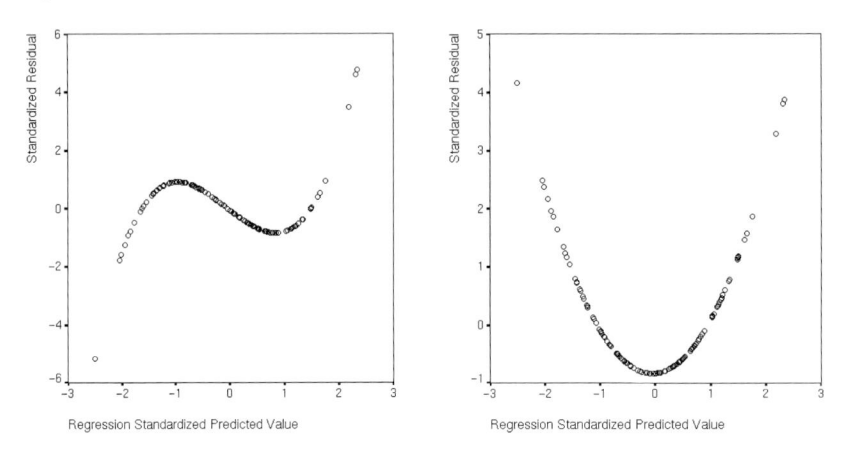

Figure 18.15 Randomly distributed residuals

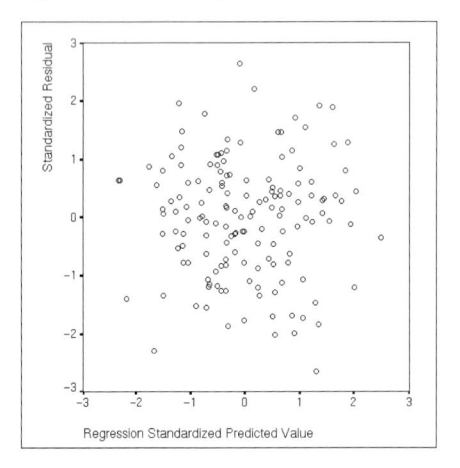

Residuals can also be plotted against individual independent variables by saving them in the Linear Regression procedure and then using the Scatter option on the Graphs menu. Again, if the assumptions are met, you should see a horizontal band of residuals. Consider as well plotting the residuals against independent variables not in the equation. If the residuals are not randomly distributed, you may want to include the variable in the equation for a multiple regression model (see "Multiple Regression Models" on p. 326).

Equality of Variance

You can also use the previously described plots to check for violations of the equality-of-variance assumption. If the spread of the residuals increases or decreases with values of the independent variables or with predicted values, you should question the assumption of constant variance of Y for all values of X.

Figure 18.16 is a plot of the Studentized residuals against the predicted values for the salary data. The spread of the residuals increases with the magnitude of the predicted values, suggesting that the variability of current salaries increases with salary level. Thus, the equality-of-variance assumption appears to be violated.

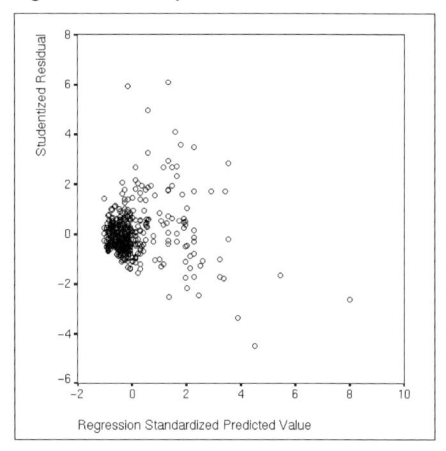

Figure 18.16 Unequal variance

Independence of Error

Whenever the data are collected and recorded sequentially, you should plot residuals against the sequence variable. Even if time is not considered a variable in the model, it could influence the residuals. For example, suppose you are studying survival time after surgery as a function of complexity of surgery, amount of blood transfused, dosage of medication, and so forth. In addition to these variables, it is also possible that the surgeon's skill increased with each operation and that a patient's survival time is influenced by the number of prior patients treated. The plot of standardized residuals corresponding to the order in which patients received surgery shows a shorter survival time for earlier patients than for later patients (see Figure 18.17). If sequence and the residual are independent, you should not see a discernible pattern.

Figure 18.17 Serial plot

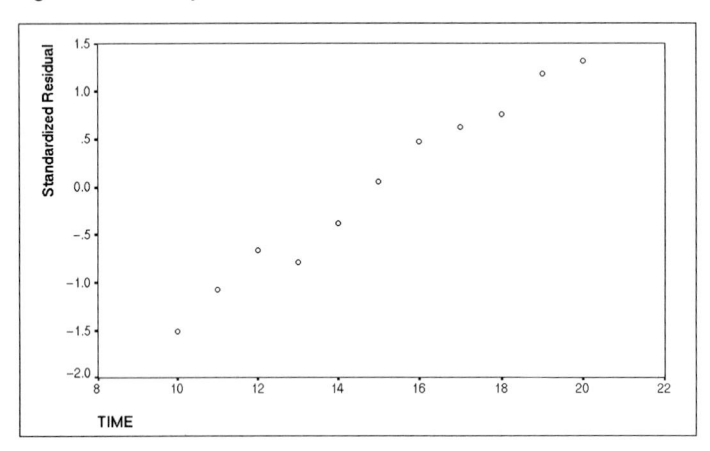

The **Durbin-Watson statistic**, a test for serial correlation of adjacent error terms, is defined as:

$$d = \frac{\sum_{t=2}^{N}(E_t - E_{t-1})^2}{\sum_{t=1}^{N} E_t^2}$$

Equation 18.23

The possible values of the statistic range from 0 to 4. If the residuals are not correlated with each other, the value of d is close to 2. Values less than 2 mean that adjacent residuals are positively correlated. Values greater than 2 mean that adjacent residuals are negatively correlated. Consult tables of the d statistic for bounds upon which significance tests can be based.

Normality

The distribution of residuals may not appear to be normal for reasons other than actual non-normality: misspecification of the model, nonconstant variance, a small number of residuals actually available for analysis, etc. Therefore, you should pursue several lines of investigation. One of the simplest is to construct a histogram of the residuals, such as the one for the salary data shown in Figure 18.18.

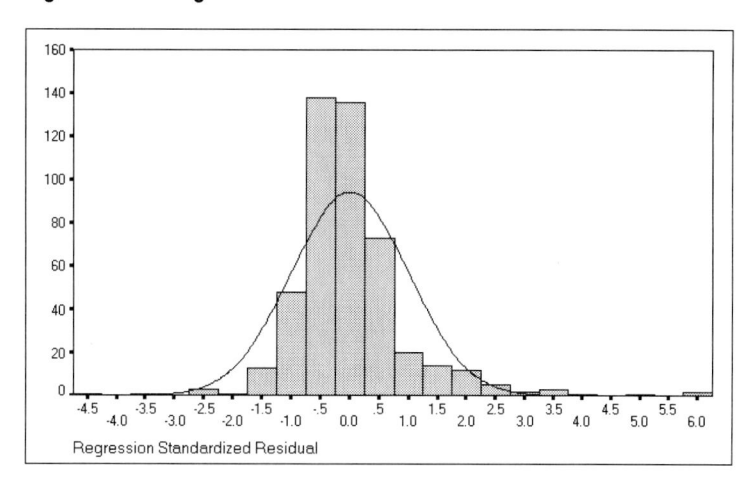

Figure 18.18 Histogram of standardized residuals

A normal distribution is superimposed on a histogram of observed frequencies (indicated by the bars). It is unreasonable to expect the observed residuals to be exactly normal—some deviation is expected because of sampling variation. Even if the errors are normally distributed in the population, sample residuals are only approximately normal.

In the histogram in Figure 18.18, the distribution does not seem normal, since there is an exaggerated clustering of residuals toward the center and a straggling tail toward large positive values. Thus, the normality assumption may be violated.

Another way to compare the observed distribution of residuals with the expected distribution under the assumption of normality is to plot the two cumulative distributions against each other for a series of points. If the two distributions are identical, a straight line results. By observing how points scatter about the expected straight line, you can compare the two distributions.

Figure 18.19 is a cumulative probability plot of the salary residuals. Initially, the observed residuals are above the "normal" line, since there is a smaller number of large negative residuals than expected. Once the greatest concentration of residuals is reached, the observed points are below the line, since the observed cumulative proportion exceeds the expected. Tests for normality are available using the Explore procedure (see Chapter 9).

Figure 18.19 Normal probability (P–P) plot

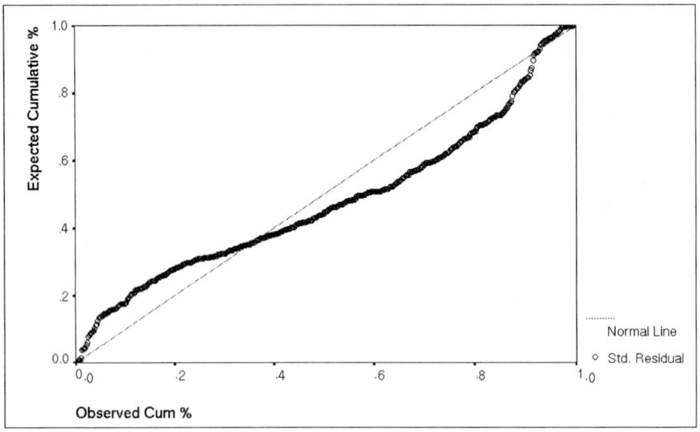

Locating Outliers

You can spot outliers readily on residual plots, since they are cases with very large positive or negative residuals. In general, standardized residual values greater than an absolute value of 3 are considered outliers. Since you usually want more information about outliers, you can use the casewise plotting facility to display identification numbers and a variety of other statistics for cases having residuals beyond a specified cutoff point.

Figure 18.20 displays information for the nine cases with standardized residuals greater than the absolute value of 3. Only two of these nine cases have current salaries less than those predicted by the model (cases 67 and 122). The others all have larger salaries, an average of $33,294, than the average for the sample, only $13,767. Thus, there is some evidence that the model may not fit well for the highly paid cases.

Figure 18.20 Casewise plot of residuals outliers

```
Casewise Plot of Standardized Residual

Outliers = 3.    *: Selected    M: Missing

            -6.    -3.   3.    6.
    Case #   0:........:  :........:O    SALNOW       *PRED        *RESID
      24     .          ..*         .     28000    17383.4949    10616.5051
      60     .          ..         *.     32000    12800.8156    19199.1844
      67     .         *..          .     26400    37043.1894   -10643.1894
     114     .          .. *        .     38800    27511.2163    11288.7837
     122     .     *    ..          .     26700    40869.7266   -14169.7266
     123     .          .. *        .     36250    24639.4039    11610.5961
     129     .          ..    *     .     33500    17383.4949    16116.5051
     149     .          ..        * .     41500    21782.8671    19717.1329
     177     .          ..   *      .     36500    23295.1513    13204.8487
```

Other Unusual Observations: Mahalanobis Distance

In the section "Outliers" on p. 300, one case was identified as an outlier because the combination of values for beginning and current salaries was atypical. This case (case 60) also appears in Figure 18.20, since it has a large value for the standardized residual. Another unusual case (case 56) has a beginning salary of $31,992. Since the average beginning salary for the entire sample is only $6,806 and the standard deviation is 3148, the case is eight standard deviations above the mean. But since the standardized residual is not large, this case does not appear in Figure 18.20.

However, cases that have unusual values for the independent variables can have a substantial impact on the results of analysis and should be identified. One measure of the distance of cases from average values of the independent variables is **Mahalanobis distance**. In the case of a regression equation with a single independent variable, it is the square of the standardized value of X:

$$D_i = \left(\frac{X_i - \bar{X}}{S_X}\right)^2 \quad \text{Equation 18.24}$$

When there is more than one independent variable—where Mahalanobis distance is most valuable—the computations are more complex.

You can save Mahalanobis distances with SPSS and display cases with the five highest and lowest values using the Explore procedure (see Chapter 9). As shown in Figure 18.21, the Mahalanobis distance for case 56 is 64 (8^2).

Figure 18.21 Mahalanobis distances

```
                    Extreme Values
                    -------  ------

5   Highest    Case #           5   Lowest     Case #
    63.99758   Case: 56             .00011     Case: 78
    29.82579   Case: 2              .00075     Case: 448
    20.32559   Case: 122            .00088     Case: 302
    14.99121   Case: 67             .00088     Case: 192
    12.64145   Case: 55             .00088     Case: 203
```

Influential Cases: Deleted Residuals and Cook's Distance

Certain observations in a set of data can have a large influence on estimates of the parameters. Figure 18.22 shows such a point. The regression line obtained for the data is quite different if the point is omitted. However, the residual for the circled point is not particularly large when the case (case 8) is included in the computations and does not therefore arouse suspicion (see the column labeled *RES_1* in Figure 18.23).

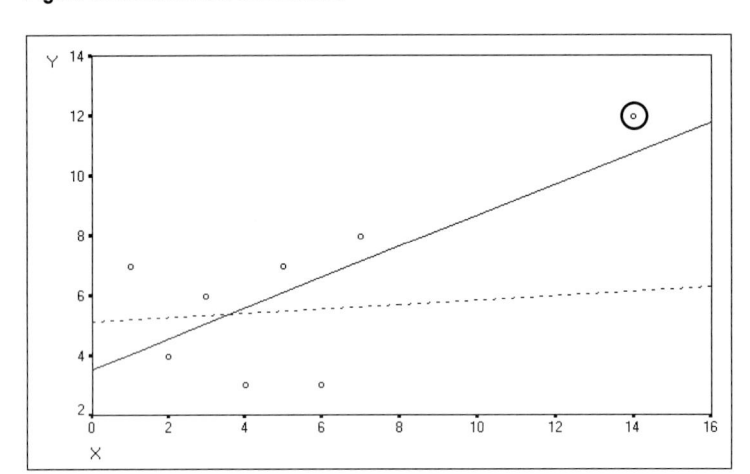

Figure 18.22 Influential observation

One way to identify an influential case is to compare the residuals for a case when the suspected case is included in the equation and when it is not. The **adjusted predicted value** for case i when it is not included in the computation of the regression line is

$$\hat{Y}_i^{(i)} = B_0^{(i)} + B_1^{(i)} X_i \qquad \text{Equation 18.25}$$

where the superscript (i) indicates that the ith case is excluded. The change in the predicted value when the ith case is deleted is:

$$\hat{Y}_i - \hat{Y}_i^{(i)} \qquad \text{Equation 18.26}$$

The residual calculated for a case when it is not included is called the **deleted residual**, computed as:

$$Y_i - \hat{Y}_i^{(i)} \qquad \text{Equation 18.27}$$

The deleted residual can be divided by its standard error to produce the **Studentized deleted residual**.

Although the difference between the deleted and ordinary residual for a case is useful as an index of the influence of that case, this measure does not reflect changes in residuals of other observations when the *i*th case is deleted. **Cook's distance** does consider changes in all residuals when case *i* is omitted (Cook, 1977). It is defined as:

$$C_i = \frac{\sum_{j=1}^{N} (\hat{Y}_j^{(i)} - \hat{Y}_j)^2}{(p+1)S^2}$$

Equation 18.28

With SPSS you can save influence measures and display them with the List Cases procedure (see Chapter 20). Influence measures for the data in Figure 18.22 are shown in Figure 18.23. The measures for case 8 (the circled point) are given in the last row. The case has neither a very large Studentized residual (*SRE_1*), nor a very large Studentized deleted residual (*SDR_1*). However, the deleted residual (*DRE_1*), 5.86, is somewhat larger than the ordinary residual (*RES_1*). The large Mahalanobis distance (*MAH_1*) identifies the case as having an *X* value far from the mean, while the large Cook's *D* (*COO_1*) identifies the case as an influential point.

Figure 18.23 Influence measures

```
CASEID  Y      RES_1     SRE_1     SDR_1     ADJ_1    DRE_1     MAH_1    COO_1

1.00    7     2.93939   1.48192   1.69900   2.90963   4.09037   1.09471  .42996
2.00    4     -.57580   -.27801   -.25543   4.73486   -.73486    .64013  .01067
3.00    6      .90910    .42617    .39506   4.90624   1.09376    .30683  .01845
4.00    3    -2.60609  -1.20001  -1.25657   6.02516  -3.02516    .09469  .11578
5.00    7      .87881    .40164    .37168   5.99502   1.00498    .00379  .01158
6.00    3    -3.63638  -1.66607  -2.07474   7.17913  -4.17913    .03410  .20715
7.00    8      .84852    .39369    .36412   6.99996   1.00004    .18559  .01384
8.00   12     1.24246   1.15294   1.19289   6.14264   5.85736   4.64016  2.46867
```

The regression coefficients with and without case 8 are shown in Figure 18.24 and Figure 18.25. Both $B_0^{(8)}$ and $B_1^{(8)}$ are far removed from B_0 and B_1, since case 8 is an influential point.

Figure 18.24 Regression coefficients from all cases

```
------------------------------ Variables in the Equation --------------------------

Variable            B         SE B    95% Confdnce Intrvl B     Beta       T    Sig T

X               .515145     .217717    -.017587    1.047877    .694761   2.366  .0558
(Constant)     3.545466    1.410980     .092941    6.997990              2.513  .0457
```

Figure 18.25 Regression coefficients without case 8

```
------------------------------ Variables in the Equation --------------------------

Variable            B         SE B    95% Confdnce Intrvl B     Beta       T    Sig T

X               .071407     .427380   -1.027192    1.170005    .074513    .167  .8739
(Constant)     5.142941    1.911317     .229818   10.056065              2.691  .0433
```

You can examine the change in the regression coefficients when a case is deleted from the analysis by saving the change in intercept and X values. For case 8 in Figure 18.26, you see that the change in the intercept (*DFB0_1*) is −1.5975 and the change in slope (*DFB1_1*) is 0.4437.

Figure 18.26 Diagnostic statistics for influential observations

```
CASEID   Y      DFB0_1      DFB1_1
1.00    7      1.30149     -.15051
2.00    4      -.20042      .02068
3.00    6       .24859     -.02131
4.00    3      -.55002      .03274
5.00    7       .13704     -.00218
6.00    3      -.37991     -.02714
7.00    8       .04546      .01515
8.00   12     -1.59748      .44374
```

When Assumptions Appear to Be Violated

When there is evidence of a violation of assumptions, you can pursue one of two strategies. You can formulate an alternative model, such as weighted least squares, or you can transform the variables so that the current model will be more adequate. For example, taking logs, square roots, or reciprocals can stabilize the variance, achieve normality, or linearize a relationship.

Coaxing a Nonlinear Relationship to Linearity

To try to achieve linearity, you can transform either the dependent or independent variables, or both. If you alter the scale of independent variables, linearity can be achieved without any effect on the distribution of the dependent variable. Thus, if the dependent variable is normally distributed with constant variance for each value of X, it remains normally distributed.

When you transform the dependent variable, its distribution is changed. This new distribution must then satisfy the assumptions of the analysis. For example, if logs of the values of the dependent variable are taken, log Y—not the original Y—must be normally distributed with constant variance.

The choice of transformation depends on several considerations. If the form of the true model governing the relationship is known, it should dictate the choice. For instance, if it is known that $\hat{Y} = AC^X$ is an adequate model, taking logs of both sides of the equation results in:

$$\log \hat{Y}_i = \underbrace{(\log A)}_{[B_0]} + \underbrace{(\log C)}_{[B_1]} X_i \qquad \text{Equation 18.29}$$

Thus, log Y is linearly related to X.

If the true model is not known, you should choose the transformation by examining the plotted data. Frequently, a relationship appears nearly linear for part of the data but is curved for the rest (for example, Figure 18.27). Taking the log of the dependent variable results in an improved linear fit (see Figure 18.28).

Figure 18.27 Nonlinear relationship

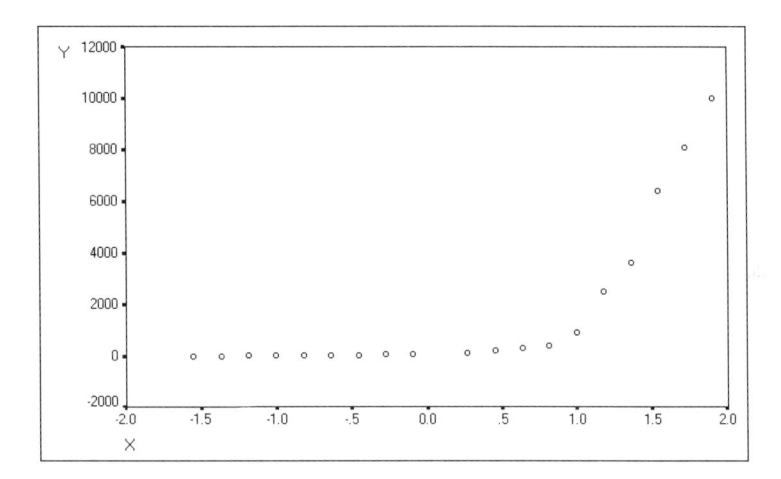

Figure 18.28 Transformed relationship

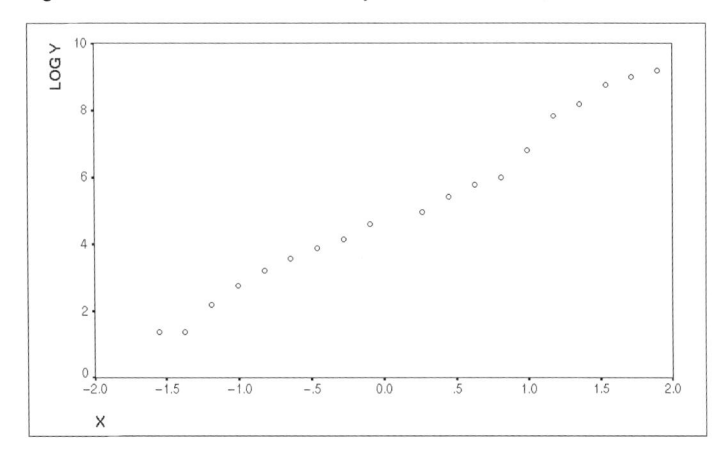

Other transformations that may diminish curvature are $-1/Y$ and the square root of Y. The choice depends, to a certain extent, on the severity of the problem.

Coping with Skewness

When the distribution of residuals is positively skewed, the log transformation of the dependent variable is often helpful. For negatively skewed distributions, the square transformation is common. It should be noted that the F tests used in regression hypothesis testing are usually quite insensitive to moderate departures from normality.

Stabilizing the Variance

If the variance of the residuals is not constant, you can try a variety of remedial measures:

- When the variance is proportional to the mean of Y for a given X, use the square root of Y if all Y_i are positive.
- When the standard deviation is proportional to the mean, try the logarithmic transformation.
- When the standard deviation is proportional to the square of the mean, use the reciprocal of Y.
- When Y is a proportion or rate, the arc sine transformation may stabilize the variance.

Transforming the Salary Data

The assumptions of constant variance and normality appear to be violated with the salary data (see Figure 18.16 and Figure 18.18). A regression equation using logs of beginning and current salaries was developed to obtain a better fit to the assumptions. Figure 18.29 is a scatterplot of Studentized residuals against predicted values when logs of both variables are used in the regression equation.

Figure 18.29 Scatterplot of transformed salary data

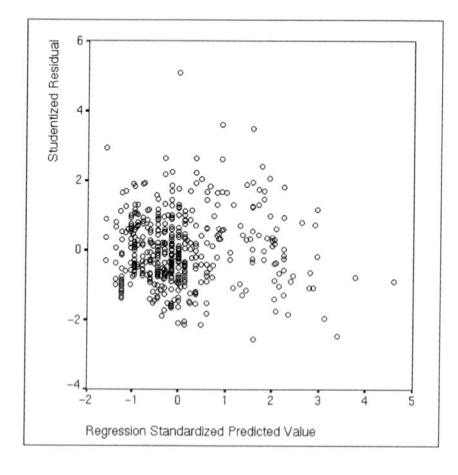

Compare Figure 18.16 and Figure 18.29, and note the improvement in the behavior of the residuals shown in Figure 18.29. The spread no longer increases with increasing salary level. Also compare Figure 18.18 and Figure 18.30, and note that the distribution in Figure 18.30 is nearly normal.

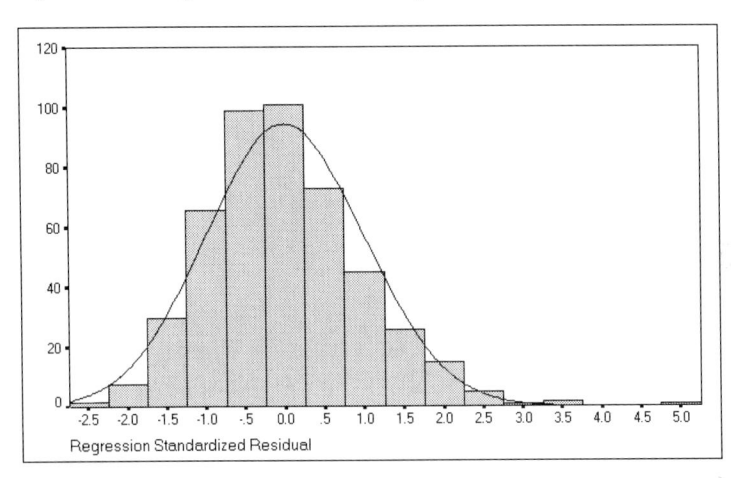

Figure 18.30 Histogram of transformed salary data

For the transformed data, the multiple R increases slightly to 0.8864, and the outlier plot contains only four cases (compare with Figure 18.6 and Figure 18.20). Thus, the transformation appears to have resulted in a better model. (For more information on transformations, see Chapter 5.)

A Final Comment on Assumptions

Rarely are assumptions not violated one way or another in regression analysis and other statistical procedures. However, this is not a justification for ignoring the assumptions. Cranking out regressions without considering possible violations of the necessary assumptions can lead to results that are difficult to interpret and apply. Significance levels, confidence intervals, and other results are sensitive to certain types of violations and cannot be interpreted in the usual fashion if serious violations exist.

By carefully examining residuals and, if need be, using transformations or other methods of analysis, you are in a much better position to pursue analyses that solve the problems you are investigating. Even if everything isn't perfect, you can at least knowledgeably gauge the potential for difficulties.

Multiple Regression Models

Beginning salary seems to be a good predictor of current salary, given the evidence shown above. Nearly 80% ($R^2 = 0.77$ from Figure 18.6) of the observed variability in current salaries can be explained by beginning salary levels. But how do variables such as education level, years of experience, race, and sex affect the salary level at which one enters the company?

Predictors of Beginning Salary

Multiple linear regression extends bivariate regression by incorporating multiple independent variables. The model can be expressed as:

$$Y_i = \beta_0 + \beta_1 X_{1i} + \beta_2 X_{2i} + \ldots + \beta_p X_{pi} + e_i \qquad \text{Equation 18.30}$$

The notation X_{pi} indicates the value of the pth independent variable for case i. Again, the β terms are unknown parameters and the e_i terms are independent random variables that are normally distributed with mean 0 and constant variance σ^2. The model assumes that there is a normal distribution of the dependent variable for every combination of the values of the independent variables in the model. For example, if child's height is the dependent variable and age and maternal height are the independent variables, it is assumed that for every combination of age and maternal height there is a normal distribution of children's heights and, though the means of these distributions may differ, all have the same variance.

The Correlation Matrix

One of the first steps in calculating an equation with several independent variables is to calculate a correlation matrix for all variables, as shown in Figure 18.31. The variables are the log of beginning salary, years of education, sex, years of work experience, minority status (race), and age in years. Variables *sex* and *minority* are represented by **indicator variables**, that is, variables coded as 0 or 1. *Sex* is coded 1 for female and 0 for male, and *minority* is coded 1 for nonwhite and 0 for white.

Figure 18.31 Correlation matrix

```
Correlation:

              LOGBEG    EDLEVEL      SEX       WORK    MINORITY     AGE
LOGBEG         1.000       .686     -.548       .040     -.173    -.048
EDLEVEL         .686      1.000     -.356      -.252     -.133    -.281
SEX            -.548      -.356     1.000      -.165     -.076     .052
WORK            .040      -.252     -.165      1.000      .145     .804
MINORITY       -.173      -.133     -.076       .145     1.000     .111
AGE            -.048      -.281      .052       .804      .111    1.000
```

The matrix shows the correlations between the dependent variable (*logbeg*) and each independent variable, as well as the correlations between the independent variables. Note particularly any large intercorrelations between the independent variables, since such correlations can substantially affect the results of multiple regression analysis.

Correlation Matrices and Missing Data

For a variety of reasons, data files frequently contain incomplete observations. Respondents in surveys scrawl illegible responses or refuse to answer certain questions. Laboratory animals die before experiments are completed. Patients fail to keep scheduled clinic appointments. Thus, before computing the correlation matrix, you must usually decide what to do with cases that have missing values for some of the variables.

Before even considering possible strategies, you should determine whether there is evidence that the missing-value pattern is not random. That is, are there reasons to believe that missing values for a variable are related to the values of that variable or other variables? For example, people with low incomes may be less willing to report their financial status than more affluent people. This may be even more pronounced for people who are poor but highly educated.

One simple method of exploring such possibilities is to subdivide the data into two groups—those with missing values for a variable and those with complete information—and examine the distributions of the other variables in the file across these two groups. SPSS crosstabulation and independent-samples *t* tests are particularly useful for this. For a discussion of other methods for detecting nonrandomness, see Frane (1976).

If it appears that the data are not missing randomly, use great caution in attempting an analysis. It may be that no satisfactory analysis is possible, especially if there are only a few cases.

If you are satisfied that the missing data are random, several strategies are available. If, for most cases, values are missing for the same few variables, consider excluding those variables from the analysis. Since this luxury is not usually available, you can alternatively keep all variables but eliminate the cases with missing values for any of them. This is termed **listwise** missing-value treatment, since a case is eliminated if it has a missing value for any variable in the list.

If many cases have missing data for some variables, listwise missing-value treatment may eliminate too many cases and leave you with a very small sample. One common technique is to calculate the correlation coefficient between a pair of variables based on all cases with complete information for the two variables, regardless of whether the cases have missing data for any other variable. For example, if a case has values only for variables 1, 3, and 5, it is used only in computations involving variable pairs 1 and 3, 1 and 5, and 3 and 5. This is **pairwise** missing-value treatment.

Several problems can arise with pairwise matrices, one of which is inconsistency. There are some relationships between coefficients that are impossible but may occur when different cases are used to estimate different coefficients. For example, if age and weight, and age and height, have a high positive correlation, it is impossible in the same sample for height and weight to have a high negative correlation. However, if the same cases are not used to estimate all three coefficients, such an anomaly can occur.

Another problem with pairwise matrices is that no single sample size can be obtained, since each coefficient may be based on a different number of cases. In addition, significance levels obtained from analyses based on pairwise matrices must be viewed with caution, since little is known about hypothesis testing in such situations.

Missing-value problems should not be treated lightly. You should always select a missing-value treatment based on careful examination of the data and not leave the choices up to system defaults. In this example, complete information is available for all cases, so missing values are not a problem.

Partial Regression Coefficients

The summary output when all independent variables are included in the multiple regression equation is shown in Figure 18.32. The F test associated with the analysis-of-variance table is a test of the null hypothesis that:

$$\beta_1 = \beta_2 = \beta_3 = \beta_4 = \beta_5 = 0$$
Equation 18.31

In other words, it is a test of whether there is a linear relationship between the dependent variable and the entire set of independent variables.

Figure 18.32 Statistics for the equation and analysis-of-variance table

```
Multiple R            .78420
R Square              .61498
Adjusted R Square     .61086
Standard Error        .09559

Analysis of Variance
                DF      Sum of Squares      Mean Square
Regression       5             6.83039          1.36608
Residual       468             4.27638           .00914

F =      149.50125      Signif F =   .0000
```

The statistics for the independent variables in Figure 18.33 are parallel to those obtained in regression with a single independent variable (see Figure 18.3). In multiple regres-

Figure 18.33 Statistics for variables in the equation

```
------------------ Variables in the Equation ------------------

Variable            B          SE B        Beta         T      Sig T

AGE            .001015    6.6132E-04     .078106      1.535    .1254
SEX           -.103576      .010318    -.336987    -10.038    .0000
MINORITY      -.052366      .010837    -.141573     -4.832    .0000
EDLEVEL        .031443      .001748     .591951     17.988    .0000
WORK           .001608    9.2407E-04     .091428      1.740    .0826
(Constant)    3.385300      .033233                 101.866    .0000
```

sion, the coefficients labeled *B* are called **partial regression coefficients**, since the coefficient for a particular variable is adjusted for other independent variables in the equation. The equation that relates the predicted log of beginning salary to the independent variables is:

logbeg = 3.3853 + 0.00102(age) − 0.10358(sex)
− 0.05237(minority) + 0.03144(edlevel)   **Equation 18.32**
+ 0.00161(work)

Since the dependent variable is in log units, the coefficients can be approximately interpreted in percentage terms. For example, the coefficient of −0.104 for *sex* when females are coded as 1 indicates that female salaries are estimated to be about 10% less than male salaries after statistical adjustment for age, education, work history, and minority status.

Determining Important Variables

In multiple regression, you sometimes want to assign relative importance to each independent variable. For example, you might want to know whether education is more important in predicting beginning salary than previous work experience. There are two possible approaches, depending on which of the following questions is asked:

- How important are education and work experience when each one is used alone to predict beginning salary?
- How important are education and work experience when they are used to predict beginning salary along with other independent variables in the regression equation?

The first question is answered by looking at the correlation coefficients between salary and the independent variables. The larger the absolute value of the correlation coefficient, the stronger the linear association. Figure 18.31 shows that education correlates more highly with the log of salary than does previous work experience (0.686 and 0.040, respectively). Thus, you would assign more importance to education as a predictor of salary.

The answer to the second question is considerably more complicated. When the independent variables are correlated among themselves, the unique contribution of each is difficult to assess. Any statement about an independent variable is contingent upon the other variables in the equation. For example, the regression coefficient *(B)* for work experience is 0.0007 when it is the sole independent variable in the equation, compared to 0.00161 when the other four independent variables are also in the equation. The second coefficient is more than twice the size of the first.

Beta Coefficients

It is also inappropriate to interpret the B's as indicators of the relative importance of variables. The actual magnitude of the coefficients depends on the units in which the variables are measured. Only if all independent variables are measured in the same units—years, for example—are their coefficients directly comparable. When variables differ substantially in units of measurement, the sheer magnitude of their coefficients does not reveal anything about relative importance.

One way to make regression coefficients somewhat more comparable is to calculate **beta weights**, which are the coefficients of the independent variables when all variables are expressed in standardized (Z score) form (see Figure 18.33). The **beta coefficients** can be calculated directly from the regression coefficients using

$$\text{beta}_k = B_k \left(\frac{S_k}{S_Y}\right) \qquad \text{Equation 18.33}$$

where S_k is the standard deviation of the kth independent variable.

However, the values of the beta coefficients, like the B's, are contingent on the other independent variables in the equation. They are also affected by the correlations of the independent variables and do not in any absolute sense reflect the importance of the various independent variables.

Part and Partial Coefficients

Another way of assessing the relative importance of independent variables is to consider the increase in R^2 when a variable is entered into an equation that already contains the other independent variables. This increase is

$$R^2_{\text{change}} = R^2 - R^2_{(i)} \qquad \text{Equation 18.34}$$

where $R^2_{(i)}$ is the square of the multiple correlation coefficient when all independent variables except the ith are in the equation. A large change in R^2 indicates that a variable provides unique information about the dependent variable that is not available from the other independent variables in the equation. The signed square root of the increase is called the **part correlation coefficient**. It is the correlation between Y and X_i when the linear effects of the other independent variables have been removed from X_i. If all independent variables are uncorrelated, the change in R^2 when a variable is entered into the equation is simply the square of the correlation coefficient between that variable and the dependent variable.

The value of *RsqCh* in Figure 18.34 shows that the addition of years of education to an equation that contains the other four independent variables results in a change in R^2 of 0.266. This value tells only how much R^2 increases when a variable is added to the regression equation. It does not indicate what proportion of the unexplained variation this increase constitutes. If most of the variation had been explained by the other variables, a small change in R^2 is all that is possible for the remaining variable.

Figure 18.34 Change in R-squared

```
Block Number 5.  Method:  Enter  EDLEVEL

Step   MultR    Rsq    AdjRsq   F(Eqn)   SigF   RsqCh    FCh     SigCh      Variable    BetaIn   Correl
   5   .7842   .6150    .6109  149.501   .000   .2662  323.554   .000   In: EDLEVEL      .5920    .6857
```

A coefficient that measures the proportional reduction in variation is:

$$Pr_i^2 = \frac{R^2 - R^2_{(i)}}{1 - R^2_{(i)}}$$

Equation 18.35

The numerator is the square of the part coefficient; the denominator is the proportion of unexplained variation when all but the ith variable are in the equation. The signed square root of Pr_i^2 is the **partial correlation coefficient**. It can be interpreted as the correlation between the ith independent variable and the dependent variable when the linear effects of the other independent variables have been removed from both X_i and Y. Since the denominator of Pr_i^2 is always less than or equal to 1, the part correlation coefficient is never larger in absolute value than the partial correlation coefficient.

Plots of the residuals of Y and X_i, when the linear effects of the other independent variables have been removed, are a useful diagnostic aid. They are discussed in "Checking for Violations of Assumptions" on p. 339.

Building a Model

Our selection of the five variables to predict beginning salary has been arbitrary to some extent. It is unlikely that all relevant variables have been identified and measured. Instead, some relevant variables have no doubt been excluded, while others that were included may not be very important determinants of salary level. This is not unusual; you must try to build a model from available data, as voluminous or scanty as the data may be. Before considering several formal procedures for model building, we will examine some of the consequences of adding and deleting variables from regression equations. The regression statistics for variables not in the equation are also described.

Adding and Deleting Variables

The first step in Figure 18.35 shows the summary statistics when years of education is the sole independent variable and log of beginning salary is the dependent variable. Consider the second step in the same figure, when another variable, *sex*, is added. The value displayed as $RsqCh$ in the second step is the change in R^2 when *sex* is added. R^2 for *edlevel* alone is 0.4702, so R^2_{change} is $0.5760 - 0.4702$, or 0.1058.

Figure 18.35 Adding a variable to the equation

```
Equation Number 1    Dependent Variable..   LOGBEG
Block Number    1.  Method:  Enter        EDLEVEL
Step    MultR    Rsq   AdjRsq   F(Eqn)    SigF   RsqCh       FCh  SigCh
  1     .6857   .4702   .4691   418.920   .000   .4702   418.920  .000

End Block Number    1   All requested variables entered.

Block Number    2.  Method:  Enter        SEX
Step    MultR    Rsq   AdjRsq   F(Eqn)    SigF   RsqCh       FCh  SigCh
  2     .7589   .5760   .5742   319.896   .000   .1058   117.486  .000

End Block Number    2   All requested variables entered.
```

The null hypothesis that the true population value for the change in R^2 is 0 can be tested using

$$F_{change} = \frac{R^2_{change}(N-p-1)}{q(1-R^2)} = \frac{(0.1058)(474-2-1)}{1(1-0.5760)} = 117.49 \quad \text{Equation 18.36}$$

where N is the number of cases in the equation, p is the total number of independent variables in the equation, and q is the number of variables entered at this step. This is also referred to as a **partial F test**. Under the hypothesis that the true change is 0, the significance of the value labeled *FCh* can be obtained from the F distribution with q and $N-p-1$ degrees of freedom.

The hypothesis that the real change in R^2 is 0 can also be formulated in terms of the β parameters. When only the ith variable is added in a step, the hypothesis that the change in R^2 is 0 is equivalent to the hypothesis that β_i is 0. The F value displayed for the change in R^2 is the square of the t value for the test of the coefficient.

When q independent variables are entered in a single step, the test that R^2 is 0 is equivalent to the simultaneous test that the coefficients of all q variables are 0. For example, if sex and age were added in the same step to the regression equation that contains education, the F test for R^2 change would be the same as the F test which tests the hypothesis that $\beta_{sex} = \beta_{age} = 0$.

Entering sex into the equation with education has effects in addition to changing R^2. For example, the magnitude of the regression coefficient for education from step 1 to step 2 decreases from 0.0364 to 0.0298. This is attributable to the correlation between sex and level of education.

When highly intercorrelated independent variables are included in a regression equation, results may appear anomalous. The overall regression may be significant, while none of the individual coefficients are significant. The signs of the regression coefficients may be counterintuitive. High correlations between independent variables inflate the variances of the estimates, making individual coefficients quite unreliable without adding much to the overall fit of the model. The problem of linear relationships between independent variables is discussed further in "Measures of Collinearity" on p. 343.

Statistics for Variables Not in the Equation

When you have independent variables that have not been entered into the equation, you can examine what would happen if they were entered at the next step. Statistics describing these variables are shown in Figure 18.36. The column labeled *Beta In* is the standardized regression coefficient that would result if the variable were entered into the equation at the next step. The t test and level of significance are for the hypothesis that the coefficient is 0. (Remember that the t test and the partial F test for the hypothesis that a coefficient is 0 are equivalent.) The partial correlation coefficient with the dependent variable adjusts for the variables already in the equation.

Figure 18.36 Coefficients for variables not in the equation

```
------------ Variables not in the Equation -------------

Variable      Beta In   Partial   Min Toler        T   Sig T

WORK          .144245   .205668    .773818     4.556  .0000
MINORITY     -.129022  -.194642    .847583    -4.302  .0000
AGE           .139419   .205193    .804253     4.545  .0000
```

From statistics calculated for variables not in the equation, you can decide what variable should be entered next. This process is detailed in "Procedures for Selecting Variables" on p. 334.

The "Optimal" Number of Independent Variables

Having seen what happens when sex is added to the equation containing education (Figure 18.35), consider now what happens when the remaining three independent variables are entered one at a time in no particular order. Summary output is shown in Figure 18.37. Step 5 shows the statistics for the equation with all independent variables entered. Step 3 describes the model with education, sex, and work experience as the independent variables.

Figure 18.37 All independent variables in the equation

```
Step    MultR     Rsq   AdjRsq    F(Eqn)    SigF    RsqCh       FCh  SigCh         Variable
  1    .6857    .4702    .4691   418.920    .000    .4702   418.920   .000   In:  EDLEVEL

Step    MultR     Rsq   AdjRsq    F(Eqn)    SigF    RsqCh       FCh  SigCh         Variable
  2    .7589    .5760    .5742   319.896    .000    .1058   117.486   .000   In:  SEX
Step    MultR     Rsq   AdjRsq    F(Eqn)    SigF    RsqCh       FCh  SigCh         Variable
  3    .7707    .5939    .5913   229.130    .000    .0179    20.759   .000   In:  WORK

Step    MultR     Rsq   AdjRsq    F(Eqn)    SigF    RsqCh       FCh  SigCh         Variable
  4    .7719    .5958    .5923   172.805    .000    .0019     2.149   .143   In:  AGE

Step    MultR     Rsq   AdjRsq    F(Eqn)    SigF    RsqCh       FCh  SigCh         Variable
  5    .7842    .6150    .6109   149.501    .000    .0192    23.349   .000   In:  MINORITY
```

Examination of Figure 18.37 shows that R^2 never decreases as independent variables are added. This is always true in regression analysis. However, this does not necessarily mean that the equation with more variables better fits the population. As the number of parameters estimated from the sample increases, so does the goodness of fit to the sample as measured by R^2. For example, if a sample contains six cases, a regression equation with six parameters fits the sample exactly, even though there may be no true statistical relationship at all between the dependent variable and the independent variables.

As indicated in "The R-squared Coefficient" on p. 306, the sample R^2 in general tends to overestimate the population value of R^2. Adjusted R^2 attempts to correct the optimistic bias of the sample R^2. Adjusted R^2 does not necessarily increase as additional variables are added to an equation and is the preferred measure of goodness of fit because it is not subject to the inflationary bias of unadjusted R^2. This statistic is shown in the column labeled *AdjRsq* in the output.

Although adding independent variables increases R^2, it does not necessarily decrease the standard error of the estimate. Each time a variable is added to the equation, a degree of freedom is lost from the residual sum of squares and one is gained for the regression sum of squares. The standard error may increase when the decrease in the residual sum of squares is very slight and not sufficient to make up for the loss of a degree of freedom for the residual sum of squares. The *F* value for the test of the overall regression decreases when the regression sum of squares does not increase as fast as the degrees of freedom for the regression.

Including a large number of independent variables in a regression model is never a good strategy, unless there are strong, previous reasons to suggest that they all should be included. The observed increase in R^2 does not necessarily reflect a better fit of the model in the population. Including irrelevant variables increases the standard errors of all estimates without improving prediction. A model with many variables is often difficult to interpret.

On the other hand, it is important not to exclude potentially relevant independent variables. The following sections describe various procedures for selecting variables to be included in a regression model. The goal is to build a concise model that makes good prediction possible.

Procedures for Selecting Variables

You can construct a variety of regression models from the same set of variables. For instance, you can build seven different equations from three independent variables: three with only one independent variable, three with two independent variables, and one with all three. As the number of variables increases, so does the number of potential models (ten independent variables yield 1,023 models).

Although there are procedures for computing all possible regression equations, several other methods do not require as much computation and are more frequently used. Among these procedures are forward selection, backward elimination, and stepwise regression. None of these variable selection procedures is "best" in any absolute sense; they merely identify subsets of variables that, for the sample, are good predictors of the dependent variable.

Forward Selection

In **forward selection**, the first variable considered for entry into the equation is the one with the largest positive or negative correlation with the dependent variable. The F test for the hypothesis that the coefficient of the entered variable is 0 is then calculated. To determine whether this variable (and each succeeding variable) is entered, the F value is compared with an established criterion. You can specify one of two criteria in SPSS. One criterion is the minimum value of the F statistic that a variable must achieve in order to enter, called **F-to-enter (FIN)**, with a default value of 3.84. The other criterion you can specify is the probability associated with the F statistic, called **probability of F-to-enter (PIN)**, with a default of 0.05. In this case, a variable enters into the equation only if the probability associated with the F test is less than or equal to the default 0.05 or the value you specify. By default, PIN is the criterion used. (In the output, SPSS generally displays t values and their probabilities. These t probabilities are equivalent to those associated with F. You can obtain F values by squaring t values, since $t^2 = F$.)

The PIN and FIN criteria are not necessarily equivalent. As variables are added to the equation, the degrees of freedom associated with the residual sum of squares decrease while the regression degrees of freedom increase. Thus, a fixed F value has different significance levels depending on the number of variables currently in the equation. For large samples, the differences are negligible.

The actual significance level associated with the F-to-enter statistic is not the one usually obtained from the F distribution, since many variables are being examined and the largest F value is selected. Unfortunately, the true significance level is difficult to compute, since it depends not only on the number of cases and variables but also on the correlations between independent variables.

If the first variable selected for entry meets the criterion for inclusion, forward selection continues. Otherwise, the procedure terminates with no variables in the equation. Once one variable is entered, the statistics for variables not in the equation are used to select the next one. The partial correlations between the dependent variable and each of the independent variables not in the equation, adjusted for the independent variables in the equation, are examined. The variable with the largest partial correlation is the next candidate. Choosing the variable with the largest partial correlation in absolute value is equivalent to selecting the variable with the largest F value.

If the criterion is met, the variable is entered into the equation and the procedure is repeated. The procedure stops when there are no other variables that meet the entry criterion.

Figure 18.38 shows output generated from a forward-selection procedure using the salary data. The default entry criterion is PIN = 0.05. In the first step, education (variable *edlevel*) is entered, since it has the highest correlation with beginning salary. The significance level associated with education is less than 0.0005, so it certainly meets the criterion for entry.

Figure 18.38 Summary statistics for forward selection

```
Step   MultR    Rsq    F(Eqn)   SigF         Variable   BetaIn
  1    .6857   .4702   418.920  .000   In:   EDLEVEL     .6857
  2    .7589   .5760   319.896  .000   In:   SEX        -.3480
  3    .7707   .5939   229.130  .000   In:   WORK        .1442
  4    .7830   .6130   185.750  .000   In:   MINORITY   -.1412
```

To see how the next variable, *sex*, was selected, look at the statistics shown in Figure 18.39 for variables not in the equation when only *edlevel* is in the equation. The variable with the largest partial correlation is *sex*. If entered at the next step, it would have a *t* value of –10.839. Since the probability associated with the *t* value is less than 0.05, variable *sex* is entered in the second step.

Figure 18.39 Status of the variables at the first step

```
----------------- Variables in the Equation ------------------

Variable              B         SE B       Beta           T    Sig T

EDLEVEL           .036424     .001780    .685719      20.468   .0000
(Constant)       3.310013     .024551                134.821   .0000


------------- Variables not in the Equation -------------

Variable     Beta In   Partial   Min Toler        T    Sig T

SEX         -.348017  -.446811    .873274    -10.839   .0000
WORK         .227473   .302405    .936316      6.885   .0000
MINORITY    -.083181  -.113267    .982341     -2.474   .0137
AGE          .157180   .207256    .921128      4.598   .0000
```

Once variable *sex* enters at step 2, the statistics for variables not in the equation must be examined (see Figure 18.36). The variable with the largest absolute value for the partial correlation coefficient is now years of work experience. Its *t* value is 4.556 with a probability less than 0.05, so variable *work* is entered in the next step. The same process takes place with variable *minority*, leaving *age* as the only variable out of the equation. However, as shown in Figure 18.40, the significance level associated with the *age* coefficient *t* value is 0.1254, which is too large for entry. Thus, forward selection yields the summary table for the four steps shown in Figure 18.38.

Figure 18.40 Forward selection at the last step

```
------------- Variables not in the Equation -------------

Variable    Beta In   Partial   Min Toler       T    Sig T

AGE         .078106   .070796    .297843     1.535   .1254
```

Backward Elimination

While forward selection starts with no independent variables in the equation and sequentially enters them, **backward elimination** starts with all variables in the equation and sequentially removes them. Instead of entry criteria, removal criteria are used.

Two removal criteria are available in SPSS. The first is the minimum F value that a variable must have in order to remain in the equation. Variables with F values less than this **F-to-remove (FOUT)** are eligible for removal. The second criterion available is the maximum **probability of F-to-remove (POUT)** that a variable can have. The default FOUT value is 2.71 and the default POUT value is 0.10. The default criterion is probability of F-to-remove.

Look at the salary example again, this time constructing the model with backward elimination. The output in Figure 18.41 is from the first step, in which all variables are entered into the equation. The variable with the smallest partial correlation coefficient, *age*, is examined first. Since the probability of its t (0.1254) is greater than the default POUT criterion value of 0.10, variable *age* is removed. (Recall that the t test and the partial F test for the hypothesis that a coefficient is 0 are equivalent.)

Figure 18.41 Backward elimination at the first step

```
----------------- Variables in the Equation ------------------

Variable              B          SE B        Beta          T      Sig T

AGE              .001015    6.6132E-04     .078106      1.535     .1254
SEX             -.103576      .010318     -.336987    -10.038     .0000
MINORITY        -.052366      .010837     -.141573     -4.832     .0000
EDLEVEL          .031443      .001748      .591951     17.988     .0000
WORK             .001608    9.2407E-04     .091428      1.740     .0826
(Constant)      3.385300      .033233                  101.866    .0000
```

The equation is then recalculated without *age*, producing the statistics shown in Figure 18.42. The variable with the smallest partial correlation is *minority*. However, its significance is less than the 0.10 criterion, so backward elimination stops. The equation resulting from backward elimination is the same as the one from forward selection. This is not always the case, however. Forward- and backward-selection procedures can give different results, even with comparable entry and removal criteria.

Figure 18.42 Backward elimination at the last step

```
----------------- Variables in the Equation ------------------

Variable              B          SE B        Beta          T      Sig T

SEX             -.099042      .009901     -.322234    -10.003     .0000
MINORITY        -.052245      .010853     -.141248     -4.814     .0000
EDLEVEL          .031433      .001751      .591755     17.956     .0000
WORK             .002753    5.4582E-04     .156592      5.044     .0000
(Constant)      3.411953      .028380                  120.225    .0000


------------- Variables not in the Equation -------------

Variable    Beta In   Partial   Min Toler       T    Sig T

AGE         .078106   .070796    .297843     1.535   .1254
```

Stepwise Selection

Stepwise selection of independent variables is really a combination of backward and forward procedures and is probably the most commonly used method. The first variable is selected in the same manner as in forward selection. If the variable fails to meet entry requirements (either FIN or PIN), the procedure terminates with no independent variables in the equation. If it passes the criterion, the second variable is selected based on the highest partial correlation. If it passes entry criteria, it also enters the equation.

After the first variable is entered, stepwise selection differs from forward selection: the first variable is examined to see whether it should be removed according to the removal criterion (FOUT or POUT) as in backward elimination. In the next step, variables not in the equation are examined for entry. After each step, variables already in the equation are examined for removal. Variables are removed until none remain that meet the removal criterion. To prevent the same variable from being repeatedly entered and removed, the PIN must be less than the POUT (or FIN greater than FOUT). Variable selection terminates when no more variables meet entry and removal criteria.

In the salary example, stepwise selection with the default criteria results in the same equation produced by both forward selection and backward elimination (see Figure 18.43).

Figure 18.43 Stepwise selection at the last step

```
Multiple R               .78297
R Square                 .61304
Adjusted R Square        .60974
Standard Error           .09573

F =      185.74958       Signif F =   .0000


------------------ Variables in the Equation ------------------

Variable              B         SE B         Beta           T    Sig T

EDLEVEL          .031433      .001751      .591755      17.956   .0000
SEX             -.099042      .009901     -.322234     -10.003   .0000
WORK             .002753    5.4582E-04     .156592       5.044   .0000
MINORITY        -.052245      .010853     -.141248      -4.814   .0000
(Constant)      3.411953      .028380                  120.225   .0000


Equation Number 1    Dependent Variable..   LOGBEG

------------ Variables not in the Equation -------------

Variable     Beta In  Partial   Min Toler        T    Sig T

AGE           .078106  .070796    .297843      1.535   .1254
```

The three procedures do not always result in the same equation, though you should be encouraged when they do. The model selected by any method should be carefully studied for violations of the assumptions. It is often a good idea to develop several acceptable models and then choose among them based on interpretability, ease of variable acquisition, parsimony, and so forth.

Checking for Violations of Assumptions

The procedures for checking for violations of assumptions in bivariate regression (see "Searching for Violations of Assumptions" on p. 312) apply in multiple regression as well. Residuals should be plotted against predicted values as well as against each independent variable. The distribution of residuals should be examined for normality.

Several additional residual plots may be useful for multiple regression models. One of these is the **partial regression plot**. For the jth independent variable, it is obtained by calculating the residuals for the dependent variable when it is predicted from all the independent variables excluding the jth and by calculating the residuals for the jth independent variable when it is predicted from all of the other independent variables. This removes the linear effect of the other independent variables from both variables. For each case, these two residuals are plotted against each other.

A partial regression plot for educational level for the regression equation that contains work experience, minority, sex, and educational level as the independent variables is shown in Figure 18.44. (Summary statistics for the regression equation with all independent variables are displayed in the last step of Figure 18.43.) The partial regression plot (created by saving residuals in the Linear Regression procedure and then using the Scatter option on the Graphs menu) shows residuals for *logbeg* on the y axis and residual values for *edlevel* on the x axis.

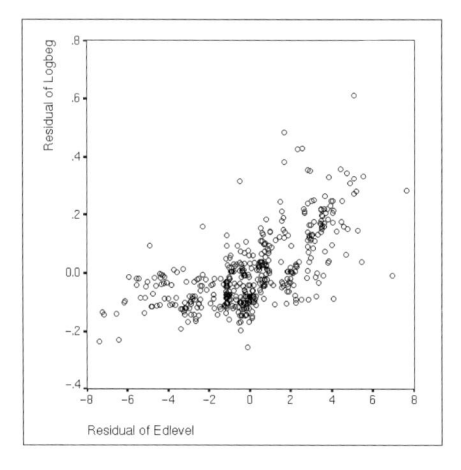

Figure 18.44 Partial regression plot

Several characteristics of the partial regression plot make it a particularly valuable diagnostic tool. The slope of the regression line for the two residual variables (0.03143) is equal to the coefficient for the *edlevel* variable in the multiple regression equation after the last step (step 4 in Figure 18.43). Thus, by examining the bivariate plot, you can conveniently identify points that are influential in the determination of the particular regression coefficient. The correlation coefficient between the two residuals, 0.638, is the partial correlation coefficient discussed in "Part and Partial Coefficients" on p. 330. The residuals from the least-squares line in Figure 18.44 are equal to the residuals from the final multiple regression equation, which includes all the independent variables.

The partial regression plot also helps you assess the inadequacies of the selected model and violations of the underlying assumptions. For example, the partial regression plot of educational level does not appear to be linear, suggesting that an additional term, such as years of education squared, might also be included in the model. This violation is much easier to spot using the partial regression plot than the plot of the independent variable against the residual from the equation with all independent variables. Figure 18.45 shows the residual scatterplot created with the Graph procedure and Figure 18.46 shows the partial regression plot produced by the Regression procedure. Note that the nonlinearity is much more apparent in the partial regression plot.

Figure 18.45 Residual plot

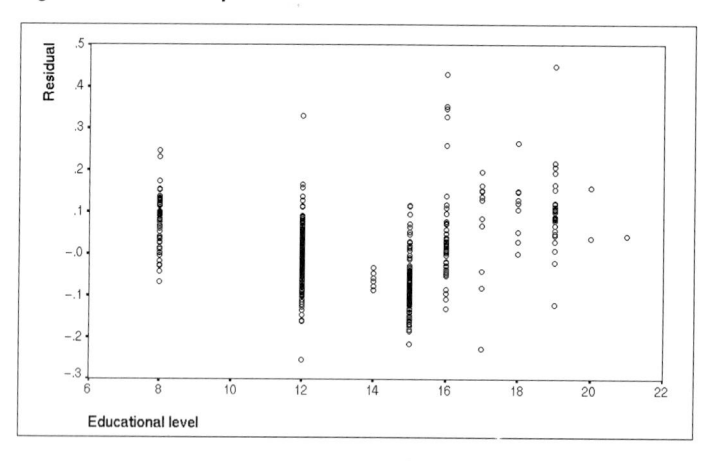

Figure 18.46 Partial regression plot

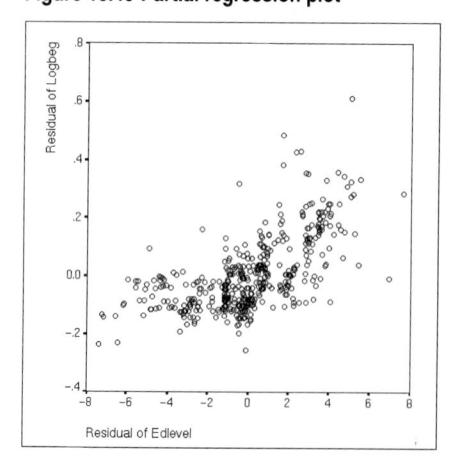

Figure 18.47 contains the summary statistics generated when the number of years of education squared is included in the multiple regression equation. The multiple R^2 increases from 0.61 (step 4 in Figure 18.43) to 0.71, a significant improvement.

Figure 18.47 Regression equation with education squared

```
Multiple R           .84302
R Square             .71068
Adjusted R Square    .70759
Standard Error       .08286

Analysis of Variance
                DF    Sum of Squares    Mean Square
Regression       5           7.89331        1.57866
Residual       468           3.21345         .00687

F =    229.91286      Signif F =   .0000
```

Looking for Influential Points

As discussed earlier, when building a regression model, it is important to identify cases that are influential, or that have a disproportionately large effect on the estimated model. (See "Locating Outliers" on p. 318.) We can look for cases that change the values of the regression coefficients and of predicted values, cases that increase the variances of the coefficients, and cases that are poorly fitted by the model.

Among the important influence measures is the **leverage** of a case. The predicted values of the dependent variable can be expressed as:

$$\hat{Y} = HY$$ **Equation 18.37**

The diagonal elements of the H matrix (commonly called the hat matrix) are called leverages. The leverage for a case describes the impact of the observed value of the dependent variable on the prediction of the fitted value. Leverages are important in their own right and as fundamental building blocks for other diagnostic measures. For example, the Mahalanobis distance for a point is obtained by multiplying the leverage value by $N-1$.

SPSS computes centered leverages. They range from 0 to $(N-1)/N$, where N is the number of observations. The mean value for the centered leverage is p/N, where p is the number of independent variables in the equation. A leverage of 0 identifies a point with no influence on the fit, while a point with a leverage of $(N-1)/N$ indicates that a degree of freedom has been devoted to fitting the data point. Ideally, you would like each observation to exert a roughly equal influence. That is, you want all of the leverages to be near p/N. It is a good idea to examine points with leverage values that exceed $2p/N$.

To see the effect of a case on the estimation of the regression coefficients, you can look at the change in each of the regression coefficients when the case is removed from the analysis. SPSS can display or save the actual change in each of the coefficients, including the intercept and the standardized change.

Figure 18.48 is a plot of standardized change values for the *minority* variable on the vertical axis against a case ID number on the horizontal axis. Note that as expected, most of the points cluster in a horizontal band around 0. However, there are a few points far removed from the rest. Belsley et al. (1980) recommend examining standardized change values that are larger than $(2/\sqrt{N})$.

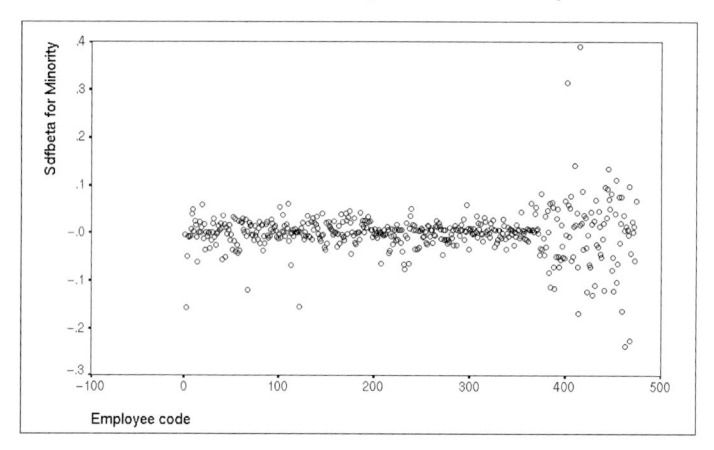

Figure 18.48 Plot of standardized change values for minority status

In addition to looking at the change in the regression coefficients when a case is deleted from an analysis, we can look at the change in the predicted value or at the standardized change. Cases with large values far removed from the rest should be examined. As a rule of thumb, you may want to look at standardized values larger than $2/\sqrt{p/N}$.

Another type of influential observation is one that influences the variance of the estimated regression coefficients. A measure of the impact of an observation on the variance-covariance matrix of the parameter estimates is called the **covariance ratio**. It is computed as the ratio of the determinant of the variance-covariance matrix computed without the case to the determinant of the variance-covariance matrix computed with all cases. If this ratio is close to 1, the case leaves the variance-covariance matrix relatively unchanged. Belsley et al. (1980) recommend examining points for which the absolute value of the ratio minus 1 is greater than $3p/N$.

You can save covariance ratios with the Linear Regression procedure and plot them using the Scatter option on the Graphs menu. Figure 18.49 is a plot of covariance ratios for the salary example. Note the circled point, which has a covariance ratio substantially smaller than the rest.

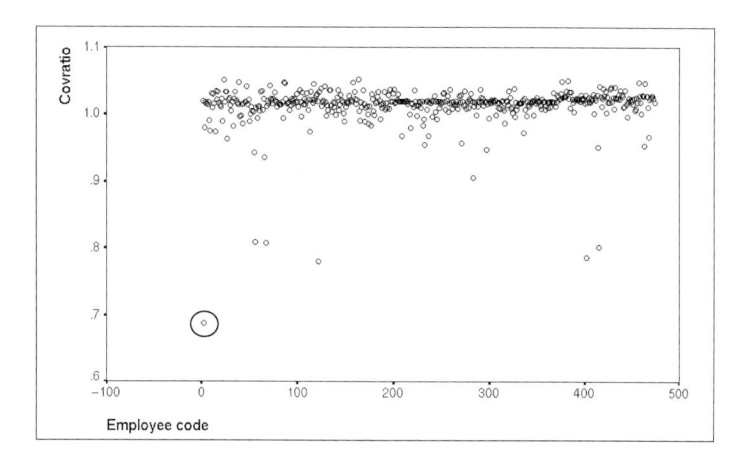

Figure 18.49 Plot of the covariance ratio

Measures of Collinearity

Collinearity refers to the situation in which there is a high multiple correlation when one of the independent variables is regressed on the others (that is, when there is a high correlation between independent variables). The problem with collinear variables is that they provide very similar information, and it is difficult to separate out the effects of the individual variables. Diagnostics are available which allow you to detect the presence of collinear data and to assess the extent to which the collinearity has degraded the estimated parameters.

The **tolerance** of a variable is a commonly used measure of collinearity. The tolerance of variable i is defined as $1 - R_i^2$, where R_i is the multiple correlation coefficient when the ith independent variable is predicted from the other independent variables. If the tolerance of a variable is small, it is almost a linear combination of the other independent variables.

The **variance inflation factor** (**VIF**) is closely related to the tolerance. In fact, it is defined as the reciprocal of the tolerance. That is, for the ith variable,

$$\text{VIF}_i = \frac{1}{(1 - R_i^2)} \qquad \text{Equation 18.38}$$

This quantity is called the variance inflation factor, since the term is involved in the calculation of the variance of the ith regression coefficient. As the variance inflation factor increases, so does the variance of the regression coefficient.

Figure 18.50 shows the tolerances and VIF's for the variables in the final model. Note the low tolerances and high VIF's for *edlevel* and *ed2* (the square of *edlevel*). This is to be expected, since there is a relationship between these two variables.

Figure 18.50 Measures of collinearity—tolerance and VIF

```
-------------------------- Variables in the Equation --------------------------

Variable              B         SE B       Beta     Tolerance      VIF        T      Sig T

WORK              .001794   4.7859E-04    .102038    .834367      1.199     3.749    .0002
MINORITY         -.038225    .009460     -.103342    .945107      1.058    -4.041    .0001
SEX              -.082503    .008671     -.268426    .776799      1.287    -9.515    .0000
EDLEVEL          -.089624    .009751    -1.687260    .018345     54.511    -9.191    .0000
ED2               .004562   3.6303E-04   2.312237    .018263     54.756    12.567    .0000
(Constant)       4.173910    .065417                                       63.804    .0000
```

Two useful tools for examining the collinearity of a data matrix are the eigenvalues of the scaled, uncentered cross-products matrix and the decomposition of regression variance corresponding to the eigenvalues.

Eigenvalues and Condition Indexes

We can compare the eigenvalues of the scaled, uncentered cross-products matrix to see if some are much larger than others. If this is the case, the data matrix is said to be **ill-conditioned**. If a matrix is ill-conditioned, small changes in the values of the independent or dependent variables may lead to large changes in the solution. The condition index is defined as:

$$\text{condition index} = \sqrt{\frac{\text{eigenvalue}_{max}}{\text{eigenvalue}_i}}$$

Equation 18.39

There are as many near-dependencies among the variables as there are large condition indexes.

Figure 18.51 shows the eigenvalues and condition indexes for the salary example. You can see that the last two eigenvalues are much smaller than the rest. Their condition indexes are 10.29 and 88.22.

Figure 18.51 Measures of collinearity—eigenvalues and condition indexes

```
Collinearity Diagnostics

Number  Eigenval    Cond    Variance Proportions
                    Index   Constant    SEX    MINORITY  EDLEVEL     ED2      WORK
  1     4.08812    1.000     .00019   .01223   .01375    .00004    .00013   .01466
  2      .79928    2.262     .00005   .08212   .65350    .00002    .00009   .04351
  3      .59282    2.626     .00001   .37219   .22139    .00003    .00022   .17437
  4      .48061    2.917     .00005   .14964   .05421    .00012    .00091   .51370
  5      .03864   10.286     .05223   .37811   .04876    .00004    .02337   .20721
  6      .00053   88.221     .94746   .00571   .00839    .99975    .97527   .04655
```

Variance Proportions

The variances of each of the regression coefficients, including the constant, can be decomposed into a sum of components associated with each of the eigenvalues. If a high proportion of the variance of two or more coefficients is associated with the same eigenvalue, there is evidence for a near-dependency.

Consider Figure 18.51 again. Each of the columns following the condition index tells you the proportion of the variance of each of the coefficients associated with each of the eigenvalues. Consider the column for the *sex* coefficient. You see that 1.22% of the variance of the coefficient is attributable to the first eigenvalue, 8.2% to the second, and 0.57% to the sixth (the proportions in each column sum to 1).

In this table you're looking for variables with high proportions for the same eigenvalue. For example, looking at the last eigenvalue, you see that it accounts for 95% of the variance of the constant, almost 100% of the variance of *edlevel*, and 98% of the variance of *ed2*. This tells you that these three variables are highly dependent. Since the other independent variables have small variance proportions for the sixth eigenvalue, it does not appear that the observed dependencies are affecting their coefficients. (See Belsley et al., 1980, for an extensive discussion of these diagnostics.)

Interpreting the Equation

The multiple regression equation estimated above suggests several findings. Education appears to be the best predictor of beginning salary, at least among the variables included in this study (Figure 18.41). The sex of the employee also appears to be important. Women are paid less than men, since the sign of the regression coefficient is negative (men are coded 0 and women are coded 1). Years of prior work experience and race are also related to salary, but when education and sex are included in the equation, the effect of experience and race is less striking.

Do these results indicate that there is sex discrimination at the bank? Not necessarily. It is well recognized that all education is not equally profitable. Master's degrees in business administration and in political science are viewed quite differently in the marketplace. Thus, a possible explanation of the observed results is that women enter areas that just don't pay very well. Although this may suggest inequities in societal evaluation of skills, it does not necessarily imply discrimination at the bank. Further, many other potential job-related skills or qualifications are not included in the model. As well, some of the existing variables, such as age, may make nonlinear as well as linear contributions to the fit. Such contributions can often be approximated by including new variables that are simple functions of the existing one. For example, the age values squared may improve the fit.

How to Obtain a Linear Regression Analysis

The Linear Regression procedure provides five equation-building methods: forward selection, backward elimination, stepwise selection, forced entry, and forced removal. It can produce residual analyses to help detect influential data points, outliers, and violations of regression model assumptions. You can also save predicted values, residuals, and related measures.

The minimum specifications are:
- One numeric dependent variable.
- One or more numeric independent variables.

To obtain a linear regression analysis, from the menus choose:

Statistics
　Regression ▶
　　Linear...

This opens the Linear Regression dialog box, as shown in Figure 18.52.

Figure 18.52 Linear Regression dialog box

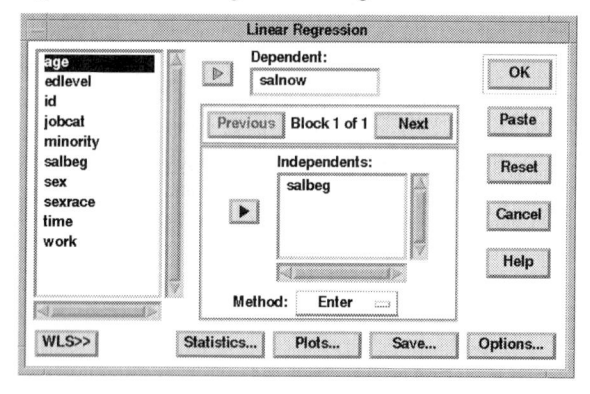

The numeric variables in your data file appear in the source list. Select a dependent variable and a block of one or more independent variables and click on OK to get the default analysis using the forced-entry method. By default, cases with missing values for any variable are excluded from the analysis.

☐ **Method.** Method selection determines the method used in developing the regression model. You can choose one of the following alternatives:

Enter. Forced entry. This is the default method. Variables in the block are entered in a single step.

Stepwise. Stepwise variable entry and removal. Variables in the block are examined at each step for entry or removal.

Remove. Forced removal. Variables in the block are removed in a single step.

Backward. Backward variable elimination. Variables in the block are entered one at a time and then removed one at a time based on removal criteria.

Forward. Forward variable selection. Variables in the block are entered one at a time based on entry criteria.

All variables must pass the tolerance criterion to be entered in the equation, regardless of the entry method specified. The default tolerance level is 0.0001. A variable also is not entered if it would cause the tolerance of another variable already in the model to drop below the tolerance criterion.

For the stepwise method, the maximum number of steps is twice the number of independent variables. For the forward and backward methods, the maximum number of steps equals the number of variables meeting entry and removal criteria. The maximum number of steps for the total model equals the sum of the maximum number of steps for each method in the model.

All independent variables selected are added to a single regression model. However, you can specify different entry methods for different subsets of variables. For example, you can enter one block of variables into the regression model using forward selection and a second block of variables using stepwise selection. To add a second block of variables to the regression model, click on Next. Select an alternate selection method if you do not want the default (forced entry). To move back and forth between blocks of independent variables, use Previous and Next. You can specify up to nine different blocks.

Optionally, you can obtain a weighted least-squares model. Click on WLS and select a variable containing the weights. An independent or dependent variable cannot be used as a weighting variable. If the value of the weighting variable is zero, negative, or missing, the case is excluded from the analysis.

Linear Regression Statistics

To control the display of statistical output, click on Statistics... in the Linear Regression dialog box. This opens the Linear Regression Statistics dialog box, as shown in Figure 18.53.

Figure 18.53 Linear Regression Statistics dialog box

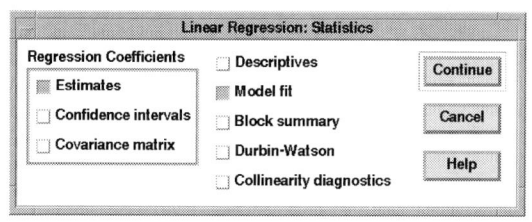

Regression Coefficients. You can choose one or more of the following:

- **Estimates.** Displays regression coefficients and related measures. These statistics are displayed by default. For variables in the equation, statistics displayed are regression coefficient B, standard error of B, standardized coefficient beta, t value for B, and two-tailed significance level of t.

  For independent variables not in the equation, statistics displayed are beta if the variable was entered, t value for beta, t probability, partial correlation with the dependent variable controlling for variables in the equation, and minimum tolerance.

- **Confidence intervals.** Displays the 95% confidence interval for each unstandardized regression coefficient.

- **Covariance matrix.** Variance-covariance matrix of unstandardized regression coefficients. Displays a matrix with covariances below the diagonal, correlations above the diagonal, and variances on the diagonal.

You can also choose one or more of the following statistics:

- **Descriptives.** Variable means, standard deviations, and a correlation matrix with one-tailed probabilities.
- **Model fit.** R, R^2, adjusted R^2, and the standard error. Also, an ANOVA table displays degrees of freedom, sums of squares, mean squares, F value, and the observed probability of F. Model fit statistics are shown by default.
- **Block summary.** Summary statistics for each step (backward, forward, or stepwise method) or block (forced entry or removal method).
- **Durbin-Watson.** Durbin-Watson test statistic. Also displays summary statistics for standardized and unstandardized residuals and predicted values.
- **Collinearity diagnostics.** Variance inflation factor (VIF), eigenvalues of the scaled and uncentered cross-products matrix, condition indices, and variance-decomposition proportions (Belsley et al., 1980). Also displays tolerance for variables in the equation; for variables not in the equation, displays the tolerance a variable would have if it were the only variable entered next.

Linear Regression Plots

To obtain scatterplots for variables in the equation, click on Plots... in the Linear Regression dialog box. This opens the Linear Regression Plots dialog box, as shown in Figure 18.54.

Figure 18.54 Linear Regression Plots dialog box

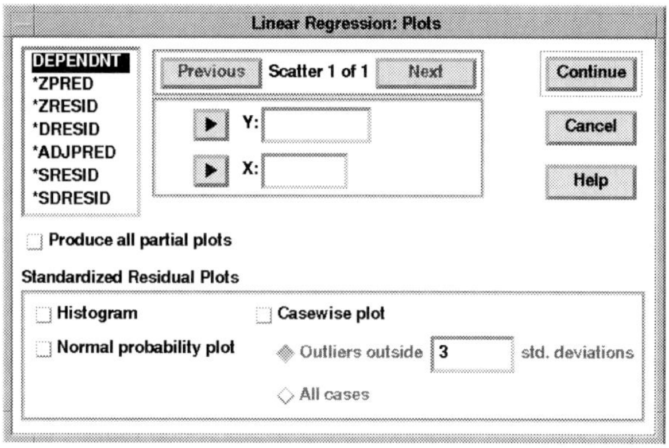

Your dependent variable and the following predicted and residual variables appear in the source list:
- *ZPRED*. Standardized predicted values.
- *ZRESID*. Standardized residuals.
- *DRESID*. Deleted residuals.
- *ADJPRED*. Adjusted predicted values.
- *SRESID*. Studentized residuals.
- *SDRESID*. Studentized deleted residuals.

Select one variable for the vertical (y) axis and one variable for the horizontal (x) axis. To request additional plots, click on Next and repeat this process. You can specify up to nine scatterplots. All plots are standardized.

Standardized Residual Plots. You can choose one or more of the following:
- **Histogram.** Histogram of standardized residuals. A normal curve is superimposed.
- **Normal probability plot.** Normal probability ($P - P$) plot of standardized residuals.
- **Casewise plot.** Casewise plot of standardized residuals accompanied by a listing of the values of the dependent and unstandardized predicted (*PRED*) and residual (*RESID*) values. For casewise plots, you can choose one of the following:
    - **Outliers outside n std. deviations.** Limits casewise plot to cases with an absolute standardized residual value greater than a specified value. The default value is 3. To override this value, enter a positive standard deviation value. For example, to display cases with residual values of more than 2 standard deviations above or be-

low the mean, enter 2. A plot is not displayed if no case has an absolute standardized residual value greater than the specified value.

◇ **All cases.** Includes all cases in the casewise plot.

If any plots are requested, summary statistics are displayed for unstandardized predicted and residual values (*PRED* and *RESID*, respectively) and for standardized predicted and residual values (*ZPRED* and *ZRESID*).

The following option is also available:

❏ **Produce all partial plots**. A partial residual plot is a scatterplot of residuals of the dependent variable and an independent variable when both variables are regressed separately on the rest of the independent variables. Plots are displayed for each independent variable in the equation in descending order of standard errors of regression coefficients. All plots are standardized. At least two independent variables must be in the equation for a partial plot to be produced.

Linear Regression Save New Variables

To save residuals, predicted values, or related measures as new variables, click on Save... in the Linear Regression dialog box. This opens the Linear Regression Save New Variables dialog box, as shown in Figure 18.55.

Figure 18.55 Linear Regression Save New Variables dialog box

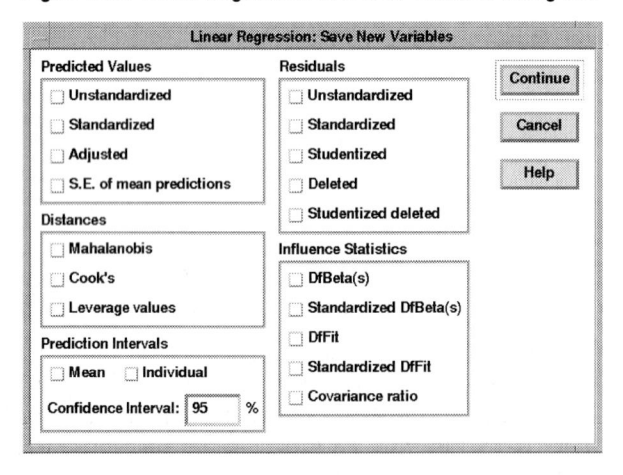

SPSS automatically assigns new variable names for any measures you save as new variables. A table in the output shows the name of each new variable and its contents.

Predicted Values. You can choose one or more of the following:
- **Unstandardized.** Unstandardized predicted values.
- **Standardized.** Standardized predicted values.
- **Adjusted.** Adjusted predicted values.
- **S. E. of mean predictions.** Standard errors of the predicted values.

Distances. You can choose one or more of the following:
- **Mahalanobis.** Mahalanobis distance.
- **Cook's.** Cook's distance.
- **Leverage values.** Centered leverage values. (See Velleman & Welsch, 1981.)

Prediction Intervals. You can choose one or both of the following:
- **Mean.** Lower and upper bounds for the prediction interval of the mean predicted response. (See Dillon & Goldstein, 1984.)
- **Individual.** Lower and upper bounds for the prediction interval for a single observation. (See Dillon & Goldstein, 1984.)

Confidence Interval. For mean and individual confidence intervals, the default is 95%. To override this value, enter a value greater than 0 and less than 100. For example, if you want 99% confidence intervals, enter 99.

Residuals. You can choose one or more of the following:
- **Unstandardized.** Unstandardized residuals.
- **Standardized.** Standardized residuals.
- **Studentized.** Studentized residuals.
- **Deleted.** Deleted residuals.
- **Studentized deleted.** Studentized deleted residuals. (See Hoaglin & Welsch, 1978.)

Influence Statistics. You can choose one or more of the following:
- **DfBeta(s).** The change in the regression coefficient that results from the exclusion of a particular case. A value is computed for each term in the model, including the constant.
- **Standardized DfBeta(s).** Standardized DfBeta values. A value is computed for each term in the model, including the constant.
- **DfFit.** The change in the predicted value when a particular case is excluded.
- **Standardized DfFit.** Standardized DfFit value.

❑ **Covariance ratio.** The ratio of the determinant of the covariance matrix with a particular case excluded to the determinant of the covariance matrix with all cases included.

If you request one or more new variables, summary statistics are displayed for the following measures:

- *ZPRED.* Standardized predicted values.
- *PRED.* Unstandardized predicted values.
- *SEPRED.* Standard errors of the mean predicted values.
- *ADJPRED.* Adjusted predicted values.
- *ZRESID.* Standardized residuals.
- *RESID.* Unstandardized residuals.
- *SRESID.* Studentized residuals.
- *DRESID.* Deleted residuals.
- *SDRESID.* Studentized deleted residuals.
- *MAHAL.* Mahalanobis distances.
- *COOK D.* Cook's distances.
- *LEVER.* Leverages.

Linear Regression Options

To control the criteria by which variables are chosen for entry or removal from the regression model, to suppress the constant term, or to control the handling of cases with missing values, click on Options... in the Linear Regression dialog box. This opens the Linear Regression Options dialog box, as shown in Figure 18.56.

Figure 18.56 Linear Regression Options dialog box

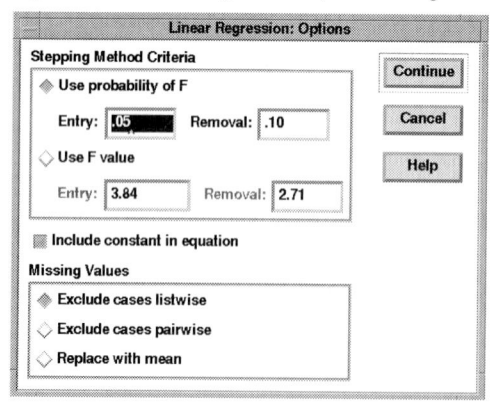

Stepping Method Criteria. The stepping method criteria apply to the forward, backward, and stepwise methods. You can choose one of the following:

- ◇ **Use probability of F.** Use probability of F-to-enter (PIN) and probability of F-to-remove (POUT) as entry and removal criteria. This is the default. The default entry value is 0.05. The default removal value is 0.10. To override these settings, enter new values. Both values must be greater than 0 and less than or equal to 1, and the entry value must be less than the removal value.
- ◇ **Use F value.** Use F values as entry and removal criteria. The default entry value (FIN) is 3.84. The default removal value (FOUT) is 2.71. To override these settings, enter new values. Both values must be greater than 0, and the entry value must be greater than the removal value.

Missing Values. You can choose one of the following:

- ◇ **Exclude cases listwise.** Only cases with valid values for all variables are included in the analyses. This is the default.
- ◇ **Exclude cases pairwise.** Cases with complete data for the pair of variables being correlated are used to compute the correlation coefficient on which the regression analysis is based. Degrees of freedom are based on the minimum pairwise N.
- ◇ **Replace with mean.** Replace missing values with the variable mean. All cases are used for computations, with the mean of a variable substituted for missing observations.

The following option is also available:

- ❑ **Include constant in equation.** Regression model contains a constant term. This is the default. To suppress this term and obtain regression through the origin, deselect this item.

Additional Features Available with Command Syntax

You can customize your regression analysis if you paste your selections to a syntax window and edit the resulting REGRESSION command syntax (see Chapter 4). Additional features include:

- Matrix facility for writing a correlation matrix or for reading a matrix in place of raw data to obtain your regression analysis (with the MATRIX subcommand).
- User-specified tolerance levels (with the CRITERIA subcommand).
- Multiple models for the same or different dependent variables (with the METHOD and DEPENDENT subcommands).
- Additional statistics (with the DESCRIPTIVES and STATISTICS subcommands).

See Appendix A for command syntax rules. See the *SPSS Base System Syntax Reference Guide* for complete REGRESSION command syntax.

19 Distribution-Free or Nonparametric Tests

Brussels sprouts and broccoli have recently joined coffee, carrots, red meat, oat bran, saccharin, tobacco, and alcohol on the ever-expanding list of substances thought to contribute to the development or prevention of cancer. This list is necessarily tentative and complicated. The two major sources of evidence—experiments on animals and examination of the histories of people with cancer—are problematic. It is difficult to predict, based on the results of giving large doses of suspect substances to small animals, the consequences for humans of consuming small amounts over a long time span.

In studies of people, lifestyle components are difficult to isolate, and it is challenging—if not impossible—to unravel the contribution of a single factor. For example, what conclusions may be drawn about the role of caffeine, based on a sample of overweight, sedentary, coffee- and alcohol-drinking, cigarette-smoking urban dwellers?

In addition to certain lifestyle factors, dietary fat is thought to play an important role in the development and progression of cancer. Wynder (1976) showed that the per capita consumption of dietary fats is positively correlated with the incidence of breast cancer and colon cancer in humans. In another study, King et al. (1979) examined the relationship between diet and tumor growth in rats. Three groups of animals of the same age, species, and physical condition were injected with tumor cells. The rats were divided into three groups and fed diets of either low, saturated, or unsaturated fat.

One hypothesis of interest is whether the length of time it takes for tumors to develop differs in two of the groups—rats fed saturated fats and rats fed unsaturated fats. If we assume a normal distribution of the tumor-free time, the independent-samples *t* test (described in Chapter 13) can be used to test the hypothesis that the population means are equal. However, if the distribution of times does not appear to be normal, and especially if the sample sizes are small, we should consider statistical procedures that do not require assumptions about the shape of the underlying distribution.

The Mann-Whitney Test

The **Mann-Whitney test,** also known as the Wilcoxon test, does not require assumptions about the shape of the underlying distributions. It tests the hypothesis that two independent samples come from populations having the same distribution. The form of the distribution need not be specified. The test does not require that the variable be measured on an interval scale; an ordinal scale is sufficient.

Ranking the Data

To compute the test, the observations from both samples are first combined and ranked from smallest to largest value. Consider Table 19.1, which shows a sample of the King data reported by Lee (1992). Case 4 has the shortest elapsed time to development of a tumor: 68 days. It is assigned a rank of 1. Case 3 has the next shortest time (81), so it is assigned a rank of 2. Cases 5 and 6 both exhibited tumors after 112 days. They are both assigned a rank of 3.5, the average of the ranks (3 and 4) for which they are tied. Case 2, with the next longest elapsed time (126 days), is given a rank of 5, and case 1, with the longest elapsed time (199 days), is given a rank of 6.

Table 19.1 Ranking the data

Saturated			Unsaturated		
Case	Time	Rank	Case	Time	Rank
1	199	6	4	68	1
2	126	5	5	112	3.5
3	81	2	6	112	3.5

Calculating the Test

The statistic for testing the hypothesis that the two distributions are equal is the sum of the ranks for each of the two groups. If the groups have the same distribution, their sample distributions of ranks should be similar. If one of the groups has more than its share of small or large ranks, there is reason to suspect that the two underlying distributions are different.

Figure 19.1 shows the output from the Mann-Whitney test for the complete King data. For each group, the mean rank and number of cases are given. (The **mean rank** is the sum of the ranks divided by the number of cases.) Note that the saturated-fats group has only 29 cases, since one rat died of causes unrelated to the experiment. The number (963) displayed under W is the sum of the ranks for the group with the smaller number of observations. If both groups have the same number of observations, W is the rank sum for the group named first in the Two-Independent-Samples Define Groups dialog box (see Figure 19.23). In this example, the value of W is 963, the sum of the ranks for the saturated-fats group.

Figure 19.1 Mann-Whitney output

```
- - - - - Mann-Whitney U - Wilcoxon Rank Sum W Test

      TUMOR
  by  DIET

     Mean Rank      Cases
         26.90        30    DIET = 0    UNSATURATED
         33.21        29    DIET = 1    SATURATED
                      --
                      59    Total
                                          Corrected for ties
            U                W                Z        2-Tailed P
          342.0            963.0          -1.4112         .1582
```

The number (342) identified in the output as U represents the number of times a value in the unsaturated-fats group precedes a value in the saturated-fats group. To understand what this means, consider again the data in Table 19.1. All three cases in the unsaturated-fats group have smaller ranks than the first case in the saturated-fats group, so they all precede case 1 in the rankings. Similarly, all three cases in the unsaturated-fats group precede case 2. Only one unsaturated-fats case (case 4) is smaller in value than case 3. Thus, the number of times the value for an unsaturated-fats case precedes the value for a saturated-fats case is $3 + 3 + 1 = 7$. The number of times the value of a saturated-fats case precedes the value of an unsaturated-fats case is 2, since case 3 has a smaller rank than both cases 5 and 6. The smaller of these two numbers is displayed in the output as U. If the two distributions are equal, values from one group should not consistently precede values in the other.

The significance levels associated with U and W are the same. They can be obtained by transforming the score to a standard normal deviate (Z). If the total sample size is less than 30, an exact probability level based on the distribution of the score is also displayed. From Figure 19.1, the observed significance level for this example is 0.158. Since the significance level is large, the hypothesis that tumor-free time has the same distribution for the two diet groups is not rejected.

Which Diet?

You should not conclude from these findings that it doesn't matter—as far as tumors are concerned—what kind of fat you (or rats) eat. King et al. found that rats fed the unsaturated diet had a total of 96 tumors at the end of the experiment, while rats fed the saturated diet had only 55 tumors. They also found that large tumors were more common in the unsaturated-diet group than in the saturated-diet group. Thus, unsaturated fats may be more hazardous than saturated fats.

Assumptions

The Mann-Whitney test requires only that the sample be random and that values can be ordered. These assumptions—especially randomness—should not be made lightly, but they are less restrictive than those for the two-sample t test for means. The t test requires further that the observations be selected from approximately normally distributed populations with equal variances.

Since the Mann-Whitney test can always be calculated instead of the t test, what determines which test should be used? If the assumptions needed for the t test are met, the t test is more powerful than the Mann-Whitney test. That is, the t test will detect true differences between the two populations more often than the Mann-Whitney test, since the t test uses more information from the data. Substituting ranks for the actual values eliminates potentially useful information. On the other hand, using the t test when its assumptions are substantially violated may result in an erroneous observed significance level.

In general, if the assumptions of the t test appear to be reasonable, it should be used. When the data are ordinal—or interval but from a markedly non-normal distribution—the Mann-Whitney test is the procedure of choice.

Nonparametric Tests

Like the Mann-Whitney test, many statistical procedures require limited distributional assumptions about the data. Collectively, these procedures are termed **distribution-free tests** or **nonparametric tests**. Like the Mann-Whitney test, distribution-free tests are generally less powerful than their parametric counterparts. They are most useful in situations where parametric procedures are not appropriate—for example, when the data are nominal or ordinal, or when interval data are from markedly non-normal distributions. Significance levels for certain nonparametric tests can be determined regardless of the shape of the population distribution, since they are based on ranks.

In the following sections, various nonparametric tests will be used to analyze some of the data described in previous chapters. Since the data were chosen to illustrate parametric procedures, they satisfy assumptions that are more restrictive than those required for nonparametric procedures. However, using the same data provides an opportunity to learn new procedures easily and to compare results obtained from different types of analyses.

One-Sample Tests

Various one-sample nonparametric procedures are available for testing hypotheses about the parameters of a population. These include procedures for examining differences in paired samples.

The Sign Test

In Chapter 13, the paired *t* test for means is used to test the hypothesis that mean buying scores for husbands and wives are equal. Remember that this test requires the assumption that differences are normally distributed.

The **sign test** is a nonparametric procedure used with two related samples to test the hypothesis that the distributions of two variables are the same. This test makes no assumptions about the shape of these distributions.

To compute the sign test, the difference between the buying scores of husbands and wives is calculated for each case. Next, the numbers of positive and negative differences are obtained. If the distributions of the two variables are the same, the numbers of positive and negative differences should be similar.

The output in Figure 19.2 shows that the number of negative differences is 56, while the number of positive differences is 39. The total number of cases is 98, including three with no differences. The observed significance level is 0.1007. Since this value is large, the hypothesis that the distributions are the same is not rejected.

Figure 19.2 Sign test

```
- - - - - Sign Test

     HSSCALE    Husband Self Scale
with WSSCALE    Wife Self Scale

         Cases

            56  - Diffs (WSSCALE LT HSSCALE)           Z =      1.6416
            39  + Diffs (WSSCALE GT HSSCALE)
             3    Ties                          2-Tailed P =       .1007
           ---
            98    Total
```

The Wilcoxon Signed-Rank Test

The sign test uses only the direction of the differences between the pairs and ignores the magnitude. A discrepancy of 15 between husbands' and wives' buying scores is treated in the same way as a discrepancy of 1. The **Wilcoxon signed-rank test** incorporates information about the magnitude of the differences and is therefore more powerful than the sign test.

To compute the Wilcoxon signed-rank test, the differences are ranked without considering the signs. In the case of ties, average ranks are assigned. The sums of the ranks for positive and negative differences are then calculated.

As shown in Figure 19.3, the average rank of the 56 negative differences is 45.25. The average positive rank is 51.95. In the row labeled *Ties*, there are three cases with the same value for both variables. The observed significance level associated with the test is large (0.3458), and once again the hypothesis of no difference is not rejected.

Figure 19.3 Wilcoxon signed-rank test

```
- - - - - Wilcoxon Matched-Pairs Signed-Ranks Test

     HSSCALE     Husband Self Scale
with WSSCALE     Wife Self Scale

     Mean Rank    Cases
         45.25       56  - Ranks (WSSCALE LT HSSCALE)
         51.95       39  + Ranks (WSSCALE GT HSSCALE)
                      3    Ties (WSSCALE EQ HSSCALE)
                    ---
                     98    Total

     Z =   -.9428            2-Tailed P =  .3458
```

The Wald-Wolfowitz Runs Test

The runs test is a test of randomness. That is, given a sequence of observations, the runs test examines whether the value of one observation influences the values for later observations. If there is no influence (the observations are independent), the sequence is considered random.

A **run** is any sequence of like observations. For example, if a coin is tossed 15 times and the outcomes are recorded, the following sequence might result:

HHHTHHHHTTTTTTT

There are four runs in this sequence: HHH, T, HHHH, and TTTTTTT. The total number of runs is a measure of randomness, since too many runs, or too few, suggest dependence between observations. The **Wald-Wolfowitz runs test** converts the total number of runs into a Z statistic having approximately a normal distribution. The only requirement for this test is that the variable tested be dichotomous (have only two possible values).

Suppose, for example, that a weather forecaster records whether it snows for 20 days in February and obtains the following sequence (1=snow, 0=no snow):

01111111010111111100

To test the hypothesis that the occurrence or nonoccurrence of snow on one day has no effect on whether it snows on later days, the runs test is performed, resulting in the output in Figure 19.4.

Figure 19.4 Runs test

```
- - - - - Runs Test

    SNOW

        Runs:    7          Test value = 1
        Cases:   5   LT 1
                15   GE 1              Z =   -.6243
                --
                20   Total 2-Tailed P =    .5324
```

Since the observed significance level is quite large (0.5324), the hypothesis of randomness is not rejected. It does not appear, from these data, that snowy (or nonsnowy) days affect the later occurrence of snow.

The Binomial Test

With data that are binomially distributed, the hypothesis that the probability p of a particular outcome is equal to some number is often of interest. For example, you might want to find out if a tossed coin was unbiased. To check this, you could test to see whether the probability of heads was equal to 1/2. The **binomial test** compares the observed frequencies in each category of a binomial distribution to the frequencies expected under a binomial distribution with the probability parameter p.

For instance, a nickel is tossed 20 times, with the following results (1=heads, 0=tails):

10011111101111011011

The output in Figure 19.5 shows a binomial test of the hypothesis that the probability of heads equals 1/2 for these data.

Figure 19.5 Binomial test

```
- - - - - Binomial Test

    HEADS

        Cases
                              Test Prop. =   .5000
            5   = 0           Obs. Prop. =   .2500
           15   = 1
           --                 Exact Binomial
           20   Total         2-Tailed P =   .0414
```

The test proportion of cases for the first value (0) is 0.5000 and the observed proportion is 0.2500; that is, 1/4 of the actual tosses were tails. The small (0.0414) observed significance level indicates that it is not likely that p equals 1/2 and it appears that the coin is biased.

The Kolmogorov-Smirnov One-Sample Test

The **Kolmogorov-Smirnov test** is used to determine how well a random sample of data fits a particular distribution (uniform, normal, or Poisson). It is based on comparison of the sample cumulative distribution function to the hypothetical cumulative distribution function.

Suppose we are analyzing the data from an evaluation of 35 beers. The beers were rated on overall quality and a variety of other attributes, such as price, calories, sodium, and alcohol content. We can use the Kolmogorov-Smirnov one-sample test to see whether it is reasonable to assume that the *alcohol* variable is normally distributed. The Kolmogorov-Smirnov output in Figure 19.6 shows an observed significance level of 0.05, small enough to cast doubt on the assumption of normality.

Figure 19.6 Kolmogorov-Smirnov test

```
- - - - - Kolmogorov - Smirnov Goodness of Fit Test
     ALCOHOL    ALCOHOL BY VOLUME (IN %)

     Test distribution  -  Normal          Mean:       4.577
                                      Standard Deviation:  .603

          Cases:   35

            Most extreme differences
       Absolute      Positive      Negative       K-S Z     2-Tailed P
        .22940        .15585        -.22940      1.3572       .0503
```

The One-Sample Chi-Square Test

In Chapter 7, frequencies of deaths for the days of the week are examined. The output suggests that all days of the week are equally hazardous in regard to death. To test this conclusion, the one-sample chi-square test can be used. This nonparametric test requires only that the data be a random sample.

To calculate the one-sample chi-square statistic, the data are first classified into mutually exclusive categories of interest—days of the week in this example—and then expected frequencies for these categories are computed. Expected frequencies are the frequencies that would be expected if the null hypothesis is true. For the death data, the hypothesis to be tested is that the probability of death is the same for each day of the week. The day of death is known for 110 subjects. The hypothesis implies that the expected frequency of deaths for each weekday is 110/7, or 15.71. Once the expected frequencies are obtained, the chi-square statistic is computed as

$$\chi^2 = \sum_{i=1}^{k} \frac{(O_i - E_i)^2}{E_i}$$

Equation 19.1

where O_i is the observed frequency for the ith category, E_i is the expected frequency for the ith category, and k is the number of categories.

If the null hypothesis is true, the chi-square statistic has approximately a chi-square distribution with $k - 1$ degrees of freedom. This statistic will be large if the observed and expected frequencies are substantially different. Figure 19.7 shows the output from the one-sample chi-square test for the death data. The observed chi-square value is 3.4, and the associated significance level is 0.757. Since the observed significance level is large, the hypothesis that deaths are evenly distributed over days of the week is not rejected.

Figure 19.7 One-sample chi-square test

```
- - - - - Chi-Square Test

     DAYOFWK   DAY OF DEATH

                                  Cases
                      Category  Observed   Expected   Residual

     SUNDAY              1         19        15.71       3.29
     MONDAY              2         11        15.71      -4.71
     TUESDAY             3         19        15.71       3.29
     WEDNSDAY            4         17        15.71       1.29
     THURSDAY            5         15        15.71       -.71
     FRIDAY              6         13        15.71      -2.71
     SATURDAY            7         16        15.71        .29
                                  ---
                        Total     110

            Chi-Square          D.F.         Significance
             3.4000               6              .7572
```

The Friedman Test

The **Friedman test** is used to compare two or more related samples. (This is an extension of the tests for paired data.) The k variables to be compared are ranked from 1 to k for each case, and the mean ranks for the variables are calculated and compared, resulting in a test statistic with approximately a chi-square distribution.

The Friedman test can be used to analyze data from a psychology experiment concerned with memory. In this experiment, subjects were asked to memorize first a two-digit number, then a three-digit number, and finally a four-digit number. After each number was memorized, they were shown a single digit and asked if that digit was present in the number memorized. The times taken to reach a decision for the two-, three-, and four-digit numbers are the three related variables of interest.

Figure 19.8 shows the results of the Friedman test, examining the hypothesis that the number of digits memorized has no effect on the time taken to reach a decision. The observed significance level is extremely small, so it appears that the number of digits does affect decision time.

Figure 19.8 Friedman test

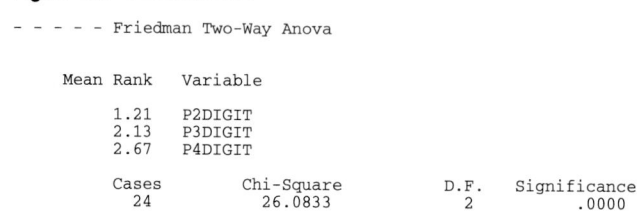

```
- - - - - Friedman Two-Way Anova

  Mean Rank    Variable
     1.21      P2DIGIT
     2.13      P3DIGIT
     2.67      P4DIGIT

     Cases       Chi-Square       D.F.    Significance
      24          26.0833          2          .0000
```

Tests for Two or More Independent Samples

A variety of nonparametric tests involve comparisons between two or more independent samples. (The Mann-Whitney test is one such test.) In this respect, these tests resemble the t tests and one-way analyses of variance described in Chapter 13 and Chapter 14.

The Two-Sample Median Test

The **two-sample median test** is used to determine whether two populations have the same median. The two samples are combined, and the median for the total distribution is calculated. The number of observations above this median, as well as the number of observations less than or equal to this median, is counted for each sample. The test statistic is based on these counts.

This test can be used to determine whether median sodium levels are the same for the highest-rated and lowest-rated beers in the beer data described earlier. The output in Figure 19.9 shows the largest possible p value, 1. Therefore, there is no reason to suspect different medians.

Figure 19.9 Median test of sodium by rating

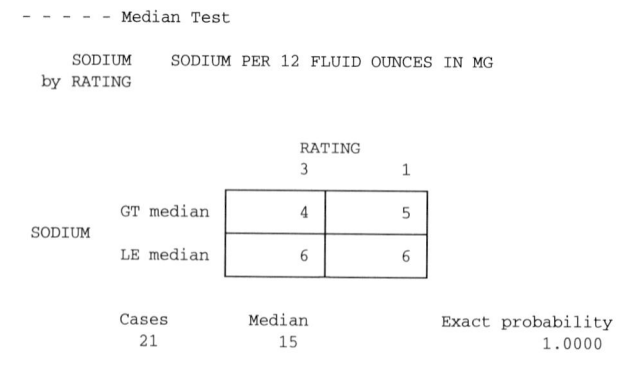

```
- - - - - Median Test

     SODIUM      SODIUM PER 12 FLUID OUNCES IN MG
  by RATING

                          RATING
                           3        1
              GT median    4        5
   SODIUM
              LE median    6        6

          Cases       Median            Exact probability
           21           15                    1.0000
```

The Two-Sample Wald-Wolfowitz Runs Test

A runs test can be used to test the hypothesis that two samples come from populations with the same distributions. To perform this test, the two samples are combined and the values are sorted. A run in this combined and sorted sample consists of a sequence of values belonging to the first sample or a sequence of values belonging to the second sample. If there are too few runs, it suggests that the two populations have different distributions.

The Wald-Wolfowitz test can be used with the beer data to compare calories for the highest-ranked and lowest-ranked beers. The output in Figure 19.10 shows an observed significance level of 0.0119. Since this is small, the distribution of calories for the highest-ranked beers appears to differ from the distribution of calories for the lowest-ranked beers.

Figure 19.10 Wald-Wolfowitz runs test

```
- - - - - Wald-Wolfowitz Runs Test

     CALORIES   CALORIES PER 12 FLUID OUNCES
  by RATING

        Cases

         10    RATING = 3   FAIR
         11    RATING = 1   VERY GOOD
         --
         21    Total
                                              Exact
                          Runs          Z     1-Tailed P
   Minimum possible:        6       -2.2335       .0119
   Maximum possible:        6       -2.2335       .0119

   Warning -- There are 1 inter-group ties involving 5 cases.
```

The Two-Sample Kolmogorov-Smirnov Test

The Kolmogorov-Smirnov test for two samples provides another method for testing whether two samples come from populations with the same distributions. It is based on a comparison of the distribution functions for the two samples.

This test can be used with the beer data to compare the alcohol content of the highest-ranked and lowest-ranked beers. Since the observed significance level in Figure 19.11 is small, the alcohol distributions do not appear to be the same. The approximation used to obtain the observed significance level may be inadequate in this case, however, because of the small sample size.

Figure 19.11 Kolmogorov-Smirnov two-sample test

```
- - - - - Kolmogorov - Smirnov 2-Sample Test

     ALCOHOL     ALCOHOL BY VOLUME (IN %)
  by RATING


        Cases

         10  RATING = 3   FAIR
         11  RATING = 1   VERY GOOD
         --
         21  Total

Warning - Due to small sample size, probability tables should be consulted.
            Most extreme differences
       Absolute        Positive         Negative         K-S Z        2-Tailed P
        .60000          .00000          -.60000          1.373           .046
```

The K-Sample Median Test

An extension of the two-sample median test, the *k*-sample median test compares the medians of three or more independent samples. Figure 19.12 shows a *k*-sample median test comparing median prices for the highest-, middle-, and lowest-quality beers. The observed significance level is fairly large (0.091), indicating no real difference in the median price of the three types of beer.

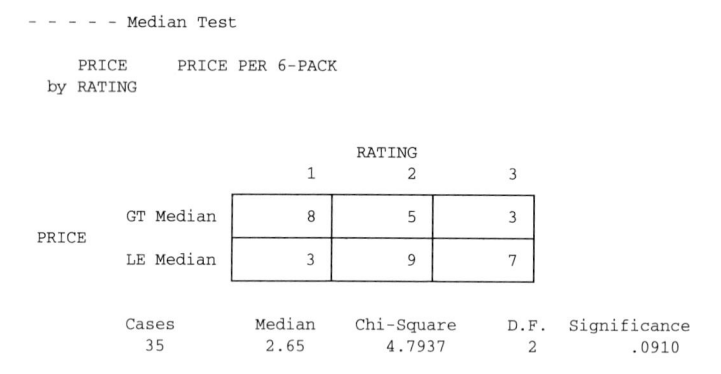

Figure 19.12 K-sample median test

```
- - - - - Median Test

     PRICE     PRICE PER 6-PACK
  by RATING

                                 RATING
                         1         2         3

              GT Median  |   8   |   5   |   3   |
     PRICE               |-------|-------|-------|
              LE Median  |   3   |   9   |   7   |

              Cases      Median    Chi-Square    D.F.    Significance
               35         2.65       4.7937       2         .0910
```

The Kruskal-Wallis Test

The experiment described at the beginning of this chapter investigates the effects of three diets on tumor development. The Mann-Whitney test was calculated to examine possible differences between saturated- and unsaturated-fats diets. To test for differences among all three diets, an extension of the Mann-Whitney test can be used. This test is known as the **Kruskal-Wallis one-way analysis of variance**.

The procedure for computing the Kruskal-Wallis test is similar to the procedure used in the Mann-Whitney test. All cases from the three groups are combined and ranked. Average ranks are assigned in the case of ties. For each group, the ranks are summed, and the Kruskal-Wallis H statistic is computed from these sums. The H statistic has approximately a chi-square distribution under the hypothesis that the three groups have the same distribution.

The output in Figure 19.13 shows that the third group, the low-fat-diet group, has the largest average rank. The value of the Kruskal-Wallis statistic is 11.1257. When the statistic is adjusted for the presence of ties, the value changes to 11.2608. The small observed significance level suggests that the time interval until development of a tumor is not the same for all three groups.

Figure 19.13 Kruskal-Wallis one-way analysis of variance output

```
- - - - - Kruskal-Wallis 1-Way Anova
     TUMOR
  by DIET

    Mean Rank     Cases

        34.12       30    DIET = 0    UNSATURATED
        43.50       29    DIET = 1    SATURATED
        56.24       29    DIET = 2    LOW-FAT
                    --
                    88    Total

                                           Corrected for ties
    Chi-Square      D.F.  Significance   Chi-Square    D.F.  Significance
      11.1257         2       .0038        11.2608       2       .0036
```

How to Obtain the Chi-Square Test

The Chi-Square Test procedure tabulates a variable into categories and computes a chi-square statistic based on the differences between observed and expected frequencies.

The minimum specification is one or more numeric variables.

To obtain the chi-square test, from the menus choose:

Statistics
  Nonparametric Tests ▶
    Chi-Square...

This opens the Chi-Square Test dialog box, as shown in Figure 19.14.

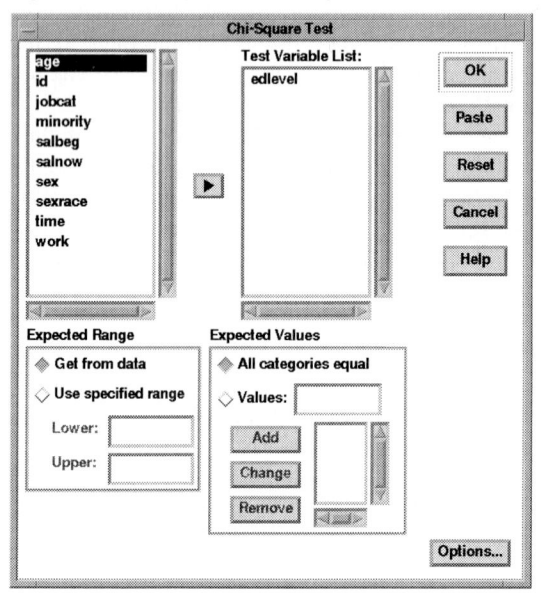

Figure 19.14 Chi-Square Test dialog box

The numeric variables in your data file appear on the source variable list. Select one or more test variables, and click on OK to obtain the default chi-square test using equal expected frequencies for each observed category of your variable(s). (See Figure 19.7.) Each variable produces a separate test. To obtain chi-square tests of the relationship between two or more variables, use the Crosstabs procedure (see Chapter 10).

Expected Range. You can choose one of the following alternatives:

◇ **Get from data.** Each distinct value encountered is defined as a category. This is the default.

◇ **Use specified range.** Enter integer values for lower and upper bounds. Categories are established for each value within the inclusive range, and cases with values outside the bounds are excluded. For example, if you specify a lowerbound value of 1 and an upperbound value of 4, only the integer values of 1 through 4 are used for the chi-square test. The lowerbound value must be less than the upperbound value, and both values must be specified.

Expected Values. You can choose one of the following alternatives:

◇ **All categories equal.** All categories have equal expected values. This is the default.

◇ **Values.** Categories have user-specified expected proportions. Enter a value greater than 0 for each category of the test variable, and click on Add. Each time you add a value, it appears at the bottom of the value list. The sequential order of the values is important, since it corresponds to the ascending order of the category values of the test variable. The first value on the list corresponds to the lowest group value of the test variable, and the last value corresponds to the highest value. Elements of the value list are summed, and then each value is divided by this sum to calculate the proportion of cases expected in the corresponding category. For example, a value list of 3, 4, 5, 4 specifies expected proportions of 3/16, 4/16, 5/16, and 4/16 for categories 1, 2, 3, and 4, respectively. To remove a value, highlight it on the list and click on Remove. To change a value, highlight it, enter a new value, and click on Change.

Chi-Square Test Options

To obtain optional summary statistics or to modify the treatment of cases with missing values, click on Options... in the Chi-Square Test dialog box. This opens the Chi-Square Test Options dialog box, as shown in Figure 19.15.

Figure 19.15 Chi-Square Test Options dialog box

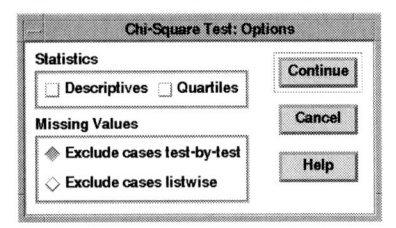

Statistics. You can choose one or both of the following summary statistics:

❑ **Descriptive.** Displays the mean, minimum, maximum, standard deviation, and the number of nonmissing cases.

❑ **Quartiles.** Displays values corresponding to the 25th, 50th, and 75th percentiles.

Missing Values. You can choose one of the following alternatives:

◇ **Exclude cases test-by-test.** When several tests are specified, each test is evaluated separately for missing values. This is the default.

◇ **Exclude cases listwise.** Cases with missing values for any variable are excluded from all analyses.

Additional Features Available with Command Syntax

You can customize your one-sample chi-square test if you paste your selections into a syntax window and edit the resulting NPAR TESTS command syntax (see Chapter 4). Additional features include:

- Specification of different minimum and maximum values or expected frequencies for different variables (with the CHISQUARE subcommand).
- Tests of the same variable against different expected frequencies or using different ranges (with the EXPECTED subcommand).

See Appendix A for command syntax rules. See the *SPSS Base System Syntax Reference Guide* for complete NPAR TESTS command syntax.

How to Obtain the Binomial Test

The Binomial Test procedure compares the observed frequency in each category of a dichotomous variable with expected frequencies from the binomial distribution.

The minimum specification is one or more numeric variables.

To obtain the binomial test, from the menus choose:

Statistics
  Nonparametric Tests ▶
    Binomial...

This opens the Binomial Test dialog box, as shown in Figure 19.16.

Figure 19.16 Binomial Test dialog box

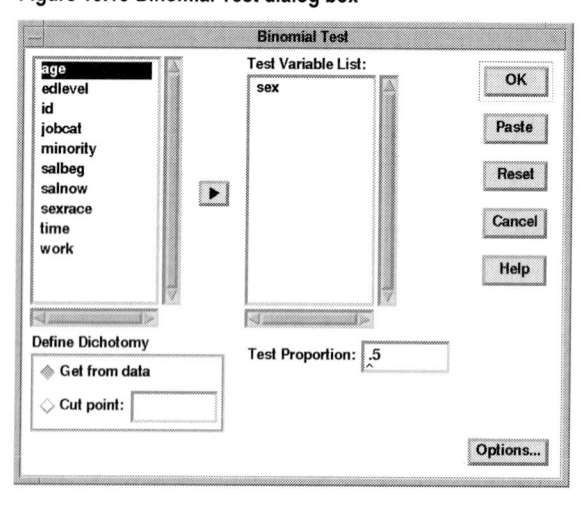

The numeric variables in your data file appear on the source variable list. Select one or more test variables to use in the binomial test. If your variables are dichotomous, you can click on OK to obtain the default binomial test using equal probabilities for each group. Otherwise, you must specify a cut point.

Define Dichotomy. You can choose one of the following alternatives:

◇ **Get from data.** Assigns cases with the lower category of a dichotomous variable to one group and cases with the higher category to the other group. This is the default.

◇ **Cut point.** User-specified cut point. Assigns cases with values less than the cut point to one group and cases with values equal to or greater than the cut point to the other group.

Test Proportion. The default null hypothesis is that the data are from a binomial distribution with a probability of 0.5 for both groups. To change the probabilities, enter a test proportion for the first group. For example, specifying .25 tests the null hypothesis that the data are from a binomial distribution with a probability of 0.25 for the first value and 0.75 for the second value. The value you specify must be between .001 and .999 and cannot include leading zeros.

Binomial Test Options

To get optional summary statistics or to modify the treatment of cases with missing values, click on Options... in the Binomial Test dialog box. This opens the Binomial Test Options dialog box, as shown in Figure 19.17.

Figure 19.17 Binomial Test Options dialog box

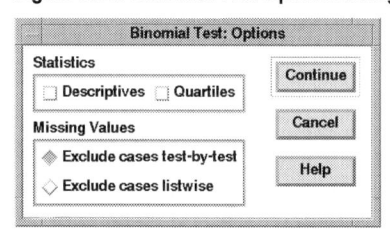

Statistics. You can choose one or both of the following summary statistics:

❏ **Descriptive.** Displays the mean, minimum, maximum, standard deviation, and the number of nonmissing cases.

❏ **Quartiles.** Displays values corresponding to the 25th, 50th, and 75th percentiles.

Missing Values. You can choose one of the following alternatives:

◇ **Exclude cases test-by-test.** When several tests are specified, each test is evaluated separately for missing values. This is the default.

◇ **Exclude cases listwise.** Cases with missing values for any variable are excluded from all analyses.

Additional Features Available with Command Syntax

You can customize your binomial test if you paste your selections into a syntax window and edit the resulting NPAR TESTS command syntax (see Chapter 4). Additional features include:

- Selection of specific groups (and exclusion of others) when a variable has more than two categories (with the BINOMIAL subcommand).
- Different cut points or probabilities for different variables (with the BINOMIAL subcommand).
- Tests of the same variable against different cut points or probabilities (with the EXPECTED subcommand).

See Appendix A for command syntax rules. See the *SPSS Base System Syntax Reference Guide* for complete NPAR TESTS command syntax.

How to Obtain the Runs Test

The Runs Test procedure tests whether the order of occurrence of two values of a variable is random. A **run** is defined as a sequence of one of the values that is preceded and followed by the other data value (or the end of the series). For example, the sequence

1 1 | 0 0 0 | 1 | 0 0 0 0 | 1 | 0 | 1|

contains seven runs (vertical bars separate the runs). For a sample of a given size, very many or very few runs suggest that the sample is not random. The Z statistic, which has an approximately normal distribution, is computed.

The minimum specification is one or more numeric variables.

To obtain the runs test, from the menus choose:

Statistics
 Nonparametric Tests ▶
  Runs...

This opens the Runs Test dialog box, as shown in Figure 19.18.

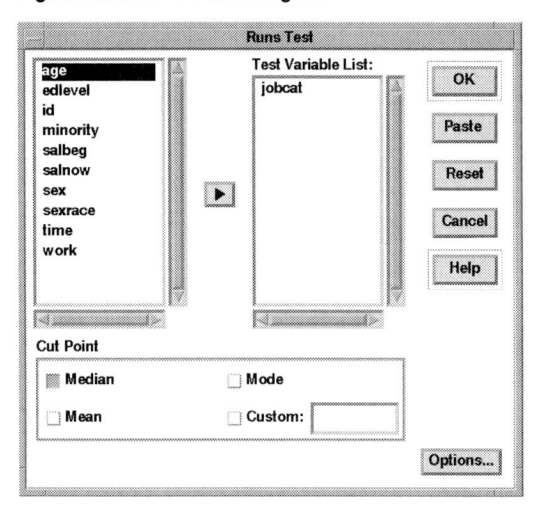

Figure 19.18 Runs Test dialog box

The numeric variables in your data file appear on the source variable list. Select one or more test variables, and click on OK to obtain the default runs test using the median to dichotomize your variable(s).

Cut Point. Assigns cases with values less than the cut point to one group and cases with values equal to or greater than the cut point to the other group. You must select at least one cut point, and one test is performed for each cut point chosen.

You can choose one or more of the following:

- **Median.** The observed median is the cut point. This is the default.
- **Mean.** The observed mean is the cut point.
- **Mode.** The observed mode is the cut point.
- **Custom.** User-specified cut point. For example, if the variable has values of 0 and 1, enter 1 as the cut point.

Runs Test Options

To get optional summary statistics or modify the treatment of cases with missing values, click on Options... in the Runs Test dialog box. This opens the Runs Test Options dialog box, as shown in Figure 19.19.

Figure 19.19 Runs Test Options dialog box

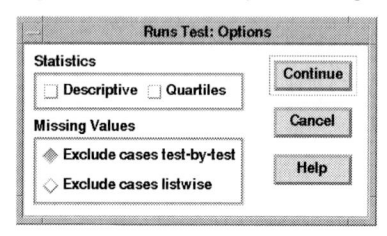

Statistics. You can choose one or both of the following summary statistics:

- **Descriptive.** Displays the mean, minimum, maximum, standard deviation, and the number of nonmissing cases.
- **Quartiles.** Displays values corresponding to the 25th, 50th, and 75th percentiles.

Missing Values. You can choose one of the following alternatives:

- **Exclude cases test-by-test.** When several tests are specified, each test is evaluated separately for missing values. This is the default.
- **Exclude cases listwise.** Cases with missing values for any variable are excluded from all analyses.

Additional Features Available with Command Syntax

You can customize your runs test if you paste your selections into a syntax window and edit the resulting NPAR TESTS command syntax (see Chapter 4). Additional features include:

- Different cut points for different variables (with the RUNS subcommand).
- Tests of the same variable against different custom cut points (with the RUNS subcommand).

See Appendix A for command syntax rules. See the *SPSS Base System Syntax Reference Guide* for complete NPAR TESTS command syntax.

How to Obtain the One-Sample Kolmogorov-Smirnov Test

The One-Sample Kolmogorov-Smirnov Test procedure compares the observed cumulative distribution function for a variable with a specified theoretical distribution, which may be normal, uniform, or Poisson. The Kolmogorov-Smirnov Z is computed from the largest difference (in absolute value) between the observed and theoretical distribution functions.

The minimum specification is one or more numeric variables.

To obtain the one-sample Kolmogorov-Smirnov test, from the menus choose:

Statistics
  Nonparametric Tests ▶
    1-Sample K-S...

This opens the One-Sample Kolmogorov-Smirnov Test dialog box, as shown in Figure 19.20.

Figure 19.20 One-Sample Kolmogorov-Smirnov Test dialog box

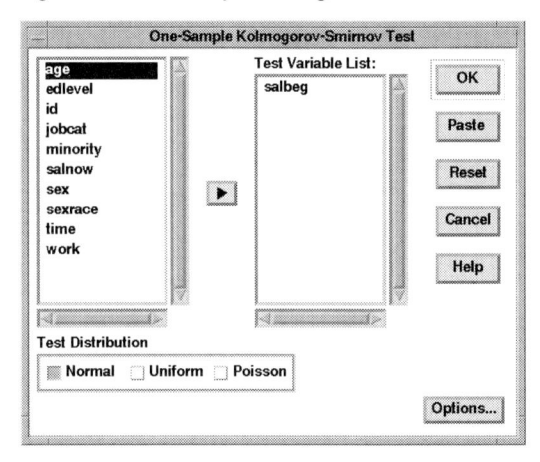

The numeric variables in your data file appear on the source variable list. Select at least one test variable, and click on OK to obtain the default (Kolmogorov-Smirnov) test using the normal distribution. Each variable produces a separate test.

Test Distribution. At least one test distribution must be selected. You can choose one or more of the following:

❑ **Normal.** The observed mean and standard deviation are the parameters. This is the default.

❑ **Uniform.** The observed minimum and maximum values define the range of the distribution.

❑ **Poisson.** The observed mean is the parameter.

Tests produced by Kolmogorov-Smirnov assume that the parameters of the test distribution are specified *in advance*. When the parameters of the test distribution are estimated from the sample, the distribution of the test statistic changes. Tests for normality that make this correction are available using the Explore procedure (see Chapter 9). See also "Additional Features Available with Command Syntax" on p. 376.

One-Sample Kolmogorov-Smirnov Options

To obtain optional summary statistics or to modify the treatment of cases with missing values, click on Options... in the One-Sample Kolmogorov-Smirnov Test dialog box. This opens the One-Sample K-S Options dialog box, as shown in Figure 19.21.

Figure 19.21 One-Sample K-S Options dialog box

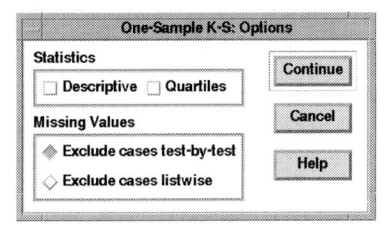

Statistics. You can choose one or both of the following summary statistics:

- **Descriptive.** Displays the mean, minimum, maximum, standard deviation, and the number of nonmissing cases.
- **Quartiles.** Displays values corresponding to the 25th, 50th, and 75th percentiles.

Missing Values. You can choose one of the following alternatives:

- **Exclude cases test-by-test.** When several tests are specified, each test is evaluated separately for missing values. This is the default.
- **Exclude cases listwise.** Cases with missing values for any variable are excluded from all analyses.

Additional Features Available with Command Syntax

You can customize your Kolmogorov-Smirnov test if you paste your selections into a syntax window and edit the resulting NPAR TESTS command syntax (see Chapter 4). As an additional feature, you can specify the parameters of the test distribution (with the K-S subcommand). See Appendix A for command syntax rules. See the *SPSS Base System Syntax Reference Guide* for complete NPAR TESTS command syntax.

How to Obtain Two-Independent-Samples Tests

The Two-Independent-Samples Tests procedure compares two groups of cases on one variable (see "The Mann-Whitney Test" on p. 355).

The minimum specifications are:
- One or more numeric test variables.
- One numeric grouping variable.
- Group values for the grouping variable.

To obtain two-independent-samples tests, from the menus choose:

Statistics
 Nonparametric Tests ▶
  2 Independent Samples...

This opens the Two-Independent-Samples Tests dialog box, as shown in Figure 19.22.

Figure 19.22 Two-Independent-Samples Tests dialog box

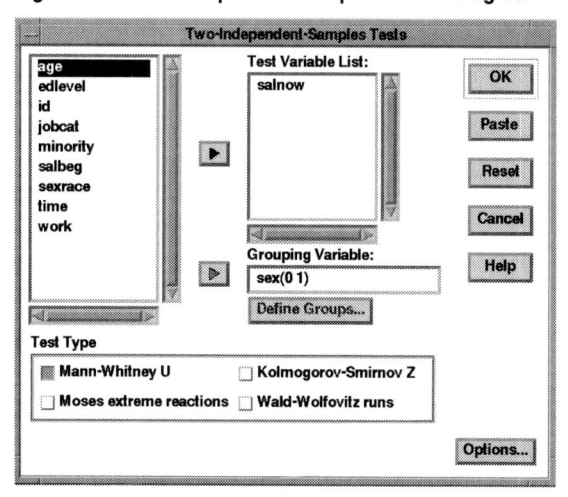

The numeric variables in your data file appear on the source variable list. Select one or more test variables and a grouping variable that splits the file into two groups or samples. After defining values of the grouping variable, click on OK to obtain the default (Mann-Whitney U) two-independent-samples test.

Test Type. At least one test type must be selected. You can choose one or more of the following:

- **Mann-Whitney U.** All cases are ranked in order of increasing size, and U (the number of times a score from group 1 precedes a score from group 2) is computed. This is the default test. If the samples are from the same population, the distribution of scores from the two groups on the ranked list should be similar; an extreme value of U indicates a nonrandom pattern. For samples with fewer than 30 cases, the exact significance level for U is computed using the Dineen and Blakesly (1973) algorithm. For larger samples, U is transformed into a normally distributed Z statistic.

- **Moses extreme reactions.** Arranges the scores from the groups in a single ascending sequence. The span of the control group is computed as the number of cases in the sequence containing the lowest and highest control scores. The exact significance level can be computed for the span. The control group is defined by the group 1 value in the Two-Independent-Samples Define Groups dialog box (see Figure 19.23). As chance outliers can easily distort the range of the span, 5% of the cases are trimmed automatically from each end. No adjustments are made for tied observations.

- **Kolmogorov-Smirnov Z.** Computes the observed cumulative distributions for both groups and the maximum positive, negative, and absolute differences. The Kolmogorov-Smirnov Z is then computed along with the two-tailed probability level based on the Smirnov (1948) formula.

- **Wald-Wolfowitz runs.** Combines observations from both groups and ranks them from lowest to highest. If the samples are from the same population, the two groups should be randomly scattered throughout the ranking. A runs test is performed using group membership as the criterion. If there are ties involving observations from both groups, both the minimum and maximum number of runs possible are calculated. If the total sample size is 30 or fewer cases, the exact one-tailed significance level is calculated. Otherwise, the normal approximation is used.

Two-Independent-Samples Define Groups

To define groups based on the values of the grouping variable, highlight the grouping variable and click on Define Groups... to open the Two-Independent-Samples Define Groups dialog box, as shown in Figure 19.23.

Figure 19.23 Two-Independent-Samples Define Groups dialog box

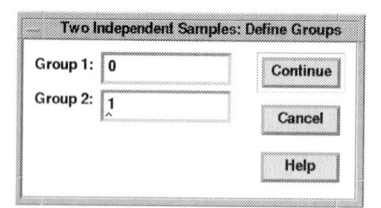

Enter integer values for group 1 and group 2. Cases with other values are excluded.

Two-Independent-Samples Options

To obtain optional summary statistics or modify the treatment of cases with missing values, click on Options... in the Two-Independent-Samples Tests dialog box. This opens the Two-Independent-Samples Options dialog box, as shown in Figure 19.24.

Figure 19.24 Two-Independent-Samples Options dialog box

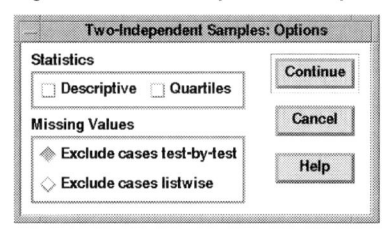

Statistics. You can choose one or both of the following summary statistics:

- **Descriptive.** Displays the mean, minimum, maximum, standard deviation, and the number of nonmissing cases.
- **Quartiles.** Displays values corresponding to the 25th, 50th, and 75th percentiles.

Missing Values. You can choose one of the following alternatives:

- **Exclude cases test-by-test.** When several tests are specified, each test is evaluated separately for missing values. This is the default.
- **Exclude cases listwise.** Cases with missing values for any variable are excluded from all analyses.

Additional Features Available with Command Syntax

You can customize your two-independent-samples tests if you paste your selections into a syntax window and edit the resulting NPAR TESTS command syntax (see Chapter 4). As an additional feature, you can specify the number of cases to be trimmed for the Moses test (with the MOSES subcommand). See Appendix A for command syntax rules. See the *SPSS Base System Syntax Reference Guide* for complete NPAR TESTS command syntax.

How to Obtain Tests for Several Independent Samples

The Tests for Several Independent Samples procedure compares two or more groups of cases on one variable.

The minimum specifications are:
- One or more numeric test variables.
- One numeric grouping variable.
- Minimum and maximum values for the grouping variable.

To obtain tests for several independent samples, from the menus choose:

Statistics
  Nonparametric Tests ▶
    K Independent Samples...

This opens the Tests for Several Independent Samples dialog box, as shown in Figure 19.25.

Figure 19.25 Tests for Several Independent Samples dialog box

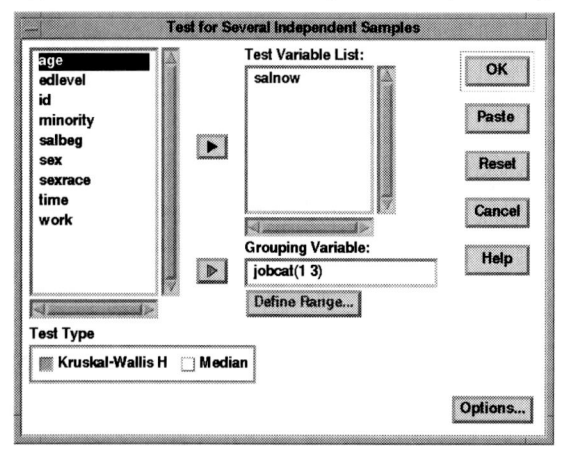

The numeric variables in your data file appear on the source variable list. Select one or more test variables and a grouping variable that splits the file into two or more groups. After defining the range of the grouping variable, click on OK to obtain the default (Kruskal-Wallis *H*) test.

Test Type. At least one test type must be selected. You can choose one or both of the following:

❑ **Kruskal-Wallis H.** Ranks all cases from the specified range in a single series, computes the rank sum for each group, and computes the Kruskal-Wallis *H* statistic, which has approximately a chi-square distribution. This is the default.

❑ **Median.** Produces a contingency table that indicates, for each group, the number of cases with values greater than the observed median and less than or equal to the median. A chi-square statistic for the table is computed.

Several Independent Samples Define Range

To define ranges based on the values of the grouping variable, highlight the grouping variable and click on Define Range... in the Tests for Several Independent Samples dialog box to open the Several Independent Samples Define Range dialog box, as shown in Figure 19.26.

Figure 19.26 Several Independent Samples Define Range dialog box

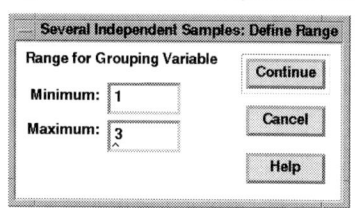

Enter values for minimum and maximum that correspond to the lowest and highest categories of the grouping variable. Both values must be integers, and cases with values outside the bounds are excluded. For example, if you specify a minimum value of 1 and a maximum value of 4, only the integer values of 1 through 4 are used. The minimum value must be less than the maximum value, and both values must be specified.

Several Independent Samples Options

To obtain optional summary statistics or modify the treatment of cases with missing values, click on Options... in the Tests for Several Independent Samples dialog box. This opens the Several Independent Samples Options dialog box, as shown in Figure 19.27.

Figure 19.27 Several Independent Samples Options dialog box

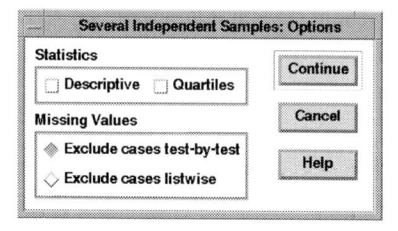

Statistics. You can choose one or both of the following summary statistics:

- **Descriptive.** Displays the mean, minimum, maximum, standard deviation, and the number of nonmissing cases.
- **Quartiles.** Displays values corresponding to the 25th, 50th, and 75th percentiles.

Missing Values. You can choose one of the following alternatives:

- **Exclude cases test-by-test.** When several tests are specified, each test is evaluated separately for cases with missing values. This is the default.
- **Exclude cases listwise.** Cases with missing values for any variable are excluded from all analyses.

Additional Features Available with Command Syntax

You can customize your test for several independent samples if you paste your selections into a syntax window and edit the resulting NPAR TESTS command syntax (see Chapter 4). As an additional feature, you can specify a value other than the observed median for the median test (with the MEDIAN subcommand). See Appendix A for command syntax rules. See the *SPSS Base System Syntax Reference Guide* for complete NPAR TESTS command syntax.

How to Obtain Two-Related-Samples Tests

The Two-Related-Samples Tests procedure compares the distributions of two variables (see "The Sign Test" on p. 359).

The minimum specification is one or more pairs of numeric variables.

To obtain two-related-samples tests, from the menus choose:

Statistics
 Nonparametric Tests ▶
  2 Related Samples...

This opens the Two-Related-Samples Tests dialog box, as shown in Figure 19.28.

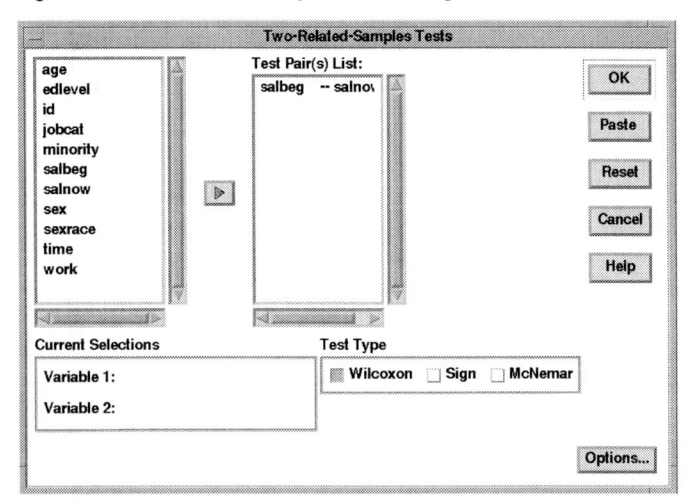

Figure 19.28 Two-Related-Samples Tests dialog box

The numeric variables in your data file appear on the source list. Select one or more pairs of variables to use in the two-related-samples tests. To select a pair:

1. Click on one of the variables. It appears as the first variable in Current Selections.

2. Click on another variable. It appears as the second variable. To remove a variable from Current Selections, click on it again.

3. Click on ▶ to move the pair to the Test Pair(s) list.

Repeat this process if you have more than one pair of variables. To obtain the default (Wilcoxon signed-rank) test for two related samples, click on OK.

Test Type. At least one test type must be selected. You can choose one or more of the following:

- **Wilcoxon.** Computes differences between pairs of variables, ranks the absolute differences, sums ranks for the positive and negative differences, and computes the test statistic Z from the positive and negative rank sums. This is the default. Under the null hypothesis, the distribution for Z is approximately normal, with a mean of 0 and a variance of 1 for large sample sizes.

- **Sign.** Analyzes the signs of the differences between two paired values. Counts the positive and negative differences between each pair of variables and ignores zero differences. Under the null hypothesis for large sample sizes, the distribution for the test statistic Z is approximately normal, with a mean of 0 and a variance of 1. The binomial distribution is used to compute an exact significance level if 25 or fewer differences are observed.

- **McNemar.** Examines the cases with different values for two dichotomous variables. Tests the hypothesis that both combinations of different values are equally likely. McNemar produces a 2 × 2 table for each pair of variables. Pairs of variables being tested must be coded with the same two values. If your variables are not dichotomous, or if they have different values, recode them (see Chapter 5). A chi-square statistic is computed for cases with different values for the two variables. If fewer than 25 cases have different values for the two variables, the binomial distribution is used to compute the significance level.

Two-Related-Samples Options

To get optional summary statistics or modify the treatment of cases with missing values, click on Options... in the Two-Related-Samples Tests dialog box. This opens the Two-Related-Samples Options dialog box, as shown in Figure 19.29.

Figure 19.29 Two-Related-Samples Options dialog box

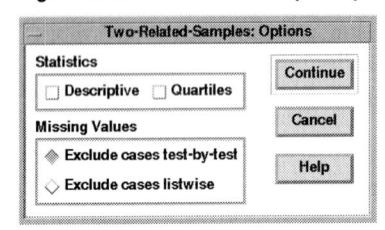

Statistics. You can choose one or both of the following summary statistics:

- **Descriptive.** Displays the mean, minimum, maximum, standard deviation, and the number of nonmissing cases.
- **Quartiles.** Displays values corresponding to the 25th, 50th, and 75th percentiles.

Missing Values. You can choose one of the following alternatives:

◇ **Exclude cases test-by-test.** When several tests are specified, each test is evaluated separately for missing values. This is the default.

◇ **Exclude cases listwise.** Cases with missing values for any variable are excluded from all analyses.

Additional Features Available with Command Syntax

You can customize your two-related-samples test if you paste your selections into a syntax window and edit the resulting NPAR TESTS command syntax (see Chapter 4). As an additional feature, you can test a variable with each variable on a list. See Appendix A for command syntax rules. See the *SPSS Base System Syntax Reference Guide* for complete NPAR TESTS command syntax.

How to Obtain Tests for Several Related Samples

The Tests for Several Related Samples procedure compares the distributions of two or more variables.

The minimum specification is two or more numeric variables.

To obtain tests for several related samples, from the menus choose:

Statistics
 Nonparametric Tests ▶
  K Related Samples...

This opens the Tests for Several Related Samples dialog box, as shown in Figure 19.30.

Figure 19.30 Tests for Several Related Samples dialog box

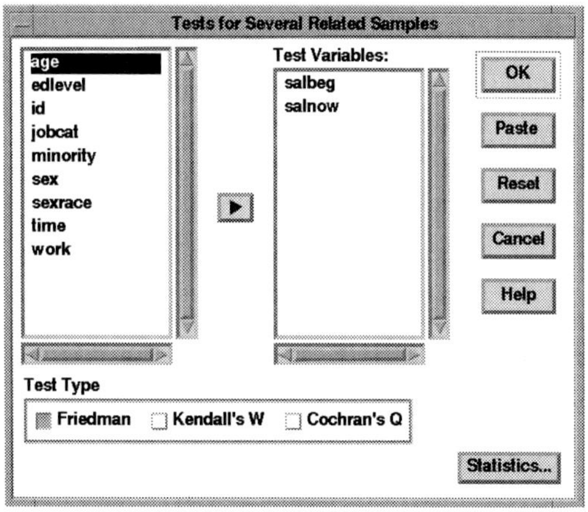

The numeric variables in your data file appear on the source variable list. Select two or more test variables, and click on OK to obtain the default (Friedman) test for several related samples. Cases with missing values for any of the variables are excluded.

Test Type. At least one test type must be selected. You can choose one or more of the following:

- **Friedman.** Ranks each variable from 1 to k for each case (where k is the number of variables), calculates the mean rank for each variable over all cases, and then calculates a test statistic with approximately a chi-square distribution. This is the default.

- **Kendall's W.** Ranks k variables from 1 to k for each case, calculates the mean rank for each variable over all cases, and then calculates Kendall's W and a corresponding chi-square statistic, correcting for ties. W ranges between 0 and 1, with 0 signifying no agreement and 1 signifying complete agreement. This test assumes that each case is a judge or rater. If you want to perform this test with variables as judges and cases as entities, you must first transpose your data matrix (see Chapter 6).

- **Cochran's Q.** Tests the null hypothesis that the proportion of cases in a particular category is the same for several dichotomous variables. Produces a $k \times 2$ contingency table (variable versus category) and computes the proportions for each variable. If your variables are not dichotomous or if they have different values, recode them (see Chapter 5). Cochran's Q statistic has approximately a chi-square distribution.

Several Related Samples Statistics

To obtain optional summary statistics, click on Statistics... in the Tests for Several Related Samples dialog box. This opens the Several Related Samples Statistics dialog box, as shown in Figure 19.31.

Figure 19.31 Several Related Samples Statistics dialog box

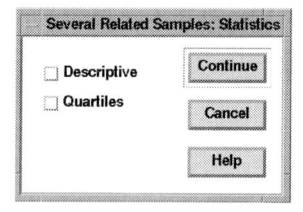

You can choose one or both of the following summary statistics:

- **Descriptive.** Displays the mean, maximum, minimum, standard deviation, and the number of nonmissing cases.
- **Quartiles.** Displays values corresponding to the 25th, 50th, and 75th percentiles.

20 Listing Cases

It is sometimes necessary or useful to review the actual contents of your data file. You may want to make sure data created in another application are being read correctly by SPSS, or you may want to verify the results of transformations or examine cases you suspect contain coding errors. You can review and print the contents of the data file using the Data Editor (see Chapter 3) or the List Cases procedure.

How to Obtain Case Listings

The List Cases procedure produces case listings of selected variables for all cases or a subset of cases.

The minimum specification is one variable.

To obtain case listings with the List Cases procedure, from the menus choose:

Statistics
  Summarize ▶
    List Cases...

This opens the List Cases dialog box, as shown in Figure 20.1.

Figure 20.1 List Cases dialog box

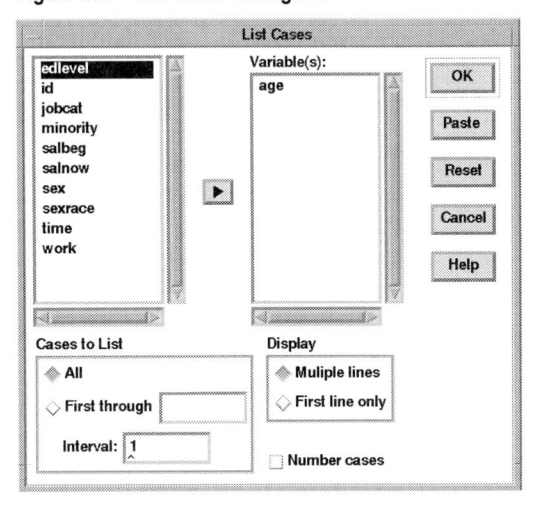

The variables in your data file are displayed on the source list. Select one or more variables for which you want case listings. To obtain the default listing of all cases in the file, click on OK.

Cases to List. You can choose one of the following:

◇ **All**. Lists all cases in the data file. This is the default.

◇ **First through n**. Lists cases from the first case to the specified number. The number represents the sequential number in the current file order, regardless of the value of any case ID variable that may exist in the file.

The following option is also available for cases to list:

Interval. Increment used to choose cases for listing. For example, if you want to see only every fifth case, enter a value of 5. The default value is 1.

Display. You can choose one of the following:

◇ **Multiple lines**. This is the default. SPSS automatically determines the format of the case listing. If all the variables can fit on one line, the variable names are used as column heads (see Figure 20.2). If it can display all variables on one line by displaying some variable names vertically, it does so (see Figure 20.3). If there is not enough room on one line to display all the requested variables, multiple lines are used for each case. SPSS generates a table indicating which variables appear on each line, and the name of the first variable on each line is displayed in the case listings (see Figure 20.4).

◇ **First line only**. If there is not enough room for all the variables on a single line, the listing is truncated to include only those variables that fit on a single line per case. Since the multiple-line format can be difficult to read, you may want to use this alternative.

The following display option is also available:

❏ **Number cases**. Displays the sequential case number in the current file order. This is the value of the system variable *$casenum*, which reflects the current order of cases in the file.

Figure 20.2   Single-line case listing with variable names displayed horizontally

```
NAME              ID  SALBEG SEX TIME    AGE SALNOW EDLEVEL  WORK JOBCAT

Delbert McManus   926   3600   0   91   53.50  12300    12    26.17    3
Karen Nigida      921   3600   1   97   60.67   6780    12    10.33    1
Kendall Newton   1010   3600   1   97   51.58   8460    15    14.25    1
Christine Martin 1096   3600   1   96   60.50   7680    15     1.92    1
Dakota Becking    741   3900   1   98   27.25   8760    12      .00    1
Kay Lewis         754   3900   1   92   55.50   6480     8      .00    1
Donna Paul        945   3900   1   86   52.00   8760    12    13.00    1
Harriet Smith     995   3900   1   86   62.00   7260    12     6.00    1
Laurie Stolarz   1107   3900   1   88   62.50   6660     8    34.33    1
Lowell George    1077   3900   0   94   29.17   9000     8     3.00    2
```

Figure 20.3 Single-line case listing with some variable names displayed vertically

```
                               S              S          J
                               A              A          O
                               L     T        L          B
                             B S     I        N          C
                             E E     M        O          A
NAME              ID         G X     E  AGE   W  EDLEVEL WORK T
Delbert McManus   926      3600 0   91  53.50 12300  12   26.17 3
Karen Nigida      921      3600 1   97  60.67  6780  12   10.33 1
Kendall Newton   1010      3600 1   97  51.58  8460  15   14.25 1
Christine Martin 1096      3600 1   96  60.50  7680  15    1.92 1
Dakota Becking    741      3900 1   98  27.25  8760  12     .00 1
Kay Lewis         754      3900 1   92  55.50  6480   8     .00 1
Donna Paul        945      3900 1   86  52.00  8760  12   13.00 1
Harriet Smith     995      3900 1   86  62.00  7260  12    6.00 1
Laurie Stolarz   1107      3900 1   88  62.50  6660   8   34.33 1
Lowell George    1077      3900 0   94  29.17  9000   8    3.00 2
```

Figure 20.4 Case listing with multiple lines

```
THE VARIABLES ARE LISTED IN THE FOLLOWING ORDER:
LINE   1: NAME ID SALBEG SEX TIME AGE SALNOW EDLEVEL WORK
LINE   2: JOBCAT MINORITY SEXRACE

      NAME: Delbert McManus    926      3600 0 91 53.50    12300 12        26
   JOBCAT:            3 1     2.00

      NAME: Karen Nigida       921      3600 1 97 60.67     6780 12        10
   JOBCAT:            1 1     4.00

      NAME: Kendall Newton    1010      3600 1 97 51.58     8460 15        14
   JOBCAT:            1 1     4.00

      NAME: Christine Martin  1096      3600 1 96 60.50     7680 15         2
   JOBCAT:            1 1     4.00

      NAME: Dakota Becking     741      3900 1 98 27.25     8760 12         0
   JOBCAT:            1 0     3.00

      NAME: Kay Lewis          754      3900 1 92 55.50     6480  8         0
   JOBCAT:            1 0     3.00

      NAME: Donna Paul         945      3900 1 86 52.00     8760 12        13
   JOBCAT:            1 0     3.00

      NAME: Harriet Smith      995      3900 1 86 62.00     7260 12         6
   JOBCAT:            1 0     3.00

      NAME: Laurie Stolarz    1107      3900 1 88 62.50     6660  8        34
   JOBCAT:            1 0     3.00

      NAME: Lowell George     1077      3900 0 94 29.17     9000  8         3
   JOBCAT:            2 1     2.00
```

Additional Features Available with Command Syntax

You can customize your descriptive statistics if you paste your selections into a syntax window and edit the resulting LIST command syntax (see Chapter 4). An additional feature is the ability to list cases beginning with any case you specify. See Appendix A for command syntax rules. See the *SPSS Base System Syntax Reference Guide* for complete LIST command syntax.

21 Reporting Results

Case listings and descriptive statistics are basic tools for studying and presenting data. You can obtain case listings with the Data Editor or the List procedure, frequency counts and descriptive statistics with the Frequencies procedure, and subpopulation statistics with the Means procedure. Each of these uses a format designed to make information clear. If you want to display the information in a different format, the Report procedure gives you the control you need over data presentation.

Basic Report Concepts

Reports can contain summary statistics for groups of cases, listings of individual cases, or a combination of both statistics and listings. The number of columns in a report is determined by the number of report variables and break variables. Each variable is displayed in a separate column. **Report variables** are the variables for which you want case listings or summary statistics. These are displayed in **data columns**. Optional **break variables** divide the data into groups. These are displayed in **break columns**, which appear on the left side of the report.

Summary Reports

Summary reports display summary statistics but do not display case listings. The summary information consists of the statistics you request for the report variables. Using break variables, you can report summary statistics for various subgroups of cases. Figure 21.1 is an example of a summary report with summary statistics reported in rows.

Figure 21.1 Summary report—summaries in rows

```
                          Report variables in
                          data columns

                                  Tenure   Tenure
                                    in       in
              Division    Age    Company   Grade   Salary--Annual

              Carpeting
                Mean      30.75    4.04     3.31       $11,754
                Minimum   22.00    2.67     2.17        $9,200
                Maximum   44.00    6.00     5.33       $19,500
              Appliances
                Mean      31.11    3.81     3.54       $12,508
                Minimum   21.00    2.67     2.08        $7,500
                Maximum   42.00    6.50     6.50       $28,300
              Furniture
                Mean      36.87    4.79     4.08       $13,255
                Minimum   25.00    3.17     3.17        $8,975
                Maximum   43.00    6.83     6.25       $17,050
```

Break variable in break column

Subgroup summary statistics

In the summary report shown in Figure 21.1:

- Age, tenure in company, tenure in grade, and salary are the report variables presented in data columns.
- Division is the break variable presented in the break column.
- Mean, minimum value, and maximum value are the summary statistics reported on summary lines for each division.

Listing Reports

Listing reports list individual cases. The case listings can display the actual data values or the defined value labels recorded for each of the report variables. As with summary reports, you divide a listing report into subgroups using break variables, as shown in Figure 21.2.

Figure 21.2 Listing report

Division	Age	Tenure in Company	Tenure in Grade	Salary--Annual
Carpeting	27.00	3.67	2.17	$9,200
	22.00	3.92	3.08	$10,900
	23.00	3.92	3.08	$10,900
	24.00	4.00	3.25	$10,000
	30.00	4.08	3.08	$10,000
	27.00	4.33	3.17	$10,000
	33.00	2.67	2.67	$9,335
	33.00	3.75	3.25	$10,000
	44.00	4.83	4.33	$15,690
	36.00	3.83	3.25	$10,000
	35.00	3.50	3.00	$15,520
	35.00	6.00	5.33	$19,500
Appliances	21.00	2.67	2.67	$8,700
	26.00	2.92	2.08	$8,000
	32.00	2.92	2.92	$8,900
	33.00	3.42	2.92	$8,900
	34.00	5.08	4.50	$15,300
	24.00	3.17	3.17	$8,975
	42.00	6.50	6.50	$18,000
	30.00	2.67	2.67	$7,500
	38.00	5.00	4.42	$28,300

Combined Reports

You can combine individual case listings and summary statistics in a single report, as shown in Figure 21.3.

Figure 21.3 Combined report with case listings and summary statistics

Division	Age	Tenure in Company	Tenure in Grade	Salary--Annual
Carpeting	27.00	3.67	2.17	$9,200
	22.00	3.92	3.08	$10,900
	23.00	3.92	3.08	$10,900
	24.00	4.00	3.25	$10,000
	30.00	4.08	3.08	$10,000
	27.00	4.33	3.17	$10,000
	33.00	2.67	2.67	$9,335
	33.00	3.75	3.25	$10,000
	44.00	4.83	4.33	$15,690
	36.00	3.83	3.25	$10,000
	35.00	3.50	3.00	$15,520
	35.00	6.00	5.33	$19,500
Mean	30.75	4.04	3.31	$11,754
Appliances	21.00	2.67	2.67	$8,700
	26.00	2.92	2.08	$8,000
	32.00	2.92	2.92	$8,900
	33.00	3.42	2.92	$8,900
	34.00	5.08	4.50	$15,300
	24.00	3.17	3.17	$8,975
	42.00	6.50	6.50	$18,000
	30.00	2.67	2.67	$7,500
	38.00	5.00	4.42	$28,300
Mean	31.11	3.81	3.54	$12,508

Multiple Break Variables

You can use more than one break variable to divide your report into groups, and you can display different summary statistics for each break variable division. In Figure 21.4, for example, each division is further divided by store location. For each store location, the minimum and maximum values are displayed, and for each division, the mean and standard deviation are presented.

Figure 21.4 Multiple break variables in a summary report

```
                              Tenure    Tenure
                Branch          in       in
Division        Store    Age   Company  Grade   Salary--Annual

Carpeting       Suburban
                Minimum  22.00  3.67    2.17     $9,200
                Maximum  35.00  6.00    5.33     $19,500

                Downtown
                Minimum  24.00  2.67    2.67     $9,335
                Maximum  44.00  4.83    4.33     $15,690
Mean                     30.75  4.04    3.31     $11,754
StdDev                    6.47   .80     .81      $3,288

Appliances      Suburban
                Minimum  21.00  2.67    2.08     $8,000
                Maximum  42.00  6.50    6.50     $28,300

                Downtown
                Minimum  30.00  2.67    2.67     $7,500
                Maximum  34.00  5.08    4.50     $15,300
Mean                     31.11  3.81    3.54     $12,508
StdDev                    6.70  1.37    1.37     $6,944
```

Grand Total Summary Statistics

In addition to reporting summary statistics for subgroups based on break variables, you can include summary statistics for all cases in the report, as shown in Figure 21.5. Overall report summary statistics are referred to as **grand totals**.

Figure 21.5 Summary report with grand totals

```
                          Tenure    Tenure
               Branch       in        in
Division       Store       Age     Company   Grade    Salary--Annual

Furniture      Suburban
               Minimum    25.00     3.17      3.17       $8,975
               Maximum    42.00     6.25      6.25      $17,050

               Downtown
               Minimum    32.00     4.42      3.50      $12,000
               Maximum    43.00     6.83      5.33      $14,400
Mean                      36.87     4.79      4.08      $13,255
StdDev                     5.71      .89       .89       $2,126

Hardware       Suburban
               Minimum    32.00     4.33      4.33      $22,500
               Maximum    32.00     4.33      4.33      $22,500

               Downtown
               Minimum    26.00     2.67      2.50       $7,450
               Maximum    44.00     6.00      6.00      $22,000
Mean                      36.20     4.60      4.57      $17,580
StdDev                     7.16     1.28      1.35       $6,103

Grand Total

Mean                      33.73     4.34      3.79      $13,179
N                            41       41        41          41
StdDev                     6.76     1.08      1.10       $4,589
```

Formatting Reports

The Report procedure offers a great deal of control over the appearance of your report. You can add titles and footnotes, change the column headings, adjust column width and alignment, and control the display of values or value labels.

Titles and Footnotes

You can add titles and footnotes to reports. You can also include the values of variables in titles and footnotes, including special variables for page number and current date, as shown in Figure 21.6.

Figure 21.6 Titles and footnotes

```
                                                                    Value label for current
Special variable   07 Apr 92   Monthly Summary Report -- Carpeting Division    value of break variable
for current date                             Tenure     Tenure
                             Branch          in         in
              Division       Store      Age  Company    Grade     Salary--Annual

              Carpeting      Suburban
                             Minimum    22.00   3.67     2.17      $9,200
                             Maximum    35.00   6.00     5.33      $19,500

                             Downtown
                             Minimum    24.00   2.67     2.67      $9,335
                             Maximum    44.00   4.83     4.33      $15,690
              Mean                      30.75   4.04     3.31      $11,754
              StdDev                     6.47    .80      .81      $3,288


                                         1 ───── Special variable for
                                                 page number
```

Column Headings

Each column in a report has a heading. By default, the variable label is used for the heading. If there is no label, the variable name is used. You can also create headings of your own and control their alignment, as shown in Figure 21.7.

Figure 21.7 User-specified column headings

```
              07 Apr 92   Monthly Summary Report -- Appliances Division
                          Store      Employee   Company   Job       Annual
              Division    Location   Age        Tenure    Tenure    Salary

              Appliances  Suburban
                          Minimum    21.00      2.67      2.08      $8,000
                          Maximum    42.00      6.50      6.50      $28,300

                          Downtown
                          Minimum    30.00      2.67      2.67      $7,500
                          Maximum    34.00      5.08      4.50      $15,300
              Mean                   31.11      3.81      3.54      $12,508
              StdDev                  6.70      1.37      1.37      $6,944
```

Displaying Value Labels

For break variables, value labels are displayed by default. For report variables in listing reports, data values are displayed by default. You can display actual data values for break variables and/or value labels for report variables in listing reports. For example, if you want to produce a personnel report that includes employee's gender, you might want to display the value labels *Male* and *Female* instead of the numeric values 1 and 2, as shown in Figure 21.8.

Figure 21.8 Displaying value labels in a listing report

```
                     Annual
Last Name    Gender  Salary   Job Grade          Shift
----------   ------  -------  -----------------  -------
Ford         Female   $9,200  Support Staff      First
Cochran      Female  $10,900  Sales Staff        First
Hoawinski    Female  $10,900  Sales Staff        First
Tygielski    Male    $19,500  Supervisory Staff  Weekend
Gates        Female  $10,000  Sales Staff        Second
Mulvihill    Male    $10,000  Sales Staff        First
Lavelle      Female  $10,000  Sales Staff        Weekend
Mahr         Female   $9,335  Sales Staff        First
Katz         Male    $10,000  Sales Staff        Weekend
Jones        Female  $15,690  Sales Staff        First
Dan          Male    $10,000  Sales Staff        Weekend
McAndrews    Female  $15,520  Supervisory Staff  First
Powell       Female   $8,700  Support Staff      Weekend
Martin       Female   $8,000  Sales Staff        First
Parris       Female   $8,975  Sales Staff        First
Johnson      Female  $18,000  Sales Staff        Second
Sanders      Male    $28,300  Managerial Staff   First
Shavilje     Male     $8,900  Sales Staff        First
Provenza     Female   $8,900  Sales Staff        First
Snolik       Male    $15,300  Sales Staff        First
Sedowski     Male     $7,500  Sales Staff        Weekend
```

How to Obtain Listing Reports and Reports with Summaries in Rows

The minimum specifications for a listing report or a report with summaries in rows are:

- One or more report variables on the Data Columns list.
- One or more summary statistics or selection of the Display cases check box.

To obtain and modify row summary reports and case listing reports, from the menus choose:

Statistics
 Summarize ▶
  Report Summaries in Rows...

This opens the Report Summaries in Rows dialog box, as shown in Figure 21.9.

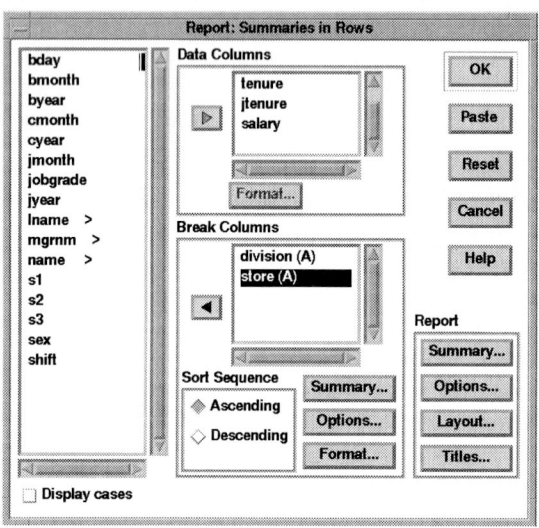

Figure 21.9 Report Summaries in Rows dialog box

Data Columns. The report variables for which you want case listings or summary statistics. You must select at least one variable for the Data Columns list.

Break Columns. Optional break variables that divide the report into groups. Each successive break variable divides the report into subgroups within groups of the previous break variable. For example, if you select *division* and then *store* as break variables, there will be a separate group for each category of *store* within each category of *division*, as shown in Figure 21.4.

> **Sort Sequence.** Sort order for categories of the break variables. Sort order is based on data values, not value labels. String variables are sorted alphabetically, and uppercase letters precede lowercase letters in sort order. For each break variable, you can choose one of the following alternatives for sort sequence:
>
> ◇ **Ascending.** Sorts break variable values by ascending order from low to high. This is the default.
>
> ◇ **Descending.** Sorts break variable values by descending order from high to low.

Report. The items in the Report group control the display of grand total summary statistics, treatment of missing values, page layout and numbering, and report titles and footers.

The following display option is also available:

- **Display cases**. Displays individual case listings. Select this option to produce listing reports, as shown in Figure 21.2.

Data Column Format

To modify data column headings, column width, and alignment of headings and data, and to control the display of value labels, select a report variable on the Data Columns list and click on Format... in the Report Summaries in Rows dialog box. This opens the Report Data Column Format dialog box, as shown in Figure 21.10.

Figure 21.10 Report Data Column Format dialog box

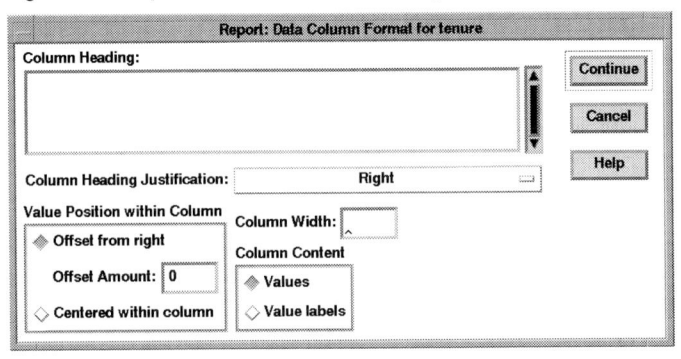

Column Heading. The heading that appears at the top of the column for the selected report variable. If you don't specify a heading, the variable label is used by default. If there is no variable label, the variable name is used. Default column headings are automatically wrapped onto multiple lines to fit in the column width. User-specified column headings are displayed on a single line unless you specify multiple-line headings. To specify a multiple-line column heading, press Ctrl-Enter at the end of each line.

- **Column Heading Justification**. Alignment of the column heading. Alignment of the column heading does not affect alignment of the data displayed in the column. You can choose one of the following alternatives:

    Left. Column headings are left-justified. This is the default for string variables.

    Center. Column headings are centered based on column width.

    Right. Column headings are right-justified. This is the default for numeric variables.

Value Position within Column. Alignment of data values or value labels within the column. Alignment of values or labels does not affect alignment of column headings. You can choose one of the following alternatives:

◇ **Offset from right/left.** Enter a number of characters for the offset amount. The default is 0. If values are displayed, the offset is from the right side of the column. If value labels are displayed, the offset is from the left side of the column. The offset value cannot exceed the defined column width.

◇ **Centered within column.** Data values or value labels are centered in the column.

Column Width. Column width expressed as a number of characters. If you don't specify a value, a default column width is determined based on the largest of the following:

- If you specify a column heading, the length of the longest line in the heading.
- If you don't specify a column heading, the length of the longest word in the variable label.
- If value labels are displayed, the length of the longest value label for the variable.

If you specify a value for column width that is shorter than the display format of the variable, numeric values that don't fit in the specified width are converted to scientific notation. If the specified width contains fewer than six characters, asterisks are displayed for numeric values that don't fit. String values and value labels are wrapped onto multiple lines to fit in the column width.

Column Content. You can choose one of the following alternatives:

◇ **Values.** Data values are displayed. This is the default for data column variables.

◇ **Value labels.** Value labels are displayed. This is the default for break column variables. If a value doesn't have a defined label, the data value is displayed.

Break Category Summary Statistics

To specify summary statistics for data column variables within categories of a break variable, select a break variable on the Break Columns list and click on Summary... in the Report Summaries in Rows dialog box. This opens the Report Summary Lines dialog box, as shown in Figure 21.11.

Figure 21.11 Report Summary Lines dialog box

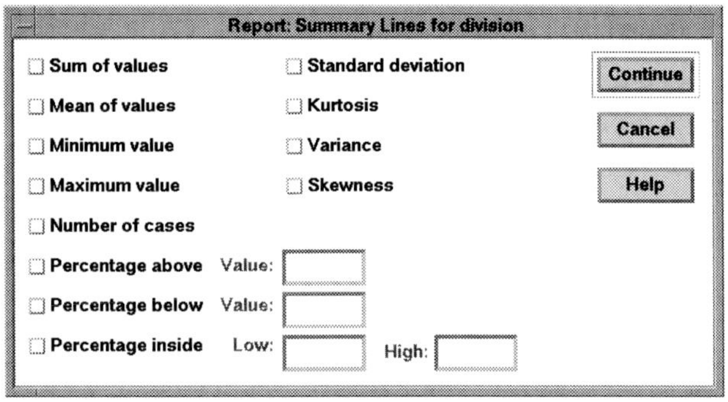

```
┌─────────────── Report: Summary Lines for division ───────────────┐
│                                                                  │
│  ☐ Sum of values        ☐ Standard deviation     [ Continue ]   │
│  ☐ Mean of values       ☐ Kurtosis                               │
│  ☐ Minimum value        ☐ Variance               [  Cancel  ]   │
│  ☐ Maximum value        ☐ Skewness               [   Help   ]   │
│  ☐ Number of cases                                               │
│  ☐ Percentage above  Value: [       ]                            │
│  ☐ Percentage below  Value: [       ]                            │
│  ☐ Percentage inside  Low: [       ]  High: [       ]            │
│                                                                  │
└──────────────────────────────────────────────────────────────────┘
```

Each summary statistic selected is calculated for all data column variables within each category of the break variable. If you choose more than one summary statistic, each statistic is displayed on a separate row in the report. You can select different summary statistics for each break variable. You can choose one or more of the following summary statistics:

- **Sum of values**. The sum of data values in the break category.
- **Mean of values**. The arithmetic average of data values in the break category.
- **Minimum value**. The smallest data value in the break category.
- **Maximum value**. The largest data value in the break category.
- **Number of cases**. Number of cases in the break category.
- **Percentage above**. Percentage of cases in the break category above a user-specified value. If you select this item, you must enter a value in the text box before you can continue.
- **Percentage below**. Percentage of cases in the break category below a user-specified value. If you select this item, you must enter a value in the text box before you can continue.
- **Percentage inside**. Percentage of cases in the break category inside a user-specified range. If you select this item, you must enter a low value and a high value before you can continue.
- **Standard deviation**. A measure of how much observations vary from the mean of values in the break category, expressed in the same units as the data.
- **Kurtosis**. A measure of the extent to which data values in the break category cluster around a central point, given their standard deviation.

❑ **Variance**. A measure of how much values vary from the mean of values in the break category, equal to the square of the standard deviation. The units are the square of those of the variable itself.

❑ **Skewness**. An index of the degree to which the distribution of data values in the break category is not symmetric.

Break Spacing and Page Options

To change the line spacing between break categories or between break headings and summary statistics, or to display each break category on a separate page, select a break variable on the Break Columns list and click on Options... in the Report Summaries in Rows dialog box. This opens the Report Break Options dialog box, as shown in Figure 21.12.

Figure 21.12 Report Break Options dialog box

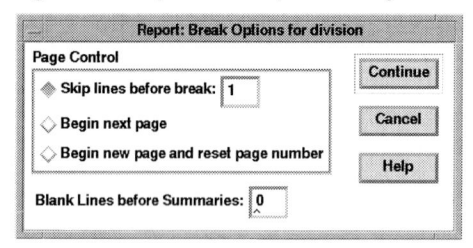

Page Control. You can select one of the following alternatives for spacing between break categories:

◇ **Skip lines before break.** The number of blank lines between break categories. The default is 1. You can specify from 0 to 20 blank lines between break categories.

◇ **Begin next page.** Starts each break category on a new page.

◇ **Begin new page and reset page number.** Starts each break category on a separate page and numbers pages for each break category separately.

Blank Lines before Summaries. The number of blank lines between the break category heading and the summary statistics. The default is 0. You can specify up to 20 blank lines between the break category heading and the rows of summary statistics.

Break Column Format

To modify break column headings, column width, and alignment of headings and data, and to control the display of value labels, select a break variable on the Break Columns list and click on Format... in the Report Summaries in Rows dialog box. This opens the Report Break Column Format dialog box, which offers selections identical to those in the Report Data Column Format dialog box, shown in Figure 21.10. See "Data Column Format" on p. 399 for information on the selections available in this dialog box.

Report Total Summary Statistics

To specify grand total summary statistics for the entire report, click on Summary... in the Report group of selections in the main dialog box. This opens the Report Final Summary Lines dialog box, which offers selections identical to those in the Report Summary Lines dialog box, shown in Figure 21.11. For more information on the available summary statistics, see "Break Category Summary Statistics" on p. 400.

Report Options

To change the treatment and display of missing values, save processing time for pre-sorted data, and control the report page numbering, click on Options... in the Report group of selections in the Report Summaries in Rows dialog box. This opens the Report Options dialog box, as shown in Figure 21.13.

Figure 21.13 Report Options dialog box

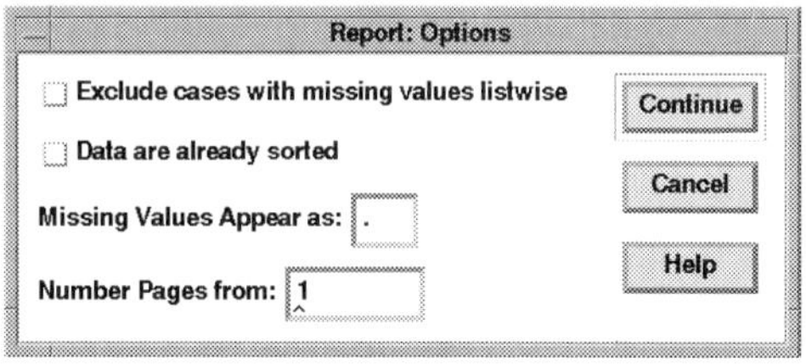

The following options are available:

- **Exclude cases with missing values listwise.** Excludes cases that have missing data for any variable in the report. By default, cases with missing data are included in the report if they have valid values for any report variable.

- **Data are already sorted.** Data are already sorted by values of the break variables. The Report procedure creates a new break category each time the value of a break variable changes in the data file. Therefore, meaningful summary reports require that the data file be sorted by values of the break variables. By default, the file is automatically sorted before the report is generated. If the data file is already sorted in the proper order, you can save processing time by selecting this option. This option is particularly useful once you have run a report and want to refine the format.

Missing Values Appear as. The character used to indicate both system- and user-missing data. By default, a period (.) is used. You can use any single character.

Number Pages from. The starting page number of the report. By default, pages are numbered from 1. The starting page number can be any integer from 0 to 99999.

Report Layout

To change the width and length of each report page and control the placement of the report on the page, click on Layout... in the Report Summaries in Rows dialog box. This opens the Report Layout dialog box, as shown in Figure 21.14.

Figure 21.14 Report Layout dialog box

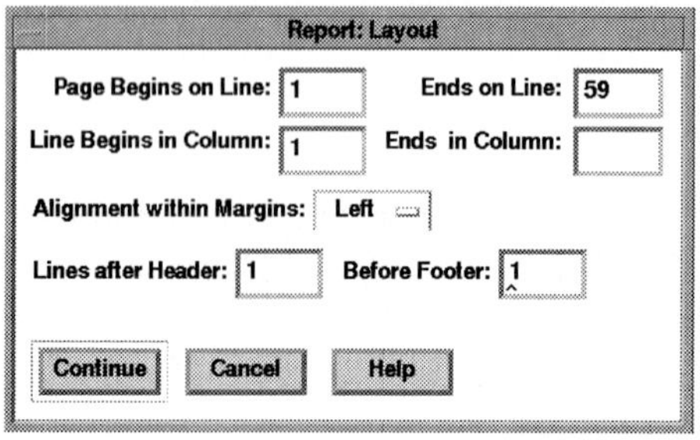

The following report layout options are available:

Page Begins on Line/Ends on Line. By default, each report page begins on the first line of the page and ends on the last line of the page as defined by the page length in the Preferences dialog box (see Chapter 29). You can specify any line number less than the defined page length, and you can specify a page length from 24 to 999 lines.

If you specify beginning and ending line values that do not provide the minimum number of lines per page required for the report, the ending line value will be overridden, and a message at the end of the report will indicate this.

Line Begins in Column/Ends in Column. The left and right margins of the report are expressed as the number of characters (columns) across the page. By default, the report begins in column 1 and ends in the column that corresponds to the page width value defined in the Preferences dialog box (see Chapter 29). You can specify a value up to 255.

If you specify beginning and ending column values that do not provide a space wide enough for the report, the report will not be generated. If you don't specify an ending column value, the Report procedure will override the default if necessary to display reports that are too wide for the default width, and a message at the end of the report will indicate this. The maximum width of a report is 255 characters.

- **Alignment within Margins.** The report can be left- or right-aligned or centered within the left and right page margins. The default is left alignment. If you don't specify beginning and ending column positions for the left and right margins, centering and right alignment have no effect.

Lines after Header/Before Footer. Indicates the number of blank lines between the report title (header) and the first line of the report, and the number of lines between the bottom of the report and any footers; by default, there is one blank line between the title and the report and one blank line between the bottom of the report and any footers.

Titles and Footers

To add titles and footers to a report, click on Titles... in the Report Summaries in Rows dialog box. This opens the Report Titles dialog box, as shown in Figure 21.15.

Figure 21.15 Report Titles dialog box

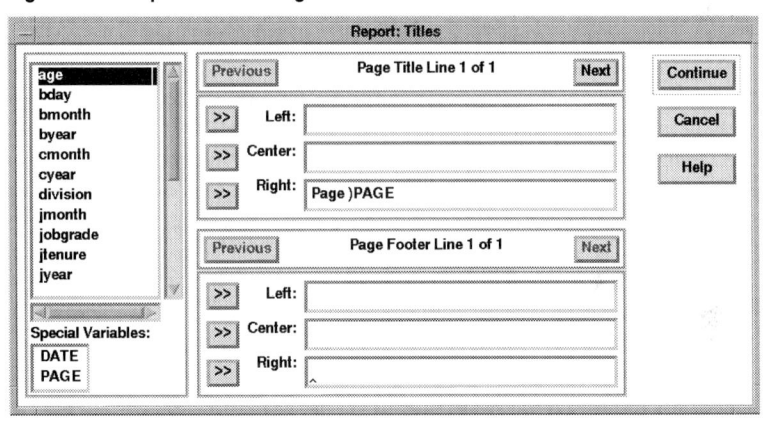

Page Titles. Titles and other text that appears above the report on each page. You can specify any combination of left, center, and right titles. To specify multiple-line titles, click on Next after each title line to specify the next line. You can have up to 10 title lines. By default, the current page number is used as the right title.

Page Footers. Text, such as footnotes, that appears below the report on each page. You can specify any combination of left, center, and right footers. To specify multiple-line footers, click on Next after each footer to specify the next footer line. You can have up to 10 footer lines.

If the combined width of the left, center, and right titles or footers exceeds the defined width of the page, the titles or footers are truncated in the report. Left and right titles and footers are truncated before center ones.

Positioning Titles and Footers

The position of titles and footers is based on the report width unless you explicitly specify left and right report margins (see "Report Layout" on p. 404). If you specify report margins, the position of titles and footers is based on alignment within those margins. For example, if you specify a right margin of 90 but the report is only 70 characters wide, center titles will not be aligned over the center of the report. You can adjust the position of titles and footers by changing the left and right margins.

Using Variables in Titles and Footers

To use a variable in a title or footer, position the cursor in the line where you want the variable to appear and click on the corresponding ▶ pushbutton. The variable name appears in the line, preceded by a right parenthesis. Two special variables, *DATE* and *PAGE*, are also available to display the current date and page number.

In titles, the value label corresponding to the value of the variable at the beginning of the page is displayed (see Figure 21.6). In footers, the value label corresponding to the value of the variable at the end of the page is displayed. If there is no value label, the actual value is displayed.

Additional Features Available with Command Syntax

You can customize your report if you paste your selections into a syntax window and edit the resulting REPORT command syntax (see Chapter 4). Additional features include:

- Control of spacing between cases in listing reports (with the FORMAT subcommand).
- Stacking of multiple report variables in a single column in listing reports (with the VARIABLES subcommand).
- Summary statistics calculated for specific data column variables instead of all data column variables (with the SUMMARY subcommand).
- Control of descriptive headings for summary statistics (with the SUMMARY subcommand).

See Appendix A for command syntax rules. See the *SPSS Base System Syntax Reference Guide* for complete REPORT command syntax.

22 Overview of the SPSS Chart Facility

High-resolution charts and plots are created by the procedures on the Graphs menu and by many of the procedures on the Statistics menu. Chapter 22 through Chapter 26 offer a systematic discussion of the various aspects of creating and enhancing charts:

- **Overview of the SPSS Chart Facility** (Chapter 22).
- **Bar, Line, Area, and Pie Charts** (Chapter 23).
- **Boxplots** (Chapter 24).
- **Scatterplots and Histograms** (Chapter 25).
- **Modifying Charts** (Chapter 26).

This chapter provides an overview of the SPSS chart facility and includes the following information:

- **Tutorial.** Detailed steps showing how to create and modify a simple chart.
- **Chart Carousel.** Discussion of the SPSS window that holds and displays charts as they are created. You can view, save, copy, and print charts from this window.
- **Chart definition global options.** Definition options that apply to all charts, including titles and subtitles, footnotes, missing data values, and templates.

How to Create and Modify a Chart

Suppose that you have recorded the temperature in your office in the early morning and late afternoon every day for a week and you want a chart that emphasizes how much the temperature varies, such as the one in Figure 22.1.

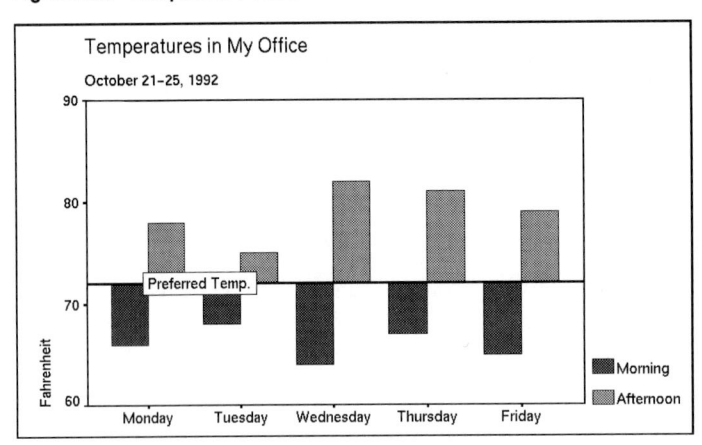

Figure 22.1 Temperature chart

First you must enter the data, then create a chart, and, finally, modify the chart to make the message clear.

Entering the Data

For the purposes of this tutorial, the data are entered directly from the keyboard. Keyboard entry is appropriate if the amount of data is small. Once the data have been entered, the basic steps for creating a chart are the same, regardless of how the data were entered or size of the data file.

1. If the Data Editor window is not active, from the Window menu choose the Data Editor window, which bears the name Newdata or the name of the data file you have already opened.

2. If an empty Newdata file is displayed, go on to step 3. If you have a data file already open, from the menus choose:

   File
   New ▶
     Data...

   This opens a Data Editor window containing the Newdata file.

3. In the Newdata file, enter the morning temperatures in the first column and the afternoon temperatures in the second column, as shown in Figure 22.2. After entering the last value, press ⏎Enter or move to another cell.

Figure 22.2 Data entered in Data Editor

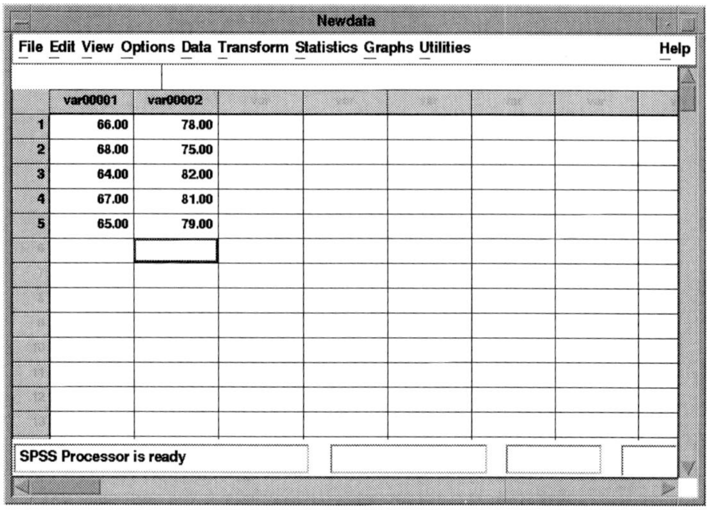

	var00001	var00002
1	66.00	78.00
2	68.00	75.00
3	64.00	82.00
4	67.00	81.00
5	65.00	79.00

You have now created two variables: *var00001* and *var00002*. Later, you may want to give them more descriptive names, such as *amtemp* and *pmtemp*. After creating a chart, you will find out how to revise the labeling within the chart.

To avoid the chore of entering the temperature data again when you want to repeat some part of this tutorial, you should save this data file now.

Creating the Chart

Now that you have entered your data, you can get on with creating a chart.

● From the menus choose:

Graphs
 Bar...

This opens the Bar Charts dialog box, as shown in Figure 22.3.

Figure 22.3 Bar Charts dialog box

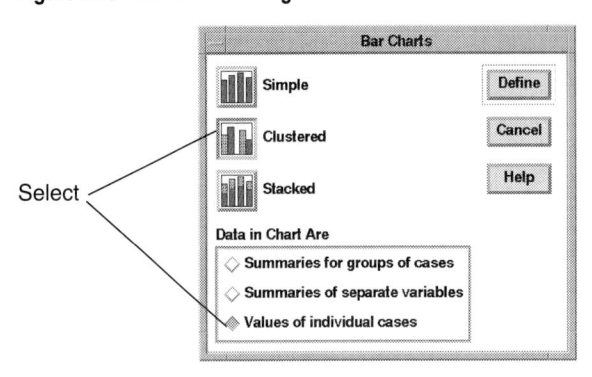

② Select the picture button Clustered.
③ Select Values of individual cases.
④ Click on Define. This opens the Define Clustered Bar Values of Individual Cases dialog box, as shown in Figure 22.4.

Figure 22.4 Define Clustered Bar Values of Individual Cases dialog box

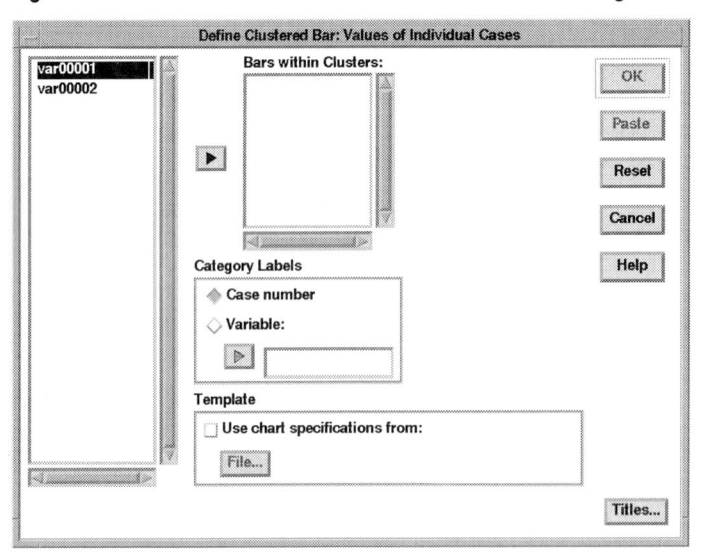

⑤ Move *var00001* and *var00002* from the variable source list to the Bars within Clusters list by highlighting them and clicking on ▶.
⑥ Click on OK. The chart appears in the Chart Carousel, as shown in Figure 22.5.

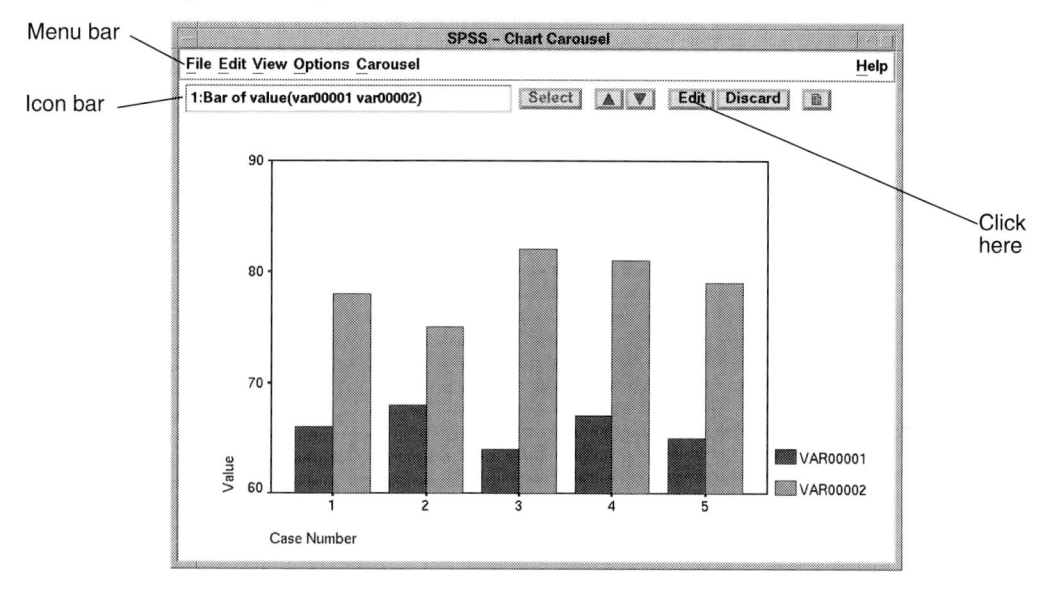

Figure 22.5 Original chart in Chart Carousel

The Chart Carousel is a holding area for newly entered charts. The Chart Carousel menu bar and a corresponding icon bar appear above the chart. The chart as it stands contains an interpretable graphic representation of the data. You could save and print this chart from the Chart Carousel and use it in a report. There are several modifications, however, that will enhance the chart so that it will deliver a clearer message.

Modifying the Chart

The first step in chart modification is to transfer the chart from the Chart Carousel to a chart window.

① Click on Edit on the icon bar. This places the chart in a chart window, as shown in Figure 22.6.

Figure 22.6 Original chart in chart window

Notice that the Chart Editor window has its own menu bar and icon bar.

❷ To edit the category axis at the base of the chart, double-click anywhere within the words *Case Number*. This opens the Category Axis dialog box, as shown in Figure 22.7. (If a different dialog box opens, click on Cancel in that dialog box and try again; you probably double-clicked too far from the category axis.)

Figure 22.7 Category Axis dialog box

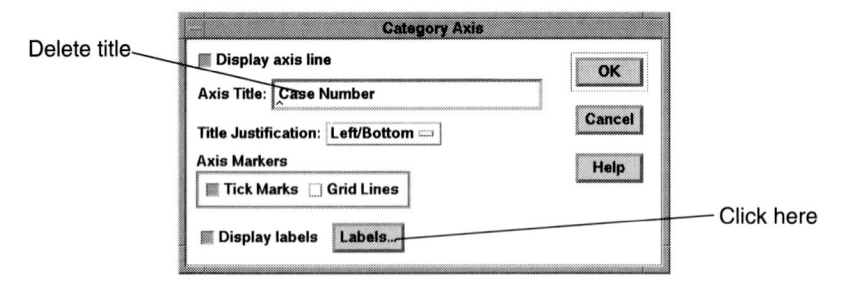

❸ Delete the axis title from the text box. It will not be meaningful when the labels are changed.

④ Click on Labels.... This opens the Category Axis Labels dialog box, as shown in Figure 22.8. The first label, the numeral *1*, is highlighted in the Label Text list and also appears in the Label text box.

Figure 22.8 Category Axis Labels dialog box

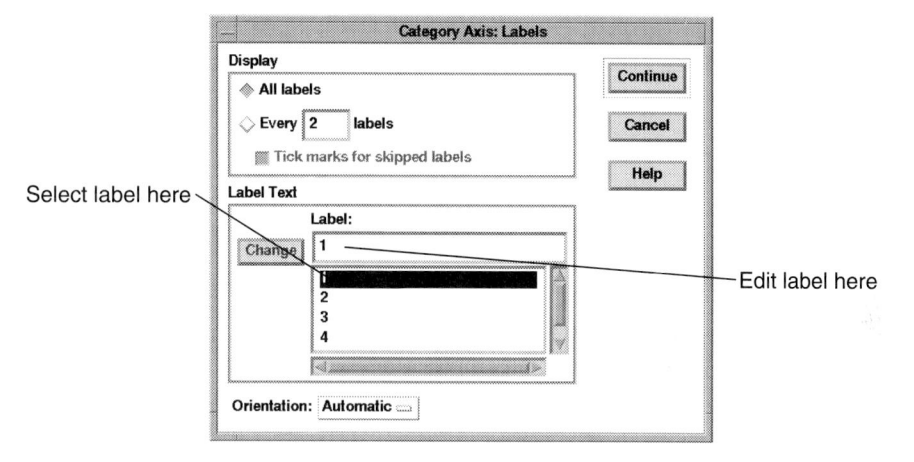

⑤ To edit the first label, delete the *1* in the text box, enter *Monday*, and click on Change.

⑥ In the same manner, click on the second label, *2*, and change it to *Tuesday*.

⑦ Click on the next label, *3*. The labels now appear as shown in Figure 22.9.

Figure 22.9 Category labels changed

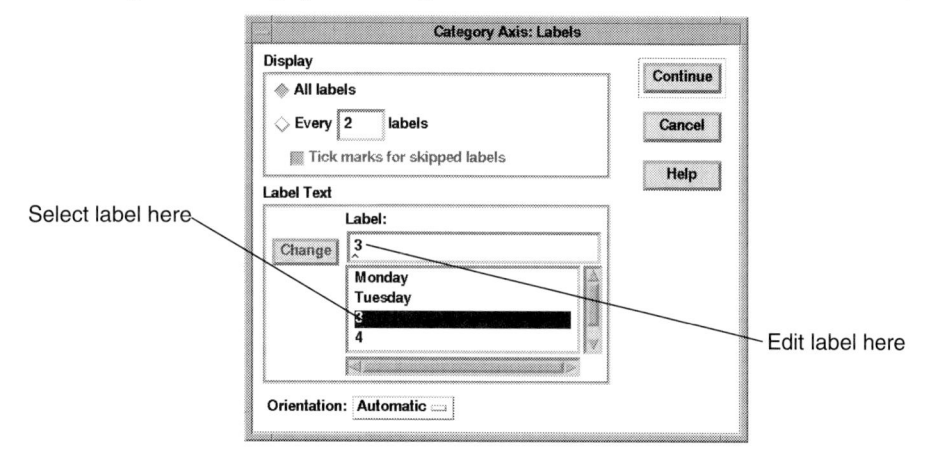

⑧ Change *3, 4,* and *5* to *Wednesday, Thursday,* and *Friday,* respectively, and click on Continue, which returns you to the Category Axis dialog box.

⑨ To return to the chart, click on OK. The results are shown in Figure 22.10.

Figure 22.10 Labeled chart

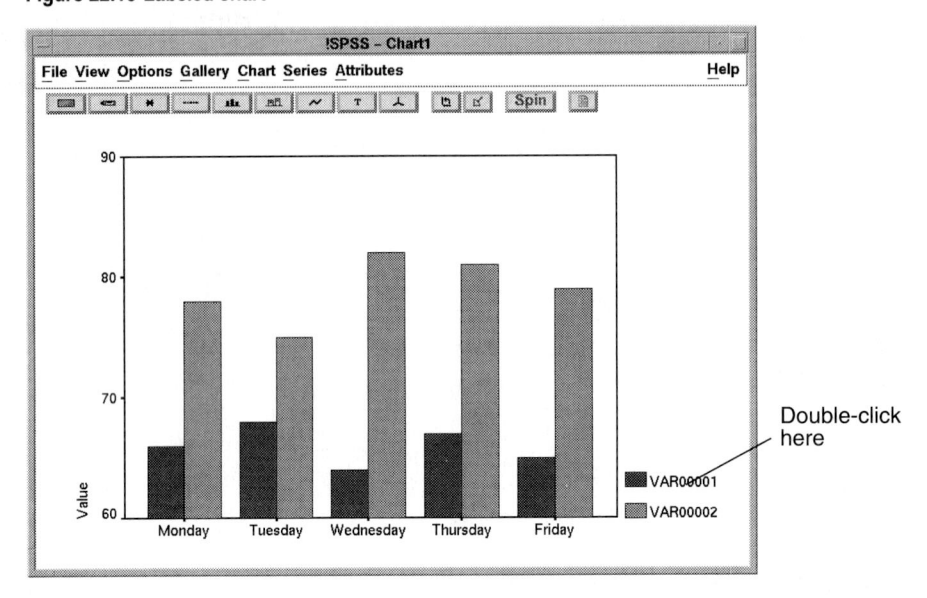

Double-click here (on legend)

⑩ To edit the legend, double-click on the legend labels. This opens the Legend dialog box, as shown in Figure 22.11.

Figure 22.11 Legend dialog box

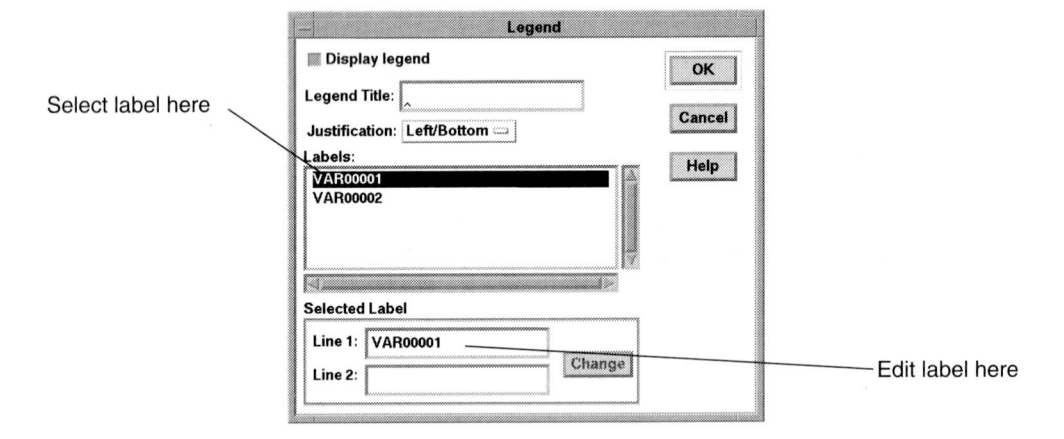

Select label here

Edit label here

⑪ In the Labels list, *var00001* is highlighted. In the text box for Line 1, delete *var00001* and type *Morning*; then click on Change.

⑫ Select *var00002* in the list of labels.

⑬ In the Line 1 text box, delete *var00002* and type *Afternoon*; then click on Change.

⑭ Click on OK to return to the chart (Figure 22.12).

Figure 22.12 Chart with edited legend

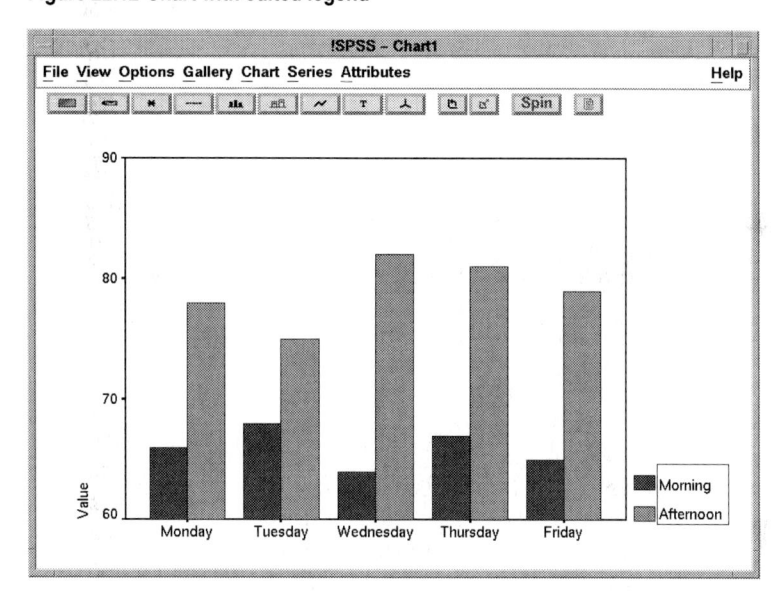

Further Enhancements

Now that the categories and subgroups are identified, you can enhance the chart for presentation.

① From the menus choose:

Chart
  Title...

This opens the Titles dialog box, as shown in Figure 22.13.

② Type a title in the Title 1 text box and a subtitle in the Subtitle text box as shown, and click on OK. The revised chart is shown in Figure 22.14.

Figure 22.13 Titles dialog box

Figure 22.14 Revised chart with title and subtitle

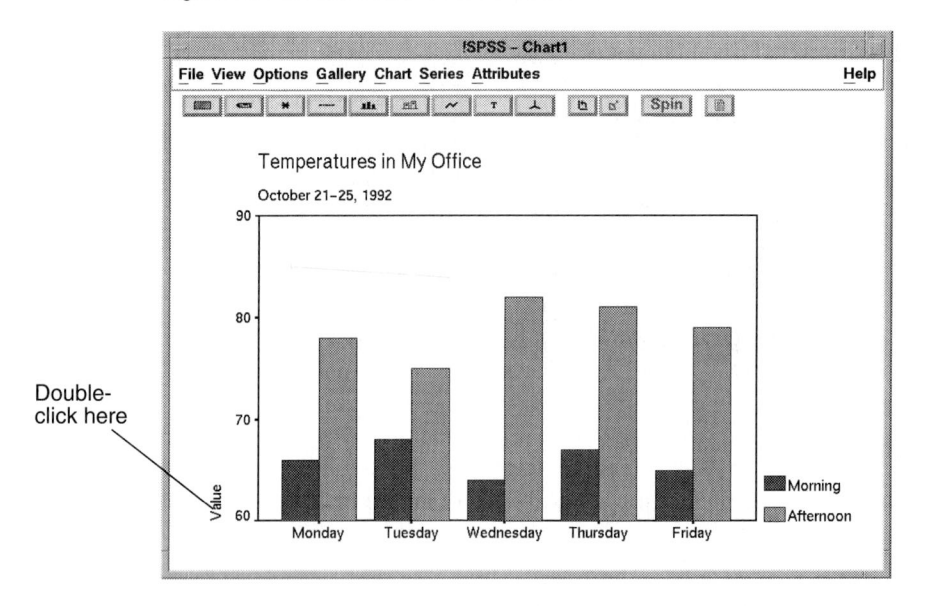

Double-click here

③ On the left side of the chart, double-click on the word *Value*. This opens the Scale Axis dialog box, as shown in Figure 22.15.

④ In the Axis Title text box, delete *Value* and enter *Fahrenheit*.

⑤ Select Bar origin line and change the value to 72.

Figure 22.15 Scale Axis dialog box

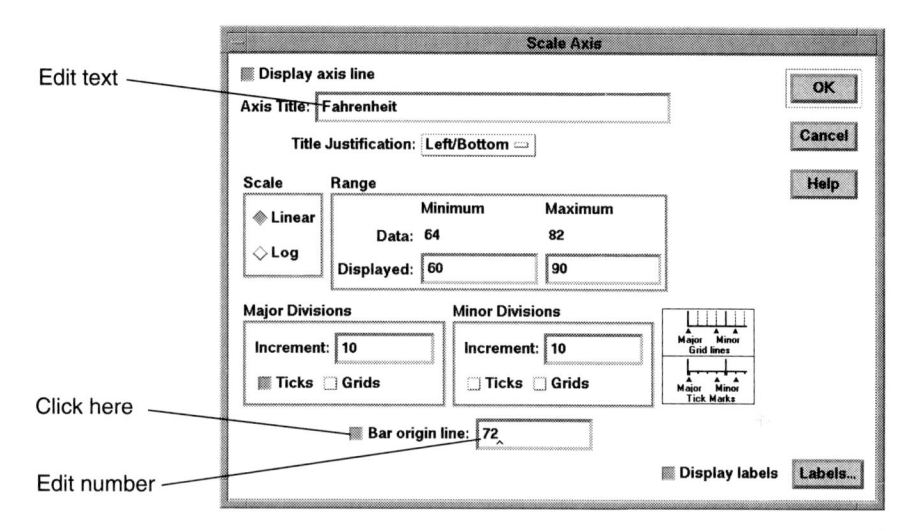

6. Click on OK. The revised chart now has hanging bars and a new axis title, as shown in Figure 22.16.

Figure 22.16 Revised chart with hanging bars and new axis title

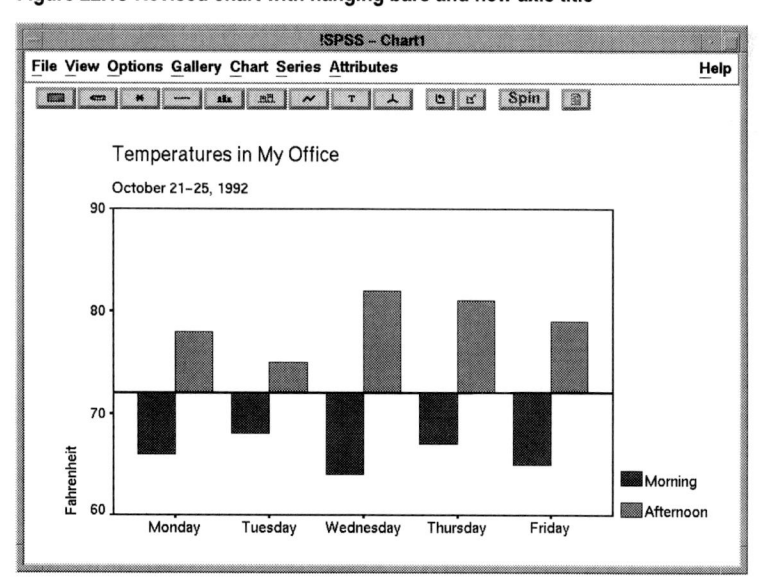

⑦ To further enhance the chart, from the menus choose:

Chart
  Annotation...

This opens the Annotation dialog box, as shown in Figure 22.17.

⑧ Enter *Preferred Temp.* in the text box, select Display frame around text, and change the Scale axis position to 72.

Figure 22.17 Annotation dialog box

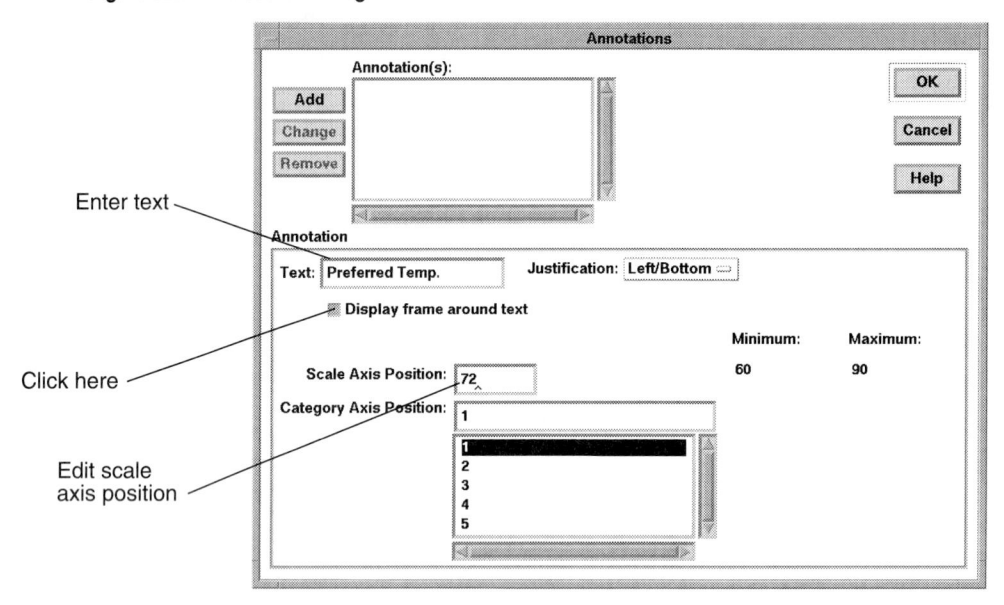

⑨ Click on Add and then OK. This displays the completed chart, as shown in Figure 22.18.

Figure 22.18 Final chart

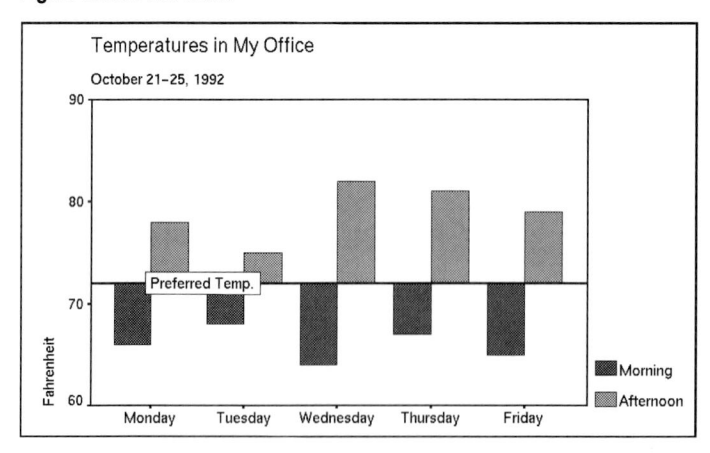

To print the chart or copy it into a document, see Chapter 27.

Chart Carousel

The tutorial showed the complete process of creating a chart. This section and the remainder of the chapter describe in detail features that apply to all or most chart types. High-resolution charts and plots are initially drawn in the Chart Carousel, shown in Figure 22.19. This is a holding area from which you can save the chart, discard it, print it, or transfer it to a chart window for editing.

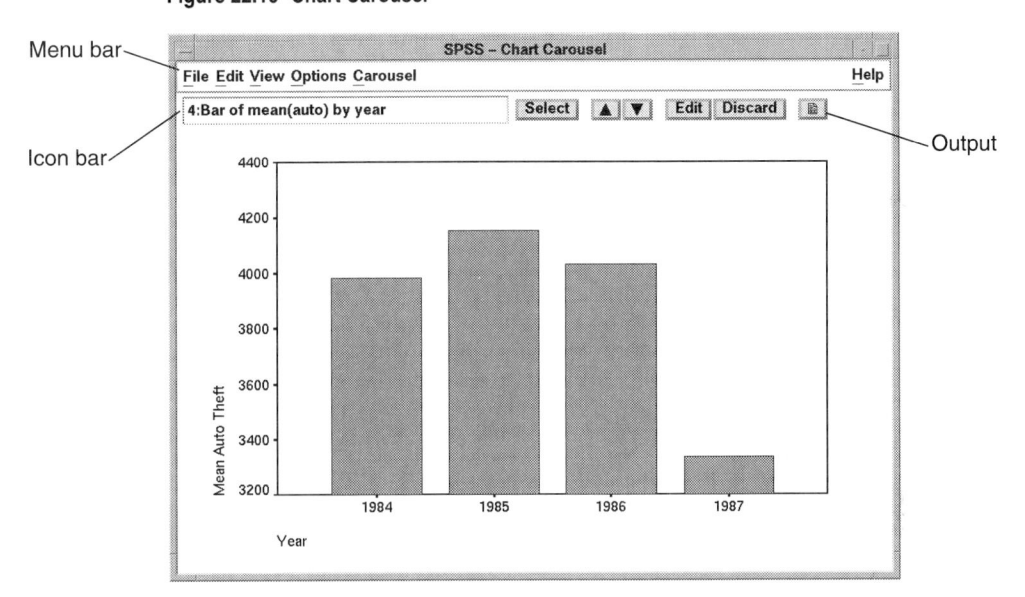

Figure 22.19 Chart Carousel

Chart Carousel Menus

The Chart Carousel window has its own menu bar and icon bar. The Chart Carousel menu bar contains five menus:

File. Use the File menu to close the Carousel, save the current chart, print the current chart, or exit from SPSS.

Save As opens the Save As dialog box, which lets you select a name and a directory for the current chart. Charts are saved in SPSS chart format. You can also save all the charts in the Carousel in one step, either when you close the Carousel or when you exit from SPSS. For more information, see "Saving Charts in the Chart Carousel" on p. 421.

Print opens the Print Chart Carousel dialog box. See Chapter 27 for more information.

Edit. Use the Edit menu to restore a discarded chart. If you have more than one chart in the Carousel and you discard a chart, you can restore the last chart discarded by selecting Undo from the Edit menu.

View. Use the View menu to refresh the screen or to raise another document window.

Options. Use the Options menu to suppress or display the icon bar.

Carousel. Use the Carousel menu to move the current chart to a chart window for editing or to move from chart to chart within the Carousel. You can also accomplish these tasks by clicking on pushbuttons on the icon bar, described in the section below.

Help. Use the Help menu to open a Help window containing information on how to use the many features of SPSS. Context-sensitive help is also available through the dialog boxes.

Chart Carousel Pushbuttons

Several pushbuttons appear on the icon bar. For the most part, they duplicate functions that can be accessed from the Carousel menu. The pushbuttons behave as follows:

Select. Opens the Carousel Select dialog box, from which you can choose one of the charts in the Carousel to be displayed. The selected chart becomes the current chart.

▲ **Previous.** Selects the previous chart in the Carousel as the current chart.

▼ **Next.** Selects the next chart in the Carousel as the current chart.

Edit. Removes the current chart from the Carousel and places it in its own chart window for editing. From the chart window you can modify most chart attributes, including colors, fonts, orientation, and type of chart displayed (see Chapter 26).

Discard. Removes the current chart from the Carousel and discards it. If the Carousel contains more than one chart, you can restore the last chart discarded by selecting Undo from the Edit menu.

Output icon. Switches to the output window, placing the cursor at the line where the currently displayed chart is listed. You can switch back by clicking on the chart icon in the output window.

Saving Charts in the Chart Carousel

The Save As Chart Carousel dialog box is shown in Figure 22.20. You can access this dialog box from the File menu, when you close the Carousel, or when you exit from SPSS.

Figure 22.20 Save As Chart Carousel dialog boxes

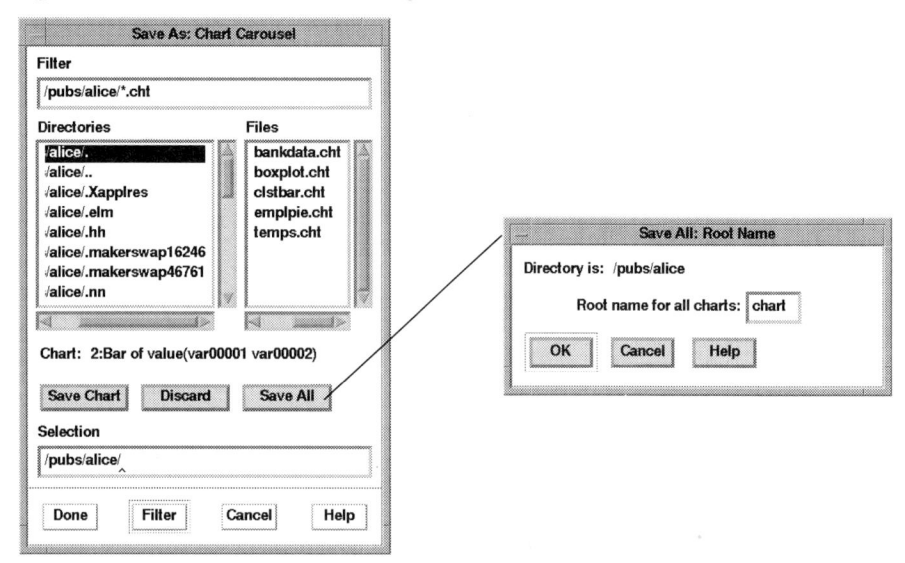

To save one chart at a time, type in a name for the current chart and click on Save Chart. The current chart is saved and the name of the next chart is displayed. You can either save or discard each chart in turn.

If you want to save all of the charts, click on Save All. This opens the Save All Root Name dialog box, as shown in Figure 22.20. Type a root name of one to five characters. SPSS will append a unique number for each chart and the extension *.cht*. For example, suppose you are working with food data and you type *food* as the root name. The filenames for the charts will be *food1.cht*, *food2.cht*, and so on. After the charts are saved, you can edit them by opening each one from the File menu.

Chart Definition Global Options

When you are defining a chart, the specific chart definition dialog box usually contains the pushbuttons Titles... and Options..., and a Template group, as shown in Figure 22.21. These global options are available for all charts, regardless of type.

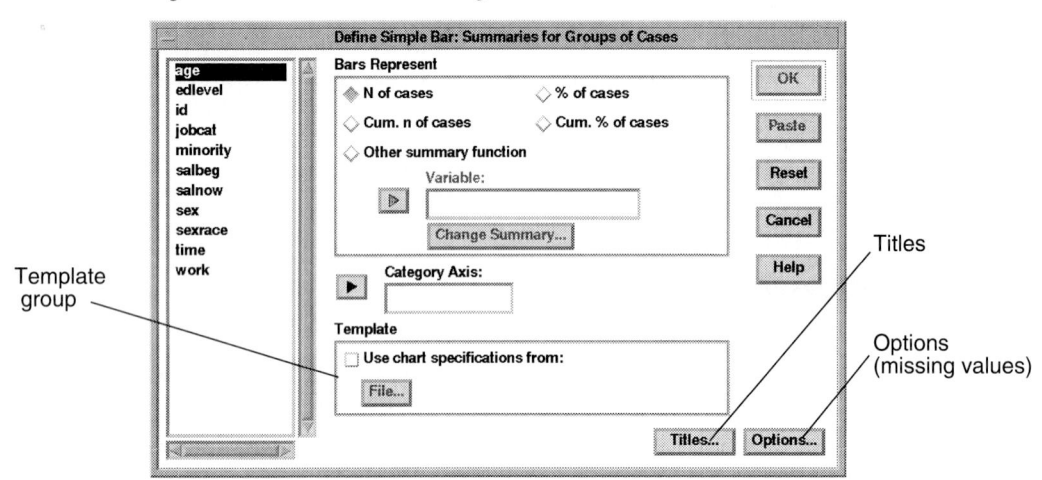

Figure 22.21 A chart definition dialog box

The Titles dialog box allows you to specify titles, subtitles, and footnotes. Clicking on Options... allows you to control the treatment of missing values. You can apply a template of previously selected attributes either when you are defining the chart or after the chart has been created. The next few sections describe how to define these characteristics at the time you define the chart.

Titles, Subtitles, and Footnotes

On any chart, you can define two title lines, one subtitle line, and two footnote lines as part of your original chart definition. To specify titles while defining a chart, click on Titles... in the chart definition dialog box, as shown in Figure 22.21. This opens the Titles dialog box, as shown in Figure 22.22.

Figure 22.22 Titles dialog box

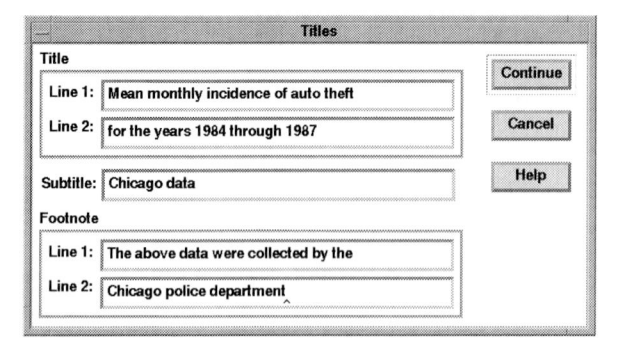

Each line can be up to 72 characters long. The number of characters that will actually fit on the chart depends upon the font and size. Most titles are left justified by default, and if too long are cropped on the right. Pie chart titles, by default, are center justified, and if too long are cropped at both ends. Figure 22.23 shows the title, subtitle, and footnote in their default font, size, and justification.

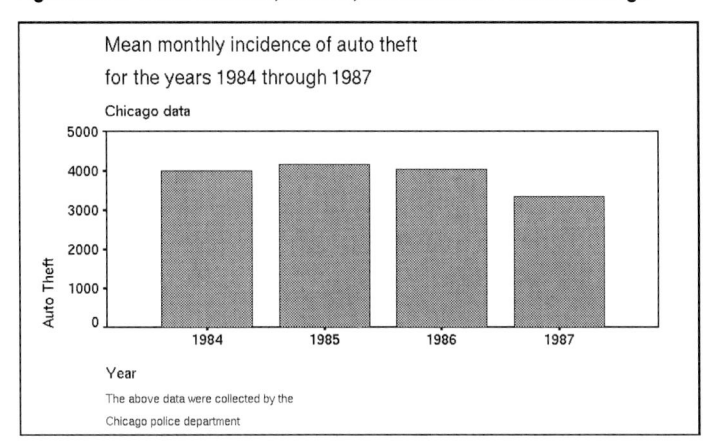

Figure 22.23 Chart with title, subtitle, and footnote in default settings

You can also add, delete, or revise text lines, as well as change their font, size, and justification, within the Chart Editor (see Chapter 26).

Missing Values

If there are missing values in the data, SPSS takes account of choices you make about treatment of missing values when it summarizes the data. To access the missing-value options available for your chart, click on Options... in the chart definition dialog box, as shown in Figure 22.21. This opens the Options dialog box, as shown in Figure 22.24. The specific options available depend on your previous choices.

Missing-value options are not available for charts using values of individual cases or for histograms.

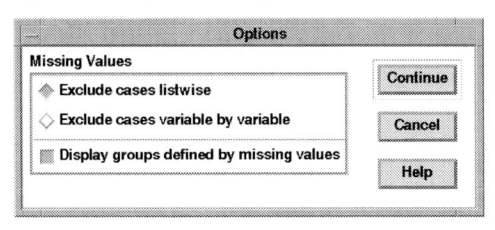

Figure 22.24 Options dialog box

Missing Values. If you selected summaries of separate variables for a categorical chart or if you are creating a scatterplot, you can choose one of the following alternatives for exclusion of cases having missing values:

◇ **Exclude cases listwise.** If any of the variables in the chart has a missing value for a given case, the whole case is excluded from the chart.

◇ **Exclude cases variable by variable.** If a selected variable has any missing values, the cases having those missing values are excluded when the variable is analyzed.

The following option is also available for missing values:

❑ **Display groups defined by missing values.** If there are missing values in the data for variables used to define categories or subgroups, user-missing values (values identified as missing by the user) and system-missing values are included together in a category labeled *Missing*. The "missing" category is displayed on the category axis or in the legend, adding, for example, an extra bar, a slice to a pie chart, or an extra box on a boxplot. In a scatterplot, missing values add a "missing" category to the set of markers. If there are no missing values, the "missing" category is not displayed.

This option is selected by default. If you want to suppress display after the chart is drawn, select Displayed... from the Series menu and move the categories you want suppressed to the Omit group. (See sections "Bar, Line, and Area Chart Displayed Data" on p. 549 through "Histogram Displayed Data" on p. 555 in Chapter 26.)

This option is not available for an overlay scatterplot or for single-series charts in which the data are summarized by separate variables.

To see the difference between listwise and variable-by-variable exclusion of missing values, consider Figure 22.25, which shows a bar chart for each of the two options. The charts were created from a version of the data file *bank.sav* that was edited to have some system-missing (blank) values in the variables for current salary and job category. In some other cases of the job category variable, the value 9 was entered and defined as missing. For both charts, the option Display groups defined by missing values is selected, which adds the category *Missing* to the other job categories displayed. In each chart, the values of the summary function, *Number of cases*, are displayed in the bar labels.

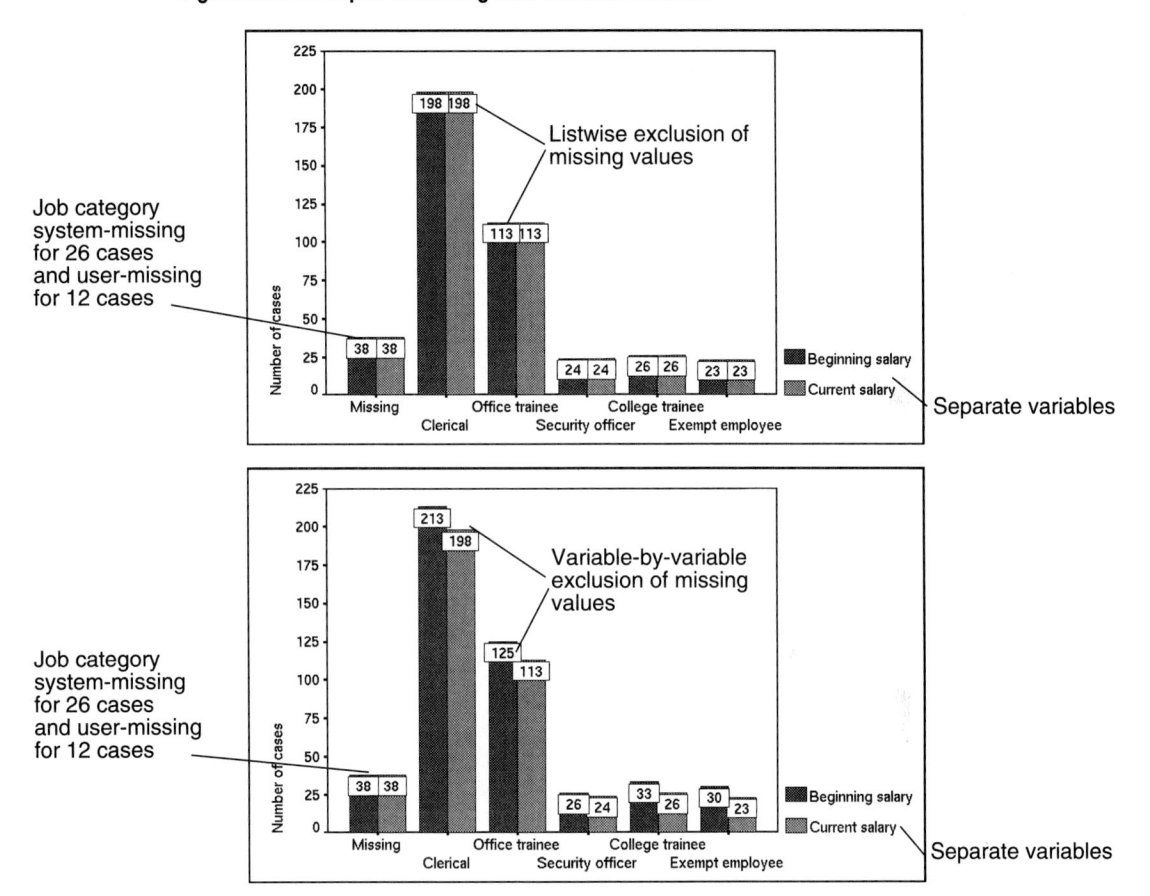

Figure 22.25 Examples of missing-data treatment in charts

In both charts, 26 cases have a system-missing value for the job category and 12 cases have the user-missing value (9). In the listwise chart, the number of cases is the same for both variables in each bar cluster because whenever a value was missing, the case was excluded for all variables. In the variable-by-variable chart, the number of nonmissing cases for each variable in a category is plotted without regard to missing values in other variables.

Display of Missing Values in a Line Chart

If you create a line chart using data that have a missing value for a category, the line connects markers across the missing category. It is easy to overlook the fact that there is no value there. Figure 22.26 shows a line chart and a bar chart, each drawn from the same data. The markers in the line chart were displayed by selecting Display Markers and Straight on the Line Interpolation dialog box (see Chapter 26).

Figure 22.26 Line chart and bar chart with missing values

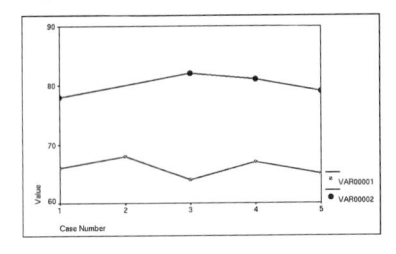

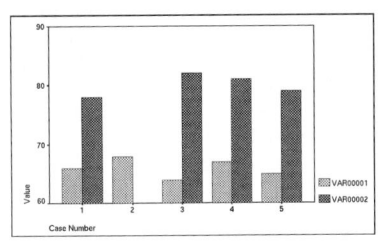

In both charts there is a missing value for case 2. In the line chart, the line connects the points on either side, while in the bar chart there is clearly a bar missing.

Chart Templates

You can apply many of the attributes and text elements from one chart to another. This allows you to modify one chart, save that chart, and then use it as a template to create a number of other, similar charts.

To use a template when creating a chart, select Use chart specifications from (in the Template group on the chart definition dialog box shown in Figure 22.21) and click on File.... This opens the Use Template from File dialog box, as shown in Figure 22.27.

Figure 22.27 Use Template from File dialog box

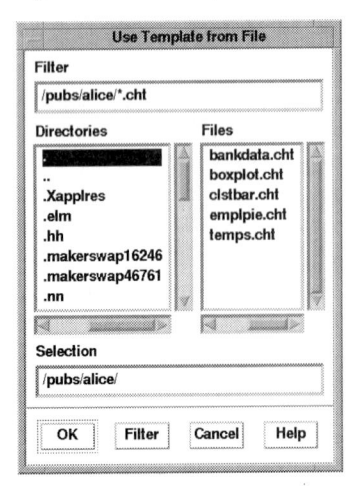

To apply a template to a chart already in a chart window, from the menus choose:

File
 Apply Chart Template...

This opens the Apply Chart Template dialog box, as shown in Figure 22.28.

Figure 22.28 Apply Chart Template dialog box

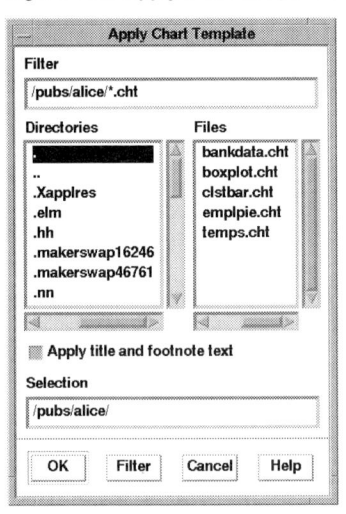

The two dialog boxes are similar. The subdirectories in the current directory are displayed in the Directories list. The chart files in the current directory are displayed in the Files list. Select a file to use as a template and click on OK. If you are creating a new chart, the filename you select is displayed in the Template group when you return to the chart definition dialog box.

A template is used to borrow the format from one chart and apply it to the new chart you are generating. In general, any formatting information from the old chart that can apply to the new chart will automatically apply. For example, if the old chart is a clustered bar chart with bar colors modified to yellow and green and the new chart is a multiple line chart, the lines will be yellow and green. If the old chart is a simple bar chart with drop shadows and the new chart is a simple line chart, the lines will not have drop shadows because drop shadows do not apply to line charts. If there are titles in the template chart but not in the new chart, you will get the titles from the template chart. If there are titles defined in the new chart, they will override the titles in the old chart.

- **Apply title and footnote text.** Applies the text of the title and footnotes of the template to the current chart, overriding any text defined in the Titles dialog box in the current chart. The attributes of the title and footnotes (font, size, and color) are applied whether or not this item is selected. This check box appears only if you are applying the template in a chart window, not when creating a new chart.

23 Bar, Line, Area, and Pie Charts

Are American cities more violent today than they were several years ago? At what time of the year do major crimes occur? Do different types of crime show similar or different patterns of increase or decrease? These are the kinds of questions that are important to police departments across the United States. And these are the kinds of questions that are often most effectively answered in categorical charts, such as bar, line, area, and pie charts.

Chicago Uniform Crime Reports Data

The Uniform Crime Reports required by the FBI show reported incidents of murder, rape, aggravated assault, armed robbery, burglary, theft, and auto theft on a month-by-month basis. The crimes for which reports are required are called **index crimes**. Each crime is recorded as a separate variable. Each case indicates the number of crimes that occurred that month. A case is identified by two variables, *month* and *year*. Two other variables, *violent* and *property*, record the total number of violent crimes (murder, rape, aggravated assault, and armed robbery) and the total number of property crimes (burglary, theft, and auto theft), respectively. Figure 23.1 shows the first seven cases of the data collected by the Chicago Police Department from 1972 to 1987.

Figure 23.1 Chicago Uniform Crime Reports data

	year	month	murder	rape	assault	robbery	burglary	theft	auto	violent	property
1	72	Jan	53	174	2061	740	2994	5972	2404	3028	11370
2	72	Feb	54	110	1671	709	2650	5791	2097	2544	10538
3	72	Mar	57	78	1541	753	2718	6435	1912	2429	11065
4	72	Apr	56	139	1728	1018	3069	7010	2578	2941	12657
5	72	May	51	138	1971	1118	3041	8233	2812	3278	14086
6	72	Jun	55	122	1770	1051	2935	9030	3083	2998	15048
7	72	Jul	73	117	2218	1200	3410	9814	3085	3608	16309

Simple Charts

In a bar chart showing the mean monthly incidence of armed robbery each year, it is immediately apparent that the number of robberies stayed fairly constant over the 11-year period between 1972 and 1982 and then sharply increased.

Figure 23.2 Simple bar chart

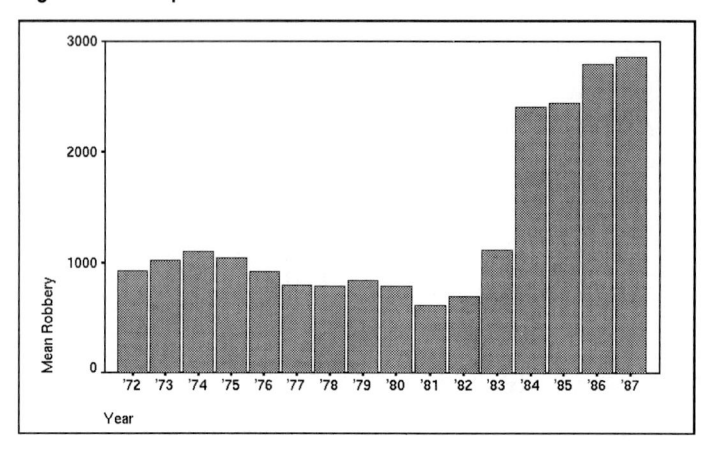

Figure 23.2 is a simple bar chart in which each bar represents the mean monthly incidence of robberies for one year. Often, a long series such as this is best displayed as a simple line chart. Although the data are the same, the chart in Figure 23.3 emphasizes the continuity from one element to the next.

Figure 23.3 Simple line chart

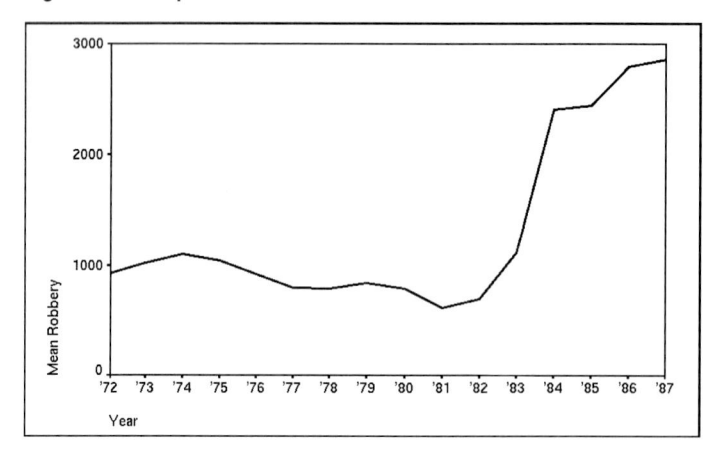

To emphasize the change, the same data might be displayed as a simple area chart, as shown in Figure 23.4. Notice that an area chart is simply a line chart with the space underneath the line filled in.

Figure 23.4 Simple area chart

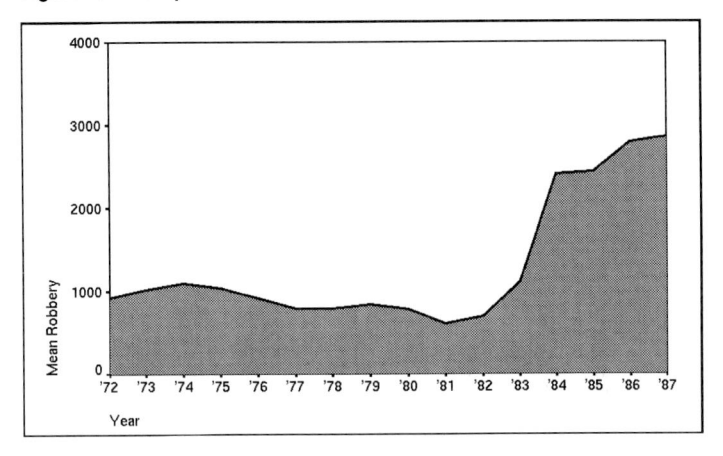

Robbery is only one crime. How does the armed robbery rate compare with that of other crimes? From a chart that shows the mean value of each crime variable as a separate bar, it can be seen that robbery is more common than murder or rape but less common than the other reported crimes (see Figure 23.5).

Figure 23.5 Simple bar chart

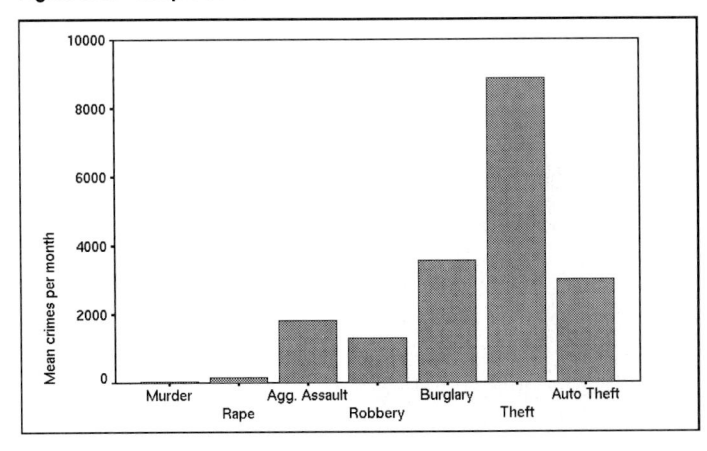

Figure 23.5 clearly shows which index crime is the least common and which is the most common. If, however, the intent is to show what proportion of the total index crimes each constitutes, a pie chart is more appropriate, as shown in Figure 23.6. While Figure 23.5 shows the average for one month in each category, Figure 23.6 shows the totals for the entire 16-year period.

Figure 23.6 Simple pie chart

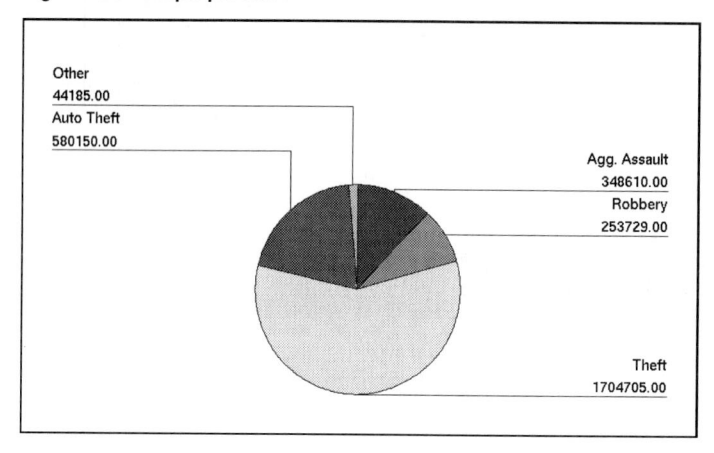

Clustered Bar and Multiple Line Charts

Theft, burglary, and auto theft are collectively known as "property crimes." In a clustered bar chart, as shown in Figure 23.7, we can show the mean monthly incidence of each property crime for each year.

Figure 23.7 Clustered bar chart

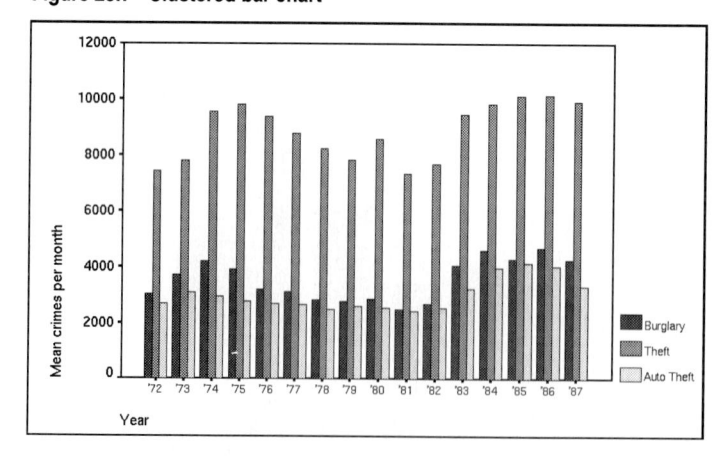

While a clustered bar chart presents the property crime data clearly, a multiple line chart can show the patterns in the same data. Figure 23.8 shows the data series in Figure 23.7 as a multiple line chart. Here you can see that the three property crimes follow a similar pattern.

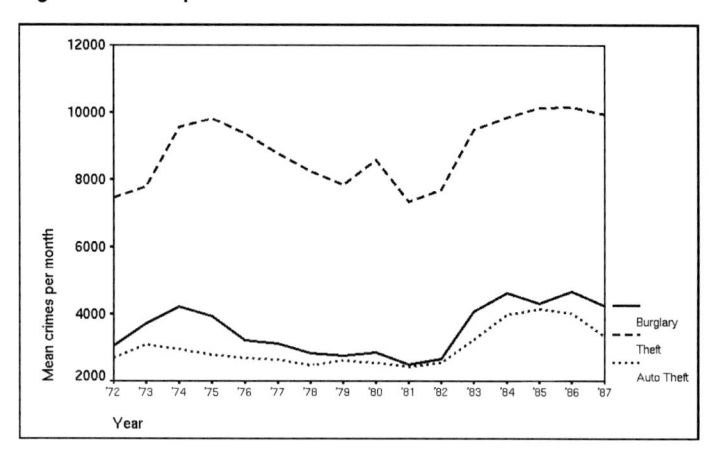

Figure 23.8 Multiple line chart

Stacked Bar and Area Charts

Three property crimes are tracked in the Chicago data. Each crime rate can be thought of as a part of a whole, which is the total recorded number of property crimes. To emphasize that these data are parts of a whole, we can display them in a stacked bar chart, as shown in Figure 23.9. The height of each bar shows the total number of property crimes committed during each year. The colored or patterned segments show the contribution of each individual property crime to that total.

Figure 23.9 Stacked bar chart

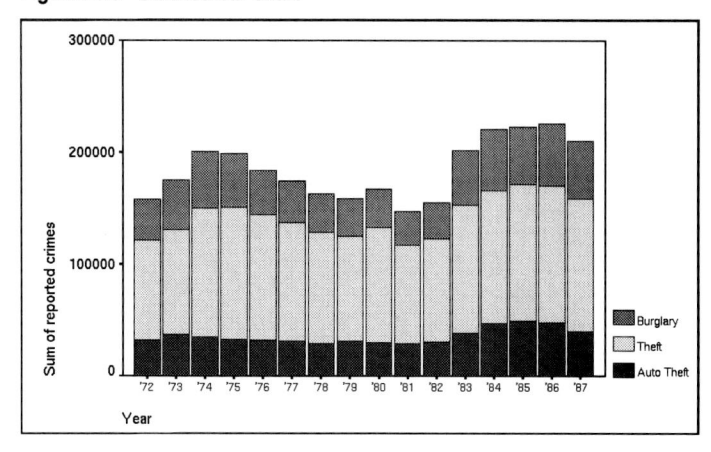

While Figure 23.9 is clear, it returns us to bars, which do not emphasize the sequential nature of the data. In Figure 23.10, the data in Figure 23.9 are shown as a stacked area chart.

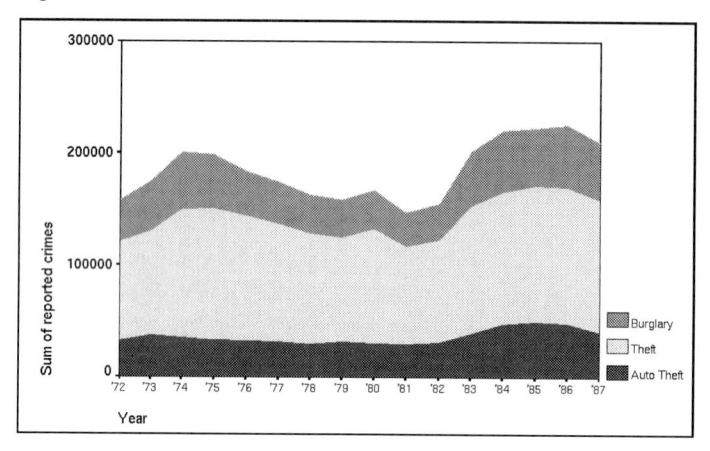

Figure 23.10 Stacked area chart

Variations on Bar, Line, and Area Charts

The following chart types require some level of modification from the basic chart types described previously. For a discussion of how to obtain these chart types with the Chart Editor, see Chapter 26.

100% Stacked Bar and Area Charts

Stacked bar and area charts show how property crimes as a whole fluctuate and at the same time how the contribution of each individual crime type changes. In some circumstances, you might simply want to show how the percentage contribution of each individual crime type changes but not how property crimes change as a whole. This type of chart is called a 100% stacked chart. A 100% stacked area chart and a 100% stacked bar chart are shown in Figure 23.11.

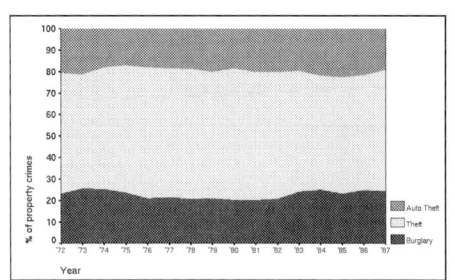

Figure 23.11 100% stacked area and bar charts

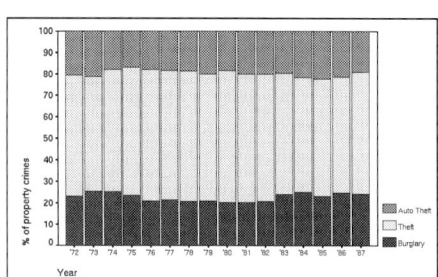

Hanging Bar Charts

A hanging bar chart is often used to show how values fluctuate around a fixed value (the **origin**), as shown in Figure 23.12.

Figure 23.12 Hanging bar chart

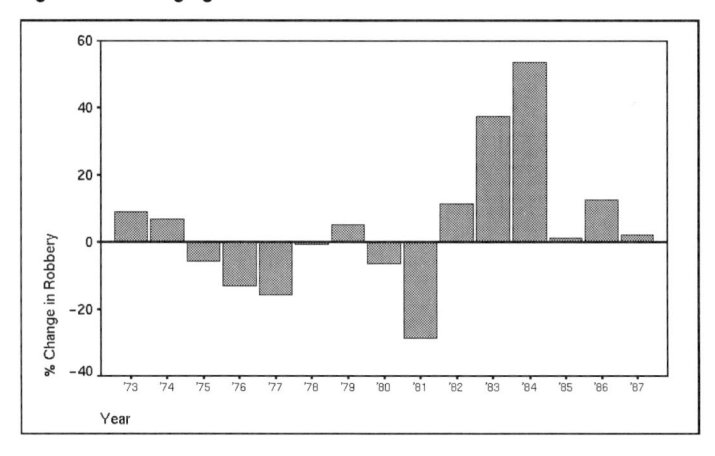

Drop-Line Charts

A drop-line chart is often used to show the difference between two or more fluctuating variables, as shown in Figure 23.13.

Figure 23.13 Drop-line chart

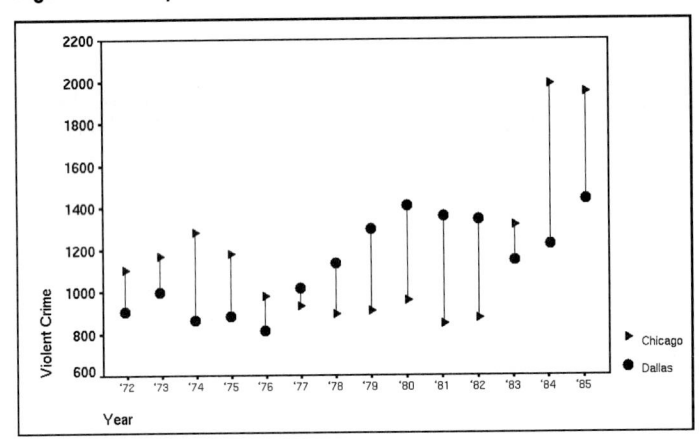

Mixed Charts

A mixed chart overlays one chart type on top of another. This is sometimes a useful way to differentiate between data that are related but somehow qualitatively different. The line and bar chart in Figure 23.14 shows national crime data as a line superimposed over Chicago crime data as bars.

Figure 23.14 Mixed line and bar chart

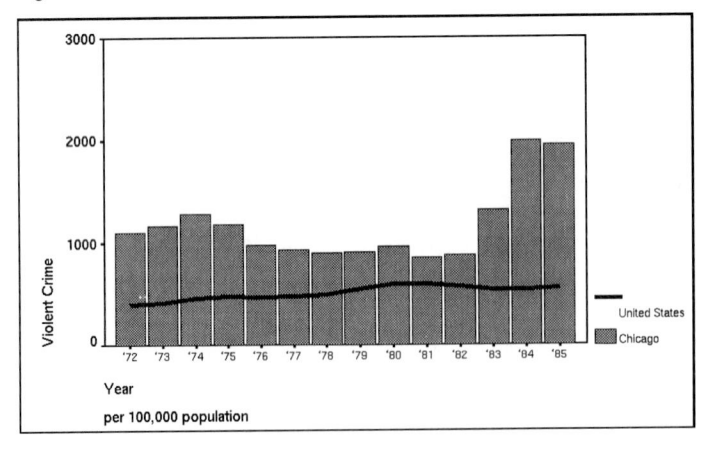

How to Obtain Bar, Line, Area, and Pie Charts

To obtain bar, line, area, or pie charts, choose the appropriate chart type from the Graphs menu, as shown in Figure 23.15.

Figure 23.15 Graphs menu

```
Graphs
Bar...
Line...
Area...
Pie...
Boxplot...
Scatter...
Histogram...
```

This opens a chart dialog box for the selected chart type, as shown in Figure 23.16 (chart dialog boxes for line, area, and pie charts are shown in Figure 23.28, Figure 23.37, and Figure 23.46, respectively).

Figure 23.16 Bar Charts dialog box

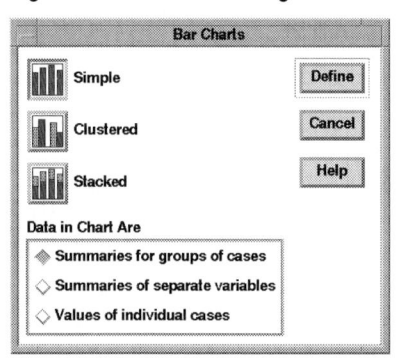

From the chart dialog box, choose the type of chart you want. Your choices depend upon the type of chart you selected on the Graphs menu. For bar charts, the choices are: simple, clustered, or stacked.

Data in Chart are. Select the choice that describes the structure of your data organization.

◇ **Summaries for groups of cases.** Cases are counted, or one variable is summarized, in subgroups. The subgroups are determined by one variable for simple charts or by two variables for complex charts.

◇ **Summaries of separate variables.** More than one variable is summarized. Simple charts summarize each variable over all cases in the file. Complex charts summarize each variable within categories determined by another variable.

◇ **Values of individual cases.** Individual values of one variable are plotted in simple charts. Values of more than one variable are plotted in complex charts.

Examples of these choices, shown with data organization structures and the charts they produce, are presented in the tables at the beginning of each section.

Bar Charts

To obtain a bar chart, from the menus choose:

Graphs
  Bar...

This opens the Bar Charts dialog box, as shown in Figure 23.16 (chart dialog boxes for line, area, and pie charts are shown in Figure 23.28, Figure 23.37, and Figure 23.46, respectively).

Select the type of bar chart you want, and select the choice that describes the structure of your data organization. Click on Define to open a dialog box specific to your selections. The choices available in the chart definition dialog box vary according to chart type and the structure of your data organization (see Table 23.1).

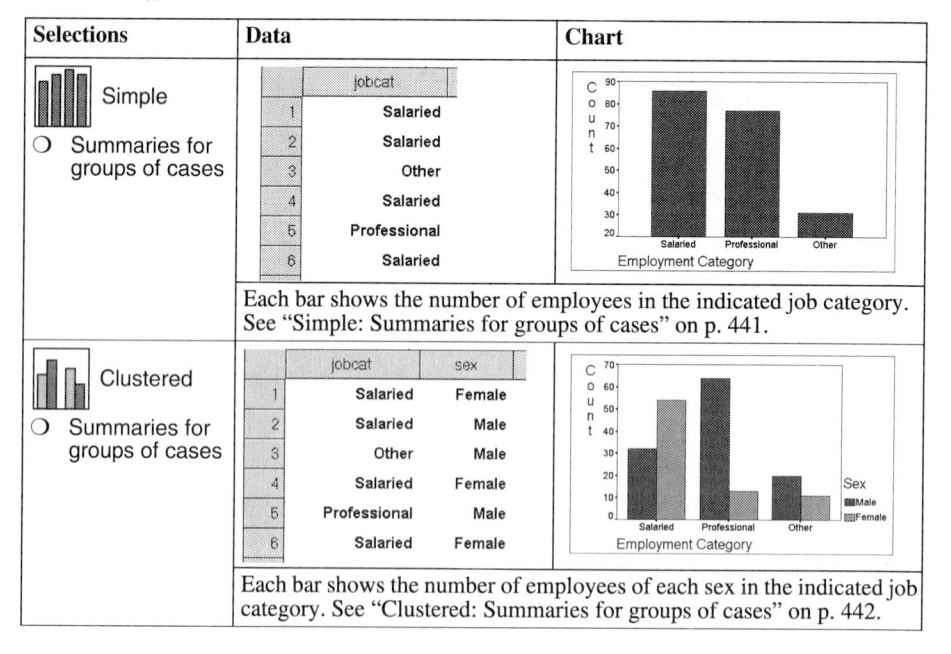

Table 23.1 Types of bar charts

Selections	Data	Chart
Simple ○ Summaries for groups of cases	jobcat: 1 Salaried, 2 Salaried, 3 Other, 4 Salaried, 5 Professional, 6 Salaried	(bar chart by Employment Category)
Each bar shows the number of employees in the indicated job category. See "Simple: Summaries for groups of cases" on p. 441.		
Clustered ○ Summaries for groups of cases	jobcat / sex: 1 Salaried Female, 2 Salaried Male, 3 Other Male, 4 Salaried Female, 5 Professional Male, 6 Salaried Female	(clustered bar chart by Employment Category and Sex)
Each bar shows the number of employees of each sex in the indicated job category. See "Clustered: Summaries for groups of cases" on p. 442.		

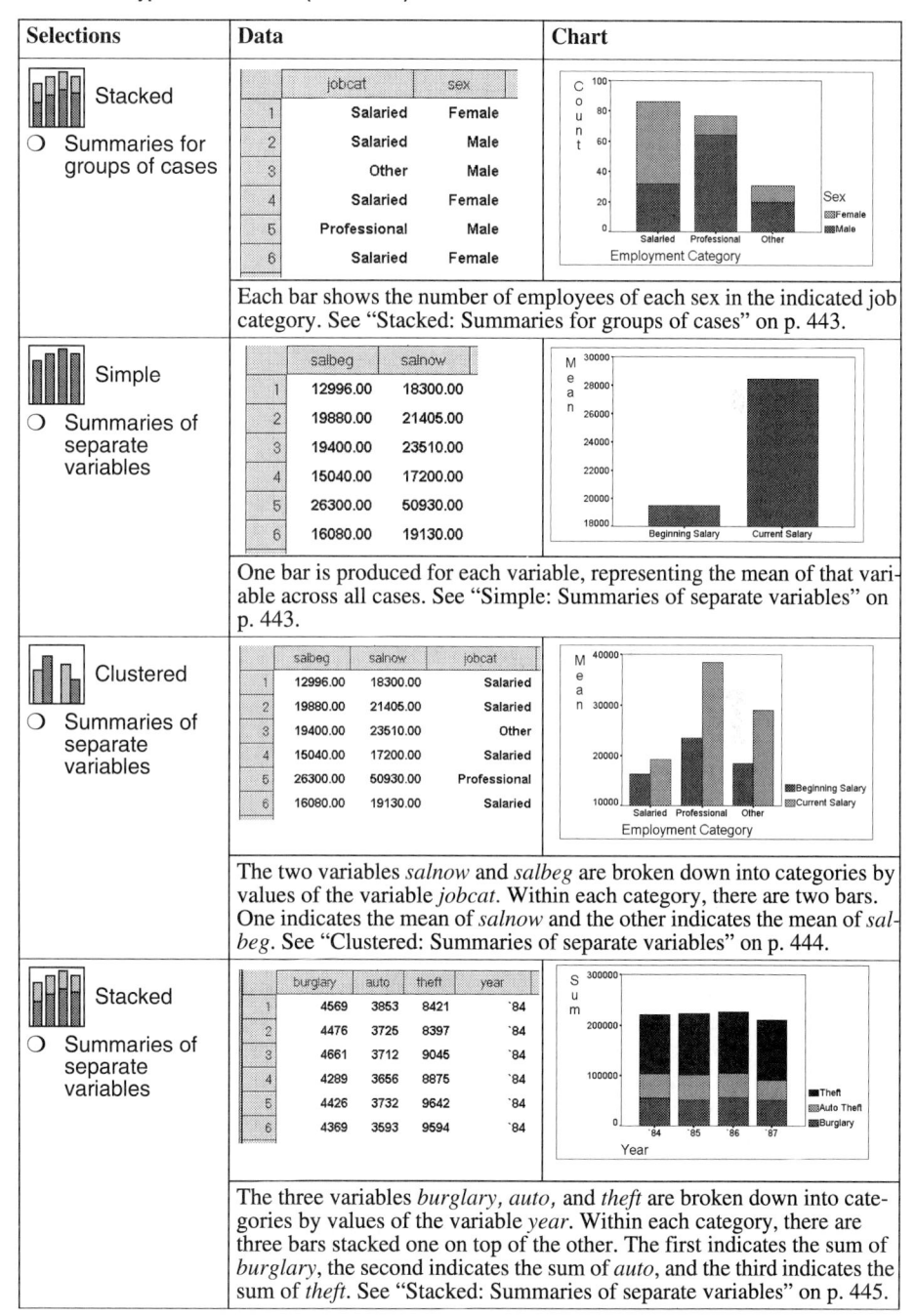

Table 23.1 Types of bar charts (Continued)

Selections	Data	Chart
Stacked ○ Summaries for groups of cases	jobcat / sex: 1 Salaried Female 2 Salaried Male 3 Other Male 4 Salaried Female 5 Professional Male 6 Salaried Female	Count by Employment Category, stacked by Sex (Female/Male)
	Each bar shows the number of employees of each sex in the indicated job category. See "Stacked: Summaries for groups of cases" on p. 443.	
Simple ○ Summaries of separate variables	salbeg / salnow: 1 12996.00 18300.00 2 19880.00 21405.00 3 19400.00 23510.00 4 15040.00 17200.00 5 26300.00 50930.00 6 16080.00 19130.00	Mean of Beginning Salary vs Current Salary
	One bar is produced for each variable, representing the mean of that variable across all cases. See "Simple: Summaries of separate variables" on p. 443.	
Clustered ○ Summaries of separate variables	salbeg / salnow / jobcat: 1 12996.00 18300.00 Salaried 2 19880.00 21405.00 Salaried 3 19400.00 23510.00 Other 4 15040.00 17200.00 Salaried 5 26300.00 50930.00 Professional 6 16080.00 19130.00 Salaried	Mean of Beginning Salary and Current Salary by Employment Category
	The two variables *salnow* and *salbeg* are broken down into categories by values of the variable *jobcat*. Within each category, there are two bars. One indicates the mean of *salnow* and the other indicates the mean of *salbeg*. See "Clustered: Summaries of separate variables" on p. 444.	
Stacked ○ Summaries of separate variables	burglary / auto / theft / year: 1 4569 3853 8421 '84 2 4476 3725 8397 '84 3 4661 3712 9045 '84 4 4289 3656 8875 '84 5 4426 3732 9642 '84 6 4369 3593 9594 '84	Sum by Year ('84–'87) stacked by Theft, Auto Theft, Burglary
	The three variables *burglary, auto,* and *theft* are broken down into categories by values of the variable *year*. Within each category, there are three bars stacked one on top of the other. The first indicates the sum of *burglary*, the second indicates the sum of *auto*, and the third indicates the sum of *theft*. See "Stacked: Summaries of separate variables" on p. 445.	

Table 23.1 Types of bar charts (Continued)

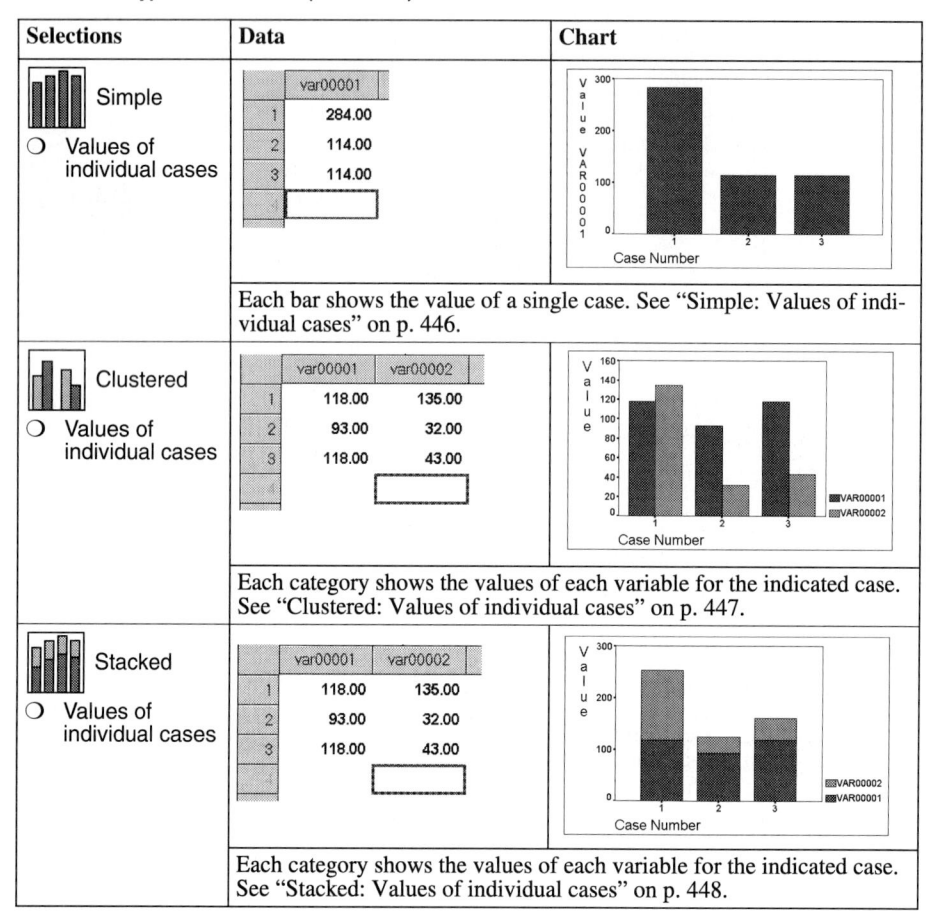

Selections	Data	Chart
Simple — Values of individual cases	var00001: 284.00, 114.00, 114.00	(bar chart showing Value vs Case Number for VAR00001)
Each bar shows the value of a single case. See "Simple: Values of individual cases" on p. 446.		
Clustered — Values of individual cases	var00001 / var00002: 118.00/135.00, 93.00/32.00, 118.00/43.00	(clustered bar chart for VAR00001, VAR00002)
Each category shows the values of each variable for the indicated case. See "Clustered: Values of individual cases" on p. 447.		
Stacked — Values of individual cases	var00001 / var00002: 118.00/135.00, 93.00/32.00, 118.00/43.00	(stacked bar chart for VAR00002, VAR00001)
Each category shows the values of each variable for the indicated case. See "Stacked: Values of individual cases" on p. 448.		

Defining Bar Charts

Each combination of chart type and data organization structure produces a different definition box. Each is discussed briefly below. The icon and section title indicate the choices that have to be made in the chart dialog box to open that chart definition dialog box. The discussion for each chart type always describes the selections required to enable the OK pushbutton. The simple chart for each data organization structure briefly describes the optional selections unique to that organizational structure. For a detailed description of optional statistics, see "Summary Functions" on p. 470.

All chart definition dialog boxes have a Titles pushbutton and Template group. These are discussed in "Titles, Subtitles, and Footnotes" on p. 422 and "Chart Templates" on p. 426, both in Chapter 22. Chart definition dialog boxes for summaries for groups of cases and for summaries of separate variables also have an Options... pushbutton. The Options... pushbutton brings up a dialog box that controls missing values options, discussed in "Missing Values" on p. 423 in Chapter 22.

Simple:
Summaries for groups of cases

Figure 23.17 shows a chart definition dialog box and the resulting simple bar chart with summaries for groups of cases.

Figure 23.17 Simple bar chart with summaries for groups of cases

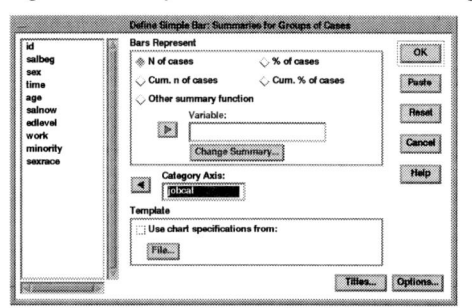

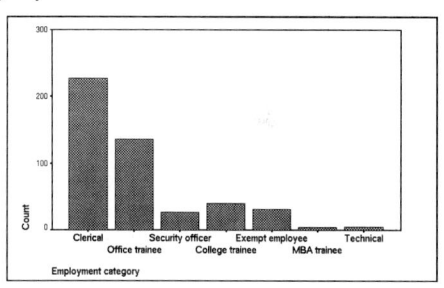

The minimum specification is a category axis variable.

The numeric, short string, and long string variables in your data file are displayed on the source variable list. Select a variable to define the category axis. To get a simple chart showing the number of cases for groups of cases in default format, click on OK.

Optionally, you can select a different summary statistic, use a template to control the format of the chart, or add a title, subtitle, or footnote. Optional summary statistics are discussed in "Summary Functions" on p. 470. The other options are discussed in detail in Chapter 22.

Category Axis. Select a variable to define the categories shown in the chart. There is one bar for each value of the variable.

If you select Other summary function in the Define Simple Bar Summaries for Groups of Cases dialog box, you must also select a variable to be summarized. Figure 23.18 shows the chart definition dialog box with a variable to be summarized and the resulting simple bar chart with a summarized variable.

Figure 23.18 Simple bar chart with summary of a variable

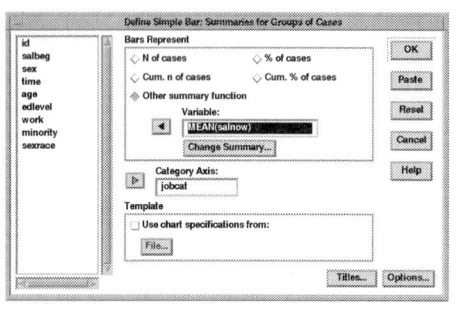

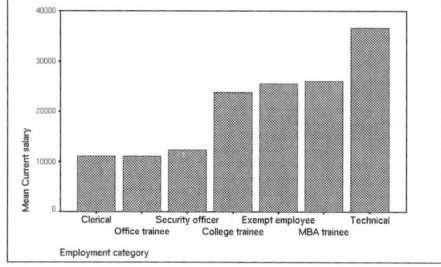

The default chart shows the mean of the selected variable within each category (determined by the category axis variable).

Clustered: Summaries for groups of cases

Figure 23.19 shows a chart definition dialog box and the resulting clustered bar chart with summaries for groups of cases.

Figure 23.19 Clustered bar chart with summaries for groups of cases

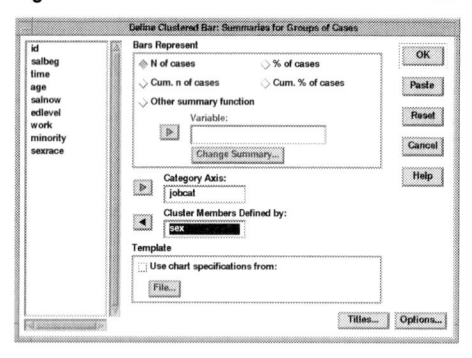

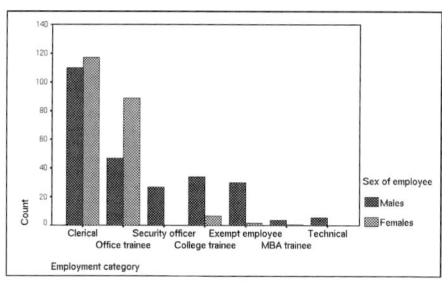

The minimum specifications are:
- A category axis variable.
- A cluster member's definition variable.

Category Axis. Select a variable to define the categories shown in the chart. There is one cluster of bars for each value of the variable.

Cluster Members Defined by. Select a variable to define the bars within each cluster. There is one set of differently colored or patterned bars for each value of the variable.

Stacked:
Summaries for groups of cases

Figure 23.20 shows a chart definition dialog box and the resulting stacked bar chart with summaries for groups of cases.

Figure 23.20 Stacked bar chart with summaries for groups of cases

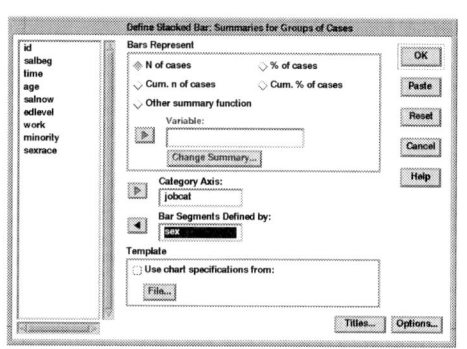

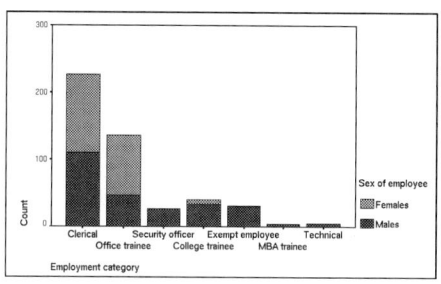

The minimum specifications are:
- A category axis variable.
- A bar segment's definition variable.

Category Axis. Select a variable to define the categories shown in the chart. There is one stack of bars for each value of the variable.

Bar Segments Defined by. Select a variable to define the bar segments within each stack. There is one bar segment within each stack for each value of the variable.

Simple:
Summaries of separate variables

Figure 23.21 shows a chart definition dialog box and the resulting simple bar chart with summaries of separate variables.

Figure 23.21 Simple bar chart with summaries of separate variables

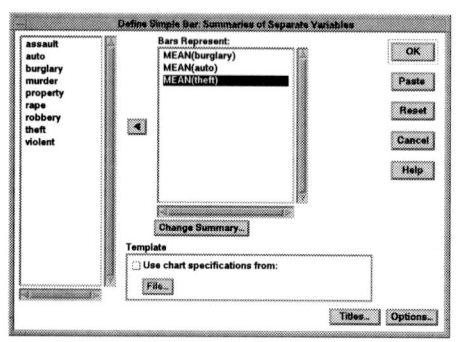

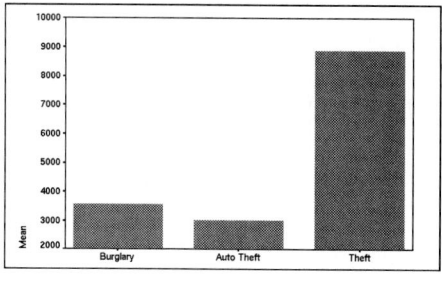

The minimum specifications are two or more bar variables.

The numeric variables in your data file are displayed on the source variable list. Select the variables you want to define the bars. To get a simple bar chart showing the mean value of each variable in default format, click on OK.

Optionally, you can select a different summary statistic, use a template to control the format of the chart, or add a title, subtitle, or footnote. Summary statistics are discussed in "Summary Functions" on p. 470. The other options are discussed in detail in Chapter 22.

Bars Represent. Select two or more variables to define the categories shown in the chart. There is one bar for each variable. By default, the bar shows the mean of the selected variables.

Clustered: Summaries of separate variables

Figure 23.22 shows a chart definition dialog box and the resulting clustered bar chart with summaries of separate variables.

Figure 23.22 Clustered bar chart with summaries of separate variables

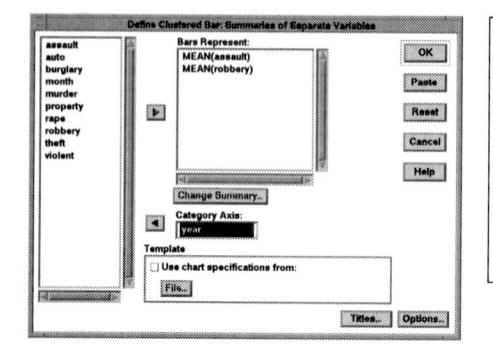

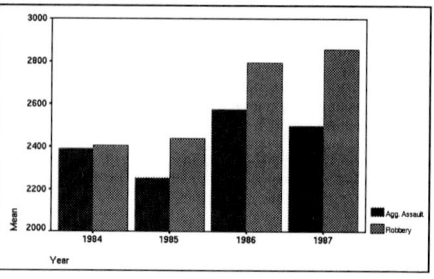

The minimum specifications are:
- Two or more bar variables.
- A category axis variable.

Bars Represent. Select two or more variables. There is one bar within each group for each variable. By default, the bars show the mean of the selected variables.

Category Axis. Select a variable to define the categories shown in the chart. There is one cluster of bars for each value of the variable.

Stacked:
Summaries of separate variables

Figure 23.23 shows a chart definition dialog box and the resulting stacked bar chart with summaries of separate variables.

Figure 23.23 Stacked bar chart with summaries of separate variables

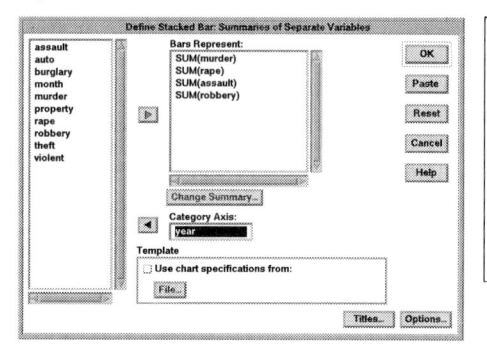

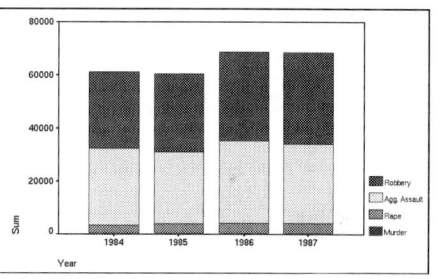

The minimum specifications are:
- Two or more segment variables.
- A category axis variable.

Bars Represent. Select two or more variables. There is one bar within each stack for each variable. By default, the bars show the sum of the selected variables.

Category Axis. Select a variable to define the categories shown in the chart. There is one stack of bars for each value of the variable.

Simple:
Values of individual cases

Figure 23.24 shows a chart definition dialog box and the resulting simple bar chart with values of individual cases.

Figure 23.24 Simple bar chart with values of individual cases

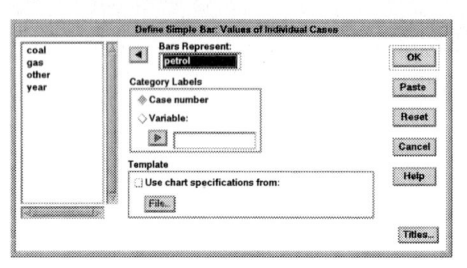

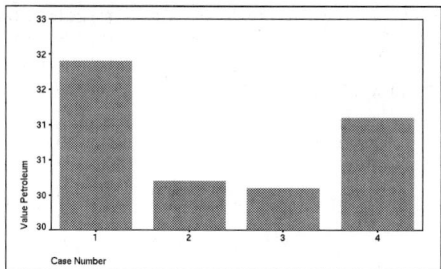

The minimum specification is a bars variable.

The numeric, short string, and long string variables in your data file are displayed on the source variable list. Select the numeric variable you want to define the bars. To get a simple bar chart showing the value of each case in the default format, click on OK.

Optionally, you can change the value labels shown in the chart, use a template to control the format of the chart, or add a title, subtitle, or footnote. These options are discussed in detail in Chapter 22.

Bars Represent. Select a numeric variable to define the bars. Each case will be displayed as a separate bar.

Category Labels. Determines how the bars are labeled. You can choose one of the following category label sources:

◇ **Case number.** Each category is labeled with the case number. This is the default.

◇ **Variable.** Each category is labeled with the current value label of the selected variable.

Figure 23.25 shows a chart definition dialog box with a label variable selected and the resulting bar chart.

Figure 23.25 Bar chart with category labels from the variable year

Clustered:
Values of individual cases

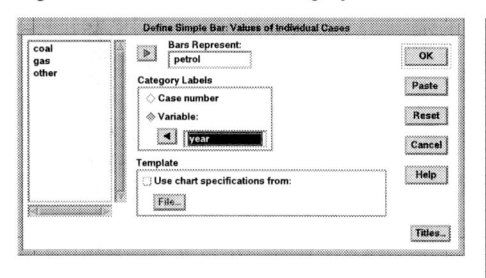

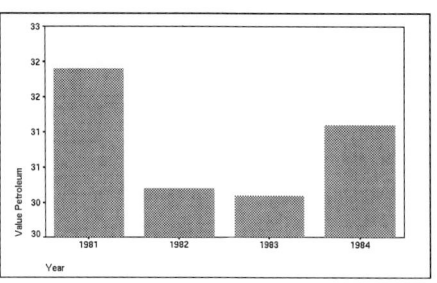

Figure 23.26 shows a chart definition dialog box and the resulting clustered bar chart with values of individual cases.

Figure 23.26 Clustered bar chart with bars as values of individual cases

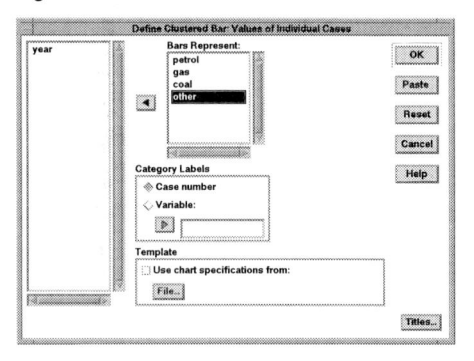

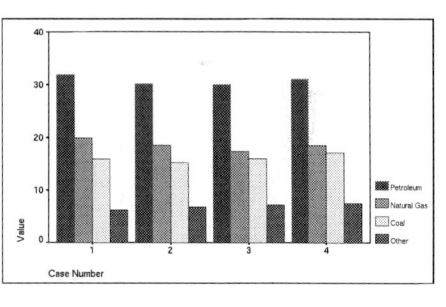

The minimum specification is two or more bar variables.

Bars Represent. Select two or more numeric variables. There is one separately colored or patterned set of bars for each variable. Each case is represented by a separate cluster of bars. The height of each bar represents the value of the variable.

Stacked:
Values of individual cases

Figure 23.27 shows a chart definition dialog box and the resulting stacked bar chart with values of individual cases.

Figure 23.27 Stacked bar chart with values of individual cases

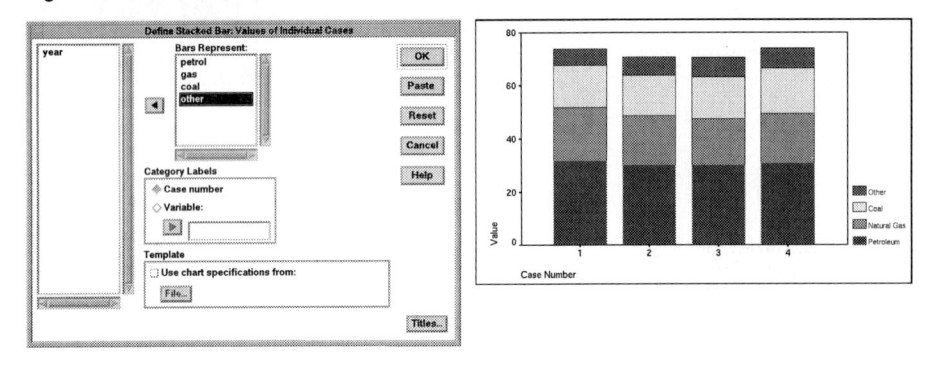

The minimum specifications are two or more segment variables.

Bars Represent. Select two or more numeric variables. There is one bar within each stack for each variable. The bars show the value of each case.

Line Charts

To obtain a line chart, from the menus choose:

Graphs
  Line...

This opens the Line Charts dialog box, as shown in Figure 23.28.

Figure 23.28 Line Charts dialog box

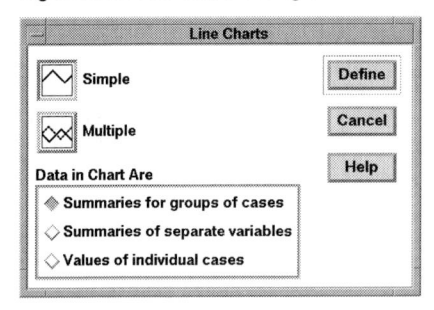

Select the type of line chart you want, and select the choice that describes the structure of your data organization. Click on Define to open a dialog box specific to your selections. The choices available in the chart definition dialog box vary according to chart type and the structure of your data organization (see Table 23.2).

Table 23.2 Types of line charts

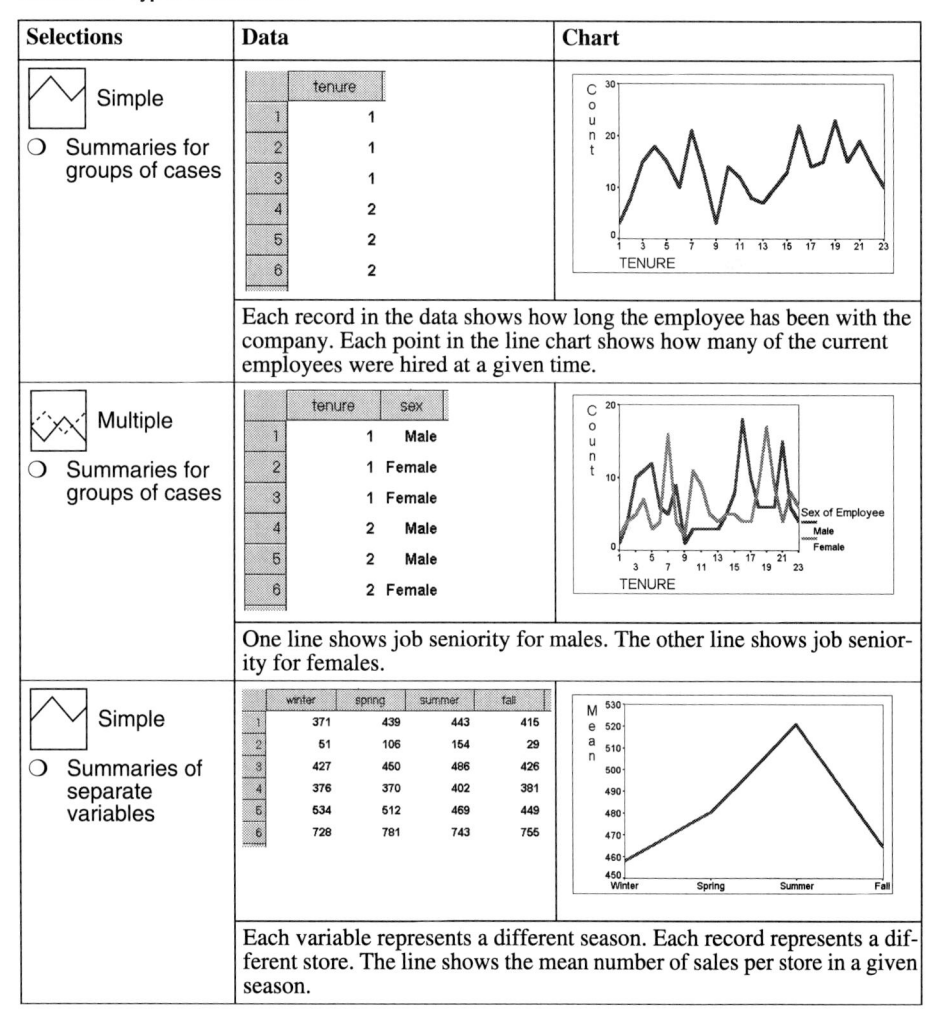

Selections	Data	Chart
Simple — Summaries for groups of cases	tenure: 1, 1, 1, 2, 2, 2	Count vs TENURE line chart
	Each record in the data shows how long the employee has been with the company. Each point in the line chart shows how many of the current employees were hired at a given time.	
Multiple — Summaries for groups of cases	tenure, sex: 1 Male, 1 Female, 1 Female, 2 Male, 2 Male, 2 Female	Count vs TENURE, by Sex of Employee (Male, Female)
	One line shows job seniority for males. The other line shows job seniority for females.	
Simple — Summaries of separate variables	winter, spring, summer, fall: 371 439 443 415; 51 106 154 29; 427 450 486 426; 376 370 402 381; 534 512 469 449; 728 781 743 755	Mean vs Winter, Spring, Summer, Fall
	Each variable represents a different season. Each record represents a different store. The line shows the mean number of sales per store in a given season.	

Table 23.2 Types of line charts (Continued)

Selections	Data	Chart
Multiple — ○ Summaries of separate variables	violent / property / year: 1: 4034, 16389, '89 2: 3634, 16424, '89 3: 4329, 17218, '89 4: 3781, 17137, '89 5: 3344, 16781, '89 6: 4198, 18162, '89	Mean vs Year line chart showing Violent Crime and Property Crimes across '89–'92
	Each of the two lines shows the mean values of one variable (either *violent* or *property*). *Year* breaks the lines into categories. There is one point on each line for each category.	
Simple — ○ Values of individual cases	var00001: 1: 284.00 2: 114.00 3: 114.00	Value of VAR00001 vs Case Number
	Each point shows the value of a single case.	
Multiple — ○ Values of individual cases	var00001 / var00002: 1: 118.00, 135.00 2: 93.00, 32.00 3: 118.00, 43.00	Value vs Case Number, showing VAR00001 and VAR00002
	Each line shows the values of a different variable. Each category shows the values of a single case. There is one point on each line for each case.	

Simple: Summaries for groups of cases

Figure 23.29 shows a chart definition dialog box and the resulting simple line chart with summaries for groups of cases.

Figure 23.29 Simple line chart with summaries for groups of cases

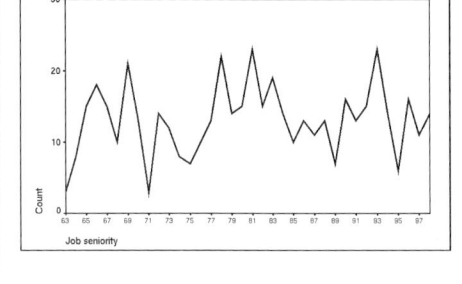

The minimum specification is a category axis variable.

The numeric, short string, and long string variables in your data file are displayed on the source variable list. Select a variable to define the category axis. To get a simple line chart showing the number of cases in each category, click on OK.

Optionally, you can select a different summary statistic, use a template to control the format of the chart, or add a title, subtitle, or footnote. Summary statistics are discussed in "Summary Functions" on p. 470. The other options are discussed in detail in Chapter 22.

Category Axis. Select a variable to define the categories shown in the chart. There is one point for each value of the variable.

If you select Other summary function in the Define Simple Line Summaries for Groups of Cases dialog box, you must also select a variable to be summarized. Figure 23.30 shows the chart definition dialog box with a variable to be summarized and the resulting chart.

Figure 23.30 Simple line chart with summary of a variable

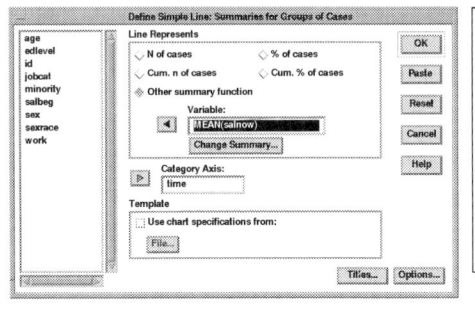

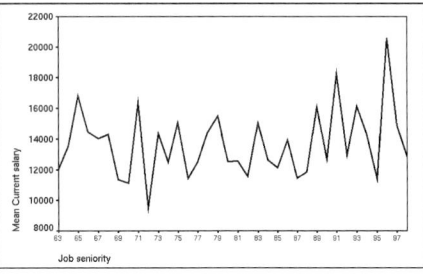

The chart generated by default shows the mean of the selected variable within each category (determined by the category axis variable).

Multiple:
Summaries for groups of cases

Figure 23.31 shows a chart definition dialog box and the resulting multiple line chart with summaries for groups of cases.

Figure 23.31 Multiple line chart with summaries for groups of cases

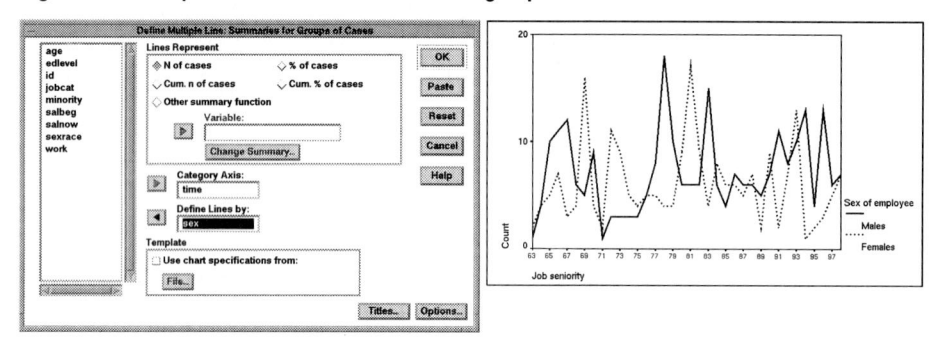

The minimum specifications are:
- A category axis variable.
- A line definition variable.

Category Axis. Select a variable to define the categories shown in the chart. There is one point on each line for each value of the variable.

Define Lines by. Select a variable to define the lines. There is one line for each value of the variable.

Simple:
Summaries of separate variables

Figure 23.32 shows a chart definition dialog box and the resulting simple line chart with summaries of separate variables.

Figure 23.32 Simple line chart with summaries of separate variables

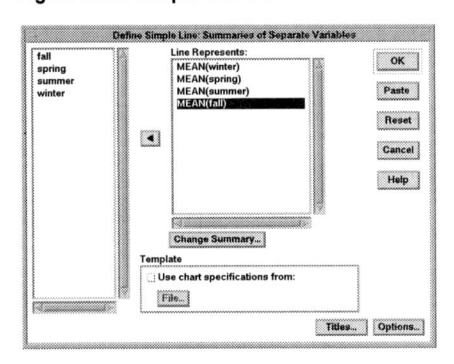

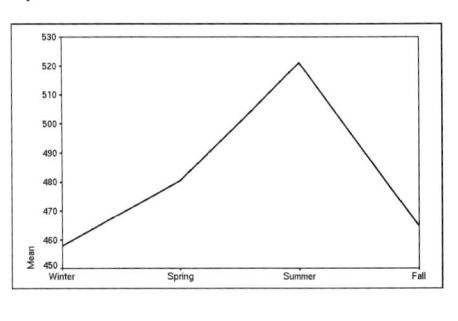

The minimum specifications are two or more point variables.

The numeric variables in your data file are displayed on the source variable list. Select the variables you want the line to represent. To get a simple line chart showing the mean value of each variable in default format, click on OK.

Optionally, you can select a different summary statistic, use a template to control the format of the chart, or add a title, subtitle, or footnote. Summary statistics are discussed in "Summary Functions" on p. 470. The other options are discussed in detail in Chapter 22.

Line Represents. Select two or more variables to define the categories shown in the chart. There is one point on the line for each variable. By default, the points show the mean of the selected variables.

Multiple:
Summaries of separate variables

Figure 23.33 shows a chart definition dialog box and the resulting multiple line chart with summaries of separate variables.

Figure 23.33 Multiple line chart with summaries of separate variables

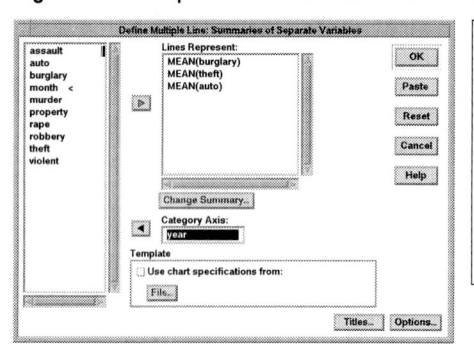

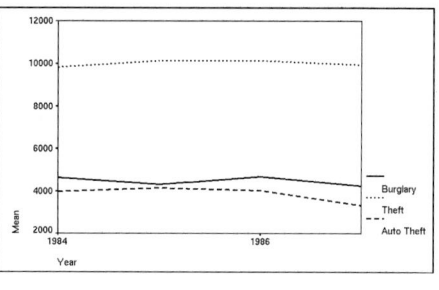

The minimum specifications are:
- Two or more line variables.
- A category axis variable.

Lines Represent. Select two or more variables to define the lines. There is one line for each variable. By default, the lines show the mean of the selected variables.

Category Axis. Select a variable to define the categories shown in the chart. There is one point on each line for each value of the variable.

Simple:
Values of individual cases

Figure 23.34 shows a chart definition dialog box and the resulting simple line chart with values of individual cases.

Figure 23.34 Simple line chart with values of individual cases

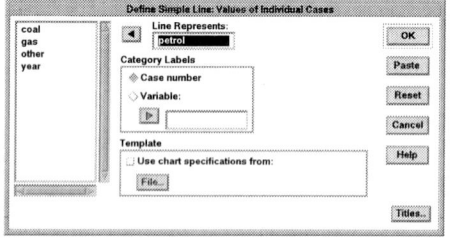

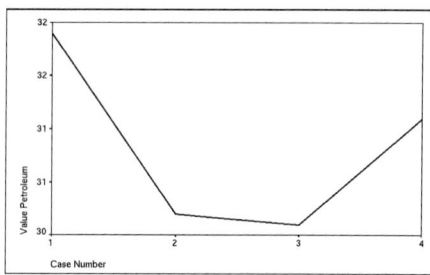

The minimum specification is a line variable.

The numeric, short string, and long string variables in your data file are displayed on the source variable list. Select the numeric variable you want to define the line. To get a simple line chart showing the value of each case in the default format, click on OK.

Optionally, you can change the value labels shown in the chart, use a template to control the format of the chart, or add a title, subtitle, or footnote. These options are discussed in detail in Chapter 22.

Line Represents. Select a numeric variable to define the line. Each case will be displayed as a point.

Category Labels. Determines how the categories are labeled. You can choose one of the following category label sources:

- **Case number.** Each category is labeled with the case number. This is the default.
- **Variable.** Each category is labeled with the current value label of the selected variable.

Figure 23.35 shows a chart definition dialog box with a label variable selected and the resulting simple line chart with category labels.

Figure 23.35 Line chart with category labels from the variable year

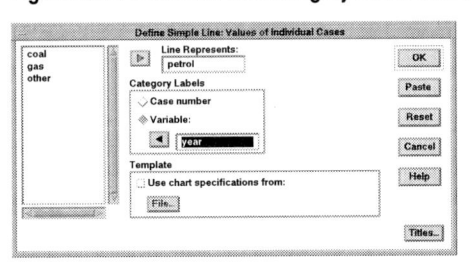

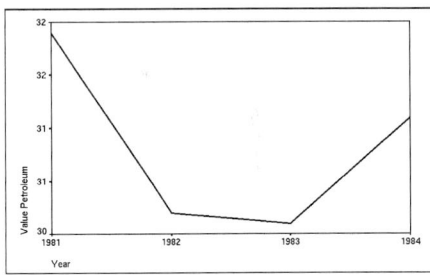

Multiple: Values of individual cases

Figure 23.36 shows a chart definition dialog box and the resulting multiple line chart with values of individual cases.

Figure 23.36 Multiple line chart with values of individual cases

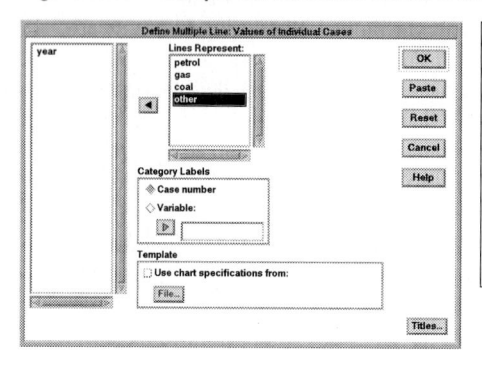

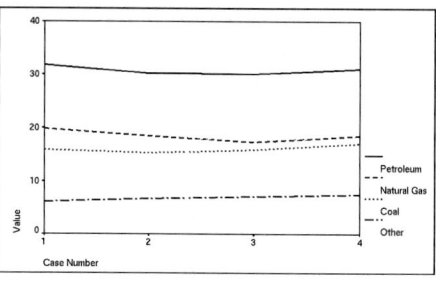

The minimum specification is two or more line variables.

Lines Represent. Select two or more numeric variables to define the lines. There is one line for each variable. There is one point on each line for each case.

Area Charts

To obtain an area chart, from the menus choose:

Graphs
  Area...

This opens the Area Charts dialog box, as shown in Figure 23.37.

Figure 23.37 Area Charts dialog box

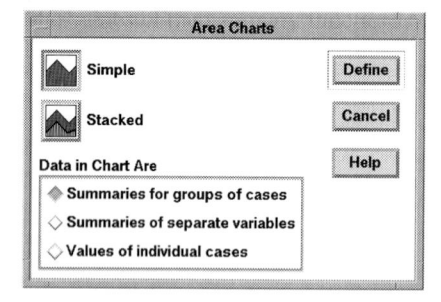

Select the type of area chart you want, and select the choice that describes the structure of your data organization. Click on Define to open a dialog box specific to your selections. The choices available in the chart definition dialog box vary according to chart type and the structure of your data organization (see Table 23.3).

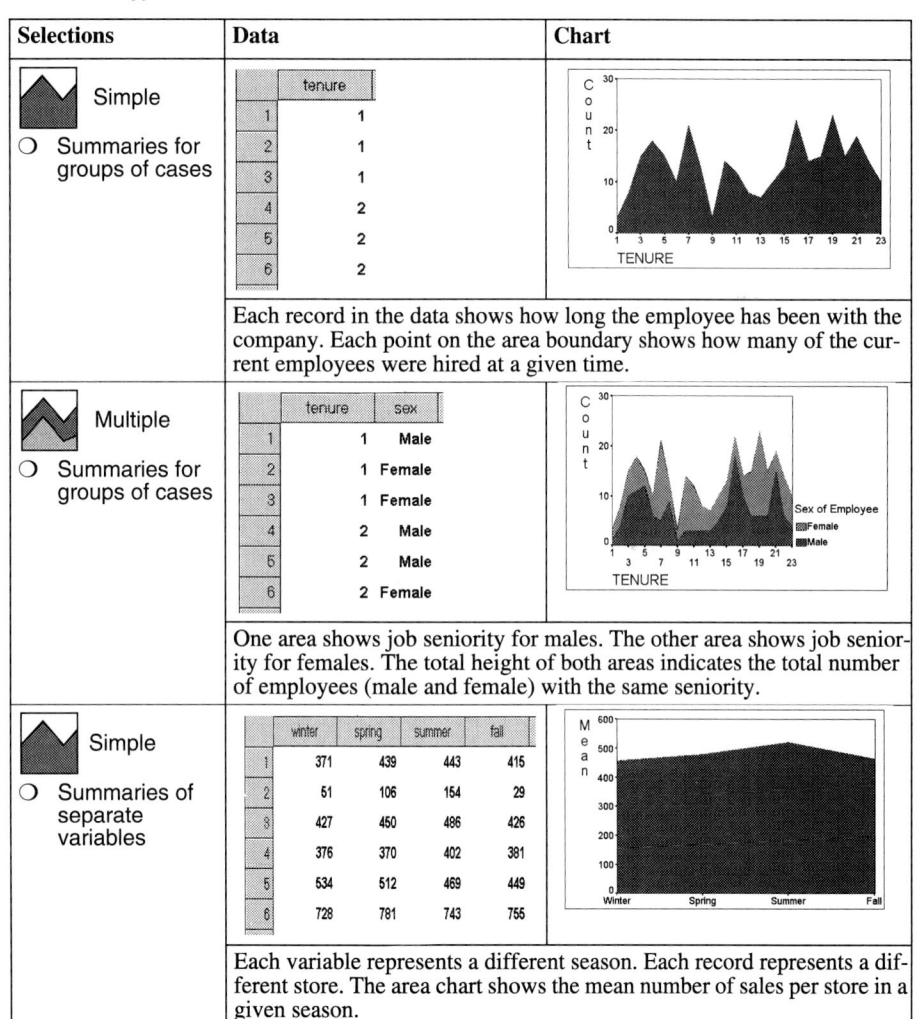

Table 23.3 Types of area charts

Selections	Data	Chart
Simple ○ Summaries for groups of cases	tenure: 1, 1, 1, 2, 2, 2	*Area chart of Count vs TENURE*
	Each record in the data shows how long the employee has been with the company. Each point on the area boundary shows how many of the current employees were hired at a given time.	
Multiple ○ Summaries for groups of cases	tenure, sex: 1 Male, 1 Female, 1 Female, 2 Male, 2 Male, 2 Female	*Area chart of Count vs TENURE by Sex of Employee (Female, Male)*
	One area shows job seniority for males. The other area shows job seniority for females. The total height of both areas indicates the total number of employees (male and female) with the same seniority.	
Simple ○ Summaries of separate variables	winter, spring, summer, fall 1: 371, 439, 443, 415 2: 51, 106, 154, 29 3: 427, 450, 486, 426 4: 376, 370, 402, 381 5: 534, 512, 469, 449 6: 728, 781, 743, 755	*Area chart of Mean by Winter, Spring, Summer, Fall*
	Each variable represents a different season. Each record represents a different store. The area chart shows the mean number of sales per store in a given season.	

Table 23.3 Types of area charts (Continued)

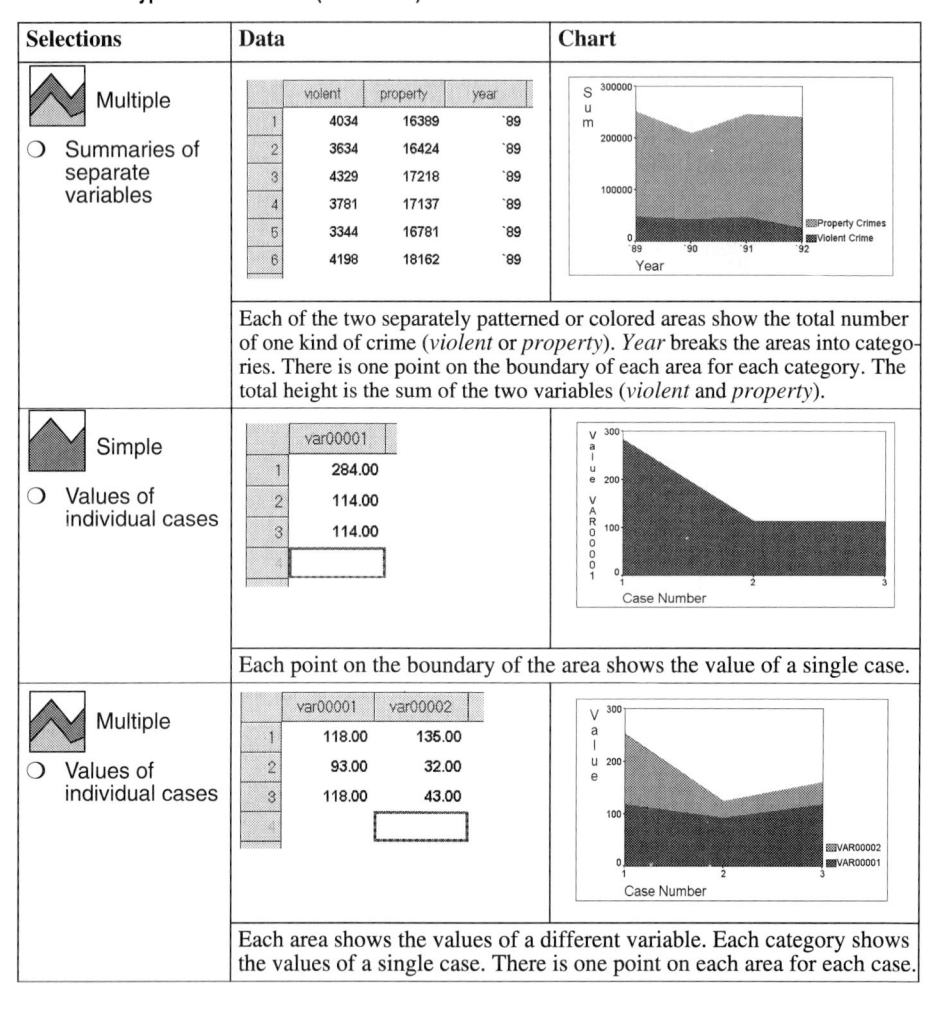

Selections	Data	Chart
Multiple ○ Summaries of separate variables	violent / property / year 1: 4034 / 16389 / '89 2: 3634 / 16424 / '89 3: 4329 / 17218 / '89 4: 3781 / 17137 / '89 5: 3344 / 16781 / '89 6: 4198 / 18162 / '89	Stacked area chart of Sum vs. Year ('89–'92) showing Property Crimes and Violent Crime
	Each of the two separately patterned or colored areas show the total number of one kind of crime (*violent* or *property*). *Year* breaks the areas into categories. There is one point on the boundary of each area for each category. The total height is the sum of the two variables (*violent* and *property*).	
Simple ○ Values of individual cases	var00001 1: 284.00 2: 114.00 3: 114.00	Area chart of VAR00001 value vs. Case Number
	Each point on the boundary of the area shows the value of a single case.	
Multiple ○ Values of individual cases	var00001 / var00002 1: 118.00 / 135.00 2: 93.00 / 32.00 3: 118.00 / 43.00	Stacked area chart of Value vs. Case Number showing VAR00002 and VAR00001
	Each area shows the values of a different variable. Each category shows the values of a single case. There is one point on each area for each case.	

Simple:
Summaries for groups of cases

Figure 23.38 shows a chart definition dialog box and the resulting simple area chart with summaries for groups of cases.

Figure 23.38 Simple area chart with summaries for groups of cases

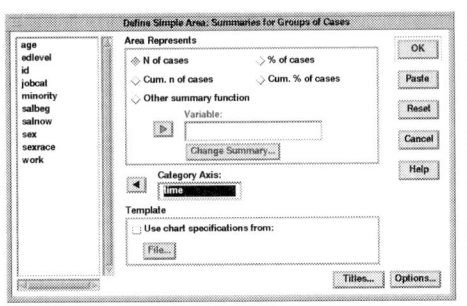

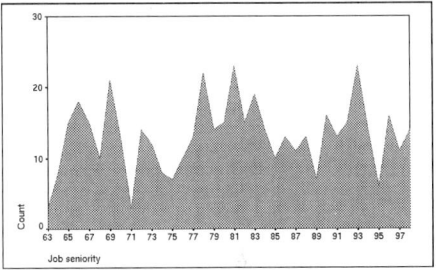

The minimum specification is a category axis variable.

The numeric, short string, and long string variables in your data file are displayed on the source variable list. Select the variable you want to define the category axis. To get a simple area chart showing the number of cases in each category, click on OK.

Optionally, you can select a different summary statistic, use a template to control the format of the chart, or add a title, subtitle, or footnote. Summary statistics are discussed in "Summary Functions" on p. 470. The other options are discussed in detail in Chapter 22.

Category Axis. Select a variable to define the categories shown in the chart. There is one point on the boundary of the area for each value of the variable.

If you select Other summary function in the chart definition dialog box, you must also select a variable to be summarized. Figure 23.39 shows the dialog box with a variable to be summarized and the resulting chart.

The chart generated by default shows the mean of the selected variable within each category (determined by the category axis variable). For a detailed description of optional statistics, see "Summary Functions" on p. 470.

Figure 23.39 Summary of a variable on a simple area chart

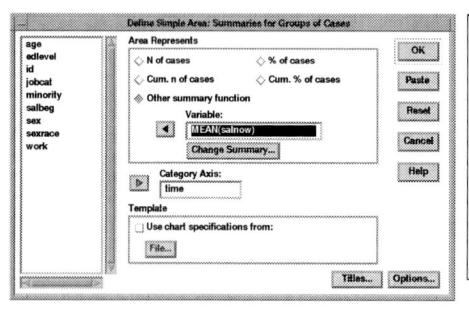

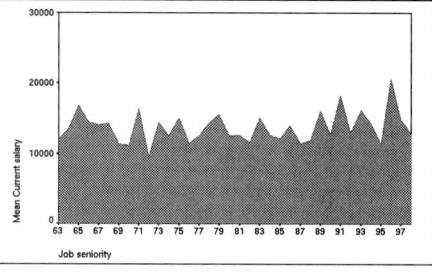

Stacked:
Summaries for groups of cases

Figure 23.40 shows a chart definition dialog box and the resulting stacked area chart with summaries for groups of cases.

Figure 23.40 Stacked area chart with summaries for groups of cases

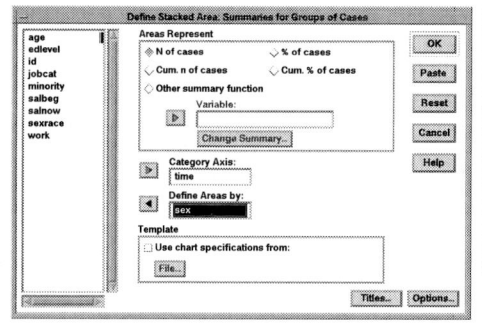

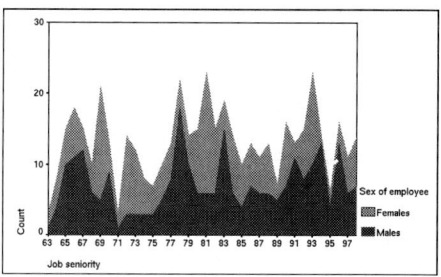

The minimum specifications are:
- A category axis variable.
- An area definition variable.

Category Axis. Select a variable to define the categories shown in the chart. There is one point on the boundary of each area for each value of the variable.

Define Areas by. Select a variable to define the areas. There is one differently colored or patterned area for each value of the variable.

Simple:
Summaries of separate variables

Figure 23.41 shows a chart definition dialog box and the resulting simple area chart with summaries of separate variables.

Figure 23.41 Simple area chart with summaries of separate variables

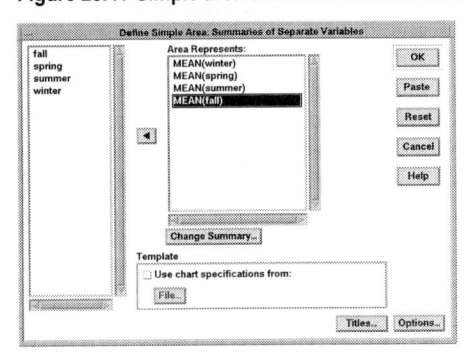

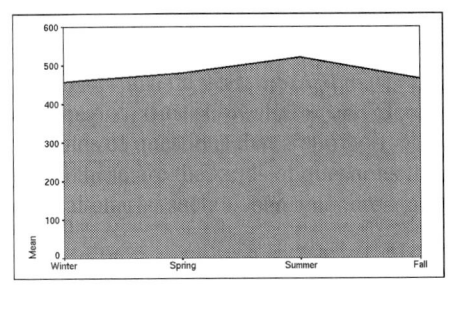

The minimum specifications are two or more point variables.

The numeric variables in your data file are displayed on the source variable list. Select the variables you want to define points on the boundary of the area. To get a simple area chart showing the mean value of each variable in default format, click on OK.

Optionally, you can select a different summary statistic, use a template to control the format of the chart, or add a title, subtitle, or footnote. Summary statistics are discussed in "Summary Functions" on p. 470. The other options are discussed in detail in Chapter 22.

Area Represents. Select two or more variables to define the categories shown in the chart. There is one point on the boundary of the area for each variable. By default, the points show the mean of the selected variables.

Stacked:
Summaries of separate variables

Figure 23.42 shows a chart definition dialog box and the resulting stacked area chart with summaries of separate variables.

Figure 23.42 Stacked area chart with summaries of separate variables

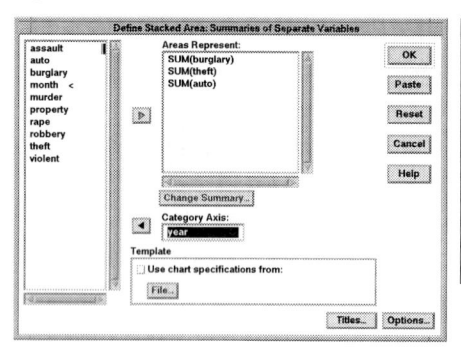

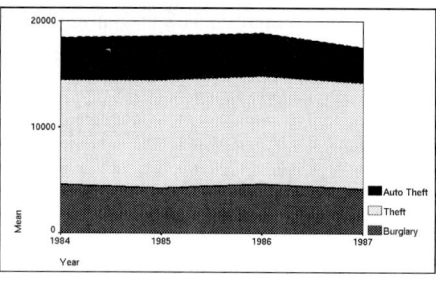

The minimum specifications are:
- Two or more area variables.
- A category axis variable.

Areas Represent. Select two or more variables to define the areas. There is one area for each variable. By default, the value axis shows the sum of the selected variables.

Category Axis. Select a variable to define the categories shown in the chart. There is one point on the boundary of each area for each value of the variable.

Simple:
Values of individual cases

Figure 23.43 shows a chart definition dialog box and the resulting simple area chart with values of individual cases.

Figure 23.43 Simple area chart with values of individual cases

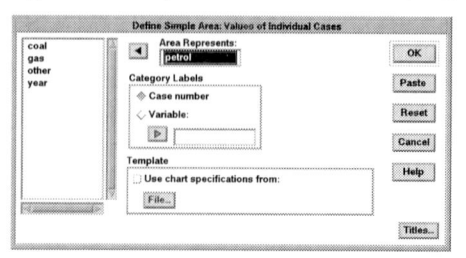

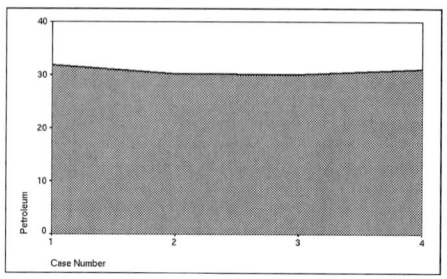

The minimum specification is an area variable.

The numeric, short string, and long string variables in your data file are displayed on the source variable list. Select the numeric variable you want to define the area. To get a simple area chart showing the value of each case in the default format, click on OK.

Optionally, you can change the value labels shown in the chart, use a template to control the format of the chart, or add a title, subtitle, or footnote. These options are discussed in detail in Chapter 22.

Area Represents. Select a numeric variable to define the area. Each case will be displayed as a category.

Category Labels. Determines how the categories are labeled. You can choose one of the following category label sources:

- **Case number.** Each category is labeled with the case number. This is the default.
- **Variable.** Each category is labeled with the current value label of the selected variable.

Figure 23.44 shows the chart definition dialog box with a label variable selected and the resulting area chart.

Figure 23.44 Area chart with category labels from the variable year

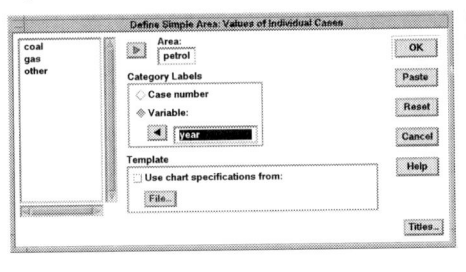

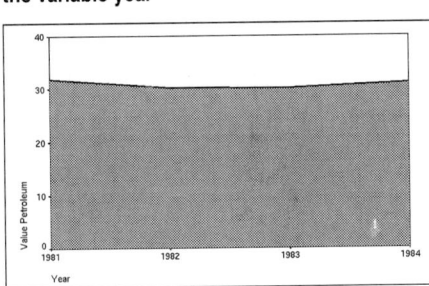

Stacked: Values of individual cases

Figure 23.45 shows the chart definition dialog box and the resulting stacked area chart with values of individual cases.

Figure 23.45 Stacked area chart with values of individual cases

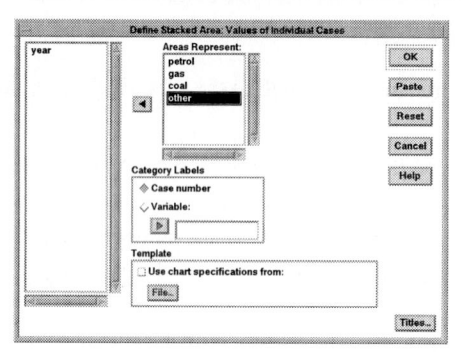

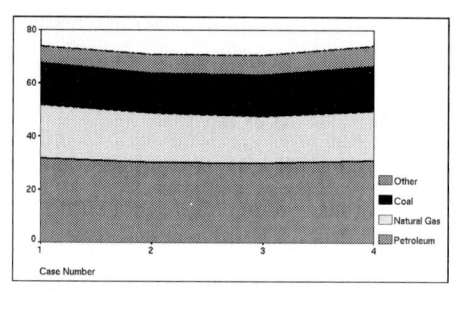

The minimum specifications are two stacked area variables.

Areas Represent. Select two or more numeric variables. There is one area for each variable. There is one point on the boundary of each area for each case.

Pie Charts

To obtain a pie chart, from the menus choose:

Graphs
  Pie...

This open the Pie Charts dialog box, as shown in Figure 23.46.

Figure 23.46 Pie Charts dialog box

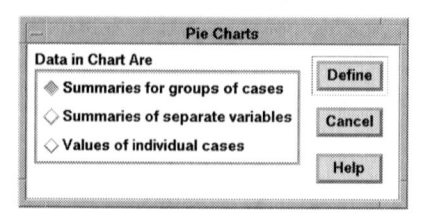

Select the choice that describes the structure of your data organization, and click on Define to open a dialog box specific to your selection (see Table 23.4).

Table 23.4 Types of pie charts

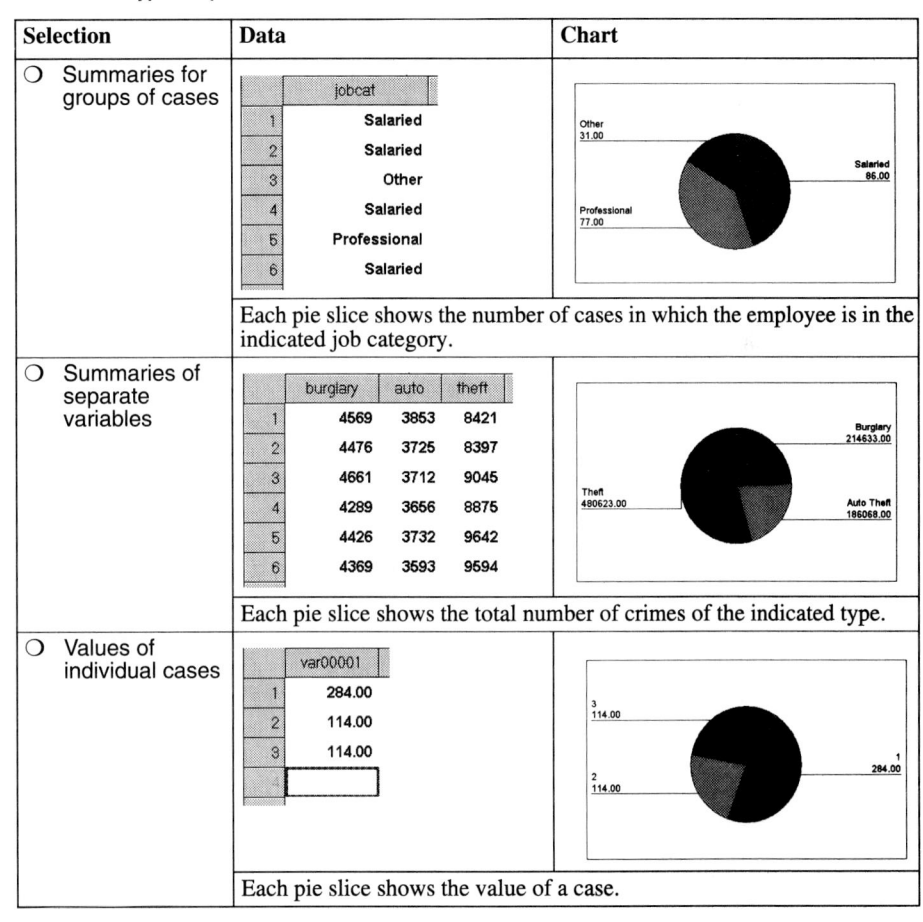

Selection	Data	Chart
○ Summaries for groups of cases	jobcat: 1 Salaried, 2 Salaried, 3 Other, 4 Salaried, 5 Professional, 6 Salaried	Pie chart: Other 31.00, Salaried 86.00, Professional 77.00
	Each pie slice shows the number of cases in which the employee is in the indicated job category.	
○ Summaries of separate variables	burglary / auto / theft 1 4569 3853 8421 2 4476 3725 8397 3 4661 3712 9045 4 4289 3656 8875 5 4426 3732 9642 6 4369 3593 9594	Pie chart: Burglary 214633.00, Theft 480623.00, Auto Theft 186068.00
	Each pie slice shows the total number of crimes of the indicated type.	
○ Values of individual cases	var00001: 1 284.00, 2 114.00, 3 114.00	Pie chart: 1 284.00, 2 114.00, 3 114.00
	Each pie slice shows the value of a case.	

Summaries for Groups of Cases

Figure 23.47 shows a chart definition dialog box and the resulting simple pie chart with summaries for groups of cases.

Figure 23.47 Pie chart with summaries for groups of cases

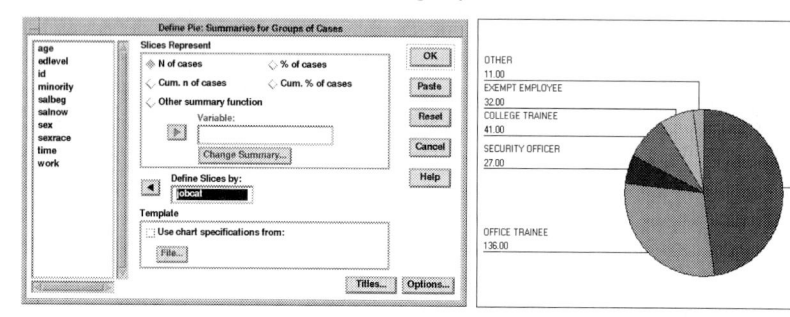

The minimum specification is a slice definition variable.

The numeric, short string, and long string variables in your data file are displayed on the source variable list. Select the variable you want to define the categories or slices. To get a simple pie chart showing the number of cases in each category, click on OK.

Optionally, you can select a different summary statistic, use a template to control the format of the chart, or add a title, subtitle, or footnote. Summary statistics are discussed in "Summary Functions" on p. 470. The other options are discussed in detail in Chapter 22.

Define Slices by. Select a variable to define the pie slices shown in the chart. There is one slice for each value of the variable. A slice definition variable must be selected to enable the OK pushbutton.

If you select Other summary function in the Define Pie Summaries for Groups of Cases dialog box, you must also select a variable to be summarized. Figure 23.48 shows the chart definition dialog box with a variable to be summarized and the resulting simple pie chart.

Figure 23.48 Simple pie chart with summary of a variable

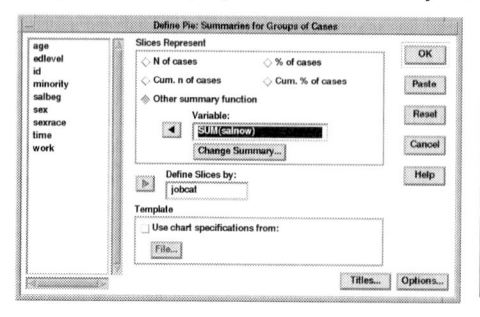

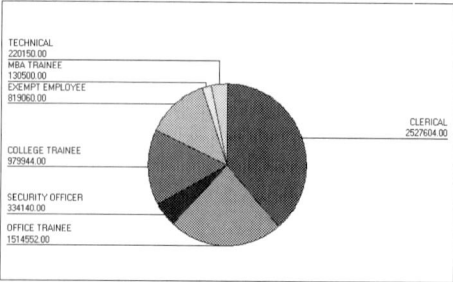

Summaries of Separate Variables

Figure 23.49 shows a chart definition dialog box and the resulting simple pie chart with summaries of separate variables.

Figure 23.49 Pie chart with summaries of separate variables

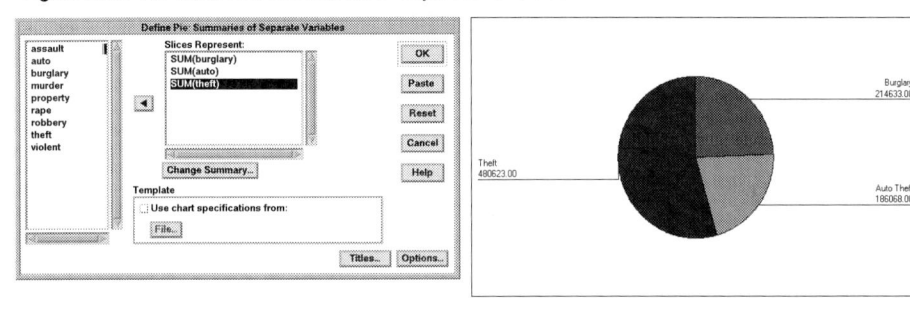

The minimum specifications are two or more slice variables.

The numeric variables in your data file are displayed on the source variable list. Select the variables you want to define the pie slices. To get a simple pie chart showing the sum of each variable in default format, click on OK.

Optionally, you can select a different summary statistic, use a template to control the format of the chart, or add a title, subtitle, or footnote. Summary statistics are discussed in "Summary Functions" on p. 470. The other options are discussed in detail in Chapter 22.

Slices Represent. Select two or more variables to define the slices shown in the chart. There is one slice for each variable. By default, the slices show the sum of the selected variables. Two or more slice variables must be selected to enable the OK pushbutton.

Values of Individual Cases

Figure 23.50 shows a chart definition dialog box and the resulting simple pie chart with values of individual cases.

Figure 23.50 Pie chart with values of individual cases

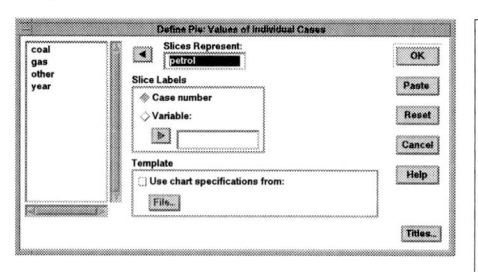

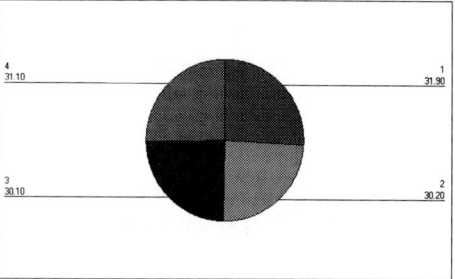

The minimum specification is a slice variable.

The numeric, short string, and long string variables in your data file are displayed on the source variable list. Select the numeric variable you want slices to represent. To get a simple pie chart showing the value of each case in default format, click on OK.

Optionally, you can change the value labels shown in the chart, use a template to control the format of the chart, or add a title, subtitle, or footnote. These options are discussed in detail in Chapter 22.

Slices Represent. Select a numeric variable to define the slices. Each case will be displayed as a separate pie slice. A variable must be selected to enable the OK pushbutton.

Slice Labels. Determines how the slices are labeled. You can choose one of the following sector label sources:

◇ **Case number.** Each slice is labeled with the case number. This is the default.

◇ **Variable.** Each slice is labeled with the current value label of the selected variable.

Figure 23.51 shows the chart definition dialog box with a label variable selected and the resulting pie chart.

Figure 23.51 Pie chart with category labels from the variable petrol

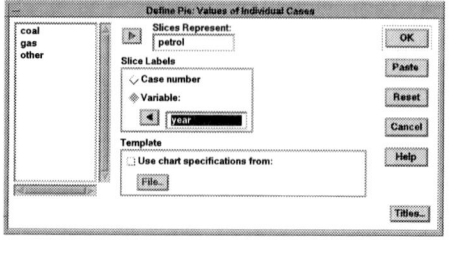

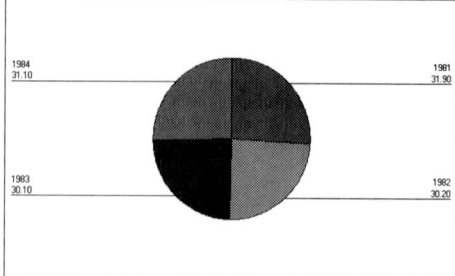

Transposed Charts

Sometimes, especially with inventory or accounting time-series data, the categories you want are defined as separate cases or values, while each date is a separate variable. For example, the inventory data in Figure 23.52 are defined this way.

Figure 23.52 Inventory data

	product	jan	feb	mar	apr	may	jun	jul	aug	sep	oct	nov	dec
1	Razors	123	97	50	67	89	56	90	45	120	110	135	79
2	Shave Cream	35	46	34	43	50	23	44	33	57	48	68	45
3	Deodorant	245	175	198	210	156	189	172	142	219	208	173	189

If you draw a line chart of these data, you get the chart in Figure 23.53.

Figure 23.53 Chart of inventory data

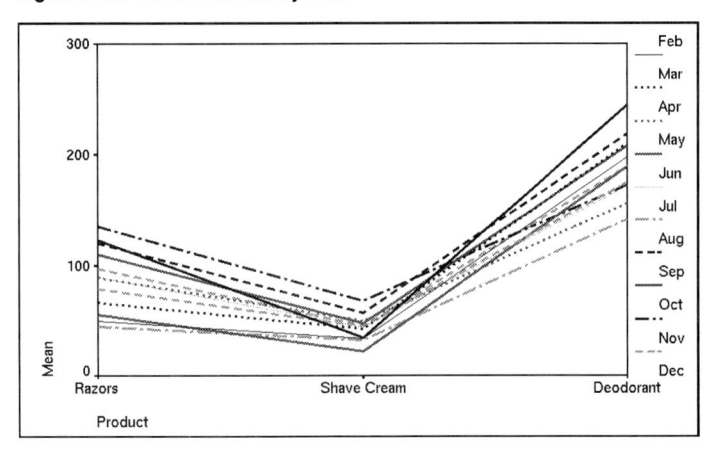

To flip this chart so that each line is a separate product and each month is a separate category, edit the chart. From the menu of the chart window select:

Series
  Transpose Data

This produces the chart shown in Figure 23.54.

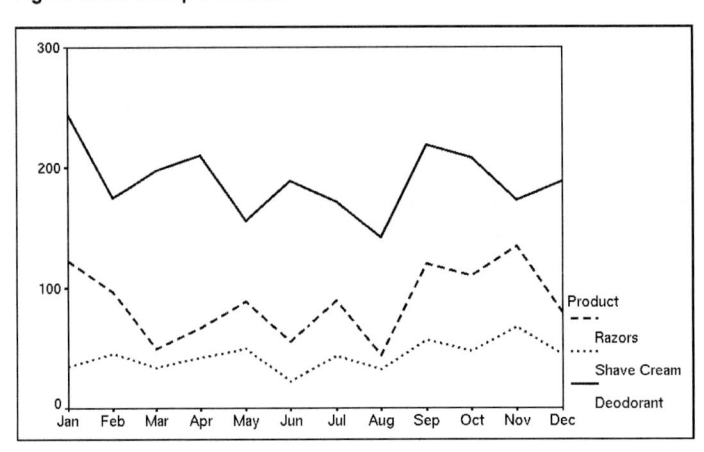

Figure 23.54 Transposed chart

You can transpose other multiple-series categorical charts, such as clustered bar charts (see "Transposing Data" on p. 555 in Chapter 26).

Summary Functions

Data can be summarized by counting the number of cases in each category or subcategory, or by calculating a statistic summarizing the values in each category or subcategory.

Count Functions

For simple summaries of groups of cases, the dialog box in Figure 23.55 shows the general layout of the chart definition dialog boxes for bar, line, area, and pie charts. For complex summaries of groups of cases, the summaries in the dialog box are similar, as shown in Figure 23.56.

Bar, Line, Area, and Pie Charts 471

Figure 23.55 Define simple summaries for groups of cases dialog box

Figure 23.56 Define multi-series summaries for groups of cases dialog box

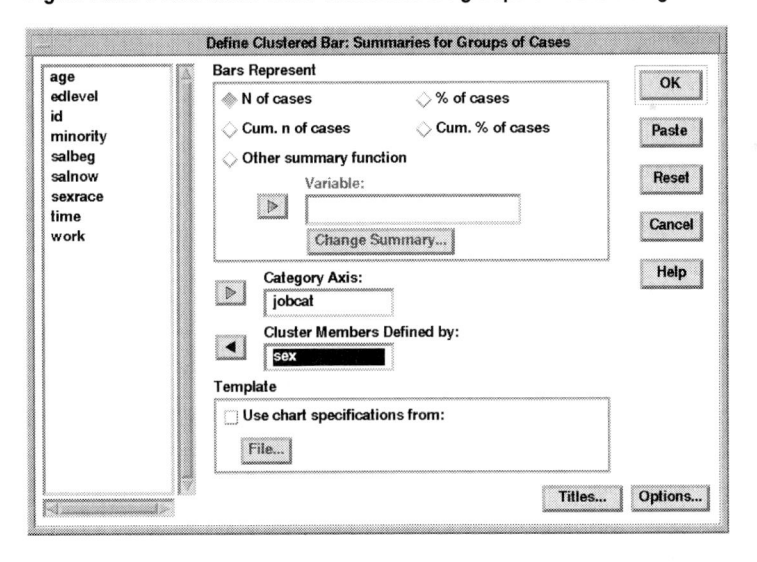

Bars/Lines/Areas/Slices Represent. Determines the summary statistic used to generate the data series illustrated by the chart. You can choose one of the following alternatives:

- **N of cases.** Each bar, point on a line, point on the boundary of an area, or pie slice represents the number of cases in a category. This is the default.
- **% of cases.** Each bar, point on a line, point on the boundary of an area, or pie slice represents the percentage of cases in a category.
- **Cum. n of cases.** Cumulative number of cases. Each bar, point on a line, point on the boundary of an area, or pie slice represents the number of cases in the current category plus all cases in previous categories. This function is not appropriate for some charts; see "Cumulative Functions" on p. 474.
- **Cum. % of cases.** Cumulative percentage of cases. Each bar, point on a line, or point on the boundary of an area represents the cumulative number of cases as a percentage of the total number of cases. This function is not appropriate for some charts; see "Cumulative Functions" on p. 474.
- **Other summary function.** The values in a series are calculated from a summary measure of a variable. In most cases, the mean of the variable is the default. For stacked bar, stacked area, and pie charts, the sum of the variable is the default.

Other Summary Functions

You can request statistical summary functions for any chart where values are summarized. When values are summarized for *groups of cases*, select Other summary function; then select a variable to summarize and click on ▶. The Variable box indicates the default summary function (mean or sum). If you want a summary function other than the default, click on Change Summary.... This opens the Summary Function dialog box, as shown in Figure 23.57.

When values are summarized for *separate variables*, first move the variables to the box for bars, lines, areas, or slices, as shown in Figure 23.21 and Figure 23.49. The default measure (mean or sum) is indicated for each variable on the list. If you want a summary function other than the default, select a variable on the list and click on Change Summary.... This opens the Summary Function dialog box, as shown in Figure 23.57. If you want the same summary function to apply to more than one variable, you can select several variables by dragging over them and then clicking on Change Summary....

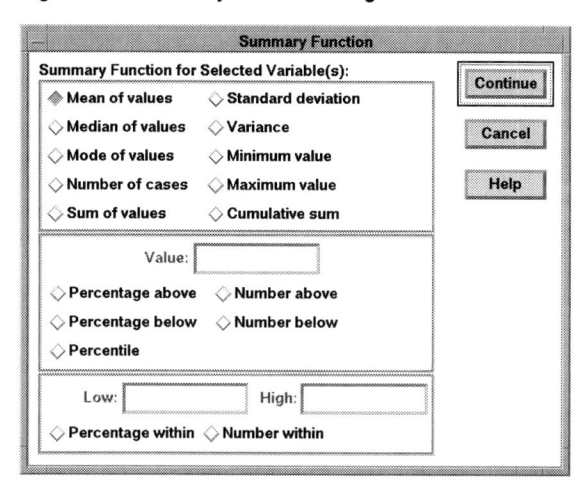

Figure 23.57 Summary Function dialog box

You can choose one of the following summary functions:

◇ **Mean of values.** The arithmetic average within the category. This is the default in most cases.

◇ **Median of values.** The value below which half the cases fall.

◇ **Mode of values.** The most frequently occurring value.

◇ **Number of cases.** The number of cases having a nonmissing value of the selected variable. If there are no missing values, this is the same as N of cases in the previous dialog box.

◇ **Sum of values.** The default for stacked bar charts, stacked area charts, or pie charts.

◇ **Standard deviation.** A measure of how much observations vary from the mean, expressed in the same units as the data.

◇ **Variance.** A measure of how much observations vary from the mean, expressed in squared units.

◇ **Minimum value.** The smallest value.

◇ **Maximum value.** The largest value.

◇ **Cumulative sum.** The sum of all values in the current category plus all values in previous categories. This function is not appropriate for some charts; see "Cumulative functions," below.

◇ **Percentage above.** The percentage of cases above the indicated value.

◇ **Percentage below.** The percentage of cases below the indicated value.

- **Percentile.** The data value below which the specified percentage of values fall.
- **Number above.** The number of cases above the specified value.
- **Number below.** The number of cases below the specified value.
- **Percentage within.** The percentage of cases with values between the specified high and low value, including the high and low values. Select this item and then type in the high and low values.
- **Number within.** The number of cases with values between the specified high and low value, including the high and low values. Select this item and then type in the high and low values.

Cumulative Functions

Cum. N of cases, *Cum. % of cases*, and *Cumulative sum* are inappropriate in pie charts. These functions are also inappropriate in stacked bar charts and area charts that have been transposed so that the cumulative function is along the scale axis. Because the Chart Editor does not recalculate summary functions, many Displayed Data operations (from the Series menu) will invalidate cumulative functions, particularly if scaled to 100%.

24 Boxplots

You can get simple boxplots either from the Explore statistical procedure or the Boxplot graphics procedure. More complex boxplots can be obtained only from the Boxplot procedure. Regardless of how you generate them, you should use boxplots to get an idea of how your data values are distributed and how the distribution of your data varies between groups. This chapter describes the boxplots that you can obtain through the Boxplot procedure. For a description of the components of a boxplot, see Chapter 9, which also describes other methods of exploratory analysis.

Chapter 9 contains an example of a simple boxplot, which is used to compare the distribution of beginning salaries for people employed in several different positions at a bank. If we break the data down further by sex, we can see the distribution of male and female salaries in different positions throughout the company. Figure 24.1 shows a clustered boxplot of beginning salary.

Figure 24.1 Clustered boxplot of beginning salary by job category and sex

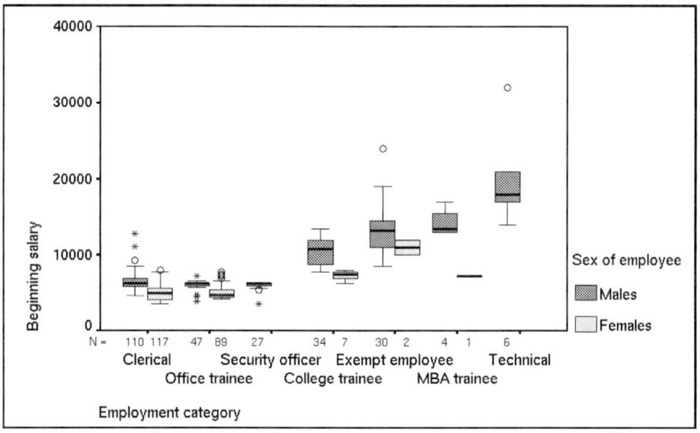

Each cluster shows both sexes. Each category shows the job category of the employees. You can see that the women's starting salaries were lower in all job categories, especially the categories with higher pay. You can also see that the men's salaries in the four higher-paid categories have similar distributions, while all the other salaries have much less variability. Also, notice how few women are in the higher-paid categories. In the college trainee, exempt employee, MBA trainee, and technical categories, there are seven, two, one, and one, respectively.

Both this example and the chart in Chapter 9 show data summarized by groups of cases. Often, we are interested in comparing the distribution of two or more different variables. For example, the starting and current salaries of bank employees are recorded as two separate variables. A simple boxplot of starting salary and current salary is shown in Figure 24.2. Here you can see that starting salary is lower and has a little less variability than current salary.

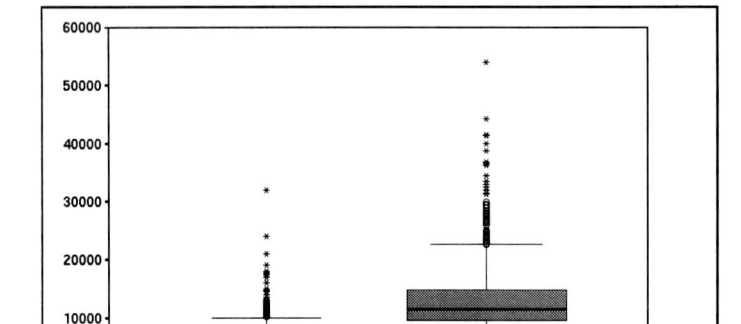

Figure 24.2 Boxplot of starting and current salaries

If you want to see beginning salary and current salary by job category, use a clustered boxplot, as shown in Figure 24.3. Here you can see that the spread of current salaries for employees in the technical, exempt, and college trainee categories is larger than for the other categories. Also, as expected, the higher categories generally show a greater difference between starting salary and current salary.

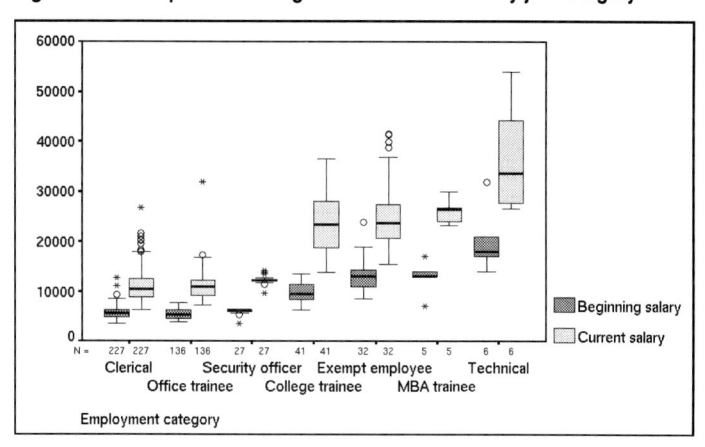

Figure 24.3 Boxplot of starting and current salaries by job category

How to Obtain a Boxplot

To obtain a boxplot, from the menus choose:

Graphs
  Boxplot...

This opens the Boxplot dialog box, as shown in Figure 24.4.

Figure 24.4 Boxplot dialog box

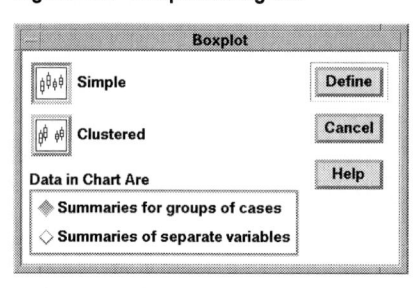

From the Boxplot dialog box, choose either simple or clustered boxplots, and then select the choice that describes the structure of your data organization.

Data in Chart are. Select the choice that describes the structure of your data organization.

- **Summaries for groups of cases.** One variable is summarized in subgroups. The subgroups are determined by one variable for simple boxplots or two variables for clustered boxplots.
- **Summaries of separate variables.** More than one variable is summarized. Simple boxplots summarize each variable over all cases in the file. Clustered boxplots summarize each variable within categories determined by another variable.

Examples of these choices, shown with data structures and the charts they produce, are presented in Table 24.1.

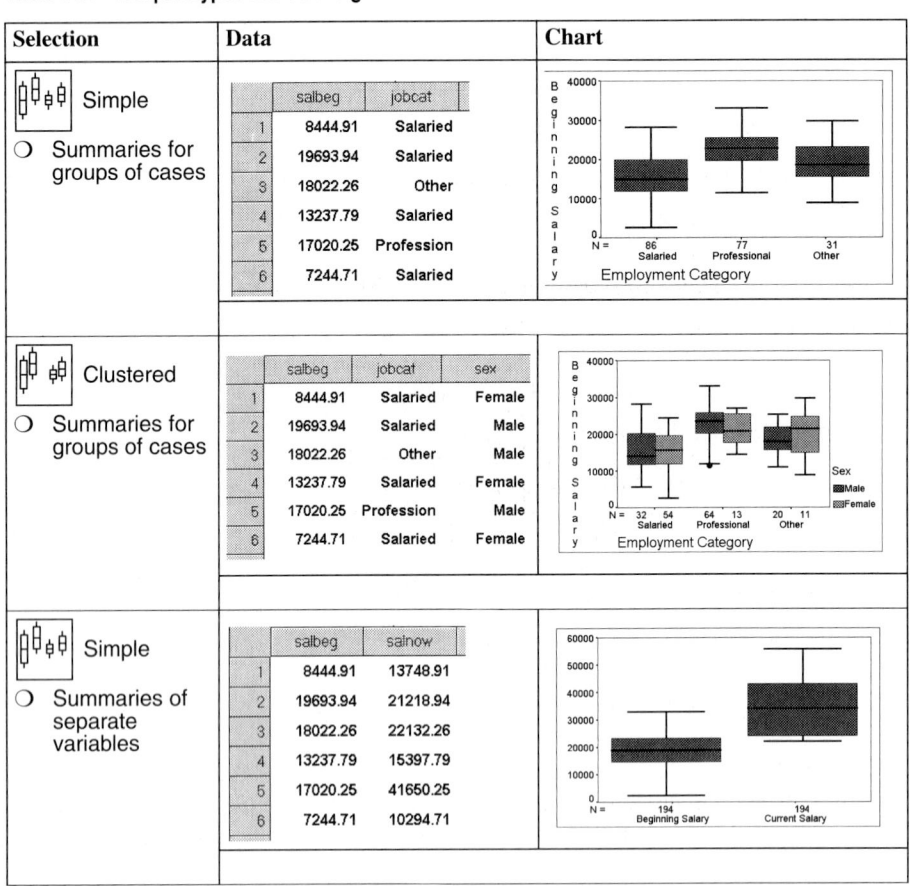

Table 24.1 Boxplot types and data organization

Selection	Data	Chart
Simple — Summaries for groups of cases	salbeg / jobcat: 8444.91 Salaried; 19693.94 Salaried; 18022.26 Other; 13237.79 Salaried; 17020.25 Profession; 7244.71 Salaried	Beginning Salary by Employment Category; N = 86 Salaried, 77 Professional, 31 Other
Clustered — Summaries for groups of cases	salbeg / jobcat / sex: 8444.91 Salaried Female; 19693.94 Salaried Male; 18022.26 Other Male; 13237.79 Salaried Female; 17020.25 Profession Male; 7244.71 Salaried Female	Beginning Salary by Employment Category, clustered by Sex (Male/Female); N = 32/54 Salaried, 64/13 Professional, 20/11 Other
Simple — Summaries of separate variables	salbeg / salnow: 8444.91 13748.91; 19693.94 21218.94; 18022.26 22132.26; 13237.79 15397.79; 17020.25 41650.25; 7244.71 10294.71	N = 194 Beginning Salary, 194 Current Salary

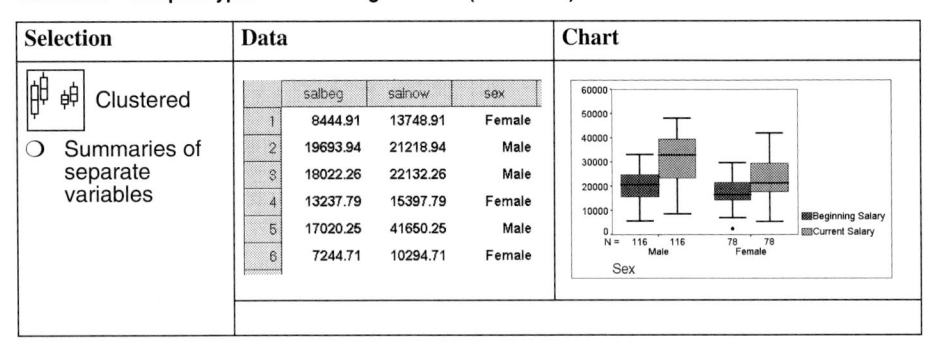

Table 24.1 Boxplot types and data organization (Continued)

Selection	Data	Chart
Clustered — Summaries of separate variables	salbeg / salnow / sex: 1 8444.91 13748.91 Female 2 19693.94 21218.94 Male 3 18022.26 22132.26 Male 4 13237.79 15397.79 Female 5 17020.25 41650.25 Male 6 7244.71 10294.71 Female	Clustered boxplot of Beginning Salary and Current Salary by Sex (N = 116 Male, 78 Female)

Defining Boxplots

Each combination of boxplot type and data structure produces a different definition dialog box. Each is discussed briefly below. The icon and section title indicate the choices that have to be made in the Boxplot dialog box to open that chart definition dialog box. The discussion for each boxplot type always describes the selection required to enable the OK pushbutton. The simple chart for each data structure briefly describes the optional selections unique to that data structure.

Simple:
Summaries for groups of cases

Figure 24.5 shows a simple boxplot with summaries for groups of cases. The specifications are on the left and the resulting chart is on the right.

Figure 24.5 Simple boxplot of groups of cases

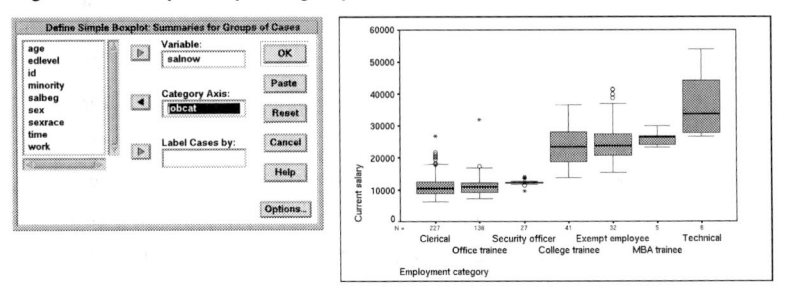

The minimum specifications are:
- A variable to be summarized.
- A category axis variable.

The numeric, short string, and long string variables in your data file are displayed on the source variable list. Select the numeric variable you want summarized and the variable you want to use to define the categories. To get a simple boxplot showing the distribution of cases in each category, click on OK.

Variable. Select a numeric variable to be summarized.

Category Axis. Select a variable to define the categories shown in the boxplot. There is one boxplot for each value of the variable.

Label Cases by. Select a variable whose value labels are to be used to label outliers and extremes. For example, if the boxplot variable is *salnow* and cases are labeled by *sex* and the third case is an outlier, the boxplot will indicate the sex of the person with that outlier salary. If this field is left blank, case numbers are used to label outliers and extremes. If two outliers or extremes have the same value but different case labels, no label is displayed. In the Chart Editor, you can turn off labels altogether, as was done in Figure 24.5.

Clustered:
Summaries for groups of cases

Figure 24.6 shows a clustered boxplot with summaries for groups of cases. The specifications are on the left and the resulting boxplot is on the right.

Figure 24.6 Clustered boxplot of groups of cases

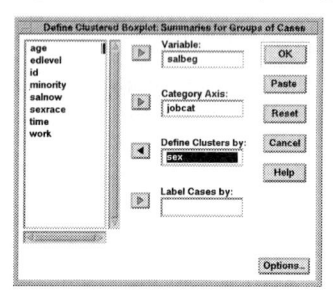

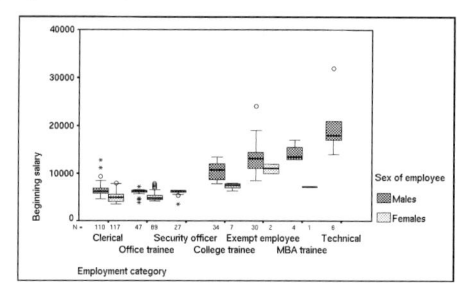

The minimum specifications are:
- A variable to be summarized.
- A category axis variable.
- A cluster variable.

Define Clusters by. Select a variable to define the boxplots within each cluster. In each cluster, there is one boxplot for each value of the variable. A cluster variable must be selected to enable the OK pushbutton.

Simple:
Summaries of separate variables

Figure 24.7 shows a simple boxplot with summaries of separate variables. The specifications are on the left and the resulting boxplot is on the right.

Figure 24.7 Simple boxplot of separate variables

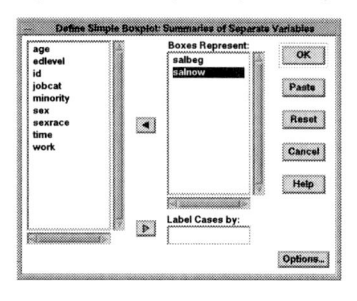

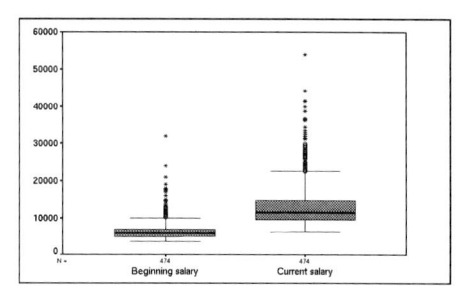

The minimum specifications are two or more box variables.

The numeric, string, and long string variables in your data file are displayed on the source variable list. Select the numeric variables you want to define the boxplots. To get a simple boxplot showing the distribution of each variable in default format, click on OK.

Boxes Represent. Select two or more variables to define the boxplots shown in the chart. There is one boxplot for each variable. Two or more box variables must be selected to enable the OK pushbutton.

Clustered:
Summaries of separate variables

Figure 24.8 shows a clustered boxplot of separate variables. The specifications are on the left and the resulting boxplot is on the right.

Figure 24.8 Clustered boxplot of separate variables

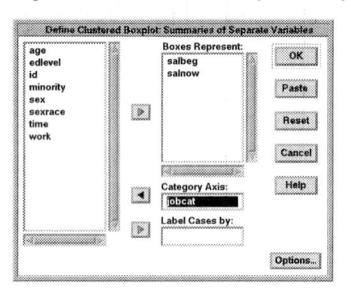

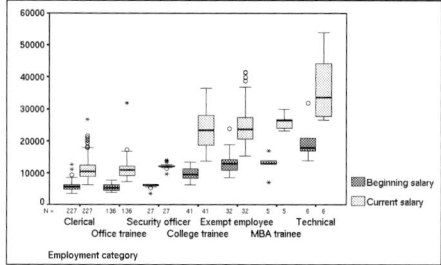

The minimum specification are:
- Two or more box variables.
- A category axis variable.

Category Axis. Select a variable to define the categories shown in the boxplot. There is one cluster of boxplots for each value of the variable. A category axis variable must be selected to enable the OK pushbutton.

25 Scatterplots and Histograms

Summaries that describe data are useful, but nothing beats taking a look at the actual values. You wouldn't consider buying a house based solely on an appraiser's report. You know that there's much more to a house than square footage and number of rooms. Similarly, you shouldn't draw conclusions about data based only on summary statistics, such as the mean and the correlation coefficient. Your data have a story that only a picture can tell.

In Chapter 7 and Chapter 9, you saw how histograms and stem-and-leaf plots (from the Frequencies and Explore procedures) are used to examine the distribution of the values of single variables. In this chapter, you'll see how plotting two or more variables together helps you untangle and identify possible relationships.

Further discussion of how to obtain histograms from the Graphs menu is also included.

A Simple Scatterplot

As American corporations come under increasing scrutiny, the compensation paid to CEO's is often described as excessive and unrelated to corporate performance. Let's look at the relationship between 1989 total yearly compensation (in thousands) and profits (in millions). The data are a sample from those published in *Forbes* (1990).

Figure 25.1 is a scatterplot of total compensation (on the vertical axis) and profits (on the horizontal axis). Total compensation does not appear to be strongly related to profits, although there does appear to be a weak positive relationship.

Figure 25.1 Scatterplot of compensation with profits

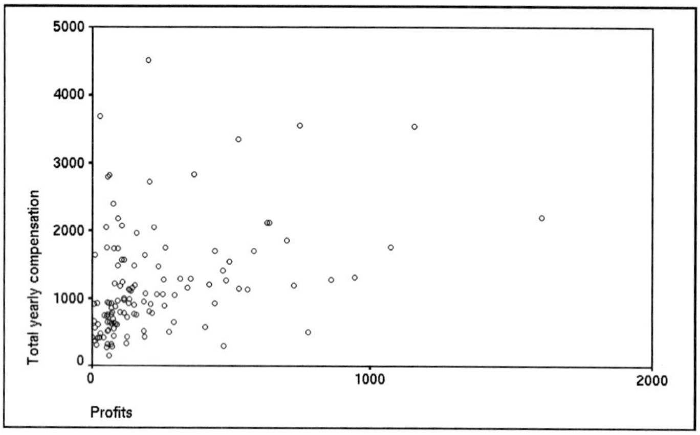

The plot is somewhat difficult to read, since many points overlap in the bottom left corner. Traditionally, in a plotting system with limited resolution, such overlapping points were represented by a numeral that indicated how many cases each point represented. Such numerals, however, don't easily translate to a visual representation of density. You still tend to "see" only one case at each point in the plot.

Cleveland and McGill (1984) proposed that overlapping or nearly overlapping points be represented by **sunflowers**. The idea is fairly simple. You divide the entire plotting grid into equal-sized regions (cells) and count the number of points that fall into each region, just as for a low-resolution plot. Instead of a numeral, you then use the sunflower symbol to display this count. If a cell contains only one point, it is represented by a small circle. If a cell has more than one point, each point is represented by a short line (a "petal") originating from the circle. Optionally, you can specify an integer larger than 1 for the number of cases represented by each petal. (For more details, see Chapter 26.)

The sunflower plot for the CEO compensation data is shown in Figure 25.2.

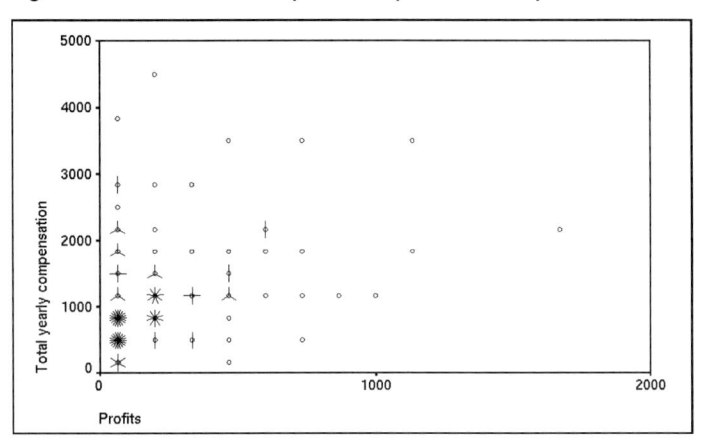

Figure 25.2 Sunflower scatterplot of compensation with profits

You can see that the overlapping points are now represented by sunflowers. It's easy to see where the cases cluster. The more petals on a sunflower, the more cases there are. However, even though it's easier to read the plot now, the relationship between CEO compensation and company profits doesn't appear to be straightforward.

Profits, Growth, and Compensation

Profits are, of course, only one indication of the success of a business, albeit an important one. Variables such as corporate growth are also indicators of a CEO who performs well. Let's look at the relationship between growth, profits, and CEO compensation. Instead of considering the actual values, we'll look at the ranks assigned to the total compensation, profits, and growth for the selected companies. (*Forbes* ranked approximately 800 companies on these variables. A rank of 1 was assigned to the best performer.)

Figure 25.3 is a scatterplot of the ranks of profit and growth for the selected companies.

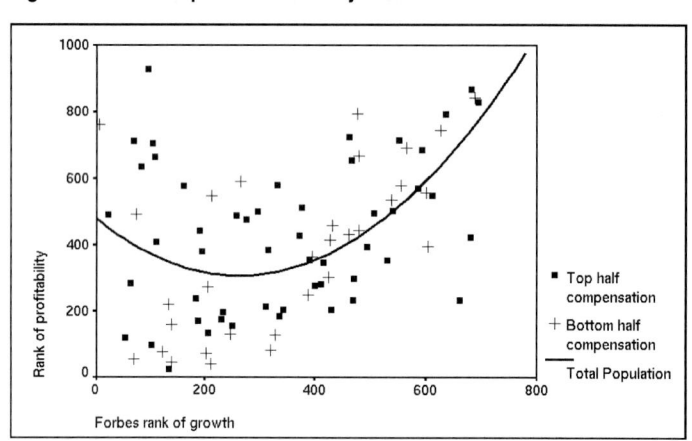

Figure 25.3 Scatterplot with summary curve

In this plot, different markers are used to identify the points in different categories. The squares are for companies with CEO's in the top half of the compensation ratings. The crosses are for companies whose CEO's are in the bottom half of compensation. There is also a summary curve drawn in the plot—a quadratic regression. From Figure 25.3, you see that the relationship between growth and profits is somewhat U-shaped. Once again, there's not a clear relationship between compensation and the other two variables.

If you think that the relationship between growth and profit ranks may be different for the two types of CEO's (high pay and "low" pay), you can draw separate summary curves for the two categories and for the total sample. These are shown in Figure 25.4.

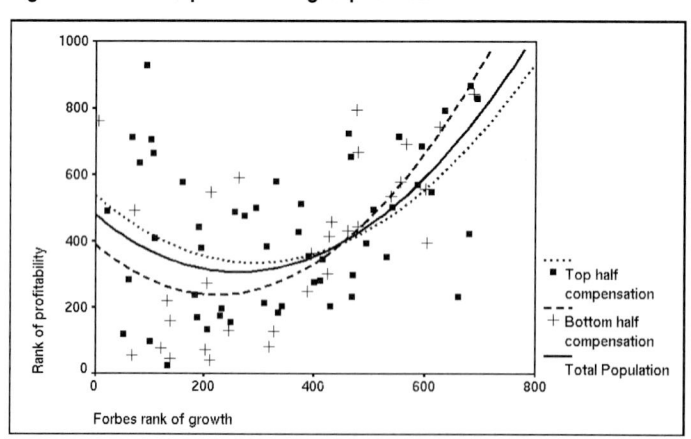

Figure 25.4 Scatterplot with subgroup curves

The relationship between ranks of growth and profits appears to be similar for each of the two categories of CEO's.

Scatterplot Matrices

When you want to examine the relationships between several pairs of variables instead of plotting all pairs separately, you can select a **scatterplot matrix**. Consider Figure 25.5, which is a scatterplot matrix of the ranks of compensation, profits, and growth.

Figure 25.5 Scatterplot matrix with lowess fit lines

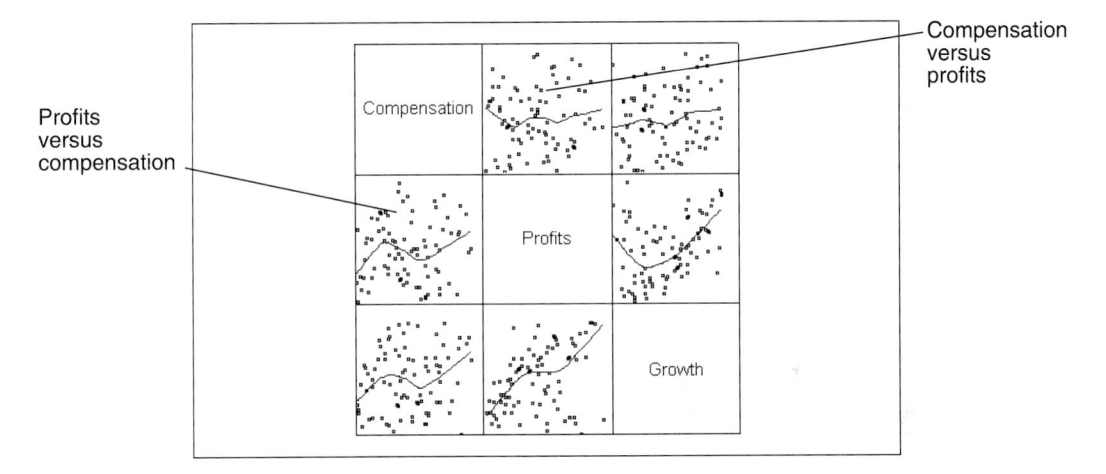

A scatterplot matrix has the same number of rows and columns as there are variables. In this example, the scatterplot matrix contains three rows and three columns. Each cell of the matrix is a plot of a pair of variables. The diagonal cells identify the variables plotted in the other cells. The first diagonal cell contains the label *Compensation*, which tells you that, for all plots in the first row, the rank of total compensation is plotted on the *y* (vertical) axis. For all plots in the first column, the rank of compensation is plotted on the *x* (horizontal) axis. Similarly, the label *Profits* is in the second diagonal cell, indicating that the rank of profits is plotted on the vertical axis for all plots in the second row and on the horizontal axis for all plots in the second column.

Look at the first plot in the first row. It is the plot of compensation (*y* axis) against profits (*x* axis). The second plot in the first row is the plot of compensation (*y* axis) against growth (*x* axis). The easiest way to read a scatterplot matrix is to scan across an entire row or column. For example, if you read across the first row, you see how total compensation relates first to profit and then to growth. The third row tells you how growth relates to compensation and then how growth relates to profitability.

Similarly, the easiest way to identify an individual plot in a scatterplot matrix is to scan up or down to find which variable is on the horizontal axis, and scan right or left to find out which variable is on the vertical axis.

In a scatterplot matrix, all possible pairs of plots are displayed. The plots above the diagonal are the same as the plots below the diagonal. The only difference is that the variables are "flipped." That is, the horizontal and vertical variables are switched. For example, above the diagonal, you see a plot of compensation and profits, where compensation is on the vertical axis and profits is on the horizontal axis. Below the diagonal, you see a plot of profits on the vertical axis and compensation on the horizontal axis.

The scatterplot matrix in Figure 25.5 reinforces our previous conclusions about compensation, profits, and growth. There appears to be little relationship between compensation and either profits or growth. However, there does appear to be a relationship between profits and growth.

Smoothing the Data

The curves added to the plots in the scatterplot matrix help you see possible trends in the data. There are many different lines and curves that can be superimposed on plots. If you know that a linear, quadratic, or cubic regression model fits your data (see Chapter 18), you can plot the appropriate model by choosing Options... from the Chart menu (see "Fit Options" on p. 519 in Chapter 26). If you don't know what kind of model fits your data, you can request lowess smoothing (Chambers et al., 1983).

Lowess smoothing doesn't require you to specify a particular model. Instead, for each value of the independent variable, it computes a predicted value using cases that have similar values for the independent variable. Points that are close to the one being predicted are assigned more importance in the computations. Lowess smoothing is robust, meaning that it isn't affected much by extreme values. That's a desirable property. Lowess smoothing requires many computations, especially for large data sets, so it may take a while for your plots to be drawn.

Plotting in Three Dimensions

So far, all of the plots you have seen in this chapter have been two-dimensional. That is, points are plotted only on two axes. You can also create scatterplots in three dimensions. Consider Figure 25.6, which is a three-dimensional plot of the ranks of compensation, growth, and profits.

Figure 25.6 3-D plot

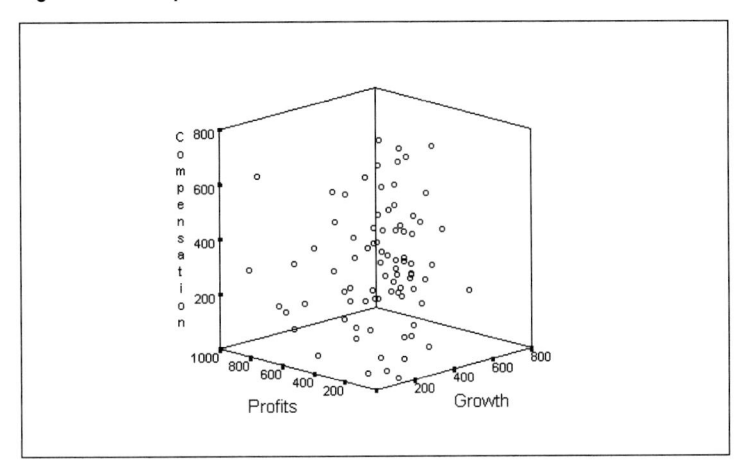

The position of each point is based on its values for all three variables. Unfortunately, since there isn't a strong relationship among the three variables, the plot is not particularly informative.

To see a more interesting three-dimensional plot, consider a hypothetical compensation strategy in which the rank of compensation is simply the average of the ranks of growth and profits. The plot of the hypothetical compensation rank is shown in Figure 25.7 for a sample including approximately a quarter of the cases. The smaller number of cases makes it easier to interpret the plot.

Figure 25.7 3-D plot with hypothetical relationship

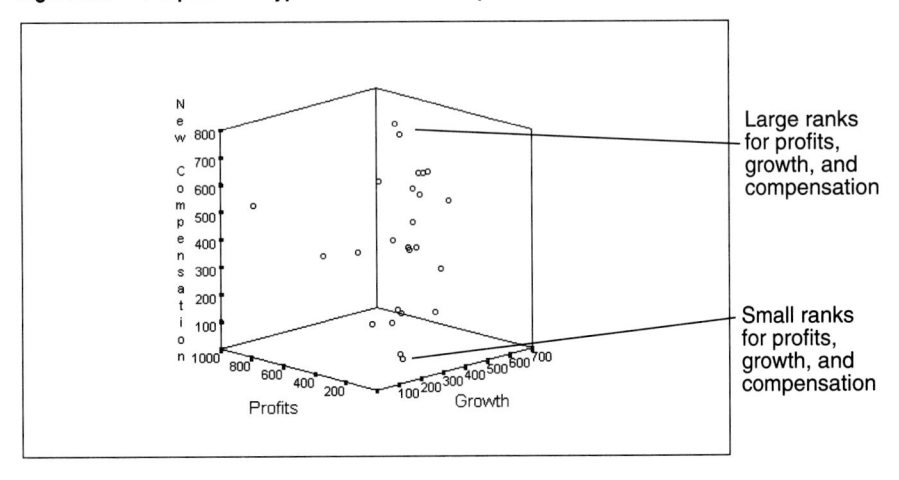

If you examine the plot carefully, you'll see the relationship between the three variables. Cases with low ranks for profits and growth have a low rank for compensation. Similarly, cases with large ranks for profits and growth have large ranks for compensation. Other cases have intermediate values.

It's easier to see the relationship between the three variables if you spin the plot until you notice a pattern. For example, if you spin Figure 25.7, you can obtain Figure 25.8. (See "Using Spin Mode" on p. 569 in Chapter 26.)

Figure 25.8 Previous 3-D plot with spin applied

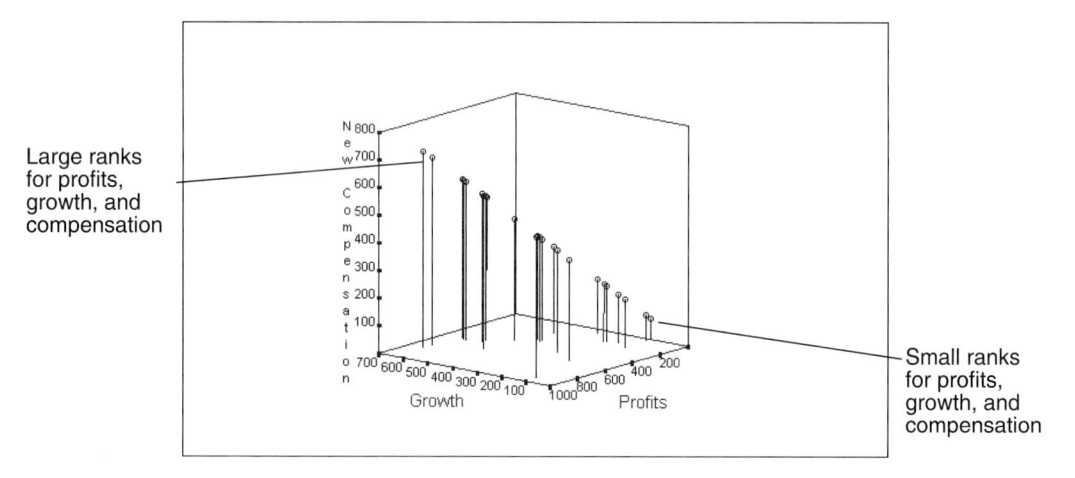

This figure has been further enhanced with **spikes** connecting each point to the floor (the bottom plane of the plot). For information on obtaining spikes, see "3-D Scatterplot Options" on p. 524 in Chapter 26. By looking at the base of a spike, you can see which point on the floor each plotted point is directly above. This strengthens the three-dimensional impression. From this figure, it's easy to see what the relationship is between compensation and the other two variables. Spinning a three-dimensional plot is useful for examining the relationships among the variables, as well as for identifying points that are far removed from the rest.

How to Obtain a Scatterplot

Scatterplots and histograms are graphical ways of looking at the actual values in a data set. In the examples in the remainder of this chapter, a survey of colleges will be used to illustrate most of the scatterplots and histograms you can obtain. Each record in this data set represents a different college. The data show SAT scores of admitted students, tuition, number of students, number of faculty, and other similar statistics. Examples that don't use the college data use the bank data.

To obtain a scatterplot, from the menus choose:

Graph
  Scatter...

This opens the Scatterplot dialog box, as shown in Figure 25.9.

Figure 25.9   Scatterplot dialog box

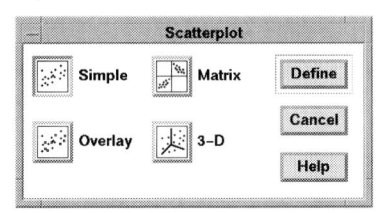

You can choose one of the following scatterplot types:

Simple. Each point represents the values of two variables for each case.

Matrix. Defines a square matrix of simple scatterplots, two for each combination of variables specified.

Overlay. Plots multiple scatterplots in the same frame.

3-D. Each point represents the value of three variables for each case. The points are plotted in a 3-D coordinate system that can be rotated.

Defining Simple Scatterplots

To obtain a simple scatterplot, select the Simple picture button in the Scatterplot dialog box and click on Define. This opens the Simple Scatterplot dialog box, as shown in Figure 25.10. The specifications are on the left and the resulting scatterplot is on the right.

Figure 25.10 Simple Scatterplot dialog box and chart

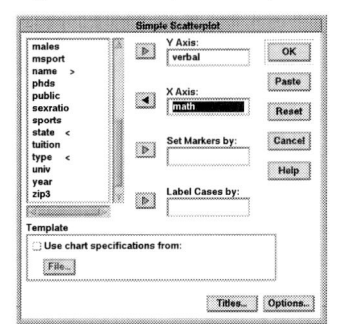

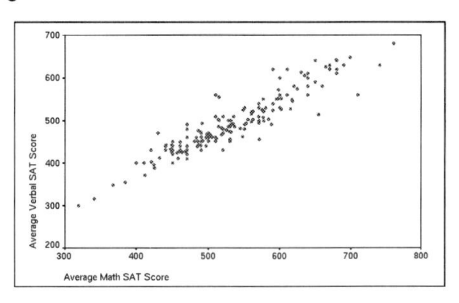

The minimum specifications are:
- An *x* axis variable.
- A *y* axis variable.

The numeric, short string, and long string variables in your data file are displayed on the source variable list. Select the numeric variables you want to define the *x* and *y* axes. To get a simple scatterplot in default format, click on OK.

Optionally, you can divide the scatterplot points into groups, label each point, use a template to control the format of the scatterplot, add a title, subtitle, or footnote, or change the missing value options.

Y Axis. Select the variable that will determine the vertical position of each point.

X Axis. Select the variable that will determine the horizontal position of each point.

Set Markers by. Select a variable to determine the categories that will be shown in the chart. Each value of the variable is a different color or marker symbol in the scatterplot.

Label Cases by. Select a variable to provide labels for each marker. The value label of each case is placed above the point in the scatterplot. If there is no value label, the actual value will be placed above the point. The value label displayed is truncated after the 20th character.

Template. You can use another file to define the format of your charts (see "Chart Templates" on p. 426 in Chapter 22).

Titles. You can add titles, subtitles, and footnotes to your charts (see "Titles, Subtitles, and Footnotes" on p. 422 in Chapter 22).

Options. You can exclude cases with missing values listwise or by variable. You can also display groups defined by missing values. For more details, see "Missing Values" on p. 423 in Chapter 22.

Defining Scatterplot Matrices

To obtain a scatterplot matrix, select Matrix in the Scatterplot dialog box and click on Define. This opens the Scatterplot Matrix dialog box, as shown in Figure 25.11. The specifications are on the left and the resulting scatterplot is on the right.

Figure 25.11 Scatterplot Matrix dialog box and chart

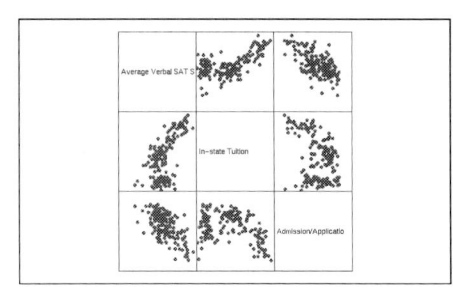

The minimum specification is two or more matrix variables.

The numeric, short string, and long string variables in your data file are displayed on the source variable list. Select two or more numeric variables to define the cells of the matrix. To get a scatterplot matrix in the default format, click on OK.

Optionally, you can show different markers for different categories, use a template to control the format of the scatterplot, or add a title, subtitle, or footnote.

Matrix Variables. Select two or more variables to define the cells of the matrix. There is one row and one column for each variable. Each cell contains a simple scatterplot of the row variable and the column variable.

Set Markers by. Select a variable to determine the categories that will be shown in the chart. Each value of the variable is a different marker symbol in the scatterplot matrix.

Label Cases by. Select a variable to provide labels for each marker. The value label of each case is placed above the point in the scatterplot. If there is no value label, the actual value will be placed above the point. The value label displayed is truncated after the 20th character.

Template. You can use another file to define the format of your charts (see "Chart Templates" on p. 426 in Chapter 22).

Titles. You can add titles, subtitles, and footnotes to your charts (see "Titles, Subtitles, and Footnotes" on p. 422 in Chapter 22).

Options. You can exclude cases with missing values listwise or by variable. You can also display groups defined by missing values. For more details, see "Missing Values" on p. 423 in Chapter 22.

Defining Overlay Scatterplots

To obtain an overlay scatterplot, select Overlay in the Scatterplot dialog box and click on Define. This opens the Overlay Scatterplot dialog box, as shown in Figure 25.12. The specifications are on the left and the resulting overlay scatterplot is on the right.

Figure 25.12 Overlay Scatterplot dialog box and chart

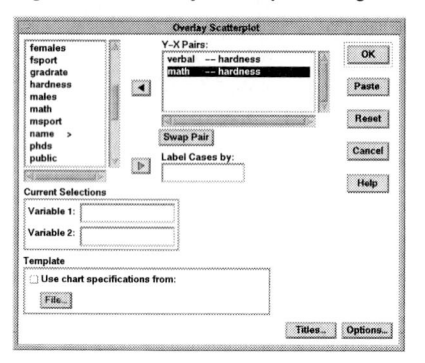

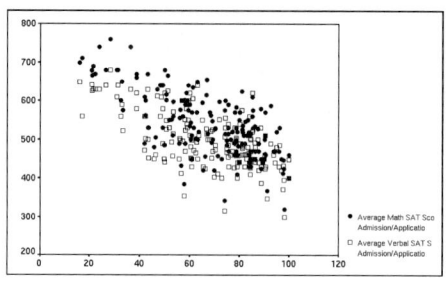

The minimum specification is two or more *y-x* pairs.

The numeric, short string, and long string variables in your data file are displayed on the source variable list. Select two or more numeric *y-x* variable pairs. To get an overlay scatterplot in default format, click on OK.

Optionally, you can label the scatterplot points, use a template to control the format of the scatterplot, or add a title, subtitle, or footnote.

Y-X Pairs. Select two or more variable pairs. Each pair of variables is plotted in the same scatterplot with a separate marker symbol. To select a variable pair, highlight two variables on the source variable list by clicking on each one. The selected variables are indicated on the Current Selections list. Click on the ▶ pushbutton. This copies the variables from the Current Selection list to the *y-x* pairs list. The same variable may be selected in multiple variable pairs. To swap the *y* and *x* variables in a *y-x* pair, highlight the pair and click on Swap Pair.

Label Cases by. Select a variable to provide labels for each marker. The value label of each case is placed beside the point in the scatterplot. If there is no value label, the actual value will be placed beside the point. The value label displayed is truncated after the 20th character.

Template. You can use another file to define the format of your charts (see "Chart Templates" on p. 426 in Chapter 22).

Titles. You can add titles, subtitles, and footnotes to your charts (see "Titles, Subtitles, and Footnotes" on p. 422 in Chapter 22).

Options. You can exclude cases with missing values listwise or by variable. You can also display groups defined by missing values. For more details, see "Missing Values" on p. 423 in Chapter 22.

Defining 3-D Scatterplots

To obtain a 3-D scatterplot, select 3-D in the Scatterplot dialog box and click on Define. This opens the 3-D Scatterplot dialog box, as shown in Figure 25.13. The specifications are on the left and the resulting 3-D scatterplot is on the right.

Figure 25.13 3-D Scatterplot dialog box and chart

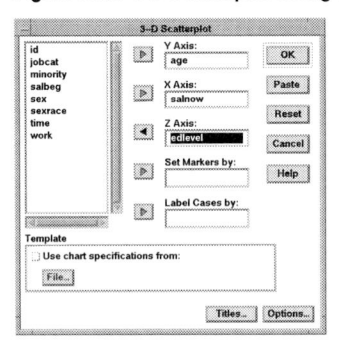

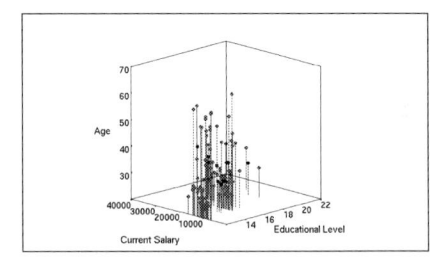

The minimum specifications are:
- A *y* axis variable.
- An *x* axis variable.
- A *z* axis variable.

The numeric, short string, and long string variables in your data file are displayed on the source variable list. Select the numeric variables you want to define the *z*, *y*, and *x* axes. To get a 3-D scatterplot in default format, click on OK.

Optionally, you can show different markers for different categories, label each point, use a template to control the format of the scatterplot, and add a title, subtitle, and footnote.

Y Axis. Select the variable that will determine the height of each point.

X Axis. Select the variable that will determine the horizontal position of each point.

Z Axis. Select the variable that will determine the depth of each point.

Set Markers by. Select a variable to determine the categories that will be shown in the chart. Each value of the variable is a different marker symbol in the scatterplot.

Label Cases by. Select a variable to provide labels for each marker. The value label of each case is placed beside the point in the scatterplot. If there is no value label, the actual value will be placed beside the point. The value label displayed is truncated after the 20th character.

Template. You can use another file to define the format of your charts (see "Chart Templates" on p. 426 in Chapter 22).

Titles. You can add titles, subtitles, and footnotes to your charts (see "Titles, Subtitles, and Footnotes" on p. 422 in Chapter 22).

Options. You can exclude cases with missing values listwise or by variable. You can also display groups defined by missing values. For more details, see "Missing Values" on p. 423 in Chapter 22.

How to Obtain a Histogram

For a discussion of how to interpret histograms, see Chapter 7. To obtain a histogram, from the menus choose:

Graphs
   Histogram...

This opens the Histogram dialog box, as shown in Figure 25.14.

Figure 25.14 Histogram dialog box and chart

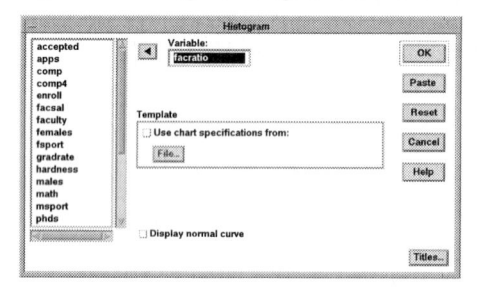

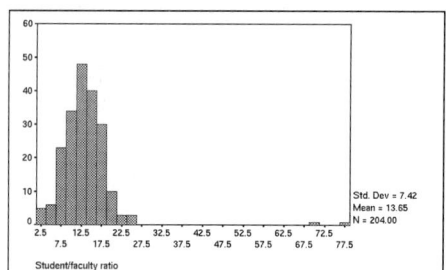

The minimum specification is a variable.

The numeric variables in your data file are displayed on the source variable list. Select the variable for which you want a histogram. To get a histogram in the default format, as shown above, click on OK.

Optionally, you can use a template to control the format of the histogram, add a title, subtitle, or footnote, or superimpose a normal curve on the histogram.

Variable. Select the variable for which you want a histogram. By default, you get bars showing the data divided into several evenly spaced intervals. The height of each bar shows the number of cases in each interval. The data series used to create the bar chart contains the individual values of each case. This means you can alter the intervals shown in the bar chart from the Chart Editor.

Template. You can use another file to define the format of your charts (see "Chart Templates" on p. 426 in Chapter 22).

Display normal curve. Select this to superimpose on the histogram a normal curve with the same mean and variance as your data.

Titles. You can add titles, subtitles, and footnotes to your charts (see "Titles, Subtitles, and Footnotes" on p. 422 in Chapter 22).

26 Modifying Charts

After creating a chart and viewing it in the Chart Carousel, you may wish to modify it either to obtain more information about the data or to enhance the chart for presentation. The chart modification capabilities of SPSS allow you to select data, change chart types, add information, and alter chart appearance to accomplish both of those goals.

Two brief examples are given in this chapter. The first example illustrates a process for exploring data relationships graphically; the second, enhancing a bar chart for presentation. Another example, the tutorial in Chapter 22, describes explicit steps for creating and enhancing a bar chart.

Following the two examples in this chapter, detailed explanations of the chart editing menus and dialog boxes are presented. A table summarizing the chapter is provided on p. 570 to help you locate information on specific chart modification facilities.

Exploring Data with the Chart Editor

Figure 26.1 shows a preliminary scatterplot matrix of graduation rate, verbal SAT score, and student-faculty ratio in 250 colleges and universities.

Figure 26.1 Scatterplot matrix of gradrate, verbal, and facratio

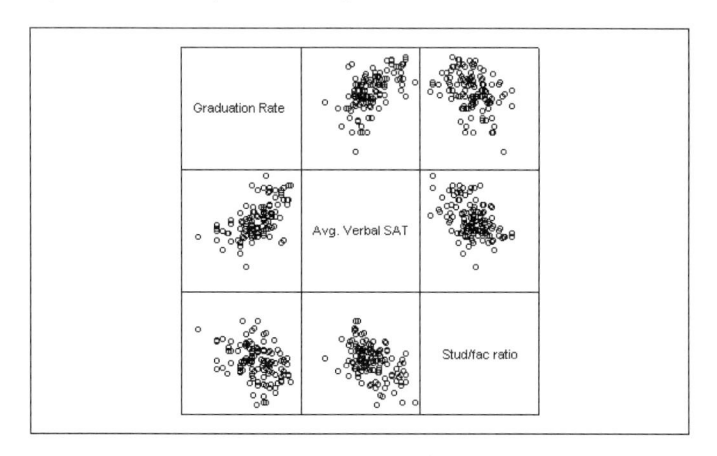

Two of the available options for scatterplots, adding axis labels and linear regression lines, help make relationships more apparent. In Figure 26.2, labels and regression lines have been added.

Figure 26.2 Scatterplot matrix with labels and regression lines

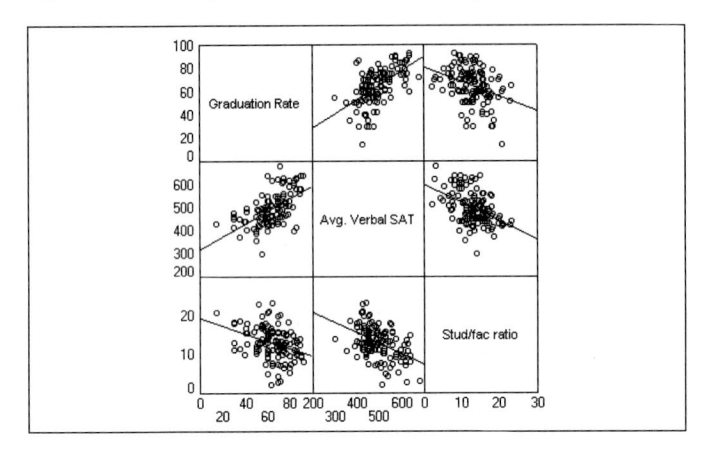

For a closer look at the relationship between schools' graduation rates and the average SAT verbal test scores of their students, we can turn to the Gallery menu and select a bivariate (simple) scatterplot of those variables. In the bivariate scatterplot, we can see more detail and display R^2 (Figure 26.3).

Figure 26.3 Scatterplot of gradrate by verbal

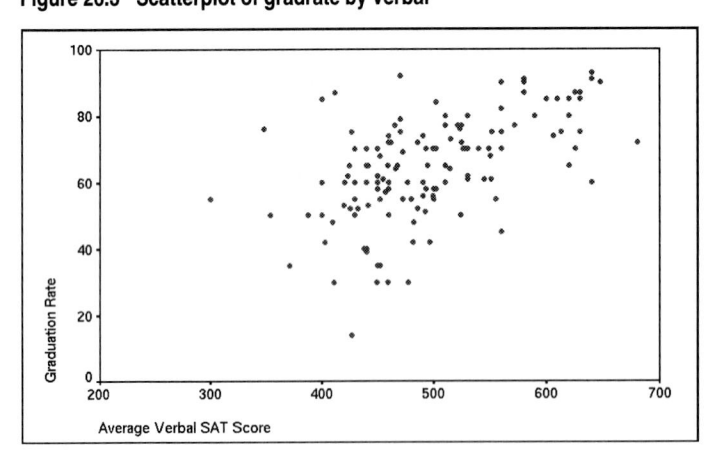

We might want to look more closely at the univariate distribution of the two variables, which we can do by returning to the Gallery menu and selecting histogram (Figure 26.4).

Figure 26.4 Histograms of verbal and gradrate

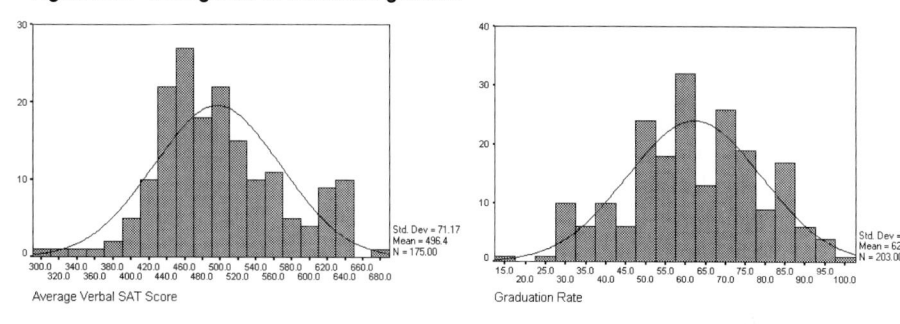

Enhancing Charts for Presentation

Although charts as originally generated by SPSS contain the requested information in a logical format, they may require some changes to make the presentation clearer or more dramatic. Figure 26.5 is the unedited clustered bar chart of *verbal* and *math* (the average verbal and math SAT scores for each university) by *comp* (level of competitiveness).

Figure 26.5 Default bar chart of verbal and math by comp

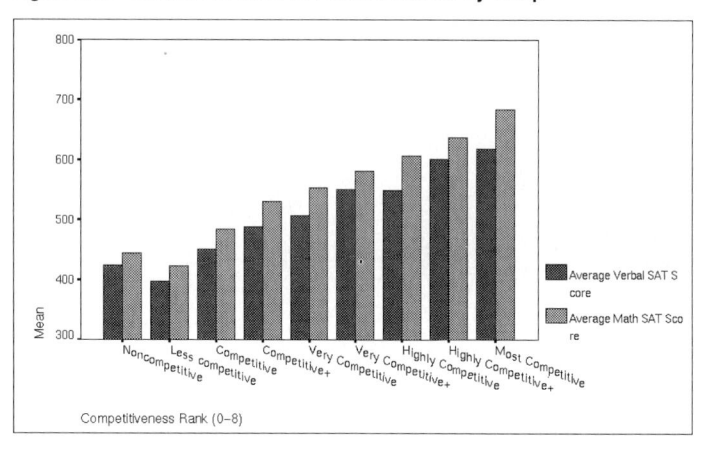

While the information is clear, at least some changes are desirable to prepare the chart for presentation. The following modifications create the chart shown in Figure 26.6:

- A title and subtitle are added.
- 3-D effect is selected for the bars.
- The cluster spacing is widened.
- Both axis titles are removed, since the information they contain appears elsewhere in the chart. This allows more room for the chart itself and the chart enlarges itself automatically.
- The noncompetitive category is removed.
- Several labels are removed from the category axis and the orientation of the remaining labels is changed. This makes the labels easier to read, and yet they still convey the essential information.
- The legend labels are edited to remove unnecessary information.
- The range of the scale axis is enlarged to start at 200, the lowest possible SAT score, in order to give a better representation of the relative differences between schools in each competitiveness level.
- Annotations are added to indicate the overall averages for the two SAT tests. (These averages are easily obtained by leaving the chart window for a moment to run descriptive statistics from the Statistics menu.)

Figure 26.6 Enhanced bar chart

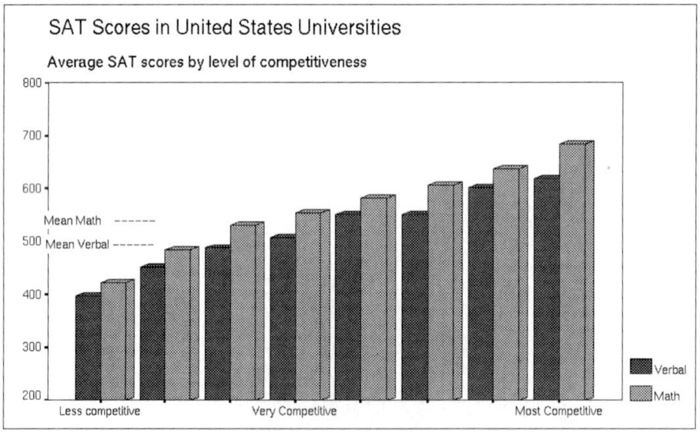

Figure 26.7 shows further bar chart variations:
- The axes, tick marks, and inner frame have been removed.
- Grid lines have been added.
- The sides and tops of the bars have been shaded a different color to enhance the 3-D effect.

- Inter-cluster spacing has been increased.
- The annotation indicating overall averages has been refined.

Figure 26.7 Another bar chart variation

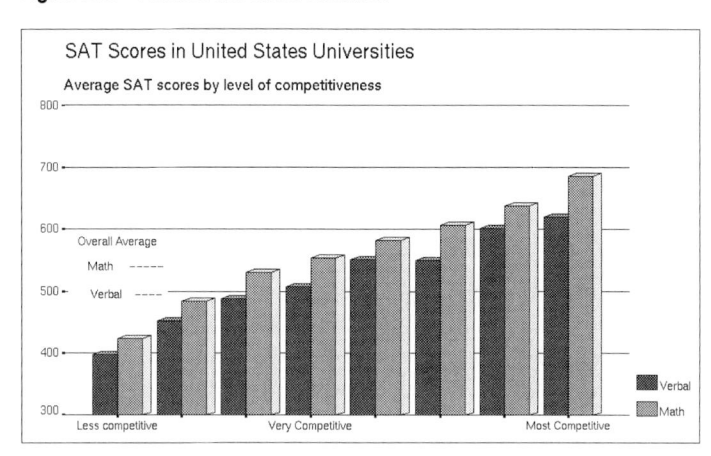

Editing in a Chart Window

All modifications to charts are done in a chart window. You open a chart window by selecting Edit from the Chart Carousel or by opening a previously saved chart from the File menu. Closing a chart window closes the chart.

Several chart windows can be open at the same time, each containing a single chart. The exact number depends on your system and on how many other windows are open at the time. If you see a message telling you there are not enough system resources, you can close some windows to free resources.

Chart Menus

A chart window displays the Chart Editor menu bar, as shown in Figure 26.8.

Figure 26.8 Chart Editor menu bar

| File View Options Gallery Chart Series Attributes | Help |

The Chart Editor menu bar contains eight menus:

File. From the File menu you can save the chart, print it, or apply specifications from an existing chart template.

If you choose Save and get an I/O error, check (without exiting from SPSS) to see if you have run out of disk space. If so, delete some files you don't need and try to save the chart again.

View. From the View menu, you can refresh the screen (that is, redraw the displayed chart). You can also bring another SPSS window to the front of the display by selecting Raise Document Window.

Options. From the Options menu, you can hide or display the icon bar.

Gallery. From the Gallery menu, you can select another compatible chart type to display the data in your chart. After selecting a new chart type, you can click on Replace to replace the current chart or click on New to create another chart in a new window. See "Changing Chart Types (Gallery Menu)" on p. 506 for more information.

Chart. From the Chart menu, you can modify many of the layout and labeling characteristics of your chart, such as the scaling and labeling of axes; all titles and labels; inner and outer frames; and whether the chart should expand to fill areas where titles are not assigned. See "Modifying Chart Elements (Chart Menu)" on p. 510 for more information.

Series. From the Series menu, you can select to display or omit data series and categories. Only data elements present in the original chart can be included. For bar, line, and area charts, you can select whether each series should be displayed as a line, an area, or a set of bars. See "Selecting and Arranging Data (Series Menu)" on p. 548 for more information.

Attributes. From the Attributes menu, you can open a set of palettes from which you can select fill patterns, colors, line styles, bar styles, bar label styles (for displaying values within bars), interpolation types, and text fonts and sizes. To use these, you must have a mouse, with which you click on the element whose attributes you want to change. Then you can make a selection from any appropriate palette. You can also swap axes of plots and rotate 3-D scatterplots. The Attributes menu choices are duplicated on the chart window icon bar so you can select them quickly with the mouse. See "Modifying Attributes (Attributes Menu)" on p. 556 for more information.

Help. The Help menu provides the same access to help as it does throughout the system.

Selecting Objects to Modify

The objects that make up a chart fall into two general categories:

- **Series objects** are the bars, lines, and markers that represent the data. They are always selected and manipulated as a series.
- **Chart objects** are the layout and labeling components of the chart—everything other than the series objects.

To modify one of these objects, double-click on it in the chart. If you double-click on a series object, the Displayed Data dialog box for the current chart type is opened (see "Selecting and Arranging Data (Series Menu)" on p. 548). If you double-click on a chart object, one of the dialog boxes from the Chart menu is opened: Axis if you have selected an axis, Title if you have selected a title, and so on (see "Modifying Chart Elements (Chart Menu)" on p. 510). If you double-click on an object for which a specific dialog box does not exist, or if you double-click away from any object, the Options dialog box for the current chart type is opened.

Instead of double-clicking on objects, you can open the series dialog boxes from the Series and Chart menus. A few items on those menus can be accessed only from the menus, not by double-clicking on an object or clicking on an icon.

The following items are available only from the Chart menu:
- Bar Spacing.
- Title, Footnote, and Annotation (when none appears in the chart).
- Toggles for the Inner Frame and Outer Frame.

The following item is available only from the Series menu:
- Transpose Data.

Both series and chart objects have **attributes** such as color and pattern. To modify the attributes of an object, select the object with a single mouse click. There is no keyboard mechanism for selecting objects. If the object is within the chart itself, **handles** (small, solid-black rectangles) indicate which object is selected. For objects outside the chart axes, such as titles or labels, a **selection rectangle** indicates that an object is selected. Selection of an inner or outer frame is indicated by handles.

Applying Attributes

After an object is selected, select a palette from the Attributes menu or from the icon bar. Figure 26.9 shows handles and the Colors palette. Select the quality (color, pattern, style, etc.) you want to apply to the selected object, and click on Apply. You can apply attributes from as many palettes as you choose; the object stays selected until you select another or click somewhere away from any object. Palettes remain open until you close them. You can leave a palette open while you select and modify different objects. See "Modifying Attributes (Attributes Menu)" on p. 556 for more details.

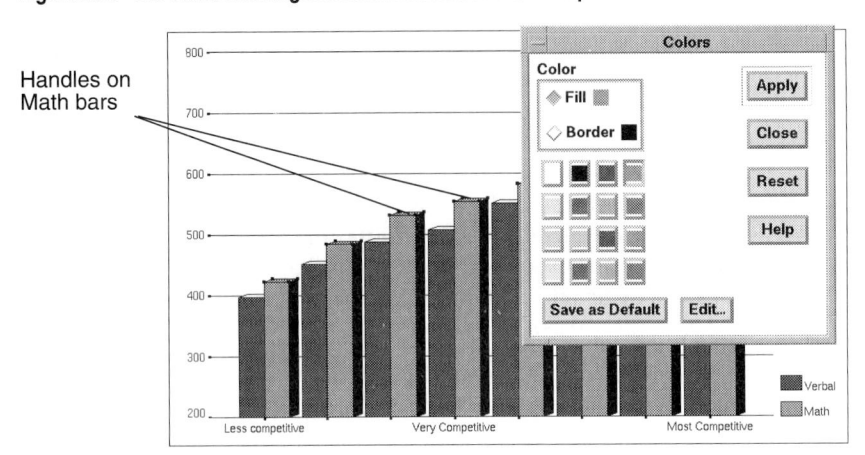

Figure 26.9 Bar chart showing selection handles and Colors palette

Changing Chart Types (Gallery Menu)

The Gallery menu allows you to change from one chart type to another. The choices are primarily the same as those available from the Graph menu, with a few additions. (See Chapter 23 to Chapter 25 for detailed descriptions of chart types.)

Additional Chart Types

Some types of charts are available only after you have created a chart. These include mixed charts, drop-line charts, and exploded pie charts.

Mixed Charts. Mixed charts are available on the Gallery menu. You can have bars, lines, and areas, all in the same chart, after defining a bar, line, or area multiple-series chart. Figure 26.10 is an example of a mixed chart with both bars and lines.

Figure 26.10 Mixed chart

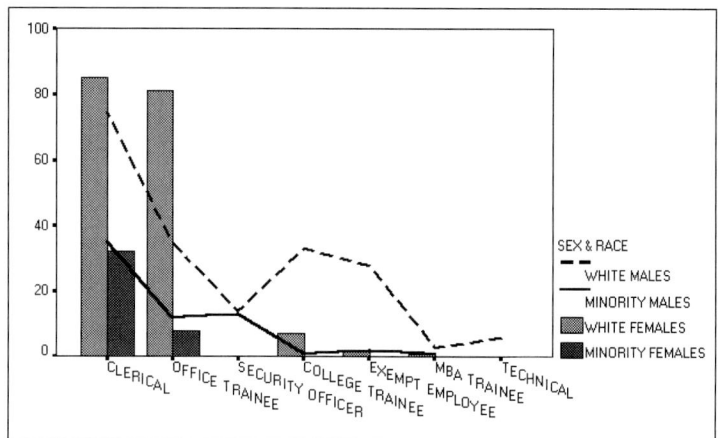

You can also define a mixed chart by choosing:

Series
 Displayed...

from the menus. For more information on mixed charts, see "Selecting and Arranging Data (Series Menu)" on p. 548.

Drop-line Charts. Drop-line charts can be generated from the Line Charts dialog box. To open the dialog box, from the menus choose:

Gallery
 Line...

A drop-line chart has no interpolation between points on a line, and vertical lines connect points in the same category. The chart in Figure 26.11 is a drop-line chart that was derived from the chart in Figure 26.6.

You can also define a drop-line chart from a multiple-line chart by suppressing the interpolation (see "Line Interpolation" on p. 563) and connecting the markers within categories (see "Bar/Line/Area Options" on p. 511).

Figure 26.11 Drop-line chart

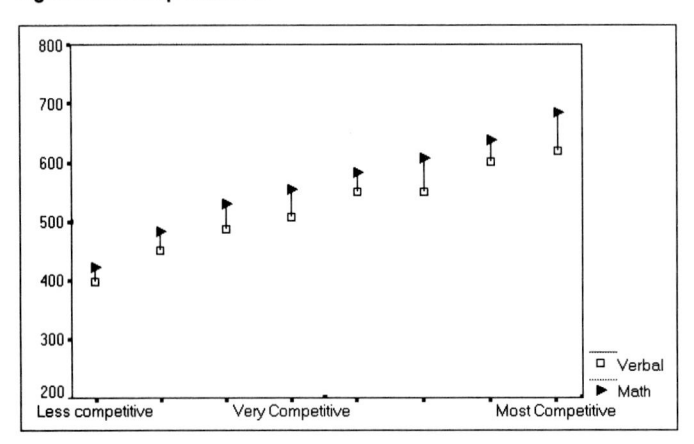

Exploded Pie Charts. Exploded pie charts can be generated from the Pie Charts dialog box. To explode all slices of a pie chart at once, from the menus choose:

Gallery
  Pie...

This opens the Pie Charts dialog box. Click on Exploded and then click on Replace or New. Each slice of the pie is moved outward from the center along a radius, as shown in Figure 26.12.

Figure 26.12 Exploded pie chart

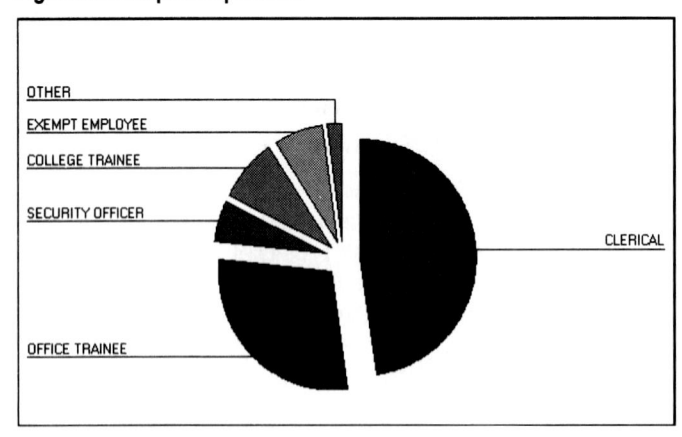

Changing Types

You can change freely among chart types, with the following restrictions:
- You must have enough data to draw the selected chart. Thus, you cannot change from a simple bar chart to a clustered bar chart if you have only one data series defined. However, if your original chart had more than one series, and you omitted all but one of those series to obtain the simple bar, you can change to a chart that requires multiple series. See "Selecting and Arranging Data (Series Menu)" on p. 548 for information on selecting series.
- You cannot change in either direction between categorical charts (bar, line, area, and pie charts) and plots based on casewise data (scatterplots and histograms).
- You cannot change from or into a boxplot. Thus, boxplot is not on the Gallery menu.

If there is an obvious transition between the display of series in the current chart and the display of series in the selected chart, the new chart is drawn automatically. If not, the Displayed Data dialog box for the new chart opens for you to indicate how to display the series. For example:
- Changing from a single-series chart such as a simple bar, simple line, or pie, to another single-series chart is automatic.
- Changing from a clustered bar chart to a simple bar chart opens a Displayed Data dialog box for you to indicate which series to plot.
- Changing from a clustered or stacked bar chart to a multiple-line chart is automatic. All series in the bar chart are plotted as lines.
- Changing from a simple bar chart to a multiple-line chart opens a Displayed Data dialog box if you have series from your original chart not displayed in the simple bar chart. See "Selecting and Arranging Data (Series Menu)" on p. 548 on omitting and restoring series.
- Changing from a 3-D scatterplot to a scatterplot matrix is automatic. Changing from a scatterplot matrix to a simple scatterplot opens Displayed Data.
- Changing into a mixed chart type always opens the Bar/Line/Area Displayed Data dialog box for you to indicate which series are to be displayed as bars, areas, or lines.

You can change among bar, line, and area charts and create mixed charts within the Bar/Line/Area Displayed Data dialog box without using the Gallery (see "Bar, Line, and Area Chart Displayed Data" on p. 549). You can create simple bar, line, or area charts from multiple versions of the charts by omitting all but one series. You can also change between stacked bars and clustered bars in the Bar/Line/Area Options dialog box (see "Bar/Line/Area Options" on p. 511). To change to a pie chart, however, you must use the Gallery.

You cannot change among scatterplot types by adding or deleting series; you must use the Gallery. For example, if you omit all but two series in a matrix scatterplot, you are left with a 2 × 2 matrix. To make a simple scatterplot from the same data, from the menus choose:

Gallery
  Scatter...
    Simple

Each type of scatterplot has its own Displayed Data dialog box. See "Bar, Line, and Area Chart Displayed Data" on p. 549 through "Histogram Displayed Data" on p. 555 for more information.

Inheritance of Attributes and Other Chart Elements

When you change from one chart type to another, if an attribute in the current chart is applicable to the new chart, it is preserved. For example, if you change from clustered bars to multiple lines, the series represented by red bars is now represented by a red line and the green bars translate to a green line.

If a change in displayed data or in chart type makes a current chart specification invalid, that specification is set to the default. For example, suppose you are changing a clustered bar chart to a stacked bar chart. The range and increment on the scale axis are no longer valid and the stacked bar defaults are used.

Modifying Chart Elements (Chart Menu)

This section explains how to modify the layout and annotation of your chart by accessing dialog boxes available from the Chart menu (Figure 26.13). For changes to data elements (removing and restoring series and/or categories), see "Selecting and Arranging Data (Series Menu)" on p. 548; for changes you can make to the color and style of objects, see "Modifying Attributes (Attributes Menu)" on p. 556.

From the Chart menu, you can:

- Alter the arrangement of the display or connect data points.
- Fit a variety of curves.
- Alter the scale, range, appearance, and labels of either axis, if appropriate.
- Adjust spacing between bars and between clusters of bars.
- Move the origin line in a bar chart to show how data values fall above and below the new origin line.
- Add or remove, outside the chart itself, a one- or two-line title, a subtitle, and footnotes, any of which can be left-justified, centered, or right-justified.
- Suppress or edit the legend.
- Add annotation text, at any position in the plot area, framed or unframed.

- Add horizontal and vertical reference lines.
- Add or remove the inner frame or outer frame.

Figure 26.13 Chart menu

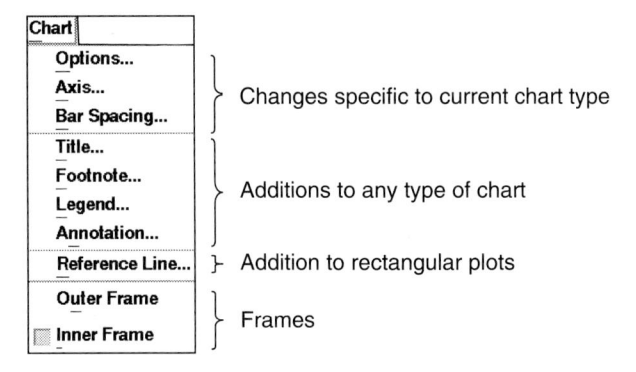

```
Chart
  Options...      ⎫
  Axis...         ⎬  Changes specific to current chart type
  Bar Spacing...  ⎭
  Title...        ⎫
  Footnote...     ⎬  Additions to any type of chart
  Legend...       ⎪
  Annotation...   ⎭
  Reference Line... ⎬ Addition to rectangular plots
  Outer Frame     ⎫
                  ⎬  Frames
  Inner Frame     ⎭
```

The three menu choices at the top of the Chart menu (Figure 26.13) help you modify the objects in the chart itself. For example, if you choose Options... when a line chart is displayed, the Bar/Line/Area Options dialog box opens, whereas if you choose Options... when a scatterplot is displayed, the Scatterplot Options dialog box opens.

The next four menu choices—Title..., Footnote..., Legend..., and Annotation...—are used to add information to many types of charts. Reference lines (the next choice) can be added to most rectangular charts.

The last two choices control the display of frames.

Accessing Chart Options

The Options dialog box appropriate to the type of chart is determined by the system. You can access options in one of two ways:

- From the menus choose:

  Chart
    Options...

  or

- Double-click in an area of the chart away from the chart objects.

Bar/Line/Area Options

To change options for a bar, line, or area chart, double-click away from the chart objects, or from the menus choose:

Chart
  Options...

This opens the Bar/Line/Area Options dialog box, as shown in Figure 26.14.

Figure 26.14 Bar/Line/Area Options dialog box (bar chart active)

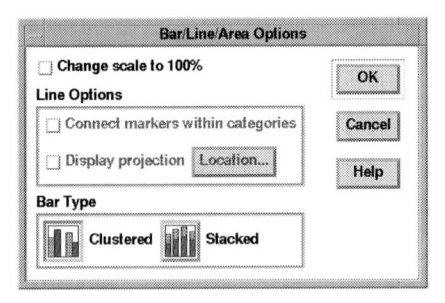

For bar or area charts, you can change the scale axis to percentage representation.

- **Change scale to 100%.** In a bar chart, this option automatically stacks the bars and changes each resulting bar to the same total length, representing 100% for the category (Figure 26.15). In an area chart, the total distance from the axis, representing 100%, is the same for each category. This feature is useful for comparing the relative percentages of different categories.

Figure 26.15 Stacked and 100% stacked bar charts

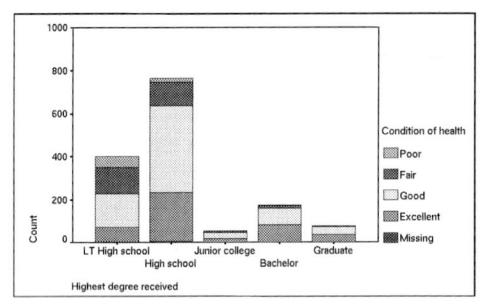

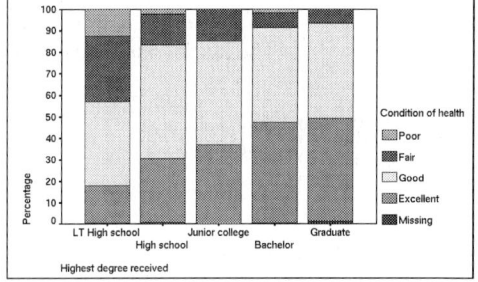

Line Options. Line options are available for line charts. You can choose one or both of the following options:

- **Connect markers within categories.** Applies to charts with more than one line. If this option is selected, vertical lines are drawn connecting the data points in the same category on different lines (different series). This option does not affect the current state of interpolation or line markers.

❏ **Display projection.** Select this option to differentiate visually between values to the left and values to the right in a line chart. To specify the category at which the projection begins, click on Location... in the Bar/Line/Area Options dialog box. This opens the Bar/Line/Area Options Projection dialog box, as shown in Figure 26.16.

Figure 26.16 Bar/Line/Area Options Projection dialog box

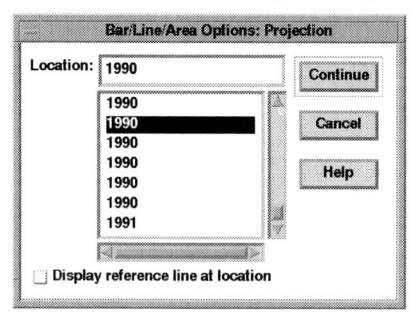

Choose the category where you want the projection line to start. The projection line will be displayed with a weight or style different from that of the original line. To make the projection stand out, you can select each part of the line individually and change its attributes. For example, the left part of the data line could be red and heavy while the right part of the data line, representing the projection, could be blue, thin, and dotted. An example is shown in Figure 26.17.

❏ **Display reference line at location.** Displays a line perpendicular to the category axis at the selected location.

Figure 26.17 Projection line chart

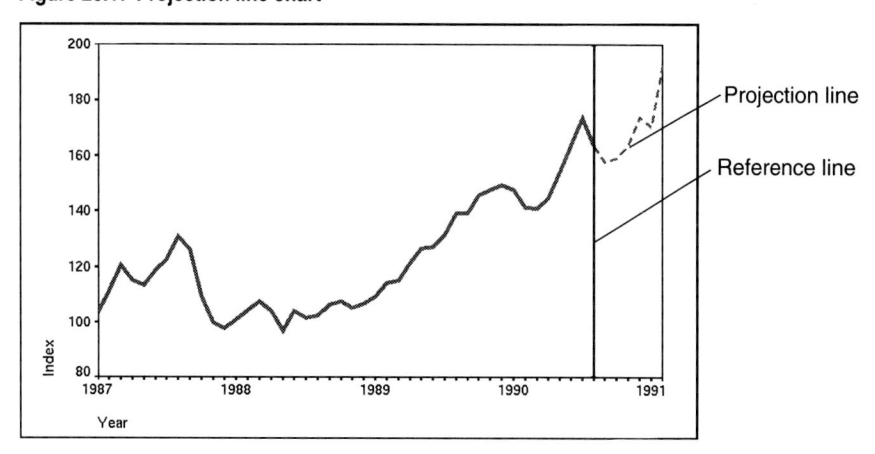

Bar Type. If two or more series are displayed in a bar chart, two bar types are available. You can choose one of the following options:

Clustered. Bars are grouped in clusters by category. Each series has a different color or pattern, identified in the legend.

Stacked. Bar segments, representing the series, are stacked one on top of the other for each category.

Pie Options

To change options for a pie chart, double-click away from the chart objects, or from the menus choose:

Chart
 Options...

This opens the Pie Options dialog box, as shown in Figure 26.18.

Figure 26.18 Pie Options dialog box

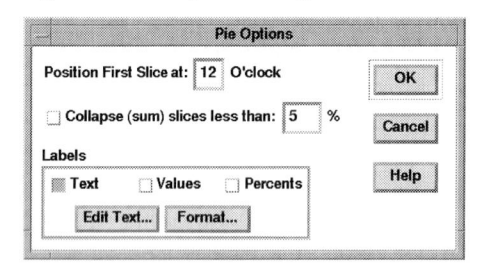

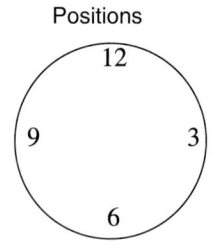

Position First Slice at n O'clock. Enter an integer from 1 to 12 to determine the position of the first "slice" of the pie. The integers represent the positions of the hours on a clock face. The default position is 12.

To combine the smallest slices into one slice labeled *Other*, select the following option:

- **Collapse (sum) slices less than n%.** Adds the values of the summary functions of the smallest slices and displays the sum as one slice labeled *Other*. This formatting option does not recalculate any statistics and is appropriate only for functions that have a meaningful sum: that is, if you defined the summary function as N of cases, % of cases, Number of cases, Sum of values, Number above, Number below, or Number within.

  If you select this option, each category for which the summary function has a value less than the specified percentage of the whole pie becomes part of the slice labeled

Other. You can enter an integer from 0 to 100. If you create another chart type from the Gallery menu, all of the original categories are available.

Labels. You can choose one or more of the following label options. You can also control the format of labels. See "Label Format," below.

- **Text.** Displays a text label for each slice. To edit the labels, see "Edit Text Labels," below.
- **Values.** Displays the value of the summary function for each slice.
- **Percents.** Displays the percentage of the whole pie that each slice represents.

Edit Text Labels

To edit text labels, click on Edit Text... in the Pie Options dialog box. This opens the Edit Text Labels dialog box, as shown in Figure 26.19.

Figure 26.19 Edit Text Labels dialog box

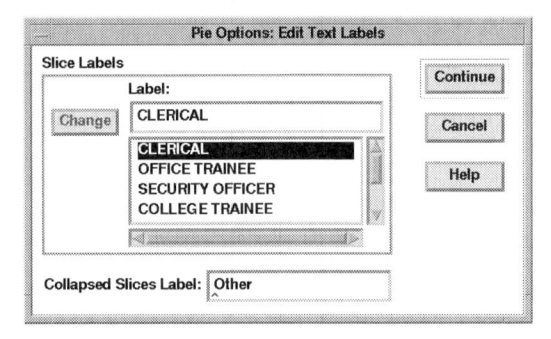

Slice Labels. To change the text of a slice label, select the label from the scroll list, edit it in the Label text box, and click on Change. Text labels can be up to 20 characters long.

Collapsed Slices Label. To change the text of collapsed slices label, edit it directly. (This label is available only if Collapse (sum) slices less than n% is selected in the Pie Options dialog box.)

When you have finished editing, click on Continue.

Label Format

To control the format of labels, click on Format... in the Pie Options dialog box. This opens the Label Format dialog box, as shown in Figure 26.20. (You can also select the labels in the chart and change the color, font, and size attributes.)

Figure 26.20 Label Format dialog box

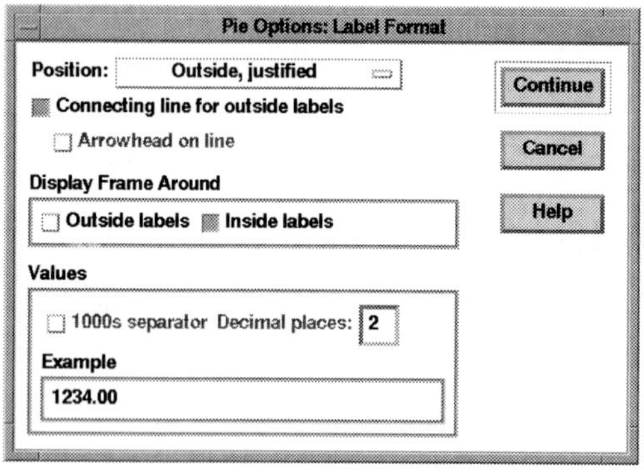

▭ **Position.** Places labels in relation to the pie. You can choose one of the following alternatives:

Outside, justified. Labels are placed outside the pie slices. Labels to the left of the pie are left-justified; labels to the right of the pie are right-justified.

Outside. Labels are placed outside the pie slices.

Inside. Labels are placed inside the pie slices.

Best fit. Labels are placed in the space available.

Numbers inside, text outside. Values and percentages are placed inside the slices; their labels are placed outside the slices.

Display Frame Around. Both inside and outside labels can have frames around them. You can select one or both sets of frames.

❑ **Outside labels.** Displays a frame around each label outside the pie.

❑ **Inside labels.** Displays a frame around each label within the pie.

Values. This group controls the format of displayed numbers. Your selections are displayed in the Example box.

❑ **1000s separator.** Displays values greater than 1,000 with the separator (period or comma) currently in effect.

Decimal places. You can specify any number of decimal places from 0 to 19 for values. However, the number of decimal places will be truncated to fit within the 20-character limit for values. If you specify 0, percentages, if selected, will also have no decimal places. If you specify an integer from 1 to 19, percentages will be shown with one decimal place.

You can also choose the following option:

- **Connecting line for outside labels.** Displays a line connecting each outside label with the slice of the pie to which it applies.
- **Arrowhead on line.** Places arrowheads on connecting lines pointing to the slices. Arrowheads are not available if the position is Outside, justified.

Boxplot Options

To change options for a boxplot, double-click away from the chart objects, double-click on one of the *n* values on the category axis, or from the menus choose:

Chart
 Options...

This opens the Boxplot Options dialog box, as shown in Figure 26.21.

Figure 26.21 Boxplot Options dialog box

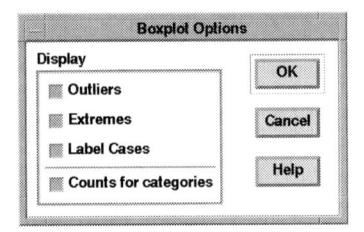

Display. Options in this group control whether outliers and extremes are shown in the chart. The height of the box is the interquartile range (IQR) computed from Tukey's hinges. You can choose one or more of the following alternatives:

- **Outliers.** Displays values that are more than 1.5 IQR's, but less than 3 IQR's, from the end of a box.
- **Extremes.** Displays values that are more than 3 IQR's from the end of a box.
- **Label cases.** Labels the outliers or extremes with case numbers or a labeling variable. Available if outliers or extremes are displayed. If two outliers or extremes have the same value but different case labels, no label is displayed.

You can also choose the following option:

- **Counts for categories.** Displays the number of cases under each category.

Scatterplot Options: Simple and Matrix

The options for a scatterplot vary according to the type of scatterplot—simple and matrix, overlay, or 3-D. To change options for a simple or matrix scatterplot, double-click away from the chart objects, or from the menus choose:

Chart
  Options...

This opens the Scatterplot Options dialog box for simple and matrix scatterplots, as shown in Figure 26.22.

Figure 26.22 Scatterplot Options dialog box for simple and matrix scatterplots

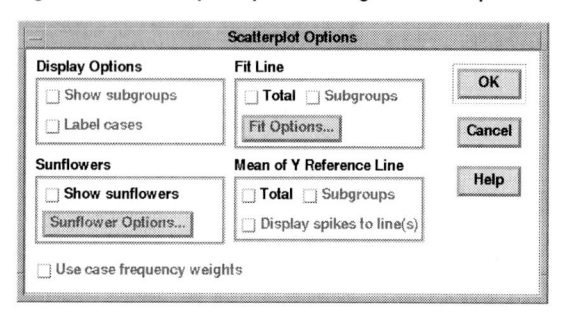

Display Options. Selected display options control how the groups and cases are differentiated. You can choose one or both of the following alternatives:

- **Show subgroups.** If a control variable was defined using Set markers by, this option is selected and markers of different colors or styles are used to differentiate the groups defined by the control variable. This option must be selected for subgroup options in other dialog boxes to be enabled.

- **Label cases.** If a label variable was defined, this option is selected and labels are attached to individual data points in the chart. This option is useful for data that are organized into a relatively small number of cases. This option is not available for a matrix scatterplot.

Fit Line. Fit Line options add one or more lines or curves to the chart, showing the best fit according to the method you select for Fit Options (see "Fit Options" on p. 519). You can choose one or both of the following alternatives:

- **Total.** Fits the total set of data points.

- **Subgroups.** Fits the selected type of curve to each subgroup. This option is enabled only if subgroups are defined and shown.

Sunflowers. The Sunflowers option allows you to group the data points into two-dimensional cells in the chart, with a sunflower in each cell. The process is similar to grouping the values for one variable into bars on a histogram. The number of cases in a cell is represented by the number of petals on the sunflower. You can also customize the display of sunflowers. See "Sunflower Options" on p. 522.

- **Show sunflowers.** To represent the data as sunflowers, select this option.

Mean of Y Reference Line. You can draw a reference line through the *y* axis at the mean of all the *y* values and reference lines at the means of defined subgroups. If you have a scatterplot matrix, any item can apply to each part of the matrix. You can choose one or more of the following alternatives:

- **Total.** Produces one line at the mean *y* value for all the data points.
- **Subgroups.** Controls whether a line is shown for the mean of each subgroup. This option is available only if you specify a control variable to define subgroups and if Show Subgroups is selected for Display Options.
- **Display spikes to line(s).** Produces a spike from each point to the appropriate mean reference line. If both Total and Subgroups are selected, spikes are drawn to the subgroup lines.

If you have defined a weight variable by selecting Weight Cases... from the Data menu, the weights are automatically applied to a simple or overlay plot.

- **Use case frequency weights.** Selected by default if a weight variable was previously defined. (The SPSS status bar indicates *Weight On*.) When weight is on, a message appears in a footnote below the chart. Weighted values are used to compute fit lines, mean of *y* reference lines, confidence limits, intercept, R^2, and sunflowers. Deselecting this option does not restore cases that were excluded from the chart because of missing or nonpositive weights.

Fit Options

To select a method for fitting the points to a line, click on Fit Options... in the Scatterplot Options dialog box. This opens the Fit Line dialog box, as shown in Figure 26.23.

Figure 26.23 Fit Line dialog box

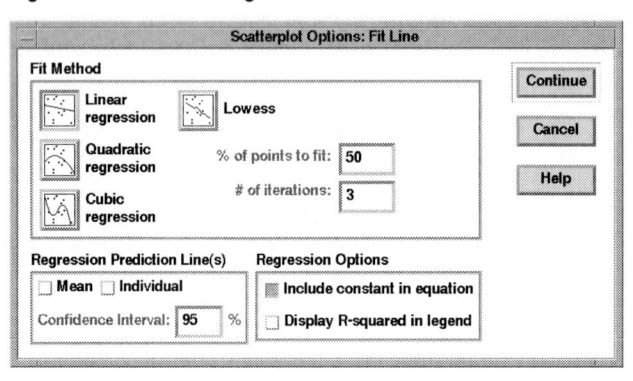

Fit Method. The picture buttons illustrate three regression types and another method for fitting the data points in a scatterplot. Examples of curves drawn by the fit methods are shown in Figure 26.24. You can choose one of the following options:

Linear regression. Produces a linear regression line that best fits the data points in a scatterplot according to the least-squares principle. This is the default fit method.

Quadratic regression. Produces a quadratic regression curve that best fits the data points in a scatterplot according to the least-squares principle.

Cubic regression. Produces a cubic regression curve that best fits the data points in a scatterplot according to the least-squares principle.

Lowess. Produces the locally weighted regression scatterplot smoothing method (Cleveland, 1979; Chambers et al., 1983). Lowess uses an iterative weighted least-squares method to fit a line to a set of points. At least 13 data points are needed. This method fits a specified percentage of the data points (the default is 50%). It also uses a specified number of iterations (the default is three).

Regression Prediction Line(s). Produces lines illustrating the confidence level that you specify. The default confidence level is 95%. These prediction lines are available only if one of the regression types is selected. You can choose one or both of the following alternatives:

❏ **Mean.** Plots the prediction intervals of the mean predicted responses.

❏ **Individual.** Plots the prediction intervals for single observations.

Confidence Interval. Specify a confidence level between 10.0 and 99.9. The default value is 95.

Regression Options. Available only if one of the regression types is selected. You can choose one or both of the following alternatives:

- **Include constant in equation.** Displays a regression line passing through the y intercept. If this option is deselected, the regression line passes through the origin.
- **Display R-squared in legend.** Displays the value of R^2 for each regression line in the legend, if it is displayed. This option is not available in matrix scatterplots. To display the legend, from the menus choose:

    Chart
      Legend...

    and select Display legend.

Figure 26.24 Examples of fit methods

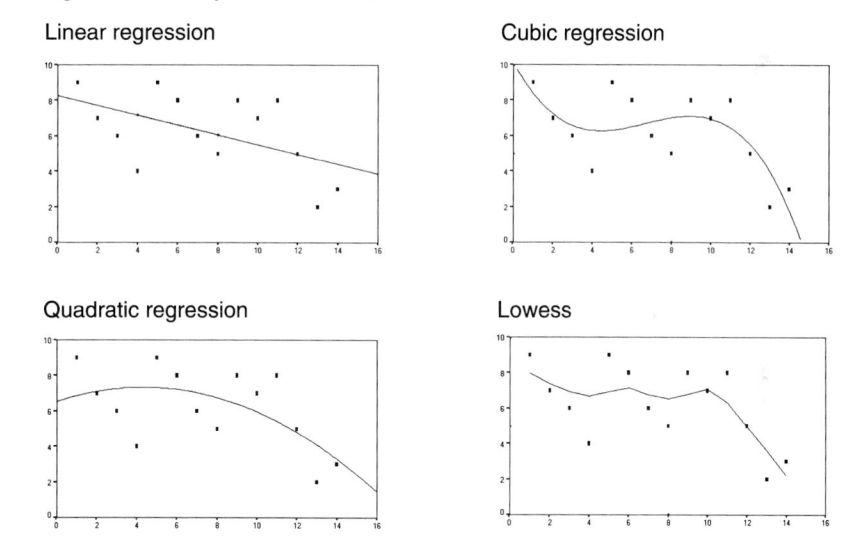

Linear regression

Cubic regression

Quadratic regression

Lowess

To access other methods of connecting the points in a scatterplot, from the menus choose:

Attributes
  Interpolation...

See "Line Interpolation" on p. 563 for more information.

Sunflower Options

To customize the display of sunflowers, click on Sunflower Options... in the Scatterplot Options dialog box. This opens the Sunflowers dialog box, as shown in Figure 26.25.

Figure 26.25 Sunflowers dialog box

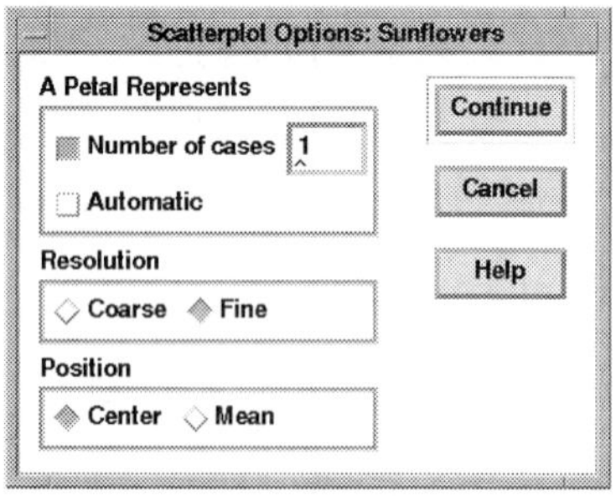

A Petal Represents. The petal number is equal to the number of cases in the cell (weighted or not) divided by the number of cases specified per petal. If the petal number is between 0 and 1.5, the center of the sunflower is displayed in the cell. If the petal number is 1.5 or greater, it is rounded, and the rounded number of petals is displayed. For example, in a nonweighted situation where each petal represents one case, a cell containing one case has only a sunflower center. A cell containing two cases has a sunflower with two petals, three cases, three petals, and so forth.

You can choose one of the following alternatives:

◇ **Number of cases.** Enter the number of cases per petal.

◇ **Automatic.** The system determines the number of cases per petal automatically.

Resolution. Controls the size of the cells. You can choose one of the following alternatives:

◇ **Coarse.** Plots cases from a large area on one sunflower. Each dimension of a sunflower cell is one-eighth of the appropriate range.

◇ **Fine.** Plots cases from a small area on one sunflower. Each dimension of a sunflower cell is one-fifteenth of the appropriate range.

Position. Controls the placement of the sunflower within the cell. You can choose one of the following alternatives:

◇ **Center.** Positions each sunflower in the center of its cell.

◇ **Mean.** Positions each sunflower at the intersection of the means for the points in the cell.

Figure 26.26 contains examples of data plotted as a simple scatterplot and the same data displayed with sunflowers.

Figure 26.26 Simple scatterplot and scatterplot with sunflowers

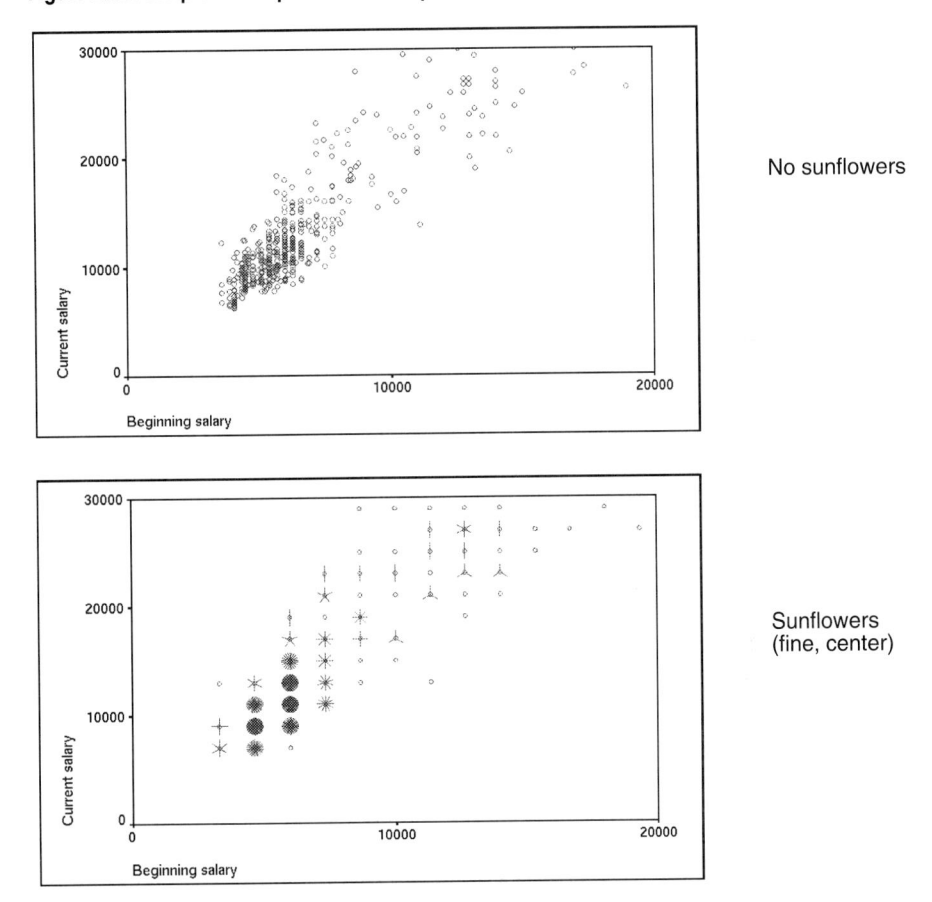

No sunflowers

Sunflowers (fine, center)

Overlay Scatterplot Options

To change options for an overlay scatterplot, double-click away from the chart objects, or from the menus choose:

Chart
  Options...

This opens the Overlay Scatterplot Options dialog box, as shown in Figure 26.27.

Figure 26.27 Overlay Scatterplot Options dialog box

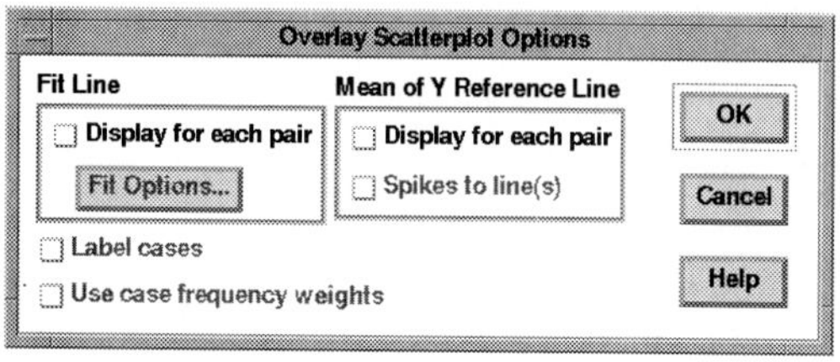

Fit Line. You can add lines or curves to the chart, showing the best fit.

- **Display for each pair.** If this item is selected, a line or curve is fitted for each pair of variables. To choose the type of line or curve, click on Fit Options... to open the Fit Line dialog box, as shown in Figure 26.23. Available options are described in "Fit Options" on p. 519.

Mean of Y Reference Line. You can request a line drawn at the mean of the y values.

- **Display for each pair.** Draws a separate reference line for each pair of variables.
- **Spikes to line(s).** Produces a spike from each point to the appropriate mean reference line. Spikes are available only if the reference lines are displayed for each pair.

You can also choose one or both of the following case options for overlay scatterplots:

- **Label cases.** If a label variable was defined in the Overlay Scatterplot dialog box, its value for each case is displayed in the chart next to the corresponding point.
- **Use case frequency weights.** Selected by default if a weight variable was previously defined by selecting Weight Cases... from the Data menu. (The status bar indicates *Weight On.*) When weighting is on, a message appears in a footnote below the chart. Weighted values are used to compute fit lines, mean of y reference lines, confidence limits, and intercepts. Deselecting this option does not restore cases that were excluded from the chart because of missing or nonpositive weights.

3-D Scatterplot Options

To change options for a 3-D scatterplot, double-click away from the chart objects, or from the menus choose:

Chart
  Options...

This opens the 3-D Scatterplot Options dialog box, as shown in Figure 26.28.

Figure 26.28 3-D Scatterplot Options dialog box

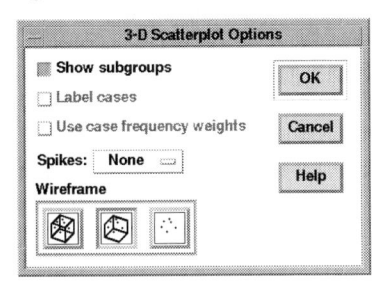

You can choose one or more of the following alternatives:

- **Show subgroups.** If a control variable was defined using Set markers by in the 3-D Scatterplot dialog box, markers of different colors or styles are used to differentiate the subgroups defined by the control variable.

- **Label cases.** If this item is selected and a variable was selected for Label cases by when the chart was defined, the selected variable is used to label each case.

- **Use case frequency weights.** Selected by default if a weight variable was previously defined by selecting Weight Cases... from the Data menu. (The status bar indicates *Weight On*.) When weighting is turned on, a message appears in a footnote below the chart. Weighted values are used to calculate the centroid. Deselecting this option does not restore cases that were excluded from the chart because of missing or nonpositive weights.

- **Spikes.** Displays a line from each data point to the location that you specify. Spikes are especially useful when printing a 3-D scatterplot. You can choose one of the following alternatives:

   None. No spikes are displayed.

   Floor. Spikes are dropped to the plane of the x and z axes of a 3-D scatterplot.

   Origin. Spikes end at the origin (0,0,0). The origin may be outside the display.

   Centroid. Spikes are displayed from each point to the centroid of all the points. The coordinates of the centroid are the weighted means of the three variables. A missing value in any one of the three variables excludes the case from the calculation. Changing the scale does not affect the calculation of the centroid.

Wireframe. The wireframe option draws a frame around the 3-D scatterplot to help you interpret it. You can choose one of the following alternatives:

The full frame shows all of the edges of a cube surrounding the data points.

The half frame shows the orientation of the three axes and their planes. This is the default wireframe.

The cloud button allows you to suppress the wireframe entirely. You may want to use this view when rotating the cloud of points while looking for a pattern.

If you select Spikes, the spikes are shown with or without a wireframe.

Histogram Options

To change options for a histogram, double-click away from the chart objects, or from the menus choose:

Chart
 Options...

This opens the Histogram Options dialog box, as shown in Figure 26.29.

Figure 26.29 Histogram Options dialog box

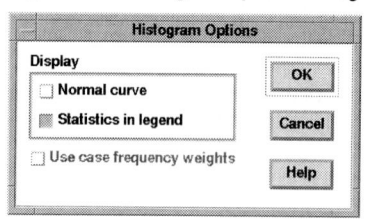

Display. You can choose one or both of the following display options:

- **Normal curve.** Superimposes a normal curve centered on the mean. The default histogram does not have a normal curve.

- **Statistics in legend.** Displays in the legend the standard deviation, the mean, and the number of cases. This item is selected by default. If you deselect the legend (see "Legends" on p. 543), the statistics display is also turned off.

The following option is also available:

- **Use case frequency weights.** Selected by default if a weight variable was previously defined by selecting Weight Cases... from the Data menu. (The SPSS status bar indicates *Weight On*.) When weighting is on, a message appears in a footnote below the chart. Weighting affects the height of the bars and the computation of statistics. Deselecting this option does not restore cases that were excluded from the chart because of missing or nonpositive weights. If the histogram was generated from the Frequencies procedure, the case weights cannot be turned off.

Axis Characteristics

You can modify, create, and change the orientation of axes in a chart. Axis dialog boxes can be opened in one of the following ways:

- Double-click near the axis.

or

- Select an axis or axis label and from the menus choose:

    Chart
    Axis...

    to open the appropriate (scale, category, or interval) axis dialog box.

or

- Without an axis selected, from the menus choose:

    Chart
    Axis...

    This opens an Axis Selection dialog box, similar to the one shown in Figure 26.30. The types of axes represented in the current chart are listed in the dialog box. Select the type of axis you want to modify and click on OK.

Figure 26.30 Axis Selection dialog box showing scale and category axes

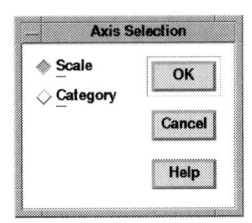

Scale Axis

If you select a scale axis, the Scale Axis dialog box appears, as shown in Figure 26.31.

Figure 26.31 Scale Axis dialog box

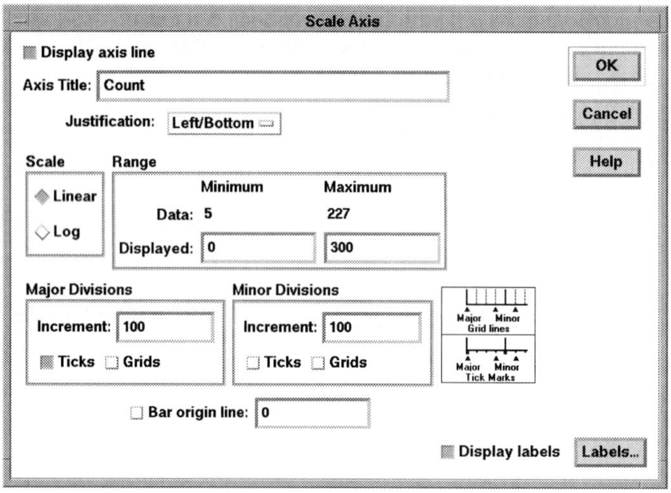

To display the axis line, select the following item:

❑ **Display axis line.** Controls the display of the axis line. Since it coincides with the inner frame, if you want no line displayed, you must also turn off the inner frame (see "Inner Frame" on p. 547). This item is not available for 3-D scatterplots.

Axis Title. You can type up to 72 characters for the axis title. To delete the title, delete all of the characters.

❑ **Title Justification.** Controls the position of the title relative to the axis. You can select one of the following alternatives:

Left/Bottom. Axis title aligns to the left for horizontal axes, at the bottom for vertical axes.

Center. Axis title is centered (applies to both horizontal and vertical axes).

Right/Top. Axis title aligns to the right for horizontal axes, at the top for vertical axes.

❑ **Title Orientation.** Available for 3-D scatterplots only. Controls the orientation of the title. You can select one of the following alternatives:

Horizontal. A horizontal title has one end near the center of the axis.

Parallel. A parallel title is parallel to the axis.

Scale. Controls whether the scale is linear or logarithmic. You can choose one of the following alternatives:

◇ **Linear.** Displays a linear scale. This is the default.

◇ **Log.** Displays a base 10 logarithmic scale. If you select this item, you can type new values for the range, or you can click on OK and then click on Yes when the program asks if you want the default range. Logarithmic is not available for boxplots.

Range. Controls the displayed range of values. The minimum and maximum actual data values are listed for your information. If you change the range, you may also want to change the increments in Major Divisions and Minor Divisions.

If the scale is logarithmic, the range values are specified in the same units as the data values. The minimum must be greater than zero and both values must be even logarithmic values (base 10)—that is, each must be an integer from 1 to 9 times a power of 10. For example, the range might be 9000 to 30000. If you enter unacceptable values, when you click on OK, the system asks if you want them adjusted.

Major Divisions/Minor Divisions. Allows you to control the marked increments along the axis. The number you enter for the increment must be positive and the range must be a multiple of the increment. The major increment must be a multiple of the minor increment. If the scale is logarithmic, you cannot change the increment.

❑ **Ticks.** If you do not want tick marks displayed, deselect this item.

❑ **Grid.** If you want grid lines displayed perpendicular to the axis, select this item.

The following option is available for bar charts:

❑ **Bar origin line.** Allows you to specify a location for the origin line from which bars will hang (vertical bars) or extend (horizontal bars). The specified value must fall within the current range. For example, two versions of a bar chart are shown in Figure 26.32, one with the origin line at 0 and the other with the origin line at 12,000. The second version emphasizes the differences in current salary for employees who have 16 or more years of education.

The following option is also available for most charts:

❑ **Display labels.** Allows you to suppress or display the labels.

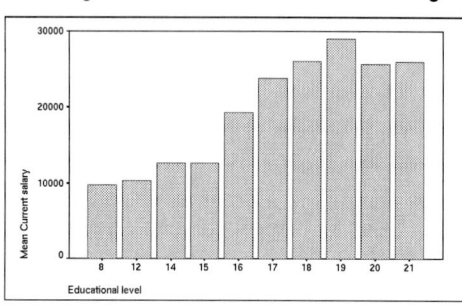

Figure 26.32 Bar charts with different origin lines

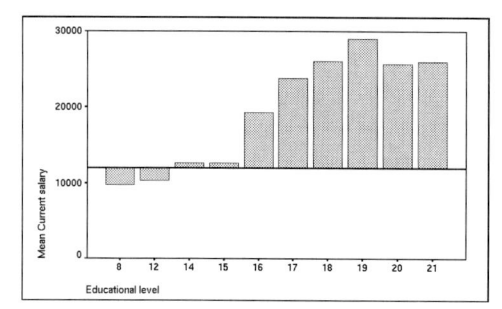

Scale Axis Labels

To modify axis labels, click on Labels... in the Scale Axis dialog box. This opens the Scale Axis Labels dialog box, as shown in Figure 26.33. Any changes you make are reflected in the Example box.

Figure 26.33 Scale Axis Labels dialog box

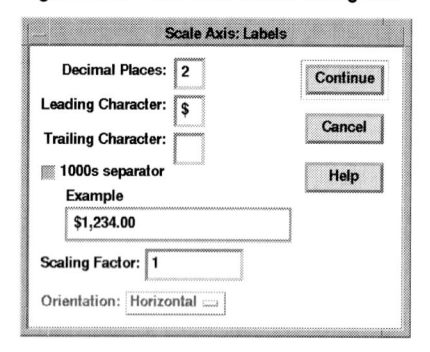

Decimal Places. Enter the number of digits you want displayed to the right of the decimal point. The number of decimal places is also applied to bar labels, if present.

Leading Character. Adds the specified character at the beginning of each axis label automatically. The most commonly used leading character is a currency symbol, such as the dollar sign ($).

Trailing Character. Adds the specified character to the end of each axis label automatically. The most commonly used trailing character is the percent sign (%).

To insert a thousands separator in numeric axis labels, select the following option:

- **1000s separator.** Displays values greater than 1,000 with the separator (period or comma) currently in effect.

Scaling Factor. Computes each label on the scale axis by dividing the original value by the scaling factor. For example, the labels 1,000,000, 2,000,000, etc., can be scaled to 1, 2, etc., and the word *millions* added to the axis title. The default value is 1. Bar labels, if present, are not affected.

- **Orientation.** Controls the orientation of axis labels. Available only for a horizontal scale axis. Not available for 3-D scatterplots. You can select one of the following alternatives:

Automatic. Selects the orientation that will give the best fit.

Horizontal. Prints axis labels horizontally.

Vertical. Prints axis labels vertically.

Staggered. Prints axis labels horizontally, but staggers them vertically.

Diagonal. Prints axis labels diagonally.

Scatterplot Matrix Scale Axes

The dialog box for scatterplot matrix scale axes is shown in Figure 26.34. You can open the dialog box in one of the following ways:

- From the menus choose:

  Chart
     Axis...

  or

- Double-click on an axis.

  or

- Double-click on one of the titles on the diagonal.

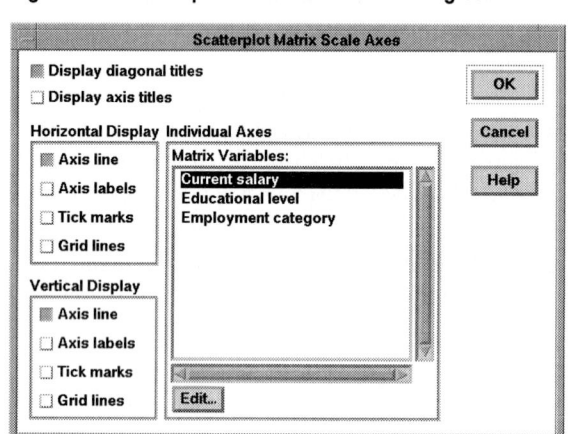

Figure 26.34 Scatterplot Matrix Scale Axes dialog box

The options at the left in the dialog box apply to all of the plots in the matrix.

To display diagonal and axis titles, choose one or both of the following alternatives:

- **Display diagonal titles.** Displays titles on the diagonal of the matrix. Diagonal titles are displayed by default.
- **Display axis titles.** Displays titles on the outer rim of the matrix.

Horizontal Display/Vertical Display. Items apply globally to all plots. Axis lines are displayed by default.

Individual Axes. Select one variable at a time and click on Edit... to edit the selected axis. (See "Edit Selected Axis," below.)

Edit Selected Axis

To edit individual scatterplot matrix axes, click on Edit... in the Scale Axes dialog box. This opens the Edit Selected Axis dialog box, as shown in Figure 26.35.

Figure 26.35 Edit Selected Axis dialog box

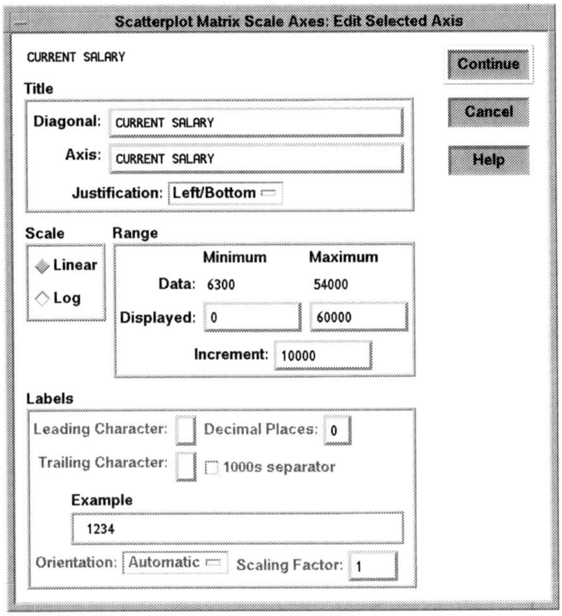

Title. Changes made to titles will be displayed only if you select the title display options in the Scale Axes dialog box. To fit titles into the space available, you can edit the text in the dialog box or select the text in the chart and change the size (see "Text" on p. 566).

Diagonal. Allows you to edit the title that appears on the matrix diagonal.

Axis. Allows you to edit the text of the axis title. With several plots in the matrix, the title for the axis often needs shortening.

- **Justification.** Controls the position of the title relative to the axis. You can select one of the following alternatives: Left/Bottom, Center, or Right/Top. Bottom and top apply to vertical axes. Left and right apply to horizontal axes. See "Axis Title" under "Scale Axis" on p. 528 for more information.

Scale. You can change the type of scale used for the axis.

- **Linear.** Displays a linear scale. This is the default.
- **Log.** Displays a logarithmic scale (base 10).

Range. Controls the displayed range of values.

Data. The minimum and maximum actual data values are displayed for your information.

Displayed. You can change the displayed range by typing the new minimum and maximum. The range must be an even multiple of the increment. If the scale is logarithmic, the minimum must be greater than zero and both values must be even logarithmic values (base 10)—that is, the values of minimum and maximum must each be an integer from 1 to 9 times a power of 10. For example, a range could be 9000 to 30000. If you enter an unacceptable value, when you click on OK, the system asks if you want the values adjusted.

Increment. The value of the increment must divide evenly into the range.

Labels. The Labels group is available only if you selected Axis labels in either horizontal display or vertical display in the Scale Axes dialog box. Any changes you make are illustrated in the Example box.

Leading Character. Adds the specified character at the start of each axis label automatically. The most common leading character is a currency symbol, such as the dollar sign ($).

Trailing Character. Adds the specified character to the end of each axis label automatically. The most commonly used trailing character is the percent sign (%).

Decimal Places. Enter the number of digits you want displayed to the right of the decimal point.

- **1000s separator.** Displays values greater than 1,000 with the separator (period or comma) currently in effect.
- **Orientation.** Controls the orientation of axis labels. Available only for a horizontal axis. You can select one of the following alternatives: Automatic, Horizontal, Vertical, Staggered, or Diagonal. See "Scale Axis Labels" on p. 530 for more information.

Scaling Factor. You can enter up to 20 characters in the box. The system divides each label by the factor. For example, the labels 1,000,000, 2,000,000, etc., can be scaled to 1, 2, etc., and the word *millions* added to the axis title. The default value is 1.

Category Axis

Selecting a category axis opens the Category Axis dialog box, as shown in Figure 26.36.

Figure 26.36 Category Axis dialog box

```
┌─────────────── Category Axis ───────────────┐
│  ▣ Display axis line                        │
│                                    ┌──────┐ │
│  Axis Title: │Employment category│  │  OK  │ │
│                                    └──────┘ │
│  Title Justification: │Left/Bottom ▾│       │
│                                    ┌──────┐ │
│  Axis Markers                      │Cancel│ │
│    ▣ Tick Marks  ☐ Grid Lines      └──────┘ │
│                                    ┌──────┐ │
│                                    │ Help │ │
│  ▣ Display labels  │ Labels... │    └──────┘ │
└─────────────────────────────────────────────┘
```

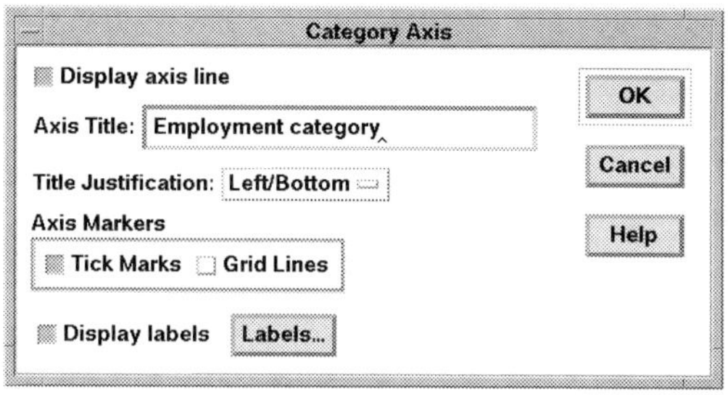

To display the category axis, select this option:

❑ **Display axis line.** Controls display of the axis line. Since it coincides with the inner frame, if you want no line displayed, you must also turn off the inner frame (see "Inner Frame" on p. 547).

Axis Title. You can type up to 72 characters for the axis title. To omit the title, delete all of the characters.

⊏ **Title Justification.** Controls the position of the title relative to the axis. You can select one of the following alternatives: Left/Bottom, Center, or Right/Top. Bottom and top apply to vertical axes. Left and right apply to horizontal axes. See "Axis Title" under "Scale Axis" on p. 528 for more information.

Axis Markers. Controls whether tick marks and grid lines are turned on or off.

❑ **Tick marks.** Controls the display of the tick marks for all categories.

❑ **Grid lines.** Controls the display of grid lines.

The following option is also available:

❑ **Display labels.** To display axis labels, select this item.

Category Axis Labels

To modify axis labels, click on Labels... in the Category Axis dialog box. This opens the Category Axis Labels dialog box, as shown in Figure 26.37.

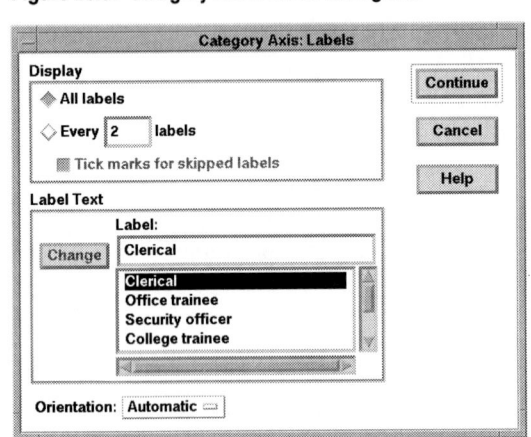

Figure 26.37 Category Axis Labels dialog box

Display. Controls the display of axis labels. You can choose one of the following alternatives:

- **All labels.** Displays a label for every category included in the display. To omit entire categories from the display, see "Bar, Line, and Area Chart Displayed Data" on p. 549.
- **Every n labels.** Allows you to specify an increment governing the number of categories not labeled between displayed labels. Enter an integer that is one greater than the number of labels to be skipped. For example, if you want to label the first category, skip the next two, and label the fourth, enter 3.
  - **Tick marks for skipped labels.** To turn off tick marks, deselect this item.

Label Text. Allows you to edit the text of labels. First select a label from the scroll list. It appears in the Label text box. Edit the text and click on Change.

- **Orientation.** Controls the orientation of axis labels. Available only for a horizontal category axis. You can select one of the following alternatives: Automatic, Horizontal, Vertical, Staggered, or Diagonal. See "Scale Axis Labels" on p. 530 for more information.

Interval Axis

The bars of a histogram extend from an interval axis. The Interval Axis dialog box is shown in Figure 26.38.

Figure 26.38 Interval Axis dialog box

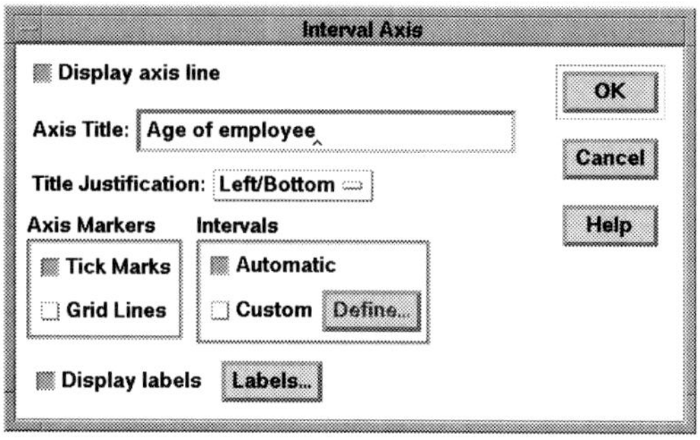

To display an axis line, select the following option:

- **Display axis line.** Turns the axis line off or on. If you want *no line* at this position, you must also turn off display of the inner frame (see "Inner Frame" on p. 547).

Axis Title. You can type up to 72 characters for the axis title. To omit the title, delete all the characters.

Title Justification. Controls the position of the title relative to the axis. You can select one of the following alternatives: Left/Bottom, Center, or Right/Top. Bottom and top apply to vertical axes. Left and right apply to horizontal axes. Justification is with respect to the ends of the displayed axis. See "Axis Title" under "Scale Axis" on p. 528 for more information.

Axis Markers. Controls whether tick marks and grid lines are turned on or off. You can choose one or both of the following alternatives:

- **Tick marks.** Controls the display of the tick marks for all categories. Tick marks are at the centers of the intervals.
- **Grid lines.** Controls the display of grid lines. Grid lines are at the bounds of intervals.

Intervals. Allows you to define the size of the intervals represented by the bars in the histogram. You can choose one of the following alternatives:

- **Automatic.** The number and size of intervals are determined automatically, based on your data. This is the default.
- **Custom.** Allows you to define the size of equal intervals. Click on Define... to change the number of intervals, the width of each interval, or the range of data displayed. See "Defining Custom Intervals," below.

The following display option is also available:

❑ **Display labels.** To display axis labels, select this item.

Defining Custom Intervals

To modify the number or width of intervals in a histogram, select Custom in the Interval Axis dialog box and click on Define... to open the Interval Axis Define Custom Intervals dialog box, as shown in Figure 26.39.

Figure 26.39 Interval Axis Define Custom Intervals dialog box

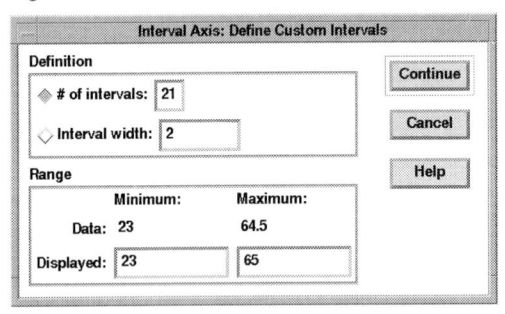

```
┌─────────────────────────────────────────────────┐
│        Interval Axis: Define Custom Intervals   │
├─────────────────────────────────────────────────┤
│ Definition                                      │
│   ◆ # of intervals: [ 21 ]       [ Continue ]   │
│                                                 │
│   ◇ Interval width: [ 2  ]       [ Cancel   ]   │
│                                                 │
│ Range                            [ Help     ]   │
│              Minimum:    Maximum:               │
│      Data:    23          64.5                  │
│   Displayed: [ 23  ]     [ 65   ]               │
└─────────────────────────────────────────────────┘
```

Definition. Two methods of specifying custom intervals are available. You can choose one of the following alternatives:

◇ **# of intervals.** You can specify the number of intervals by entering an integer greater than one. The system calculates the width of each interval, based on the range.

◇ **Interval width.** You can enter a width for each interval, starting at the minimum listed under Range. The system calculates the number of intervals, based on the range.

Range. Allows you to adjust the range of data displayed. The minimum and maximum data values are listed for your information. You can adjust the range when you change the number of intervals or the interval width. For example, if you specify 10 intervals and a range of 20 to 70, the intervals start at 20 and are 5 units wide. (See Figure 26.40.) You can get the same result by specifying 5 as the interval width, along with the range of 20 to 70.

Figure 26.40 Histogram with custom intervals

Modifying Interval Labels

Labels on an interval axis can be suppressed or modified. To modify the labels on the interval axis, click on Labels... in the Interval Axis dialog box. This opens the Interval Axis Labels dialog box, as shown in Figure 26.41. Any changes you make are illustrated in the Example box.

Figure 26.41 Interval Axis Labels dialog box

Display. Controls the display of axis labels.

◇ **All labels.** Displays a label for every interval included in the display.

◇ **Every n labels.** Allows you to specify an increment governing the number of intervals not labeled between displayed labels. Enter an integer that is one greater than the number of labels to be skipped. For example, if you want to label the first interval, skip the next two, and label the fourth, enter 3.

❏ **Tick marks for skipped labels.** To turn off tick marks, deselect this item.

Type. Allows you to select whether each label will denote the midpoint or the range of the interval.

◇ **Midpoint.** Displays the midpoint of each interval as the label.

◇ **Range.** Displays the lower and upper bounds of each interval as the label.

Decimal Places. You can specify the number of decimal places. Enter a value from 0 to 19.

To insert a thousands separator in numeric axis labels, select the following option:

❏ **1000s separator.** Displays values greater than 1,000 with the separator (period or comma) currently in effect.

Scaling Factor. You can enter up to 20 characters. The system divides each label by the factor. For example, the labels 1,000,000, 2,000,000, etc., can be scaled to 1, 2, etc., and the word *millions* added to the axis title. This factor does not affect the scale axis or bar labels.

▢ **Orientation.** Controls the orientation of axis labels. Available only for a horizontal axis. You can select one of the following alternatives: Automatic, Horizontal, Vertical, Diagonal, or Staggered. See "Scale Axis Labels" on p. 530 for more information.

Bar Spacing

To adjust the spacing of the bars in a bar chart or histogram, from the menus choose:
Chart
  Bar Spacing...

The Bar Spacing dialog box for a bar chart is shown in Figure 26.42.

In a bar chart, you can change the margin spacing at both ends of the series of bars, the inter-bar spacing, and the inter-cluster spacing. The system adjusts the size of the bars to meet the new specifications.

For a histogram, the Bar Spacing dialog box contains only the bar margin specification.

Figure 26.42 Bar Spacing dialog box (bar chart)

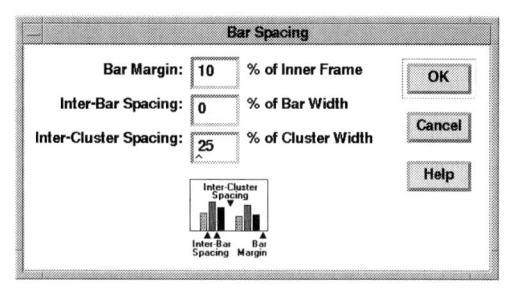

Bar Margin: n% of Inner Frame. The percentage (0 to 99) of the inner frame left blank on both sides of the series of bars. This percentage is split equally between the two sides. The default is 10% for bar charts and 0% for histograms.

Inter-Bar Spacing: n% of Bar Width. The distance between bars within a cluster or the distance between bars in a simple bar chart. Enter the percentage of the bar width (0 to 100) that you want left blank between bars. The default is 0% for a clustered bar chart or 20% for a simple bar chart.

Inter-Cluster Spacing: n% of Cluster Width. The distance between clusters. Enter the percentage of the cluster width (0 to 100). The default is 25%.

Adding or Changing Explanatory Text

Explanatory text can be added to charts in the form of titles, footnotes, a legend, and text annotation.

Titles

To add a title to the top of a chart, from the menus choose:

Chart
 Title...

This opens the Titles dialog box, as shown in Figure 26.43. If you already have a title for the chart, you can double-click on it to open the dialog box.

Figure 26.43 Titles dialog box

Title 1/Title 2. You can enter up to 72 characters for each title. The amount of the title that is displayed depends on the length of the title and the size of the type font selected.

- **Title Justification.** Both titles are justified together. You can choose one of the following alternatives: Left/Bottom, Center, or Right/Top. Left aligns the first character with the axis on the left; right aligns the last character with the right side of the inner frame.

Subtitle. You can enter up to 72 characters for the subtitle.

- **Subtitle Justification.** A subtitle can be left-justified, centered, or right-justified, independent of titles 1 and 2. The default font size for the subtitle is smaller than the font size for titles 1 and 2. You can choose one of the following alternatives: Left/Bottom, Center, or Right/Top.

To delete any title, delete all of the characters in its text box.

Footnotes

To add up to two footnotes to a chart, from the menus choose:

Chart
  Footnote...

This opens the Footnotes dialog box, as shown in Figure 26.44. If you already have a footnote, you can double-click on it to open the dialog box.

Figure 26.44 Footnotes dialog box

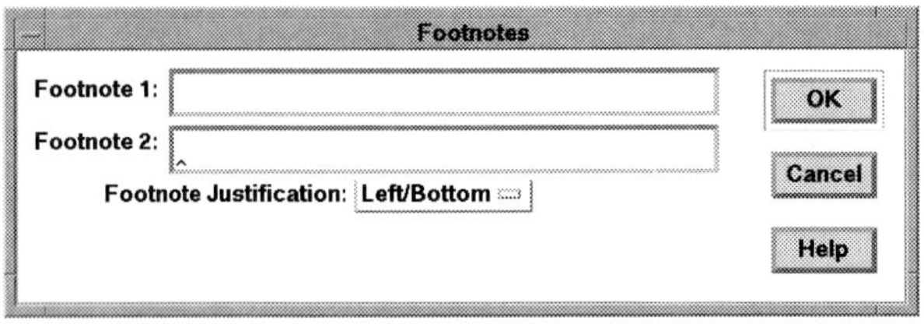

Footnote 1/Footnote 2. You can enter up to 72 characters for each footnote. The portion of a footnote displayed depends on the length of the footnote and the size of the type font selected.

- **Footnote Justification.** Footnotes are justified relative to the inner frame. You can choose one of the following alternatives: Left/Bottom, Center, or Right/Top. Left aligns the first character with the axis on the left; right aligns the last character with the right side of the inner frame.

To delete a footnote, delete all of the characters in its text box.

Legends

If you have more than one series in a chart, the system provides a legend to distinguish between the series. A legend is also displayed automatically if you have statistics displayed for a histogram or R^2 for a regression line in a scatterplot. To make changes to the legend, double-click on the legend, or from the menus choose:

Chart
 Legend...

This opens the Legend dialog box, as shown in Figure 26.45. The legend resulting from the specifications is shown in Figure 26.46.

Figure 26.45 Legend dialog box

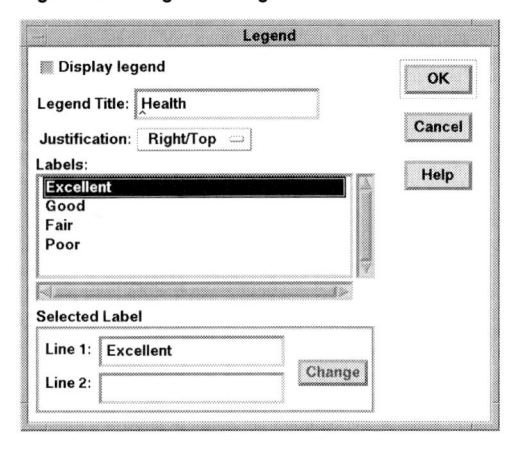

Figure 26.46 Legend example

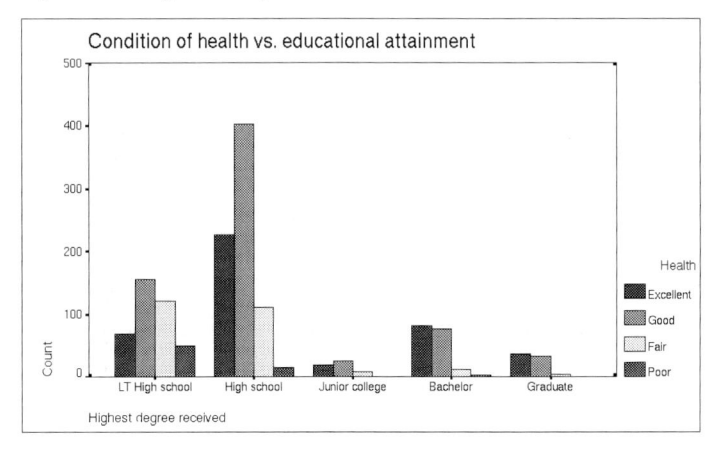

544   Chapter 26

To display a legend for your chart, select the following option:

❑ **Display legend.** Controls whether the legend is displayed.

Legend Title. You can edit the legend title or add one if none exists. The legend title can be up to 20 characters long.

▱ **Justification.** Aligns the legend title within the area occupied by the legend. You can choose one of the following alternatives: Left/Bottom, Center, or Right/Top. Left aligns the first character at the left of the legend area; right aligns the last character with the right side of the legend area.

Labels. The labels in the legend are listed. When you select one of the labels from the list, it appears starting in Line 1 of the Selected Label group. You can edit the text and add a second line if it is not already there. Each line can be up to 20 characters long. When you have finished editing the label, click on Change.

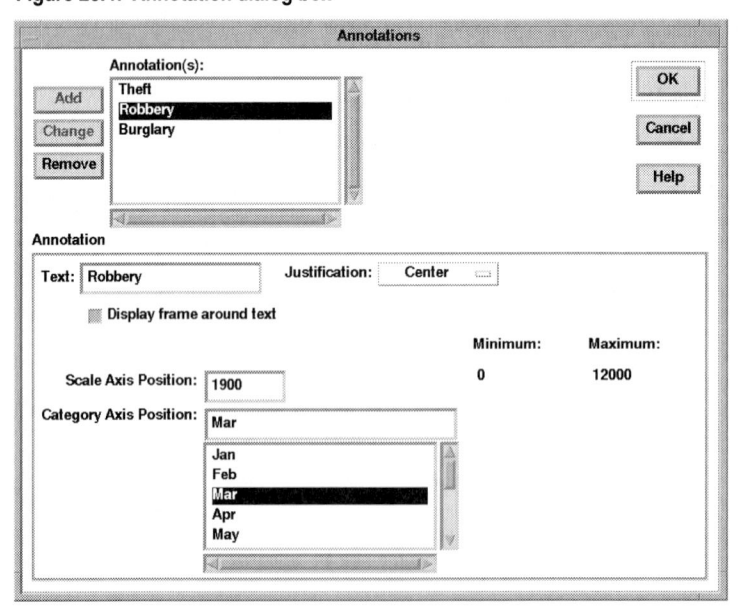

Annotation

Annotation places text within the chart area, anchored to a specific point within the chart. To add annotation to the chart or edit existing annotation, from the menus choose:

Chart
  Annotation...

This opens the Annotation dialog box, as shown in Figure 26.47. The annotations resulting from these specifications are shown in Figure 26.48.

Figure 26.47 Annotation dialog box

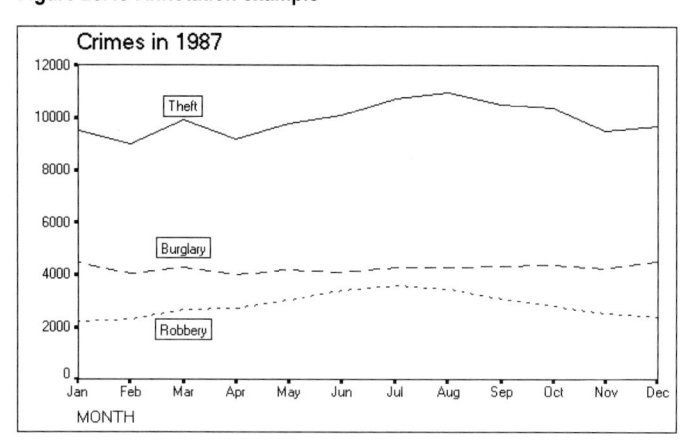

Figure 26.48 Annotation example

[Chart titled "Crimes in 1987" showing three lines labeled Theft, Burglary, and Robbery across months Jan–Dec, with scale 0 to 12000. Annotations positioned above Mar tick mark.]

If you already have an annotation in the chart, you can edit it or add others by double-clicking on it. Since you position annotations at axis coordinates, the form of the Annotation dialog box depends on the kind of axes in your chart. Figure 26.47 shows an annotation dialog box for a chart containing a scale axis and a category axis.

For a new annotation, when the text and coordinates have been specified, click on Add and then OK. To make changes to an existing annotation, select the annotation in the list at the top, edit the text or position, and click on Change.

Annotation. The default position for annotation is the intersection of the displayed axes (the lower left corner).

> **Text.** You can type up to 20 characters in the text box.
>
> ▫ **Justification.** The choices available on the drop-down list are Left/Bottom, Center, or Right/Top. The default is left, indicating that the leftmost character of the annotation will be positioned at the selected coordinates. In Figure 26.48, the annotations are centered above the tick mark for Mar.
>
> ❏ **Display frame around text.** Adds a frame around the annotation text.
>
> **Scale Axis Position.** The scale axis position is a number between the minimum and maximum values.
>
> **Category Axis Position.** If you have a category axis, the annotation will be positioned at the category you select from the scroll list. In Figure 26.48, all annotations are positioned at the Mar category, appearing directly above one another.

Adding Reference Lines

To add a horizontal or vertical reference line, or both, from the menus choose:

Chart
 Reference Line...

This opens an Axis Selection dialog box appropriate for your chart. Category Axis Reference Line and Scale Axis Reference Line dialog boxes are shown in Figure 26.49.

Figure 26.49 Reference Line dialog boxes

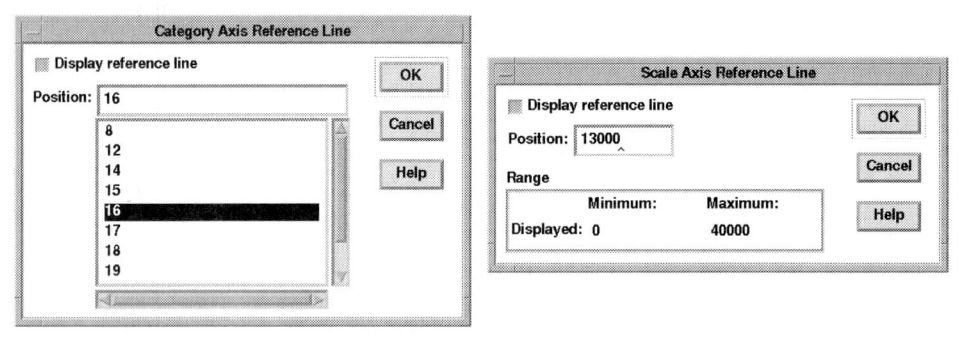

To display a reference line, select the following option:

- **Display reference line.** Controls whether a reference line is displayed perpendicular to the current axis. For a category axis, select the position on the axis from the scroll list; for a scale axis, type the position. For a scale axis, the value specified for Position must be within the displayed range. To modify or delete a reference line, double-click on it to open the dialog box.

Figure 26.50 shows the chart that has a reference line perpendicular to each axis, as specified in the dialog boxes in Figure 26.49. You can display one horizontal and one vertical reference line. If you already have a reference line displayed, you can open the dialog box by double-clicking on it.

Figure 26.50 Reference Lines

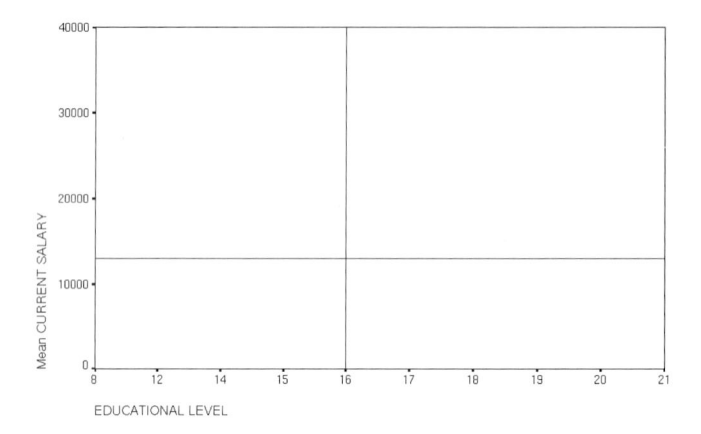

Inner and Outer Frames

A chart has an inner frame and an outer frame. You can select either one by clicking on it and you can change its attributes. If you want a fill color within a selected frame, be sure the selection in the Fill Pattern dialog box is a pattern other than empty. Both frames are displayed in Figure 26.51. To set the default display for either frame, from the menus choose:

Options
  Preferences...

and click on Graphics.

Figure 26.51 Inner and outer frames

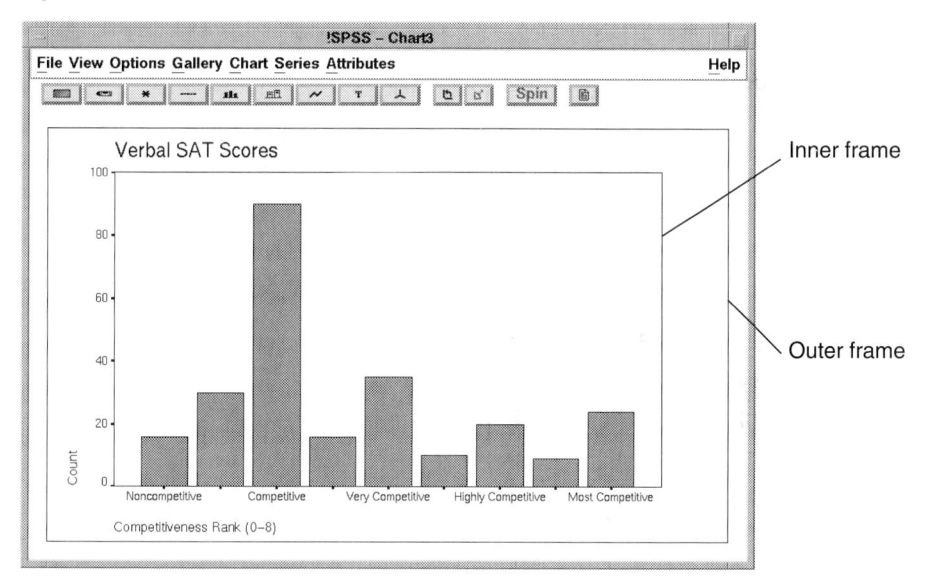

Inner Frame

The inner frame completes a rectangle, two sides of which coincide with the two axes. For most charts, the inner frame is displayed by default. To suppress or display the inner frame, from the menus choose:

Chart
  Inner Frame

When it is displayed, a check button appears to the left of Inner Frame on the Chart menu.

Outer Frame

The outer frame encloses the titles, footnotes, and legend, as well as the chart. To display or suppress the outer frame, from the menus choose:

Chart
 Outer Frame

When it is displayed, a check button appears to the left of Outer Frame on the Chart menu.

Selecting and Arranging Data (Series Menu)

The Series menu allows you to modify your chart by selecting data and reassigning data elements within the chart. All of the data must exist within the original chart; you cannot add new data in the Chart Editor. You also cannot change values within the data. The options available vary by chart type:

- For bar, line, and area charts, you can omit data series and categories as long as enough data remain to generate the chart, and change the order of series and categories. You can specify for each series individually whether it is to be displayed as a bar, line, or area. You can also transpose the data so that series become categories and categories become series.
- For pie charts, you can omit categories (slices). If the original chart defined more than one data series, you can select the series to be displayed.
- For boxplots, series operations are not available.
- For scatterplots, you can reassign series to axes, omitting those not needed in the plot. You cannot omit individual values within a series. Since the assignment of series to axes differs for each type of scatterplot, there are different Displayed Data dialog boxes for each type of scatterplot.
- For histograms, if the original chart was a scatterplot with more than one series, you can select which one of the series is to be displayed.

All of these options, except transposing data, are specified in Displayed Data dialog boxes, which are specific to the chart type and are discussed in the following sections. When you choose

Series
 Transpose Data

data transposition takes place without further query.

Cumulative Distributions in Charts

Data distributions are never recalculated in the chart editor. Thus, removing categories from a cumulative distribution, for example, will not change the values of the remaining categories. Cumulative distributions in pie charts, or in the scale dimension of stacked bar and area charts, will yield charts whose interpretation is unclear.

Bar, Line, and Area Chart Displayed Data

To arrange the data in a bar, line, area, or mixed chart, from the menus choose:

Series
 Displayed...

This opens a Bar/Line/Area Displayed Data dialog box. Figure 26.52 shows the Bar/Line/Area Displayed Data dialog box for the bar chart in Figure 26.6.

Figure 26.52 Bar/Line/Area Displayed Data dialog box

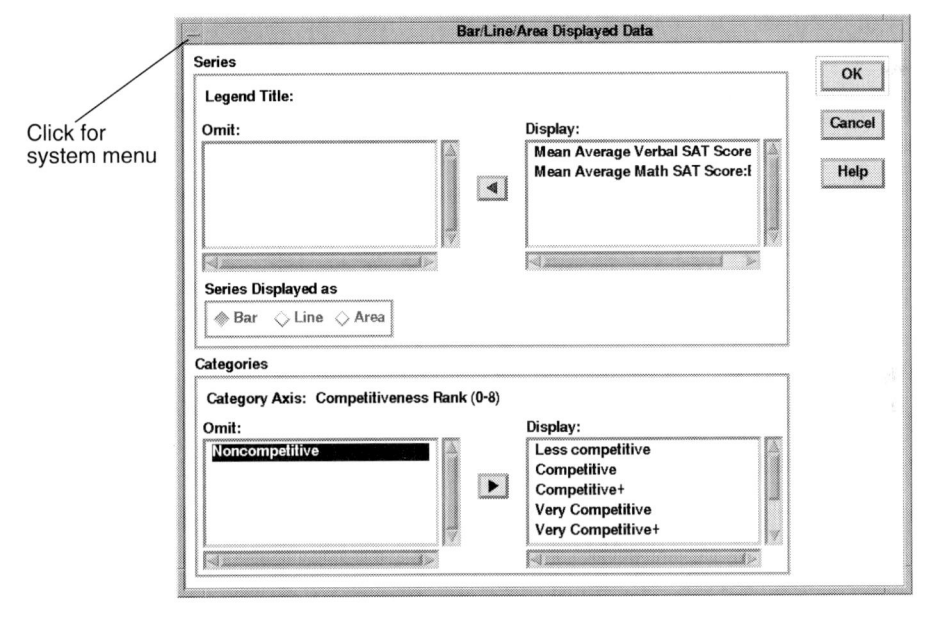

The controls in the Bar/Line/Area Displayed Data dialog box fall into two groups: those having to do with series and those having to do with categories.

Series. The legend title, if any, is listed for your information. (To change it, see "Legends" on p. 543.) Since multiple series are identified in the legend, this title may help to clarify what the series represent. The series are displayed in two list boxes: those omitted from the chart and those displayed in the chart. To move a series from one list box to the other, select it and click on ▶ or ◀. You must have at least one series displayed for the OK pushbutton to be enabled.

The order of series in the Display list controls the order of bars within clusters, the order of segments within stacked bars, the order of stacked areas, and the order of legend items for all bar, area, and line charts. You can reorder the Display list by selecting a variable and using the system menu to move your selection up or down (see Chapter 28). In mixed charts, lines appear in the legend above areas and areas above bars.

Series Displayed as. In the list of series, each series name is followed by a colon and the word *Bar*, *Line*, or *Area* to indicate how it will be displayed when the chart is next drawn. To change the display for a series, select the series and then select one of the Series Displayed as alternatives. The chart in Figure 26.53 was derived from the chart in Figure 26.10 by changing the lines to areas and stacking the bars.

Categories. You can select categories to omit or display in the same way you select series. Displayed categories form the category axis in the order listed. You can reorder the Display list by selecting a category and using the system menu (see Chapter 28).

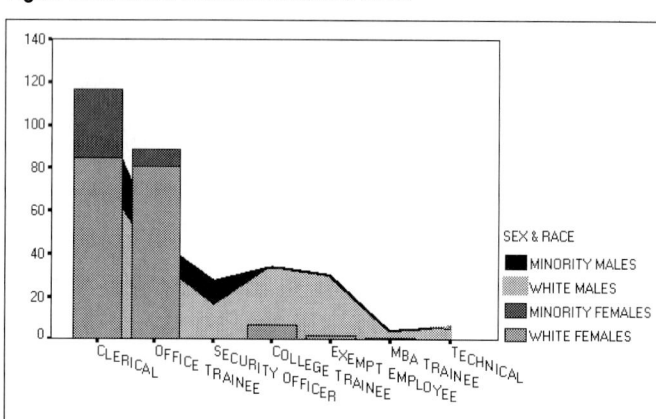

Figure 26.53 Mixed chart with bars and areas

Pie Chart Displayed Data

To adjust the display of series and categories in a pie chart, from the menus choose:
Series
 Displayed...

This opens the Pie Displayed Data dialog box, as shown in Figure 26.54.

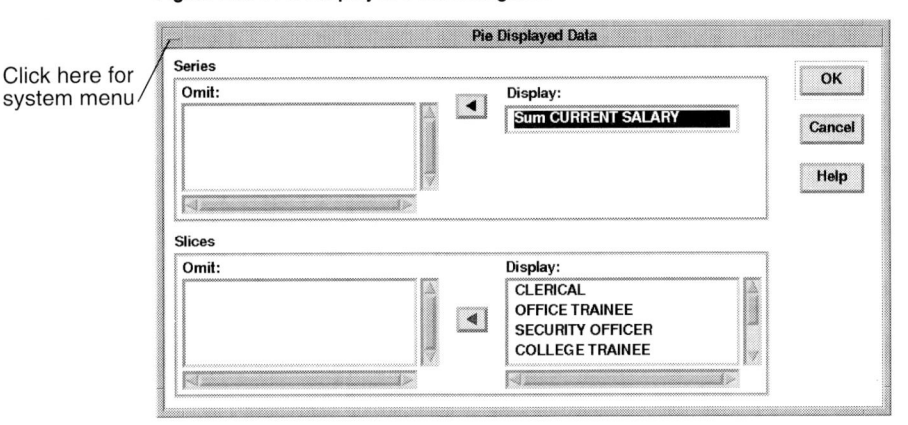

Figure 26.54 Pie Displayed Data dialog box

Click here for system menu

Series. If you created the chart as a pie chart, there is only one series listed. If you selected Pie from the Gallery menu with a multiple-series chart, there are several series in the Omit group and one under Display. If you don't want the selected series, first move the series to the Omit group. Then select the series you want.

Slices. You can reorder the Display list by selecting a category and using the system menu to move your selection up or down (see Chapter 28). You can delete categories from the display by moving them to the Omit list in the Slices group. If you omit any categories, the size of each slice is recalculated, using only the categories to be displayed.

Simple Scatterplot Displayed Data

To adjust the display of data series on a simple scatterplot, from the menus choose:

Series
 Displayed...

This opens the Simple Scatterplot Displayed Data dialog box, which controls the assignment of data series to the axes. You can use it to swap axes in a simple scatterplot. In changing to a simple scatterplot from a chart that includes more than two series, you can select the series you want to display on each axis. For example, suppose you have produced the overlay scatterplot shown in Figure 26.55, and you want to plot the verbal score against the math score.

Figure 26.55 Overlay scatterplot of SAT scores and tuition

From the menus choose:

Gallery
  Scatter...

Then click on Simple and New. The Simple Scatterplot Displayed Data dialog box appears, as shown in Figure 26.56.

Figure 26.56 Simple Scatterplot Displayed Data dialog box

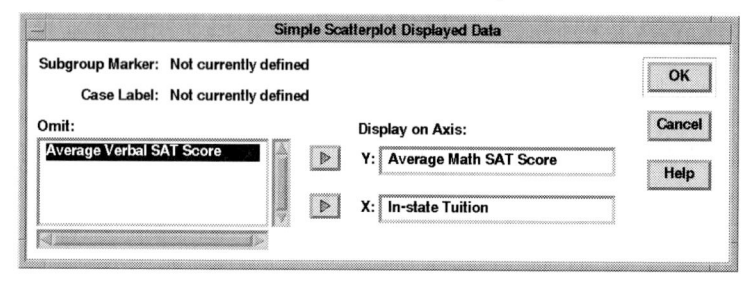

The variable that determines subgroup markers and the variable that supplies case labels (if either is assigned) are listed for your information. (Display of subgroup markers and case labels is controlled in Scatterplot Options. See "Overlay Scatterplot Options" on p. 523.)

To create a simple scatterplot where average verbal SAT is on the x axis and average math SAT is on the y axis, first select In-state Tuition in Display on Axis for X and click on ◄ to move it to the Omit list box. Then select Average Verbal SAT Score and click on ► to move it to Display on Axis for Y. Both Y and X must be specified for the OK pushbutton to be enabled.

If the current chart data are limited to two variables, you can use this dialog box to swap the *x* and *y* axes by first moving the variables to the Omit box and then back to the appropriate Y and X text boxes. When you have finished specifying variables, click on OK to display the new chart.

Overlay Scatterplot Displayed Data

To manipulate the display of series in an overlay scatterplot, from the menus choose:

Series
 Displayed...

This opens a dialog box similar to the one in Figure 26.57.

Figure 26.57 Overlay Scatterplot Displayed Data dialog box

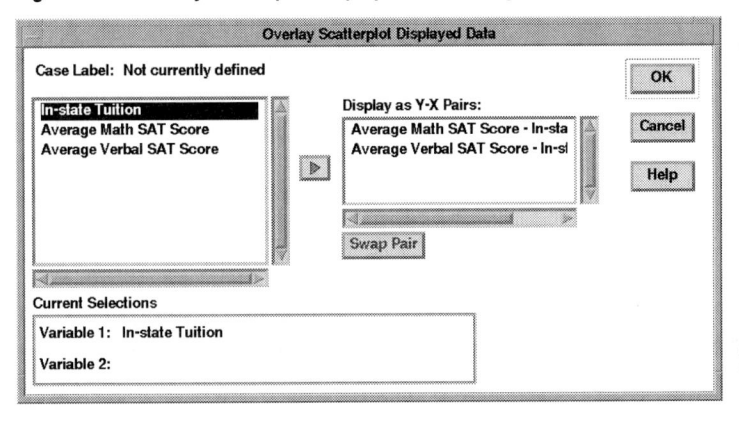

The case label variable, if any, is listed for your information. Underneath it is a box containing a list of the variables available for the chart. You cannot add any other variables. In the box labeled Display as Y-X Pairs are the pairs of variables plotted in the current chart. To remove a pair, select it and click on ◀.

You can add pairs selected from the available variables. When you select one variable, it appears in the Current Selections group in the first position. The next variable you select appears in the second position. To deselect a variable, click on it again. When a pair of variables is in the Current Selections group and you click on ▶, the pair appears in the Display box. For example, you might add the pair Average Math SAT Score- Average Verbal SAT Score. However, if you want the plots overlaid, you should consider the range on each axis. In the example just considered, the first two pairs listed have Tuition, which ranges into the thousands. SAT scores are in the hundreds, and the plot will look like a narrow line on the scale of thousands.

Clicking on Swap Pair reverses the axis assignments of a selected pair.

Scatterplot Matrix Displayed Data

If your chart is a scatterplot matrix, to change which series and categories are displayed, from the menus choose:

Series
 Displayed...

This opens a dialog box similar to the one shown in Figure 26.58.

Figure 26.58 Scatterplot Matrix Displayed Data dialog box

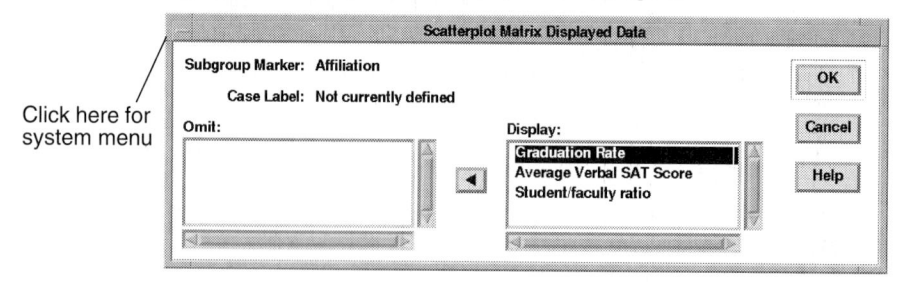

Click here for system menu

The subgroup marker and case label variable, if any, are listed for your information. The Display list box shows a list of available variables. To remove a variable from this list, select it and click on ◄ so that it moves to the Omit box. There must be at least two variables in the Display list box for the OK button to be enabled.

You can reorder the Display list by selecting a variable and using the system menu to move your selection up or down (see Chapter 28).

3-D Scatterplot Displayed Data

To change the series displayed on a 3-D scatterplot, from the menus choose:

Series
 Displayed...

This opens the dialog box shown in Figure 26.59. This box is also displayed if you change to a 3-D scatterplot from the Gallery menu.

Figure 26.59 3-D Scatterplot Displayed Data dialog box

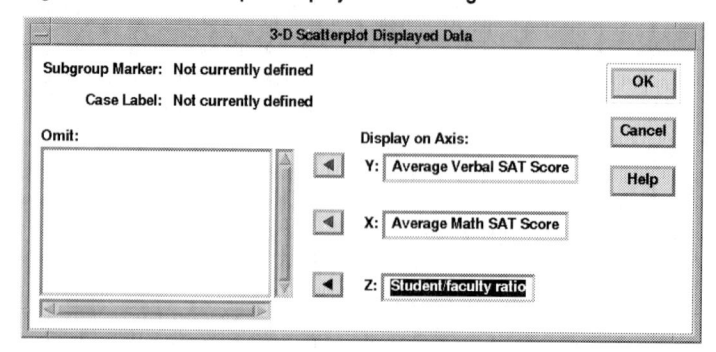

The subgroup marker and case label are listed for your information. The variable for each axis is listed under Display on Axis. To move a variable to the Omit list box, select it and click on [◀]. You can swap the axes by moving the variables to the Omit list box and then moving them back to the axes you want. In the default position, the y axis is vertical and perpendicular to the plane formed by the x and z axes.

Histogram Displayed Data

If a scatterplot is displayed (as in Figure 26.1), to obtain a histogram of one of the variables, from the menus choose:

Gallery
  Histogram...

This opens the Histogram Displayed Data dialog box, as shown in Figure 26.60. It can also be opened when a histogram is displayed by choosing:

Series
  Displayed...

Figure 26.60 Histogram Displayed Data dialog box

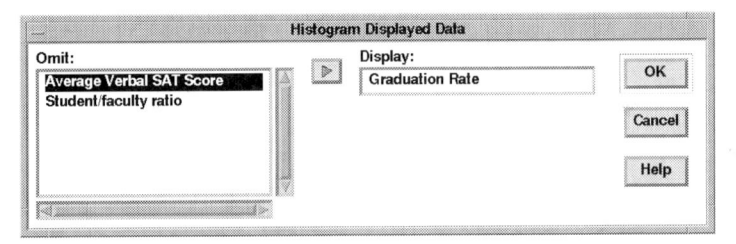

If you want to change the variable selected for display in the histogram, first select the variable in the Display box and move it to the Omit list box. Then select another variable in the Omit list box and move it to the Display box.

Transposing Data

In a multiple bar, line, or area chart, you can transpose series and categories. For example, in a clustered bar chart, the categories (designated on the category axis) become series (designated in the legend) and the series become categories. To do this, from the menus choose:

Series
  Transpose Data

The system redraws the chart if possible. If there are too many data or the assignment is ambiguous, the appropriate Displayed Data dialog box is displayed.

An example is shown in Figure 26.61. The difference between transposing data and swapping axes is illustrated in "Swapping Axes on Two-Dimensional Charts" on p. 567. Data transposition is not available for boxplots, scatterplots, or histograms.

Figure 26.61 Example of transposing data

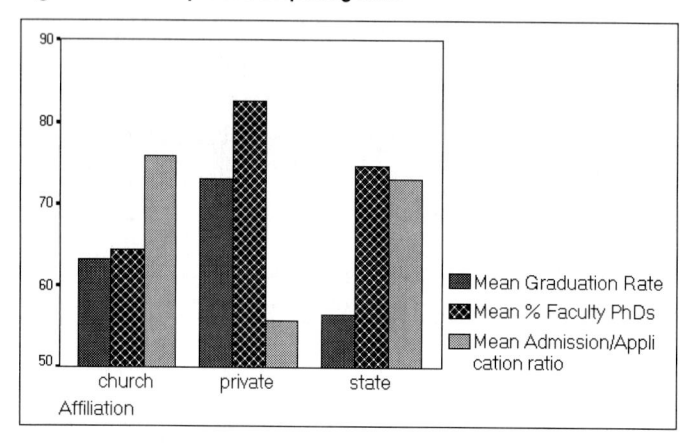

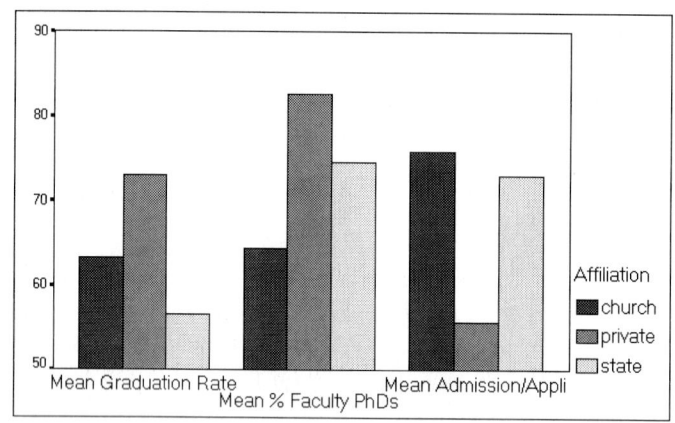

Modifying Attributes (Attributes Menu)

The objects that make up a chart have attributes that can be modified:
- Almost all objects have color.
- Lines, including data lines, axes, and the borders surrounding areas, have style and weight.
- Areas have fill pattern.
- Markers have style (shape) and size.

- Bars have bar style (normal, drop-shadows, or 3-D effect) and labels that indicate the exact values they represent along the scale axis.
- Data lines have interpolation style.
- Text items have font and size.
- Pie slices have position (normal or exploded).
- Axes have orientation that can be swapped (for two-dimensional charts) or rotated (for three-dimensional charts).

Modifying these attributes requires a mouse. With the mouse you select an object to modify and then make selections from palettes (see "Selecting Objects to Modify" on p. 504). The quickest way to select a palette or perform an Attributes menu action is to click on the appropriate button on the chart window icon bar. The attributes and their corresponding icon buttons are shown in Figure 26.62.

Figure 26.62 Attributes menu and chart window icon bar

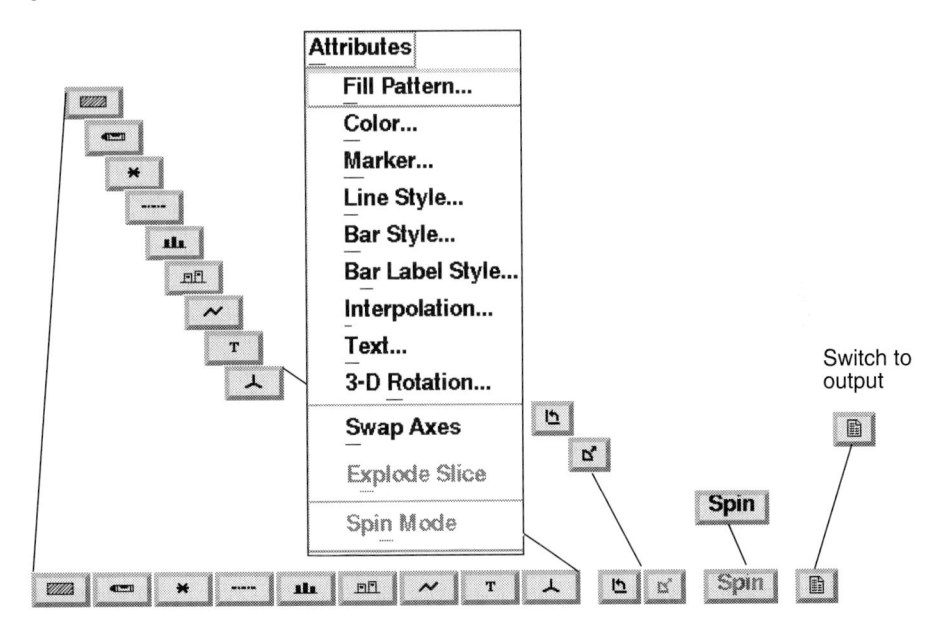

Palettes

When you select an item from the Attributes menu or click on the corresponding button on the icon bar, a palette or dialog box opens. It contains picture buttons illustrating the patterns or styles and several action buttons.

- If you click on Apply, the selected picture button is applied to the currently selected series or object.

- If you click on Apply All, the selected picture button is applied to all series in the chart.
- If you click on Close, the palette is closed without applying the selection.
- If you click on Help, the SPSS Help window for the palette opens.

The pattern or style of the selected chart object is highlighted by a box drawn around a picture button. If you select a different object in the chart while the palette is open, the attribute of the new selection is highlighted in the palette.

You can drag the palette anywhere on the screen, and you can have more than one palette open at a time.

Fill Patterns

To fill in enclosed areas such as bars, areas under lines, and background area, from the menus choose:

Attributes
 Fill Pattern...

or click on [icon]. This opens the Fill Patterns palette, as shown in Figure 26.63.

Figure 26.63 Fill Patterns palette

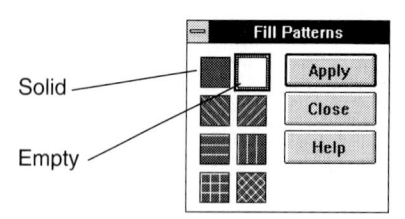

You can use a fill pattern to make distinctions between the areas, especially if the chart is to be presented in black and white or a limited number of colors. In the palette itself, patterns appear in only one color, but your pattern selection is applied to whatever color is in the selected area.

The white picture button represents an empty area. If this fill pattern is selected, the selected object will appear white or have the same color as the background, no matter what color is selected on the Colors palette.

If the bar style is drop-shadow or 3-D effect, you can select any surface of a series of bars and change the fill pattern. For example, you can select the top surface of the 3-D bars for one pattern and the right side for another pattern.

Colors

You can change the color of chart objects, including areas, lines, markers, and text. To change a color, select the object you want to change, and from the menus choose:

Attributes
 Color...

or click on [icon]. This opens the Colors palette, as shown in Figure 26.64.

Figure 26.64 Colors palette

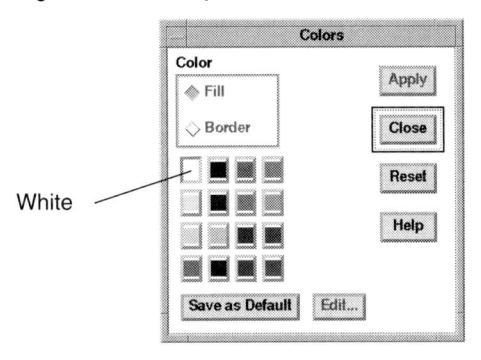

The color of a chart object is associated with a position in the palette and takes on whatever color is currently in that position.

Color. You can change the fill color or the border color (if the object has a border).

- **Fill.** Specifies the color inside the element if it is an area, or the color of other elements such as lines or text. To change the fill color, select an object in the chart, choose Fill, and then click on the color you want. When you click on Apply, the selected element changes to the color at the position you clicked on. Be sure that a non-empty fill pattern was previously selected and applied.

- **Border.** Specifies the color of the border of an enclosed area. To change the border color, select an area in the chart, choose Border, and then click on a color from the palette. When you click on Apply, the color of the border of the selected area changes.

Save as Default. If you change the colors in the palette, you can save the palette as the default palette. Then whenever you click on Reset, the saved default palette will appear and colors of chart objects change to match their associated positions in the palette.

Reset. If you have edited the color palette but have not saved it, clicking on Reset restores the colors in the default palette. It also changes the colors of elements in the chart to match the ones in the default palette.

Edit. If you want to customize a color in the palette, select the color you want to replace in the Colors palette shown in Figure 26.64 and click on Edit..., which opens the Colors Edit Color dialog box, as shown in Figure 26.65. White and black cannot be edited.

Figure 26.65 Colors Edit Color dialog box

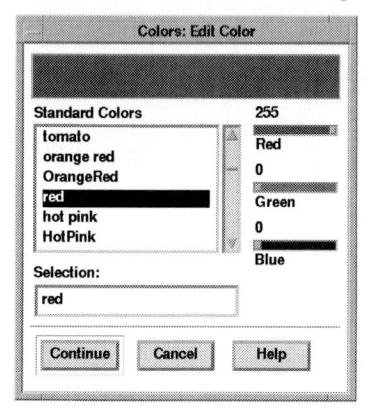

The bar at the top of the dialog box displays the current color. There are two ways to specify a color: either choose from the list or specify amounts of red, green, and blue.

Standard Colors. You can select a standard color from the list.

Red/Green/Blue. A custom color can be specified by adjusting the three scroll bars on the right. As you move a scroll-bar slider, the number above the scroll bar indicates the amount of red, green, or blue. The numbers range between 0 and 255. Specifications for common colors are in Table 26.1. This type of specification is commonly used to specify a color to be used in a light-emitting device, such as a video display. After specifying the color, click on Continue.

Table 26.1 Common color specifications

Color	Red	Green	Blue
Black	0	0	0
White	255	255	255
Red	255	0	0
Yellow	255	255	0
Green	0	255	0
Cyan	0	255	255
Blue	0	0	255
Magenta	255	0	255

Markers

Markers are used to indicate the location of data points in a line chart, area chart, or scatterplot. To change the size or style of markers in a chart, from the menus choose:

Attributes
  Marker...

or click on [✳]. This opens the Markers palette, as shown in Figure 26.66.

Figure 26.66 Markers palette

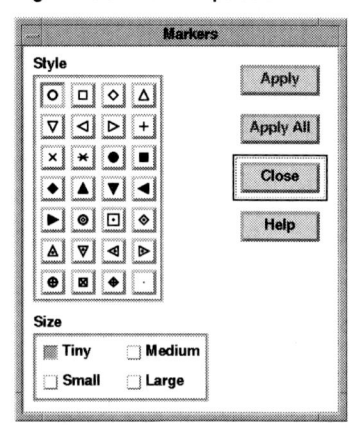

You can change the marker style and size for a single series or for all the series at once. By default, each series appears in a different color or with a different marker style according to how your graphic preferences are set.

If you have a line chart in which the markers are not displayed, open the Line Interpolation palette (see "Line Interpolation" on p. 563) and select Straight (or another interpolation style) and then Display Markers.

Line Styles

The lines in a chart, including the data lines and the axes, can have different weights and different styles. To change the weight or style of a line, select it and from the menus choose:

Attributes
  Line Style...

or click on [----]. This opens the Line Styles palette, as shown in Figure 26.67.

Figure 26.67 Line Styles palette

Style. Controls the pattern of the line. The default is solid.

Weight. Controls the thickness of the line. The default is thin.

Bar Styles

To add a drop-shadow or a 3-D effect to a bar chart, from the menus choose:

Attributes
  Bar Style...

or click on [icon]. This opens the Bar Styles palette, as shown in Figure 26.68. Bars for every series in a chart have the same bar style.

Figure 26.68 Bar Styles palette

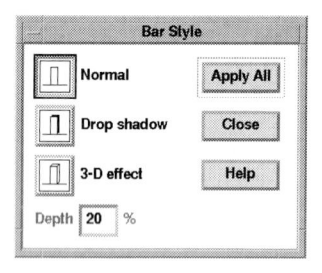

Normal. No shadows or 3-D effect. This is the default.

Drop shadow. Displays a shadow behind each bar. You can specify the depth of the shadow as a positive or negative percentage of the width of each original bar. The default is 20%. Positive depth places the shadow to the right of the bar, negative to the left.

3-D effect. Displays each bar as a rectangular solid. You can specify depth as a percentage of the width of each original bar. The default is 20%. Switching from positive to negative depth changes the perspective of the viewer. With a positive value, you see the tops and right sides of the bars. With a negative value, you see the left sides.

If you have already changed the color or pattern of the original bars, the new block surfaces are displayed in the default color and pattern, while the front surface retains the attributes you selected previously. Once the shadows or 3-D bars are displayed, you can change the color and pattern of each type of individual surface, including the shadows or the side and top surfaces for each series.

Bar Label Styles

To label each bar in a bar chart with its numerical value, from the menus choose:

Attributes
　Bar Label Style...

or click on ▣▣. This opens the Bar Label Styles palette, as shown in Figure 26.69.

Figure 26.69 Bar Label Styles palette

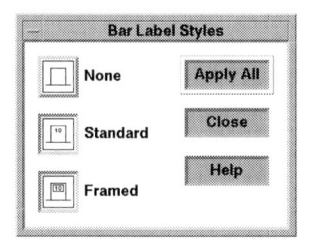

The bar label style applies to all of the bars in the chart. In a bar chart, the number of decimal places in the bar labels is the same as the number of decimal places in the scale axis labels.

None. No values appear on the bars. This is the default.

Standard. Displays a value at the top of each bar. It may or may not be easy to read, depending on the color and pattern of the bar. You can change the color, font, or size of the value text.

Framed. Displays the values in white frames at the tops of the bars. You can change the color, font, or size of the value text and the color of the frames.

Line Interpolation

In a line chart or scatterplot, to select a method used to connect the data points, from the menus choose:

Attributes
　Interpolation...

or click on ∿. This opens the Line Interpolation palette shown in Figure 26.70. The Step, Jump, and Spline picture buttons each have a drop-down list. Examples of various types of interpolation are shown in Figure 26.71.

Figure 26.70 Line Interpolation palette

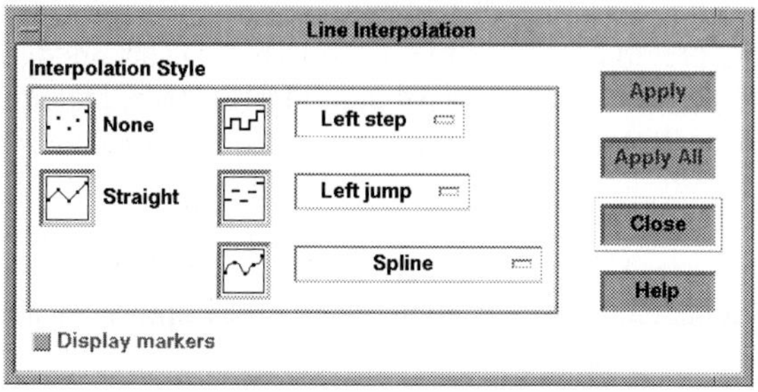

The following options are available for line interpolation style:

None. No lines connect the points.

Straight. The data points are connected in succession by straight lines. This is the default for line charts.

- **Step.** Each data point has a horizontal line drawn through it, with vertical risers joining the steps. Selecting Left step, Center step, or Right step from the drop-down list specifies the location of the data point in the horizontal line.

- **Jump.** Each data point has a horizontal line drawn through it, with no risers. Selecting Left jump, Center jump, or Right jump from the drop-down list specifies the location of the data point in the horizontal line.

- **Spline.** The data points are connected by a cubic spline. Lines are always drawn from left to right. For scatterplots, the parametric cubic form is used, and lines are drawn in order of data entry. On the Spline drop-down list are two more types of interpolation:

   3rd-order Lagrange. Produces third-order Lagrange interpolations in which the third-order polynomial is fitted through the closest four points. The parametric cubic form is used with scatterplots.

   5th-order Lagrange. Produces fifth-order Lagrange interpolations in which the fifth-order polynomial is fitted through the closest six points. The parametric form is used with scatterplots.

The following option is also available:

- **Display markers.** Displays markers at the data points. To change the style and size of the markers, see "Markers" on p. 561.

For scatterplots, to obtain more interpolation types, from the menus choose:

Chart
 Options...

Then select Total or Subgroups and click on Fit Options.

Figure 26.71 Examples of line interpolation with markers displayed

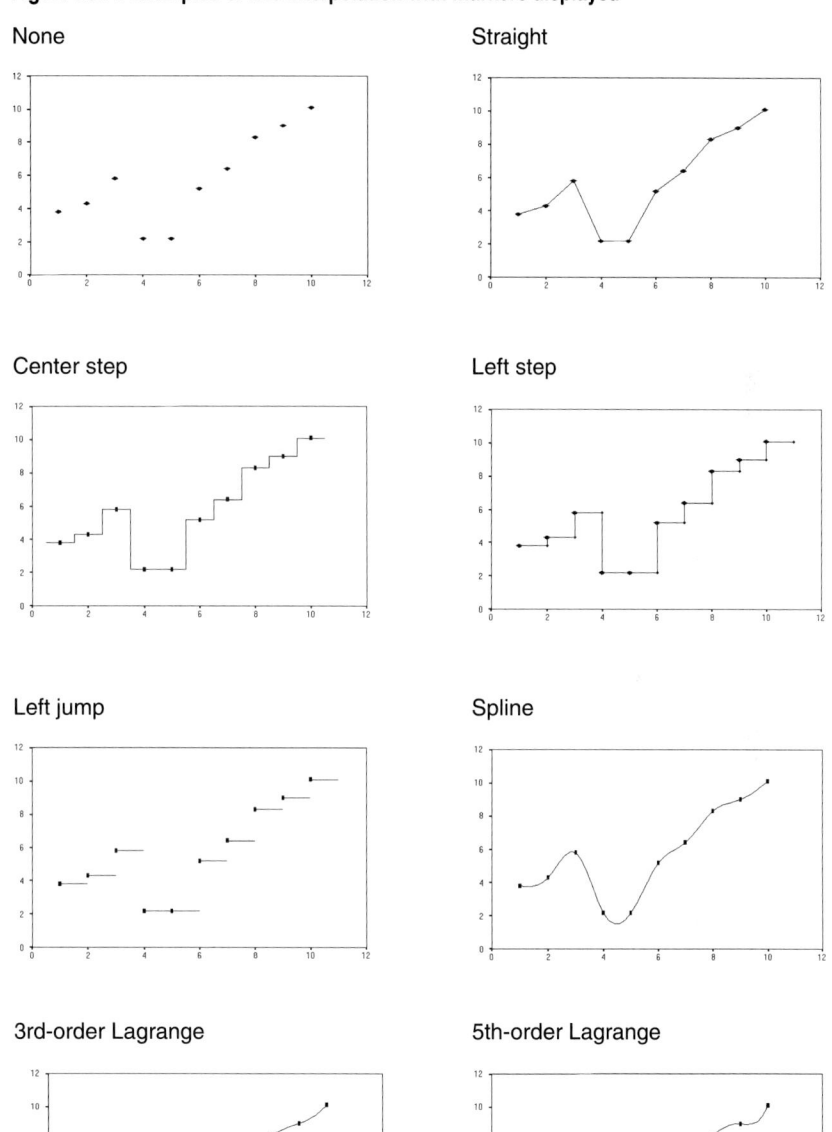

None

Straight

Center step

Left step

Left jump

Spline

3rd-order Lagrange

5th-order Lagrange

Text

To change the font or size of a text element of the chart, such as an axis label, select the text and from the menus choose:

Attributes
  Text...

or click on [T]. This opens the Text Styles palette, as shown in Figure 26.72.

Figure 26.72 Text Styles palette

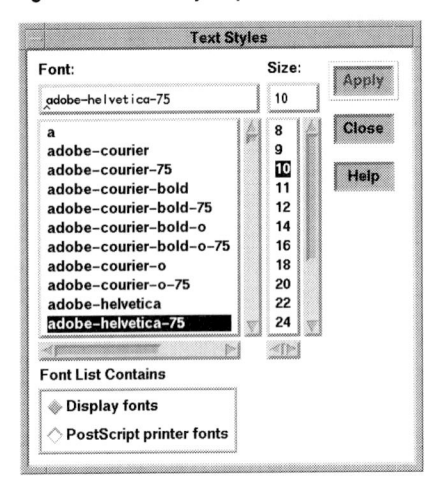

Font. The scroll list contains a list of fonts installed on your system. To change the font, select it from the list.

Size. To change the font size, select the size from the list or type it.

Font List Contains. Controls the fonts displayed in font list. You can choose one of the following alternatives:

◇ **Display fonts.** All display fonts available in your font path.

◇ **PostScript printer fonts.** Standard PostScript printer fonts plus PostScript fonts supplied in *$SPSS_ROOT/AFM (/usr/lpp/SPSS/bin/AFM)*.

Exploding Pie Chart Slices

You can **explode** (separate) one or more slices from a pie chart for emphasis (see Figure 26.73).

Figure 26.73 Pie chart with exploded slice selected

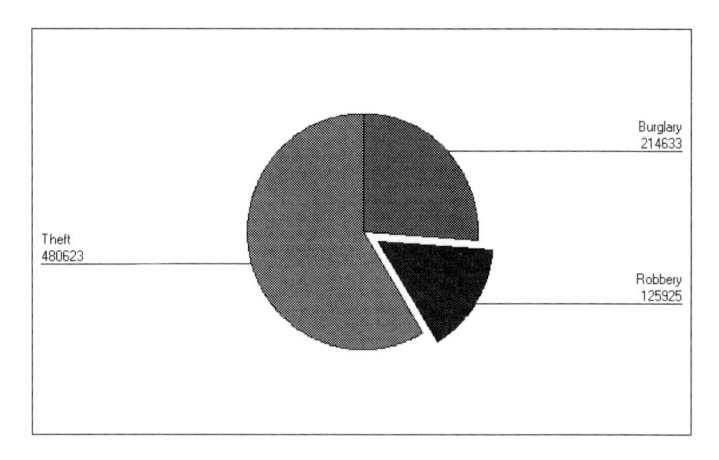

[Pie chart showing: Burglary 214633, Robbery 125925, Theft 480623, with the Robbery slice exploded]

To explode a slice, select it and from the menus choose:

Attributes
  Explode Slice

or click on [icon]. To reverse the explosion, select the slice and click on the icon or menu choice again. A check mark on the menu indicates the currently selected slice is exploded. You can explode two or more slices, one at a time.

To explode the whole pie, from the menus choose:

Gallery
  Pie...

and then click on Exploded.

Changing or Rotating the Axes

You can change the perspective of a chart by swapping axes or rotating the chart.

Swapping Axes on Two-Dimensional Charts

Category charts, boxplots, and histograms. In a 2-D bar chart, line chart, area chart, or mixed chart with one scale axis, you can swap the axes, which changes the orientation between vertical and horizontal. The bars, lines, or areas still represent the same values.

568   Chapter 26

This is different from transposing, where the categories change places with the series named in the legend (see "Transposing Data" on p. 555). The difference between swapping axes and transposing data is illustrated in Figure 26.74.

Figure 26.74 Swapping axes and transposing data

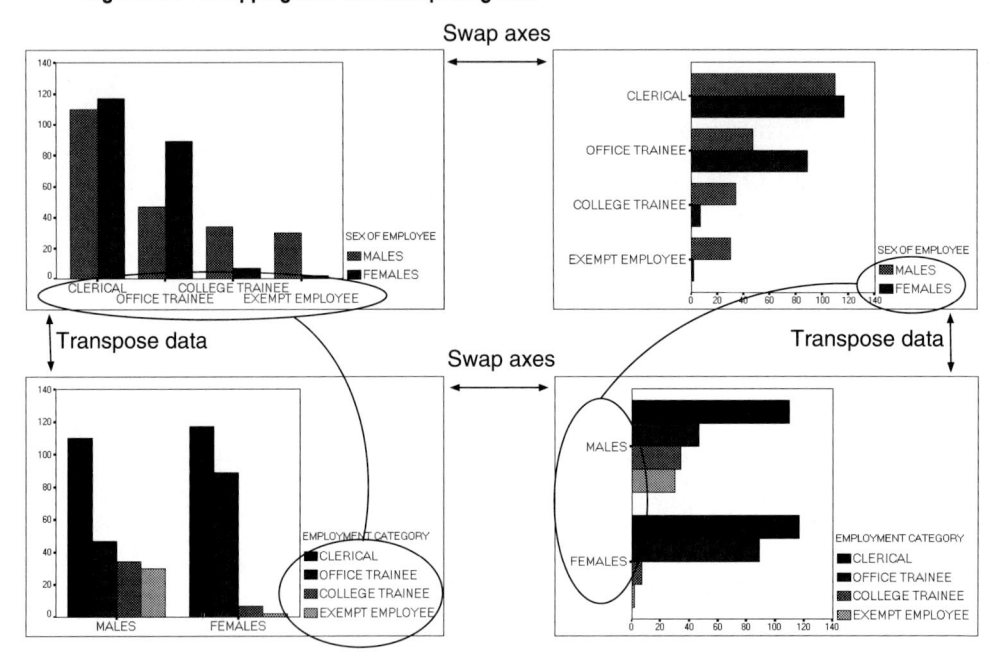

To swap axes, from the menus choose:

Attributes
  Swap Axes

or click on 🔄. You can also use this procedure for boxplots and histograms.

Scatterplots. To swap the axes in a scatterplot, from the menus choose:

Series
  Displayed...

and assign the variables to different axes, as described in "Simple Scatterplot Displayed Data" on p. 551.

Rotating a 3-D Chart

If the current chart is a 3-D scatterplot, you can rotate in six directions. To rotate a 3-D scatterplot, from the menus choose:

Attributes
　3-D Rotation...

or click on ⊥. This opens the 3-D Rotation dialog box, as shown in Figure 26.75.

Figure 26.75 3-D Rotation dialog box

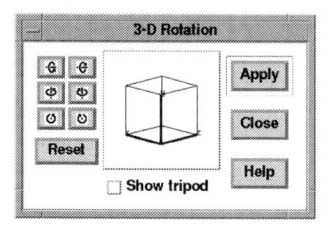

The direction of rotation is indicated on each button. Rotation is about one of three lines: a horizontal line in the plane of the screen, a vertical line in the plane of the screen, or a line perpendicular to the plane of the screen. You can click on a rotation button and release it, or you can click and hold the mouse button until you get as much rotation as you want. The rotation is illustrated in the center of the dialog box. When you have reached the orientation you want, click on Apply and then click on Close. Clicking on the Reset pushbutton returns the chart to the default orientation.

❏ **Show tripod.** Displays a tripod composed of lines parallel to the x, y, and z axes, with their intersection at the center of the wireframe.

Using Spin Mode

For another way to rotate 3-D charts, from the menus choose:

Attributes
　Spin Mode

or click on **Spin**. This displays the chart with a new icon bar having the same rotation buttons as the 3-D Rotation dialog box. However, in this mode, the chart is stripped down for the duration of spinning. Only the tripod is shown and solid markers are hollow.

　Spin mode allows you to watch the pattern of the points change while you spin the chart. As in the other rotation mode, you can click on a rotation button and release it, or you can hold it down while the chart spins. When you are satisfied with the chart orientation, click on End Spin. The rotated chart is returned to the full version in the new position with its other attributes and options restored. The Reset button returns the chart to its default orientation.

Finding Information in This Chapter

The following table summarizes the chapter contents by menu selection, section reference, and comments, to help you locate specific chart modification facilities.

Table 26.2 Finding information in this chapter

Menu Selection	Reference	Comments
	"Editing in a Chart Window" on p. 503	Summary of menu functions
	"Selecting Objects to Modify" on p. 504	How to select various chart objects
View/Refresh	"Chart Menus" on p. 503	Redrawing a chart
Gallery	"Changing Chart Types (Gallery Menu)" on p. 506	Standard plus additional chart types (mixed, drop-line, and exploded pie)
Gallery/ Bar, Line, Area, Mixed, Pie		Change type among bar, line, area, mixed, and pie charts
Gallery/ Scatter, Histogram		Change between types of scatterplots and histograms
Chart/Options	"Bar/Line/Area Options" on p. 511	100% scale, connect markers, projection line, clustered/stacked bars
	"Pie Options" on p. 514	Position slices, collapse slices, labels
	"Boxplot Options" on p. 517	Outliers, extremes, labels, counts
	"Scatterplot Options: Simple and Matrix" on p. 518 "Overlay Scatterplot Options" on p. 523 "3-D Scatterplot Options" on p. 524	Subgroups, fit line, sunflowers, mean reference line, label cases, case frequency weights, spikes, prediction lines, intercept, R^2, wireframe (3-D)
	"Histogram Options" on p. 526	Normal curve, statistics, weights
Chart/Axis	"Scale Axis" on p. 528	Axis title, scale, range, divisions, labels, tick marks, grid lines, hanging bars
	"Scatterplot Matrix Scale Axes" on p. 531	Axis title, diagonal title, labels, tick marks, grid lines
	"Category Axis" on p. 534	Axis title, markers, labels
	"Interval Axis" on p. 536	Axis title, markers, intervals, labels
Chart/Bar Spacing	"Bar Spacing" on p. 540	Spacing of bars and bar clusters
Chart/Title	"Titles" on p. 541	Adding or editing chart titles
Chart/Footnote	"Footnotes" on p. 542	Adding or editing chart footnotes
Chart/Legend	"Legends" on p. 543	Adding or editing chart legend
Chart/Annotation	"Annotation" on p. 544	Adding or editing text within the chart area
Chart/ Reference Line	"Adding Reference Lines" on p. 546	Adding or deleting horizontal and vertical reference lines
Chart/Outer Frame	"Outer Frame" on p. 548	Frame outside titles and footnotes
Chart/Inner Frame	"Inner Frame" on p. 547	Frame coincident with axes

Table 26.2 Finding information in this chapter (Continued)

Menu Selection	Reference	Comments
Series/ Displayed	"Bar, Line, and Area Chart Displayed Data" on p. 549 "Pie Chart Displayed Data" on p. 550 "Simple Scatterplot Displayed Data" on p. 551 "Overlay Scatterplot Displayed Data" on p. 553 "Scatterplot Matrix Displayed Data" on p. 554 "3-D Scatterplot Displayed Data" on p. 554 "Histogram Displayed Data" on p. 555	Omitting or displaying series and categories
Series/ Transpose Data	"Transposing Data" on p. 555	Transposing series between the category axis and the legend
Attributes (Also pushbuttons on the icon bar)	"Palettes" on p. 557	Changing fill patterns, colors, markers, line styles, bar styles, bar label styles, line interpolation, text styles
Attributes/ Swap Axes	"Swapping Axes on Two-Dimensional Charts" on p. 567	Swapping axes
Attributes/ Explode Slice	"Exploding Pie Chart Slices" on p. 567	Exploding pie slices
Attributes/Spin Mode	"Rotating a 3-D Chart" on p. 569 "Using Spin Mode" on p. 569	Rotating or spinning a 3-D scatterplot

27 Printing

You can print text files from output and syntax windows, data files from the Data Editor window, and chart files from chart windows.

Printers

SPSS supports PostScript printers and ASCII text printers.

- The contents of output and syntax windows and the Data Editor window can be printed on a PostScript or ASCII text printer.
- High-resolution charts in chart windows can be printed only on PostScript devices.

Printing a Syntax or Output File

You can print a whole syntax or output file, or a selected portion. To print a syntax or output text file:

1. Make the window containing the file the active window.
2. From the menus choose:

    File
      Print...

    This opens the Print dialog box, as shown in Figure 27.1. The name of the file is shown in the dialog box. The printer name is also displayed.

    Figure 27.1   Print dialog box for text

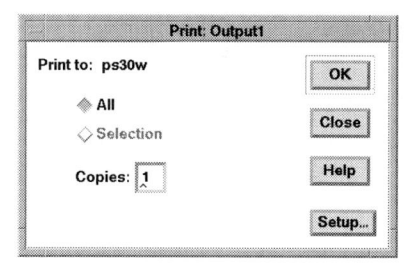

3. To print the file, click on OK.

The following print options are available:

◇ **All**. Prints the entire file. This is the default.

◇ **Selection**. Prints a selected area of the file. To select an area for printing, use the click-and-drag technique to highlight the area. If there is no highlighted area in the file, this option is disabled.

Copies. By default, one copy is printed. If you want multiple copies, enter the number of copies you want to print.

Text Printer Setup

You can also change the selected printer, change the page orientation for PostScript printing, or print to a file. Click on Setup... in the Print dialog box to open the Text Printer Setup dialog box, as shown in Figure 27.2.

Figure 27.2 Text Printer Setup dialog box

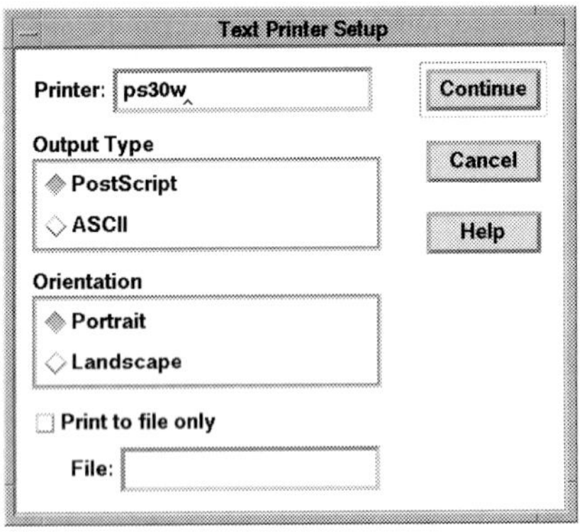

Printer. To override the default printer, enter the name of the printer you want to use. (See Appendix F for information on changing the default printer used by SPSS.)

Output Type. Select the appropriate output type for the selected printer.

◇ **PostScript**. This is the default. If the selected printer is not a PostScript printer, this option will produce raw PostScript code (probably not what you want).

◇ **ASCII**. Select this option if you are using an ASCII text printer. If the selected printer is not an ASCII text printer (for example, a PostScript printer), an error will result.

Orientation. If you are using a PostScript printer, you can also specify the page orientation.

- **Portrait.** Vertical orientation (the length is greater than the width). This is the default.
- **Landscape.** Horizontal orientation (the width is greater than the length).

The following option is also available:

- **Print to file only.** Prints to a file in the specified output form. Enter a filename in the text box. If you do not specify a path, the file is placed in the directory from which you started SPSS.

Determining the Correct Width and Length for Printed Output

In SPSS, output width and length are based on the number of characters per line and the number of lines per page as specified in the Preferences Output dialog box (see Chapter 29). Width and length selections generally should be consistent with font size and printer setup options, such as page orientation. For example, if you specify a font size or line length greater than the default values, you may need to change the page size or orientation in your printer setup to avoid truncating printed output.

Using Page Headers to Format Printed Output Pages

By default, SPSS puts as much output as possible on each page and doesn't insert any additional space between pages. To insert space between pages and begin printing output from each procedure on a new page, select Page headers in the Preferences Output dialog box. This also prints any output page titles or subtitles you have specified. For more information on page titles, see Chapter 28 and Chapter 29.

Printing a Data File

To print a data file, follow the same steps used to print a syntax or output file. The name of the file and the printer are shown in the Print dialog box. You can print the entire file or a selected area.

Options for Data Files

You can print or suppress grid lines that outline data cells. You can also print actual data values or value labels that have been defined.

A data file is printed as it appears on screen. Whether grid lines and value labels are printed depends on whether they appear in the Data Editor window.

Grid Lines

By default, grid lines are displayed. To turn grid lines off and on:

1. Make the Data Editor window the active window.
2. From the menus choose:

    View
      Grid Lines

Value Labels

By default, value labels are not displayed. To turn value labels on and off:

1. Make the Data Editor window the active window.
2. From the menus choose:

    View
      Value Labels

When value labels are turned on, all values for which a label is defined appear as the label. A label wider than the cell in which it appears is truncated.

Format of Printed Data Files

Printed data files are paginated from left to right and top to bottom. Page numbers in the form *row–column* are displayed. For example, page 1–1 contains the top rows of data in the first set of columns from the left. Page 2–2 contains data in the second set of rows from the top in the second set of columns from the left. Variable names and case numbers are printed on every page.

Printing a Chart File

To print a chart file:

1. Make the chart window or the chart carousel the active window. If you activate the chart carousel, the currently displayed chart is printed.
2. From the menus choose:

    File
      Print...

This opens the Print dialog box for charts, as shown in Figure 27.3. The name of the file is displayed. The printer name is also displayed. You can print only the entire chart, not just a selected portion.

Figure 27.3 Print dialog box for charts

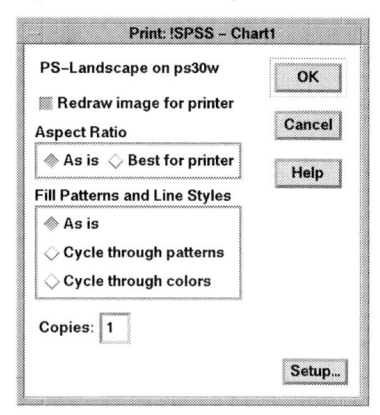

3. To print the file, click on OK.

The following options are available for printing charts:

- **Redraw image for printer**. Redraws chart to adjust for printer fonts. If your chart uses fonts or font sizes that are not loaded in the printer, the printer uses the closest available font and size, and text may be truncated or may not be aligned properly with the chart unless the chart is first redrawn for the printer. This option produces the best printed results, but it can be slow. Deselect this default option if you want only a quick draft or if your chart uses only printer fonts.

Redrawing a chart for printing also allows you to adjust the following chart features:

Aspect Ratio. The width-to-height ratio of the outer frame of the chart. You can choose one of the following alternatives:

- **As is**. Uses the chart aspect ratio as it appears in the chart on the screen. (Chart aspect ratio is controlled from the Preferences Graphics dialog box. See Chapter 29.)
- **Best for printer**. Makes full use of an 8 1/2 × 11-inch page in landscape (horizontal) mode.

Fill Patterns and Line Styles. You can choose one of the following alternatives:

- **As is**. Uses the colors and/or patterns as they appear on the chart. If you are using a black-and-white PostScript printer, colors appear as shades of gray.
- **Cycle through patterns**. Substitutes patterns for colors in graphic elements, such as bars, lines, and pie sectors. For line charts, the cycle includes four line styles within four line weights to make sixteen possible combinations. For bar charts, area charts, and pie charts, the cycle includes seven fill patterns (including solid). For scatterplots, the cycle includes 28 available marker types. Any existing patterns, line styles,

or marker types in the chart are ignored. This option also converts all text to solid black and backgrounds to white.

◇ **Cycle through colors**. Substitutes colors for patterns, line styles, and marker styles. The default palette of 14 colors is used. If more than 14 colors are required, patterns are added to the colors. Any existing colors or patterns are ignored. This option also converts all text to solid black and backgrounds to white.

Copies. By default, one copy is printed. If you want multiple copies, enter the number of copies you want to print.

Chart Printer Setup

You can also change the selected printer, change the page orientation, or print the chart to an encapsulated PostScript (EPS) file. Click on Setup... in the Print dialog box. This opens the Chart Printer Setup dialog box, as shown in Figure 27.4.

Figure 27.4 Chart Printer Setup dialog box

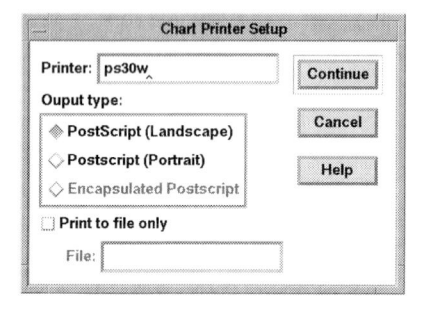

Printer. To override the default printer, enter the name of the printer you want to use. (See Appendix F for information on changing the default printer used by SPSS.)

Output Type. You can choose one of the following options:

◇ **PostScript (Landscape)**. Horizontal orientation (the width is greater than the length). This is the default for charts.

◇ **PostScript (Portrait)**. Vertical orientation (the length is greater than the width).

◇ **Encapsulated PostScript**. Prints to a file in EPS format. This option is available only if you select Print to file only.

The following option is also available:

❏ **Print to file only.** Prints to a file in the specified output form. Enter a filename in the text box. If you do not specify a path, the file is placed in the directory from which you started SPSS.

Font Mapping

For PostScript printing in output and syntax windows and in the Data Editor window, the screen display font is mapped to a standard PostScript printer font using the settings in the file *$SPSS_ROOT/PSstd.fonts*. The files *$SPSS_ROOT/AFM/*.afm* contain font characteristics that can be downloaded. There is one *.afm* file for each font family. You can modify the *PSstd.fonts* file to include additional mappings, provided that a *.afm* file is available for the printer font. If no printer font mapping exists for the display font, the Courier font is used and a warning message is issued.

For PostScript printing of charts, the settings in *$SPSS_ROOT/gefonts.map* are used to map display fonts to printer fonts.

28 Utilities

This chapter describes the functions found on the Utilities menu, as well as two additional features: reordering target variable lists and stopping the SPSS processor.

Command Index

If you are familiar with SPSS command syntax, you can quickly find the corresponding dialog boxes using the Command Index. From the menus choose:

Utilities
  Command Index...

This opens the Command Index dialog box, as shown in Figure 28.1.

Figure 28.1 Command Index dialog box

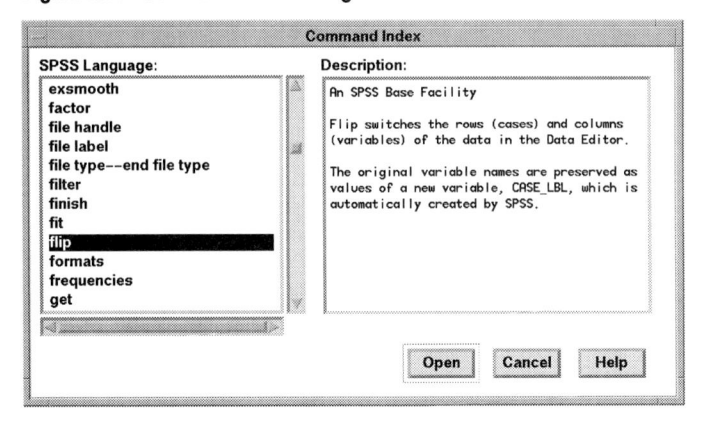

SPSS Language. Displays a complete list of SPSS commands in alphabetical order. To search for a particular command, use the scroll bar or type the first letter of the command name. This scrolls through the list to the first command that starts with that letter. Repeatedly typing the letter will cycle through all commands that begin with that letter. To go to the corresponding dialog box for a command, select the command from the list and click on Open... (or double-click on the command name).

Description. Provides a brief description of the command and its availability. Some commands are not part of the Base system and require add-on options; others cannot be accessed through dialog boxes. The description identifies optional features and commands that can be run only by entering syntax in a syntax window.

Variable Information

To obtain information on individual variables, copy and paste variable names into command syntax, or go to a specific variable in the Data Editor window, from the menus choose:

Utilities
  Variables...

This opens the Variables dialog box, as shown in Figure 28.2.

Figure 28.2 Variables dialog box

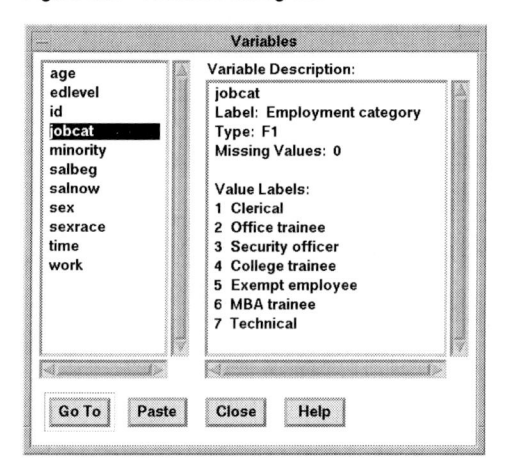

The Variable Information box displays variable definition information for the currently selected variable, including:

- Data format
- Variable label
- User-missing values
- Value labels

You can modify the definition of a variable using the Define Variable dialog box (see Chapter 3).

In addition to variable information, the following options are available:

Go To. To find the selected variable in the Data Editor window, click on Go To. This closes the Variables dialog box and makes the Data Editor the active window.

Paste. To paste variable names into command syntax:

1. If you have more than one syntax window open, make the syntax window in which you want to paste the variable names the designated syntax window.
2. Position the cursor where you want the variable names to be pasted.
3. Highlight the variables in the Variables dialog box and click on Paste. You can also paste individual variables simply by double-clicking on them.

Variable Sets

You can restrict the variables that appear on dialog-box source variable lists by defining and using variable sets.

Defining Variable Sets

To define variable sets, from the menus choose:

Utilities
　Define Sets...

This opens the Define Variable Sets dialog box, as shown in Figure 28.3.

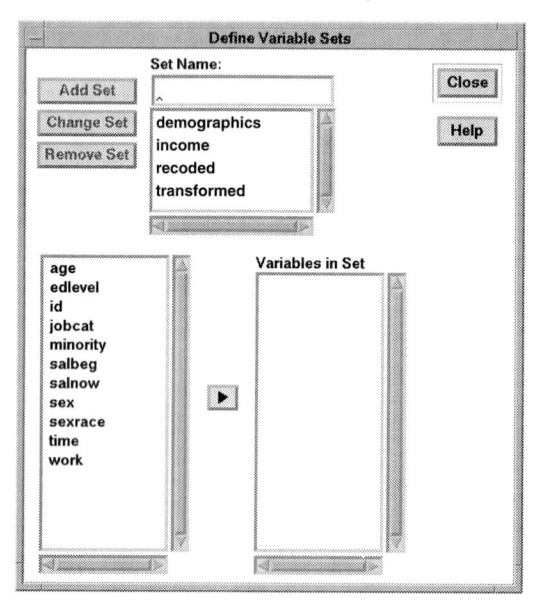

Figure 28.3 Define Variable Sets dialog box

You can create new sets, modify existing sets, and remove sets.

- To create a new set, enter a set name, select the variables to include in the set, and click on Add Set.
- To modify an existing set or change the set name, select the set name from the list of sets, make the changes, and click on Change Set.
- To remove a set, select the set name from the list of sets and click on Remove Set.

Set Name. Set names can be up to 12 characters long. Any characters, including blanks, can be used. Set names are not case-sensitive. If you enter the name of an existing set, Add Set is disabled and Change Set is enabled, indicating that the new set definition will replace an existing set.

Variables in Set. Any combination of numeric, short string, and long string variables can be included in a set. The order of variables in the set has no effect on the display order of the variables on dialog box source lists. A variable can belong to multiple sets.

Using Variable Sets

To use variable sets, from the menus choose:

Utilities
 Use Sets...

This opens the Use Sets dialog box, as shown in Figure 28.4.

Figure 28.4 Use Sets dialog box

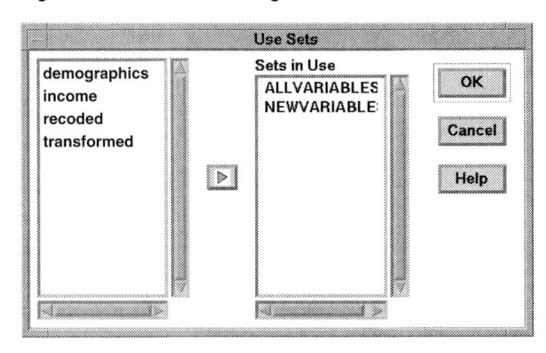

The source list contains any defined variable sets for the data file.

Sets in Use. Displays the sets used to produce the source variable lists in dialog boxes. Variables appear on the source lists in alphabetical or file order. The order of sets and the order of variables within a set have no effect on source list variable order. By default, two system-defined sets are in use:

- **ALLVARIABLES**. This set contains all variables in the data file, including new variables created during a session.
- **NEWVARIABLES**. This set contains only new variables created during the session.

You can remove these sets from the list and select others, but there must be at least one set on the list. If you don't remove the ALLVARIABLES set from the Sets in Use list, any other sets you include are more or less irrelevant.

File Information

To display complete dictionary information for every variable in the currently open data file, from the menus choose:

Utilities
 File Info

The following information is displayed in the output window:

- Variable name.
- Descriptive variable label (if any).
- Print and write formats. The data type is followed by a number indicating the maximum width and the number of decimal positions (if any). For example, F8.2 indicates a numeric variable with a maximum width of 8 columns, including one column for the decimal point and two columns for decimal positions.
- Descriptive value labels (if any) for different values of the variable. Both the value and the corresponding label are displayed.

Reordering Target Variable Lists

Variables appear in dialog box target lists in the order in which they are selected from the source list. If you want to change the order of variables in a target list—but you don't want to deselect all the variables and reselect them in the new order—you can move variables up and down in the target list with the following key combinations:

- (Alt) + plus sign moves the selected variables down one position in the target list.
- (Alt) + minus sign moves the selected variables up one position in the target list.

You can select and move multiple variables at the same time provided they are contiguous (not separated by other variables).

Stopping the SPSS Processor

If you inadvertently select a statistical analysis that you don't want, you can stop the SPSS processor. This is particularly useful if you are working with a large data file or have requested statistics for a large number of variables and the procedure takes a long time to execute. To halt the execution of a procedure, from the menus choose:

File
　Stop SPSS Processor

29 Preferences

Many of the SPSS default settings can be replaced by user-specified values. Most of these changes remain in effect only for the duration of the session. However, some changes can be persistent across SPSS sessions. These persistent default modifications are called **preferences**, and you can customize these preferences to meet your specific needs. These preferences include:

- Content and location of the SPSS journal file.
- Working memory allocation.
- Custom currency formats.
- Plot symbols used in character-based charts and plots.
- Colors, patterns, and other default preferences for high-resolution charts.
- Output page width and length.
- System information displayed in output windows.

Preferences Dialog Boxes

The first time you start an SPSS session, the SPSS Startup Preferences dialog box, shown in Figure 29.1, opens automatically.

Figure 29.1 SPSS Startup Preferences dialog box

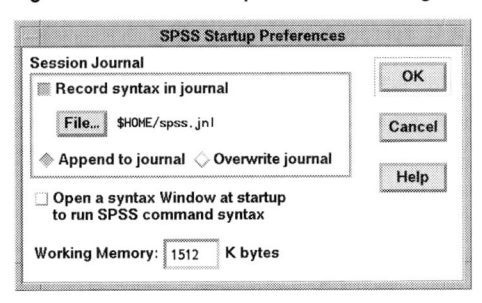

The startup preferences are a subset of the preferences available with the Preferences dialog box. Since you can modify the preference settings at any time, and the new settings remain in effect across SPSS sessions, in most cases you can simply accept the default startup preferences.

To modify the SPSS preference settings during a session, from the Data Editor menus choose:

Options
  Preferences...

This opens the Preferences dialog box, as shown in Figure 29.2.

Figure 29.2 Preferences dialog box

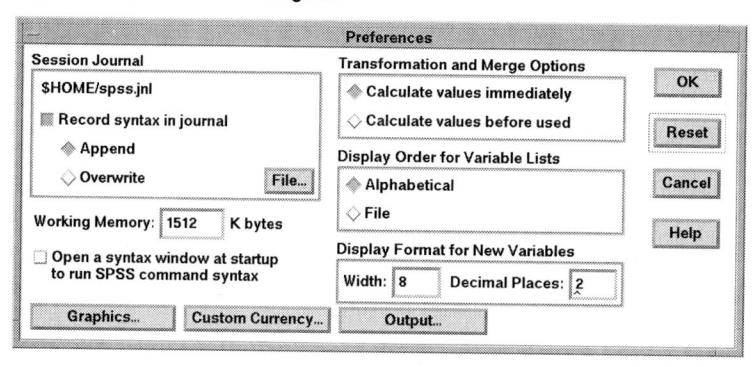

Session Journal

SPSS automatically creates and maintains a journal file of all commands run in an SPSS session. This includes commands entered and run in syntax windows and commands generated by dialog box choices. You can edit the journal file and use the commands again in other SPSS sessions.

- **Record syntax in journal.** Any SPSS command syntax generated in the session is recorded in the journal file. This is the default. You can turn the journal off and on during the session, saving selected sets of commands.

    - **Append.** Saves a journal of all SPSS sessions. The command syntax for each successive SPSS session is appended to the bottom of the journal file. This is the default.

    - **Overwrite.** Saves a journal of only the most recent SPSS session. Each time you start a new session, the journal file is overwritten.

Journal Filename and Location

By default, SPSS creates a journal file named *spss.jnl* in your home directory. To change the filename or directory location, click on File... in the Preferences dialog box. This opens the Preferences Journal File dialog box, as shown in Figure 29.3.

Figure 29.3 Preferences Journal File dialog box

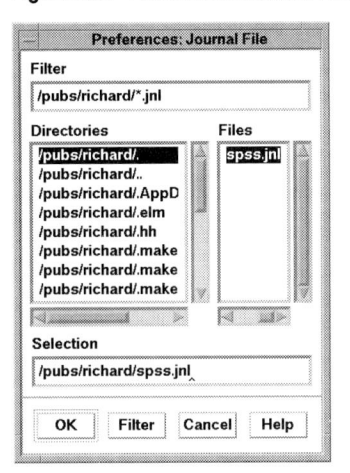

Filter. To display a list of files that match a wildcard search or change the directory location, enter the directory path and wildcard specification and click on Filter. By default, SPSS looks for all files in the current directory with the extension *.jnl* and displays them on the Files list.

Directories. You can also use the Directories list to change the directory location. To change directories, select the name of the directory on the Directories list and click on Filter or double-click on the directory name. To move up a directory level, select the directory path that ends with a slash and two periods (/..).

Files. All files in the directory that match the wildcard search appear on the Files list. If you select a file from the list, SPSS asks you if you want to replace the existing file.

Selection. Enter the directory path and filename and click on OK. If you select a directory and file from the lists, the information is entered automatically. If you enter the information directly, you can bypass the filter process. If you enter a filename without a directory path, the journal file is saved in the directory from which you started SPSS.

Working Memory

You can increase the allocation of virtual memory for workspace. The default is 1512K. This is sufficient for most purposes. Unless SPSS tells you that there is insufficient memory to run a procedure, increasing the working memory allocation is usually not recommended, since this can actually decrease performance (that is, make your computer slower) under some circumstances.

The new workspace allocation does not take effect until the next SPSS session. If the workspace allocation exceeds the available contiguous memory, SPSS allocates the available memory and indicates the amount in an alert box.

Opening a Syntax Window at Startup

Syntax windows are text file windows used to enter, edit, and run SPSS commands. If you frequently work with command syntax, select Open a syntax window at startup to automatically open a syntax window at the beginning of each SPSS session. This is useful primarily for experienced SPSS users who prefer to work with command syntax instead of dialog boxes.

Transformation and Merge Options

Each time SPSS executes a command, it reads the data file. Some data transformations (for example, Compute, Recode) and file transformations (Add Variables and Add Cases) do not require a separate pass of the data, and execution of these commands can be delayed until SPSS reads the data to execute another command, such as a statistical procedure command. There are two alternatives for the treatment of these transformations:

- **Calculate values immediately.** Executes the requested transformation and reads the data file. This is the default. If the data file is large and you have multiple transformations, this may be time-consuming.

- **Calculate values before used.** Delays execution of all transformations until SPSS encounters a command that requires a data pass. If the data file is large, this can save a significant amount of processing time. However, pending transformations limit what you can do in the Data Editor (see Chapter 3).

  This option can also save time when reading large SQL database files into SPSS. If you select this option and then read an SQL database file, the variable names will appear in the Data Editor window, but the data values will not be displayed until SPSS runs a command that requires a data pass, such as a statistical procedure.

Display Order for Variable Lists

There are two alternatives for the display order of variables in the dialog box source variable lists:

- **Alphabetical.** Displays variables in alphabetical order. This is the default.
- **File.** Displays variables in file order. This is the same order in which variables are displayed in the Data Editor window.

A change in variable display order takes effect the next time you open a data file. Display order affects only source variable lists. Selected variable lists always reflect the order in which variables were selected.

Display Format for New Variables

The default display format for new variables applies only to numeric variables. There is no default display format for new string variables.

Width. Total display width (including decimal positions) for new numeric variables. The maximum total width is 40 characters. The default is eight.

Decimal Places. Number of decimal positions for new numeric variables. The maximum number of decimal positions is 16. The default is two.

If a value is too large for the specified display format, SPSS first rounds decimal places and then converts values to scientific notation. Display formats do not affect internal data values. For example, the value 123456.78 may be rounded to 123457 for display, but the original unrounded value is used in any calculations.

Graphics

To specify new default setting for high-resolution graphics (charts and plots that appear in the Chart Carousel and chart windows), click on Graphics... in the Preferences dialog box. This opens the Preferences Graphics dialog box, as shown in Figure 29.4.

Figure 29.4 Preferences Graphics dialog box

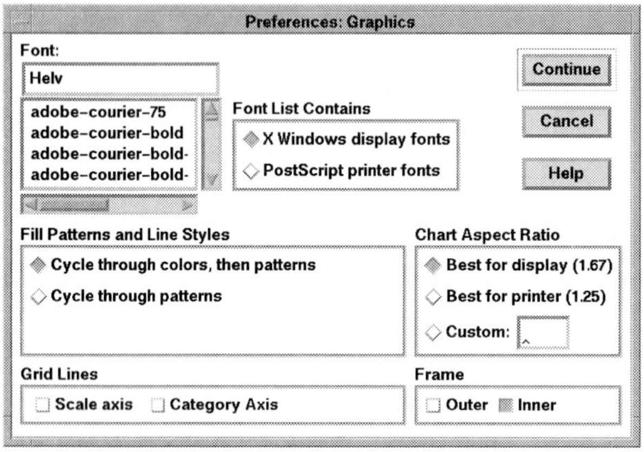

With the exception of changes in Chart Aspect Ratio, any changes you make in the default settings affect only new charts and charts still in the Chart Carousel. Charts in chart windows are not affected.

Font. The initial type font for new charts. Select a font from the list.

> **Font List Contains**. Controls the fonts displayed in font list. You can choose one of the following alternatives:
>
> ◇ **X Windows display fonts**. All display fonts available in your font path. To display your current font path, at the UNIX prompt type: xset -q.
>
> ◇ **PostScript printer fonts**. Standard PostScript printer fonts plus PostScript fonts supplied in *$SPSS_ROOT/AFM* (*/usr/lpp/SPSS/bin/AFM*).

Fill Patterns and Line Styles. The initial assignment of colors and/or patterns for new charts. You can choose one of the following alternatives:

◇ **Cycle through colors, then patterns**. Uses the default palette of 14 colors and then adds patterns to colors.

◇ **Cycle through patterns**. Uses patterns only. Does not use colors. This is recommended for monochrome and grayscale monitors. For line charts, the cycle includes four line styles within four line weights to make 16 possible combinations. For bar charts, area charts, and pie charts, the cycle includes seven fill patterns (including solid). For scatterplots, the cycle includes 28 available marker types.

Grid Lines. You can choose one or both of the following:

Preferences   593

❑ **Scale axis**. Displays horizontal grid lines on the scale axis.

❑ **Category axis**. Displays vertical grid lines on the category axis.

Chart Aspect Ratio. The width-to-height ratio of the outer frame of charts. Charts displayed in chart windows, as well as new charts and charts in the Chart Carousel, are affected by a change in the Chart Aspect Ratio box. You can choose one of the following for the width-to-height ratio of charts:

◇ **Best for display (1.67)**. This makes full use of the available space in a maximized window.

◇ **Best for printer (1.25)**. This makes full use of an 8 1/2 × 11-inch page in landscape (horizontal) mode.

Custom. You can specify your own width-to-height ratio from 0.5 to 2.0. Values below 1 make charts that are taller than they are wide. Values over 1 make charts that are wider than they are tall. A value of 1 produces a square chart.

Frame. You can choose one or both of the following:

❑ **Outer**. Draws a frame around the entire chart, including titles and legends.

❑ **Inner**. Draws a frame around the graphic portion of the chart.

Custom Currency Formats

You can specify up to five custom currency display formats. To create a custom currency format, click on Custom Currency... in the Preferences dialog box. This opens the Preferences Custom Currency Formats dialog box, as shown in Figure 29.5.

Figure 29.5   Preferences Custom Currency Formats dialog box

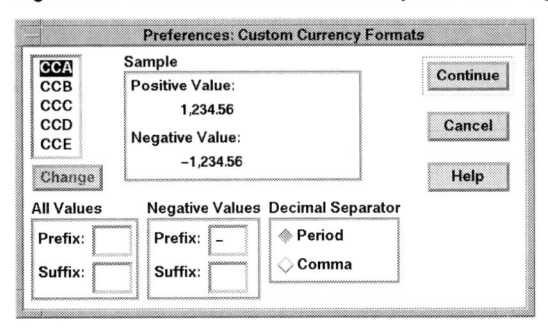

The five custom currency format names are CCA, CCB, CCC, CCD, and CCE. You cannot change the format names or add new ones. By default, all five custom currency formats use a minus sign for the negative prefix and do not have a negative suffix. To modify a custom currency format, select the format name from the source list, make the desired changes, and then click on Change.

All Values. Prefix and suffix specifications appear with both positive and negative values.

Negative Values. Prefix and suffix specifications appear only with negative values. For example, you may want to indicate negative values with parentheses instead of a leading minus sign.

Decimal Separator. The decimal indicator can be either a period or a comma.

Output

Output preferences affect the text-based results of your SPSS session displayed in the output windows. Changes to output preferences affect all output windows. Changes to output preferences affect only output generated after the modification is made; output generated earlier in the session is not affected.

To modify the display of system information, page size specifications, symbols used in character-based plots, and borders for tabular data, click on Output... in the Preferences dialog box. This opens the Preferences Output dialog box, as shown in Figure 29.6.

Figure 29.6 Preferences Output dialog box

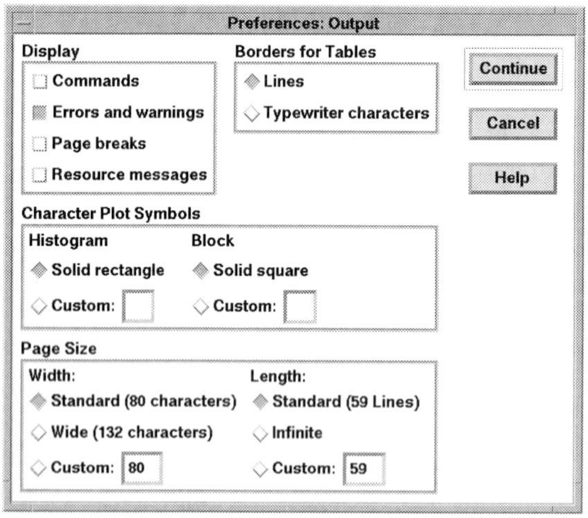

Display. In addition to the results of statistical procedures, SPSS can also display page titles and a variety of system information in the output windows.

- **Commands.** Displays SPSS command syntax in the output window. Most dialog box choices generate underlying SPSS command syntax, and it is often helpful to have a record of how certain results were obtained.
- **Errors and warnings.** Displays all SPSS error and warning messages in the output window. These are displayed by default. Deselect this item to suppress the display of error and warning messages.
- **Page headers.** Displays output page titles and subtitles, inserts space between pages, and begins printing output from each procedure on a new page.
- **Resource messages.** Displays resource utilization messages, including elapsed time, available memory, and memory required to run each statistical procedure.

Borders for Tables. You can use either extended ASCII characters or standard typewriter characters to create borders around crosstabulations and other tabular output.

- **Lines.** Uses graphical characters to create solid horizontal and vertical lines for tables. This is the default.
- **Typewriter characters.** Uses standard typewriter characters to create horizontal and vertical borders for tables. The dash (—) is used for horizontal lines, the vertical bar symbol (|) is used for vertical lines, and the plus sign (+) is used for the intersection of vertical and horizontal lines. Select this option if you want to open the output file later in another software application.

Character Plot Symbols. For low-resolution, character-based charts and plots, you can select the plot symbols used in the output display.

Histogram. You can choose one of the following alternatives for histogram plot characters:

- **Solid rectangle.** Uses graphical characters to display a solid rectangle. This is the default.
- **Custom.** Uses user-specified, standard typewriter character. Only one character can be specified. For example, each bar of the histogram can be represented by a string of asterisks.

Block. You can choose one of the following alternatives for block characters used in bar charts and icicle plots:

- **Solid square.** Uses graphical characters to display solid squares for bar charts and icicle plots. This is the default.
- **Custom.** Uses user-specified, standard typewriter character. Only one character can be specified. For example, each bar can be represented by a string of pound signs (#).

Use the Custom options for plotting symbols to specify standard typewriter characters if you want to open the output file later in another software application.

Page Size. In SPSS, page size is defined by number of characters per line and number of lines per page. The default settings of 80 characters per line and 59 lines per page are based on the default font size (10 pt) and the default paper size and orientation (8 1/2 × 11, portrait). For more information on fonts and printing, see Chapter 27.

Width. You can choose one of the following alternatives for width:

◇ **Standard.** 80 characters per line. This is the default.

◇ **Wide.** 132 characters per line.

◇ **Custom.** User-specified number of characters per line. The minimum is 80. The maximum is 255.

Length. You can choose one of the following alternatives for length:

◇ **Standard.** 59 lines per page. This is the default.

◇ **Infinite.** Output appears as one continuous page.

◇ **Custom.** User-specified number of lines per page. The minimum is 24. The maximum is 9999.

Using SPSS Graphical Characters

SPSS uses a special graphical character set not available with other software applications. If you copy output that contains graphical characters from SPSS into another application via the clipboard, SPSS automatically converts these graphical characters to standard typewriter characters.

- Table borders are converted to a dash (—) for horizontal lines, a vertical bar symbol (|) for vertical lines, and a plus sign (+) for the intersection of vertical and horizontal lines.
- The solid rectangle used in character-based histograms is converted to an asterisk (*).
- The solid square used in character-based bar charts and icicle plots is converted to a capital letter X.

If you save an SPSS output file that contains special graphical characters and then open it in another application (rather than cutting or copying and pasting), no conversion takes place, and you'll probably end up with something that looks like hieroglyphics.

Saving Preferences

Changes to preference settings only last for the duration of the session unless you save the new settings. To save your new preference settings, from the Data Editor menus choose:

Options
  Save Settings

If you make preference changes and don't save the new settings, at the end of the session SPSS asks if you want to save the changes.

Note: SPSS views any change to the preferences file (*.spssrc*) as a preference change, and this file can be affected by settings outside the Preferences dialog boxes, such as display of grid lines or value labels and SET commands run from syntax windows.

Preferences File (.spssrc)

Preferences are stored in your home directory in a file named *.spssrc*. This file contains all the user-controllable settings that are used in SPSS Motif sessions, including:

- Any selections made in the Preferences dialog boxes.
- View and Options menu settings for grid lines, value labels, and status bar.
- Default chart color palette settings saved from the Colors dialog box.
- Any SET commands run from a syntax window.

Figure 29.7 shows the initial settings in the *.spssrc* file the first time you start SPSS. Figure 29.8 shows a modified *.spssrc* file after various changes to settings during an SPSS session.

Figure 29.7   Initial contents of .spssrc file

```
[SPSSWIN]
Journal='/pubs/richard/spss.jnl'
Append=1
WorkSpace=1512
OpenInput=0

[SET]
Journal=ON
```

Figure 29.8   Modified .spssrc file

```
[SPSSWIN]
JOURNAL='/pubs/richard/spss.jnl'     ← Preferences dialog box settings
Append=1
WorkSpace=1512
OpenInput=0
ExecTrans=1
Record=1
TypeFace=adobe-helvetica             ← Preferences Graphics dialog box settings
UsePrinterFonts=1
CycleThru=1
GridScaleAxis=1
GridCategoryAxis=0
FrameOuter=1
FrameInner=1
ChartAspect=1.25
DEValueLabels=1
TempDir=/bigdisk/temp                ← Directory location for SPSS temporary files (manually entered in file)

[SET]
JOURNAL=ON                           ← Preferences dialog box settings
FORMAT=F8.2
ERRORS=ON
HEADER=ON
MESSAGES=OFF
BOX=X'939495969798999A9B9C9D'
HISTOGRAM=X'9F'                      ← Preferences Output dialog box
BLOCK=X'9E'
LENGTH=100
WIDTH=90
CCA='-,$,,  '                        ← Preferences Custom Currency dialog box settings
CCB='(,$,, )'
```

(SET command specifications bracket on right side)

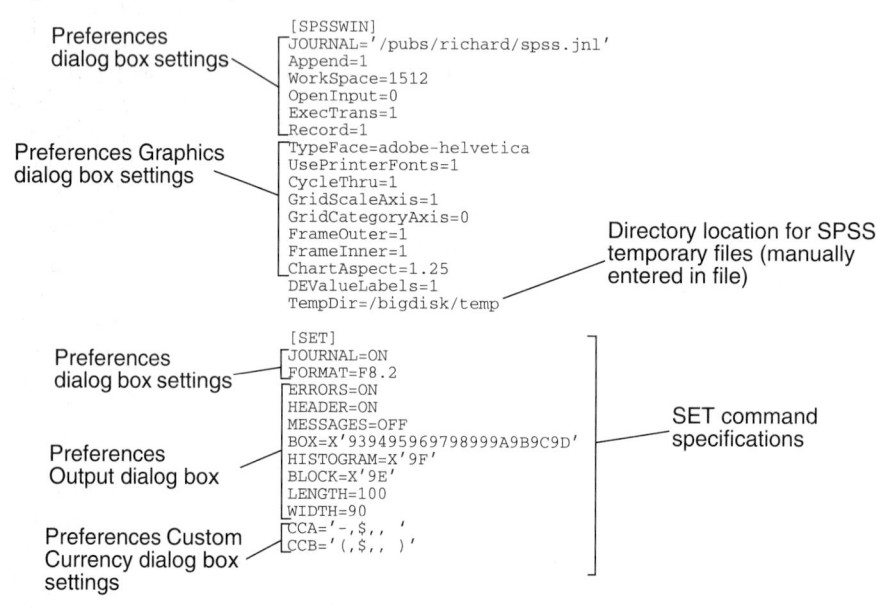

Editing the Preferences File (.spssrc)

The *.spssrc* file is a simple text file that can be edited with any text editor. Most settings can be easily modified by making dialog box and menu selections in an SPSS session, which is the recommended method for changing those settings. The only valid additional settings are SET subcommand specifications not available in dialog boxes and the directory location for SPSS temporary files.

SPSS is fairly tolerant of invalid specifications in the *.spssrc* file, either ignoring them or ignoring the entire file and using the initial default settings. If you somehow manage to alter the file in a manner that makes it impossible for SPSS to run, simply delete the file and restart SPSS. If there is no *.spssrc* file, SPSS opens the Startup Preferences dialog box and creates a new *.spssrc* file.

SET Command Specifications

The [SET] section of the *.spssrc* file contains any settings from the Preferences dialog boxes that also have SET command equivalents. You can add any additional SET subcommands that are valid in SPSS. Each subcommand must appear on a separate line (without a preceding slash).

Preferences and Profile (.profile.sps)

The *.spssrc* preferences file is only used when you run SPSS with the Motif graphical user interface. If you run batch jobs or use the character-based SPSS Manager, you may also have an automatic profile called *.profile.sps* that contains commands you want to execute each time you start SPSS. If you have both an *.spssrc* file and a *.profile.sps*, the settings in both files are used in Motif sessions. If there are any conflicting settings, the *.spssrc* settings override those in *.profile.sps*.

Multiple Sessions

Running more than one session of SPSS at the same time can affect both the preferences file and the journal file.

Preferences

Changes to preferences in one SPSS session do not affect the preference settings in concurrent sessions. However, SPSS only saves one permanent version of your preference settings. If you save preference settings in concurrent sessions, the last one saved overwrites your *.spssrc* file and determines the preferences in effect the next time you start SPSS.

Journal File (spss.jnl)

By default, the SPSS Motif interface appends session journal information to the file *spss.jnl* in your home directory. If you run multiple concurrent sessions, commands from each session are appended to the journal file in sequential order, which means commands from one session may be interspersed between commands from another session.

If your preference settings overwrite the journal file, only commands from the last session started are recorded in the journal. You cannot regain journaling in any concurrent sessions started previously.

While neither of these outcomes is likely to be desirable, they do not pose any serious problems either—unless you need meaningful journal records. If you run multiple concurrent sessions and also need useful journal files, specify the journal filename *spss.jnl.$$* in the Preferences Journal File dialog box.

The shell variable *$$* expands to a unique number, providing a unique name for each session journal file, such as *spss.jnl.46458*.

30 Getting Help

SPSS Motif interface uses a hypertext-based Help system to provide information on how to use SPSS and how to interpret your statistical results. This chapter is a brief description of the Help system.

The best way to find out more about the Help system is to use it. You can access Help in several ways:

- Select Help from the menu bar in any SPSS window to open the Help menu.
- Press F1 at any time in SPSS to open the table of contents of the Help system.
- Click on the Help pushbutton in an SPSS dialog box for information on the dialog box and its functions.
- Click on the Glossary pushbutton in an SPSS output window for definitions of statistical and other terms used in SPSS output.
- Click on the Syntax pushbutton in a syntax window for a syntax diagram of the SPSS command you are trying to enter or edit.

The Help system contains a huge body of information to meet the needs of all kinds of users. At the same time, it provides adequate means to facilitate the search for a specific topic. To familiarize yourself with the Help system, it is useful to go through the Help menu. To obtain specific information, it is usually faster to use the Help pushbutton in the dialog box.

The Help Menu

You can open the Help menu by selecting Help on the far right side of the menu bar in an SPSS window. The Help menu contains the following selections:

On Help. Provides information on the Help system. For the first-time user of online help, it is useful to walk through the help on Help.

Contents. Displays the table of contents of the Help system. Each topic listed is a hypertext link, which appears as an underlined term. You can click on any underlined item to move to a more detailed discussion of that topic.

How to Use SPSS. Displays a list of topics on how to run SPSS. Each topic listed is a hypertext link. You can click on any item to move to a more detailed discussion of that topic.

The Data Editor. Provides information on operations of the Data Editor. Related topics are also available as hypertext links.

On Commands. Displays a list of all menus available in SPSS windows. You can select a menu to find information about a specific command on that menu or select Overview to obtain a brief description of each command on that menu.

What Commands Do. Displays a list of all menus available in SPSS windows. You can select a menu to display a brief description of all the commands on that menu. The same information is displayed when you select On Context and then a menu command.

On Keys. Provides information on running SPSS from the keyboard. Also available is a list of various SPSS windows. You can click on one of them to find out accelerator key or key combinations used for that window.

Glossary. Displays the same glossary index you can obtain by clicking on the Glossary pushbutton in an output window. (See "Output Glossary" on p. 607.)

On Syntax. Displays an index to syntax diagrams. Each command listed there functions as a menu item. Select one of them to see the syntax diagram of that command. You can also obtain a context-sensitive syntax diagram by clicking on the Syntax pushbutton in a syntax window. (See "SPSS Command Syntax Charts" on p. 607.)

On Version. Displays information about the software in the About box you see when you start SPSS.

Help Text

The Help system displays help text in a Help window. When a Help window is active, you have access to both hypertext links and pushbuttons across the top of the window (see Figure 30.1).

Figure 30.1 Help window

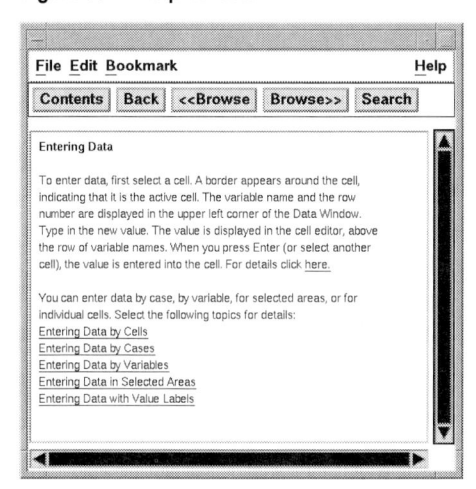

Hypertext Links

Within the text of a Help window, there are hypertext links that lead to related topics. Hypertext links appear as underlined words and may be in color. To move to a topic you want to read more about, just click on an underlined word.

Clicking on a link underlined with a solid line causes the Help system to display another topic. You can use the pushbuttons and the hypertext links in the new text to move to other related topics. To return to the current display, click on the Back pushbutton.

Clicking on a link underlined with a dotted line causes a display box to "pop up" in front of the Help window. The box usually contains a short definition or discussion of the underlined term. Clicking the mouse or pressing a key closes the display box and returns you to the current display.

Pushbuttons

You can use the pushbuttons across the top of the Help window to move from topic to topic:

Contents. Moves to the table of contents of the Help system.

Back. Moves back to the topics you have just viewed, one at a time. Available only when you have moved from one topic to another.

<<Browse. Moves backward to related topics. Not available when you have reached the first of a group of topics.

Browse>>. Moves forward to related topics. Not available when you have reached the last of a group of topics.

Search. Opens the Search dialog box, as shown in Figure 30.2.

Figure 30.2 Search dialog box

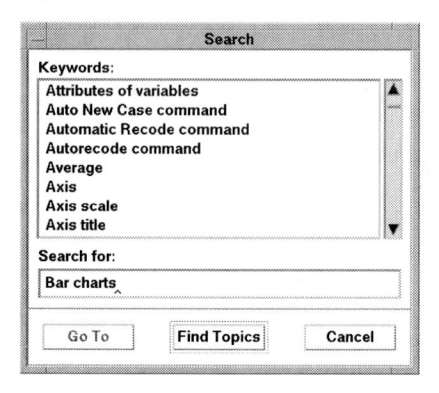

You can type a word or short phrase when the Search dialog box is active. You do not have to type an entire word. The Help system matches the characters you type as closely as possible with the available keywords regardless of case.

The keywords are all listed in the list box and they scroll up and down when you continue typing. When you stop, the closest match is highlighted. Alternatively, you can scroll through the list to find a topic.

When a keyword is selected, you can click on Find Topics to list all topics related to the keyword. For example, if you type

```
Bar charts
```

and click on Find Topics, the Search dialog box displays a list of topics, as shown in Figure 30.3.

Figure 30.3 Topics in Search dialog box

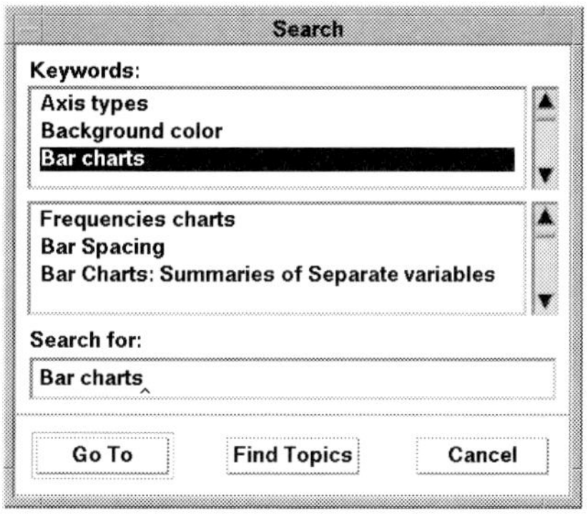

```
┌─────────────── Search ───────────────┐
│ Keywords:                            │
│ ┌──────────────────────────────────┐ │
│ │ Axis types                       │ │
│ │ Background color                 │ │
│ │ Bar charts                       │ │
│ └──────────────────────────────────┘ │
│ ┌──────────────────────────────────┐ │
│ │ Frequencies charts               │ │
│ │ Bar Spacing                      │ │
│ │ Bar Charts: Summaries of Separate variables │ │
│ └──────────────────────────────────┘ │
│ Search for:                          │
│ ┌──────────────────────────────────┐ │
│ │ Bar charts                       │ │
│ └──────────────────────────────────┘ │
│   [ Go To ]  [ Find Topics ]  [ Cancel ] │
└──────────────────────────────────────┘
```

Select a topic you want to read about and then click on Go To. The text on the selected topic is displayed in the Help window.

Note that the selected keyword is used to invoke all topics that have information on it. If more than one are listed, you must select one of the topics and click on Go To to move to that topic.

The Help Window Menu

The Help window has its own menu bar, as shown in Figure 30.1. The menu selections provide additional facilities for using the Help system. This section discusses the most useful features provided by the menu selections.

Copying Help Text

The Help window allows you to copy any Help topic to an SPSS output or syntax window, or to another application. To copy help text, from the Help window menu choose:

Edit
  Copy...

The entire text of the Help topic is copied to the clipboard. You can then paste the help text to an output or syntax window or to any application that supports the clipboard.

Annotating a Help Topic

You can annotate a Help topic by choosing:

Edit
  Annotate...

A Help Annotation dialog box appears for you to enter the note you want to attach to the Help topic. Type the note in the text box and click on OK. A note icon appears in front of the topic as a hypertext link. When you move to this topic in future, you can click on the note icon to read your annotation. You can also move to the annotation, append to it, edit it, or delete it. When you click on Delete, the note icon disappears from the Help topic.

The ability to annotate a Help topic allows you to personalize the Help system.

Marking Most Frequently Consulted Topics

You can move most frequently consulted Help topics to the Bookmark menu and have ready access to them through the Bookmark menu. To add a topic to the Bookmark menu, move to the topic and choose:

Bookmark
 Define...

The Bookmark dialog box appears, as shown in Figure 30.4. You can accept the default Bookmark Name specification, which is the topic in the Help window. To do so, click on OK. Otherwise, specify the topic that you want on the menu and then click on OK.

Figure 30.4 Bookmark dialog box

When a topic is included on the Bookmark menu, you can directly access information on it by selecting it from the menu. Nine Bookmark topics can be displayed directly on the Bookmark menu. If you have defined more than nine topics, the Bookmark menu displays More... as the last selection. You can click on it to have a complete list of marked topics.

To delete a marked topic from the Bookmark menu, select the topic from the list box in the Bookmark dialog box and click on Delete. You can delete as many topics as you like before clicking on OK to return to the Help window.

Marking most frequently consulted topics is another way to personalize the Help system.

SPSS Command Syntax Charts

Syntax diagrams for the SPSS command language are available to you if you work with command syntax in a syntax window. Click on the Syntax pushbutton in the syntax window and then select a command on the scrolling list. If the window already contains command syntax, the Syntax pushbutton takes you directly to the diagram for the command you are working on. Figure 30.5 shows the syntax diagram of FREQUENCIES.

Figure 30.5 Syntax Help window

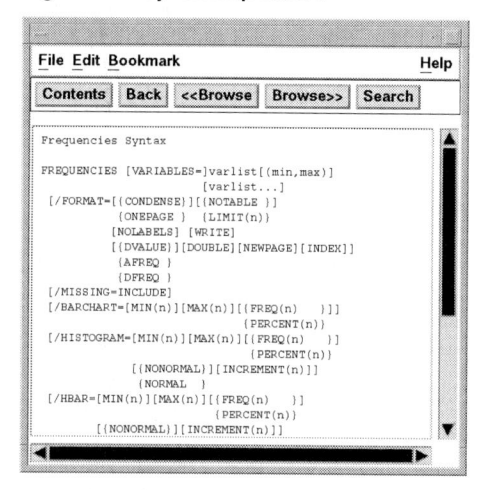

```
File Edit Bookmark                                    Help
Contents  Back   <<Browse  Browse>>  Search

Frequencies Syntax

FREQUENCIES [VARIABLES=]varlist[(min,max)]
                              [varlist...]
 [/FORMAT=[(CONDENSE)][(NOTABLE )]
          (ONEPAGE ) (LIMIT(n))
          [NOLABELS] [WRITE]
          [(DVALUE)][DOUBLE][NEWPAGE][INDEX]]
          (AFREQ )
          (DFREQ )
 [/MISSING=INCLUDE]
 [/BARCHART=[MIN(n)][MAX(n)][((FREQ(n)    )]]
                              (PERCENT(n))
 [/HISTOGRAM=[MIN(n)][MAX(n)][((FREQ(n)   )]
                              (PERCENT(n))
          [(NONORMAL)][INCREMENT(n)]]
          (NORMAL  )
 [/HBAR=[MIN(n)][MAX(n)][((FREQ(n)    )]
                         (PERCENT(n))
          [(NONORMAL)][INCREMENT(n)]]
```

If you prefer, you can copy the syntax diagram (see "Copying Help Text" on p. 605) and paste it into the SPSS syntax window for reference or for editing. Don't try to run the syntax diagram, though!

To obtain syntax diagrams, you can also select On Syntax from the Help menu (see "The Help Menu" on p. 601).

Output Glossary

The SPSS Glossary contains definitions of terms that appear in the statistical output displayed by SPSS. There are two ways to access an index to output glossary.

- Click on the Glossary pushbutton in an SPSS output window.
- Open the Help menu and select Glossary.

When the glossary index appears in the Help window, as shown in Figure 30.6, use the Search pushbutton to search for the closest match of the term in the index. Each listed term is a hypertext link that leads to a discussion of the term.

Figure 30.6 Help window with glossary index

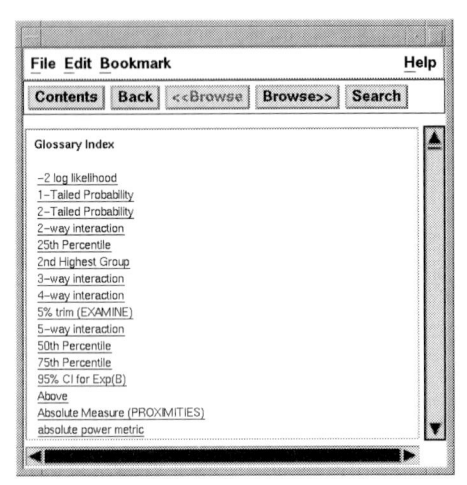

Alternatively, you can scroll down the list of terms and select the one you want to read about. It is time-consuming, though, since there are more than a thousand terms in the glossary.

When you have moved to the definition or discussion of the statistical term, you can print it or copy and paste it to another window, as you do with any other help text.

Appendix A
Command Syntax

This appendix provides an overview of SPSS command syntax. For detailed information on specific commands, see the *SPSS Base System Syntax Reference Guide*.

A Few Useful Terms

All terms in the SPSS command language fall into one or more of the following categories:
- **Keyword.** A word already defined by SPSS to identify a command, subcommand, or specification. Most keywords are, or resemble, common English words.
- **Command.** A specific instruction that controls the execution of SPSS.
- **Subcommand.** Additional instructions on SPSS commands. A command can contain more than one subcommand, each with its own specifications.
- **Specifications.** Instructions added to a command or subcommand. Specifications may include subcommands, keywords, numbers, arithmetic operators, variable names, and special delimiters.

Each command begins with a command keyword (which may contain more than one word). The command keyword is followed by at least one blank space and then any additional specifications. For example:

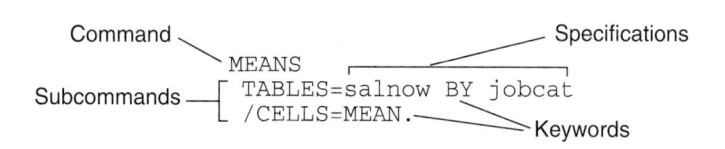

```
            Command              Specifications
                  \             /
                   MEANS
    Subcommands ─┬─ TABLES=salnow BY jobcat
                 └─ /CELLS=MEAN.
                                  \
                                   Keywords
```

Syntax Rules

Keep in mind the following simple rules when editing and writing command syntax:
- Each command must begin on a new line and end with a period (.).

- Most subcommands are separated by slashes (/). The slash before the first subcommand on a command is usually optional.
- Variable names must be spelled out fully.
- Text included within apostrophes or quotation marks must be contained on a single line.
- Each line of command syntax cannot exceed 80 characters.
- A period (.) must be used to indicate decimals, regardless of your *LANG* environment variable setting.
- Variable names ending in a period can cause errors in commands created by the dialog boxes. You cannot create such variable names in the dialog boxes, and you should generally avoid them.

SPSS command syntax is case-insensitive, and three-letter abbreviations can be used for many command specifications. You can use as many lines as you want to specify a single command. You can add space or break lines at almost any point where a single blank is allowed, such as around slashes, parentheses, arithmetic operators, or between variable names. For example:

```
FREQUENCIES
 VARIABLES=JOBCAT SEXRACE
 /PERCENTILES=25 50 75
 /BARCHART.
```

and

```
freq var=jobcat sexrace /percent=25 50 75 /bar.
```

are both acceptable alternatives that generate the same results.

Batch Mode and Include Files

For SPSS command files run in batch mode (see Appendix C) or via the SPSS INCLUDE command, the syntax rules are slightly different:

- Each command must begin in the first column of a new line.
- Continuation lines must be indented at least one space.
- The period at the end of the command is optional.

If you generate command syntax by pasting dialog box choices into a syntax window, the format of the commands is suitable for modes of operation.

Commands Available Only with Syntax

The commands in Table A.1 cannot be obtained through the dialog box interface. They can be obtained only by typing command syntax in a syntax window.

Table A.1 SPSS commands available only with command syntax

Command	Alternative
ADD VALUE LABELS	Data menu: Define Variable
BEGIN-END DATA	Enter data in Data Editor
BREAK	
CLEAR TRANSFORMATIONS	
COMMENT	
DO IF	
DO REPEAT	
DOCUMENT	
DROP DOCUMENTS	
END CASE	
END FILE	
ERASE	
EXECUTE	
FILE HANDLE	
FILE LABEL	
FILE TYPE	
FORMATS	Data menu: Define Variable
GET SAS	
INCLUDE	
INPUT PROGRAM	
LEAVE	
LOOP-END LOOP	
Macro facility (!DEFINE)	
MATRIX DATA	
MCONVERT	
N OF CASES	Transform menu: Select Cases
NUMERIC	Data menu: Define Variable
PLOT	Graph menu: Scatter
PRESERVE	
PRINT	
PRINT EJECT	
PRINT FORMATS	Data menu: Define Variable
PRINT SPACE	
PROCEDURE OUTPUT	
RECORD TYPE	

Table A.1 SPSS commands available only with command syntax (Continued)

Command	Alternative
REFORMAT	Data menu: Define Variable
RENAME VARIABLES	Data menu: Define Variable
REPEATING DATA	
REREAD	
RESTORE	
SET	Edit menu: Preferences
SHOW	Edit menu: Preferences
STRING	Data menu: Define Variable
TEMPORARY	
UPDATE	
VECTOR	
WRITE FORMATS	Data menu: Define Variable
XSAVE	

Appendix B
Commands Not Available in SPSS for UNIX

The following tables list commands not available in SPSS for UNIX and commands not available in the SPSS Motif interface.

Table B.1 Commands not available in SPSS for UNIX

GET TRANSLATE	NUMBERED
GET BMDP	SAVE SCSS
GET SCSS	SAVE TRANSLATE
NUMBERED	UNNUMBERED
HELP	

Table B.2 Commands not available in SPSS Motif interface

EDIT
KEYED DATA LIST
POINT

Table B.3 SET subcommands not available in SPSS Motif interface

ENDCMD
DUMP
NULLINE
MXERRS

Appendix C
Batch Processing

In **batch mode**, you submit a command syntax file for execution, and SPSS produces an output file and any charts requested. SPSS runs unattended and terminates after executing the last command, so you can perform other tasks while it runs. Batch mode is useful if you often run the same set of time-consuming analyses, such as weekly reports. Batch mode requires some knowledge of SPSS command syntax (see Appendix A).

Running SPSS in Batch Mode

To run a command syntax file in batch mode, at the UNIX prompt type:

```
spss -m [filename]
```

Do *not* use the -S (capital S) switch before the filename to indicate a syntax file. The filename that follows the -m switch is assumed to be a command syntax file, regardless of its extension. You can use the -s (lower case) switch to allocate workspace. The syntax command filename must come last, as in:

```
spss -m -s 1512 batchjob.sps
```

Syntax Rules

The following syntax rules apply to SPSS command files run in batch mode:
- Each command must begin in the first column of a new line.
- Continuation lines must be indented at least one space.
- The period at the end of the command is optional.

Output File

By default, SPSS sends the text-based output results to the window from which you executed the job. You can also direct the output to a file, as in:

```
spss -m batchjob.sps > batchjob.lst
```

Chart Files

Each high-resolution chart generated by the batch job is saved in a separate file in the directory from which you executed the job. Chart filenames are assigned by adding a sequential number and the extension *.cht* to the prefix *chfil*, as in *chfil1.cht*, *chfil2.cht*, *chfil3.cht*, and so on.

Character-based Charts

If you don't have a graphics terminal that supports the SPSS Motif interface, you cannot view or edit high-resolution charts. To produce character-based charts, use the SPSS command:

```
SET HIGHRES OFF.
```

If you put this command in a file called *.profile.sps* in your home directory, it will automatically be executed each time you run an SPSS job. On operating systems that don't use the SPSS Motif interface, this command may be included in a system profile.

Building a Command Syntax File

A command syntax file containing SPSS commands is required to run SPSS in batch mode, and the command syntax file must specify the data file to use, as in:

```
get file '/users/beeblebrox/bank.sav'.
frequencies variables=jobcat
 /barchart.freq.
```

One way to build a command syntax file is to manually enter syntax and save the file. You can do this in a syntax window in an SPSS session or by using any text editor or word processing software that saves files in text format.

There are several ways in which SPSS can help build your command syntax file. These methods are usually faster than manually entering commands, and they minimize the chance of syntax errors. Each method involves running SPSS in interactive mode and saving and editing the command syntax generated in the session.

Pasting Syntax from Dialog Boxes

The easiest way to build command syntax is to paste dialog box selections into a syntax window in an SPSS Motif session. To do so, make dialog box choices for the analyses you want to perform. When you click on Paste, command syntax based on your dialog box choices is pasted into a syntax window. You can then save the contents of the syntax window as a command syntax file. (For more information on pasting command syntax, see Chapter 4.)

Editing Syntax in an Output File

You can also save command syntax in an output file from an SPSS session that performs the analyses you want. To use this method, display of command syntax in the output must be selected in the Preferences Output dialog box (see Chapter 29). When SPSS runs your dialog box choices, it writes command syntax to an output file along with the results of your analyses.

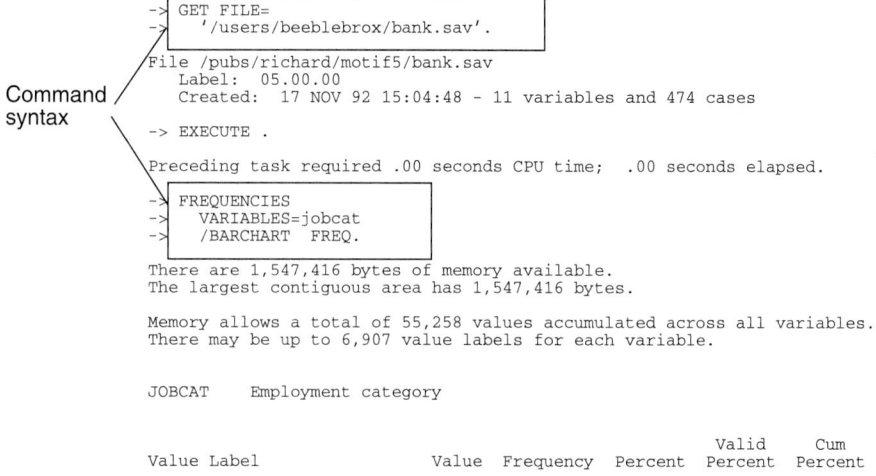

Figure C.1 Unedited output file

```
-> GET FILE=
->    '/users/beeblebrox/bank.sav'.
File /pubs/richard/motif5/bank.sav
   Label:  05.00.00
   Created:   17 NOV 92 15:04:48 - 11 variables and 474 cases
-> EXECUTE .

Preceding task required .00 seconds CPU time;  .00 seconds elapsed.

-> FREQUENCIES
->    VARIABLES=jobcat
->    /BARCHART   FREQ.

There are 1,547,416 bytes of memory available.
The largest contiguous area has 1,547,416 bytes.

Memory allows a total of 55,258 values accumulated across all variables.
There may be up to 6,907 value labels for each variable.

JOBCAT      Employment category

                                                Valid     Cum
Value Label              Value  Frequency  Percent  Percent  Percent

Clerical                   1        227     47.9     47.9     47.9
Office trainee             2        136     28.7     28.7     76.6
Security officer           3         27      5.7      5.7     82.3
College trainee            4         41      8.6      8.6     90.9
Exempt employee            5         32      6.8      6.8     97.7
MBA trainee                6          5      1.1      1.1     98.7
Technical                  7          6      1.3      1.3    100.0
                                -------  -------  -------
                       Total        474    100.0    100.0
```

Command syntax is indicated by the boxed commands (GET FILE, EXECUTE, FREQUENCIES) preceded by -> arrows.

To create a command syntax file, save only the command syntax to a file. You can do this by cutting and pasting the command syntax into another file or deleting everything but the command syntax from the output file. Make sure to remove any headers, titles, error and warning messages, and the right arrows (–>) that precede command syntax. Note, however, that any errors in the output must be resolved prior to the batch mode run or the run will not complete successfully.

Editing Syntax in a Journal File

By default, SPSS records all commands executed during a Motif session in a journal file named *spss.jnl*, located in your home directory. In Manager and prompted sessions, the default location of the journal file is the current directory (the one from which you started SPSS).

The journal file is a text file that can be edited like any other text file, and you can create a syntax file by editing the journal file. Remove any error or warning messages. Note, however, that any errors must be resolved prior to the batch run or the run will not complete successfully.

Save the edited journal file with a different filename. Since SPSS automatically appends or overwrites the journal file for every session—including batch runs—attempting to use the same filename for a syntax file and the journal file may yield some unexpected and unwanted results.

Figure C.2 shows a journal file for an SPSS run that opens a data file, creates a variable *y* based on the values of variable *x*, and displays descriptive statistics for each variable. In addition to the SPSS command syntax, there is a data-specific warning message.

Figure C.2 Unedited journal file

```
GET FILE='/users/marvin/mydata.sav' .
EXECUTE .
COMPUTE y = 10 / x .
EXECUTE .
>Warning # 511
>A division by zero has been attempted on the indicated command.  The result
>has been set to the system-missing value.
DESCRIPTIVES
 VARIABLES=x y
 /FORMAT=LABELS NOINDEX
 /STATISTICS=MEAN STDDEV MIN MAX
 /SORT=MEAN (A) .
```

The warning message has been deleted in Figure C.3. Only SPSS command syntax remains in the file, which can be specified as the syntax file on the command line.

Figure C.3 Edited journal file

```
GET FILE='/users/marvin/mydata.sav' .
EXECUTE .
COMPUTE y = 10 / x .
EXECUTE .
DESCRIPTIVES
 VARIABLES=x y
 /FORMAT=LABELS NOINDEX
 /STATISTICS=MEAN STDDEV MIN MAX
 /SORT=MEAN (A) .
```

Appendix D
Keyboard Movement and Accelerator Keys

Although a mouse is recommended, you can accomplish most tasks in SPSS with the keyboard. This appendix provides a summary of accelerator and navigation keys.

Menus

Table D.1

Action	Keys
Move to the menu bar	F10
Move between menus and submenus	→ ←
Move up and down selected menu	↑ ↓
Select the highlighted menu item	Enter or Space
Select a menu from the menu bar	Alt + underlined letter in menu name
Select an item from an open menu	Underlined letter in item name
Close menu or submenu	Esc
Open Use Sets dialogbox	F7
Help	F1

Dialog Boxes

Table D.2

Move between items	Tab / Shift+Tab
Select highlighted item	Space
Select OK or Continue	Enter
Select Cancel	Esc

Table D.2   (Continued)

Move up and down variable list or list box	↑ ↓
Move in a check box or radio button group	↑ ↓
Select multiple variables from list	Shift + up and down arrow keys
Move selected variables up one position in list	Alt + minus sign on typewriter keys (−)
Move selected variables down one position in list	Alt + plus sign on typewriter keys (+)
Open the window menu	Alt+Space
Help	F1

Data Editor

Table D.3

Move and select one cell down	↓ or ←Enter
Move and select one cell up	↑
Move and select once cell right or left	→ ← or Tab→ / Shift+Tab→
Select first cell in case (row)	Ctrl+←
Select first cell in case or selected area	Home
Select last cell in case	Ctrl+→
Select last cell in case or selected area	End
Select first case in variable (column)	Ctrl+↑
Select last case in variable	Ctrl+↓
Select entire case (entire row)	Shift+Space
Select entire variable (entire column)	Ctrl+Space
Select first cell in the data file	Ctrl+Home
Select last cell in the data file	Ctrl+End
Extend selection	Shift + cursor movement
Scroll up or down the height of the window	PgUp PgDn
Scroll left or right the width of the window	Ctrl+PgUp / Ctrl+PgDn
Copy from selected cells	Ctrl+Ins
Cut from selected cells	Shift+Del
Paste into selected cells	Shift+Ins
Display value label list for data entry	Shift+F2
Search for data	Alt+F5
Help	F1
Edit Mode	
Switch to Edit Mode	F2
Move one character right or left	→ ←

Table D.3 (Continued)

Extend selection	⇧Shift + cursor movement
Move to beginning of value	Home
Move to end of value	End
Select to beginning of value	⇧Shift+Home
Select to end of value	⇧Shift+End

Syntax and Output Windows

Table D.4

Move one character right or left	→ ←
Move one word right or left	Ctrl+→ / Ctrl+←
Move down or up one line	↑ ↓
Move to start of line	Home
Move to end of line	End
Move to start of file	Ctrl+Home
Move to end of file	Ctrl+End
Select text	⇧Shift + arrow keys
Search for text	F5
Replace text	⇧Shift+F5
Copy selected text	Ctrl+Ins
Cut selected text	⇧Shift+Del
Paste copied or cut text	⇧Shift+Ins
Designate window	Ctrl + !
Help	F1
Output Window Icon Bar	
Pause	Ctrl+S
Scroll	Ctrl+Q
Round	Ctrl + 0 (zero)
Glossary	Ctrl+G
Go to chart	Ctrl+J
Syntax Window Icon Bar	
Run	Ctrl+A
Syntax	Ctrl+N

Chart Carousel

Table D.5

Open Carousel Select dialog box	Ctrl+P
Discard selected chart	Ctrl+D
Edit selected chart	Ctrl+E
Go to next chart	Ctrl+F
Go to previous chart	Ctrl+B
Go to output	Ctrl+J

Chart Window[1]

Table D.6

Refresh chart	Ctrl+L

Window Control

Table D.7

Cycle through open windows	Ctrl+Tab→ or Ctrl+F6
Close active window	Alt+F4

---

1. A mouse is required for some features of the Chart Editor.

Appendix E
Command Line Switches

Command line switches are optional parameters that you can specify when you start SPSS. With command line switches, you can tell SPSS to perform a variety of tasks at startup, including:

- Run SPSS in Manager, prompted, or batch modes.
- Open data, output, syntax, and chart files.
- Control colors and fonts for SPSS windows and dialog boxes.
- Allocate workspace (virtual memory).

You can use multiple command line switches with the spss command. For example:

```
spss -data inventory.dat -C lastmonth.bar -S charts.com
```

starts SPSS and opens the data file *inventory.dat*, the chart file *lastmonth.bar*, and the command syntax file *charts.com*.

Motif Graphical User Interface

To run SPSS with the Motif graphical user interface, at the UNIX prompt type:

```
spss
```

The following optional specifications are also available for Motif sessions:

-bordercolor *color* or **-bd** *color*. Sets the border color. Specify the color you want by name after the switch. For example, to run the SPSS Motif interface with red borders, at the UNIX prompt type:

```
spss -bd red
```

-background *color* or **-bg** *color*. Sets the background color. Specify the color you want by name after the switch.

-borderwidth *width* or **-bw** *width*. Sets the width of the border. Specify the border width in pixels after the switch.

-C *chart filename.* Opens a chart file. Specify the directory path and name of the chart after the switch. This may be used multiple times to open multiple chart files. For example:

```
spss -C /users/fred/wilma.cht -C /users/barney/betty.cht
```

-Ci *chart filename.* Opens a chart file and iconifies it. Specify the directory path and name of the chart after the switch. This may be used multiple times to open multiple chart documents.

-data *data filename.* Opens a data file. Specify the directory path and name of the data file after the switch. Only one data file may be opened. For example:

```
spss -data /bulwinkle/moose/bank.sav
```

-display *device.* Tells SPSS the name of your display device. If you want your output to appear on a device other than the one specified for *$DISPLAY*, enter the new display device after the switch.

-fg *color.* Sets the foreground color. Specify the color you want by name after the switch.

-font *font* or **-fn** *font.* Sets the font to be used on menus and in dialog boxes. Any standard Motif font may be used.

-iconic. Starts SPSS with all windows iconified.

-name *startup.* Changes the name of SPSS on startup. Specify the new startup name after the switch. This changes the name of the SPSS resource file that controls the appearance of menus and dialog boxes. By default, SPSS uses the settings in *SPSS*. For example, if you specify

```
spss -name spss2
```

SPSS uses the resource settings in *spss2*. In this way, you can run multiple SPSS sessions with different preferences (such as fonts and colors). For more about preferences and multiple sessions, see Chapter 29. For more about the SPSS resource file, see Appendix F.

-O *[output file].* Opens an additional output window. If you specify a filename after the switch, that file opens in the output window. You may specify the switch multiple times to open multiple output windows.

-Oi *[output file].* Opens an output window and iconifies it. If you specify a filename after the switch, that file opens in the output window. You may specify the switch multiple times to open multiple output windows.

-S *[syntax filename].* Opens a syntax window. If you specify a filename after the switch, that file opens in the syntax window. You may specify the switch multiple times to open multiple syntax windows.

-Si *[syntax filename].* Opens a syntax window and iconifies it. If you specify a filename after the switch, that file will be in the syntax window. You may specify the switch multiple times to open multiple syntax windows. GUI mode.

-s *workspace.* Specifies the number of bytes SPSS uses as working storage. Specify a number followed by k (kilobytes) or m (megabytes). The default is 1512K.

-xrm *resource.* Sets the specified X resource before starting SPSS. This overrides settings in the SPSS resource file (see Appendix F).

*filename.***cht.** If your chart file has the extension *.cht*, you do not need the -C switch to open it. For example:

```
spss sample.cht
```

*filename.***lst.** If your output file has the extension *.lst*, you do not need the -O switch to open it. For example:

```
spss test.lst
```

*filename.***sav.** If your data file has the extension *.sav*, you do not need the -data switch to open it. For example:

```
spss test.sav
```

*filename.***sps.** If your syntax file has the extension *.sps*, you do not need the -S switch to open it. For example:

```
spss test.sps
```

Manager Mode

To use SPSS with the character-based Manager interface, use the +m switch, as in:

```
spss +m
```

You can also start SPSS in Manager mode with a command syntax file in the input window, as in:

```
spss +m comfile.sps
```

The following optional specifications, in conjunction with the +m switch, are available for SPSS in Manager mode:

-a *on/off.* Sets autoview on or off. With autoview on, your output automatically displays in the upper Manager window.

-c *command.* Specifies the command to be used to start the SPSS Processor. This switch can be used to start the SPSS Processor on another computer, using the rsh (remote shell) command. If so, the remote shell should execute spssrem. Any switches used on the spss command are appended to the additional options defined for the spssrem command. For example:

```
rsh otherbox
spss +m -c spssrem
```

-d *macro.* Defines a simple string-substitution macro in the form macroname=text. Spaces are not allowed on either side of the equals sign. If the macro contains spaces, the entire macro definition must be enclosed in apostrophes or quotation marks. Use apostrophes if there are no variable substitutions in the definition. Use quotation marks if the definition contains shell filenames or variable substitutions. Any number of -d options defining different macros can be used. For example,

```
spss +m -d 'sesvars=age sex educ religion'
```

defines the macro *sesvars* to stand for the variables *age*, *sex*, *educ*, and *religion*.

-e *filename.* Starts an editing session in the Manager and loads the specified file for editing. The Processor is not available for this session. This means you can perform all of the Manager's functions except those for running commands.

-g *on/off.* Determines whether the Manager session begins in menu mode. The default is off, which means the Manager is in edit mode.

-s *workspace.* Specifies the number of bytes SPSS uses as working storage. Specify a number followed by k (kilobytes) or m (megabytes). The default is 512K.

-u *lines.* Sets the number of lines in the upper Manager window. This changes the default size for the Input and Output windows at the beginning of the session. On most terminals, the number of lines can be any value from 7 to 14, and 11 is the default. The range and default vary according to the type of terminal you have.

-x *on/off.* Determines if the Manager menu system shows extended choices. The default is off, which means the menus omit keywords that are seldom used and provide standard choices.

Prompted Mode

To run SPSS in a prompted session (see Appendix H), use the -m switch, as in:

```
spss -m
```

The following optional specifications, in conjunction with the -m switch, are available for SPSS in prompted mode:

-c *command.* Specifies the command to be used to start the SPSS Processor. This switch can be used to start the SPSS Processor on another computer, using the rsh (remote shell) command. If so used, the remote shell should execute spssrem, as in:

```
rsh otherbox
spss -m -c spssrem
```

Any switches used on the spss command are appended to the additional options defined for the spssrem command.

-p. Displays output on the terminal one screen at a time. This is the same as the MORE facility in UNIX.

-s *workspace.* Specifies the number of bytes SPSS uses as working storage. Specify a number followed by k (kilobytes) or m (megabytes). The default is 512K.

-t *filename.* Specifies an output file. When you specify this switch, output goes to your screen and the file you specify. By default, in prompted mode, output goes to the screen only; it is not saved to a file.

Batch Processing

To run an SPSS command syntax file in batch mode, use the -m switch followed by a command filename, as in:

```
spss -m comfile.sps
```

For more information on batch processing, see Appendix C.

Appendix F
Customizing the SPSS Resource File

You can control many aspects of the way SPSS windows and dialog boxes appear on the screen, including:
- Font style and size.
- Position and size of windows.
- Number of items that appear in the visible portion of source variable lists.
- Key combinations for accelerator keys.
- Foreground and background colors and other standard resource settings.

The SPSS Resource File

The default settings that determine the appearance of SPSS windows and dialog boxes are stored in an X Windows resource file. The easiest way to create a customized SPSS resource file is to start with the system default version that comes with SPSS. This file is called *SPSS*, and it should be located in the */usr/lib/XII/app-defaults* directory. Copy this file, or the portions you want to modify, into your applications resources directory (see "Applications Resources Directory" on p. 633). Do not change the name of the file, and make sure the filename *SPSS* is in all capital letters.

Figure F.1 shows selected portions of the SPSS resource file. The actual file is much larger, containing initial settings for all accelerator keys and many dialog box source lists. Comments in the file (lines that begin with an exclamation point) make it easy to identify what each setting controls. You do not need to have a complete copy of the resource file in your applications resources directory. Your copy needs to contain only the settings that you want to change. Any settings not found in your resource file will be taken from the system default version.

Figure F.1 Portions of the SPSS resource file

```
! Default Printers

SPSS*textPrinter: ps30w
SPSS*chartPrinter: pubst1

! These resources control intial window placement and size

SPSS*OutputWindow.geometry: 800x525+100+100
SPSS*SyntaxWindow.geometry: 800x525+160+160
SPSS*DataWindow.geometry: 865x525+220+220
SPSS*ChartWindow.geometry: 600x400+50+50
SPSS*ChartCarousel.geometry: 600x400+50+50
```
— Initial size and placement for windows

```
! Fonts

SPSS*.fontList: -*-helvetica-bold-r-normal--12-*-*-*-p-*-iso8859-1
SPSS*DataWindow.fontList: -*-helvetica-medium-r-normal--12-*-*-*-p-*-iso8859-1
SPSS*OutputWindow.fontList: -*-courier-medium-r-normal--14-*-*-*-m-*-iso8859-1
SPSS*SyntaxWindow.fontList: -*-courier-medium-r-normal--14-*-*-*-m-*-iso8859-1
```
— Font used in text windows, menus, and dialog boxes

```
! Accelerator Keys

! Interrupt SPSS Processor Accelerator
SPSS*Spss_IDM_INT_SPSS.acceleratorText: Control + C
SPSS*Spss_IDM_INT_SPSS.accelerator: Ctrl<Key>C

! Undo Accelerator
SPSS*Spss_IDM_EDIT_UNDO.accelerator: Alt<Key>BS
SPSS*Spss_IDM_EDIT_UNDO.acceleratorText: Alt + Backspace
```
— Key bindings for accelerators

```
! The following resouces control the number of variables displayed
! in a source variable list, and in turn controls the height
! of the Dialogs

SPSS*SelectCasesSourceList.visibleItemsCount: 24
SPSS*SortCasesSourceList.visibleItemCount: 20
SPSS*RankSourceList.visibleItemCount: 20
SPSS*FrequenciesSourceList.visibleItemCount: 15
```
— Number of items on source variable lists

```
! Appearance Resources

SPSS*.background: grey75
SPSS.foreground: black
SPSS*XmPushButton.background: lightgrey
SPSS*XmToggleButton.selectColor: black
SPSS*OutputWindow.background: white
SPSS*OutputWindow.foreground: black
SPSS*SyntaxWindow.background: white
SPSS*SyntaxWindow.foreground: black
SPSS*shadowthickness: 3
```
— Colors for windows, dialog boxes, pushbuttons, etc.

Window Size and Position

For each type of SPSS window, you can control the initial size and position on the screen:

SPSS*OutputWindow.geometry controls the size and placement of output windows.

SPSS*SyntaxWindow.geometry controls the size and placement of syntax windows.

SPSS*DataWindow.geometry controls the size and placement of the Data Editor window.

SPSS*ChartWindow.geometry controls the size and placement of chart windows.

SPSS*ChartCarousel.geometry controls the size and placement of the Chart Carousel.

Fonts

You can control the font used to display text in output and syntax windows, data in the Data Editor window, as well as the font used in menus and dialog boxes.

SPSS*.DataWindow.fontList controls the font used for data in the Data Editor window.

SPSS*.OutputWindow.fontList controls the font used for text in output windows. The font must be a fixed-pitch font (for example, Courier). If you specify a proportional font, a warning message is issued and a system default font called "fixed" is used.

SPSS*.SyntaxWindow.fontList controls the font used for text in syntax windows. The font must be a fixed-pitch font (for example, Courier). If you specify a proportional font, a warning message is issued and a system default font called "fixed" is used.

SPSS*.fontList controls the font used in SPSS menus and dialog boxes. For example,

```
SPSS*.fontList: -*-helvetica-bold-r-normal--14-*-*-*-p-*-iso8859-1
```

specifies 14 point Helvetica bold as the font. The size of dialog boxes and all items within the dialog boxes automatically adjust to accommodate the specified font size. The font must be one recognized by your server; otherwise, the system default font is used.

Note: If you don't explicitly specify fonts for text windows (output and syntax) or the Data Editor window, the font specified on SPSS*.fontList is used. If this is not a fixed-pitch font, a warning message is issued and a system font called "fixed" is used.

Accelerator Keys

You can change any of the accelerator keys defined in the SPSS resource file. (For example, you might want to change the accelerator keys for cutting and pasting text to be consistent with other applications you use.) Each accelerator key definition contains two lines: one to specify the key combination and one to specify the text that appears next to the item on the SPSS menus. For example,

```
SPSS*Spss_IDM_EDIT_CUT.accelerator: Shift<Key>Delete
SPSS*Spss_IDM_EDIT_CUT.acceleratorText: Shift + Del
```

defines the key combination Shift-Delete for Cut on the Edit menu, and the text Shift + Del appears next to the item on the menu.

Source Variable List Length

SourceList.visibleItemCount controls the number of variables that appear in the visible portion of the source variable list in many dialog boxes. If you change the visibleItemCount value, the size of the dialog box will automatically be adjusted to accommodate the new source variable list box length. For example,

```
SPSS*FrequenciesSourceList.visibleItemCount: 12
```

specifies that the Frequencies dialog box should display 12 variables in the visible portion of the source variable list.

Only dialog boxes with a SourceList.visibleItemCount entry in the SPSS resource file have an adjustable source variable list length.

Default Printer

The default printer is determined by the setting for the environment variable *PRINTER*. You can override this setting with separate default printers for printing text and printing charts.

SPSS*textPrinter specifies the default printer for text from output and syntax windows, and data from the Data Editor window.

SPSS*chartPrinter specifies the default printer for high-resolution charts from chart windows.

Colors

The SPSS resource file provides color schemes appropriate for color, grayscale, and monochrome monitors. All of these settings are disabled (each line begins with an exclamation point) in the default version of the resource file, and the system default colors are used. To use one of the color schemes in your customized resource file, simply remove the exclamation points from the beginning of the settings you want to use. You can also change the specified colors to any colors recognized by your system.

Other Settings

You can also change other aspects of SPSS windows and dialog boxes, such as pushbutton and scroll bar attributes, using standard resource settings preceded by `SPSS*`. For example, to change the shadow thickness on dialog box pushbuttons, you could specify:

```
SPSS*XmPushButton.shadowThickness: 4
```

Applications Resources Directory

To use your customized SPSS resource file, the file must be in your applications resource directory. To see if you have a defined applications resources directory, at the UNIX prompt type:

```
echo $XAPPLRESDIR  ↵Enter
echo $XUSERFILESEARCHPATH  ↵Enter
```

If a directory path is displayed in response to either of these commands, you already have a defined applications resources directory, and that is where you should put your SPSS resource file. If no directory path is displayed, you don't have a defined applications resources directory, and you should make one.

Setting the XAPPLRESDIR or XUSERFILESEARCHPATH Environment Variable

If you don't have a previously defined applications resources directory, you also need to set the environment variable *XAPPLRESDIR* or *XUSERFILESEARCHPATH* for the directory you want to use.

If you are using the Bourne or Korn shell, use the following UNIX commands:

```
XAPPLRESDIR=[directory location]
export XAPPLRESDIR
```

or

```
XUSERFILESEARCHPATH=[directory location]
export XUSERFILESEARCHPATH
```

If you are using the C shell, use the following command:

```
set env XAPPLRESDIR=[directory location]
```

or

```
set env XUSERFILESEARCHPATH=[directory location]
```

This tells SPSS (and other applications) to look in the specified directory for your application resource files. You should put this command in your *.profile* or whatever file you use to define environment variables.

Using the .Xdefaults File

Instead of using an applications resource directory and a customized resource file, you can specify SPSS settings in your *.Xdefaults* file. However, this is not as efficient as using an application-specific resource file.

Appendix G
Running SPSS through the Manager

The SPSS Manager is a character-based interactive interface designed to help you build and run SPSS commands. The Manager does not require Motif, a window manager, or a graphics terminal.

SPSS Manager

To start an SPSS Manager session, at the UNIX prompt type:

```
spss +m
```

When you press ⏎Enter, the SPSS Manager appears, as shown in Figure G.1.

Figure G.1   SPSS Manager

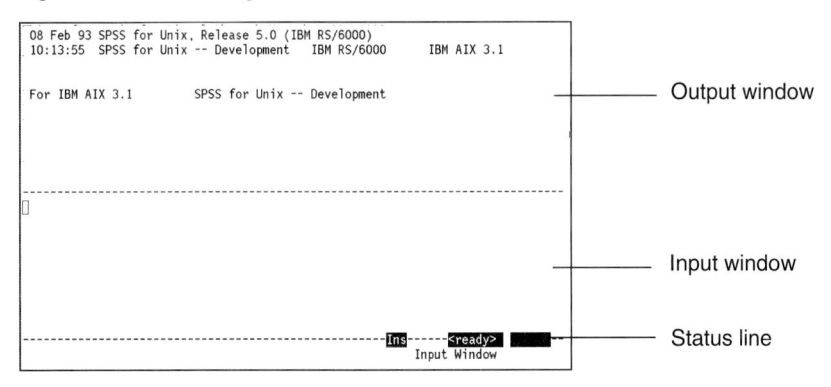

```
08 Feb 93 SPSS for Unix, Release 5.0 (IBM RS/6000)
10:13:55  SPSS for Unix -- Development     IBM RS/6000      IBM AIX 3.1

For IBM AIX 3.1       SPSS for Unix -- Development
```
— Output window

— Input window

`Ins----<ready>` — Status line
Input Window

The SPSS Manager is a text editor especially designed to let you
- Enter, edit, and save SPSS commands.
- Run SPSS commands by submitting them to the SPSS Processor.
- View, edit, and save SPSS output.

The following sections introduce some of the Manager's features and ways to access them. Because UNIX installations use many different keyboards, the key combinations mentioned in these sections may not work on your keyboard.

Mini-Menus and Keyboard Shortcuts

You can control your SPSS Manager session using either the mini-menus or key combinations. A **mini-menu** is a menu you open at the bottom of your screen in the SPSS Manager to perform Manager functions. To open a mini-menu, press [Esc] (or its equivalent on your keyboard) followed by a number. If your keyboard has function keys, you can use the corresponding function key; that is, [F1] for [Esc] [1], [F2] for [Esc] [2], and so on. Table G.1 lists options available on the mini-menus. Figure G.2 shows the Information mini-menu.

Table G.1   Options on mini-menus

Key Combination	Mini-Menu	Menu Options
[Esc] [1]	Information	Manager Help, Menus, Variable List, File List, Glossary, Syntax
[Esc] [2]	Windows	Switch, Change Size, Zoom
[Esc] [3]	Input Files	Edit Different File, Insert File
[Esc] [4]	Lines	Insert After, Insert Before, Delete, Undelete
[Esc] [5]	Find/Change	Forward Find, Backward Find, Forward Change, Backward Change
[Esc] [6]	Go To	After Submitted Line, Output Page
[Esc] [7]	Mark/Unmark	Lines, Rectangle, Command
[Esc] [8]	Block Action	Copy, Move, Delete, Round
[Esc] [9]	Output File	Write Block, Write File, Delete, Append Block
[Esc] [0]	Run/Exit	Run from Cursor, Run Marked Area, Exit, Autoview New Off

Figure G.2   Information mini-menu in menu mode

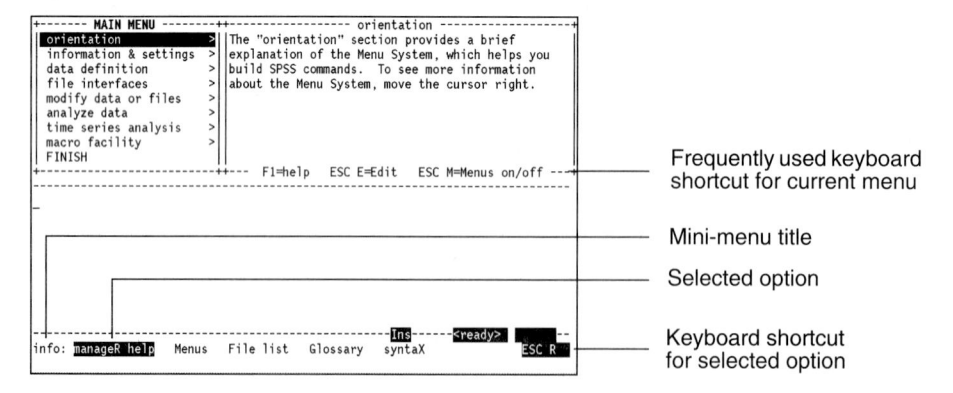

```
+------- MAIN MENU --------++---------------- orientation ------------------+
              orientation         >  The "orientation" section provides a brief
              information & settings  >  explanation of the Menu System, which helps you
              data definition         >  build SPSS commands. To see more information
              file interfaces         >  about the Menu System, move the cursor right.
              modify data or files    >
              analyze data            >
              time series analysis    >
              macro facility          >
              FINISH
+--------------------------++---- F1=help   ESC E=Edit   ESC M=Menus on/off ---+
-
-
-
-------------------------------------------Ins------<ready>-------
info: manageR help   Menus   File list   Glossary   syntaX            ESC R
```

— Frequently used keyboard shortcut for current menu

— Mini-menu title

— Selected option

— Keyboard shortcut for selected option

Choosing an Option from Mini-Menus

There are two ways to choose an option from a mini-menu:

- Press the letter capitalized for the option on the menu. For example, to choose SyntaX from the Information menu, press X, the character in upper case as shown on the screen. This is the quickest way to choose the option.
- Use the arrow keys (→ or ←) to select the option you want, and then press ↵Enter.

Accelerator Keys

As an alternative to using the mini-menus, you can perform most of the Manager's functions with the accelerator keys. For example, to switch the cursor between windows, you can open the Windows mini-menu and choose Switch. Alternatively, you can press the key combination Esc S on most keyboards without having to open a mini-menu. Using the accelerator keys can speed your work for frequently used commands.

The key combinations shown throughout this manual work on most keyboards. If they do not work on yours, you can easily determine which combinations do work. The Manager tells you the keys to use on your keyboard by displaying them in one of three places, depending on your current task:

- If a mini-menu is open, you can use arrow keys to highlight the option you want from the menu and then look in the bottom right corner of your screen to find out the keyboard shortcut for the selected option. For example, in Figure G.2, the key combination displayed in the lower right corner of the Information mini-menu, ESC R, indicates that the accelerator key combination for Manager Help is Esc R. You can request Manager Help by simply pressing Esc and then R in the input or output window without having to open the Information mini-menu.
- If you are in menu mode, the keys you are most likely to use are displayed below the menu description box. Use the keys displayed on your screen rather than the keys shown in this manual.
- Key combinations are also displayed in Manager Help.

Obtaining Help for Keyboard Shortcuts

If the key you need is not displayed on your screen, you can request Manager Help by pressing Esc R on most keyboards. There are two Help screens in Manager Help, each of which provides a table of key combinations that are functional on your keyboard. See "Manager Help" on p. 649.

Edit Mode and Menu Mode

By default, the Manager is in **edit mode**, which lets you type, review, and edit your commands in the input window (see Figure G.1). You can switch to **menu mode**, which lets you select commands from menus and then paste them into the input window (see Figure G.3). To switch between edit mode and menu mode, press [Esc] [M].

Editing with the Manager

The SPSS Manager provides all the editing features you need for working with SPSS command files and output files (see "Command and Output Files" on p. 660). Though you can use the SPSS editor to create, edit, or browse through any text file, it was not designed to be your principal editor.

Finding and Changing Text

You can find and then make changes to text preceding the cursor (Backward Find/ Backward Change) or to text after the cursor (Forward Find/Forward Change). To find and then change text in the active window:

1. Open the Find/Change mini-menu ([Esc] [5] on most keyboards).

2. To find or change text preceding the cursor, choose Backward Find or Backward Change. To find or change text after the cursor, choose Forward Find or Forward Change. This opens an entry field so you can enter the text string you want to find.

3. The search string most recently specified is displayed by default. If you want to search for another string, just type it in. You can type the string with or without capital letters. The Manager will find the first occurrence of the string, whether that occurrence is in lower, upper, or mixed case. When you are done, press [↵Enter].

4. If you select Forward Find or Backward Find, the cursor returns to the active window, and the first occurrence of the search string is highlighted. To find the next occurrence, go back to Step 1.

   If you select Forward Change or Backward Change, an entry field opens, requesting the replacement text you want to use. The text you most recently specified for replacement is displayed by default. If you want to use another replacement string, just type it in. You must type the replacement text exactly as you want it to appear in the file, upper case for upper case and lower case for lower case. When you are done, press [↵Enter].

5. If the Manager finds the string you typed in Step 3, you can respond to the Manager's prompt by pressing one of the following keys:

C	Changes this occurrence of the string, finds the next occurrence, and then waits for instructions.
A	Changes all occurrences of the string without waiting for additional instructions.
N	Does not change this occurrence of the string but continues to find the next occurrence and then waits for instructions.
S	Cancels the change request and returns the cursor to the active window.
K	Changes this occurrence of the string, cancels the change request, and returns the cursor to the active window.

- If no occurrence of the search string is found, the Manager displays Not Found at the bottom of the screen.
- If multiple strings are replaced, the Manager displays the number of changes made at the bottom of the screen.

Marking Text

In the SPSS Manager, you can mark a block of text and perform block copy, move, and delete operations. In addition, you can mark a command or a number of commands to execute and lines or rectangles to save part of the content in the input or output window into a separate file. The marked area remains marked until you unmark it, even if you have moved or copied it. When a marked area exists, invoking the Mark/Unmark mini-menu (Esc 7 on most keyboards) automatically unmarks it.

Marking a Command. You can mark a command in the input window to copy, delete, move, or execute it. To mark a command:

1. Position the cursor anywhere within the command you want to mark.

2. Open the Mark/Unmark mini-menu (Esc 7 on most keyboards) and choose Command.

The command, including all subcommands and keyword specifications, is highlighted on your screen. To find the beginning of a command, SPSS searches up in the input window from the current cursor position until it finds a command terminator. It then uses the line below the terminator as the first line of the current command. If the terminator is missing on the previous command, SPSS will merge the previous command with the current command, which results in a syntax error.

Marking Lines. You can mark a single line or multiple lines to copy, delete, move, or save. To mark one or more lines:

1. Position the cursor anywhere on the line you want to mark.

2. Open the Mark/Unmark mini-menu ([Esc] [7] on most keyboards) and choose **Lines**. The Manager displays a message telling you that it is waiting for the second line mark.

3. Move the cursor to the bottom line or the top line you want to mark and press [Esc] [7] again (or the key combination you pressed to choose the first line).

This highlights the selected line(s) on your screen. The Manager displays a message telling you the number of lines marked.

Marking a Rectangle. You can also mark a rectangle, such as a chart or a column of numbers. To mark a rectangle:

1. Position the cursor where you want the rectangle to start.

2. Open the Mark/Unmark mini-menu ([Esc] [7] on most keyboards) and choose **Rectangle**. This marks one corner of the rectangle. The Manager displays a message that tells you it is waiting for the second rectangle mark.

3. Use any combination of arrow keys to move the cursor to the corner diagonally opposite the corner you marked in Step 2.

4. Press [Esc] [7] again (or the key combination you pressed to mark the first corner).

This highlights the rectangle on your screen. The Manager displays a message telling you the area is marked.

Copying or Moving Text

You can copy or move a block of text after it is marked. When you copy or move text, lines do not wrap automatically. Thus, if the text you copy or move would cause a line to extend off your screen, the Manager issues an error message and does not copy the text.

Copying Text. To copy text:

1. Position the cursor where you want the copied text to go. The position does not have to be in the current window. For example, the original text can be in the input window, and the place to which you want to copy it can be in the output window.

2. Open the Block Action mini-menu ([Esc] [8] on most keyboards) and choose **Copy**.

This copies the text to the cursor position. The text you marked remains marked, and you can copy it again or unmark it.

Moving Text. To move text:

1. Position the cursor where you want to move the text. The position does not have to be in the active window. For example, the original text can be in the input window, and the place to which you want to move it can be in the output window.
2. Open the Block Action mini-menu ([Esc] [8] on most keyboards) and select Move.

This moves the text. The text you have moved is still marked. You can move it again or unmark it.

Deleting Text

There are a number of ways to delete text in edit mode.
- To delete a character before the cursor, press [←Backspace] on most keyboards.
- To delete a character at the cursor, press [Ctrl] [D] on most keyboards.
- To delete a single line, position the cursor on the line, open the Lines mini-menu ([Esc] [4] on most keyboards), and select Delete.
- To delete a marked area, open the Block Action menu ([Esc] [8] on most keyboards) and select Delete.

Using Menus

The menus in the menu system are context-sensitive and can be used in either of two ways:
- If you know the command you want to use, type as much of the command as you can remember into the input window and then open the menus. The menus will open at the appropriate level for you to enter more subcommands for that command.
- If you do not know the command you want to use, add a new line to the input window and then open the menus without typing anything on the line. This will access menus at the top of their hierarchy. You can then use the menus as a guide to finding the command you want.

Figure G.3 shows a menu invoked after typing the command EXAMINE in the input window.

Figure G.3 Menu mode

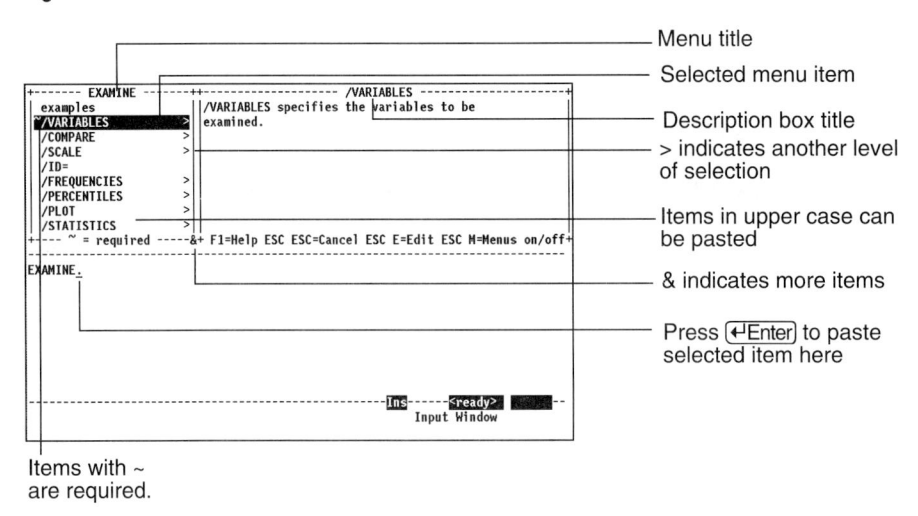

```
+------ EXAMINE ---++-------------------- /VARIABLES -------------------+
| examples         || /VARIABLES specifies the variables to be           |
| /VARIABLES     > || examined.                                          |
| /COMPARE       > ||                                                    |
| /SCALE         > ||                                                    |
| /ID=             ||                                                    |
| /FREQUENCIES   > ||                                                    |
| /PERCENTILES   > ||                                                    |
| /PLOT          > ||                                                    |
| /STATISTICS    > ||                                                    |
+--- ~ = required -----&+ F1=Help ESC ESC=Cancel ESC E=Edit ESC M=Menus on/off+
EXAMINE.

-------------------------------------------------Ins-----<ready>-------
                                                      Input Window
```

- Menu title
- Selected menu item
- Description box title
- \> indicates another level of selection
- Items in upper case can be pasted
- & indicates more items
- Press (↵Enter) to paste selected item here

Items with ~ are required.

In menu mode, you can verify that a selected command or subcommand is the one you want by reading the text in the **description box** that describes the currently selected menu item.

Visual Cues in Menu Mode

When the Manager is in menu mode, as shown in Figure G.3, it uses visual cues on your screen to communicate information. The cues are:

Case. Selections on the menus that can be pasted are always in uppercase letters. Selections that cannot be pasted are in lowercase letters.

Keys. The bottom line of the description box displays the key combinations for the most common functions.

Titles. Titles above the menus tell you the selection you made to reach the current menu level. Titles above the description box tell you the topic or keyword that is being described in the window.

Arrowhead (>). An arrowhead to the right of a menu selection indicates there is another menu level below that selection.

Tilde (~). A tilde preceding a menu selection indicates that the selection is required by its associated command.

Parentheses ( ). A set of parentheses on a menu means the current keyword requires parentheses on some of its settings. When you select the parentheses, the Manager opens an entry field so you can type a value or string, depending on the context of your selection. The parentheses are automatically added to the entry you type in the entry field.

Ampersand (&). An ampersand on the right border of a menu indicates that there are more selections available on that menu. An ampersand on the right border of the description box indicates that there is more information you can scroll to. The ampersand is displayed in the bottom corner if you must scroll down to see the additional information, and in the top corner if you must scroll up to see it. The Manager displays the key combination you can use to scroll up or down.

Extended Menus

By default, the menus omit keywords that are seldom used and provide only the standard choices. If you think you need all SPSS keywords on your menu, press Esc Y on most keyboards to turn on the **extended menus**, which list all keywords on the menus. When extended menus are on, an X is displayed on the right side of the status line.

Incremental Search for Menu Items

The Manager has an incremental search function. When you are in menu mode, simply type the menu item you would like to select. The highlight on the menu moves to the item that most closely matches what you have already typed. For example, in Figure G.4, the highlight indicates that orientation is currently selected. If you press M, the highlight moves to modify data or files and the bottom of your screen displays the current search string as M. If the menu item you want to select is macro facility, just keep typing. When you press A, the highlight moves to macro facility and the search string becomes MA. The Manager searches forward and backward on the menu for a match closest to the search string. Incremental search is a quick way to select a menu item.

Figure G.4 Incremental search in menu mode

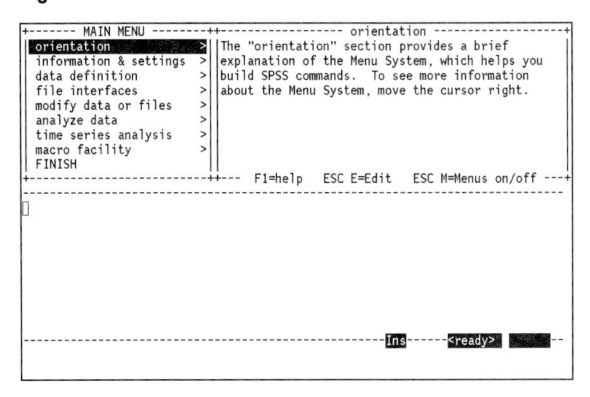

```
+------- MAIN MENU --------++------------------ orientation ------------------+
| orientation            > || The "orientation" section provides a brief      |
| information & settings > || explanation of the Menu System, which helps you |
| data definition        > || build SPSS commands.  To see more information   |
| file interfaces        > || about the Menu System, move the cursor right.   |
| modify data or files   > ||                                                 |
| analyze data           > ||                                                 |
| time series analysis   > ||                                                 |
| macro facility         > ||                                                 |
| FINISH                    ||                                                |
+--------------------------++--- F1=help   ESC E=Edit   ESC M=Menus on/off ---+
-----------------------------------------------------------------------------
[]




                                                          Ins------<ready>-------
```

Navigating the Menus

In addition to incremental search, you can navigate the menus with the following keys (the keys may be different on your keyboard):

- ↑ moves to the previous menu item.
- ↓ moves to the following menu item.
- → or Tab→ moves down one level in the menu system while pasting the selected item into the holding area, if the item can be pasted.
- ← or Esc Esc or Esc Tab→ moves up one level in the menu system while removing the item pasted in the holding area by a previous → or Tab→.
- Esc J jumps to the Main Menu.
- Esc H opens and closes the description box.

If a menu has more selections or the description box has more text than can be displayed at once, an ampersand (&) in the lower right corner appears. The bottom line of the menu or description box tells you how to scroll down.

Pasting Selections

You can use the Manager to paste your menu selections into the input window. Before pasting, be sure the cursor is positioned where you want the selection to go in the input window.

There are two ways to paste a selection into the input window:

- Highlight the selection you want to paste and then press ↵Enter. This pastes the selection into the input window and proceeds to the next menu level (if any).
- Paste selections into the holding area using → or Tab→ (see "Navigating the Menus," above) and press ↵Enter to paste the whole group into the input window.

Using the holding area allows you to collect selections in the holding area and then paste them together into the input window. This reduces the chance of syntax errors. It is also easier to remove a selection from the holding area than to delete it from the input window.

The commands, subcommands, and various specifications are pasted following these rules:

- Command names are always pasted into the input window at the beginning of the next line below the current command. If a command already exists on that line, it is moved down to make room for the command being pasted.
- SPSS subcommands and keywords are pasted into the input window to the right of the word at the current cursor position, shifting everything else on the line to the right.

- You can paste selections where you want them and in the order you choose. SPSS does not check for correct syntax until you run a command. If command syntax is incorrect, the Processor generates a warning or error message.
- If you paste the BEGIN DATA command into the input window, the Manager automatically pastes the END DATA command for you, positioning the cursor between the two. It also puts you in edit mode so that you can enter the data.
- The Manager automatically adds apostrophes or parentheses to selections that require them.

Windows

In the Manager, you use windows to control your session. You can

- Switch the cursor between the input and output windows to make either window active.
- Change the size of input and output windows and enlarge either window to full-screen size.
- Open the Files window to see a list of the files in any of your directories.
- Open the Variables window to see a list of the variables in your data or to paste variable names into the input window.

Input and Output Windows

The **output window,** at the top of your screen, is where SPSS displays output during the session. The **input window**, at the bottom of your screen, is where you enter commands. In the output window, you scroll up and down through the output, open new or existing output files, edit output files, and save them. In the input window, you scroll up and down to review the commands already entered, open new or existing command files, edit command files, and save them. The input and output windows are always open in the Manager, though both are not always visible.

Switching between Windows

To switch the cursor between windows, open the Windows mini-menu (Esc 2 on most keyboards) and choose Switch. The keyboard shortcut is Esc S on most keyboards.

If the Manager is in edit mode, the cursor switches between the input window and the output window and remains in edit mode. If the Manager is in menu mode, the cursor switches between the menus and the output window. The Manager enters edit mode when the cursor switches to the output window but returns to menu mode when the cursor switches back to the menus.

Changing Window Sizes

To change the size of the input and output windows:

1. Open the Windows mini-menu (Esc 2 on most keyboards) and choose Change Size.

2. Type the number of lines you want for the upper window and press Enter. On most terminals, you can specify any value from 7 to 14. The default is 11. The range and default vary according to the type of terminal you have.

Zooming a Window

You can **zoom** either the input or the output window. This enlarges the window to full-screen size, so you can see the maximum amount of text. To zoom a window:

1. Switch the cursor to the window you want to zoom.

2. Open the Windows mini-menu (Esc 2 on most keyboards) and choose Zoom. The keyboard shortcut is Esc Z on most keyboards.

Figure G.5 shows a full-size output window. To un-zoom, see the instructions on your screen. On the terminal illustrated, it is Esc Esc.

Figure G.5   Zoomed output window

```
COMPANY    TYPE  PRICE  METHOD  YEAR  REVENUE  INCOME  RATIO

SUPER       2    $90.0    2     1987  $41.50   $7.88   2.17%
DATAIBE     1    $188.4   2     1983  $70.12   $7.31   1.55%
ALPHA       1    $110.7   1     1983  $51.17   $7.23   2.16%
DISK        2    $54.8    2     1987  $89.16   $4.81    .61%
MEGABYTE    2    $17.0    1     1986  $38.10   $3.20    .45%
HARDCORE    2    $26.0    2     1986  $17.20   $3.20   1.51%
VALUE       3    $43.4    2     1985  $38.09   $2.45   1.14%
BINARY      1    $9.3     2     1984  $13.25   $2.26    .70%
GRAND       1    $27.5    1     1987  $29.52   $1.73    .93%

Number of cases read:  9    Number of cases listed:  9
0
09:47:20  SPSS Inc Official Field System IBM RS/6000      AIX 3.1

Preceding task required .02 seconds CPU time;  .00 seconds elapsed.
-----------------------------------------------Ins------<ready>  --
ZOOMview: press ESC ESC to unZOOM.                  Output Window
```

Files Window

The Files window displays a list of files from a specified directory. From the listing, you can select a filename and paste it into the input window. This is useful for making a file reference on a FILE, OUTFILE, MATRIX, or WRITE subcommand. To request a directory listing:

1. Place the cursor where you want to paste a filename.
2. Open the Windows mini-menu (Esc 2 on most keyboards) and select File List. The keyboard shortcut on most keyboards is Esc F.
3. Enter the file specification in the entry field that appears. Use wildcards to list the type of files that have either same extension or similar filenames, for example, *.sav or report*.dat. You can also specify a path, if the file is located in a directory other than the current one.
4. Press ←Enter to open the Files window.

Figure G.6 shows the Files window for a request of *.sav from the current directory.

Figure G.6 Files window

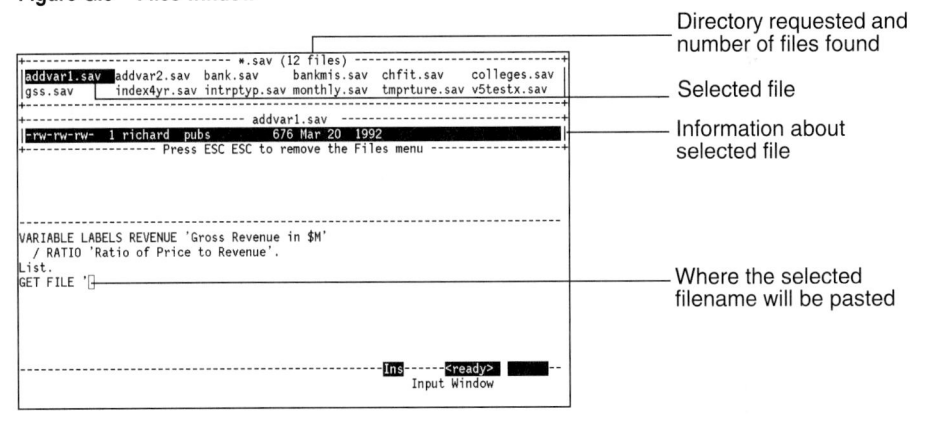

```
+-------------------- *.sav (12 files) --------------------+
|addvar1.sav addvar2.sav bank.sav   bankmis.sav chfit.sav  colleges.sav|
|gss.sav      index4yr.sav intrptyp.sav monthly.sav tmprture.sav v5testx.sav|
+----------------------------------------------------------+
+-------------------- addvar1.sav -------------------------+
|-rw-rw-rw-  1 richard  pubs         676 Mar 20  1992      |
+--------------- Press ESC ESC to remove the Files menu ---+



VARIABLE LABELS REVENUE 'Gross Revenue in $M'
   / RATIO 'Ratio of Price to Revenue'.
List.
GET FILE '[]



---------------------------------------------Ins------<ready>-------
                                              Input Window
```

- Directory requested and number of files found
- Selected file
- Information about selected file
- Where the selected filename will be pasted

Navigating the Files Window

Filenames are listed in the top box; information about the selected file is displayed in the bottom box. To see file information about any file on the list, select the filename. You can use the arrow keys to move to a specific file. You can use the Manager's incremental search function (see "Incremental Search for Menu Items" on p. 643) to move directly to the file you want to examine or use.

Pasting a Filename

To copy a filename into the input window, select the filename you want and then press ←Enter. You can paste a filename either in edit mode or in menu mode. The difference is that in menu mode, the filename is first pasted into the entry field below the information box and then pasted into the input window when you press ←Enter a second time.

Variables Window

The Variables window displays all variables in the working data file. When the data have been defined for a working file, you can open a Variable window to look up variable names and labels and also to paste variable names into the input window.

You can open the Variables window whether the Manager is in edit mode or menu mode. To do so, open the Information mini-menu ([Esc] [1] on most keyboards) and choose Variable List. The keyboard shortcut is [Esc] [V] on most keyboards. To close the Variables window, press [Esc] [Esc] on most keyboards. Figure G.7 shows a Variables window after the commands in the input window have been executed.

Figure G.7   Variables window

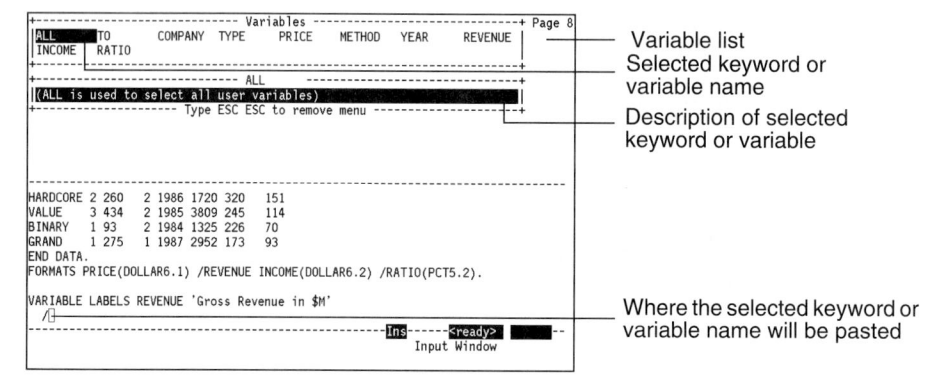

```
+------------------------------ Variables ------------------------------+ Page 8
|ALL      TO         COMPANY TYPE      PRICE      METHOD   YEAR   REVENUE  |
|INCOME   RATIO                                                             |
+---------------------------------------------------------------------------+
+------------------------------ ALL ----------------------------------------+
|(ALL is used to select all user variables)                                 |
+------------------- Type ESC ESC to remove menu ---------------------------+


HARDCORE 2 260    2 1986 1720 320   151
VALUE    3 434    2 1985 3809 245   114
BINARY   1  93    2 1984 1325 226    70
GRAND    1 275    1 1987 2952 173    93
END DATA.
FORMATS PRICE(DOLLAR6.1) /REVENUE INCOME(DOLLAR6.2) /RATIO(PCT5.2).

VARIABLE LABELS REVENUE 'Gross Revenue in $M'
 /|
----------------------------------------------Ins------<ready>   --
                                                     Input Window
```

— Variable list
— Selected keyword or variable name
— Description of selected keyword or variable

— Where the selected keyword or variable name will be pasted

Navigating the Variables Window

The lower box in the Variables window displays the variable label for the variable currently selected in the top box, or a description of the keyword if one is selected. You can navigate the menus with the arrow keys. You can use the Manager's incremental search function (see "Incremental Search for Menu Items" on p. 643) to move directly to the variable you want to examine or use.

Pasting a Variable List

When the Variables window is open, you can paste a variable list to the cursor location, including the keyword ALL or TO. By default, the keyword ALL is selected for pasting all variable names into the input window.

- To paste individual variable names, select the variable you want to paste and then press [↵Enter]. Repeat this process for each variable you want to paste.
- You can paste keyword TO between two variable names to imply a list of variables.

Online Help

The SPSS Manager provides various online help.

- Manager Help shows you the keys you can press to perform the Manager functions.
- Syntax Help displays online syntax charts.
- Context-sensitive Glossary Help provides definitions for statistical terms or terms in SPSS output.

Manager Help

To see the key combinations you can use to perform the Manager's functions, open the Information menu ([Esc] [1] on most keyboards) and choose Manager Help.

Your screen should look similar to Figure G.8.

Figure G.8   Guide to function keys and menu commands

```
+---------------------- Guide to Manager Function Keys ----------------------+
|Information    F1   Manager Help and Menus, Variable and File Lists, Glossary|
|Windows        F2   Switch, Change Size, Zoom                                |
|Input Files    F3   Insert File, Edit Different File                         |
|Lines          F4   Insert, Delete, Undelete                                 |
|Find&Replace   F5   Find Text, Replace Text                                  |
|Go To          F6   Area, Output Page, After Last Line Executed, New Output  |
|Define Area    F7   Mark/Unmark Lines, Rectangle, or Command                 |
|Area Actions   F8   Copy, Move, Delete, Round Numbers, Copy Glossary Entry   |
|Output File    F9   Write Area or File, Delete File                          |
|Run           F10   Run Commands from Cursor or Marked Area, Exit SPSS       |
+---------------------- Guide to Menu Commands ------------------------+
    |ENTER     Paste Selection & Move Down One Level in Menu          |
    |TAB       Temporarily Paste Selection & Move Down One Level      |
    |ESC ESC   Remove Last Temporary Paste & Move Up One Level        |
    |ESC J     Jump to Main Menu                                       |
    |ESC K     Kill All Temporary Pastes                               |
    |ESC T     Get Typing Window                                       |
    |ESC E     Switch to Edit Mode                                     |
    |ESC M     Remove Menus                                            |
    |ESC Y     Switch between Standard and Extended Menus              |
    +----------------------------------------------------------------+
       Enter command or press ESC R for more help, or ESC ESC to continue.
```

- To perform one of the available functions, press the corresponding key combination. For example, Figure G.8 tells you that [F9] is the function key to press when you want to write a file. The combination may be different on your keyboard, but the Manager Help always tells you the correct one.
- To see another Help screen, follow the instructions on your screen. For example, in Figure G.8, [Esc] [R] takes you to the next Help screen, which should look similar to Figure G.9:

Figure G.9 Motion Commands

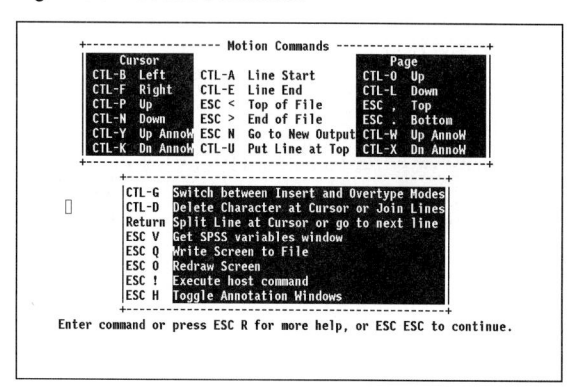

```
+--------------------- Motion Commands ---------------------+
|    Cursor                                  Page           |
| CTL-B  Left       CTL-A  Line Start    CTL-O  Up          |
| CTL-F  Right      CTL-E  Line End      CTL-L  Down        |
| CTL-P  Up         ESC <  Top of File   ESC ,  Top         |
| CTL-N  Down       ESC >  End of File   ESC .  Bottom      |
| CTL-Y  Up AnnoW   ESC N  Go to New Output CTL-W Up AnnoW  |
| CTL-K  Dn AnnoW   CTL-U  Put Line at Top  CTL-X Dn AnnoW  |
+-----------------------------------------------------------+
      | CTL-G   Switch between Insert and Overtype Modes |
   □  | CTL-D   Delete Character at Cursor or Join Lines |
      | Return  Split Line at Cursor or go to next line  |
      | ESC V   Get SPSS variables window                |
      | ESC Q   Write Screen to File                     |
      | ESC O   Redraw Screen                            |
      | ESC !   Execute host command                     |
      | ESC H   Toggle Annotation Windows                |
      +--------------------------------------------------+
  Enter command or press ESC R for more help, or ESC ESC to continue.
```

Syntax Help

Syntax Help displays online syntax charts for SPSS commands. If you request syntax for a command that is not in this Help system, the syntax window displays a chart for the command with the closest alphabetical match. The window's title line indicates the command whose syntax is currently displayed.

To see the syntax chart for a command, press [Esc] [X] to open a request box and then type the name of the command whose chart you want to see.

An ampersand (&) in the bottom right corner of the syntax window indicates there are more lines of syntax. Press [↓] to scroll down in the window. Press [↑] to scroll up again.

Once the syntax window is on your screen, you can scroll up and down in the system to see the syntax chart of other commands. The bottom line of the syntax window tells you which commands precede or follow the current command, and also the key combinations to use to see syntax for those commands. Or you can press [Esc] [X] again to make another specific request. Figure G.10 shows the syntax chart for FREQUENCIES.

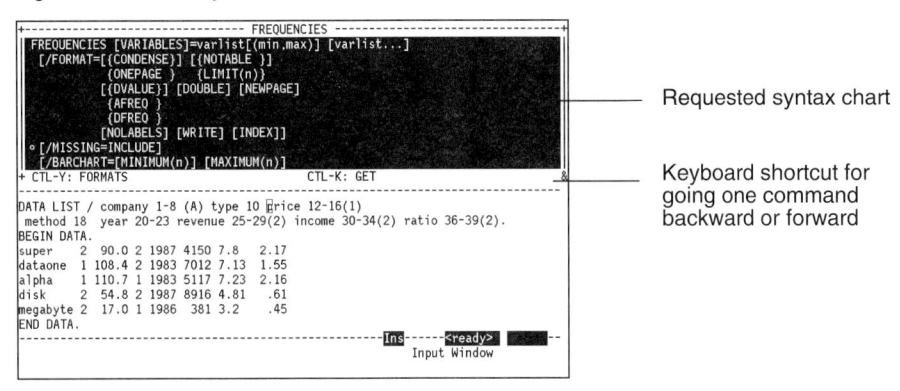

Figure G.10 Online syntax chart for FREQUENCIES

```
+--------------------------------- FREQUENCIES ---------------------------------+
| FREQUENCIES [VARIABLES]=varlist[(min,max)] [varlist...]                       |
|   [/FORMAT=[{CONDENSE}] [{NOTABLE }]                                          |
|             {ONEPAGE }  {LIMIT(n)}                                            |
|            [{DVALUE}] [DOUBLE] [NEWPAGE]                                      |
|             {AFREQ }                                                          |
|             {DFREQ }                                                          |
|            [NOLABELS] [WRITE] [INDEX]]                                        |
| o [/MISSING=INCLUDE]                                                          |
|   [/BARCHART=[MINIMUM(n)] [MAXIMUM(n)]                                        |
|+ CTL-Y: FORMATS                              CTL-K: GET                     &|
+-------------------------------------------------------------------------------+
DATA LIST / company 1-8 (A) type 10 price 12-16(1)
 method 18   year 20-23 revenue 25-29(2) income 30-34(2) ratio 36-39(2).
BEGIN DATA.
super     2  90.0 2 1987 4150 7.8   2.17
dataone   1 108.4 2 1983 7012 7.13  1.55
alpha     1 110.7 1 1983 5117 7.23  2.16
disk      2  54.8 2 1987 8916 4.81   .61
megabyte  2  17.0 1 1986  381 3.2    .45
END DATA.
------------------------------------------------------------Ins-----<ready>----
                                                               Input Window
```

— Requested syntax chart

— Keyboard shortcut for going one command backward or forward

Glossary Help

Glossary Help displays definitions of statistical terms used in SPSS output. You can use the Glossary window in two ways:

- If there is a term in the output that you do not understand, you can use the arrow keys to position the cursor anywhere within the term and press [Esc] [G] to bring up the request box. The term is automatically displayed in the box. Press [←Enter] again to open the Glossary window and read about the term.

- You can also press [Esc] [G], enter the statistical term you want to read about, and press [←Enter] to open the Glossary window.

Figure G.11 shows the glossary box defining a statistical term in the output.

Figure G.11 Glossary Help

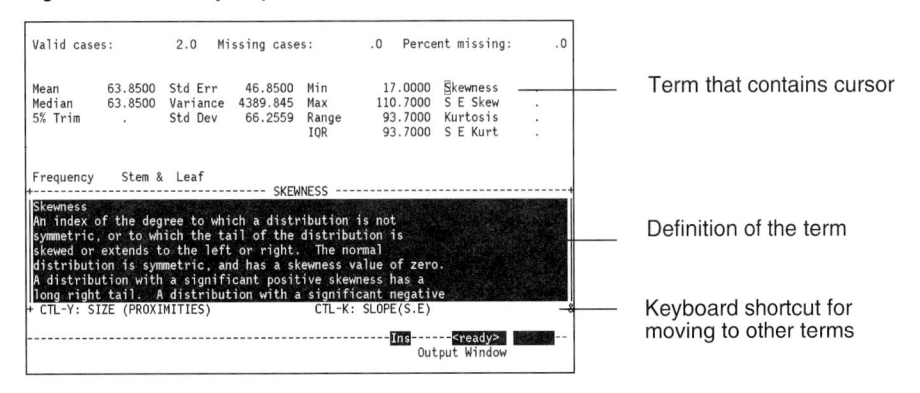

```
Valid cases:      2.0  Missing cases:     .0  Percent missing:    .0

Mean       63.8500  Std Err   46.8500  Min     17.0000  Skewness
Median     63.8500  Variance 4389.845  Max    110.7000  S E Skew    .
5% Trim        .    Std Dev   66.2559  Range   93.7000  Kurtosis
                                       IQR     93.7000  S E Kurt    .

Frequency    Stem & Leaf
+------------------------------ SKEWNESS ----------------------------------+
|Skewness                                                                  |
|An index of the degree to which a distribution is not                     |
|symmetric, or to which the tail of the distribution is                    |
|skewed or extends to the left or right.  The normal                       |
|distribution is symmetric, and has a skewness value of zero.              |
|A distribution with a significant positive skewness has a                 |
|long right tail.  A distribution with a significant negative              |
|+ CTL-Y: SIZE (PROXIMITIES)          CTL-K: SLOPE(S.E)                   &|
+--------------------------------------------------------------------------+
------------------------------------------------------------Ins-----<ready>----
                                                              Output Window
```

— Term that contains cursor

— Definition of the term

— Keyboard shortcut for moving to other terms

Once you are in the glossary box, you can use simple key combinations (your screen tells you the combinations) to scroll through the definitions of other terms. An ampersand (&) in the bottom right corner of the glossary box indicates that there are more lines in the definition. Press ⤓ to scroll down in the window. Press ↑ to scroll up again. Or, you can press [Esc] [G] again to make another specific request.

You can also copy the glossary definition into the active window. To do so:

1. Position the cursor on the line *preceding* the line where you want the glossary entry to go.

2. Instruct the Manager to copy the glossary term ([Esc] [8] on most keyboards).

The entire definition is copied into the active window, beginning on the line below the current cursor position. The definition is copied as a marked area.

Other Functions

The SPSS Manager has other features to facilitate your work. They include:
- Go To function.
- Rounding.
- Writing current screen to a file.
- Redrawing the screen.

Go To Function

You can quickly position the cursor in one of three places with the Go To function.
- The end of the command line of the last command you ran (this option is not available until you run a command).
- The top left corner of a marked area (this option is not available unless there is a marked area).
- A specific page of output (this option is available only when the output window is active).

To go to one of the three positions listed above:

1. Open the Go To mini-menu ([Esc] [6] on most keyboards).

2. Choose the option you want.

3. If you choose Output Page, type the page number and press [⏎Enter].

Rounding Numbers

To round numbers:

1. Mark the numbers you want to round off by opening the Mark/Unmark mini-menu (Esc 7) and following the process of marking a rectangle (see "Marking Text" on p. 639).

2. Open the Block Action mini-menu (Esc 8 on most keyboards) and choose Round.

3. Specify the number of decimal positions when asked and press ↵Enter.

All numbers within the selected rectangle are rounded to the specified decimal places. The number of decimal places you specify becomes the default for the next use.

Write Current Screen to a File

At any time during a session, you can write the contents of your current screen to a file. This is like taking a snapshot of the screen; everything visible on your screen is copied to the file.

Note that this is different from writing the contents of the active window to a file. When you write the contents of the active window to a file, only contents of the active window are written, including contents that may not be visible on the screen. Anything on the screen that is not within the active window is not written to the file.

To write the current screen to a file:

1. Press Esc Q. This opens an entry field that lets you name the file. If you have already written screen contents to a file, the Manager automatically enters the name of that file into the entry field.

2. To accept the filename (if any) provided by the Manager, press ↵Enter. To write the screen to a different file, type the name of the file and then press ↵Enter.

Caution: If the name you assign in Step 2 is not unique, the screen you write from the Manager is appended to the end of the existing disk file with the same name. The Manager *does not* issue a warning that it is appending screen contents to an existing file.

Redrawing the Screen

Occasionally while you are working, someone might send you a message that is flashed on your screen. To clear the message away, you must redraw the screen by pressing Esc O on most keyboards.

Status Line Messages

The status line of the Manager (see Figure G.1) reports on the status of your session. Messages that are displayed on or below the status line fall into two categories:

- Some messages report on the Manager. For example, if you are in menu mode and press [Tab→] to enter a selection into the temporary holding area, the left end of the status line displays the selections that are currently in the holding area.
- Some messages report on the SPSS Processor. For example, the message <loop> tells you that the Processor has processed the LOOP command and will interpret all subsequent commands as part of the loop until you run the END LOOP command. Messages that report on the Processor's input status always appear in lowercase letters and are displayed between angle brackets (< >).

Messages you will see most often for the Manager status are:

- STARTING. You have just started the session and the Processor is being loaded.
- Input Window. The input window is active. If you write the contents of the window to disk or edit a different file, this message changes to the name of the file you write or edit.
- Output Window. The output window is active. If you write the contents of the window to disk or edit a different file, this message changes to the name of the file you write or edit.
- Ins. The Manager is in insert mode. If you switch the Manager to overtype mode, no message is displayed.
- ESC-. To perform functions in the Manager, you press [Esc] (or its equivalent on your keyboard) plus a second key, which varies according to the function you want to perform. The ESC- message indicates that you have pressed [Esc] and that the Manager is waiting for you to press the second key. (If your keyboard uses a different key in place of [Esc], the name of that key is displayed on the status line in place of ESC-.)
- MORE. The Autoview New feature (see "Autoview New" on p. 658) is off and the Processor has sent new output to the output window since you last made the output window active.
- X. An X in the right corner of the status line means the extended menus are on. When the extended menus are off, there is no message or screen cue. By default, extended menus are off.

Messages you will see most often for the Processor are:

- <ready>. The Processor is ready for a new command.
- <data>. You have run the BEGIN DATA command and the Processor is ready to read data. The Processor continues to expect data until you run the END DATA command.

- <usrcod>. You have started an SPSS user procedure (userproc) and the Processor is ready to process more commands as part of that procedure. The Processor continues to interpret commands as part of the userproc until it reaches the command you have defined as the end of the procedure.
- <define>. You have run the !DEFINE command to begin a macro definition and the Processor is ready to process more commands within the macro. The Processor continues to interpret commands as part of the macro until you run the !ENDDEFINE command.
- <matrix>. You have run the MATRIX command to begin a matrix program and the Processor is ready to process more commands within that program. The Processor continues to interpret commands as part of the matrix program until you run the END MATRIX command.

Running an SPSS Manager Session

In a typical Manager session, you can:
- Enter commands in the input window, either by typing them directly or selecting them from the menus.
- Run the commands, either individually or as a group.
- View the results in the output window.
- Save data files and output files.

Beginning the Session

To begin an SPSS Manager session:

1. Change your directory to the directory you want to use as the default directory during your SPSS session.

2. At the UNIX prompt type

```
spss +m
```
⏎Enter

You can specify input and output files and use various switches on the command line to define your session. See Appendix E for information on command line switches.

Opening Input and Output Files Automatically

You can begin an SPSS Manager session and automatically open an existing SPSS command syntax file in the input window by specifying a filename. For example, the specification

```
spss +m value.sps
```

begins a Manager session and loads the command file *value.sps* into the input window.

To open an existing output file as well as a command file, specify the output file after the command file. For example, the specification

```
spss +m value.sps value.lst
```

begins an SPSS session and loads the command file *value.sps* into the input window and the output file *value.lst* into the output window.

Using an Automatic Profile

If there are SPSS commands that you want to run every time you start a session (such as SET commands), you can put them into a file called *.profile.sps*, and SPSS will run them automatically each time you start an SPSS session. This file is a simple text file that contain SPSS command syntax. The *.profile.sps* file must be located in your home directory.

Running SPSS Commands

During an SPSS Manager session, you enter and run commands through the Manager. When you save those commands, you create an SPSS command syntax file, which you can open and run at another SPSS session. See Appendix A for command syntax rules.

Entering Commands

You can enter commands using either edit mode or menu mode. During a session, you will usually use a combination of both modes to enter commands.

- By default, the Manager is in edit mode. This means you can type commands directly into the input window. All of the Manager's editing functions are available in edit mode.
- As an alternative to typing commands into the input window, you can select commands from menus and paste them into the input window. This is convenient when you cannot remember SPSS command syntax.
- At any time while in menu mode, you can enter edit mode without closing the menus. On most keyboards, the key combination is [Esc] [E]. Once in edit mode, you can type as many command lines as you like and then quickly return to the menus by pressing [Esc] [Esc].
- In menu mode, you can get a typing window. On most keyboards, [Esc] [T] opens the typing window. The typing window lets you type a single line. When you press [↵Enter] to enter the line into your input window, control returns to the menus.

Selecting Files and Variables

In menu mode, the Manager automatically opens a Files window if you paste a selection that requires a filename as an argument. Similarly, it automatically opens a Variables window if you paste a selection that requires at least one variable name. You can highlight a displayed file or variable name (or a relevant keyword in the Variables window) and press ⏎Enter. The selection is pasted where you have placed the cursor. See "Variables Window" on p. 648 and "Files Window" on p. 646.

Running Commands

Entering a command into the input window in the Manager does not execute it. You must instruct SPSS to run the commands you have entered using either the mini-menu or the keyboard shortcut (see "Mini-Menus and Keyboard Shortcuts" on p. 636 and "Accelerator Keys" on p. 637).

- Once the Manager runs the command(s), it automatically switches to edit mode.
- You can run one command or a group of commands. Multiple commands are run sequentially as though they were run one at a time.

Running All Commands from the Cursor

To execute a group of SPSS commands you have just typed or pasted, place the cursor on the first command and open the Run mini-menu by pressing Esc 0 on most keyboards. When the Run mini-menu appears, press ⏎Enter to select Run from Cursor.

- When running all commands from the cursor line, the cursor can be anywhere within the first command. For example, if the first command you want to run occupies three lines of the input window, the cursor can be positioned anywhere within those three lines.
- If there is any line in the input window preceding the first command to be executed, it must have a command terminator. If there is no terminator, SPSS will merge the previous input line with the current command, which results in a syntax error.

Running a Marked Block of Commands

To execute a command or a group of commands you have entered earlier, you can move back and mark the command(s) and then execute the marked block. To mark a command, select Command on the Mark/Unmark mini-menu. To mark a group of commands, select Lines in the Mark/Unmark mini-menu.

To run the marked block, press Esc 0 to open the Run mini-menu and select Run marked area.

If there is no marked area in the input window, the Run marked area selection is unavailable on the Run mini-menu. Using the keyboard shortcut for the selection (Esc A on most keyboards) produces an error.

Viewing Output

When you run SPSS commands through the Manager, you can view output immediately after the commands are run. To view output, you can

- Set the width of the output window (available only if your terminal can emulate a workstation).
- Specify whether the cursor is automatically switched to the output window after a command is run, or whether it remains in the input window.

Output Width

The default width for output in SPSS for UNIX is 80 columns. If you use the SET WIDTH command to set the width of your SPSS output anywhere from 80 to 132 columns, the output window automatically widens to display that output provided that either of the following is true:

- You have a terminal that is capable of 132-column display and you have a proper entry set up for it in the file *spsstermcap*. (SPSS provides a proper entry for VT100 terminals. If you do not have a VT100 terminal, you must modify *spsstermcap* yourself.)
- You are using a UNIX workstation. At the beginning of an SPSS session, the Manager measures the length and width of the application window (if any) opened for SPSS on the workstation. It assumes that the length and width of that application window will not change during the SPSS session. Thus, if you plan to display SPSS output beyond column 80, open an application window that is wide enough to display that output *before* you begin the SPSS session. You should not change the length or width of the application window during the SPSS session.

If neither of the above is true, the width specified on SET WIDTH will not affect the width of the Manager's output window, and you will be able to view only the first 80 columns in the output window. To see output in columns 81 to 132, you must save contents of the output window into an output file (see "Saving Files" on p. 661) and then print the output file (printing instructions should be available at your site).

Autoview New

By default, the Manager turns the Autoview New feature on when you start a session. This means that each time you run a command, the Manager displays new output in the output window, scrolling the output through the window (if necessary). It also automatically switches the cursor to the output window so you can view the new output.

If you prefer not to have the cursor switch to the output window each time you run a command, or if you find it distracting to see output scrolling on your screen while you work, you can turn this feature off. Then you cannot see any of your output, not even error messages, until you request to see it. (The Manager tells you the key you should use to see the new output.)

To turn off the Autoview New feature, open the Run mini-menu (`Esc` `O` on most keyboards) and choose **autoviewNew off**. To turn on the Autoview New feature again, open the Run menu and choose **autoviewNew on**.

Interrupting Commands that are Running

You can interrupt command processing at any time (that is, you can stop commands that are running and return SPSS to an idle state) by pressing `Ctrl` `C`.

Following an interrupt, you may want to check the data dictionary and data transformations in the SPSS working data file to see what has been updated. If a complete data pass did not occur prior to the interrupt, there may not be working data file following the interrupt. This might be the case if none of the prior commands caused the data to be read (see the *SPSS Base System Syntax Reference Guide*).

Executing UNIX Commands during an SPSS Manager Session

To suspend the SPSS session and run UNIX commands, follow these steps:

1. Open the UNIX Command entry field (by pressing `Esc` `!` on most keyboards). The Manager automatically enters the name of your current shell into the entry field.

2. To execute more than one UNIX command, press `⏎Enter`. This turns control over to UNIX, and you can execute as many UNIX commands as you like.

3. To return to the SPSS session, exit from the UNIX session (by pressing `Ctrl` `D` at most installations) and then press `⏎Enter` when prompted to do so.

To execute only one UNIX command, simply type the UNIX command you want to execute after the displayed name of the current shell and then press `⏎Enter`. This executes the UNIX command. To resume the SPSS session, press `⏎Enter` when prompted to do so.

Ending an SPSS Session

To end an SPSS session:

1. Save any changes you want from the input and/or the output window. (For ways to save files, see "Saving Files" on p. 661.)

2. Open the Run menu ([Esc] [0] on most keyboards) and choose **Exit**.

If there are unsaved changes in the input window or the output window, the Manager queries whether it should discard them.

Command and Output Files

When you begin a session, SPSS opens a new input window (essentially a temporary command file) and a new output window (essentially a temporary output file). These files are not created on disk unless you explicitly save them at some point during your session. When the Manager is in edit mode, you can do any of the following:

- Create files.
- Delete files.
- Edit an existing file.
- Insert contents from an existing file into the current file.
- Request a file list.
- Save files.

For reading, modifying, and writing data files, see the *SPSS Base System Syntax Reference Guide*.

Opening Files

To open a file:

1. Switch the cursor to the input window to create a new command file, or to the output window to create a new output file.

2. Open the Input Files menu ([Esc] [3] on most keyboards) and choose **Edit different file**.

3. If there are unsaved changes in the current file, the Manager queries whether it should discard them.

4. After you save or discard the changes, type the name of the file in the File to edit entry field and press [↵Enter]. Type a new name if you want to create a new file.

When the command or output file is open or a new file is created, the current command or output file is cleared. This, however, does not affect the working data file even if one is open.

As an alternative to creating a command file within SPSS, you can use a text editor to create the command file and open it in the input window.

Deleting Files

To delete a file from any directory:

1. Open the Output File menu ([Esc] [9] on most keyboards) and choose Delete. This opens an entry field that lets you name the file.

2. Type the name of the file you want to delete and then press [←Enter]. This deletes the entire file. If the Manager cannot find the file, it displays the message Delete failed.

To clear the contents of the current input window or output window without saving them, follow the instructions in "Creating Files" earlier. Answer yes when the Manager asks if it should discard changes.

Inserting from Files

To insert contents from an existing file into the current file:

1. Position the cursor on the line *preceding* the line where you want the insertion to go.

2. Open the Input Files menu ([Esc] [3] on most keyboards) and choose Insert file.

3. Type the name of the existing file in the File to insert entry field and press [←Enter].

All contents from the requested file are entered into the active window, beginning on the line below the cursor line. If the Manager cannot find the file, it displays the message File not found.

Saving Files

You can save all contents of the active window or a marked block. To save a file:

1. Switch the cursor to the input window to save contents of a command file, or to the output window to save contents of an output file.

2. If you want to save a marked area, mark the area (see "Marking Text" on p. 639). Otherwise, skip this step.

3. Open the Output File menu ([Esc] [9] on most keyboards).

4. Select Write File to save all contents of the active window, Write Block to save only the marked area, or Append Block to append the marked area to the end of an existing file.

5. A filename entry field appears after you make the selection. If there is already an open file in the current window, the Manager automatically enters the name of that file into the entry field. You can use this file to save all contents of the active window; you cannot use it to save a marked area.

6. To accept the filename (if any) provided by the Manager, press ⏎Enter. To write the changes to a different file, type the name of the file you want to save and then press ⏎Enter.

- When SPSS writes output to the output window, it *does not* automatically save that output in a disk file, unless you use the -t switch when you begin the SPSS session.
- If the name you assign in the filename entry field is not unique and you have chosen Write File or Write Block, the file you write from the Manager replaces the existing disk file with the same name. The Manager *does not* issue a warning that an existing file is being replaced.

Saving the Journal File

By default, SPSS creates a journal of the commands you use during a session. This journal file lets you recover commands you did not save during the session.

- An edited journal file can be used as a command file in SPSS. It can be edited in the Manager or with a text editor.
- For Manager sessions, the default name of the journal is *spss.jnl*, and it is created in the directory where you started the SPSS session. You can assign a different name and location for the journal file with the SET command.
- A journal file that has the default name *spss.jnl* is replaced the next time you run an SPSS Manager session. To prevent this journal file from being replaced, rename it with the UNIX command mv after your session.

For more information about the journal file, see Chapter 29.

Appendix H
Running an SPSS Prompted Session

This appendix is for experienced users who prefer to run SPSS for UNIX from prompts rather than from the Motif interface or the SPSS Manager. It is assumed that you are already familiar with SPSS syntax.

An SPSS Prompted Session

During a prompted session, SPSS prompts you and you respond with commands or data. When you terminate a command, it is run immediately and the results are displayed on your screen. They are not copied to an output file unless you use the -t switch when you start the session.

By default, SPSS keeps a journal of the commands that you use during the session. You can recall and use these commands in other SPSS sessions.

Starting a Prompted Session

To begin a prompted session, add the -m switch to the spss command, which you issue from the UNIX prompt, as in:

```
spss -m
```

During a prompted session, your commands are processed as you issue them, and SPSS output and messages are displayed on your screen as you work.

Using an Automatic Profile

If there are SPSS commands that you want to run every time you start a session (such as SET commands), you can put them into a file called *.profile.sps*, and SPSS will run them automatically each time you start an SPSS session. This file is a simple text file that contains SPSS command syntax. The *.profile.sps* file must be located in your home directory.

Output Files

During a prompted session, output is displayed on your screen as you work. To write the output to an output file as well, use the -t switch followed by a filename. For example,

```
spss -m -t value.lst
```

begins a prompted session and saves the output from the session to a file called *value.lst*. The output file is sent to the current directory, unless you include a directory path with the filename.

You can also create an output file after you start an SPSS session by using the SET LISTING command. For example,

```
SPSS> SET LISTING test1.out
```

saves the output of the prompted session to a file named *test1.out*. For more information on the SET command and the LISTING subcommand, see the *SPSS Base System Syntax Reference Guide*.

Journal File

By default, SPSS keeps a journal of the commands you run in a session in a file called *spss.jnl* in the current directory. In prompted sessions, the journal file is overwritten each time you start a new session. So, if you want to save the commands from a previous session, use the UNIX mv or cp command to save the old journal file under a different filename. You can also use the SET JOURNAL command in an SPSS session to assign a unique name to the journal file and turn journaling on and off during the session.

Three settings are available for the SET JOURNAL command:

- **ON** *Turn journaling on.* All subsequent commands are copied into the journal file.
- **OFF** *Turn journaling off.* Journaling is suspended. Subsequent commands are not copied into the journal file. The file is still available and stores commands again if journaling is turned on.
- **file** *Open a new journal file, using the specified filename.* If you include a directory or capital letters in the filename, enclose the file specification in quotes or apostrophes.

For example,

```
SPSS> SET JOURNAL '/u2/stats/job.one'.
```

opens the new journal file *job.one* in the directory */u2/stats*. Commands that follow this setting are copied into this journal file. The command

```
SPSS> SET JOURNAL OFF.
```

suspends journaling, so that commands that follow this setting are not copied into the journal file. The command

```
SPSS!> SET JOURNAL ON.
```

resumes journaling. You can turn journaling on and off as often as you like during a session. When journaling is suspended with OFF, the current journal file is still available and is used again when you resume journaling with ON. To close the current journal file and open a new one, specify a new file on the SET JOURNAL command.

SPSS Prompts

Prompted SPSS presents one of following prompts, depending on the status of your command entries:

SPSS> is the command level prompt. The system expects an SPSS command.

CONTINUE> is the continuation line prompt. The system expects you to continue your command from the previous line because you omitted the command terminator. You can either continue with your command or just press ⏎Return if you forgot to type a command terminator on your previous command.

DATA> is the inline data prompt. The system expects you to enter data. Issue the END DATA command to return to the SPSS> prompt.

DEFINE> is the prompt used for the MACRO facility. Additional MACRO text or the command !ENDDEFINE is expected. The MACRO facility is explained in the *SPSS Base System Syntax Reference Guide*.

USRCOD> is the prompt used for a user procedure. All input is interpreted as part of the user procedure until you run the command that you have defined as the end of the user procedure.

Command Line Continuation

Do not type past column 80 of your screen. Some of the information contained in column 81 and beyond will be lost, and SPSS may interpret the command incorrectly. Instead, find a natural breaking point in your command, press ⏎Return, and continue on the next line, as in:

```
SPSS> frequencies variables=testvar1 testvar2 testvar4 ⏎Return
CONTINUE> testvar7 testvar11 /statistics=all. ⏎Return
```

You cannot break a line in the middle of a word or quoted string.

Command Terminator

The command terminator informs SPSS that a command is complete. The default terminator is a period (.), which can be changed with the SET ENDCMD subcommand. A blank line (nulline) also functions as a terminator but can be turned off with the SET NULLINE subcommand.

Using UNIX Commands

Use the HOST command to execute UNIX commands from within an SPSS prompted session without affecting the session. For example,

SPSS> HOST ls val*.

requests a listing of all files in the current directory with filenames that begin with *val*.

When you type HOST plus a UNIX command (as above), you are automatically returned to your SPSS session once the UNIX command is executed. When you type HOST by itself, as in

SPSS> HOST.

the SPSS> prompt is replaced with the UNIX prompt and you remain in UNIX. You can issue as many UNIX commands as you like. To return to the SPSS session, press Ctrl-D, or issue the command you use to log off your system (most UNIX systems use the exit command to log off).

Interrupting a Prompted Session

You can cancel SPSS command execution by pressing Ctrl-C. This feature provides a mechanism for "bailing out" of SPSS processing. For example, you may want to cancel the execution of a LIST command if it is listing more information than you need.

- When you press Ctrl-C, SPSS stops whatever it is currently doing and returns to the SPSS> prompt. The working data file returns to its state after the last complete data pass.
- Following an interrupt, you may want to check the data dictionary and data transformations in the SPSS working data file to see what has been updated. If a complete data pass did not occur prior to the attention interrupt, there may not be a working data file following the interrupt. This might be the case if none of the prior commands caused the data to be read (data definition and transformation commands such as DATA LIST, VALUE LABELS, COMPUTE, and RECODE do not cause the data to be read). Because SPSS creates a journal file, you can recover such lost commands.
- SPSS informs you if it returns to an earlier version of the working data file or if it discards the working data file. Since some SPSS procedures involve more than one pass of the data, SPSS issues a message indicating the exact time that the SPSS working data file was last updated.
- If you press Ctrl-C at a blank prompt line, SPSS simply returns the prompt.

Ending a Prompted Session

To end a prompted session, run the FINISH command.

Bibliography

Anderson, R., and S. Nida. 1978. Effect of physical attractiveness on opposite and same-sex evaluations. *Journal of Personality*, 46:3, 401–413.

Beard, C. M., V. Fuster, and L. R. Elveback. 1982. Daily and seasonal variation in sudden cardiac death, Rochester, Minnesota, 1950–1975. *Mayo Clinic Proceedings*, 57: 704–706.

Belsley, D. A., E. Kuh, and R. E. Welsch. 1980. *Regression diagnostics: Identifying influential data and sources of collinearity.* New York: John Wiley and Sons.

Benedetti, J. K., and M. B. Brown. 1978. Strategies for the selection of log-linear models. *Biometrics*, 34: 680–686.

Berk, K. N. 1977. Tolerance and condition in regression computation. *Journal of the American Statistical Association*, 72: 863–866.

_____. 1978. Comparing subset regression procedures. *Technometrics*, 20: 1–6.

Bishop, Y. M. M., S. E. Fienberg, and P. W. Holland. 1975. *Discrete multivariate analysis: Theory and practice.* Cambridge, Mass.: MIT Press.

Blalock, H. M. 1979. *Social statistics.* New York: McGraw-Hill.

Blom, G. 1958. *Statistical estimates and transformed beta variables.* New York: John Wiley and Sons.

Borgatta, E. F., and G. W. Bohrnstedt. 1980. Level of measurement once over again. *Sociological Methods and Research*, 9:2, 147–160.

Cedercreutz, C. 1978. Hypnotic treatment of 100 cases of migraine. In: *Hypnosis at Its Bicentennial*, F. H. Frankel and H. S. Zamansky, eds. New York: Plenum.

Chambers, J. M., W. S. Cleveland, B. Kleiner, and P. A. Tukey. 1983. *Graphical methods for data analysis.* Belmont, Calif.: Wadsworth, Inc.; Boston: Duxbury Press.

Churchill, G. A., Jr. 1979. *Marketing research: Methodological foundations.* Hinsdale, Ill.: Dryden Press.

Cleveland, W. S. 1979. Robust locally weighted regression and smoothing scatterplots. *Journal of the American Statistical Association*, 74: 829–836.

Cleveland, W. S., and R. McGill. 1984. The many faces of a scatterplot. *Journal of the American Statistical Association*, 79: 807–822.

Cohen, J. 1960. A coefficient of agreement for nominal scales. *Educational and Psychological Measurement*, 20: 37–46.

Conover, W. J. 1974. Some reasons for not using the Yates continuity correction on 2 × 2 contingency tables. *Journal of the American Statistical Association*, 69: 374–376.

_____. 1980. *Practical nonparametric statistics.* 2nd ed. New York: John Wiley and Sons.

Cook, R. D. 1977. Detection of influential observations in linear regression. *Technometrics*, 19: 15–18.

Daniel, C., and F. Wood. 1980. *Fitting Equations to Data.* Rev. ed. New York: John Wiley and Sons.

Davis, H., and E. Ragsdale. 1983. Unpublished working paper. Graduate School of Business, University of Chicago.

Davis, J. A. 1982. *General social surveys, 1972–1982: Cumulative codebook.* Chicago: National Opinion Research Center.

Dillon, W. R., and M. Goldstein. 1984. *Multivariate analysis: Methods and applications.* New York: John Wiley and Sons.

Dineen, L. C., and B. C. Blakesley. 1973. Algorithm AS 62: A generator for the sampling distribution of the Mann-Whitney U statistic. *Applied Statistics*, 22: 269–273.

Draper, N. R., and H. Smith. 1981. *Applied regression analysis.* New York: John Wiley and Sons.

Duncan, O. D. 1966. Path analysis: Sociological examples. *American Journal of Sociology*, 72: 1–16.

Everitt, B. S. 1977. *The analysis of contingency tables.* London: Chapman and Hall.

Fienberg, S. E. 1977. *The analysis of cross-classified categorical data.* Cambridge, Mass.: MIT Press.

Fox, J. 1984. *Linear statistical models and related methods.* New York: John Wiley and Sons.

Frane, J. W. 1976. Some simple procedures for handling missing data in multivariate analysis. *Psychometrika*, 41: 409–415.

———. 1977. A note on checking tolerance in matrix inversion and regression. *Technometrics*, 19: 513–514.

Goodman, L. A., and W. H. Kruskal. 1954. Measures of association for cross-classification. *Journal of the American Statistical Association*, 49: 732–764.

Haberman, S. J. 1978. *Analysis of qualitative data.* Vol. 1. New York: Academic Press.

Hansson, R. O., and K. M. Slade. 1977. Altruism toward a deviant in city and small town. *Journal of Applied Social Psychology*, 7:3, 272–279.

Hoaglin, D. C., and R. E. Welsch. 1978. The hat matrix in regression and ANOVA. *American Statistician*, 32: 17–22.

Hoaglin, D. C., F. Mosteller, and J. W. Tukey. 1983. *Understanding robust and exploratory data analysis.* New York: John Wiley and Sons.

Hocking, R. R. 1976. The analysis and selection of variables in linear regression. *Biometrics*, 32: 1–49.

Hogg, R. V. 1979. An introduction to robust estimation. *Robustness in Statistics*, 1–18.

Judge, G. G., W. E. Griffiths, R. C. Hill, H. Lutkepohl, and T. C. Lee. 1985. *The theory and practice of econometrics.* 2nd ed. New York: John Wiley and Sons.

Kendall, M. G., and A. Stuart. 1973. *The advanced theory of statistics.* Vol. 2. New York: Hafner Press.

King, M. M., et al. 1979. Incidence and growth of mammary tumors induced by 7,12-dimethylbenz(a) anthracene as related to the dietary content of fat and antioxidant. *Journal of the National Cancer Institute*, 63:3, 657–663.

Kleinbaum, D. G., and L. L. Kupper. 1978. *Applied regression analysis and other multivariable methods.* Boston, Mass.: Duxbury Press.

Kleinbaum, D. G., L. L. Kupper, and H. Morgenstern. 1982. *Epidemiological research: Principles and quantitative methods.* Belmont, Calif.: Wadsworth, Inc.

Kraemer, H. C. 1982. Kappa coefficient. In: *Encyclopedia of Statistical Sciences*, S. Kotz and N. L. Johnson, eds. New York: John Wiley and Sons.

Lee, E. T. 1992. *Statistical methods for survival data analysis.* New York: John Wiley and Sons.

Lehmann, E. L. 1975. *Nonparametrics: Statistical methods based on ranks*. San Francisco: Holden-Day.

Loether, H. J., and D. G. McTavish. 1976. *Descriptive and inferential statistics: An introduction*. Boston: Allyn and Bacon.

Lord, F. M., and M. R. Novick. 1968. *Statistical theories of mental test scores*. Reading, Mass.: Addison-Wesley.

Mantel, N. 1974. Comment and a suggestion on the Yates continuity correction. *Journal of the American Statistical Association*, 69: 378–380.

Mantel, N., and W. Haenszel. 1959. Statistical aspects of the analysis of data from retrospective studies of disease. *Journal of the National Cancer Institute*, 22: 719–748.

Meyer, L. S., and M. S. Younger. 1976. Estimation of standardized coefficients. *Journal of the American Statistical Association*, 71: 154–157.

Neter, J., W. Wasserman, and R. Kutner. 1985. *Applied linear statistical models*. 2nd ed. Homewood, Ill.: Richard D. Irwin, Inc.

Nunnally, J. 1978. *Psychometric theory*. 2nd ed. New York: McGraw-Hill.

Olson, C. L. 1976. On choosing a test statistic in multivariate analysis of variance. *Psychological Bulletin*, 83: 579–586.

Overall, J. E., and C. Klett. 1972. *Applied multivariate analysis*. New York: McGraw-Hill.

Paul, O., et al. 1963. A longitudinal study of coronary heart disease. *Circulation*, 28: 20–31.

Rabkin, S. W., F. A. Mathewson, and R. B. Tate. 1980. Chronobiology of cardiac sudden death in men. *Journal of the American Medical Association*, 244:12, 1357–1358.

Roberts, H. V. 1979. An analysis of employee compensation. *Report 7946*, October. Center for Mathematical Studies in Business and Economics, University of Chicago.

———. 1980. Statistical bases in the measurement of employment discrimination. In: *Comparable Worth: Issues and Alternatives*, E. Robert Livernash, ed. Washington, D.C.: Equal Employment Advisory Council, 173–195.

Siegel, S. 1956. *Nonparametric statistics for the behavioral sciences*. New York: McGraw-Hill.

Sigall, H., and N. Ostrove. 1975. Beautiful but dangerous: Effects of offender attractiveness and nature of the crime on juridic judgment. *Journal of Personality and Social Psychology*, 31: 410–414.

Smirnov, N. V. 1948. Table for estimating the goodness of fit of empirical distributions. *Annals of Mathematical Statistics*, 19: 279–281.

Snedecor, G. W., and W. G. Cochran. 1967. *Statistical methods*. Ames: Iowa State University Press.

Somers, R. H. 1962. A new symmetric measure of association for ordinal variables. *American Sociological Review*, 27: 799–811.

Speed, M. F. 1976. Response curves in the one way classification with unequal numbers of observations per cell. *Proceedings of the Statistical Computing Section*, American Statistical Association.

SPSS Inc. 1991. *SPSS statistical algorithms*. 2nd ed. Chicago: SPSS Inc.

Stevens, S. S. 1946. On the theory of scales of measurement. *Science*, 103: 677–680.

Tatsuoka, M. M. 1971. *Multivariate analysis*. New York: John Wiley and Sons.

Theil, H. 1967. *Economics and information theory*. Chicago: Rand McNally.

Tukey, J. W. 1962. The future of data analysis. *Annals of Mathematical Statistics*, 33: 22.

Velleman, P. F., and R. E. Welsch. 1981. Efficient computing of regression diagnostics. *American Statistician*, 35: 234–242.

Winer, B. J., D. R. Brown, and K. M. Michels. 1991. *Statistical principles in experimental design*. 3rd ed. New York: McGraw-Hill.

Wright, S. 1960. Path coefficients and path regressions: Alternative or complementary concepts? *Biometrics*, 16: 189–202.

Wynder, E. L. 1976. Nutrition and cancer. *Federal Proceedings*, 35: 1309–1315.

Wyner, G. A. 1980. Response errors in self-reported number of arrests. *Sociological Methods and Research*, 9:2, 161–177.

Index

This is a combined subject index for the *SPSS for UNIX Base System User's Guide* and the *SPSS Base System Syntax Reference Guide*. Information located in the *SPSS Base System Syntax Reference Guide* is denoted with the prefix R before the page number.

absolute value function, 95
accelerator keys, 619–622
   customizing, 631
   in SPSS Manager, 637
active cell, 63
active system file, R23, R25
Add Cases procedure, 120–125, R74–R81
   case source variable, 122, R79–R80
   dictionary information, 125, R76
   key variables, R78–R79
   limitations, R76
   removing variables, 123, R79
   renaming variables, 124–125, R77–R78
   selecting variables, 122–123, R79
   unpaired variables, 121–122, R76
   variables in the new file, 122, R80–R81
Add Variables procedure, 126–131, R382–R389
   case source variable, 128, R388
   dictionary information, R383–R384
   duplicate cases, R386
   excluded variables, 128, R387–R388
   file sort order, 126, 128, R384, R385
   key variables, 128–129, R385–R386
   keyed tables, 128, R386
   limitations, R384
   renaming variables, 130–131, R387
   variables in the new file, 128, R389
adjusted predicted values, 320
adjusted R^2, 306
aggregating data, 134–138, R85–R94
   aggregate functions, 135–136, R90–R92
   aggregate variables, 134, R91–R92
   break variables, 134, R85, R88–R89
   saving files, 137–138, R88

   variable labels, 137, R90
   variable names, 137, R89–R90
agreement measures, 204–205
Akaike information criterion
   in Linear Regression procedure, R538
Ameniya's prediction criterion
   in Linear Regression procedure, R538
analysis of variance, 259, 271–280, R95–R103, R461–R470
   degrees of freedom, 273
   explained sum of squares, 273
   in Linear Regression procedure, 348, R538
   in Means procedure, 224, R418
   in regression, 306
   interaction effects, 274–275
   main effects, 273
   nonorthogonal designs, 275
   observed significance level, 274
   sums of squares, 273
   See also one-way analysis of variance, One-Way ANOVA procedure, Simple Factorial ANOVA procedure
annotating charts, 544
ANOVA. *See* analysis of variance
application resource directory
   defining, 633
arcsine function, 96, R47
arctangent function, 96, R47
area charts, 456–464
   100% stacked, 434
   category labels, 463
   displayed data, 549
   means for groups of cases, 459
   options, 511–512

671

percentage scale, 512
simple, 459, 461, 462
stacked, 460, 462, 464
summaries for groups of cases, 459–460
summaries of separate variables, 461–462
swapping axes, 567
values of individual cases, 462–464
arguments
complex, R46
defined, R46
arithmetic functions, 95–96, R122–R123
arithmetic operators, 94, R45, R122
arrays. *See* vectors
ASCII text data files
data types, 40–43
defining fixed-format variables, 39–44
defining freefield variables, 44–45
fixed-format, 38, 39–44
freefield format, 38
reading, 36–45
saving, 50
value assigned to blanks, 38
See also raw data files
assignment expression
computing values, R119
association measures, 199–208
asymptotic standard error, 205
attributes
of chart objects, 505
automatic profile, 656, 663
axes
category axes, 534–536
changing scale, 533
defining intervals, 538
displaying line, 528, 535, 537
grid, 529, 535, 537
interval axes, 536–540
labels, 534, 535, 538, 539
linear scale, 533
logarithmic scale, 533
modifying, 527–540
range, 529, 533, 538
scale axes, 528–534
scatterplot matrix, 531–534
ticks, 529, 535, 537
titles, 528, 532, 533, 535, 537

background color, 623
backward elimination, 337
in Linear Regression procedure, 347, R536
bar charts, 147, 438–448, R321
100% stacked, 434
bar label styles, 563
bar spacing, 540–541
bar styles, 562
category labels, 446
clustered, 442, 444, 447, 514
displayed data, 549
in Frequencies procedure, 153, R273–R274, R275
interval width, R273–R274
means for groups of cases, 441
moving origin line, 529
options, 511–513
percentage scale, 512
scale, R273–R274
simple, 441, 443, 446
stacked, 443, 445, 448, 514
summaries for groups of cases, 441–443
summaries of separate variables, 443–445
swapping axes, 567
values of individual cases, 446–448
batch processing, 615–618, 627
chart files, 616
output files, 615
syntax rules, 610
beta coefficients, 330
in Linear Regression procedure, 348
between-groups mean square, 261
between-groups variability, 261
binomial test
in Binomial Test procedure, R444–R445
Binomial Test procedure, 370–372, R444–R445
dichotomies, 371
expected proportions, R445
missing values, 371
observed proportions, R444–R445
statistics, 371
Bivariate Correlation procedure, 288–290, R127–R132, R436–R441, R471–R478
case count, R438
control variables, R473
correlation coefficients, 289, R127
format, R130, R436, R439, R475
limitations, R128, R437, R472
matrix input, R476–R478

matrix output, R130–R132, R436, R440–R441, R476–R478
missing values, 290, R130, R439, R475, R477
order values, R473
random sampling, R436, R439
rank-order coefficients, R436–R441
significance level, R438–R439
significance levels, 289, R129, R436, R474
statistics, 290, R129–R130, R438–R439, R474
blank
 delimiter, R17
blank data fields
 treatment of, R633
blank lines
 displaying, R504–R505
 See also printing cases
Blom's transformation, R512
BMDP files
 conversion to SPSS, R284–R285, R529–R530
 format specification, R529
 numeric variables, R529
 reading, R283–R288
 string variables, R529
Bonferroni test, 263
 in One-Way ANOVA procedure, 268
border color, 623
border width, 623
box-and-whiskers plots. *See* boxplots
boxplots, 175–177, 475–482
 comparing factor levels, 187, R225–R226
 comparing variables, 187, R225–R226
 extreme values, 175
 identifying outliers, R227
 in Explore procedure, 187, R229
 options, 517
 outliers, 175
 scale, R226
 series operations, 548
 simple, 479, 481
 stacked, 480, 482
 summaries for groups of cases, 479–480
 summaries of separate variables, 481–482
 swapping axes, 568
 type changes, 509
break variables, 391

calculator pad, 94–95
case identification variable, R525–R526
case selection, 139–142, R433–R434
 See also subsets of cases
case-control studies
 estimating risk, 210
cases, 51
 finding, 72
 limiting, R433–R434
 listing, 387–389, R368–R371
 sampling, 142, R608–R610
 selecting, 139–142, R433–R434, R625–R629
 sorting, 117–118, R648–R649
 weighting, 143–144, R685–R687
casewise plots, 311
 in Linear Regression procedure, 349
categorical charts, 429–474
category axes
 modifying, 534–536
cell editor, 63
cell frequency, 192
cells, 191
 in Data Editor, 51
central tendency measures, 162–163
character sets, R711–R717
Chart Carousel, 3, 419–421
 menus, 419
 pushbuttons, 420
 saving charts, 421
chart files
 opening at startup, 624
 printing, 576–579
charts, 21–24, R317–R336
 annotating, 544
 applying attributes, 557
 area, 456–464
 area options, 511–512
 aspect ratio, 593
 Attributes menu, 556–569
 bar, 438–448, R321
 boxplot, 475–482
 categorical, 429–474
 changing types, 506–510
 Chart menu, 505, 510–548
 colors, 559
 controlling default format, 591–593
 count functions, R318

displayed data, 549–555
drop-line, 507
enhancing, 501–503
exploring data, 499–500
fill patterns, 558
fonts, 566
footnotes, 422, 542
Gallery menu, 506–510
handles, 505
histograms, 496–497, R333
inheriting attributes, 510
inner frames, 547
jump interpolation, 564
Lagrange interpolation, 564
legend, 543
line, 448–456, R326
line styles, 561
marker styles, 561
markers displayed, 564
menus, 503–504
missing values, 423–426
mixed, 436
modifying axes, 527–540
modifying charts, 499–569
options, 511–527
outer frames, 548
palettes, 557
pie, 464–468, R329
printing, 419
reference lines, 546
refreshing screen, 504
resolution, R642
rotating, 569
saving, 421, 504
scatterplots, 483–496, R330
selecting objects, 504–506
Series menu, 505, 548–556
simple, 430–432
step interpolation, 564
subtitles, 422
summaries for groups of cases, 430–431
summaries of separate variables, 431–434
summary functions, 470–474, R318
templates, 426, R334
text styles, 566
titles, 422, 541
transposing data, 469, 555–556
tutorial, 407–418
View menu, 504
See also area charts, axes, bar charts, boxplots, mixed charts, pie charts, scatterplots

check buttons, 15
chi-square, 196–199, 247
   degrees of freedom, 198
   Fisher's exact test, 199
   in Chi-Square Test procedure, R445–R446
   in Crosstabs procedure, 212, R141
   likelihood ratio, 198
   Mantel-Haenszel, 206
   nonparametric tests, 362–363
   observed significance level, 198
   Pearson, 197
   Yates' correction, 198
Chi-Square Test procedure, 367–369, R445–R446
   expected proportions, R446
   missing values, 369
   observed proportions, R445–R446
   statistics, 369
chi-square-based measures, 200–201
Clear
   in Data Editor, 70
   in output windows, 87
   in syntax windows, 87
closing files
   data files, 50, 76
Cochran's Q
   in Tests for Several Related Samples procedure, 386, R446–R447
coefficient of contingency, 200
coefficient of determination, 306
coefficient of variance function, 96
coefficient of variation, R47
Cohen's kappa. *See* kappa
cohort studies
   estimating risk, 208–209
collinearity, 343–345
   in Linear Regression procedure, 348
color
   background, 623
   border, 623
   foreground, 624
column headings, R498–R500
   See also page ejection
column percentages, 192–193
   in Crosstabs procedure, 214, R140
column variable, 192
column width
   in Data Editor, 60
   vs. variable width, 60

column-style format specifications, R160
combined reports, 393
comma
　delimiter, 594, R17
comma format, 54
command
　order, R17–R19
　syntax, R13–R15
command files, R21, R350–R351
　See also syntax files, syntax windows
command index, 581–582
command line switches, 623–627
command order, R703–R710
command pushbuttons, 11, 15
command syntax, 609–612
　batch processing, 610
　in Help window, 607
　INCLUDE files, 610
　See also syntax windows
command terminator
　specifying, R640
commands
　processed through your operating system, R14–R15
　run within SPSS, R13–R14
　that read data, R18–R19
　that take effect immediately, R18–R19
　See also syntax windows, batch processing
comments
　in commands, R116
complex data files, R520–R528
　case identification variable, R525–R526
　defining, R520–R528
　duplicate records, R527
　grouped files, R520
　missing records, R526–R527
　mixed files, R520
　nested files, R520
　repeating groups, R520
　skipping records, R524–R525
　spreading values across cases, R527–R528
　undefined records, R523–R524
complex files
　defining, R202–R203, R213–R216, R216–R217
complex raw data files, R718–R731
　defining, R242–R256
　grouped, R247

mixed, R247
nested, R247
computing values, 93–100, R117–R126
　arithmetic functions, 95–96, R122–R123
　arithmetic operators, 94, R122
　assignment expression, R119
　calculator pad, 94–95
　conditional expressions, 98–99, R196–R198, R340–R342
　cross-case functions, R124
　date and time functions, R125
　formats of new variables, R121–R122
　functions, 95–97, R117–R119
　if case satisfies condition, 98–99, R195–R203, R340–R345
　logical expressions, R196–R198, R340–R342
　logical functions, 96–97, R124
　logical operators, 95, R195, R340
　loop structures, R372–R381
　missing values, 97, R121
　missing-value functions, R123–R124
　nested functions, 97
　new variables, 99–100
　random-number functions, 97, R124–R125
　relational operators, 94, R195, R340
　statistical functions, 96, R123
　string data, 100, R120, R121–R122
　string functions, R126
　subsets of cases, 98–99
　syntax rules, 100, R120–R121
　target variable, 94, R119
concordant pairs, 206
condition index
　in Linear Regression procedure, R538
conditional expressions, 98–99
　See also logical expressions
conditional transformations, 98–99, R195–R203, R340–R345
　conditional expressions, 98–99, R196–R198, R340–R342
　formats of new variables, R197, R342
　logical expressions, 98–99, R196–R198, R340–R342
　logical operators, 99, R195, R340
　missing values, R198, R342
　nested, R202
　relational operators, 99, R195, R340
　string data, R196, R197, R341, R342

confidence intervals
 in Linear Regression procedure, 348, 351, R539, R541, R551
 in One-Way ANOVA procedure, 269
 in regression, 305
 one-way analysis of variance, 258
confidence levels
 specifying, 520
consecutive integers
 converting numeric data, 114–115, R108–R111
 converting string data, 114–115, R108–R111
constants, R45–R46
contingency coefficient, 200
 in Crosstabs procedure, 213, R141
contour plots, R482
contrasts
 analysis of variance, R463–R464
 in One-Way ANOVA procedure, 267
control variables, 193–195
 in Crosstabs procedure, 212, R139
 in Partial Correlations procedure, 296
converting data files. *See* data files
Cook's distance, 319–322
 in Linear Regression procedure, 351, R551
Copy
 in Data Editor, 66–69
 in output windows, 87
 in syntax windows, 87
Copy Table
 in output windows, 87
 in syntax windows, 87
correlation, R127–R132
 bivariate, 281–290
 crosstabulation, 205
 in Linear Regression procedure, R539, R544
 in multiple regression, 326–328
 nonparametric measures, 285, 287
 partial, 291–298
 scatterplots, 281–283
 zero-order, 292
 See also Bivariate Correlation procedure
cosine function, 96
counting occurrences, 101–104, R133–R134
 defining values, 103–104, R133
 if case satisfies condition, 104
 missing values, R134
 subsets of cases, 104

counts
 in Report Summaries in Rows procedure, R592, R593
covariance
 in Linear Regression procedure, 348, R538, R544
covariance ratio, 342
 in Linear Regression procedure, 352, R551
Cp. See Mallow's *Cp*
Cramér's *V*, 200
 in Crosstabs procedure, 213, R141
cross-case functions, R124
cross-product deviation
 in Linear Regression procedure, R544
Crosstabs procedure, 211–216, R135–R145
 boxes around cells, 215, R143
 column percentages, 214, R140
 control variables, 212, R139
 expected count, 214, R141
 general mode, R139
 index of tables, 215, R143
 integer mode, R140
 labels, 215, R143
 layers, 212, R139
 missing values, R142
 observed count, 214, R140
 reproducing tables, R145
 residuals, 214, R141
 row order, 215, R143
 row percentages, 214, R140
 statistics, 212–214, R141–R142
 suppressing tables, 212, R143
 table format, 215, R142–R143
 total percentage, 214, R141
 writing tables, R143–R145
crosstabulation, 191–210, R135–R145
 agreement measures, 204–205
 association measures, 199–208
 case-control studies, 210
 cell frequency, 192
 cells, 191
 chi-square, 196–199
 chi-square-based measures, 200–201
 cohort studies, 208–209
 column percentages, 192–193
 column variable, 192
 control variables, 193–195
 correlation, 205
 data screening, 195–196
 degrees of freedom, 198

Index

dependent variable, 193
expected count, 196
graphical representation, 195
in Means procedure, R416–R417
independent variable, 193
interval data measures, 208
marginals, 192
multiple response, 228–229, 234–237, R427–R430
nominal measures, 199–205
observed count, 196
ordinal measures, 205–208
percentages, 192–193
proportional reduction in error, 201–204
residuals, 197
row percentages, 192–193
row variable, 192
statistics, 196–210
table percentage, 192
writing to a file, R506–R507
See also Crosstabs procedure
cumulative distribution function, R48
cumulative percentage, 146
custom currency formats
creating, 593–594, R637–R638
in Data Editor, 55
customizing resource file, 629–633
Cut
in Data Editor, 66–69
in output windows, 87
in syntax windows, 87

d. See Somers' *d*, R142
data
inline, R112–R113, R149, R150
invalid, R633
data compression
scratch files, R639
data conversion
in Data Editor, 67, 71
Data Editor, 3, 18–21, 51–77
blank cells, 51
cases, 51
cells, 51
column format, 59–60
column width, 60
converting data type, 67, 71

copying data, 66–69
cutting data, 66–69
data types, 54–56
data value restrictions, 65
decimal indicator, 56
defining variables, 52–63
deleting cases, 70–71
deleting variables, 70–71
displaying value labels, 73
editing data, 20–21, 65–69
entering data, 18–20, 63–65, 73
file structure, 51
finding cases, 72
finding data values, 72
finding variables, 72
fonts, 74, 631
grid lines, 74
inserting cases, 69
inserting variables, 69–70
keyboard navigation, 76–77
missing values, 58–59
moving variables, 71
pasting data, 66–69
printing, 75
system-missing value, 51
templates, 60–63
text alignment, 60
value labels, 57–58
variable labels, 57
variables, 51
data files, 29–50
aggregating, 134–138, R85–R94
applying data dictionary, 132–133, R104–R107
ASCII text, 36–45, 50
BMDP, R283–R288, R529–R530
closing, 50, 76
complex, R213–R216, R242–R256, R520–R528, R718–R731
converting, R619–R624
Data Editor window, 45
dBASE, R311–R312, R619–R624
default file extension, R639–R640
direct access, R360–R365
documents, R193–R194, R209
Excel, R310–R311, R619–R624
file information, 46–48, R190–R192, R657
grouped, R520
Informix, 32–36
Ingres, 32–36
keyed, R360–R365, R487–R490

labels, R241
Lotus 1-2-3, R310–R311, R619–R624
master files, R667–R673
merging, 119–131, R74–R81, R382–R389
mixed, R520
Multiplan, R310–R311
nested, R520
opening, 29–36, R279–R282
opening at startup, 624
Oracle, 32–36
OSIRIS, R293–R298
printing, 575–576
raw, R147–R164
reading, 29–45, R148, R279–R316, R346–R349, R360–R365
repeating data groups, R520
SAS, R299–R304
save as different format, 48–50
save as new file, 48–50
saving, 48–50, 75, R611–R615, R696–R701
SCSS, R305–R308, R616–R618
split-file processing, 138–139, R650–R652
spreadsheet, R310–R311, R620–R621
SPSS, 31, 50, R279
SPSS portable, 31, 50, R234–R239, R346
SPSS/PC+, R346
SQL database, 31–36
subsets of cases, 139–142, R257–R258, R625–R629
Sybase, 32–36
SYLK, R310–R311, R619–R624
tab-delimited, R312, R621
text, 36–45
transaction files, R667–R673
transformations, 117–144
updating, R667–R673
weighting cases, 143–144
data formats. *See* data types; display formats; input formats; output formats
Data menu. *See* Data Editor, file transformations
data records
 defining, 40–44, R153–R154, R520–R528
data selection
 in charts, 548–556
data transformations, 93–115
 arithmetic functions, 95–96, R122–R123
 arithmetic operators, 94, R122
 calculator pad, 94–95
 clearing, R115
 computing values, 93–100, R117–R126
 conditional, 98–99, R195–R203, R340–R345
 conditional expressions, 98–99, R196–R198, R340–R342
 consecutive integers, 114–115, R108–R111
 controlling calculation, 115, 590
 converting strings to numeric, 114–115, R108–R111, R518–R519
 counting occurrences, 101–104, R133–R134
 counting the same value across variables, 101–104, R133
 cross-case functions, R124
 date and time functions, R125
 functions, 95–97, R117–R119
 if case satisfies condition, 98–99, R195–R203, R340–R345
 logical expressions, 98–99, R196–R198, R340–R342
 logical functions, 96–97, R124
 logical operators, 95, R195, R340
 loop structures, R372–R381
 missing-value functions, R123–R124
 nested functions, 97
 new variables, 99–100
 pending, 115, 590
 random-number functions, 97, R124–R125
 random-number seed, 101
 ranking data, 110–113
 recoding values, 104–110, R108–R111, R514–R519
 relational operators, 94, R195, R340
 repeating, R204–R208
 statistical functions, 96, R123
 string functions, R126
 subsets of cases, 98–99
 syntax rules, 100
data transposition
 in charts, 555, 556
data types, 40–43, 54–56, R147–R148
 American date, 41
 comma, 42, 54
 conversion, 67
 custom currency, 55, 593–594, R637–R638
 date, 40–41, 55
 date and time, 41
 day and time, 42
 day of week, 42
 display formats, 56
 dollar, 40, 55
 dot, 42, 55

European date, 41
implied decimal, 40
input formats, 56
Julian date, 41
month, 42
month and year, 41
numeric, 40, 44, 54
quarter and year, 41
scientific notation, 55
string, 40, 44
time, 42, 55
week and year, 41
database files, 31–36, R621
date and time functions, R125
date formats, 40–42, 55
   in Data Editor, 56
date functions, R59–R73
dates, R59–R73
dBASE files
   reading, R309–R316
   saving, R622
decimal indicator
   in command syntax, 610
   in custom currency formats, 594
   in Data Editor, 56
   LANG environment variable, 56
   specifying, R638
decimal places
   implied, 40, R161–R163
Define Multiple Response Sets procedure, 231–232, R425–R426
   categories, 232, R425–R426
   dichotomies, 232, R425–R426
   set labels, 232, R425–R426
   set names, 232, R425–R426
defining variables, 52–63
degrees of freedom
   analysis of variance, 273
deleted residuals, 319–322
   in Linear Regression procedure, 351
deleted variables
   in dialog boxes, 70–71
deleting
   cases, 70–71
   variables, 70–71

delimiter, R17
   blank, R17
   comma, R17
   special, R17
dependent variable, 193
descriptive statistics, 157–170, R183–R189
   in Explore procedure, R230
   See also Descriptives procedure
Descriptives procedure, 167–170, R183–R189
   display order, 170, R188–R189
   format options, 168, R186–R187
   index of variables, 168, R187
   limitations, R184
   missing values, R189
   output width, R186–R187
   saving Z scores, 168, R185–R186
   statistics, 169–170, R187–R188
deselecting variables, 13
Designate Window
   output window, 81
   syntax window, 86
designated window, 4
detrended normal plots, 179
   in Explore procedure, 188, R229
dfBeta
   in Linear Regression procedure, 351, R551
dfFit
   in Linear Regression procedure, 351, R551
dialog boxes, 10–18
   check buttons, 15
   colors, 632
   command pushbuttons, 11, 15
   customizing, 632
   deselecting variables, 13
   fonts, 631
   option menus, 17
   radio buttons, 16–17
   selected variable lists, 11
   selecting variables, 12
   source variable list, 11
   text boxes, 16
direct-access files
   reading, R360–R365
discordant pairs, 206
dispersion measures, 163–164
display file, R25

display formats, R265–R268, R501–R503
    in Data Editor, 56
    vs. input formats, 56
displayed data
    in charts, 549–555
documentation
    online, R352–R355
documents
    dropping, R209
    for SPSS data files, R193–R194
    retaining in aggregated files, R89
dollar format, 40, 55
domain errors
    defined, R48
    numeric expressions, R48–R57
dot format, 55
drop-line charts, 436, 507
Duncan's multiple range test
    in One-Way ANOVA procedure, 268
Durbin-Watson statistic
    in Linear Regression procedure, 348, R553

editing
    in Data Editor, 20–21, 65–69
    in output windows, 86–90
    in syntax windows, 86–90
eigenvalues, 344
    in Linear Regression procedure, 348, R538
elementary variables, 226
encapsulated PostScript
    printing to a file, 578
end-of-file control
    in input programs, R154–R156
entering data
    by case, 64
    by column, 64
    by row, 64
    by variable, 64
    in Data Editor, 18–20, 63–65
    in selected area, 64
    restrictions, 65
    using value labels, 73
EPS format
    printing to a file, 578

equality of variance
    in regression, 302, 315
erasing files, R222
errors
    displaying, 595, R634–R635
    maximum number, R633–R634
eta, 208
    in Crosstabs procedure, 213, R142
    in Means procedure, 224, R418
evaluating assumptions, 177–181
exact-size sample, R608
examining data, 171–189, R223–R232
    See also Explore procedure, exploring data
Excel files
    read range, R314–R315
    read variable names, R314
    reading, R309–R316
    saving, R622
expected count, 196
    in Crosstabs procedure, 214, R141
expected value, 241
Explore procedure, 185–189, R223–R232
    factor variable, 185, R225
    frequency tables, 187, R227–R228
    grouped frequency table, 187
    limitations, R224
    missing values, 189, R231–R232
    plots, 187–188, R229–R230
    scaling plots, R226
    statistics, 186–187, R228, R230–R231
exploring data, 171–189, R223–R232
    boxplots, 175–177
    detrended normal plots, 179
    displaying data, 172–177
    evaluating assumptions, 177–181
    extreme values, 174
    histograms, 172, 501
    normal probability plots, 179
    normality tests, 179–181
    outliers, 175
    robust measures, 181–184
    scatterplots, 499–500
    spread-and-level plots, 178–179
    stem-and-leaf plots, 173–175
    See also Explore procedure, 171
exponent function, 95

extended menus
  SPSS Manager, 626
extreme values, 174
  boxplots, 175
  in Explore procedure, 186, R230

F ratio
  analysis of variance, 273
  in Linear Regression procedure, R538, R539
  in Means procedure, 224, R418
  one-way analysis of variance, 262
F test
  in Linear Regression procedure, 348
  partial, 332
file, R21
file definition, R21
file handle, R240
file information, 585–586
  SPSS data files, 47–48, R657
  working data file, 46–47, R190–R192
file specifications, R240
file transformations, 117–144, R667–R673
  aggregating, 134–138, R85–R94
  applying data dictionary, 132–133, R104–R107
  merging files, 119–131, R74–R81, R382–R389
  sorting cases, 117–118
  subsets of cases, R625–R629
  transposing cases and variables, 118–119
  weighting cases, 143–144
Fisher's exact test, 199
  in Crosstabs procedure, 212, R141
fit methods
  in charts, 519–521, 563–564
fixed format, 38, R149, R149–R150, R151–R152, R157–R158
fonts, 624
  Data Editor, 74, 631
  dialog boxes, 631
  in charts, 566
  mapping for printing, 579
  menus, 631
  output windows, 90, 631
  resource file, 631
  syntax windows, 90, 631
footnotes
  in charts, 422, 542

forced entry
  in Linear Regression procedure, 346, R536
forced removal
  in Linear Regression procedure, 347, R537
foreground color, 624
foreign files
  input files, R23
formats, R34–R44
  of new variables, R121–R122, R197, R342
  See also data types; display formats; input formats; output formats
FORTRAN-like format specifications, R160–R161
forward entry
  in Linear Regression procedure, R536
forward selection, 335–336
  in Linear Regression procedure, 347
frames
  in charts, 547
freefield format, 38, 44–45, R149, R150, R151–R152, R158–R159
  commas as delimiters, 45
  international setting, 45
  missing data, 45
Frequencies procedure, 150–155, R269–R278
  charts, 153–154, R273–R275
  condensed format, 154, R272
  display order, 154, R272
  general mode, R270–R271
  index of tables, 155, R273
  integer mode, R270–R271
  limitations, R271
  missing values, R278
  page format, 154–155, R272
  statistics, 151–153, R277–R278
  suppressing tables, 155, R273
  value labels, 155, R272
  writing tables, R273
frequency tables, 145–155, R270–R273
  format, R272–R273
  in Explore procedure, 187, R227–R228
  increment, R227–R228
  percentages, 146
  screening data, 150
  starting value, R227–R228
  values, 145
  writing to a file, R506–R507
  See also Frequencies procedure

Friedman test
  in Tests for Several Related Samples procedure, 386, R447
F-to-enter, 335
  in Linear Regression procedure, 353, R540
F-to-remove, 337
  in Linear Regression procedure, 353, R540
functions, 95–97, R117–R119
  absolute value, 95
  arcsine, 96
  arctangent, 96
  arithmetic, 95–96
  coefficient of variance, 96
  cosine, 96
  count, in charts, 470
  examples, R122–R126
  exponent, 95
  logarithm, 95–96
  logical, 96–97
  maximum, 96
  mean, 96
  mean, in charts, 441, 451, 459
  minimum, 96
  missing values in, 97, 97–98, R121
  nested, 97
  numeric variables, R46–R57
  random-normal, 97
  random-number, 97
  random-number seed, 101
  random-uniform, 97
  range, 96
  remainder, 95
  round, 95
  sine, 96
  square root, 95
  standard deviation, 96
  statistical, 96
  string variables, R49–R52
  sum, 96
  sum, in charts, 466
  summary, in charts, 472
  syntax rules, 100
  truncate, 95
  variance, 96

gamma, 207
  in Crosstabs procedure, 213, R142

general mode
  Crosstabs procedure, R139
  Frequencies procedure, R270–R271
  Means procedure, R412, R413, R416
glossary
  in Help window, 607
Go to Case, 72
Goodman and Kruskal's gamma. *See* gamma
Goodman and Kruskal's lambda. *See* lambda
Goodman and Kruskal's tau, 203–204
  in Crosstabs procedure, 213, R141
goodness of fit
  in regression, 305–308
grand totals, 394
graphs
  See charts
grid lines
  in Data Editor, 74
grouped files, R247, R520

H. *See* Kruskal-Wallis *H*
handles
  for chart objects, 505
hanging bar charts, 435
harmonic average
  in One-Way ANOVA procedure, 268
harmonic means
  in analysis of variance, R466
help, 601–607, R337–R338
  command syntax, 607
  copying Help text, 605
  F1 key, 601
  glossary, 607
  SPSS Manager help, 649
hidden relationships, 294
hierarchical files. *See* nested file
high-resolution charts, 407
histograms, 148–149, 172, 496–497, R333
  adding normal curves, 526
  displayed data, 555
  in Explore procedure, 188, R229
  in Frequencies procedure, 153, R274–R275
  in Linear Regression procedure, 349, R552–R553
  interval width, R274

options, 526–527
scale, R226, R274
statistics in legend, 526
swapping axes, 568
weighting cases, 526
with normal curve, R275
homogeneity-of-variance
  in One-Way ANOVA procedure, 269
HOST (command)
  during a prompted session, 666
hypothesis testing, 239–250
  assumptions, 250
  chi-square, 247
  correlation, 285–286
  in analysis of variance, 259
  in regression, 304–305
  preparing for, 172

icon bars
  output windows, 6
  syntax windows, 6
ill-conditioned matrix, 344
implied decimal format, 40, R161–R163
INCLUDE files
  syntax rules, 610
independence
  in regression, 303
independence of error, 315–316
independent variable, 193
Independent-Samples T Test procedure, 250–253, R663–R666
  defining groups, 251–252
  dependent variables, R665
  grouping variables, 251, R665
  limitations, R664
  missing values, 253, R666
  string variables, 252
  variable labels, R666
independent-samples t test. *See* t test
indexing clause
  in loop structures, R374–R379
indexing strings, R52
indicator variables, 122, 326
Informix database
  reading, 32–36

Ingres database
  reading, 32–36
initialization
  scratch variables, R34
  suppressing, R366–R367
initializing variables, R459–R460, R653–R654
  formats, R459, R460, R653–R654
  numeric variables, R459–R460
  scratch variables, R459
  string variables, R653–R654
inline data, R112–R113, R149, R150
inner frames
  in charts, 547
input data, R22
  file, R21
input formats, R147–R148, R159–R164
  column-style specifications, R160
  FORTRAN-like specifications, R160–R161
  numeric, R161–R163
  string, R163–R164
  vs. display formats, 56
input programs, R356–R359
  end-case control, R212–R219
  end-of-file control, R154–R156, R220–R221
  examples, R155–R156, R203, R206, R213–R219, R221, R358–R359, R376–R378, R379, R380–R381, R460, R488–R489, R682–R683
input state, R357
inserting
  cases, 69
  variables, 69–70
integer mode
  Crosstabs procedure, R140
  Frequencies procedure, R270–R271
  Means procedure, R412, R413, R416
interaction effects
  analysis of variance, 274–275, R98
interpolation
  in charts, 563
interrupting a prompted session, 666
interval axes
  modifying, 536–540
interval measurement, 160
invalid data
  treatment of, R633

journal file, 588–589, 599, R21, R641
    Manager session, 662
    multiple SPSS sessions, 599
    prompted sessions, 664–665

kappa, 205
    asymptotic standard error, 205
    in Crosstabs procedure, 213, R142
Kendall's tau-*a*, 206
Kendall's tau-*b*, 206, 285
    in Bivariate Correlation procedure, 289, R438
    in Crosstabs procedure, 213, R141
Kendall's tau-*c*, 207
    in Crosstabs procedure, 213, R141
Kendall's *W*
    in Tests for Several Related Samples procedure, 386, R450–R451
key variables, 128, R667–R673
keyboard navigation, 28, 619–622
    chart windows, 622
    Data Editor, 76–77, 620
    dialog boxes, 28, 619
    menus, 28, 619
    output windows, 621
    syntax windows, 621
    window control, 622
keyed data files, R487–R490
    defining, R487–R490
    file handle, R489
    file key, R487, R488–R489, R489–R490
keyed files
    reading, R360–R365
keyed tables, 128, R386
keywords
    reserved, R32
    syntax, R16
Kolmogorov-Smirnov *Z*
    in One-Sample Kolmogorov-Smirnov Test procedure, 374, R448–R449
    in Two-Independent-Samples Tests procedure, 378, R449
Kruskal-Wallis *H*, 367
    in Tests for Several Independent Samples procedure, 380, R449–R450

kurtosis, 165
    in Descriptives procedure, 170, R188
    in Explore procedure, 186, R230
    in Frequencies procedure, 153, R277
    in Report Summaries in Rows procedure, 401, R592

lambda, 203
    in Crosstabs procedure, 213, R141
landscape printing, 575, 578
least squares, 301
least-significant difference
    in One-Way ANOVA procedure, 268
legends
    in charts, 543
leptokurtic distribution, 165
level of measurement, 159–160
Levene test, 177, 260
    in Explore procedure, 188, R229
    in One-Way ANOVA procedure, 269
leverage values, 341
    in Linear Regression procedure, 351, R551
likelihood-ratio chi-square, 198
    in Crosstabs procedure, 212, R141
Lilliefors test, 180
    in Explore procedure, 188, R229
limitations. *See* individual procedures
line charts, 448–456, R326
    category labels, 455
    connecting markers, 512
    displayed data, 549
    interpolation styles, 563
    line styles, 561
    marker styles, 561
    means for groups of cases, 451
    multiple, 452, 454, 456
    options, 511–513
    projection display, 513
    simple, 450, 453, 454
    summaries for groups of cases, 450–452
    summaries of separate variables, 453–454
    swapping axes, 567
    values of individual cases, 454–456
line fitting
    in scatterplots, 518–521, 524

line interpolation, 563–564
  in charts, 563
linear association, 281–290
  scatterplots, 281–283
linear regression, R531–R548
  See also Linear Regression procedure
Linear Regression procedure, 346–353, R531–R548, R549–R557
  blocks, 346
  case selection, R544–R545
  casewise plots, R553–R554
  constant term, R541–R542
  dependent variables, R535
  format, R547–R548
  histograms, R552–R553
  matrix input, R545–R547
  matrix output, R545–R547
  missing values, 353, R546–R547
  model criteria, R539–R541
  normal probability plots, R553
  partial residual plots, R555
  plots, 348–350
  residuals, 348–352, R549–R557
  saving new variables, 350–352, R556
  scatterplots, R554–R555
  statistics, 347–348, R537–R539, R543–R544
  tolerance, 347, R539, R540, R541
  variable selection methods, 346–347, R536–R537
  weights, 347, R542–R543
linear regression. *See* regression
linearity
  in regression, 303, 313–314
linearity test
  in Means procedure, 224, R418
List Cases procedure, 387–389, R368–R371
listing cases, 387–389, R368–R371
listing files, 91
listing reports, 392
local documentation, R352, R354
logarithm function, 95–96
logical expressions, 98–99, R49, R52–R58, R196–R198, R340–R342
  defined, R52
  in END LOOP, R53
  in LOOP, R53
  in loop structures, R374
  in SELECT IF, R53
  missing values, R56, R57

order of evaluation, R55
selecting cases, R625
string variables, R49
See also conditional transformations
logical functions, 96–97, R53, R124
logical operators, 95, R54, R55, R195, R340, R625
  defined, R55
  in conditional expressions, 99
  missing values, R56, R198, R342
logical variables
  defined, R52
long string variables, 40, 55, R42
loop structures, R372–R381
  increment value, R378–R379
  indexing variable, R374–R379
  initial value, R375
  logical expression, R374
  macro facility, R180–R182
  terminal value, R375
looping structures
  terminating, R114
loops
  maximum number, R634
Lotus 1-2-3 files, R622
  read range, R314–R315
  read variable names, R314
  reading, R309–R316
lower case
  specifying, R636–R637

macro facility, R165–R182
  assigning defaults, R175–R176
  conditional processing, R180
  display macro commands, R641–R642
  examples, R732–R746
  keyword arguments, R170–R171
  loop structures, R180–R182
  macro call, R167
  macro definition, R166–R167
  macro expansion, R641–R642
  positional arguments, R171–R172
  SET command, R178–R179
  string functions, R176–R178
  tokens, R172–R175

Mahalanobis distance, 319
   in Linear Regression procedure, 351, R551
Mallow's *Cp*
   in Linear Regression procedure, R538
Manager mode. *See* SPSS Manager
Mann-Whitney test, 355
Mann-Whitney *U*
   in Two-Independent-Samples Tests procedure, 378, R451
Mantel-Haenszel chi-square, 206
   in Crosstabs procedure, 212, R141
marginals, 192
master files, R667–R673
matrices
   correlation, 286, R127–R132, R436–R441, R471–R478
   covariance, R129–R130
   split-file processing, R651
matrix data files
   converting correlation to covariance, R409–R411
   converting covariance to correlation, R409–R411
   raw, R390–R408
   See also raw matrix data files
matrix system files, R26, R28, R30
   format, R30
   matrix input, R28
maximum, 163
   in Descriptives procedure, 169, R188
   in Explore procedure, 186, R230
   in Frequencies procedure, 152, R278
   in Report Summaries in Rows procedure, 401, R592
maximum function, 96
MCA. *See* multiple classification analysis
McNemar test
   in Two-Related-Samples Tests procedure, 384, R452
mean, 163
   comparing, 217–222, 239–250
   in Descriptives procedure, 169, R188
   in Explore procedure, 186, R230
   in Frequencies procedure, 152, R277
   in Linear Regression procedure, R543
   in Means procedure, 223, R417
   in One-Way ANOVA procedure, 269
   in Report Summaries in Rows procedure, 401, R592
   subgroup, 217–222

   testing differences, 239–250
   trimmed, 182
mean function, 96
mean reference line
   in scatterplots, 519, 524
mean substitution
   in Linear Regression procedure, R547
Means procedure, 222–224, R412–R419
   crosstabulation, R416–R417
   general vs. integer mode, R412, R413, R416
   labels, 224, R418–R419
   layers, 223, R416
   missing values, R418
   statistics, 223–224, R417–R418
measurement level, 159–160
measures of association, 199–208
median, 162
   in Explore procedure, 186, R230
   in Frequencies procedure, 152, R277
   in Report Summaries in Rows procedure, R592
median test
   in Tests for Several Independent Samples procedure, 380, R452–R453
memory, 590, 625, 626, 627
menus, 4–5
merging data files, 119–131
   files with different cases, 120–125, R74–R81
   files with different variables, 126–131, R382–R389
   raw data files, R77, R385
   See also Add Cases Procedure, Add Variables procedure
M-estimators, 182–184
   in Explore procedure, 186, R230–R231
minimum, 163
   in Descriptives procedure, 169, R188
   in Explore procedure, 186, R230
   in Frequencies procedure, 152, R278
   in Report Summaries in Rows procedure, 401, R592
minimum function, 96
missing values
   and aggregated data, R92–R94
   and logical operators, R198, R342
   counting occurrences, 103, R134
   defining, 58–59, R420–R422
   functions, R55, R56
   in Binomial Test procedure, 371

in Bivariate Correlation procedure, 290
in charts, 423–426
in Chi-Square Test procedure, 369
in correlation matrices, 286–287, 327–328
in Data Editor, 51, 58–59
in Explore procedure, 189
in functions, 97, 97–98, R121
in Independent-Samples T Test procedure, 253
in Linear Regression procedure, 353
in logical expressions, R56, R57
in loop structures, R380
in Multiple Response Crosstabs procedure, 237, R430–R431
in Multiple Response Frequencies procedure, 233, R430–R431
in numeric expressions, R48
in One-Sample Kolmogorov-Smirnov Test procedure, 376
in One-Way ANOVA procedure, 269
in Paired-Samples T Test procedure, 255
in Partial Correlations procedure, 297
in Report Summaries in Rows procedure, 403
in Runs Test procedure, 374
in Tests for Several Independent Samples procedure, 382
in transposed data files, 119
in Two-Independent-Samples Tests procedure, 379
in Two-Related-Samples Tests procedure, 384
listwise deletion, 286, 327
MISSING function, R56–R57
NMISS function, R57
pairwise deletion, 286, 327
recoding, 105, 108–109
SYSMIS function, R57
system-missing, 58, R420
user-missing, 58–59, R420–R422
VALUE function, R56
with logical operators, R56
See also individual procedures
missing-value functions, R123–R124
mistakes
identifying, 171
mixed charts, 506
mixed files, R247, R520
mode, 162
in Frequencies procedure, 152, R277
in Report Summaries in Rows procedure, R593
Moses test
in Two-Independent-Samples Tests procedure, 378, R453–R454

Multiplan files
read range, R314–R315
read variable names, R314
reading, R309–R316
saving, R622
multiple classification analysis
analysis of variance, R103
in Simple Factorial ANOVA procedure, 279
multiple comparisons, 262–264
analysis of variance, R464–R466
in One-Way ANOVA procedure, 267–268
multiple *R*, 325
in Linear Regression procedure, R538
multiple regression, 326–345, R531–R548
backward elimination, 337
beta coefficients, 330
building a model, 331–334
collinearity, 343–345
correlation matrix, 326–328
determining important variables, 329–331
forward selection, 335–336
indicator variables, 326
influential points, 341–342
part correlation, 330–331
partial correlation, 330–331
partial *F* test, 332
partial regression coefficients, 328
selecting independent variables, 333–338
stepwise selection, 338
variables not in equation, 333
violations of assumptions, 339–341
See also Linear Regression procedure
multiple response analysis, 225–237, R423–R432
counted values, 226
crosstabulation, 228–229, 234–237
defining sets, 231–232, R423–R424
elementary variables, 226
frequency tables, 232–234
multiple category, 226, R423–R424
multiple dichotomy, 225, 226, R423–R424
See also Define Multiple Response Sets procedure, Multiple Response Crosstabs procedure, Multiple Response Frequencies procedure
Multiple Response Crosstabs procedure, 234–237, R427–R430
cell percentages, 237, R429–R430
defining value ranges, 236, R426–R427
matching variables across response sets, 237, R429
missing values, 237, R430–R431

percents based on cases, 237, R430
percents based on responses, 237, R430
value labels, R431
Multiple Response Frequencies procedure, 232–234, R427
  missing values, 233, R430–R431
  table format, R431–R432
  value labels, R431
multiple SPSS sessions, 599
  journal file, 599
  preferences, 599
multipunch data, R240

nested conditions, R202
nested files, R247, R520
nested functions, 97
nominal measurement, 159
nominal measures, 199–205
noninteger weights, R686
nonparametric tests, 355–386
nonprintable numeric formats, R41
normal curves
  in histograms, 526
normal distribution, 164–166
normal probability plots, 179
  in Explore procedure, 188, R229
  in Linear Regression procedure, 349, R553
normality
  in regression, 302, 316–317
normality tests, 179–181
  in Explore procedure, 188
null hypothesis, 249
numeric data, 44
  input formats, R147–R148, R161–R163
  output formats, R265–R268, R501–R503, R693–R695
numeric expressions, R45–R49
  missing values, R48

observed count, 196
  in Crosstabs procedure, 214, R140
  in Linear Regression procedure, R544
observed significance level, 198, 244, 246, 274

odds ratio, 210
One-Sample Kolmogorov-Smirnov Test procedure, 374–376, R448–R449
  missing values, 376
  statistics, 376
  test distribution, 375, R448
one-sample test
  chi-square, 362–363
one-tailed test, 246
one-way analysis of variance, 257–270
  assumptions, 260
  between groups variability, 261
  hypothesis testing, 259
  multiple comparisons, 262–264
  within groups variability, 261–262
One-Way ANOVA procedure, 264–269, R461–R470
  contrasts, 267, R463–R464
  defining factor ranges, 265–266, R462, R463
  display labels, R466
  factor variables, 265, R462, R463
  harmonic means, R466
  limitations, R462
  matrix input, R467–R470
  matrix output, R467–R470
  missing values, 269, R467, R469
  multiple comparisons, 267–268, R464–R466
  orthogonal polynomials, R463
  polynomial contrasts, 266–267
  sample size estimates, 268
  statistics, 269, R466–R467
online documentation, R352–R355
online help, 601–607, R337–R338
  See also help
opening files
  at startup, 624
  data files, 29–36, R279–R282
  output files, 79–81
  syntax files, 83–84
option menus, 17
options, R630–R643
  displaying, R644–R647
  See also preferences
Options pushbutton, 423
Oracle database
  reading, 32–36
order of commands, R17–R19

order of operations
  numeric expressions, R45–R46
ordinal measurement, 160
ordinal measures, 205–208
orthogonal polynomials
  analysis of variance, R463
OSIRIS files
  conversion to SPSS, R294–R295
  reading, R293–R298
outer frames
  in charts, 548
outliers
  boxplots, 175
  identifying, 175, R227
  in Explore procedure, 186
  in Linear Regression procedure, 349, R553, R554
  in regression, 318–322
  scatterplots, 300
output files
  borders for tables, R643
  chart characters, R642–R643
  destination of, R634–R635
  display command syntax, R634–R635
  display output page titles, R637
  letter case, R636–R637
  opening at startup, 624
  page size, R635–R636
  printing, 573–575
  See also output windows
output formats, R149, R501–R503, R693–R695
  custom currency, R265, R501, R693
  displaying, R502, R694
  format specification, R501, R693
  print (display), R265–R268
  string data, R265
  write, R265–R268, R693–R695
  See also data types
output page titles, 82–83
  displaying, 82–83
  See also titles, subtitles
output windows, 3, 79, 79–82
  borders for tables, 595
  clearing text, 87
  controlling default format, 594–596
  copying tables, 87
  copying text, 87
  cutting text, 87
  designated window, 6, 81

display command syntax, 595
display output page titles, 595
editing files, 86–90
existing files, 80–81
finding charts, 6, 81
fonts, 90, 631
glossary, 81
graphical characters, 596
multiple windows, 81
new files, 79
opening, 79–81
page size, 596
pasting text, 87
pause display, 81
rounding numbers, 81, 89–90
saving files, 90–92
saving selected areas, 92
scroll display, 81
search and replace text, 88, 88–89
overlay plots, R482

padding strings, R52, R53
page ejection, R498–R500
  missing values, R499
  variable list, R499
page orientation
  for printing, 575
page size, 596, R635–R636
  effect on printing, 575
paired samples, 248–249
Paired-Samples T Test procedure, 253–255, R663–R666
  limitations, R664
  missing values, 255, R666
  selecting paired variables, 254
  variable labels, R666
  variable list, R665
paired-samples *t* test. *See t* test
part correlation, 330–331
  in Linear Regression procedure, R539
partial correlation, 291–298, 330–331, R471–R478
  hidden relationships, 294
  in Linear Regression procedure, 348, R539
  significance test, 292
  spurious correlations, 292
  See also Bivariate Correlation procedure

Partial Correlations procedure, 295–298
    control variables, 296
    missing values, 297
    statistics, 297
    zero-order correlations, 297
partial regression coefficients, 328
Paste
    in Data Editor, 66–69
    in output windows, 87
    in syntax windows, 87
Pearson chi-square, 197
    in Crosstabs procedure, 212, R141
Pearson correlation coefficient, 208, 282–284
    hypothesis testing, 285–286
    in Bivariate Correlation procedure, 289, R127
    in Crosst\abs procedure, 213, R142
    linear association, 283
Pearson's *r*. *See* Pearson correlation coefficient
percentages, 146
    cummulative, 146
    in Crosstabs procedure, 214, R140–R141
    in Report Summaries in Rows procedure, R593
    valid, 146
percentiles, 149–150
    break points, R228
    estimating from grouped data, 153, R275–R276
    in Explore procedure, 186, R228
    in Frequencies procedure, 152, R276–R277
    methods, R228
persistence, 17
phi, 200
    in Crosstabs procedure, 213, R141
pie charts, 146, 464–468, R329
    displayed data, 550
    exploding sectors, 567
    options, 514–516
    summaries for groups of cases, 466
    summaries of separate variables, 467
    titles, 423
    values of individual cases, 467
platykurtic distribution, 165
plot symbols, 595–596
polynomial contrasts
    in One-Way ANOVA procedure, 266–267
pooled-variance *t* test. *See t* test
population, 240
    estimate, 240
    parameter, 240

portable files. *See* SPSS portable files
portrait printing, 575, 578
post hoc multiple comparisons. *See* multiple comparisons
post-hoc tests. *See* multiple comparisons
PostScript
    printing, 574, 578
predicted values
    adjusted, 320, R550
    in Linear Regression procedure, 351
    in regression, 308–312
    standard errors, R551
    standardized, R551
    unstandardized, R550
preferences, 587–599, R630–R643
    blank data fields, R633
    borders for tables, 595, R643
    charts, 591–593, R642
    command terminator, R640
    custom currency formats, 593–594, R637–R638
    data compression, R639
    data transformations, 590
    decimal indicator, R638
    default file extension, R639–R640
    default variable format, 591, R636
    display errors, R634–R635
    display macro commands, R641–R642
    display resource messages, R634–R635
    display statistical results, R634–R635
    display warnings, R634–R635
    displaying, R644–R647
    errors, R633–R634
    graphics, 591–593, R642, R642–R643
    invalid data, R633
    journal file, 588–589, R641
    letter case, R636–R637
    macro expansion, R641–R642
    maximum loops, R634
    multiple SPSS sessions, 599
    open syntax window, 590
    output, 594–596, R634–R635, R637
    output page size, 596, R635–R636
    plot symbols, 595–596
    preserving, R491, R607
    random number seed, R638–R639
    restoring, R491, R607
    saving, 597
    sort program, R639
    .spssrc file, 597–599

startup, 587
thousands separator, R638
warnings, R633–R634
working memory, 590
preferences file, 597–599
print formats. *See* output formats
printer setup
    chart files, 578–579
    text files, 574–575
printing, 573–579
    ASCII, 574
    chart files, 576–579
    charts, 419
    data files, 75, 575–576
    default printer, 632
    font mapping, 579
    in Data Editor, 75
    landscape, 575, 578
    output files, 573–575
    page orientation, 575
    page size, 575
    portrait, 575, 578
    PostScript, 574, 578
    printer setup, 574–575, 578–579
    syntax files, 573–575
    to a file, 575, 579
printing cases, R492–R497, R504–R505
    column headings, R498–R500
    displaying blank lines, R504–R505
    formats, R492, R494, R690
    missing values, R493
    number of records, R496
    output file, R492, R496–R497, R504
    page ejection, R498–R500
    strings, R492, R495
    summary table, R492, R497
probability of F-to-enter
    in Linear Regression procedure, 353, R540
probability of F-to-remove
    in Linear Regression procedure, 353, R540
procedure output
    output file, R506–R507
    writing to a file, R506–R507
procedures
    update documentation, R354
.profile.sps, 656, 663
    with .spssrc, 599
program states, R703–R710

prompted mode. *See* prompted sessions
prompted sessions, 627, 663–666
    automatic profile, 663
    command line continuation, 665
    command terminator, 665
    ending a session, 666
    interrupting a session, 666
    journal file, 664–665
    output files, 664
    prompts, 665
    starting, 663
    using UNIX commands during a session, 666
prompts
    CONTINUE>, 665
    DATA>, 665
    DEFINE>, 665
    SPSS>, 665
    USRCOD>, 665
proportional reduction in error, 201–204
proportional sample, R608
prospective studies, 209
pushbuttons, 11, 15

Q. *See* Cochran's Q
quartiles, 150
    in Frequencies procedure, 152

R
    in Linear Regression procedure, 348
    in Means procedure, 224, R418
r, 208, 282–284
    See also Pearson correlation coefficient
R^2, 306–308
    adjusted, 306
    displaying in scatterplots, 500, 521
    explained variance, 308
    in Linear Regression procedure, 348, R538
radio buttons, 16–17
random number seed
    specifying, R638–R639
random sample, 240
    in nonparametric tests, R458
    selecting from data file, 142
random-number functions, 97, R124–R125

random-number seed, 101
  in data transformations, 101
  in functions, 101
range, 163
  in Descriptives procedure, 169, R188
  in Explore procedure, R230
  in Frequencies procedure, 152, R278
range function, 96
rank correlation coefficient. *See* Spearman correlation coefficient
ranking data, 110–113, R508–R513
  fractional rank, 111
  method, 111–112, R510–R511
  missing values, R513
  new variable names, 111, R511–R512
  normal scores, 112–113
  ntiles, 112
  order, 111, R509
  proportion estimate method, 112–113
  proportion estimates, 112–113, R512–R513
  Savage scores, 111
  sum of case weights, 112
  tied values, 113, R512
  within subgroups, 110, R509
rank-order correlation coefficients
  in Bivariate Correlation procedure, R436
raw data files
  blanks, R149–R150
  data types, R147–R148
  fixed format, R149, R149–R150, R151–R152, R157–R158
  freefield format, R149, R150, R151–R152, R158–R159
  reading, R147–R164
  variable definition, R156–R164, R520–R528
  See also ASCII text data files
raw matrix data files, R390–R408
  factors, R402–R404, R406–R407
  format, R390–R391, R393–R401
  N, R408
  record types, R404–R408
  split files, R401–R402
  within-cells records, R404, R406–R407
recoding values, 104–110, R514–R519
  conditional, 106
  converting strings to numeric, 109, R108–R111, R518–R519
  defining values to recode, 105–106, 108–110
  if case satisfies condition, 106, 110

  into different variable, 107–110
  into same variable, 104–106
  limitations, R516
  missing values, 105, 108–109, R515–R516
  numeric variables, R515–R519
  string variables, R516–R519
  subsets of cases, 106, 110
  target variable, R517–R518
records
  defining, R153–R154, R520–R528
  duplicate, R527
  missing, R526–R527
  skipping, R524–R525
  types, R520–R528
reference lines
  adding to charts, 546
  mean, in scatterplots, 519, 524
regression, 299–353
  adjusted predicted values, 320
  analysis of variance, 306
  casewise plots, 311
  confidence intervals, 305
  equality of variance, 302, 315
  explained variance, 308
  goodness of fit, 305–308
  hypothesis testing, 304–305
  independence, 303
  independence of error, 315–316
  least squares, 301
  linear transformations, 322–323
  linearity, 303, 313–314
  multiple, 326–345
  normality, 302, 316–317
  outliers, 300, 318–322
  population parameters, 304
  predicted values, 308–312
  regression line, 301–302
  residuals, 307, 312–313, 319–322
  scatterplots, 300
  standard error, 309
  standardized regression coefficient, 302
  sums of squares, 308
  violations of assumptions, 312–317
  See also Linear Regression procedure, multiple regression
regression coefficients
  in Linear Regression procedure, 348, R538
regression line, 301–302
regression plots, R482–R483
  in Linear Regression procedure, 348

regression prediction lines, 520
relational operators, 94, R54, R195, R340, R625
 defined, R54
 in conditional expressions, 99
relative risk ratio, 208
 in Crosstabs procedure, 213, R142
remainder function, 95
renamed variables
 in dialog boxes, 54
repeating data, R560–R573
 case identification, R572–R573
 defining variables, R568
 input file, R568–R569
 repeating groups, R567–R569
 starting column, R566–R567
 summary table, R573
repeating data groups, R520
repeating fields. *See* repeating data
Replace
 in output windows, 88
 in syntax windows, 88
Report Summaries in Rows procedure, 397–406, R574–R600
 break spacing, 402
 column contents, R584–R585, R588
 column heading alignment, 399
 column headings, 399, R575, R585, R588–R589
 column spacing, R576
 column width, 400, R576, R576, R585–R586, R589
 data value alignment, 400
 defining subgroups, 398, R587–R591
 footnotes, 405–406, R598–R599
 format, R580–R582
 grand totals, 403
 limitations, R579–R580
 listing reports, 399
 margins, 404
 missing values, 403, R576, R578, R600
 output file, R578, R582–R584
 page control, 402
 page layout, R582
 pre-sorted data, 403
 print formats, R596–R598
 report alignment, 404
 report layout, 404–405
 report types, R578
 sorting data, 403
 string variables, R586–R587
 summary statistics, 400–402, R578, R591–R598
 summary titles, R595–R596
 titles, 405–406, R598–R599
 value labels, 400
 variable list, R584–R586
 variables in titles, 406
reports, 391–406, R574–R600
 break columns, 391
 break variables, 391
 column headings, 396
 combined reports, 393
 data columns, 391
 footnotes, 396
 formatting, 395–397
 grand totals, 394
 listing reports, 392
 multiple break variables, 394
 report variables, 391
 summary reports, 391
 titles, 396
 value labels, 397
 See also Report Summaries in Rows procedure
re-reading records, R601–R606
 input file, R604–R605
 starting column, R605–R606
residual sum of squares, 308
residuals, 197
 deleted, 319–322, R550
 in Crosstabs procedure, 214, R141
 in Linear Regression procedure, 351
 in regression, 307, 312–313
 standardized, 313, R551
 Studentized, 313, R551
 Studentized deleted, 320, R551
 unstandardized, R550
resistant measures, 181
resource file, 629–633
 accelerator keys, 631
 applications resource directory, 633
 colors, 632
 default printer, 632
 default version, 629
 fonts, 631
 source lists, 632
 window position, 630
 window size, 630
robust estimators, 181–184

Round
   in output windows, 88
   in syntax windows, 88
round function, 95
row percentages, 192–193
   in Crosstabs procedure, 214, R140
row variable, 192
Run Pending Transforms, 115
running commands, 85
   batch mode, 615–618, R14–R15
   interactive mode, R13–R14
runs test
   in Runs Test procedure, R454–R455
Runs Test procedure, 372–374, R454–R455
   cut points, 373
   cutting point, R455
   missing values, 374
   statistics, 374

sample, 240
   exact-size, 142, R608
   proportional, 142, R608
sample size estimates
   in One-Way ANOVA procedure, 268
sampling cases, 142, R608–R610
   See also Select Cases procedure, subsets of cases
sampling distribution, 241–244
   expected value, 241
   of mean, 242–244
   standard error, 241
SAS files
   conversion to SPSS, R300–R304
   reading, R299–R304
Savage scores, 111
saving files
   aggregated data files, 137–138, R88
   ASCII text data files, 50
   charts, 421
   data compression, R615, R700–R701
   data files, 48–50, R611–R615, R696–R701
   dBASE format, R619–R624
   dropping variables, R613–R615, R698–R699
   Excel format, R619–R624
   keeping variables, R613–R615, R698–R699
   Lotus 1-2-3, R619–R624
   output files, 90–92
   renaming variables, R614–R615, R699–R700
   SCSS format, R616–R618
   spreadsheet format, R619–R624
   SPSS data files, 50
   SPSS portable files, 50, R234–R239
   SYLK format, R619–R624
   syntax files, 90–92
   tab-delimited data files, R619–R624
   variable map, R700
saving SCSS data files, R616–R618
   dropping variables, R617–R618
   keeping variables, R617–R618
   missing values, R617
   numeric precision, R617
   output file, R617
   renaming variables, R618
   string variables, R617
scale axes
   modifying, 528–534
scatterplot matrix
   modifying, 499–500
scatterplots, 483–496, R330, R479–R486
   3-D, 488–490, 495–496
   3-D options, 524–527
   bivariate, 483, 500
   case labels, 518, 524
   changing types, 509
   contour plots, R482
   control variables, R481–R482
   cutpoints, R483–R484
   displayed data, 551
   displaying R^2, 500, 521
   fitting a line, 518–521, 524, 563
   horizontal axis, R481, R485–R486
   interpolation styles, 563
   limitations, R480–R481
   lowess fit, 488, 520
   marker categories, 492, 493, 495
   marker labels, 492, 493, 494, 496
   marker styles, 561
   matrix, 487–488, 492–493
   matrix axes, 531–534
   mean reference line, 519
   missing values, R486
   options, 518–527
   overlay, 494–495
   overlay options, 523–524
   overlay plots, R482
   plot resolution, R479

plot scaling, R485–R486
plot types, R480
regression curves, 486, 520
regression plots, R482–R483
rotating 3-D, 569
simple, 483–487, 491–492
spikes, 490, 519, 524, 525
subgroups, 518, 525
sunflowers, 484, 519–522
swapping axes, 568
symbols, R483–R484
titles, R486
vertical axis, R481, R485–R486
weighting cases, 519, 524
wireframes, 525
Scheffé test
  in One-Way ANOVA procedure, 268
Schwarz Bayesian criterion
  in Linear Regression procedure, R538
scientific notation, 55
scratch variables
  defined, R34
screening data, 150
SCSS files
  conversion to SPSS, R305–R306
  reading, R305–R308
  saving data files as, R616–R618
Search
  in Data Editor, 72
  in output windows, 88
  in syntax windows, 88
Search for Data, 72
seed. *See* random-number seed
Select All
  in output windows, 88
  in syntax windows, 88
Select Cases procedure, R608–R610
  exact-size sample, R608
  limitations, R609
  proportional sample, R608
  temporary sample, R608
selected variable lists, 11
selecting cases, 139–142
  See also subsets of cases
selecting variables, 12–13
semi-partial correlation. *See* part correlation

series objects
  in charts, 504
settings, R630–R643
  displaying, R644–R647
  See also preferences
Shapiro-Wilks' test, 180
  in Explore procedure, 188, R229
short string variable, R42
short string variables, 40, 55
sign test, 359
  in Two-Related-Samples Tests procedure, 383, R455–R456
signed-ranks test, 359
significance level
  in Linear Regression procedure, R544
  t test, 246
Simple Factorial ANOVA procedure, 276–280
  covariates, 277, 279, R98, R98
  defining factor ranges, 277, R97–R98
  display labels, 280, R103
  factor variables, 276, R97–R98
  full factorial model, 277
  interaction effects, 279–280, R98
  limitations, R96–R97
  methods, 278, R98–R100
  missing values, R103
  multiple classification analysis, 279, R103
  statistics, 279, R100–R103
  sums of squares, R98–R100, R101
  treatment effects, R103
sine function, 96
skewness, 165
  in Descriptives procedure, 170, R188
  in Explore procedure, 186, R230
  in Frequencies procedure, 153, R277
  in Report Summaries in Rows procedure, 402, R592
Somers' d, 207
  in Crosstabs procedure, 213, R142
sorting cases, 117–118, R648–R649
  sort keys, R648
  sort order, 118, R648
  specifying sort program, R639
source variable list, 11, 11
Spearman correlation coefficient, 205, 285, 287
  in Bivariate Correlation procedure, 289, R438
  in Crosstabs procedure, 213, R142

Spline, 564
split-file processing, 138–139, R650–R652
  break variables, R650
  matrices, R651
  scratch variables, R650
  system variables, R650
  temporary, R658–R659
  with matrix system files, R28
spread-and-level plots, 178–179
  determining transformation, 178–179
  in Explore procedure, 188, R229
spreadsheet files
  read ranges, R314–R315
  read variable names, R314
  reading, R309–R316
  saving, R619–R624
SPSS
  exiting, 27
  multiple sessions, 599
  performing statistical analysis, 7–18
  starting, 1
spss (command)
  batch processing, 627
  command line switches, 623–627
  prompted sessions, 663–666
  starting a Manager session, 625
  starting a prompted session, 627
SPSS data files
  documents, R193–R194, R209
  reading, 31, R279–R282
  saving, 50
SPSS Manager, 625–626, 635–662
  automatic profile, 656
  building commands from menus, 644
  changing text, 638–639
  changing window sizes, 646
  copying text, 640
  deleting files, 661
  deleting text, 641
  edit mode, 638–641
  entering commands, 656
  exiting, 659
  extended menus, 626, 643
  Files window, 646
  finding text, 638–639
  glossary help, 651
  go to function, 652
  incremental search, 643
  input window, 645
  inserting files, 661
  interrupting commands, 659
  journal file, 662
  marking commands, 639
  marking lines, 639
  marking rectangles, 640
  marking text, 639–640
  menu mode, 641–648
  mini-menus, 636
  moving between windows, 645
  moving text, 641
  online help, 649
  opening files, 660
  output width, 658
  output window, 645
  pasting menu selections, 644
  redrawing screen, 653
  rounding numbers, 653
  running commands, 656–658
  running UNIX commands, 659
  saving files, 661
  selecting files, 646
  selecting variables, 648
  starting, 635, 655
  status line, 654
  syntax help, 650
  Variables window, 648
  viewing output, 658
  writing current screen, 653
  zooming windows, 646
SPSS portable files, R23
  reading, 31, R346–R349
  saving, 50, R234–R239
SPSS resource file. *See* resource file
SPSS/PC+ files
  reading, R346–R349
.spssrc file, 597–599, 624
  adding SET subcommands, 598
  editing, 598
spurious correlations, 292
SQL database files
  reading, 31–36
square root function, 95, R46–R47
stacked area charts, 460, 462, 464
stacked bar charts, 443, 445, 448
standard deviation, 164
  in Descriptives procedure, 169, R188
  in Explore procedure, 186, R230

in Frequencies procedure, 152, R277
in Linear Regression procedure, R544
in Means procedure, 223, R417
in Report Summaries in Rows procedure, 401, R592
standard deviation function, 96, R47
standard error, 241
  in Explore procedure, 186, R230
  in Linear Regression procedure, R538, R539
  in regression, 309
standard error of the estimate, 304, 311
standard error of the mean
  in Descriptives procedure, 169, R188
  in Frequencies procedure, 152, R277
standard scores, 166
standardized regression coefficient, 302
standardized residuals, 313
  in Linear Regression procedure, 349–350, 351
stand-in variable, R204–R205
starting SPSS, 1
  command line switches, 623–627
startup preferences, 587
statistical functions, 96, R123
status bar, 7
stem-and-leaf plots, 173–175
  in Explore procedure, 188, R229
  scale, R226
stepwise selection, 338
  in Linear Regression procedure, 347, R536
Stop SPSS Processor, 586
string data, 40, 44, 55, 56
  computing values, R120, R121–R122, R125–R126
  conditional transformations, R196, R197, R341, R342
  converting to numeric, 109, 114–115, R108–R111
  in Data Editor, 56
  input formats, R147–R148, R163–R164
  long string, 40, 55
  missing values, R420
  output formats, R265, R501–R502, R693–R694
  right-padding, 56
  short string, 40, 55
  value labels, R83–R84, R674
string expressions
  defined, R49
string functions, R49–R52, R126
  macro facility, R176–R178

string variables
  in logical expressions, R49
Studentized residuals, 313
  in Linear Regression procedure, 351
Student-Newman-Keuls test
  in One-Way ANOVA procedure, 268
subcommand
  syntax, R16
subgroup means, 217–222
subgroups
  splitting data files into, R650–R652
subpopulation, 217–222
subsets of cases
  conditional expressions, 141–142, R625–R626
  deleting unselected cases, 141
  filter status, 141, R257–R258
  filtering unselected cases, 140, R257–R258
  if condition is satisfied, 141–142, R625–R629
  random sample, 142
  selecting, 139–142, R625–R629
  selection variable, 140
substrings, R52
subtitles, 82–83, R655–R656
  apostrophes in, R655
  length, R655
  quotation marks in, R655
  suppressing, R655
  with inline data, R655
sum
  in Descriptives procedure, 169, R188
  in Frequencies procedure, 152, R278
  in Report Summaries in Rows procedure, 401, R592
sum function, 96
summary reports, 391
summary statistics, 161–164
sums of squares
  in regression, 308
survival tables
  writing to a file, R506–R507
sweep matrix
  in Linear Regression procedure, R538
Sybase database
  reading, 32–36
SYLK files
  read ranges, R314–R315
  read variable names, R314

reading, R309–R316
saving, R622
syntax, 609–612, R11–R20
syntax charts, R11–R12
   in Help window, 607
syntax files
   opening at startup, 625
   printing, 573–575
syntax windows, 4, 79, 83–86
   clearing text, 87
   copying tables, 87
   copying text, 87
   cutting text, 87
   designated window, 86
   editing commands, 24–26
   editing files, 86–90
   existing files, 83–84
   fonts, 90, 631
   multiple windows, 86
   new files, 83
   open at startup, 590
   opening, 83–84
   pasting commands, 24–26, 84–85
   pasting text, 87
   pasting variable names, 85
   running commands, 24–26, 84–85
   saving files, 90–92
   saving selected areas, 92
   search and replace text, 88, 88–89
system files. *See* data files
system variables, R33
system-missing value, R420
   in Data Editor, 58

t test
   in Independent-Samples T Test procedure, 250–253, R663
   in Paired-Samples T Test procedure, 253–255, R663
   independent samples, 244–248
   one-tailed, 246
   paired samples, 248–249
   pooled-variance, 245
   significance level, 246
   two-sample, 244–248
   two-tailed, 246

tab-delimited files
   reading, R309–R316
   saving, R621, R622
table lookup files, 128, R386
table percentage, 192
target variable
   computing values, 94
   counting values, R133, R134
target variable lists, 11
   reordering, 586
target variables
   computing values, R119
   formats, R121–R122
   in COMPUTE command, R49
tau. *See* Goodman and Kruskal's tau
tau-*a*. *See* Kendall's tau-*a*
tau-*b*. *See* Kendall's tau-*b*
tau-*c*. *See* Kendall's tau-*c*
templates
   in charts, 426, R334
   in Data Editor, 60–63
temporary transformations, R658–R660
temporary variables, R658
Tests for Several Independent Samples procedure, 379–382, R449–R450, R452–R453
   grouping variables, 380, R450, R453
   missing values, 382
   statistics, 381
Tests for Several Related Samples procedure, 385–386, R446–R447, R450–R451
   statistics, 386
text alignment
   in Data Editor, 60
text boxes, 16
text data files. *See* ASCII text data files
thousands separator
   specifying, R638
tied pairs, 206
time formats, 42, 55
   in Data Editor, 56
time functions, R59–R73
time intervals, R59–R73
titles, 82–83, R661–R662
   apostrophes in, R661
   displaying, R637
   in charts, 422, 541

length, R661
  quotation marks in, R661
  with inline data, R661
  See also subtitles, R661
tolerance, 343
  in Linear Regression procedure, 348, R539, R540, R541
total percentage
  in Crosstabs procedure, 214, R141
transaction files, R667–R673
Transform menu. *See* data transformations
transformations
  data, 93–115
  file, 117–144
  temporary, R658–R660
translating data files. *See* data files
transposing cases and variables, 118–119, R261–R264
treatment effects
  analysis of variance, R103
trimmed mean, 182
  in Explore procedure, 186, R230
truncate function, 95
Tukey's *b*
  in One-Way ANOVA procedure, 268
Tukey's transformation, R512
Two-Independent-Samples Tests procedure, 377–379, R449, R451, R453–R454, R456
  defining groups, 378
  grouping variables, 377, R449, R451, R454, R456
  missing values, 379
  outlier trimming, R454
  statistics, 379
Two-Related-Samples Tests procedure, 382–384, R452, R455–R456, R457
  missing values, 384
  statistics, 384
two-sample *t* test. *See t* test
two-tailed test, 246

U. *See* Mann-Whitney *U*
uncertainty coefficient
  in Crosstabs procedure, 213, R141
update documentation, R352, R354

updating data files, R667–R673
  dropping variables, R672
  flag variables, R672–R673
  input files, R670
  keeping variables, R672
  key variables, R667–R673
  limitations, R669
  master files, R667–R673
  raw data files, R670
  renaming variables, R671–R672
  transaction files, R667–R673
  variable map, R673
upper case
  specifying, R636–R637
user-missing values, 58–59, R420–R422

V. *See* Cramér's *V*
valid percentage, 146
value
  syntax, R16–R17
value labels, 57–58, R82–R84, R674–R676
  adding, R674–R676
  apostrophes in, R674
  concatenating strings, R674, R675
  displaying, 73
  length, R674
  revising, R82–R84
  string data, R83–R84, R674
  using for data entry, 73–74
Van der Waerden's transformation, R513
variability, 157
variable labels, 57, R677–R678
  apostrophes in, R677
  concatenating strings, R677, R678
variable sets, 583–585
  defining, 583–584
  using, 585
variable types. *See* data types
variables, 51
  controlling default format, 591, R636
  defining, 39–45, 52–63, R156–R164, R459–R460, R520–R528, R653–R654
  deselecting, 13
  dictionary information, 582–583
  finding, 72, 583
  labels, 57

moving, 71
naming rules, 39, 53–54, R156–R157
renaming, 54
selecting, 12–13
sets, 583–585
temporary, R658
variance, 163
   in Descriptives procedure, 169, R188
   in Explore procedure, 186, R230
   in Frequencies procedure, 152, R277
   in Linear Regression procedure, R538, R544
   in Means procedure, 223, R417
   in Report Summaries in Rows procedure, 402, R592
variance function, 96
variance inflation factor, 343
   in Linear Regression procedure, 348, R538
vectors, R679–R684
   index, R679, R683–R684
   variable list, R679
virtual memory, 590

W. See Kendall's *W*
Wald-Wolfowitz test
   in Two-Independent-Samples Tests procedure, 378, R456
warnings
   displaying, 595, R634–R635
   maximum number, R633–R634
weighted least-squares
   in Linear Regression procedure, 347, R542
weighting cases, 143–144, R685–R687
   in histograms, 526
   in scatterplots, 519, 524
Wilcoxon signed-rank test, 359
Wilcoxon test
   in Two-Related-Samples Tests procedure, 383, R457
windows
   colors, 632
   position, 630
   size, 630
within-groups variability, 261–262

working memory, 590, 625, 626, 627
workspace, 590, 625, 626, 627
write formats, R693–R695

XAPPLERESDIR (environment variable), 633
XUSERFILESEARCHPATH (enviroment variable), 633

Yates' correction for continuity, 198
   in Crosstabs procedure, 212, R141

Z scores, 166
   in Descriptives procedure, 168, R185–R186
   saving as variables, 168, R185–R186
zero-order correlations, 292
   in Partial Correlations procedure, 297